MINNESOTA
WISCONSIN
MICHIGAN
NEW YORK
MAINE
VT.
N.H.
MASS.
CONN.
R.I.
IOWA
ILLINOIS
INDIANA
OHIO
PENNSYLVANIA
N.J.
MD.
DEL.
WEST VIRGINIA
WASHINGTON D.C.
VIRGINIA
MISSOURI
KENTUCKY
NORTH CAROLINA
TENNESSEE
ARKANSAS
SOUTH CAROLINA
MISSISSIPPI
ALABAMA
GEORGIA
LOUISIANA
FLORIDA
ATLANTIC OCEAN
GULF OF MEXICO

Political and Social Growth
of the American People
1865–1940

BY ARTHUR MEIER SCHLESINGER

FRANCIS LEE HIGGINSON PROFESSOR OF HISTORY AT HARVARD UNIVERSITY

THIRD EDITION

New edition of *Political
and Social Growth of the
United States, 1852-1933*

The Macmillan Company

New York

First and second editions copyrighted and published 1925 and 1933
By The Macmillan Company

FOREWORD

$\mathbf{A}$MERICAN history has a triple value. It is worth knowing for its own sake; it helps to explain the present state of the nation; and it affords clues to the future. Youth has been known to cry, "Let bygones be bygones!" and even a contemporary poet has disdainfully written, "I tell you the past is a bucket of ashes." But sooner or later young people come to realize that they are the heirs of a living tradition, that if they could succeed in blotting out the memory of their forebears, they would be like a ship without rudder and compass. As for the poet, was it in a mood of expiation that he devoted many wearisome years to preparing a massive six-volume study of Abraham Lincoln?

The history of the American people has been beaten out on the anvil of experience. The story reveals both failures and successes, confused aims and clearness of direction, ruthless self-seeking and disinterested devotion. The great men of the Republic usually possessed great faults as well as great virtues; and each generation contained countless obscure persons who were indifferent to the public weal as well as countless others ready to sacrifice their ease for causes bigger than themselves. Yet the record as a whole sums up a people who, despite the ills to which mankind is prey, managed to fashion a way of life and system of government which at every period of American history served as a beacon light for struggling humanity everywhere. So viewed, the story is one of ceaseless effort and unflinching idealism. He who drinks at the springs of the American past will never resign himself to injustice or inequality of opportunity, to intolerance or corruption, to the cruelty of man to man, any more than the medical scientist resigns himself to the existence of diseases supposedly incurable.

The present volume seeks without sentimentality or cynicism to trace the course of United States history from the close of the Civil War through the presidential election of 1940. These years were crammed with incident, aspiration and broadening interests. The nation completed the peopling of its continental area and unfurled the Stars and Stripes over distant dependencies. The Economic Revolution altered all the lineaments of American life and hastened the inpouring of millions from every quarter of the globe. Urbanization replaced the frontier as the dominant force in American society. New problems arose which Lincoln's generation had never known. Democracy was viewed not as a finished achievement but as a continuing effort to adjust government to the nation's changing needs.

At the same time the people found increasing time to cultivate the concerns of the mind and spirit. They began to forge ahead rapidly in the arts and sciences, to promote humanitarian reforms, to adapt religion to new conditions, to enlarge their contribution to literature, to learn the uses of leisure. All these interests were interwoven with one another and with influences emanating from the outside world. The main lines of endeavor coincided with comparable tendencies abroad. Though politicians continued to declaim against "entangling alliances," the country's material, intellectual and artistic growth proved that, in nonpolitical spheres at least, "isolation" was neither possible nor desirable. Even in matters of government, the experience of Western Europe often pointed the way for America.

The lapse of seven years since the second edition of this work has afforded an opportunity to expand somewhat on the earlier treatment, continue the narrative to the present and revise certain judgments in the light of later evidence. Because of limitations of space the bibliographical references are confined to studies of book length. Notes on the illustrations will be found in the pages immediately following the Table of Contents. Among the persons whose suggestions have improved the volume I wish particularly to thank my colleagues Professor Paul H. Buck and Dr. Richard W. Leopold, Professor Fred A. Shannon of the University of Illinois and Mr. Arthur M. Schlesinger, Jr., of the Society of Fellows of Harvard University. I am also indebted to Miss Elizabeth F. Hoxie for her help in seeing the manuscript through the press and for compiling the index. At every point I have had the encouragement and coöperation of my wife Elizabeth Bancroft.

A. M. S.

CAMBRIDGE, MASS.
November 8, 1940

CONTENTS

ix

Due to wartime conditions all black and white half-tone illustrations are inserted at the end of the text.

ILLUSTRATIONS

MAPS, TABLES AND CHARTS

Political and Social Growth
of the American People
1865–1940

PART ONE
THE RISE OF MODERN AMERICA

Chapter I

THE POSTWAR SOUTH, 1865–1877
THE PROBLEMS OF PEACE

THE close of the Civil War saw modern America in the making. The four years' struggle had demonstrated the supremacy of the national will throughout the land. Whatever the theoretical merits of the states' rights contention, the issue had been resolved in favor of an indissoluble Union. Assured of the nation's geographic unity, the triumphant North could now turn to the stupendous task of developing the country's unexploited material resources in the confident knowledge that the agrarian slaveholding South could no longer halt its efforts. A sense of power and a spirit of arrogant self-assurance reigned, heralding a new era in the history of the American people. The heightened nationalism expressed itself not only in domestic affairs but also, for a time, in foreign relations.

But before these newly released energies could find untrammeled sway, certain questions left over from the war demanded attention. The eleven ex-Confederate states must be accorded their ancient position in the federal system; the defeated people must adopt an unwelcome conception of race relations; and if American nationality was to be more than an exclusive sentiment of the North, they must somehow learn again to love the Union which they had tried to destroy. At the same time, the government faced an unprecedented war debt of $2,750,000,000, and means had to be found of revising taxation and currency policies to suit peace-time conditions. Finally, the presence of several million ex-soldiers among the voters injected a new element into the political life of both North and South, one which would long keep alive the dying embers of sectional ill will. Though the problems of statecraft altered radically as the Civil War receded, Republican leaders found it good politics on every occasion to brand the opposition with the odium of secession, and in every election throughout the rest of the century the party chose its presidential nominee, with a single exception, from men who had been officers in the Union army. As a further bait to the old-soldier vote, the Republicans, beginning as early as 1862, voted pensions on increasingly generous terms, at a total charge to the taxpayers of over $2,500,-000,000 by the end of the century and of $2,500,000,000 more by 1917.

Neither the South nor the North was in a fit mood in 1865 to undertake the delicate task of mending the torn fabric of the Union. In both sections the emotional tension was great. The ex-Confederate people were broken in spirit and confronted with economic disaster as well. The later years of the war had wrought vast destruction in important Southern centers. Charleston, wrote a Northern visitor, was "a city of ruins, of desolation, of vacant houses, of widowed women, of rotting wharves." Richmond, Columbia, Atlanta and Mobile presented similar scenes. Moreover, in every part of the South plantations had been laid waste or had fallen into decay. The South Carolina back country "looked for miles like a broad black streak of ruin and desolation—the fences all gone; lonesome smoke stacks, surrounded by dark heaps of ashes and cinders, marking the spots where human habitations had stood." The transportation system was prostrate. "Bridges were burnt," said a Northern observer, "rails were torn up and twisted for miles and miles; the companies themselves were utterly impoverished." At the same time, the emancipation of the Negroes had deranged the only labor system that the dominant race had ever known, while whole fortunes had been wiped out by the confiscation of slave property, valued at over two billion dollars in 1860, and by the collapse of Confederate bonds and currency.

Some Southerners in their bitterness resolved to quit the scene of their humiliation. In the few years after Appomattox eight thousand or more, including a number of generals and high officials, settled in Mexico, Central America and especially in Brazil where the presence of Negro slavery proved an attraction. But many of the refugees, disillusioned by their experiences, presently returned to the United States. Judah P. Benjamin, who had served in the Confederate cabinet, fled to England, where he became Queen's counsel and practiced law with great distinction. The vast majority of Southerners, however, had neither the opportunity nor the desire to leave. Some of them sullenly accepted their lot, but the greater number hearkened to the advice of Robert E. Lee to "unite in honest efforts to obliterate the effects of war, and to restore the blessings of peace." Lee himself accepted the post of president of Washington College at Lexington, Virginia, and spent the five remaining years of his life in educating the rising generation. "I am satisfied," asserted General Ulysses S. Grant in December, 1865, "that the mass of thinking men of the South accept the present situation of affairs in good faith."

The immediate fate of the South, however, rested with the twenty-five Northern states. The people there could not forget that the struggle had been no ordinary one. It had been a "Brothers' War," Americans fighting Americans. Now that the territorial integrity of the nation was assured and the evil of slavery ended, a strong sentiment favored forgiveness of the past and the return of the seceded states with the least possible delay or friction. This spirit was best embodied in President Lincoln, and it later guided the actions of his successor, Andrew Johnson. But to other Northerners, the attempt of their fellow Americans to dismember the Union revealed a malignity of heart and a diabolical mentality which called for stern measures. Members of Congress like Benjamin Wade, Thaddeus Stevens and Charles Sumner were actuated in part by vengeance and in part by a determination to safeguard the fruits of victory. In place of the healing methods advocated by conservative Republicans and Northern Democrats, they prescribed the surgeon's knife. They assumed the name of Radicals to signify the thoroughgoing policy which they deemed necessary.

This conflict of purposes provides the key to an understanding of the maze of executive acts and congressional decisions that charted the devious and protracted course of Southern reconstruction. The framers of the Constitution had not foreseen such a contingency; and even had they done so, men were lacking in Washington, once Lincoln was removed from the scene, to supervise the process with the sagacity and skill which the circumstances required. At no other critical juncture in American history has the quality of statesmanship fallen so low; and at no other time have the difficulties confronting the government been more complex.

The Southern problem was threefold in character. On its humanitarian side it involved a temporary oversight of the three and a half million former slaves. In its governmental phases it involved reviving the normal political life of the states and reattaching them to the federal framework. In its economic aspects it meant, or should have meant, some active concern for the chaos into which Southern agriculture and trade had fallen. But the postwar psychology prevented the working out of any coördinated plan. Negro welfare began as an object of private philanthropists and ended as a football for politicians. From the outset political reconstruction excited fierce factional differences within the majority party and, as the months passed, increasingly antagonized the more substantial elements among the Southerners. As for economic rehabilitation, neither Congress nor the President gave it a thought, leaving the vanquished people to work out their salvation unhindered and unhelped.

THE PRESIDENTIAL SOLUTION OF RECONSTRUCTION

Before the collapse of the Confederacy in April, 1865, progress had already been made in dealing with the Southern problem. From the early months of the war, when slaves began flocking into the Union camps in Virginia and elsewhere, the American Missionary Association and other Northern groups had carried on relief work among the fugitives. Presently more than three thousand men and women were engaged in this service, including agents of the war-time Sanitary Commission and of British benevolent societies. They not only provided material aid, but organized schools for teaching the refugees how to read and write, and also gave them religious instruction. As the federal troops occupied additional territory, however, the scope of the work became too vast for private agencies to handle efficiently, and the chief responsibility inevitably fell upon the government. In response to this need, Congress with Lincoln's approval created the Freedmen's Bureau early in March, 1865, to continue for one year after the war. It was to perform humanitarian work among the Negroes, relieving immediate distress and, when possible, allotting them small farms from abandoned estates, which the tenants after occupying at a low rental for three years might buy.

Under Major General Oliver O. Howard the Bureau established local branches, coördinated the activities of the private societies and assumed a general guardianship over the freedmen. The difficulties were great, for the Negroes were dazed and distracted by their new-found freedom and wholly unprepared for its responsibilities, while the Southern whites watched the Northern interference with distrust and resentment. The Bureau officials strove to impress on the ex-slaves that liberty did not mean idleness, and it protected them in making working arrangements with the former master class. The local agents often proved overzealous, however, and in some instances betrayed their trust by raising fantastic hopes of sudden prosperity in the breasts of their wards. Despite such shortcomings, the Freedmen's Bureau rendered notable service in the difficult period of transition from servitude to freedom. Though various complicating factors prevented the distribution of much land to members of the race, the Bureau in its eventual four and a half years of life issued 15,500,000 rations to the starving, spent more than $5,000,000 on schools, and gave medical aid to nearly half a million patients. The death rate among the Negro refugees fell from thirteen per cent in 1865 to two in 1869.

Important steps were also taken during the war for reestablishing loyal governments in the South. President Lincoln assumed the initiative in these proceedings, for he held that as commander-in-chief of the army and navy he, rather than Congress, possessed the authority to fix the conditions of withdrawing military law. He based his course of action upon the view that the South had fallen temporarily under the power of insurrectionary elements and that a minority of loyal citizens in a state provided a sufficient basis for erecting an acceptable government. As fast as the success of the federal arms permitted, Lincoln put this plan into practice.

He recognized as legal the makeshift government of Virginia, which had been contrived in the summer of 1861 to sanction the separation of West Virginia. When Tennessee, Louisiana and Arkansas passed under Union control in 1862 and 1863, he appointed military governors to take charge until suitable civil governments could be formed. In order to facilitate such action, he outlined a general procedure for the Southern people in a proclamation of December 8 of the latter year. Excluding certain classes of persons such as prominent Confederate officials, he announced that all others might recover the right of suffrage by taking an oath to support the Constitution and to abide by the measures against slavery. As soon as a tenth of the number who had voted in the presidential election of 1860 in any state took this step, they might establish a state government which he would recognize as the "true government." Under this "ten-per-cent plan" constitutional conventions were held and state governments set up during 1864 in Tennessee, Louisiana and Arkansas. Though these governments were but "as the egg is to the fowl," Lincoln believed "we shall sooner have the fowl by hatching the egg than by smashing it."

Congress watched these proceedings with growing concern. In view of its constitutional right to judge the qualifications of its own members, it declined to regard reconstruction as a presidential function. As a matter of fact, Lincoln in his proclamation of December 8, 1863, had explicitly recognized this right to reject members; but he hoped that Congress would accept his achievements as a *fait accompli*. Moreover, the more radical Republicans thought that the President's terms were too soft, little calculated to discourage treasonable movements in the future. Though the lines were not as sharply drawn as they soon would be, Congress in July, 1864, laid down its own specifications in the Wade-Davis bill. This measure would have hampered political rehabilitation by demanding a more drastic disfranchisement of Southerners, delaying action until a majority of whites had qualified as voters, and requiring rigorous assurances of loyalty from the newly formed governments. Lincoln by a pocket veto prevented the Wade-Davis bill from becoming a law, but he tactfully recommended it nevertheless as "one very proper plan for the loyal people of any State choosing to adopt it."

His action is an augury of how he might have dealt with Congress when the return of peace made reconstruction the paramount issue. But hardly had Lee surrendered when an assassin's bullet removed Lincoln from the scene. Attending a Washington theater to witness a performance of "Our American Cousin" on the night of April 14, 1865, he was shot through the head by a pro-Southern fanatic. Only that very afternoon Lincoln had reiterated to his cabinet, "We must extinguish our resentments if we expect harmony and union." Little wonder that Clement C. Clay, a prominent ex-Confederate, upon hearing the news of the murder exclaimed, "God help us! If that is true, it is the worst blow that has yet been struck the South."

The tragic event brought to the White House a man ill fitted by temperament and training to take over the responsibilities at so critical a juncture. Andrew Johnson's rise from humble origins had been even more remarkable than that of Lincoln himself. Starting in poverty and ignorance as a tailor's apprentice, unable to write until taught by his wife, he had fought his way upward by sheer pluck and native ability against tremendous odds and the scorn of the planting aristocracy. When scarcely of age, he was chosen mayor of his little mountain village in eastern Tennessee, an event which proved the first step in a political ascent that took him to the state legislature, the national House of Representatives, the governor's chair and, in 1857, to the United States Senate. Thick-set, swarthy, somber of visage, he had many of Andrew Jackson's mental traits: pugnacity, self-assurance and an immovable loyalty to duty as he conceived it. He stoutly resisted the secession of Tennessee, and his selection as Lincoln's running mate in 1864 was a sop to the War Democrats in the party. Long experience in public life wore off some of his rough edges, revealing sterling traits of intellectual courage and inflexible purpose. Unfortunately, the situation before him called also for tact, patience and political skill, and these qualities were utterly foreign to his make-up.

Lincoln's murder put the North in an ugly humor. While the excitement was at fever heat, Johnson offered rewards for the arrest of Jefferson Davis and certain other Southern leaders as accomplices in the terrible deed. Radical chieftains, misled by this passionate action, confidently expected the new President to pursue a vindictive course toward the South, and in their intimate circles they referred to Lincoln's martyrdom as a "godsend to the country." Even the pastor of St. George's Church in New York told his great congregation, "I do not know but God intended that Lincoln should be removed in order that the proper punishment should be imposed upon the authors of the Rebellion," while Ralph Waldo Emerson, aroused from his philosophic calm in distant Concord, believed that "what remained to be done required new and uncommitted hands."

Johnson disappointed such expectations. As the days passed and his humane instincts rose to the surface again, he adopted the essentials of Lincoln's good-will policy. He announced his acceptance of the Lincoln governments in Virginia, Tennessee, Louisiana and Arkansas, retained his predecessor's cabinet intact, and proceeded to hasten the reconstruction of the remaining states, though insisting on a somewhat wider disfranchisement than Lincoln had required. When the conventions assembled, he made known his wish that they should disavow the ordinances of secession and repudiate their war debts, and that their first legislatures should ratify the pending Thirteenth Amendment. This amendment, proposed by Congress in January, 1865, carried the Emancipation Proclamation to its logical conclusion and precluded the future reëstablishment of slavery. The reorganization of the seven commonwealths proceeded along these lines, and when Congress gathered on December 4, 1865, for the first time under the new executive, all the states save one had substantially complied with the terms. The Thirteenth Amendment was declared a part of the Constitution two weeks later. Texas completed its process of restoration the following April.

CONGRESS INTERVENES

The next move now belonged to the legislative branch. Congress, confronted with the question of admitting members from the Southern states, declined to do so. It resented the President's effort to minimize its rôle in reconstruction and, at the same time, it scorned his lenient conditions. In particular, the Radicals censured his failure to require Negro enfranchisement. As a matter of fact, both Lincoln and Johnson would have welcomed action by the Southern states to grant the suffrage to educated Negroes and ex-soldiers, but they considered the vast bulk of the former slaves unprepared for the responsibility.[1] They could not forget that freedom had been brought about by violence, not by natural evolution or by the race's own exertions. But Radical leaders such as Charles Sumner regarded the ballot as an inherent human right, while Thaddeus Stevens saw in the measure a means of extending and intrenching the Republican party in the South. This latter need was all the greater because abolition, by canceling the constitutional provision for counting only three fifths of the slaves for purposes of representation,

[1] On this point a Negro historian, Carter G. Woodson, writing in 1922, said: "Had there been a close coöperation among the best whites in the South and a gradual incorporation of the intelligent freedmen into the electorate, many of the mistakes made would have been obviated." At the time, even William Lloyd Garrison disapproved action by Congress to force Negro suffrage on the South, and so also did Harriet Beecher Stowe, whom Lincoln called "the little woman who wrote the book that made this great war."

involved an increase of Southern membership both in the House and in the electoral college. It was deemed imperative, therefore, that a black electorate be created to counteract the white electorate. If the South was to have home rule, the Radicals were resolved to make sure as to who would rule at home. They were not deterred by the fact that Negroes could vote in but six Northern commonwealths—New York and five of the New England states.

Nor did the conduct of the newly organized state governments excite confidence in the President's conditions or in the defeated people's penitence. Prominent ex-Confederates, such as Alexander H. Stephens who had just been chosen Senator from Georgia, were again entering politics, while the so-called loyal legislatures were adopting "black codes" which, in Northern eyes, seemed singularly like the old slave codes. This legislation, while extending to freedmen such ordinary civil rights as making contracts and owning property, aimed at the same time to discourage idleness, vagrancy and race friction. In general, it imposed special penalties on Negroes for breaking labor contracts or committing criminal offenses, forbade them to serve on juries or to carry arms, and prohibited marriages between the races. Mississippi went so far as to fine unemployed freedmen and to provide that in default of payment they must work out the fines in the service of an employer. However justifiable such regulations were from the standpoint of the former master class, they seemed to Radicals a deliberate attempt to undo the result of the war.

The Congress which passed these matters under review contained conservative, moderate and radical Republicans. If Johnson had been prudent enough to conciliate the moderates by slight concessions, he might have preserved the essentials of his plan with the help of the conservatives and of the Democratic minority. But the insolence of the extremists stung him beyond endurance, arousing all his qualities of combativeness and dogmatism. As a result, many of his natural allies were soon driven into league with Stevens and Sumner, iron-willed, imperious men who for two years dictated the course of affairs.

The two houses, after setting up a joint committee on reconstruction to formulate Congress's terms for the South, proceeded at once to take action for safeguarding the exslaves against the black codes. As a first move in this direction, Congress in February, 1866, passed a bill extending the Freedmen's Bureau indefinitely and enlarging its powers so that it might employ military aid to protect the Negro's rights. The President promptly rejected the bill as an unconstitutional exercise of the war power in time of peace, and in an intemperate speech he classed Stevens and Sumner with Jefferson Davis as traitors to the American system of government. This was Johnson's last victory over Congress. Never again was he able to thwart the will of the opposition. In April Congress adopted over his veto the civil-rights act, which accomplished the purpose of the earlier bill but in a more thorough way. It declared all persons born in the United States (excluding untaxed Indians) to be citizens of the United States and, as such, entitled to the same legal rights as white persons, any "statute . . . to the contrary notwithstanding." Besides inflicting heavy penalties for violations, the statute authorized the use of the troops to secure enforcement. Three months later Congress retrieved its earlier defeat by prolonging the life of the Freedmen's Bureau.

Meanwhile the joint committee on reconstruction had been taking evidence on Southern conditions, and on the last day of April it reported its conclusions in the form of a proposed constitutional amendment. With some changes at the hands of Congress this eventually became the Fourteenth Amendment. It dealt with every important phase of the Southern problem. The first section firmly imbedded the principles of the civil-rights act in the Constitution, thereby setting at rest all question of its possible unconstitutionality.[1] The second section sought to coerce the states into granting Negro suffrage by giving them the option of enfranchising all adult male citizens or suffering a proportionate reduction of representation in Congress. The next section, designed to check the rapid return of the old leaders into politics, barred from officeholding ex-Confederates who had been federal or state officials before the war, until they should be pardoned by a two-thirds vote of Congress. The fourth section declared that the war debt of the South should never be paid nor that of the Union repudiated, and further stipulated that former masters should never be compensated for their slaves.

In June, 1866, the amendment was sent to the states. Johnson was quick to point out that, though the Southern governments were not deemed eligible for membership in Congress, the Radicals were nevertheless willing to have them ratify a constitutional amendment. On July 19 Tennessee, where the well-disposed William G. ("Parson") Brownlow was governor, took the desired step, and five days later Congress declared her entitled to representation. The other Southern legislatures rejected the amendment by decisive majorities.

Both Congress and the executive had now indicated their conceptions of a proper reconstruction policy, and the fall elections of 1866 gave the people a chance to choose between them. The President's friends sought to attract the support of the moderates of both political parties, but their promis-

---

[1] For the precise wording of this section, see page 248. Though evoked by the necessities of the freedmen, its chief effect, as we shall see, has been to enable the federal courts to protect corporations ("persons") by the due-process clause from state and local regulation. This purpose, it appears, was in the minds of a few members of the joint committee, notably John A. Bingham of Ohio.

ing efforts were unwittingly defeated by Johnson himself
when he undertook a "swing round the circle," making a
series of blustering extemporaneous speeches in many of the
leading cities of the East and Midwest. His cause was further
injured by a bloody race riot in New Orleans on July 30, an
affray which convinced many Northerners that the South did
not intend to deal fairly with the freedmen. Both factions
exerted themselves to win the soldier vote by assembling special conventions of the veterans—efforts which may be said to
mark the formal entry of the old-soldier influence into postwar politics. In the end, the Radicals won an overwhelming
triumph, securing more than two thirds of each branch of
Congress. If the President had stayed in Washington, the
outcome might have been different. As it was, the Radicals
acclaimed the result as a popular mandate to pursue a harsh
course toward the South.

THE REIGN OF THE RADICALS

When Congress met shortly after the election, the Radicals
lost no time in working out a new and more drastic program.
Thaddeus Stevens drove through the House a bill imposing
complete military rule on the unreconstructed states without
any provision for its termination; but the Senate amended
the measure by designating a procedure of restoration on the
basis of immediate Negro suffrage. Congress's new plan was
set forth in the basic reconstruction law of March 2, 1867,
and in supplementary acts of March 23 and July 19 and of
March 11, 1868. It proceeded on the view that no lawful
governments existed in the ten states. These commonwealths
were to be divided into five military districts under the command of generals who should preserve order and continue or
supplant civil officials as they saw fit. The people of a state
might regain representation in Congress upon complying
with certain conditions: a constitutional convention, chosen

by voters of both races (excluding those disfranchised as former rebels), must frame a constitution establishing Negro
suffrage; this constitution must be approved by the same
electorate and by Congress; the new legislature must ratify
the Fourteenth Amendment; and then the state must wait
until a sufficient number of other ratifications made the
amendment a part of the federal Constitution.

Meanwhile, the feeling between the President and Congress had grown constantly more vindictive. Johnson vainly
vetoed all the important reconstruction measures and, in
turn, Congress set about to hamper and defeat his purposes
in every conceivable way. One of its efforts, the tenure-of-
office act of March 2, 1867, declared the President guilty of a
"high misdemeanor" if he removed an officeholder without
the Senate's consent. The statute specifically included cabinet officers who, unless the Senate agreed to their dismissal,
were to hold office "during the term of the President by
whom they may have been appointed and for one month
thereafter." Johnson in his ineffectual veto branded the act
unconstitutional. Not content with halfway measures, the
Radicals determined to depose the President. In their inflamed state of mind, his stubborn resistance to the measures
they deemed necessary amounted to disloyalty. The House judiciary committee labored for months to find evidence to
justify impeachment on one of the grounds named in the
Constitution—"treason, bribery, or other high crimes and
misdemeanors"—and in December, by a vote of five to four,
reported in favor of such action. But the House decided to
await more convincing proof of misconduct.

The opportunity came on February 21, 1868, when Johnson, without consulting the Senate, removed the Secretary of
War, Edwin M. Stanton, who had long been acting in secret
league with the Radicals. Three days later the House amid
intense excitement voted to impeach the President "of high

crimes and misdemeanors." The eleven verbose articles of
the indictment contained much duplication and confusion
of thought, with the principal emphasis placed on Johnson's
dismissal of Stanton, which was asserted to constitute a "high
misdemeanor" under the tenure-of-office act. The trial in the
Senate began on March 30 and lasted until May 26, with
Chief Justice Salmon P. Chase presiding. It soon appeared
that Johnson had not actually violated the tenure-of-office
act, for Stanton, a Lincoln appointee, had continued in service nearly three years after the term of the President who
had named him. Nothing daunted, the Radicals turned their
efforts toward ousting the chief executive for reasons of party
expediency.

The excitement throughout the North was intense, with
popular sentiment against Johnson. Even the General Conference of the Methodist Church, then in session at Chicago,
set aside an hour of prayer that the Senators might be directed to do their "high duty." When the crucial vote was
taken on May 16, the Senate stood 35 to 19 for conviction,
one vote short of the necessary two thirds. Seven Republicans defied public opinion to join with the Democratic minority in making this result possible. To posterity it is clear
that Johnson had done nothing to merit removal. As Senator
Lyman Trumbull said before casting his ballot for acquittal,
"Once set the example of impeaching a President for what,
when the excitement of the hour shall have subsided, will be
regarded as insufficient causes . . . and no future President
will be safe who happens to differ with a majority of the
House and two thirds of the Senate on any measure deemed
by them important."

While these stormy scenes were being enacted at Washington, Congress's scheme of military reconstruction had gone
into effect in the South. Johnson, despite his deep-seated objections, designated the district commanders as required by

law, and these officers proceeded to establish the paramount authority of the federal government in the ten states. Wherever possible, they coöperated with the local civil officials, but when this proved difficult, they did not hesitate to remove governors (as in Louisiana, Texas, Georgia and Mississippi), or to substitute military tribunals for the civil courts. In due course, they took the necessary steps for holding constitutional conventions. In Georgia the registered voters were about equally divided between the two races; in South Carolina, Florida, Alabama, Mississippi and Louisiana the blacks actually outnumbered the whites.

The elections that ensued produced the most extraordinary constituent assemblies in American history. All the conventions contained Negroes bewildered by their sudden political prominence; in South Carolina they formed a majority. A more influential element consisted of the so-called Carpetbaggers, newcomers from the North, most of whom were intent on political plunder. They were popularly alleged to have carried all their worldly goods to their adopted states in carpetbags. Allied with them were a small number of Southern whites—the hated Scalawags—who for various reasons had forsaken their neighbors to espouse the Radical cause. The bulk of the Negro members counted for little except as pawns in the hands of white or black leaders. During the late winter and spring of 1868 the conventions completed their handiwork in all the states but Texas. Surprisingly enough, the constitutions formed under these unpromising conditions embraced many excellent features, notably the provisions for setting up free public school systems and for reforming the machinery of local government. All the constitutions also guaranteed the civil and political equality of the two races, and some of them carried the principle of disfranchising ex-Confederates beyond any previous limits.

To the old master class the new frames of government seemed a reversal of the natural order of society. Acclaiming themselves defenders of "Caucasian civilization" against the inroads of "African barbarism," they worked hard to prevent ratification; but the odds were too heavy against them. Only in Mississippi, where the white-disfranchisement clause was unusually harsh, did a majority of those voting reject the constitution. Elsewhere—in Arkansas, the Carolinas, Georgia,

THE PROCESS OF CONGRESSIONAL RECONSTRUCTION, 1866-1877

Alabama, Florida and Louisiana—the constitutions were approved, and the newly installed legislatures promptly ratified the Fourteenth Amendment. Though the amendment did not become a part of the federal Constitution until the next month, Congress in June, 1868, authorized the readmission of the seven states on the "fundamental condition" that they forever retain Negro suffrage. As Virginia and Texas had not yet completed the process of adopting constitutions, these two states, along with Mississippi, continued under martial rule. An important reason for hurrying action in the case of the other seven had been the Radical desire to secure their electoral support in the impending presidential election.

GRANT AND THE RADICALS

On May 20, 1868, while President Johnson's fate still hung in the balance before the Senate, the Radicals, calling themselves the National Union Republican party, met in Chicago to nominate his successor. Their unanimous choice fell on Ulysses S. Grant, with Schuyler Colfax of Indiana, Speaker of the House, for Vice-President. Thanks to their arrogant conduct in office, the Radicals needed all the popular support that Grant's war record would bring to the ticket; and since Andrew Jackson's time the electorate had accepted the idea that any military hero was capable of holding any office. As a matter of fact, Grant's political affiliations, so far as he had had any, had been Democratic, but shortly before the impeachment trial he had become friendly with the Radicals as a result of a bitter quarrel with Johnson. The platform praised congressional reconstruction and, anticipating the stand of the Democrats, pledged payment of the national debt in gold.

The opposition party faced a more difficult situation. Discredited by Southern secession and Northern Copperheadism, the Democrats stood at a parting of the ways. To recover their former strength, they must develop new leaders and new issues, a task hardly to be accomplished in one or even two presidential campaigns. There was an uncomfortable amount of truth in the remark of Kate Chase, the political-minded daughter of the Chief Justice, that "when the South seceded, the brains of the party went with it." Meeting in New York on July 4, the Democrats set about to clear their skirts of past offenses and strike out along fresh lines—a course which in time became known in party circles as the "New Departure."

The platform declared the questions of slavery and secession "settled for all time," pronounced Radical reconstruction "unconstitutional" and "revolutionary" and, as a bid for new support, advocated adoption of what was popularly called the "Ohio Idea." In this last demand the party leaders took advantage of a condition created by the fact that certain war-time bonds about to fall due had been issued under a statute requiring the interest to be paid in coin, the principal in "dollars." Hard times in the Midwest, especially in 1867, had caused the farmers to insist that the "bloated bondholders" be paid off in depreciated greenback dollars such as they themselves used. "The same currency for the bondholder and the ploughholder" was their cry, and in the Democrat, George H. Pendleton of Ohio, they found an able champion. The "Ohio Idea" appealed also to those Democrats who regarded the war debt as having been incurred in an unrighteous cause. Andrew Johnson had some support for the nomination, Pendleton and Thomas A. Hendricks of Indiana considerably more; but the Eastern Democrats, bent on undoing the mischief of the financial plank, succeeded on the twenty-second ballot in naming a sound-money man, ex-Governor Horatio Seymour of New York, who reluctantly accepted. The second place went to Francis P. Blair, Jr., of Missouri.

The campaign was savagely contested. Republican orators sidestepped the debt issue by insisting on the "treasonable" character of the Democratic party—a device that was soon to be known as "waving the bloody shirt." The Republicans enjoyed the advantage of the support of a multitude of office-holders and of the Carpetbag governments in the South, while the opposition suffered from internal discord over the financial question. Moreover, though both parties had promised pensions to the ex-soldiers, naturally the Republican pledge was looked upon as more certain of results. In the end, Grant secured 214 electoral votes to 80 for Seymour, but the actual state of public sentiment is better reflected by the fact that the winner received only 53 per cent of the popular votes (3,013,000) to 47 per cent (2,703,000) for his opponent. A careful analysis of the results shows that without the Negro vote Grant would have failed to poll a popular majority.

The new President was purely a product of the war. A graduate of West Point, he had left the army in 1854 rather than stand trial on a charge of drunkenness. He had turned next to farming, then to real estate, but without success. At the outbreak of the war he was working in his father's leather store at Galena, Illinois, for eight hundred dollars a year. This short, slouchy, taciturn man knew neither the theory nor the practice of politics. He had scarcely visited a state capital unless to capture it. Yet no President ever took over the reins with greater self-confidence. "The responsibilities of the position I feel," he said in his brief inaugural address, "but accept them without fear." As chief magistrate, he seemed to regard his office as a reward for past services rather than as a solemn public trust. Unfortunately, he turned for advice to men who had selfish and often corrupt interests to serve. Honorable himself, loyal to a fault to his friends, Grant retained unshaken his hold on the public, which continued to revere him as the "Hero of Appomattox."

The new administration proceeded at once to deal with the two questions raised by the campaign: the debt issue and the completion of reconstruction. The first was settled on March 18, 1869, when Congress formally pledged payment of the public debt in coin. As regards the Southern problem, Grant inclined at first to follow his own independent judgment, but he soon fell under the sway of the extremists, notably Benjamin F. Butler of Massachusetts, an unscrupulous politician who had mysteriously amassed a fortune while in the army. Taught by the recent election how necessary the Negro vote was for the predominance of their party, the Radicals proposed a Fifteenth Amendment providing that the right of suffrage should not be denied "on account of race, color, or previous condition of servitude." This amendment, of course, rendered mandatory what the Fourteenth Amendment had left optional. Congress imposed the requirement of ratification on the unreconstructed states of Virginia, Mississippi and Texas, and in the first three months of 1870 they were declared entitled to representation. But the process of reconstruction was not yet completed, for the newly installed Georgia legislature, dominated by the Democrats, had aroused the ire of the Radicals by expelling all the Negro members. Egged on by Butler, Congress in December, 1869, placed that state once more under military rule and, after requiring it to ratify the Fifteenth Amendment, admitted it to membership the following July. The Fifteenth Amendment had gone into effect nearly four months before.

THE SOUTHERN STRUGGLE FOR WHITE DOMINION

Though all the ex-Confederate states were now back in Congress, the Radical leaders had no thought of allowing them to manage their affairs without further interference. Reconstruction had resulted in standing the social pyramid on its apex; left alone, it would be sure to try to right itself. From the standpoint of the former dominant class, the forcible remaking of Southern life and politics was a process monstrous and intolerable. Even as a penalty for rebellion it seemed senseless since martial rule and Negro suffrage were imposed two or more years after the peace. Nor was the resentment lessened by the behavior of the ex-slaves. Though the rank and file went quietly about their tasks, delusions of grandeur dazzled others who, abetted by mulatto and white leaders from the North, did their utmost to stir the race to self-assertiveness. One outcome was the widespread formation of "Union Leagues," secret oath-bound societies composed mostly of Negroes and pledged to maintaining the new order of things. These bands often resorted to violence toward the old master class, waylaying men and burning houses and barns. All the latent Southern fears of a bloody race conflict revived, with the whites uncertain of survival. The better elements were at first driven to anger, then to genuine alarm.

In politics the fruits of the new racial equality appeared in the actions of the state governments installed as armed rule was withdrawn. These governments were dominated by Carpetbaggers in the higher offices, by Scalawags and Negroes in the lower. In the seven states reconstructed in 1868, four of the governors and ten of the United States Senators had never seen their respective commonwealths before the war. Every legislature contained a substantial contingent of Negroes, South Carolina's a majority. In a well-known contemporary account James S. Pike, a Northern newspaper man, described the lawmakers of Calhoun's state: "The Speaker is black, the Clerk is black, the door-keepers are black, the little pages are black, the chairman of the Ways and Means is black, and the chaplain is coal-black. . . . Every one esteems himself as good as his neighbor, and puts in his oar, apparently as often for love of riot and confusion as for anything else." But, he added, "underneath all this shocking burlesque upon legislative proceedings" lay "something very real to this uncouth and untutored multitude. . . . Seven years ago these men were raising corn and cotton under the whip of the overseer. Today they are raising points of order and questions of privilege." No wonder it was "their day of jubilee."

The new ruling class had, for the most part, no large property interests; in Alabama the taxes paid by the legislators were said to total less than a hundred dollars. Since the taxes would fall upon the hated aristocracy, the lawmakers saw no reason for staying their hand. Besides, there was real need of unusual expenditures for repairing roads, bridges and government buildings and for setting up a public school system. The mounting costs, however, were due chiefly to other reasons—the irresponsible character of those in power, their ignorance of the rudiments of finance and, most of all, downright corruption and fraud. A conservative estimate in 1872 put the increased indebtedness of the eleven states at about $132,000,000, much of it due to loans and guarantees to wildcat railroad enterprises. The orgy rose highest in Louisiana and South Carolina. In the latter state, a free restaurant and bar was maintained for the members, and among the articles purchased as legislative supplies were hams, perfumes, suspenders, bonnets, champagne and a coffin. The state's printing bills during the eight years of Carpetbag rule exceeded by nearly $718,000 the total amount expended for that purpose since 1789.

Southern whites, trained in a different school, stood aghast at the social and political chaos that threatened to engulf everything in life most dear to them. How could their proud civilization be saved from "Africanization"? From Congress no relief could be expected, and the Supreme Court, when appealed to, had turned a deaf ear to their pleas.[1] They therefore resorted to that form of secret terroristic resistance of which history offers so many parallels in the case of oppressed minorities. The Ku Klux Klan, the best known of these organizations, started innocently in 1866 at Pulaski, Tennessee, as a means of providing diversion for local youths

---

[1] In the cases of Mississippi *v.* Johnson, Georgia *v.* Stanton and *Ex parte* McCardle, all in 1867.

bored after the excitements of army life. When they observed that their weird nocturnal ceremonies aroused the superstitious dread of the Negroes, the members quickly took advantage of the fact. Appareled in ghostly manner and riding white-sheeted horses with muffled hoofs, they would visit the homes of unruly blacks and obnoxious whites at dead of night and warn them to behave or flee. The Pulaski idea spread like wildfire, causing similar groups or "dens" to spring up elsewhere in Tennessee and in the near-by states. A secret meeting at Nashville in May, 1867, joined the dens in a unified system under the name of the Invisible Empire of the South, with officers bearing awe-inspiring titles.

The use of violence increased as time passed. In many instances the midnight riders whipped and maimed their victims, or even killed them. Criminal bands, too, found it useful to don the eerie disguise for purposes of loot or private vengeance. The situation had already gotten out of hand when in March, 1869, the men at the head of the order decreed its disbandment. But this only made matters worse, for many of the dens refused to obey, and the withdrawal of conservative members gave the turbulent elements full sway. Through a misapprehension of the true state of affairs, Northerners applied the term "Ku Klux" to all secret movements of terrorism in the South. In reality, scores of others existed, including the powerful Knights of the White Camelia, which operated in the states from Texas to the Carolinas under nominal control of a supreme council at New Orleans.

Northern radicals saw in this lawlessness not evidence of their own folly, but fresh proof of the South's incorrigibility. Ben Butler, rising to his feet to demand stern repressive action, brandished before the House of Representatives a nightshirt stained with the blood of a flogged Carpetbagger in Mississippi. This incident gave rise to the expression, "waving the bloody shirt," and suggests the spirit in which Congress proceeded to deal with the Southern disorders. A series of measures—the force act of May, 1870, the federal elections law of February, 1871, and the Ku Klux act two months later—conferred on the President the power to break up the undercover societies and assure to the Negroes the civil and political equality guaranteed by the Fourteenth and Fifteenth amendments. For these purposes he might appoint commissioners to supervise congressional elections, employ armed force and suspend the writ of habeas corpus. As a result, hundreds of men were haled before the federal courts on charges of conspiracy, troops reappeared in many parts of the South and, for a time in the fall of 1871, the privilege of habeas corpus was denied in nine South Carolina counties. By 1872 "Ku Kluxing" had virtually disappeared. It is a sufficient commentary on the zeal of the Radicals surrounding Grant that the essential provisions of the force and Ku Klux acts were later found unconstitutional by the Supreme Court.[1]

Despite these many handicaps steady strides were made toward the recovery of white rule. As early as 1869 the Tennesseans turned out the obnoxious "Parson" Brownlow government. The federal legislation of 1870–1871, though it stopped the physical suppression of colored voters, taught the whites to substitute craft for force. A mere threat of violence had the desired effect of frightening Negroes from the polls and usually left no trace on which to base hostile court action. In 1870 and 1871 the Carpetbag governments toppled in North Carolina, Virginia and Georgia. In May of the next year Congress, in the general amnesty act, restored the right of officeholding to most of those disqualified under the Fourteenth Amendment, thereby allowing nearly one hundred

[1] U. S. v. Cruikshank (1875). U. S. v. Reese (1875) and U. S. v. Harris (1882).

thousand of the South's ablest citizens to return to active political life. Meanwhile the Scalawags, wearying of their alliance with ex-slaves and Northern adventurers, began to make common cause with their white neighbors. Aided by these circumstances, Alabama, Arkansas, Texas and Mississippi were "redeemed" in 1874 and 1875.

Only the presence of federal bayonets enabled the Carpetbaggers to retain their hold on the remaining commonwealths. During the presidential campaign of 1876 the opposing political elements contended fiercely for supremacy, with the result that the electoral votes of the three states were in doubt and the whole nation was thrown into confusion (see page 94). The seating of Samuel J. Tilden, the Democratic candidate, would have insured the removal of the troops, but, as it happened, his opponent's elevation had the same effect, for Rutherford B. Hayes represented that wing of the Republican party which had grown desperately tired of federal interference in Southern politics. Even before Hayes entered office the Carpetbag government fell in Florida, and early in 1877, with the withdrawal of the troops from South Carolina and Louisiana, those states lapsed back into native white control.

In this fashion the tortuous course of Reconstruction at last reached an end. Even more than the crushing defeat on the battlefield, Congress's high-handed procedure left rankling scars in Southern breasts. For a decade, more or less, the Radical Republicans had withheld the essentials of self-government from the South, causing that section to experience what the nation had never before known: military rule in time of peace. Moreover, Northern influences had degraded the traditional political standards, and retarded the progress of the Negroes toward responsible citizenship for at least a generation. Southerners who had endured the nightmare of Reconstruction could not easily forgive and forget.

Besides discouraging the revival of their former love of country, it arrayed the mass of whites against the Republican
party as an alien and "nigger" party, and helped make the
ex-Confederate states thick-and-thin supporters of the Democrats, an example which the old border slave states usually
followed. Out of a total of 369 electoral votes in 1880, the
"Solid South" cast 95, the border states 35 more—a substantial nucleus about which the Democrats of the North might
hope to rebuild their shattered strength.

Only in after years did the people come to realize that,
however galling Reconstruction had been, it might have
been worse. The collapse of the sectional war for independence had placed the South wholly at the mercy of its con-
queror; and the conditions imposed by Congress amounted
to what in an international conflict would have been the
terms of the peace treaty. Compared with the practice of
many other countries in dealing with vanquished minorities,
the Radicals had avoided the crowning blunders, for they
confiscated virtually no enemy land and put no one to death
for a political offense; and within seven years of Lee's surrender they granted amnesty to all but four or five hundred
of their recent foe. Even Jefferson Davis, though never pardoned, was left to his own devices after being held for two
years as a state prisoner. It was the considered opinion of
James Bryce in his great work *The American Commonwealth* that "there was never a civil war or rebellion . . . followed by so few severities." Nor did the Southern states ever
actually pay the full financial cost of Carpetbag misgovern-
ment. With the native whites once more in control, they proceeded to repudiate most of the bonded indebtedness, including in some instances part of the honestly incurred
prewar obligations. In this way they shook off approximately
$138,000,000. Only Mississippi and Texas refrained from
this dubious course.

ECONOMIC RECONSTRUCTION

The war required a remaking of the economic as well as the political fabric of the South. A transition had to be effected from a semifeudal order of society based on slavery to a modern system based on free labor. Ruined by the war, the great planters nevertheless tried to reëstablish agriculture on its former large-scale basis. That they should fail was inevitable, for they had to operate on borrowed capital, and they were hampered by the excessive taxation of the Carpetbag governments as well as by the shiftless character of their Negro labor. Salvation seemed possible only through a break-up of the great estates. Accordingly, the plan was widely adopted of disposing of small tracts to Negroes and poor whites. These people, unable to pay cash for the land, usually became share-croppers, receiving implements, seed and other aid from the landlords and giving in return a third or a half of what they grew.

From 1860 to 1880 the number of farm holdings in Dixie more than doubled, reaching a total of 1,500,000, with 300,-000 added in the next decade. As farms increased in number, the average holding shrank in size—from 335 acres at the beginning of the war to 214 in 1870, 153 in 1880 and 139 ten years later. Southern agriculture began to take on the appearance of the Northern small-farm system. But there were significant differences. Most of the farmers were tenants living in dire poverty, and in many cases the landlord, through his control over them, managed a whole group of farms as a unit, thus preserving many of the economic advantages of large-scale operation. Moreover, the tenants were constantly tempted to borrow from local money lenders at heavy rates of interest in anticipation of their harvest. This "lazy descent into hell," as Ben Tillman called it, plunged many into a bog of debt-peonage from which extrication proved heart-breakingly difficult.

Yet, in the long run, the subdivision of the big estates was to make possible an independent economic footing for both Negroes and poor whites, the two classes which, according to Hinton R. Helper's *The Impending Crisis,* had borne the yoke of slavery. Under the share-crop system any tenant could, and many did, save money and eventually buy their properties. But the new scheme more immediately benefited the small yeoman farmers, whose greater resources enabled them to buy the choicer lands without waiting. It was this latter element which, as the old gentry retired from the countryside to the towns, was to seize the reins of political power and, in the 1880's, give Southern public life a distinctly plebeian cast (see page 223). The agricultural reconstruction of the South involved the emancipation of the white masses in as real a sense as the Thirteenth Amendment had that of the Negroes.

Nor, in the long run, were the economic results harmful. Though the South continued to lag behind the North in agricultural methods, a larger number of farmers than before sought to conserve the soil through crop rotation and the use of fertilizers. Already by 1870 the average cotton yield an acre was greater than in 1860, and in eight years more the total crop exceeded that at the start of the war. Though cotton remained the principal reliance, increased attention was paid to other products—tobacco, fruits, vegetables, wheat, hay—so that in time the total value of these minor crops came to outstrip that of cotton. Moreover, the quickened spirit of enterprise made Southerners vision the possibility of developing manufactures. "If we have lost the victory on the field of fight," declared a South Carolina newspaper in 1881, "we can win it back in the work shop, in the factory, in an improved agriculture and horticulture, in our mines and in our schoolhouses." The industrializing trend of the eighties and nineties, however, formed part of an economic revolution that was transforming the whole nation, and will be considered in that connection.

THE DIPLOMATIC AFTERMATH

The successful conclusion of the Civil War freed the government's hands for a more active rôle in foreign affairs. In this new climate of opinion the old sentiment of "Manifest Destiny" reasserted itself, but now as a demand of Northerners—not of Southerners thirsting for additional slave territory. The heightened national feeling accounts for this expansionist zeal, but its particular direction was determined largely by the need, felt during the war, for adequate naval bases in the West Indies from which to cope with Confederate blockade runners. That these efforts at expansion failed was due mainly to Congress's reluctance to shoulder new burdens in the Caribbean while engaged in trying to solve the vexatious problem of race relations in the Southern states. In 1867 Johnson's Secretary of State, William H. Seward, negotiated a treaty to buy the Danish West Indies (the Virgin Islands) for $7,500,000, only to find that the Senate would not do its part. Grant as President pushed hard for the annexation of Santo Domingo, another of Seward's projects; but the treaty, when submitted to the Senate in 1870, failed of ratification. American expansion into the Caribbean had to await a time when new economic forces would dictate a more adventurous policy.

Yet the postwar zeal was not without effect, though the only substantial addition of territory occurred in a quite different latitude. Ever since 1861, when the Czar had freed the serfs, the Northern people had felt a sympathetic bond with Russia, and this sentiment had been strengthened by the appearance of her fleets in American waters two years later at a time when the United States still feared intervention by Great Britain and France. Hence Secretary Seward, shortly after the war, eagerly accepted Russia's offer to sell Alaska. The territory was unfamiliar to the American public, and one wag, wishing to compliment its best-known inhabitants as well as the parent nation, proposed calling it "Walrussia." The Senate in 1867 ratified the treaty by an almost unanimous vote, paying $7,200,000 for the acquisition. As the future was to disclose, the United States had unwittingly made a noble purchase.

A contributing motive in the annexation was the desire to prevent Alaska from falling eventually into the hands of England, whose Dominion of Canada lay next door. Anti-British feeling was intense because of that country's policy of friendly neutrality toward the Confederacy during the war. This sentiment helps to explain the popular attitude toward the activities of the Fenians, a secret brotherhood of Irish Americans who believed they might win freedom for their homeland by seizing Canada as a hostage. They raised large sums through appeals to the public; and in 1866, and again in 1870, they launched quixotic attacks against Canada despite the attempted vigilance of the United States authorities. The lesson was not lost on Great Britain. As mistress of many subject peoples, she had a striking demonstration of the importance of strict neutral conduct by other countries when her own sovereign authority should be challenged by civil strife.

The first effort to iron out Anglo-American differences, the Johnson-Clarendon convention in January, 1869, was overwhelmingly rejected by the Senate because the treaty contained no specific provision for defraying the damages which had been inflicted on United States commerce by the *Alabama* and other Confederate raiders. In an impassioned speech Senator Sumner, not content with asking $15,000,000 for these injuries, went on to claim $2,110,000,000 more for indirect damages due to the decline of the merchant marine, assistance given Confederate raiders in British colonial ports, and the effect of the premature recognition of Confederate belligerency on prolonging the conflict. His purpose was to induce Britain to meet this enormous debt by ceding Canada. Sumner's extravagant demands accorded with the expansionist mood of the moment, but for the time being chilled British ardor for reaching a settlement. In the end, however, the treaty of Washington was signed in May, 1871, providing for an adjustment of all outstanding difficulties.

This comprehensive document, after settling certain matters relating to the fisheries and the use of waters of common concern to Canada and the United States, referred the more contentious questions to a series of arbitral tribunals. A dispute over the international boundary along the channel separating Vancouver Island from the state of Washington was submitted to the German Emperor, who later decided in favor of the United States. In like manner the claims of British subjects for damages suffered from military operations during the Civil War were referred to a tribunal, which eventually made an award of nearly $2,000,000. As for the so-called *Alabama* claims, the thorniest problem of all, the treaty contained a frank expression of British "regret" for what had happened, and laid down certain principles which were to guide the court of arbitration and also to govern the observance of neutrality in the future. This court included one member each from Switzerland, Italy, Brazil, Britain and America. Meeting at Geneva, the members ruled out Sumner's indirect claims from consideration, and in September, 1872, granted direct damages of $15,500,000 for the *Alabama* and other depredations. The outcome was a signal triumph for the cause of international peace and good will.

Two great nations had found a better method than the sword for settling their differences.

SELECT BIBLIOGRAPHY

The Rise of Modern America. The changing American scene from 1865 to 1900 receives detailed treatment in Oberholtzer, *History of the United States since the Civil War,* and Rhodes, *History of the United States from the Compromise of 1850 to the McKinley-Bryan Campaign of 1896,* and in the large-scale co-operative works: Hart, ed., *American Nation;* Johnson, ed., *Chronicles of America Series;* and Schlesinger and Fox, eds., *History of American Life,* the last emphasizing social and cultural development. Individual volumes of these series are cited later in appropriate connections. Historical aspects of American civilization are presented pictorially in Gabriel, ed., *Pageant of America.* Hacker, Modley and Taylor, *The United States, a Graphic History,* illuminates the subject by means of "pictorial statistics." Among the standard biographical series are Morse, ed., *American Statesmen;* Oberholtzer, ed., *American Crisis Biographies;* and Nevins, ed., *American Political Leaders.* For briefer reference, the *Dictionary of American Biography,* edited by Allen Johnson and Dumas Malone, is indispensable. The most useful historical atlas is Paullin, *Atlas of the Historical Geography of the United States.*

Political Reconstruction. The general surveys include the accounts in Dunning, *Reconstruction Political and Economic;* Fleming, *Sequel of Appomattox;* Henry, *Story of Reconstruction;* Oberholtzer, *History,* I-III; Randall, *Civil War and Reconstruction;* Rhodes, *History,* IV-VII; and Schouler, *History,* VII. The constitutional aspects are considered in Hockett, *Constitutional History,* II; Lewis, *History of American Political Thought;* McLaughlin, *Constitutional History;* and Warren, *Supreme Court in United States History,* II. Among the biographies of leading figures are Winston, *Andrew Johnson;* Woodburn, *Thaddeus Stevens;* Haynes, *Charles Sumner;* Hesseltine, *U. S. Grant;* Mitchell, *Horatio Seymour;* Dyer, *William M. Evarts;* and Coulter, *William G. Brownlow.* For a thrilling portrayal of Lincoln's assassination, see Eisenschiml, *Why Was Lincoln Murdered?* Buck, *Road to Reunion,* analyzes the state of the public mind in the postwar years, while Hill, *Confederate Exodus to Latin America*, treats a little-known episode.

Peirce, *Freedmen's Bureau*, gives a short factual account of relief activities. Milton, *Age of Hate*, is a thoroughly documented study, concerned primarily with Johnson's rôle in Reconstruction. The same theme receives attention in Dewitt, *Impeachment and Trial of Andrew Johnson*, the standard work on this subject. In the *Critical Year* Beale argues the thesis that the South was kept from representation in order that Northern industrial interests might more easily accomplish their designs. The origins of the Fourteenth Amendment are studied in Kendrick, *Journal of the Joint Committee of Fifteen on Reconstruction*, and Flack, *Adoption of the Fourteenth Amendment*. Coleman treats the Grant-Seymour campaign in the *Election of 1868*. The Radical reorganization of the South is described in a host of monographs emphasizing the political effects in different states. Among the best of these special studies are Lonn, *Reconstruction in Louisiana*; Patton, *Unionism and Reconstruction in Tennessee*; Ramsdell, *Reconstruction in Texas*; Hamilton, *Reconstruction in North Carolina*; and Thompson, *Reconstruction in Georgia*. Of a broader scope is Simkins and Woody, *South Carolina during Reconstruction*, which traces social and economic as well as political changes. A corrective from the Negro point of view is provided by Taylor's two monographs: *Negro in South Carolina during Reconstruction*, and *Negro in the Reconstruction of Virginia*. Du Bois, *Black Reconstruction*, is a provocative interpretation. A neglected phase is developed in Knight, *Influence of Reconstruction in the South*. The secret movements of opposition to Carpetbag rule form the theme of Horn, *Invisible Empire*.

Economic Reconstruction.   The general lines of development are set forth in Chandler and others, *South in the Building of the Nation*, esp. VI; Thompson, *New South*; Bruce, *Rise of the New South*; and Nevins, *Emergence of Modern America*. On particular phases, see Hammond, *Cotton Industry*; Wesley, *Negro Labor*; Brooks, *Agrarian Revolution in Georgia*; Shugg, *Origins of Class Struggle in Louisiana*; and Scott, *Repudiation of State Debts*.

The Diplomatic Aftermath.   The principal trends are discussed in Bailey, *Diplomatic History*, and Bemis, *Diplomatic History*, as well as in the general works by Rhodes and Oberholtzer. The more detailed treatments include Smith, *Republican Expansionists of the Early Reconstruction Era;* Tansill, *Purchase of the Danish West Indies,* and his *United States and Santo Domingo;* Farrar, *Annexation of Russian America;* Shippee, *Canadian-American Relations;* and Callahan, *American Foreign Policy in Canadian Relations.* For the diplomacy of Grant's presidency Nevins, *Hamilton Fish,* is important.

Chapter II

THE ECONOMIC REVOLUTION,
1860–1890

NEW FORCES AT WORK

WHILE the smoke still lingered over the battlefields of the Civil War and the Carpetbaggers ran their piratical course, irresistible forces beneath the surface of events were altering the whole character of American life. The emergence of these new energies marked the advent of the Economic Revolution in the United States. In its lasting effects this transformation proved more significant than the war itself, for it wrought changes so sudden, so profound, so far-reaching, that even today the nation has scarcely learned to adjust itself to them. The Economic Revolution had its remote origins in eighteenth-century England, when inventors began to apply steam power and machinery to the making of textiles. In the early years of the next century ingenious Yankees availed themselves of the new methods, and contributed an important device of their own by introducing the principle of interchangeable parts into the manufacture of guns, plows, sewing machines and certain other articles, thus laying the foundations for the system of mass production. Before the Civil War, scattered mill districts sprang up in the East, and to some extent manufacturing secured a footing in the Midwest and even in parts of the South. The vast bulk of the people, however, continued to be engaged in other pursuits.

The prewar manufacturing establishments were nearly always of limited size and represented small outlays of capital. About two hundred companies in different parts of the land made mowers and reapers; approximately a thousand mills turned out cotton goods; and after petroleum was discovered in 1859 in Pennsylvania, the refining of oil also fell promptly into the hands of small producers. The dressing of meat was perhaps the most decentralized business of all. Every town had at least one slaughterhouse, New York City more than two hundred. In the nation's metropolis, the street now known as Fifth Avenue was oftentimes choked with cattle wending their way toward vast inclosures, where today stand hotels, apartment houses and fine retail shops. The better grades of manufactured goods generally came from abroad. Even large supplies of coal and copper were imported, so little had been done to develop America's own splendid resources. Nor did railway development pass much beyond the period of its infancy despite the great activity in the fifties. The little wheezy engines, the unheated, dimly lighted coaches, the iron rails, wooden bridges and single tracks, indicate the progress yet to be made. The typical fortunes before the war were small compared with later standards, and represented the profits reaped from shipping, real estate and merchandising rather than from manufactures, railroads, mines and stock manipulation.

On these tender industrial growths the Civil War had the effect of a hothouse. The government's military needs, currency inflation and the repeated additions to the protective tariff acted as a powerful stimulus. Nearly every branch of business grew lustily, with the most notable gains in woolen and leather goods and ready-to-wear clothing. Pittsburgh, lying in an area rich in coal, petroleum and natural gas, moved rapidly ahead in iron manufactures, while Chicago as the principal rail center of Middle America now took the lead in meat packing and certain other lines. The hot breath of war seemed also to quicken inventive talent. Though many of the inventions were for war purposes, the vast majority were

for the pursuits of peace. The number of patents issued in
1866 was twice as great as in 1860. Meanwhile, the discovery
of precious metals, beginning with the famous Comstock
Lode in Nevada in 1859, foreshadowed the enormous mineral development of the Far West.

To the generation that had saved the Union these war-
time advances acted as a mighty spur. Everywhere an intensely
materialistic spirit reigned—the urge to exploit new sources
of wealth, to make fortunes, to grasp power. The absence of
Southern members from Congress for nearly a decade after
1861 expedited such plans. It is not necessary to believe that
the Northern industrial and agrarian classes deliberately
blocked the South's return in order more easily to impose
their will upon the nation; but there can be no doubt that
they seized the opportunity to enact far-reaching legislation
of a kind which Southern opposition had earlier prevented.
From these years date the revival of high protection and its
conversion into a peace-time policy, the inauguration of free
homesteads for settlers, and the adoption of lavish federal aid
for the building of transcontinental railways.

What had gone before seemed pale by comparison. Evolution became revolution. Backed by a friendly federal government, businessmen bestirred themselves to meet the heavy
demands levied by the rapidly peopling West and by the necessities of the prostrate South, while they vigorously developed new markets in the North. Many circumstances contributed to the success of their efforts: brilliant industrial
leadership, inventive genius, abundant capital (largely from
abroad), the country's unmatched physical resources, the
wide extension of methods of mass production, and a plentiful supply of cheap labor. To these factors one may well add,
in the words of the census officials of 1900, America's favored
position as the largest area in the world "unrestricted by
customs, excises. or national prejudice," containing a people

who, because of their high standard of living, had "a larger consuming capacity than that of any other nation."

Within a single generation the United States changed from a country employing simple methods of tillage and importing the bulk of its manufactures from abroad into an industrialized nation with an export trade in farm and factory products that reached the outer fringes of the globe. "In short," asserted David A. Wells in *Recent Economic Changes* (1889), "to one whose present memory and life-experiences do not extend over a period of time more extensive than . . . a generation, the recital of the economic experiences and industrial conditions of the generation next preceding is very much akin to a recurrence to ancient history." Another economist, Edward Atkinson, writing two years later, added: "There has never been in the history of civilization a period, or a place, or a section of the earth in which science and invention have worked such progress or have created such opportunity for material welfare as in these United States in the period which has elapsed since the end of the civil war."

So swift and momentous a transition could not take place without uprooting established ways of life and necessitating profound economic and social readjustments. Never before had American society suffered from such a severe attack of "growing pains." The issues arising from the Civil War were soon submerged by the new interests of the nation. Southern Reconstruction touched only one part of the Union; the reconstruction imposed by the Economic Revolution affected the entire country. In the quarter of a century following Appomattox, the machine rose to its dominant place in industry, the dynamic modern city upset the ancient balance of American life, the rift between capital and labor dangerously widened, while inventions and conveniences galore came to relieve the drudgery of everyday living.

	1860	1880	1890
POPULATION AND WEALTH			
No. of people	31,443,321	50,155,783	62,622,250
Population per sq. mile	10.4	16.6	20.7
National wealth	$16,159,616,000	$43,642,000,000	$65,037,091,000
Wealth per capita	$513.9	$850.2	$1,038.6
AGRICULTURE			
No. of farms	2,044,077	4,008,907	4,564,641
Improved farm land in acres . .	163,110,720	284,771,042	357,616,755
Value of all farm property . . .	$7,980,493,063	$12,180,501,538	$16,082,267,689
Value of farm implements . . .	$246,118,141	$406,520,055	$494,247,467
Value of farm products	?	$2,212,540,927	$2,460,107,454
Wool production in pounds . .	60,264,913	232,500,000	276,000,000
Wheat production in bushels . .	173,104,924	498,549,868	399,262,000
Corn production in bushels . .	838,792,740	1,717,434,543	1,489,970,000
Cotton production in bales . . .	4,861,292	5,761,252	7,311,322
Cane sugar production in tons .	119,040	92,802	136,503
MANUFACTURING			
No. of plants	140,433	253,852	355,415
Value of domestic manufactures . .	$1,885,861,676	$5,369,579,191	$9,372,437,283
Capital invested in manufactures .	$1,009,855,715	$2,790,272,606	$6,525,156,486
No. of wage-earners	1,311,246	2,732,595	4,251,613
Importation of manufactures . .	$261,264,310	$423,699,010	$230,685,581
Exportation of manufactures . . .	$48,453,008	$121,818,298	$178,982,042
No. of patents issued in year named .	4,778	13,947	26,292
TRANSPORTATION			
Vessels built for foreign trade (tons) .	2,546,237	1,352,810	946,695
Vessels built for domestic purposes (tons)	2,807,631	2,715,224	3,477,802
Railway mileage in operation . . .	30,626	93,267	163,597
MINING			
Production of gold	$46,000,000	$36,000,000	$32,845,000
Silver production (commercial value)	$156,800	$34,717,000	$57,242,100
Tons of coal mined	13,044,680	63,822,830	140,866,931
Gallons of petroleum mined . .	21,000,000	1,104,017,166	1,924,552,224
Production of pig iron (tons) . .	821,223	3,835,191	9,202,703
Production of steel (tons) . . .	———	1,247,335	4,277,071
Production of copper (tons) . . .	7,200	27,000	115,966
COMMUNICATION			
No. of post offices	28,498	42,989	62,401
Mileage of post routes	227,908	343,888	427,990
Postal receipts	$8,518,067	$33,315,479	$60,882,098
No. of telegrams sent	?	29,215,509	63,258,762
BANKS AND SAVINGS			
No. of national banks	———	2,045	3,214
National bank capital	———	$454,606,073	$607,428,365
Deposits in national banks . . .	———	$833,701,034	$1,521,745,665
No. of savings banks	278	629	921
Deposits in savings banks . . .	$149,277,504	$819,106,973	$1,524,844,506
No. of depositors in savings banks . .	693,870	2,335,582	4,258,893

The social, political and intellectual consequences of the Economic Revolution form the central themes of American history since the Civil War. Industrial monopoly, the money question, tariff protection, political corruption, immigration, labor discontent, agrarian unrest, the turn to imperialism, the unequal distribution of wealth—such questions, new in kind or new in degree, illustrate the variety and gravity of the problems that beset society. In the long run, the nation had to decide whether political agencies and instrumentalities, devised in the eighteenth century for a few million people living under rural conditions with easy means of livelihood, could be adapted to the vital needs of a teeming population fast becoming urbanized and industrialized. The far-reaching character of the transformation can best be understood by examining its effects on the different sections of the country.

THE CHANGING WEST

In 1865 the frontier line ran northward through central Texas and followed in a general way the western limits of the states bordering the Mississippi, bulging outward to include the near-by parts of Kansas and Nebraska. East of this thin edge of settlement still lay much unoccupied land, and to the west stretched the unfenced prairies till they merged in the gray, sagebrush plains that extended to the foothills of the Rockies. Then, for nearly a thousand miles, the mountains lifted their enormous bulk, embosoming huge treasures of silver, gold and other metals. On the Pacific side lay more plains and deserts, reaching to the wooded coast ranges and the ocean. Settled districts adjoined San Francisco and San Diego, with others in the Willamette and Columbia valleys. Apart from scattered outposts of whites and notably the Mormon commonwealth in Utah, the vast inland region was inhabited by wild buffaloes and yet wilder Indians. It took twenty-five days to make the overland trip from St. Joseph on the Missouri by the stagecoach line, inaugurated in 1858, and more than ten days to carry mail to San Francisco by the swift pony express, established two years later. The Americans of 1865 looked upon this imperial expanse as a well-nigh inexhaustible reserve which would afford room for growth and provide farms and natural resources for generations to come. Yet, a quarter of a century later, virtually all the country was carved into states and territories, and what was regarded as the last of the arable lands had passed from the government into private possession. Never before had so far-flung a frontier been so quickly overrun by civilization.

Three factors speeded the white penetration of the Great West. One of these, the homestead act adopted by Congress in 1862, bestowed free farms of a hundred and sixty acres on persons who were citizens, or who had taken out naturalization papers, on condition that they occupy and improve the land for five years. The original statute was supplemented in the 1870's by acts making it possible for settlers to acquire additional acreage in unwooded and arid regions.[1] This legislation had a double purpose. On the one hand, it was designed to hurry settlement and develop the nation's resources; on the other, it served as a species of federal work relief for persons who found it difficult to make a living in the older parts of the country. By 1883 twenty-six million acres had been granted under the homestead act alone.

[1] The timber-culture act of 1873, in effect until 1891, authorized a grant of 160 acres on condition that a part of it be planted with trees. The desert-land law of 1877 provided for selling 640 acres at $1.25 an acre to anyone who would undertake their irrigation. In addition, an act of 1878 enabled settlers to buy, at $2.50 an acre, tracts of 160 acres that were valuable chiefly for stone and timber. A further 160 acres might be secured under the pre-emption law of 1841 (repealed in 1891) at $1.25 an acre. By the homestead act and these other enactments an individual might conceivably acquire a holding of 1280 acres or two square miles. Much fraud developed in the actual operation of this legislation.

The two other influences that hastened occupation were the construction of the transcontinental railways and the taming of the redskins. A rail line to the Pacific had long been agitated, but sectional rivalries in the 1850's had prevented agreement as to its location. In 1862 Congress decided on a central route and intrusted the undertaking to two companies: the Union Pacific, which should build westward from the Missouri River at Council Bluffs, Iowa; and the Central Pacific, a California corporation, which should build eastward toward an undetermined junction point. The law provided for heavy federal subsidies. As revised in 1864, it offered each company, in addition to a free right of way through the public domain, ten alternate sections (square miles) on each side of the track and a loan of United States bonds at the rate of $16,000, $32,000 or $48,000 a mile according as the roadbed traversed plain, plateau or mountain.

The active work of grading and track laying began in 1866, being directed at the one end by the Crédit Mobilier, a company formed by leading stockholders of the Union Pacific, and at the other by a similar construction company organized by Leland Stanford, president of the Central Pacific. Grenville M. Dodge was the chief engineer of the Union Pacific, and Theodore D. Judah of the Central Pacific. The Orient made its contribution toward success, for Stanford drew his laborers from Chinese coolies who, picturesquely garbed in basket hats and flapping pantaloons, performed even heavier toil in the mountain country than did the Irish "paddies" and ex-soldiers on the plains of Nebraska and Wyoming. Because of Indian hostility, every mile of the work required the protection of scouts, and the laborers at a moment's notice had to be ready to drop their picks and shovels for rifles and revolvers. The engineering difficulties often proved appalling. In traversing the Sierra Nevadas frequent tunnels and deep rock-cuttings were necessary, or long, high trestles had to be flung across ravines and gorges. Moreover, the construction gangs worked without steam shovels, steam derricks and other modern appliances. The road was almost literally handmade.

The imagination of the whole country was stirred as the two lines steadily closed the gap between them. Greedy for the federal subsidies, each group tried to outstrip the other in the amount of trackage laid. The results were often hasty and wasteful construction, a failure to follow the shortest route, and other practices sufficiently scandalous to provoke a later congressional investigation. Finally, on May 10, 1869, the two tracks met at Promontory Point, northwest of Ogden, Utah, a "wedding of the rails" celebrated with pomp and circumstance. Special arrangements made it possible for the blows of the silver sledge, which drove gold spikes into the connecting rails, to be recorded in telegraph stations throughout the land. The great adventure was at an end. Of the completed line, the Union Pacific had built 1086 miles, the Central Pacific 689. The two oceans, hitherto sundered by a month of laborious travel, now lay within a week's reach of each other.

The zeal for transcontinental roads did not spend itself with the Union Pacific. Even before it was completed, Congress had authorized the building of three others, one to the north of the original line and two to the south. Though these enterprises lacked the Union Pacific's advantage of direct financial aid from the government, they received even more princely land subsidies. In all, the public land given to the four lines amounted to a hundred and sixty-four thousand square miles, a total area twice the size of Minnesota. Some of it, however, had later to be forfeited because of noncompliance with the terms of grant. By 1884 four main roads joined the great central valley with the West Coast: the Northern Pacific, the Union Pacific, the Santa Fé (Atchison,

Topeka and Santa Fé) and the Southern Pacific. In addition, the Canadian Pacific, paralleling these tracks beyond the international border, furnished a route which American settlers often found it convenient to use.

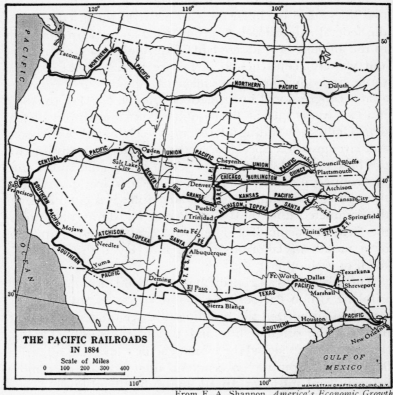

THE PACIFIC RAILROADS
IN 1884

Scale of Miles
0   100   200   300   400

From F. A. Shannon, *America's Economic Growth*

(The map shows only the principal lines)

The rival companies left no stone unturned to populate the Great West, for settled communities meant bigger revenues both from passenger and freight traffic and from the sale of railroad lands. They scattered boom literature and established agencies in the Eastern states and in Europe. They offered reduced rates of transportation and sometimes carried settlers free of charge. "Without the railroad," de-clared an enthusiastic Dakotan in the mid-eighties, "it would have required a century to accomplish what has been done in five years under its powerful influence."

Meanwhile, marked progress had been made in allaying the Indian peril. The story is not one to excite pride in the vaunted American spirit of fair play, but it amply illustrates the inexorable character of the conflict between two civiliza-tions, the one dynamic and acquisitive, the other static and satisfied with simple wants. In 1860 there were perhaps two hundred and twenty-five thousand Indians scattered through the Western country. In return for the government's annual gifts of food, munitions and clothing, the bulk of them had agreed to keep the peace, stay within their preserves and al-low migration along their trails. But as settlers penetrated into the region these solemn treaty stipulations proved mere scraps of paper. The land-hungry or gold-crazy whites viewed the redskin as a bar to the introduction of their "superior" way of life, and, whenever it suited their purpose, they seized his lands without further ado. In the end, the "Great White Father" at Washington acquiesced, removing the native bands to less desirable tracts. "Many, if not most, of our Indian wars," President Hayes told Congress in 1877, "have had their origin in broken promises and acts of injustice on our part."

Almost incessant conflict harassed the relations of the two races from 1862 to 1886, with an interlude of mere scatter-ing outbursts between 1867 and 1875. This tangled skein of petty wars there is no need to unravel in detail. Stung to re-prisals by white encroachments or the exactions of unprin-cipled government agents, the tribesmen would suddenly take to the warpath, burning, scalping and slaying. Savagery, unhappily, was not always on the one side. In November,

1864, a force under Colonel J. M. Chivington fell upon an unsuspecting Cheyenne village on Sand Creek in Colorado, killing and mutilating men, women and children. Like most frontier fighters, he shared General "Phil" Sheridan's senti-ment: "There are no good Indians but dead Indians." Partly as a result of the Chivington massacre, the govern-ment set up a commission, which in 1867–1868 succeeded not only in clearing away all legal obstacles to the building of railways through Indian country, but also in inducing most of the Apache, Comanche and Kiowa bands to remove to Indian Territory and other tribes to diminish their reser-vations or accept new ones off the beaten tracks. On the initiative of President Grant, an advocate of peace on the plains, Congress in 1869 created a Board of Indian Com-missioners to supervise government expenditures for the tribesmen. Though waste and graft were not eliminated, a temporary improvement of relations resulted.

A new source of friction presently appeared, however, causing hostilities to break out with renewed ferocity. This was the destruction of the buffalo herds, the Indian's main-stay of existence. From the buffalo or bison he obtained food, clothing, bowstrings and harness; the sale of hides provided his principal source of ready cash. Fifteen million of these great, ungainly beasts, it is estimated, were roving the plains at the close of the Civil War. The laborers on the railroads subsisted in large part on buffalo meat, William F. Cody winning his nickname of "Buffalo Bill" for killing forty-two hundred and eighty in eighteen months while a scout in the employ of the Kansas Pacific. The worst slaughter, however, occurred at the hands of hunters who, for the sake of what they called sport, killed them by the tens of thousands, leav-ing their carcasses for coyotes and buzzards. By the end of 1875 the vast southern herd had been virtually wiped out and, with the building of the Northern Pacific a few years

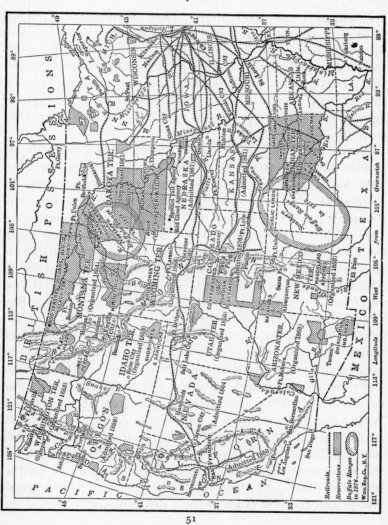

THE INDIAN COUNTRY
OF THE GREAT WEST
IN 1876

51

later, a similar fate befell the smaller northern herd. Already alarmed by the inroads of the white man, the Plains Sioux under Sitting Bull donned their war paint in 1876 to repel the onrush of gold prospectors into the Black Hills, which lay within their reservation. They annihilated General George A. Custer's command of two hundred and sixty-five men in a battle on the Little Big Horn in June, but they were soon quelled by superior force and dispossessed of the Black Hill country. Other notable uprisings took place among the Nez Percé Indians of the Pacific Northwest in 1877 and among the Apache in Arizona and New Mexico from 1882 to 1886.

Never before had the United States carried on such extensive Indian warfare. A list of the engagements between 1868 and 1882 alone fills over a hundred pages. Success depended on eternal watchfulness, instant preparedness and dauntless personal daring. One never knew when, out of the vast treeless expanse, murderous bands would swoop down on the border settlements. No names perhaps stand higher in the annals of plains fighting than those of Nelson A. Miles, George Crook and Ranald S. Mackenzie, all Civil War veterans. The savages counted among their great heroes Red Cloud, Crazy Horse and Sitting Bull of the Sioux and Geronimo of the Apache, who were true patriots from the red man's point of view. Every mile of Western railroad increased the military advantage of the whites, while the wanton destruction of game gave the red men little choice but to accept a dependent existence in government reservations. As the eighties drew toward a close, the Indian question had become less a military problem than one of how the tribesmen might be assimilated to American civilization. From the standpoint of settlement, the quarter-century of conflict had made the Great West safe for the more advanced people and placed the best lands at their disposal.

The first great rush of population resulted from the discovery of valuable metals in the mountainous regions. The Comstock Lode in Nevada, which yielded $145,000,000 worth of gold and silver ore in a little more than a decade after 1859, was but the most fabulous of these strikes. In the same year as its discovery prospectors found gold in Colorado, precipitating a stampede of perhaps a hundred thousand persons from all parts of the country for "Pike's Peak or Bust!" Some of the Argonauts set out on foot across the plains, shouldering packs; others pulled handcarts laden with meager supplies; still others went on horseback or in covered wagons. Subsequent years saw the opening of rich mineral deposits in eastern Washington and Oregon, western Montana, Idaho, New Mexico and Arizona.

In the wake of these finds boom towns sprang up like mushrooms in a lush soil. Of Virginia City, Montana, an inhabitant later wrote: "This human hive, numbering at least ten thousand people, was the product of ninety days. Into it were crowded all the elements of a rough and active civilization. . . . Gold was abundant, and every possible device was employed by the gamblers, the traders, the vile men and women that had come with the miners to the locality, to obtain it. Nearly every third cabin was a saloon. . . . Not a day or night passed which did not yield its full fruition of vice, quarrels, wounds, or murders." These lawless conditions, of course, represented only a passing phase, difficult to control because of remoteness from the seats of law and authority. In many cases, the more substantial elements of the community took the law into their own hands, forming bands of "vigilantes" to overthrow the reign of the badman and the desperado. Most of the adventurers failed to "strike it rich" or to gain anything at all but experience; but many of them stayed on in the new region, finding an unexpected source of livelihood in ranching and agriculture. Despite the vast mineral discoveries the new country itself benefited little, for the lion's share of the profits went to California mining corporations and stock speculators in the East.

Meanwhile, almost as powerful a magnet was drawing population into the plains region lying east of the Rockies. Cattle raising had long been an important industry in Texas; after the war enterprising men took advantage of the fact that, if Texas longhorns were driven north across the unfenced public domain, feeding as they went, they would arrive at the railway shipping points in Kansas and beyond fatter than when they started. Soon the "Long Drive" became a regular event, with herds of from one to ten thousand cattle moving ceaselessly northward. It is estimated that nearly four million reached Kansas between 1867 and 1880. Dodge City, on the newly built Santa Fé, became the greatest of the "cow towns," the focus of a reckless, turbulent life that won it a dubious repute as the "Bibulous Babylon of the Frontier." At the same time, the cattle industry spread rapidly into the Northern Great Plains, thanks to the demand of railway laborers and mining camps for fresh beef and to the improved marketing facilities afforded by the completion of the railroads and the introduction of the refrigerator car. Immense ranches appeared overnight, as it were, in Colorado, Wyoming, Montana, Kansas, Nebraska and Dakota, while Western cities began to flourish as centers for the slaughter and dressing of meat.

Ranching introduced a stirring and colorful mode of existence, with the picturesque cowboy as its central figure. "We led a free and hardy life, with horse and with rifle," Theodore Roosevelt wrote in fond memory of his own experiences in Dakota. "We worked under the scorching midsummer sun, when the wide plains shimmered and wavered in the heat; and we knew the freezing misery of riding night guard round the cattle in the late fall round-up. . . . But we felt the beat of hardy life in our veins and ours was the glory of work and the joy of living." The huge profits of the "cattle kings" fruited from the benevolent neglect of the government. After branding their animals the cowboys allowed them to range at will over the public domain, and then, at the spring round-up, sought them out for the drive to market. Cattle, costing only a few dollars, raised in vast numbers, fed on free pasturage and requiring few men to tend them, could be sold a few years later for five or six times the original investment. Peace did not always dwell on the ranges. The ranchers often waged petty wars with one another over cattle stealing, the changing of brands, and other such matters. Sometimes, to vary the routine, they made common cause against the sheep herders, who soon appeared to appropriate their share of free land and free grass.

By the late eighties the halcyon days of the cattlemen had passed. Not far behind the rancher creaked the covered wagon of the farmer or "nester," bringing his womenfolk and children, his draft horses, cows and pigs. Under the homestead act he staked off his claim, fenced it with barbed wire and, backed by the government, ousted the ranchman from the lands of which the latter held illegal possession. The crisscrossing lines of railroad further limited the freedom of the cattle kings, while quarantine measures adopted by various legislatures impeded the movement of herds following the Long Drive. Moreover, the immense profits had caused stock raising to expand far beyond market demands. Money had flowed into the business not only from Chicago, New York and other Eastern cities, but also from Great Britain, Germany and elsewhere. Of twenty great companies in Wyoming in 1884, half were English or Scotch, representing a combined capital of nearly $20,000,000. To make matters worse, the bitter winters of 1885–1886 and 1886–1887 killed vast numbers of the animals on the open range.

As a result, the romantic cattle kingdom began rapidly to give way to settled communities and prosaic fields of wheat, corn and oats. "It was right and necessary that this life should pass," declared Roosevelt in retrospect, "for the safety of our country lies in its being made the country of the small home-maker." In order to survive, the stock grower had to reorganize his business on a new basis—own his grazing grounds, provide winter feed, and breed better cattle. As a matter of fact, the inclosure of land led to no decline of the industry, for the total number of beef cattle in the United States nearly doubled between 1880 and 1900.

Abetted by the spread of farming in the West, the agricultural revolution swiftly gathered momentum. In the single decade from 1870 to 1880 the farms of the nation increased by an area as large as the British Isles and Sweden combined, and the next two decades added an amount equal to the British Isles and the three Scandinavian countries, with Holland, Belgium and Switzerland thrown in for good measure. Citrus fruits throve in California and Florida. Wisconsin took the lead in dairy products. Wheat growing was the main reliance in Dakota and Minnesota. South of the wheat belt, corn predominated in Iowa, Nebraska and Kansas, going to market either as grain or in the converted form of hogs. Many of the farmers were immigrants from Germany and the Scandinavian states, who settled in the new lands in groups. Between 1860 and 1880 the production of wheat and corn doubled, and it doubled again by the end of the century. Already by 1880 the United States had become the greatest wheat-exporting country in the world. One of the major causes of agrarian unrest grew out of the difficulties occasioned by crop surpluses.

The enormous agricultural production resulted in part from better methods of farming. With nearly every husbandman a landholder, mechanical power was necessary to make up for the dearth of hired labor. Improvement followed improvement, invention followed invention, causing many a homestead to be mortgaged to secure the new labor-saving implements. As early as 1860 steam engines were used in threshing. Improved windmills, suitable for semiarid regions, appeared on the market shortly after the Civil War. Particularly noteworthy was the twine binder, patented in 1878 and 1879 by John F. Appleby of Wisconsin, for, by increasing the speed of harvesting, this device correspondingly enlarged the amount of wheat that could profitably be grown. Meanwhile, through the establishment of the federal Department of Agriculture (1862) and the passage of the Morrill act the same year, the government did what it could to change husbandry from a traditional folk exercise to a science. The Morrill act offered each state a generous land grant as endowment for a college devoted chiefly to teaching agriculture and the mechanic arts. In this fashion the government disposed of over eleven million acres, aggregating an area nearly half as big as Indiana. The states applied the gift either to enlarging old institutions or to founding new ones. In the Hatch act of 1887 Congress went even further by subsidizing state experiment stations for carrying on agricultural research. Soon important discoveries began to be made in regard to soil fertility, animal breeding, and the methods of combating insect pests and the diseases of plants and animals. America led the world in developing scientific principles of farming.

The various influences that had quickened the westward flow of settlement from the early sixties led to the organization of the frontier country into self-governing communities. The number of inhabitants increased so amazingly as to provoke the saying that one couldn't tell the truth about the West without lying. From 1870 to 1890 Idaho grew sixfold, Montana and Wyoming each sevenfold, Colorado tenfold,

Washington fifteenfold. Already in the 1860's territorial governments had been erected in Nevada, Colorado, Dakota, Arizona, Idaho, Montana and Wyoming, leaving only the so-called Indian Territory without the usual provision. This tract, bounded by Kansas, Texas and Arkansas, represented the last remnant of the old Indian country and it lacked any government except that of the tribes. New states were also created, Nevada attaining this boon somewhat prematurely in 1864 because of Lincoln's need of support for his policies in Congress. Three years later Nebraska achieved statehood; Colorado followed in 1876; and in 1889–1890 six more states entered the Union: North and South Dakota, Montana, Washington, Idaho and Wyoming. Utah was denied the privilege until 1896, when the Mormon Church finally satisfied Congress that the national laws against polygamy were being enforced.

Meanwhile, the pressure of events had opened another territory to white occupation. For many years Westerners had cast hungry eyes on that section of Indian Territory known as Oklahoma, and from time to time troops ejected invading bands of "boomers." At last, in 1889, the government decided to begin opening it to settlement. For weeks before April 22, the appointed day, thousands of people gathered along the borders, held back by the soldiers. At exactly high noon a bugle shrilled, the troops stood aside, and the impatient throng—afoot, on horseback, in buggies and buckboards—began the pell-mell race for lands. By nightfall Guthrie, a tented city of ten thousand inhabitants, had sprung into being, while over the countryside flickering camp fires told of farm homes in the making. The district held sixty thousand people before the year closed. In 1890 Congress created the territory of Oklahoma. Besides an irregular area in the western part of Indian Territory, it included "No Man's Land," a narrow rectangular strip bordering the northernmost section of Texas. Statehood was denied until the twentieth century, as was also the case with New Mexico and Arizona, two much older territories.

Though public lands still remained for occupancy, the unbroken frontier was gone by 1890 and the best sites had passed into private hands. From earliest times the existence of undeveloped natural resources, open to all, had served as an insurance policy of national prosperity. By draining off the restless spirits from the older parts of the country, the West had also acted as a safety valve of discontent. The rugged individualism and incurable optimism which the frontier engendered became a part of the national habit of mind. Thus, what had been a great historic force, shaping American life and ideals from the first days of colonization, was slowing to a halt. Yet there occurred no sudden shock to the economic and social structure. The years ahead would reveal unsuspected vistas for husbandry as Americans learned the secret of dry farming and the government reclaimed countless acres through irrigation and drainage. The fact is that more land was patented for homestead and grazing purposes in the generation after 1890 than in the one before. Moreover, apart from the free government grants, an abundance of privately owned cheap land was available, while across the international border lay a vast pioneer zone open to those willing to cast in their lot with Canada. But most important of all was the rush of employment and opportunity afforded by the growth of urban centers and the launching of colossal new industries. Even in the 1870's and 1880's the city was beginning to cast its spell over men of spirit and ambition, an enchantment which presently came to exceed that exerted by the "lure of the sunset regions." If the townward drift meant turning American thought and energy in a different direction, at least it provided equally challenging opportunities for individual initiative, enterprise and achievement.

THE ONRUSH OF INDUSTRIALISM

Just as the agricultural revolution transformed the nation's traditional industry, so the revolution in manufacturing, mining and transportation girded the American people for even greater undertakings. Though the Great West contributed to these newer fields of endeavor, the principal activity took place in the older parts of the country. The progress in manufacturing since the Civil War, according to the United States Industrial Commission in 1902, was "probably the most rapid change in the methods of industry observable at any time in history." Through the substitution of machinery for men, the widespread introduction of steam for water power, and an ever greater application of the system of interchangeable parts, factory production grew at an unparalleled pace. The records of the Patent Office shed some light upon the rôle played by invention. With less than sixty-two thousand patents granted in the entire period before 1865, the number during the remainder of the century reached nearly six hundred and thirty-eight thousand.

Until the 1880's farming continued to be the chief fount of national wealth, but the census of 1890 gave first place to manufacturing, and ten years later the value of manufactured products had risen to more than twice that of agricultural. From less than two billion dollars in 1860, the output of American mills and shops had trebled by 1880. The rate of growth in particular industries was even more astonishing. The share of labor-saving machinery in this advance appears in the fact that, while from 1860 to 1890 the number of factory hands increased threefold, the total product increased fivefold. By 1894 the United States had jumped from fourth place as a manufacturing nation, its rank in 1860, to first in all the world. At that time its output exceeded the combined total of Great Britain and Germany.

The chief development occurred in the East, where southern New England, eastern and southern New York and large sections of Pennsylvania and New Jersey became thoroughly industrialized. New England excelled in textiles, the finer grades of paper, and boots and shoes; Pennsylvania in tanning and iron and steel products; New Jersey in silks; New York state in the bewildering variety and total value of her wares. At the same time factories spread into the Midwest in such numbers as to cause the center of manufactures in the nation to shift from western Pennsylvania in 1860 to northeastern Ohio (near Canton) in 1890. Broadly speaking, Middle America specialized in the fabrication of farm implements, railway supplies, building materials, furniture, prepared foods and drinks. Chicago, the center of a great network of transportation facilities, possessed nearly eight hundred woodworking establishments, machine shops and metal works by 1880, besides more than a hundred breweries and distilleries.

During these years, too, the factory system began its extensive invasion of Dixie, attracted by abundant raw materials, cheap labor and cheap power. "Bring the mills to the cotton!" was the cry that rang through the seaboard South in the 1880's. Soon the fall line of the rivers became dotted with factories built out of the meager savings of the people near by and manned by poor whites—men, women and children—from the foothill and mountain country. Between 1880 and 1890 the number of spindles and looms almost trebled, and another decade found nearly half the nation's cotton mills clustered there. The manufacture of iron, equally favored by natural conditions, made as notable progress. Great beds of ore were discovered near deposits of coal and limestone, as if Nature had purposely associated the necessary ingredients for reducing the crude metal. During the eighties fifty new blast furnaces were erected in Alabama,

Tennessee and Virginia. Cottonseed mills, tobacco factories, furniture establishments, vehicle factories and canneries represented other important businesses. The prime movers in Southern industrialization were usually of the old yeoman strain rather than of the class which had ruled in prewar days, and Northern capital played a negligible part until toward the end of the century when the certainty of profits had been clearly demonstrated. An observer in 1889 scarcely needed to point out that "the nonsense that it is beneath the dignity of any man or woman to work for a living is pretty much eliminated from the Southern mind."

The revolution in manufacturing everywhere rested on the exploitation of vast fields of coal and iron, the two minerals that have most vitally affected modern industrial civilization. Large coal beds were uncovered along the Appalachian system and also in Ohio, Indiana and Illinois. With improved transportation facilities and an increased use of steam-driven machinery, production grew tenfold from 1860 to 1890. Meantime, to meet the voracious demands of industry, the yield of iron ore in western Pennsylvania advanced by leaps and bounds, and in the 1880's great ranges in the Lake Superior region began to be developed. Besides being extremely rich and pure, these new deposits lay near the surface, which made it possible to mine them with labor-saving machines. From 1860 to 1890 pig-iron production multiplied elevenfold. At the same time, the manufacture of iron and steel products was speeded by new methods of smelting, notably the Bessemer process, which forced a cold blast through the molten metal, thereby eliminating carbon impurities.[1]

[1] This process, named after Henry Bessemer, was introduced into the United States from England in 1864. It had been discovered independently in 1851 by William Kelly of Kentucky. Toward the end of the century it was supplanted by the Siemens-Martin or open-hearth process, which is superior for less pure ores.

The newest source of subsurface wealth, petroleum, underwent an even more spectacular development. Thanks to the
introduction of tank cars and pipe lines and to the discovery
of new uses for oil and its derivatives, the output increased
ninetyfold in the three decades. Still other stores of minerals
came from the Great West. In the eighties copper mines
were opened in Arizona and Montana, rivaling the product
hitherto furnished by Michigan. Large-scale silver mining
was another venture, growing out of the discoveries in Nevada, Colorado and elsewhere. From a value of $157,000 in
1860, the yield reached $36,000,000 in 1873, with an even
larger return in the years to follow—a fact which was to
have important political reverberations. Gold production,
on the other hand, having reached its peak in 1854, steadily
declined from 1872 to 1893.

Meanwhile, all over the land, a spider web of rails was
being spun to draw the remotest outposts into the common
whole and everywhere to stimulate commercial enterprise.
From thirty thousand miles of track in 1860, the number
trebled by 1880, reaching a total of a hundred and sixty-four
thousand ten years later. Not only in the new West but also
in the older North the railroads multiplied, and pushed
southward to spur the industrial development of Dixie.
Moreover, expansion in mileage was attended by great improvements in service. Iron rails were replaced with steel in
order to insure both heavier carrying capacity and greater
safety. The inventor George Pullman in 1864 added to the
comfort of travel through his ingenious "palace cars," described by one enthusiast as "gorgeous traveling hotels."
Four years later he contrived the separate diner. In 1872
George Westinghouse took out his first patent on the automatic air brake, a device which permitted the engineer, by
means of a steam-driven air pump, to set the brakes simultaneously throughout the whole train. Automatic car coup-

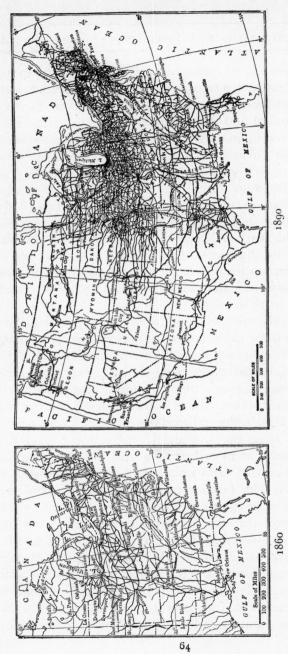

THE REVOLUTION IN RAIL TRANSPORTATION, 1860–1890

In these thirty years the railway attained an importance greater than in any other country. "It is the locomotive," wrote William Barrows in *The United States of Yesterday and of To-morrow* (1887), "which has hauled up the United States to the front in the procession of the nations."

ling came into use at about the same time. As more and
more short roads were linked into through lines and a standard gauge of track was adopted, another betterment of service
resulted. A traveler from the Atlantic Seaboard to the Mississippi before 1870 might have been obliged to change
trains a half-dozen times. Now this inconvenience came to be
the exception rather than the rule.

No less profound were the new strides in communication
—a revolution based less on steam than on electricity, whose
possibilities were just beginning to be glimpsed. In harness-
ing electric power to the service of mankind Americans led
the way, notably Thomas A. Edison who from 1868 to 1900
took out nearly eight hundred patents, mostly in this field.
His invention of quadruplex telegraphy in 1874 allowed two
messages to be sent simultaneously from opposite ends of the
same line, thus multiplying the carrying capacity of the
wires. In 1866 the principle of the telegraph was applied,
after several unsuccessful trials, to cable communication
with Europe, a great engineering feat for which Cyrus W.
Field was responsible.

Ten years later a new marvel, the telephone, was invented
by Professor Alexander Graham Bell of Boston University as
a by-product of his interest in teaching the deaf to talk.
Though at first it was hardly more than a mechanical curiosity—the London *Times* called it the "latest American hum-
bug"—improvements by Edison, Francis Blake, John J. Carty
and others soon rendered the telephone an efficient instrument. The invention of a multiple switchboard by Leroy B.
Firman in 1879 greatly extended its usefulness and assured
the telephone's commercial success. From 1880 to 1890 the
number of subscribers rose from fifty thousand to two hundred and fifty. At the same time the reach of the telephone
grew constantly greater. By 1892 Boston and New York were
chatting with Washington, Chicago and Milwaukee. As

presidential candidate in 1896 William McKinley talked from his home at Canton, Ohio, with his campaign managers in thirty-eight states. When the century ended, the United States had twice as many telephones as all Europe.

Meanwhile the postal service was placed on a modern basis. Free delivery was introduced in the larger cities in 1863, the system of money orders a year later. In 1883 the rate for single letters was cut from three to two cents a half-ounce and, in 1885, to two cents an ounce. It would be diffi-cult to overestimate the importance of the improved means of transportation and communication. They not only pro-moted business development, but they also helped to break down regional isolation and contributed in a thousand ways to greater social solidarity.

THE URBAN TREND

If the plantation was the typical unit of prewar Southern society and the small farm of the Northern agricultural sys-tem, so the modern city was the nerve center of the rising industrial order. Within its borders were concentrated all the new economic forces: the huge accumulations of capital, the business and financial institutions, the sprawling railroad yards, the gaunt smoky factories, the white-collar middle classes, the motley army of wage-earners. Recruited from the countryside and from lands across the sea, villages grew into towns and towns sprang into cities almost overnight. Urban centers, said a contemporary, "start like Jonah's gourd, but grow and endure like the oaks of Bashan, and promise to live like the cedars of Lebanon." In 1830 one out of every fifteen persons dwelt in places of 8000 or over; in 1860 nearly one out of every six; and in 1890 three out of ten. Moreover, considerably more than half of this increasing horde of city folk had come to reside in communities of 25,000 or more. The older rural districts of the Midwest and

the East suffered shocking losses, due to the attractions of
the near-by city or of free farms on the frontier. From 1880
to 1890, 755 townships out of 1316 in Ohio declined in
population; 800 out of 1424 in Illinois. Two fifths of Pennsylvania and nearly seven tenths of New York state experienced a similar eclipse. In New England the townward
exodus, greater than elsewhere, left mute witnesses in deserted hill villages and abandoned farms. "The crumbling
ruins of the foundations only are left to mark the site,"
wrote one observer, "or perchance . . . the tottering well
sweep and perennial lilac bush still stand as mementoes of
once happy homes."

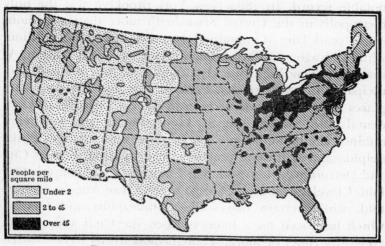

People per
square mile

░ Under 2

▨ 2 to 45

■ Over 45

DISTRIBUTION OF POPULATION IN 1890

Though the postwar years beheld the movement at greatly
increased tempo, the trend to the city had long been in
process. In the century from 1790 to 1890 the urban inhabitants of the republic had grown 139-fold while the total
population had increased but 16-fold—this despite the titanic
energies that had gone into subduing the wilderness. The

forces responsible for the rise of cities were world-wide in their sweep. By 1891 London and Paris had doubled their population of mid-century and Berlin had more than quadrupled hers; and in all these countries the number of rural dwellers had lost ground. Everywhere the causes were the same: the superior opportunities of urban life; the extension of railways, which not only made cities easier of access, but also simplified the problem of feeding masses of people collected at a single point; and, finally, the dwindling profits of agriculture which, with the increased use of labor-saving implements, hastened the townward exodus.

Even as compared with Europe, American cities scored a notable record. In 1860 New York-Brooklyn was the only metropolis in the United States with more than a million; thirty years later it contained over two and a half million, while Chicago and Philadelphia each exceeded a million. At that time New York-Brooklyn (which became a single municipality in 1898) rivaled Paris in size, and the two other places ranked sixth and seventh in the constellation of Occidental cities. Meanwhile, St. Louis, Boston and Baltimore attained the half-million class. In these three decades Philadelphia and Baltimore doubled in population, Kansas City and Detroit grew fourfold, San Francisco and Memphis fivefold, Cleveland sixfold, Chicago tenfold, Los Angeles twentyfold, while certain places like Minneapolis and Omaha, which had been mere hamlets when the Civil War began, grew fifty times or more. Though most towns were smaller, everywhere they sought to copy the enterprise and ways of the bigger ones. In Josiah Strong's phrase, the city was "the mighty heart of the body politic, sending its streams of life pulsating to the very finger-tips of the whole land." As the centers of wealth and economic power, moreover, the great cities molded business institutions and transportation facilities to suit their own particular needs and advantage, thus

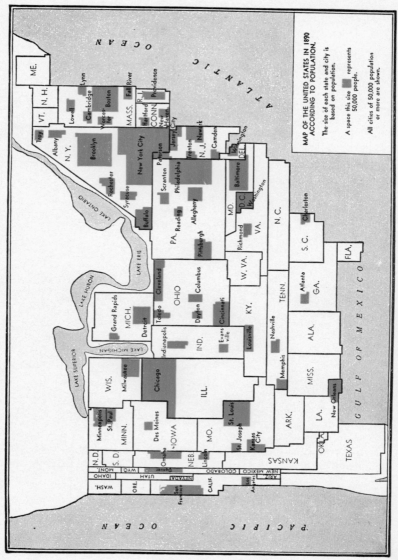

THE POPULOUS STATES IN 1890

MAP OF THE UNITED STATES IN 1890
ACCORDING TO POPULATION.

The size of each state and city is
based on population.

A space this size represents
50,000 people.

All cities of 50,000 population
or more are shown.

increasing the difficulties from which the farm dwellers suffered during these years.

Earlier American cities had been hardly more than overgrown villages; now, as urban populations thickened, they began to change into modern municipalities. In some measure European experience furnished a guide, but in other respects, notably rapid transit and lighting, the United States pointed the way for the Old World. Volunteer fire companies were abandoned by New York in 1865 and by Philadelphia in 1871 in order to make way for full-time, paid fire departments. The urgent need for swifter conveyance, no longer adequately met by horse cars, led New York in 1868 to introduce steam-drawn trains on elevated rails high above the streets. Five years later San Francisco demonstrated the utility of the cable car, contrived by Andrew S. Hallidie and operated by means of a grappling device reaching downward to an endless steel cable moving in a slotted trench between the tracks. Somewhat later came the even more successful trolley car, first installed for public use in 1888 at Richmond, Virginia, and adopted within three years by fifty-one towns. In 1895 Boston began the construction of the first American subway.

Great activity also occurred in building bridges in order to link more closely those parts of cities separated by water. The most notable achievement, the Brooklyn Bridge, required thirteen years for its completion in 1883. A monument to the engineering genius of Washington A. Roebling, the majestic structure was over a mile in length. City streets, hitherto ill paved when paved at all, showed great improvement as asphalt and brick surfacing passed into more general use. Serious attention was also given, for the first time, to problems of sewage and garbage disposal, and from 1860 to 1890 the number of public waterworks increased nearly thirteenfold.

Meanwhile, better illumination came to the aid of city dwellers, helping to dispel much of the darkness of night life as well as some of its dangers. Improving upon the efforts of others, Charles F. Brush of Cleveland in 1878 devised a feasible system of arc lights suitable for streets and public squares. The problem of indoor illumination, however, remained unsolved until Edison two years later patented the first practicable incandescent electric light. Advances were also made in gas illumination, notably after Thaddeus S. C. Lowe's discovery in 1873 of the process of manufacturing water gas. Though some municipalities were quicker than others in adopting the new facilities, urban life everywhere assumed a different aspect, causing towns on the advancing frontier to flaunt conveniences and comforts of living which the noblest centers had lacked a generation before.

The nation's pride in these new accomplishments found expression in two great urban expositions, the first of the kind ever to be held in the United States: the Philadelphia Centennial Exhibition in 1876, and the World's Fair at Chicago in 1893. The earlier one was designed to commemorate the centenary of American independence. The later marked the four-hundredth anniversary of Columbus's discovery, though a year tardy in doing so. Behind these historical occasions, however, lay the desire to offer visual evidence that in the arts and technology of modern life the United States could court comparison with the most progressive countries of Europe. At Philadelphia, Machinery Hall particularly entranced the visitors, who in this and other buildings could see a thousand articles manufactured before their eyes. Chicago, without neglecting mechanical prowess, accented the nation's progress in artistic and cultural fields. That the second and greater of these spectacles took place in the midland metropolis signalized the westward sweep of urbanization, and awakened Easterners to the new significance of Middle

America in the national life. Moreover, to these fairs flocked
nearly fifteen million Americans, many of whom had never
been more than a buggy's drive away from home. There, for
the first time, they saw the wonders of their own and other
lands. As a result, the two expositions quickened the spread
of better standards of taste and improved ways of life.

These gorgeous displays, unhappily, evidenced only the
hopeful aspects of urban achievement. City life in undress
offered a different picture, due to haste of growth and the
low state of public morals. The larger places presented startling contrasts of poverty and riches, squalor matching splendor, urban vice contending with civic virtue. New York reminded one English visitor of "a lady in ball costume, with
diamonds in her ears, and her toes out at her boots." In the
slums huddled the newly arrived immigrant families, living
under conditions which made for diseased minds as well as
diseased bodies. Organized crime, long characteristic of frontier communities, now shifted to the great population centers, thanks to the concentration of wealth there and the
inadequacy of police protection. It may not be without significance that the bloody repulse of the James Boys' attempt
to loot the bank at Northfield, Minnesota, in 1876 was followed two years later by the first great urban criminal exploit, the successful robbery of the Manhattan Savings Institution in New York of nearly three million dollars by
"Western George" Leslie and his gang. The increase of lawlessness was due, in part, to the collusion of municipal officials with the wrongdoers.

During these years the boss and the machine, fostered by
the most vicious elements in city life, rose to a position of
dominance. As in national politics, predatory men found
opportunities for illicit gain in lax law enforcement, and particularly in obtaining control, by whatever means, of the expanding public utilities. "Where the carcass is," Francis

Parkman bitterly observed, "the vultures gather together." Contracts for street paving and other public works provided one source of graft, but more profitable were the municipal franchises granted to private individuals and companies for supplying water, light and rapid transit, usually with few or no safeguards for the public. One of the sensations of Grant's first term was the exposure of the Tweed Ring in New York, whose members in two and a half years swelled the city's debt by $70,000,000, most of it going into their own pockets. Though Tweed himself was finally brought to justice, most of his confederates escaped, and later years found New York again suffering from Tammany misrule. Other places fared hardly better—Philadelphia with its Gas Ring, Minneapolis under the corrupt "Doc" Alonzo Ames, San Francisco under "Blind Boss" Buckley.

As James Bryce wrote in 1888, "There is not a city with a population exceeding 200,000 where the poison germs have not sprung into a vigorous life; and in some of the smaller ones, down to 70,000, it needs no microscope to note the results of their growth." He called municipal government "the one conspicuous failure of the United States." The truth is that, while long experience had taught Americans how to rule populations scattered over large areas, they had yet to learn how to govern densely packed urban centers. Fortunately, as will be seen later, this failure did not prevent cities from exerting a fructifying influence on cultural life.

SELECT BIBLIOGRAPHY

New Forces at Work. Faulkner, *Economic History,* Kirkland, *History of American Economic Life,* and Shannon, *America's Economic Growth,* deal briefly with the principal aspects of the Economic Revolution. Much relevant material also appears in Nevins, *Emergence of Modern America.*

The Changing West. Among the general treatments are

Paxson, *History of the American Frontier;* Clark, *West in American History;* Webb, *Great Plains;* and Rister, *Southwestern Frontier.* The study of particular phases of post-Civil War Western history has produced a large and growing literature. For the operation of federal land legislation Hibbard, *History of Public Land Policies,* is helpful. The more useful works on the transcontinental roads include Riegel, *Story of the Western Railroads;* Haney, *Congressional History of Railways;* Smalley, *History of the Northern Pacific Railroad;* Hedges, *Henry Villard and the Railways of the Northwest;* and Sabin, *Building the Pacific Railway.* Leading figures in the Central Pacific form the subject matter of Clark, *Leland Stanford,* and Lewis, *Big Four.* For border warfare the student should turn to Macleod, *American Indian Frontier;* Paxson, *Last American Frontier;* Wellman, *Death on the Prairie,* and *Death in the Desert;* Hyde, *Red Cloud's Folk;* and Vestal, *Sitting Bull.* Branch, *Hunting the Buffalo,* treats a special aspect of the Indians' plight.

The mining development of the Far West comes in for attention in Trimble, *Mining Advance into the Inland Empire;* Rickard, *History of American Mining;* Quiett, *Pay Dirt;* and Wilson, *Silver Stampede.* DeVoto, *Mark Twain's America,* affords vivid glimpses of life in the mining regions. Notable among the works dealing with the cattle kingdom, its economic and social significance, are Branch, *Cowboy and His Interpreters;* Dale, *Range Cattle Industry;* Osgood, *Day of the Cattleman;* Pelzer, *Cattlemen's Frontier;* Rister, *Southern Plainsmen;* Streeter, *Prairie Trails and Cow Towns;* Wellman, *Trampling Herd;* and Wright, *Dodge City.* Information concerning the agricultural revolution appears in Schmidt and Ross, *Readings in the Economic History of American Agriculture.* The opening of Indian Territory supplies the theme of Gittinger, *Formation of the State of Oklahoma.* Dick, *Sod-House Frontier,* and Briggs, *Frontiers of the Northwest,* give lively pictures of pioneer days and ways.

The Onrush of Industrialism. Clark, *History of Manufactures,* the standard general work, devotes one volume to the years 1860–1914. Special studies include Allen, *Shoe Industry;* Clemen, *American Livestock and Meat Industry;* Cole, *American Wool Manufacture;* Copeland, *Cotton Manufacturing Industry;* Giddens, *Birth of the Oil Industry;* Holbrook, *Iron Brew;* Kuhlman, *Development of the Flour-Milling Industry;* Lawrence, *Petroleum*

Comes of Age; Smith, *Story of Iron and Steel;* and Woodworth, *American Tool Making.* Hutchinson, *McCormick,* portrays the leading figure in the manufacture of farm machinery. Southern industrial advance is the special concern of Bruce, *Rise of the New South,* Armes, *Story of Coal and Iron in Alabama,* and Mitchell, *Rise of Cotton Mills,* with biographical sidelights provided by Jenkins, *James B. Duke,* and Winston, *Builder of the New South* (D. A. Tompkins). Among the best surveys of technological progress are Byrn, *Progress of Invention,* Burlingame, *Engines of Democracy,* and Kaempffert, *Popular History of American Invention,* which should be supplemented by such detailed accounts as Casson, *History of the Telephone;* Husband, *Story of the Pullman Car;* and Martin and Coles, *Story of Electricity.* Lives of outstanding inventors include Dyer and Martin, *Edison;* Mackenzie, *Bell;* and Prout, *Westinghouse.*

The Urban Trend.   Schlesinger, *Rise of the City,* treats many phases of the theme, while Weber, *Growth of Cities,* considers it in its world-wide aspects. Wilson, *Hill Country of Northern New England,* depicts the disastrous effects of the rural exodus in New England. Schuyler, *Roeblings,* tells of two notable bridge builders. For the Tweed Ring, see Paine, *Th. Nast,* and Flick, *Samuel J. Tilden.*

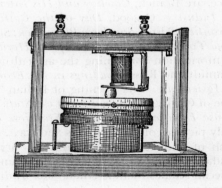

Chapter III

POLITICAL TRANSITION, 1869-1877

PUBLIC MORALS AND NATIONAL POLITICS

GRANT'S eight years in the White House marked a significant transition in national politics. As questions concerning Southern Reconstruction receded into the background, new issues growing out of the changing economic order thrust themselves forward. "To the great mass of our population," Francis Parkman wrote in 1869, "the clearing of trees, the acquiring of new territory, the building of cities, the multiplication of railroads, steamboats, and telegraph lines, the growth of trade and manufactures, the opening of mines, with the resulting fine houses, fine clothes, and sumptuous fare, constitute the real sum and substance of progress and civilization." Aspiring men, thirsty for wealth and power, demanded special privileges from the national, state and local governments, and cared not about the means they used to gain their ends. They embarked upon their schemes at a time when the country was suffering a moral relapse from the lofty idealism of war days, and when the upswing of prosperity continuing from the war made people careless as regards official rectitude. Tweedism in the cities and Carpetbaggery in the Southern states illustrated on a local scale the diseased condition of national political life.

"The power of wealth, individual and associated, concentrated and diffused, constitutes the new danger that is threatening us with its portentous and increasing dimensions," declared Senator Henry Wilson of Massachusetts, ancient foe of the "Slave Power," in 1869. Another early

Republican, George W. Julian of Indiana, pointed to the "railway power," possessing a "consolidated capital of $5,-000,000,000," and "sapping and mining its way through the consciences" of those vested with political authority. "Men buy their way into the Senate," wrote James Russell Lowell, "and, of course, expect a profit on their investment." As if to corroborate such views, a congressional investigating committee reported in 1873: "The country is fast becoming filled with gigantic corporations wielding and controlling immense aggregations of money and thereby commanding great influence and power. It is notorious in many state legislatures that these influences are often controlling."

(President Grant possessed neither the experience nor the will to stem the materialistic tide in politics. As a man who had himself striven vainly against poverty, he readily accepted financial success as the "sum and substance of progress and civilization," and hence he viewed the new tendencies with complacency.) Though his personal integrity was undoubted, he and members of his family received loans from the banks of Jay Cooke at a time when the Northern Pacific and other concerns in which Cooke was interested wanted governmental favors. Grant, moreover, openly consorted with "Jim" Fisk, an unscrupulous stock manipulator, and accepted costly gifts from persons whose motives were dubious, if not corrupt.

Nor, aside from a few members, did his cabinet contribute much to the statesmanlike quality of his presidency. His first appointee as Secretary of State, an old personal friend, fortunately resigned shortly, making way for Hamilton Fish of New York, a man of real ability, who gained merited laurels for his part in negotiating the treaty of Washington (see page 35). As head of the Treasury, Grant named Alexander T. Stewart, a New York merchant prince who ranked third among America's richest men; but when an old statute came to light forbidding the choice of a businessman for this responsible post, Stewart was replaced with George S. Boutwell, a Massachusetts politician with no special fitness for the office. Of the remaining members only Jacob D. Cox of Ohio, Secretary of the Interior, and E. Rockwood Hoar of Massachusetts, Attorney-General, possessed the qualifications usually expected.[1]

Grant's entry into office coincided with the rise of a new generation of political leaders. The giants of the Civil War era were fast passing away. Stevens died in 1868, Stanton in 1869, Seward in 1872, Chase in 1873, Sumner (with whom Grant parted company as early as 1870 because of the Massachusetts Senator's opposition to the annexation of Santo Domingo) in 1874, and Johnson in 1875. Their places were taken by men of lesser stature and of dissimilar interests and aims. In Henry Adams's opinion, "No period so thoroughly ordinary had been known in American politics since Christopher Columbus first disturbed the balance of American society." It is not unlikely that the men of creative vision and organizing genius—the natural leaders of the time—felt the challenge of the transforming economic life of the country, and renounced politics to become architects of the new capitalist order. At any rate, the men who now seized the reins in Congress—Roscoe Conkling of New York, James A. Garfield of Ohio, James G. Blaine of Maine, Samuel J. Randall and William D. ("Pig-Iron") Kelley of Pennsylvania, and their like—hastened the exploitation of the nation's resources through lavish subsidies, charter grants and tariffs, and were often themselves personally interested as stockholders or lawyers in corporate enterprises which might be affected by their votes as legislators.

[1] Besides the three named above, the original cabinet consisted of Elihu Washburne of Illinois, Secretary of State; John A. Rawlins of Illinois, Secretary of War; Adolph E. Borie of Pennsylvania, Secretary of the Navy; and John A. J. Creswell of Maryland, Postmaster-General.

At the same time the civil service was thoroughly demoralized. The spoils system, introduced when Jackson was President, had never before borne such evil fruit as during and after the Civil War when the rapid expansion of the public service brought into office an unusual number of worthless persons. Grant was accused by the *Nation* of making not only "bad appointments but probably some of the worst ever made by a civilized Christian government." The *New York World* ironically suggested that each applicant be asked: "Were you a contributor to either of Grant's three houses in Philadelphia, Washington or Galena, or have you made gifts to him or to any member of his family?" At the instigation of his political cronies the President in 1870 got rid of Attorney-General Hoar and Secretary of the Interior Cox because of their unwelcome zeal in resisting the demands of spoilsmen and job seekers.

The administration's blatant disregard of decent standards of officeholding caused increasing criticism and threatened to alienate the better elements in the Republican party. In the end, therefore, Grant asked Congress to enact a law for basing federal appointments upon personal fitness as determined by competitive examinations. Such a system, already in operation in England, France and Prussia, had been urged since 1865 by Congressman Thomas A. Jenckes of Rhode Island, and more recently by Carl Schurz, who early in 1870 entered the Senate from Missouri. In March, 1871, Congress granted the desired authority; and the President declared the new rules effective in the federal offices at Washington and New York from January 1, 1872. Grant's interest in the matter undoubtedly smacked of eleventh-hour virtue in anticipation of the coming presidential election. Indeed, he soon chafed under the restrictions, and in 1873 Congress declined to renew the appropriation for the supervisory commission upon which the success of the plan depended. The achievement of civil-service reform had to await a more auspicious occasion.

Meanwhile, the government dealt with the problem of reorganizing the national finances on a peace basis. These efforts, initiated under President Johnson, involved the conversion of the war debt into bonds at lower interest rates, a steady reduction of internal-revenue duties, and a lessening of the income tax until in 1872 it was abolished. Proposals to lower import duties, however, aroused the ire of the manufacturing interests suckled by the war-time tariff, for they were resolved to increase rather than decrease protection. Beginning in 1866, swarms of lobbyists descended upon Washington ready to do battle at an instant's notice for the industries they represented. Shrewdest among them was John L. Hayes, agent of the newly formed National Association of Wool Manufacturers, who brought together the wool-growing and wool-manufacturing groups in a combined demand for higher rates.

The results of such pressure tactics soon appeared. Though no Republican national platform had yet advocated protection apart from a passing mention in 1860, Congress raised the duties on wool and woolens in 1867, on copper in 1869, and on steel rails, nickel and marble in 1870. As a hostile critic said, the country had advanced from the five and ten-per-cent protection of Alexander Hamilton to the twenty and thirty-per-cent tariff of Clay and Webster, and now, though the duties extended all the way up to five hundred per cent, the industrialists clamored for still steeper rates.

In granting these increases the Republican leaders had reckoned without their farming constituencies, which complained of the rise of prices. So strong was the Western dissatisfaction that Congress felt obliged to make a gesture toward tariff reduction. The resulting act of 1870 failed to allay the discontent, however, for it affected chiefly tea, coffee, spices and certain other articles in which no domestic manufacturing interest was involved. As the presidential election drew closer, the party chieftains, deeming discretion the better part of valor, took a somewhat more decisive step. In acts of May and June, 1872, Congress imposed a horizontal cut of ten per cent on the principal imported manufactures. The concession proved only temporary, however, for the deficit in revenue caused by the Panic of 1873 led to a restoration of the protective duties in 1875. At this point they were permitted to remain until the general tariff revision of 1883.

Though the most shocking misdeeds of the administration remained as yet undisclosed, certain elements among Grant's following were already beginning to distinguish between the "Hero of Appomattox" and the peace-time incumbent of the White House. As early as 1870 a Republican faction in Missouri, led by Schurz and aided by the Democrats, carried the state elections. The Liberal Republicans, as they called themselves, favored a more generous treatment of their fellow citizens who had taken the Southern side during the war and, in addition, demanded civil-service reform and tariff revision. The Missouri incident was like a spark to a powder train. As similar bolts from the party occurred in other states, the anti-Grant movement assumed nation-wide proportions. "I tremble for my country," wrote Charles Sumner, "when I contemplate the possibility of this man being fastened upon us for another four years."

With high hopes the Liberal Republicans assembled at Cincinnati on May 1, 1872, to nominate candidates for the forthcoming election. The convention contained diverse elements: tariff reductionists, civil-service reformers, opponents of federal intervention in the South and disgruntled politicians nursing personal grudges. The proceedings quickly became snarled in a tangle of personalities and politics, greatly to the glee of the Republicans, who derided the gathering as the "Convention of Cranks." The platform, after a savage arraignment of the administration, declared for civil service reform and home rule in the South, but, in consequence of frankly confessed "irreconcilable differences," it was noncommittal on the tariff. For President the convention made the preposterous mistake of naming Horace Greeley, lifelong foe of the Democrats and a rabid protectionist. Governor B. Gratz Brown of Missouri was chosen to run with him. Though it was a bitter pill for them to swallow, the Democrats when they convened saw nothing better to do than to indorse the ticket. The Republicans, meeting on June 5, unanimously renominated Grant, associating with him Henry Wilson of Massachusetts. Their platform, after justifying the administration's Southern policy, pledged tariff protection and paid sanctimonious respects to civil-service reform.

The outcome was never in doubt. Many Democrats stayed at home rather than vote for Greeley, who had long castigated them in the columns of the *New York Tribune*. Yet even with a stronger candidate, the Liberal Republican movement could hardly have triumphed, for the average Republican continued to see Grant with his war-time halo, and the Carpetbag governments, still prevailing in seven Southern states, were certain to support him. Republican spellbinders vigorously waved the bloody shirt and told the voters that Grant's defeat would mean pensions for the ex-Confederate veterans, if not the peaceable secession of the South. Indicative of the new trend of politics, the great business and financial interests of the country contributed generously to the Republican campaign, Jay Cooke's subscription alone totaling over fifty thousand dollars.

Grant won an electoral vote of 286 to 62 and a popular majority of almost 56 per cent (3,600,000 votes) to 44 per cent (2,835,000) for his opponent. Greeley died a broken-hearted man a few weeks later. In the history of the Republican party the campaign was notable as marking the formal adoption of tariff protection as an article of party faith. The campaign also signalized the entry of labor into politics in the guise of the short-lived Labor Reform party. No presidential contest since has been without one or more minor parties devoted to the welfare of urban or rural workers.

ECONOMIC COLLAPSE AND POLITICAL BETRAYAL

(Six months after Grant's second inauguration the feverish prosperity that had infected the country chilled suddenly to depression, unemployment and despair. Men in their mad strife for gain had forgotten the distinction between possible and impossible. The unnatural stimulus given by the Civil War, the inflated currency and an illimitable credit had caused millions of capital to pour into factories and mills until their productive capacity far outstripped existing needs.) In the decade after the incorporation of the Union Pacific well over a billion was sunk in rail construction alone. Only the future growth of the country could make many such enterprises profitable, and in the meantime indebtedness piled up beyond ability to pay. Moreover, much of the speculation was sheer dishonesty, foisted on the gullible public by rascals. It was to these years that Mark Twain and Charles Dudley Warner referred in their book *The Gilded Age.* "Beautiful credit!" they jibed, citing a "speculator in lands and mines" who boasted, "I wasn't worth a cent two years ago, and now I owe two million dollars." Even the farmers felt the contagion, heavily mortgaging their lands for implements and additional acreage.

The economic collapse was precipitated by conditions of world-wide extent. Other countries besides the United States had been experiencing a period of fungus growth and excessive speculation. A halt was inevitable. In May, 1873, a panic in Vienna, spreading to other money centers of the Old World, sounded a general alarm. The results, wrote David A. Wells, were "grievous in old communities like England and Germany, and equally so in Australia, South Africa, and California, which represent the new." Much of the American business expansion had been financed from abroad, and the money stringency in Europe now caused a withdrawal of a great part of this support. American bankers, already over-burdened, were unprepared to carry the additional load. In September came the crash, hastened by the failure of Jay Cooke and Company, America's leading banking firm, which had invested too heavily in the projected Northern Pacific Railroad.

A frenzy of excitement and fear gripped the business world. The Grant administration was helpless before the storm, and the foundations of credit began to crumble. Financial and business houses toppled, eighty-nine railroads defaulted on their bonds, and the industrial regions were stricken as by a paralysis. In all, more than five thousand concerns failed during the Panic year with an aggregate loss of about $228,500,000. Meantime, upwards of three million wage-earners were thrown out of work; and the Western and Southern farmers, their crops a drug on the market, found themselves unable to meet their mortgage payments. Cotton declined twenty per cent; wheat fell about fifteen cents a bushel, and flour fifty cents a barrel.

Five years were to follow the Panic of 1873 before normal conditions returned—years rendered more disheartening by the revelations of the knavery and dishonor that honeycombed the federal government. In the opinion of George F. Hoar, Republican Senator from Massachusetts, corruption "never got so dangerous a hold upon the forces of the Government, or upon a great political party, as in the Adminis-

tration of General Grant." Early in 1873 investigating committees of the House and Senate disclosed that Schuyler Colfax, the outgoing Vice-President, and a number of Congressmen, including James A. Garfield and "Pig-Iron" Kelley,
owned stock in the Crédit Mobilier, construction company
for the Union Pacific. These shares had been given them
free of charge by Congressman Oakes Ames, an officer of the
company, who had told his business associates he would place
the holdings where they would "protect us" and "do the
most good" in averting an inquiry into the company's affairs. The House, accepting the committee's view that most
of the Congressmen implicated had acted without "any corrupt motive or purpose," contented itself with censuring
Ames and another member.

Other exposures followed with almost clocklike regularity.
Among the more notorious was Postmaster-General Creswell's admission that he had authorized the payment of
nearly $500,000 for services which the claimant himself later
estimated to be worth $176,000. Another cabinet officer,
William A. Richardson, was found to have grossly abused his
authority as Secretary of the Treasury in order to divert
some of the department's funds, through unearned commissions, into the pockets of a political henchman of Ben Butler.
In May, 1874, Richardson hurriedly resigned to avoid a vote
of censure by the House.

The public, racked by the hard times but as yet unaware
how far the moral poison had spread, turned on its rulers in
the fall elections, giving the Democrats their first victory
since before the war. While the Senate remained in control
of the party in power, the House changed from two-thirds
Republican to three-fifths Democratic, a fact which would
give the administration chieftains sleepless nights when the
time came to count the returns of the next presidential election. In addition, the Democrats swept twenty-three states

out of thirty-five, including New York where Samuel J.
Tilden, an active participant in the assault against the
Tweed Ring, was chosen governor on a platform of political
reform.

But this stinging popular rebuke came too late to undo
the damage. In 1875 Benjamin H. Bristow, Richardson's successor as head of the Treasury, exposed the rascality of a
"whisky ring" made up of wealthy distillers and revenue
officers who since 1870 had been defrauding the government
of millions in taxes. Grant's private secretary, Orville E.
Babcock, who was implicated in this conspiracy, escaped punishment only through the President's unwise intervention
on his behalf. On the heels of these disclosures, in March,
1876, Secretary William W. Belknap of the War Department precipitately resigned in order to avoid impeachment
on the charge of having received an annual bribe since 1870
from an officeholder anxious to escape removal.

A few weeks later came another scandal, involving one of
the most promising of the younger Republican leaders,
James G. Blaine. The investigation showed that, while
Speaker of the House, he had acted as bond salesman for a
land-grant railway, and that later he had permitted the
Union Pacific and certain other land-grant corporations to
relieve him of a large block of the securities at a sum far in
excess of their market value. By a trick Blaine got possession
of the incriminating evidence, the so-called Mulligan letters,
and though he refused to allow the documents to be examined, he made a brilliant speech in the House, which, if it
left the skeptical unsatisfied, at least convinced orthodox Republicans of his innocence. But Blaine's penalty was to be a
heavy one, for his connection with this affair was to prevent
him from ever attaining the goal of his ambition, the White
House.

THE GRANGER MOVEMENT AND THE MONEY QUESTION

Meanwhile, the economic depression continued to spread its black wings over the nation. In the industrial centers hordes of the jobless crowded the bread lines, while speakers on the street corners demanded that the government find work for the idle and stop evictions for failure to pay rent. Private charities stretched their resources to the limit, and New York, Boston, Chicago and certain other municipalities provided food and, in some instances, work relief in the form of wood chopping and road building. Immigrants departed for Europe by the tens of thousands, while many native wage-earners turned hobo, wandering aimlessly about the country—pathetic caricatures of the restless, hardy pioneers who had helped to conquer the wilderness. Criminality increased, and the violence attending the railroad strikes of 1877 (see page 148) further attested the spread of radicalism and despair. These grim years gave impetus to many a scheme of social and economic redemption—labor solidarity, consumers' and producers' coöperatives, "free silver," socialism, the "single tax" and the like—while rendering clamorous the demands for railway regulation and greenback inflation.

As early as 1869 Massachusetts had established a commission with advisory power to deal with the unfair practices of railroads within the state. The chief victims of such abuses, however, were the Midwestern farmers. Already afflicted with low prices for their crops, and obliged to pay middlemen excessive charges for tools and other supplies, they considered the rates demanded for hauling their products unwarrantably high. As a matter of fact, the railroads did not hesitate to impose extortionate charges, or even to discriminate against certain communities and shippers in favor of others. In 1867 a secret ritualistic order, named the Patrons of Husbandry but usually known as the Grange, had appeared among the farmers originally for the purpose of fostering a pleasanter social life among rural dwellers of both sexes. The movement to curb the railroads is always associated with the rise of this organization, though the Grange was avowedly nonpolitical and grew but slowly until the hard times after 1873 suddenly swelled its membership to two and a half million. From the first, however, it provided a common meeting ground for farmers and, as it increased in strength, the Grange played an important, if indirect, part in politics.

Inspired by "Farmers' Declarations of Independence" and pledged to emancipate "white slaves from the Slave-Power of Monopoly," local agrarian parties sprang up in the Midwest and bent the legislatures to their will. "The State must either absorb the railroads or the railroads will absorb the State," was their cry. Acts were passed for regulating railroad rates either by direct legislative decree or through official commissions set up for the purpose. Illinois and Minnesota led the way in 1870 and 1871. Ohio and Michigan followed in the Panic year, and Iowa, Wisconsin and Missouri in the next two years. These laws were based upon the then novel principle that railways should be treated as public-service enterprises, not as mere private businesses for the enrichment of their stockholders. Some of the acts were ill wrought or tinged with a spirit of vengeance; but the fury of the rail magnates was directed less against the kind of legislation than against the constitutionality of any interference by the state. Facing ruin because of the depression, they further believed that statutory regulation would frighten investors from putting money into the transportation business.

The so-called Granger cases, decided in 1877, settled the question of constitutionality, and later years revealed the groundlessness of the financial fear. In Munn *v.* Illinois, the

Supreme Court found in the state's police power (that is, its inherent right to protect the health, welfare and safety of its citizens) ample authority to regulate businesses "clothed with a public interest." "Property," asserted the judges, "does become clothed with a public interest when used in a manner to make it of public consequence and affect the community at large." [1] In Peik *v.* Chicago and Northwestern Railway, the court dismissed a further objection by declaring that, until Congress acted under the interstate-commerce clause, states might even fix rates on shipments passing beyond their limits.

Not content merely with lower transportation rates, the Grangers through their own devices attacked the evil of high middlemen's charges. They set up their own agencies for the sale of farm produce; and in several states coöperative creameries and grain elevators saved Grange members many thousands of dollars. By pooling their funds farmers also effected great economies through ordering in wholesale lots directly from manufacturers. In Iowa the State Grange established its own factories for making plows and harvesters, which were sold to members at cost. But by 1876 most of these undertakings were abandoned, having failed for lack of adequate support or proper business direction or because of the unfair practices of competitors. Yet the widespread interest in coöperation was not without result. Besides making middlemen less ready to ask exorbitant prices, it brought about the first Chicago mail-order house, which with Grange sanction proceeded to do business directly with rural dwellers over the heads of local dealers. As the seventies drew toward a close, this first farmers' uprising started to decline.

Meanwhile, an increasing number of agrarian leaders had

[1] Though this case really involved an Illinois law of 1871 for regulating grain warehouses, the principle applied equally to railway regulation, and was so construed by the court in the Peik and other decisions.

turned to currency inflation as a remedy for their ills. Since the early days of the war commercial transactions had been carried on largely in depreciated greenbacks which the government declined to redeem at face value in gold. When peace came, the substantial business classes in the East demanded the withdrawal of this "cheap money," or at least of enough of it to restore conditions under which all forms of currency would have full gold value. In 1866 Congress authorized a reduction of the greenbacks by gradual stages, but this process had to be discontinued two years later, when the amount stood at $356,000,000, because of the outcry from the Midwestern agricultural regions. Many farmers saw in contraction the chief cause of the low crop prices. Moreover, since a large number of farms were heavily mortgaged, they felt intolerably handicapped if, before their debts fell due, the volume of currency diminished. With less money in circulation greenbacks became harder to get, or, to put it differently, their value increased. If paper dollars, borrowed when they were worth sixty-five cents in gold, were repaid in paper dollars worth ninety-five or one hundred cents in gold, the debtor was repaying in principal considerably more than he had received. Many members of the "debtor class" began to insist that the greenbacks be retained permanently.

During the Panic of 1873 the Secretary of the Treasury, as a temporary measure of relief, reissued $26,000,000 worth of the greenbacks that had been retired. This action only whetted the demand, and in April, 1874, Congress passed a bill to increase the total volume to $400,000,000. In great alarm delegations of businessmen hurried to Washington to bring influence to bear on President Grant, who had been talking on both sides of the inflation question. In the end, he vetoed the measure. When the fall elections assured the Democrats control of the next House, the Republicans under business pressure made use of their remaining months to enact a plan for the renewal, or resumption, of specie payments. The resumption act of January 14, 1875, has been called, not inaptly, the "deathbed repentance of the Republican party."

John Sherman of Ohio was its principal author. Far from drastic in its terms, the statute sought to appease both the greenback notions of the West and the gold-standard sentiment of the East. It provided that from January 1, 1879, the government should stand ready to exchange gold dollars for greenback dollars, and that meanwhile, in preparation for the event, the government should retire part of the greenbacks and at the same time accumulate a gold reserve through the sale of bonds. The purpose of this last provision was to assure the full specie value of the greenbacks left in circulation. The gold reserve was subsequently fixed at $100,000,-000, and Congress decided in 1878 that $346,681,016 of greenbacks should form a permanent part of the monetary system. The plan proved entirely feasible, for, as it happened, the time of its execution coincided with the return of prosperity. After the date of resumption the full value of the greenback in terms of gold was firmly established.

Grant's veto of the inflation bill incensed the small group of extreme greenbackers in the country, and the passage of the resumption act increased their anger. These persons subscribed to the doctrine of "absolute money"; that is, they contended that money derived its value solely from the stamp (or fiat) of the government, not from its intrinsic value or the fact that it was exchangeable for gold or some other precious metal. Hopeless of winning support from either of the old parties, they organized the National Greenback party in May, 1875, which presented candidates in the next three presidential elections. Their platform called for the repeal of the resumption act and for the establishment of a legal-tender currency redeemable only in low-interest United

States bonds. Though winning some followers in the Midwest and in Eastern labor centers, and polling a million votes in the congressional elections of 1878, the party never cast an electoral vote. It gradually succumbed to the rising tide of sentiment in favor of unlimited silver coinage.

THE DISPUTED ELECTION OF 1876

(Satisfied for the time being with Congress's disposition of the money question, the mass of voters were thinking of other things as the campaign of 1876 drew near.) Already in December, 1875, two thirds of the Republican members of the House had voted with the Democratic majority in condemning the principle of a third presidential term. While this rebuke checked the scheme of Roscoe Conkling and the spoilsmen to continue Grant in the White House, it also helped fix public attention anew upon the malodorous record of the party in power. What could the Republicans do to avert disaster in the election? Blaine, himself the chief contender for the nomination, pointed the way in January, 1876, when he delivered in the House a violent bloody-shirt speech which goaded Southern members into passionate and ill-considered replies. The Republicans took prompt advantage of the opportunity to frighten voters with the spectacle of an unrepentant South about to ride into office on the back of the Democratic party.

When the Republicans assembled in Cincinnati on June 14, Blaine was at first the favorite in the balloting, but he failed of success, thanks to opposition both from the reform elements and from Conkling, who cherished an invincible personal dislike for him. Instead, the prize went on the seventh ballot to Rutherford B. Hayes, a Civil War veteran of irreproachable character, then serving a third term as governor of Ohio. William A. Wheeler of New York was named for Vice-President. The platform bristled with bloody-shirt allusions and, as four years before, declared for tariff protection and civil-service reform.

The Democrats, meeting two weeks later in St. Louis, decided on the second ballot in favor of Samuel J. Tilden. As governor of New York Tilden had destroyed the corrupt "Canal Ring," which had looted many millions of state funds through the manipulation of public-works contracts; and this feat, together with his earlier activities against the Tweed Ring, had won him nation-wide renown as a reformer. Moreover, as a wealthy corporation lawyer he enjoyed the confidence of many conservative Easterners. The second place fell to Thomas A. Hendricks of Indiana. The paramount issue, declared the Democratic platform, was reform—financial, tariff and governmental—a duty which could not safely be intrusted to a party "honey-combed with incapacity, waste, and fraud."

In the ensuing campaign the Democrats strove valiantly to rivet attention upon the crying need for reform. Their principal assets were the popular disgust with "Grantism," the continuing depression and the encouragement afforded by the victories in the 1874 elections. As Hayes wrote one of his Republican associates, "Our strong ground is the dread of a solid South, rebel rule, etc., etc. . . . It leads people away from 'hard times,' which is our deadliest foe." But his campaigners needed no such prompting. In the words of James Russell Lowell, a Hayes supporter, "the worst element of the Republican party has got hold of the canvass, and everything possible is done to stir up the old passions of the war." On the morning after the election Tilden's victory was almost universally conceded by the newspapers, but the Republican national headquarters stoutly claimed Hayes's success. Within a few days it became clear that, with 185 electoral votes necessary for election, Tilden had unquestioned right to 184, including the usually decisive states of New York, New Jer-

sey, Connecticut and Indiana, and that Hayes in like manner
had won 165. Twenty votes—one from Oregon, seven from
South Carolina, four from Florida and eight from Louisiana
—were in doubt. Tilden's popular majority was 4,285,000
(49.9 per cent) to 4,034,000 (47.9 per cent) for Hayes.

The difficulty in Oregon grew out of the fact that after the
election one of the successful Republican electors was discovered to be disqualified by the constitutional provision forbidding federal officeholders to serve as electors. The state

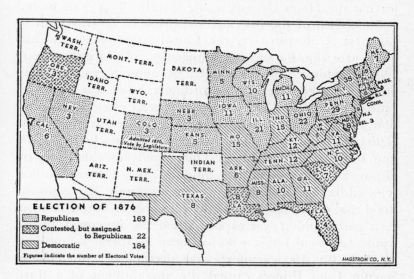

ELECTION OF 1876
Republican   163
Contested, but assigned
    to Republican   22
Democratic   184
Figures indicate the number of Electoral Votes

HAGSTROM CO., N.Y.

law stipulated that the remaining electors should fill the
vacancy, but the Democratic governor insisted that the highest Democratic candidate for elector should have the place.
In the three Southern states the question was more complicated. There the native whites, engaged in a final desperate
effort to dislodge the Carpetbaggers, had in countless instances frightened Negroes from the polls by intimidation
and violence. But the state election machinery, headed by

the famous or infamous "returning boards," was controlled by the Carpetbaggers, who from their seats of power could manipulate the election results as they pleased. The worst conditions prevailed in Louisiana, where the four members of the returning board refused to add a Democratic member as required by law, offered at one stage to sell out to Tilden for a million dollars, and ended up by rejecting Democratic votes in wholesale lots in order to create the desired majority for Hayes. They actually threw out 13,213 Tilden votes, leaving the Hayes electors a safe margin of 3437 or more.[1]

From each of the four states two sets of returns went to Congress. Unfortunately, the Constitution makes no adequate provision for such a contingency and, since the Senate and the House were controlled by opposite parties, compromise proved necessary. Accordingly, a law was passed on January 29, 1877, which created a special electoral commission of five Senators, five Representatives and five members of the Supreme Court, the fifth Justice to be chosen by the four specified in the statute. The commission's decisions on disputed returns should be binding upon Congress unless rejected by the two branches voting separately. It was understood that seven members of the commission would be from each party, and it was expected that the unnamed Justice would be David Davis, who had been a Liberal Republican in 1872. But Davis's unexpected election as United States Senator from Illinois caused the appointment of a third Republican Justice, Joseph P. Bradley, the most acceptable to the Democrats of the remaining members of the bench.

[1] To give an appearance of fairness, they also rejected 2415 Republican votes. President Grant believed that Tilden was entitled to Louisiana and hence to election. James Ford Rhodes concludes his discussion of the situation by saying, "if Hayes had envisaged the facts as I now do he would have refused to accept the presidency from the Louisiana Returning-Board." But Paul L. Haworth, another historical student, while conceding "grossly partisan and illegal acts," expresses the belief that "in an absolutely fair and free election the state would have gone Republican by five to ten thousand."

The electoral commission sat throughout the month of February. The time was drawing perilously near to inauguration day and newspapers of both parties carried inflammatory utterances. Tense excitement pervaded the country, the bad economic conditions aroused fears of violence, and Grant strengthened the military forces about Washington. Bent on averting the possibility of another civil war, forty-two ex-Confederates in the House took a solemn pledge to oppose all attempts to prevent the electoral count. Meantime the commission took cognizance, in turn, of the cases of Florida, Louisiana, Oregon and South Carolina. On all crucial points the decision favored the Hayes electors by a vote of eight to seven.[1] (On March 2 Hayes was formally pronounced the victor with an electoral majority of 185 to 184. The disappointment of the Democrats is indescribable, but with angry mutterings they yielded grudging acquiescence. It is hardly too much to say that, in the peaceful acceptance of Hayes's election, the supremacy of the law won the greatest victory in the history of popular government.)

SELECT BIBLIOGRAPHY

Political Transition, 1869–1877. The general histories by Rhodes, Schouler and Oberholtzer treat the principal events and outstanding political scandals, as do also Dunning, *Reconstruction Political and Economic,* Nevins, *Emergence of Modern America,* and Josephson, *Politicos.* The following biographies are helpful: Hesseltine, *Grant;* Linn, *Greeley;* Muzzey, *Blaine;* Williams, *Hayes;* Flick, *Tilden;* and Nevins, *Abram S. Hewitt* (Tilden's campaign manager). Barclay, *Liberal Republican Movement in Missouri,* and Ross, *Liberal Republican Movement,* present special studies of the election of 1872, while Haworth,

[1] There is good reason to believe that Mr. Justice Bradley, who held the balance of power in the commission, decided originally in favor of the Tilden returns from Florida, but changed his mind overnight because of the pleas of two Republican friends and his wife, who contended that a Democratic triumph would mean national disaster.

Hayes-Tilden Disputed Election, performs a similar service for the campaign of 1876.

Dewey, *Financial History,* is a convenient reference work for one aspect of postwar economic reorganization. Tarbell, *Tariff in Our Times,* emphasizes the political and social forces in tariff making; Stanwood, *American Tariff Controversies,* is especially good for the legislative history of tariff measures; and Taussig, *Tariff History,* approaches the subject from the standpoint of an economist. The Panic of 1873 receives attention in Burton, *Financial Crises;* Oberholtzer, *Jay Cooke,* II; Larson, *Jay Cooke;* and Feder, *Unemployment Relief in Periods of Depression.* The standard account of the Midwestern farmers' uprising is Buck, *Granger Movement.* Political aspects of the Greenback movement are sketched in Buck, *Agrarian Crusade,* and Haynes, *Third Party Movements;* the technical aspects in Barrett, *Greenbacks and Resumption of Specie Payments,* and Mitchell, *History of the Greenbacks.*

Chapter IV

OLD ISSUES AND NEW ATTITUDES, 1877–1897

REPUBLICANS AND REFORM

THE narrowness of the Republican victory in 1876 frightened the party chieftains, who had hitherto believed they had an unshakable hold on popular favor. By the same token, it gave a strategic advantage to those members who wished to purify the party. Each age has its own abuses that call for cure and, as might be expected, the political reformers of the 1870's and 1880's strove, above all else, for the honest, efficient and economical conduct of public affairs. Alarmed by the ominous creaking of the governmental machinery as operated by unskilled or unscrupulous hands, they feared lest the theory of democracy be defeated by its practices. Therefore they sought civil-service reform, prompt punishment of delinquent officials and the abolition of campaign assessments on officeholders; some of them also labored for tariff reform. Chief among the leaders were Carl Schurz, George W. Curtis, editor of *Harper's Weekly,* Edwin L. Godkin, editor of the *Nation,* and Dorman B. Eaton, a New York lawyer and publicist.

If to a later generation these reformers seem to have occupied themselves with symptoms rather than with the seat of the disease, they at least attacked evils that challenged all civic decency. Most of them were Republicans by preference, but they placed their purposes above party, assuming an attitude of independence whenever occasion demanded. Their potential freedom from party restraints, their insistence that parties were merely instruments for the public

97

good rather than ends in themselves, enraged the professional politicians. Roscoe Conkling spoke for many of his kind when he denounced these "carpet knights of politics" for "cracking their whips over Republicans and playing schoolmaster to the Republican party." But their example helped gradually to fashion a tradition of independent voting at a period when the fetish of party regularity was stronger than at any other time in American history.

Though President Hayes gained office under dubious circumstances, he earnestly sought to live up to the maxim, announced in his inaugural address, that "he serves his party best who serves his country best." A simple, dignified man, conscientious and hard working but lacking in personal magnetism, he gathered about him an unusually able group of advisers, including William M. Evarts of New York as Secretary of State and John Sherman of Ohio as head of the Treasury. To the horror of Conkling and the practical politicians who had surrounded Grant, Hayes also appointed to his official family Carl Schurz, civil-service reformer and in 1872 an anti-Grant campaigner, as Secretary of the Interior, and David M. Key, a Tennessee Democrat and ex-Confederate veteran, as Postmaster-General.[1] They found equally unpalatable other of the President's early acts, such as his refusal to lend further military support to the Carpetbag governments, and particularly his determination to reduce the ravages of the spoils system. Soon they began to refer to him as only a "halfbreed" Republican in contrast to their own "stalwart" Republicanism. The names, Halfbreed and Stalwart, clung to the two wings of the party throughout this administration and the next.

President Hayes made a resolute effort to secure adminis-

[1] The other members of the cabinet were George W. McCrary of Iowa, Secretary of War; Richard W. Thompson of Indiana, Secretary of the Navy; and Charles Devens of Massachusetts, Attorney-General.

tration efficiency and to weed out dishonesty. He early informed Secretary Sherman, "Party leaders should have no more influence in appointments than other equally respectable citizens. No assessments for political purposes on officers or subordinates should be allowed. No useless officer or employee should be retained." But Congress turned a deaf ear to his repeated appeals to renew the civil-service appropriation which Grant had allowed to lapse, and Hayes had to make what progress he could under his executive authority. With the President's encouragement Schurz placed the Department of the Interior on a merit basis; and other department heads, though with less enthusiasm, took similar action.

In the teeth of bitter opposition from the Stalwarts, Hayes also applied the reform to the federal offices in New York City. Besides reappointing as local postmaster Thomas L. James, an ardent civil-service champion, he dealt strongly with the situation in the New York customhouse, where an investigating committee had reported incompetency, graft and political favoritism. When other measures failed, he ousted Chester A. Arthur and Alonzo B. Cornell, respectively collector and naval officer. Both men were powers in New York state politics, Arthur as Republican boss of New York City and Cornell as chairman of the state committee. The Senate, egged on by Conkling, declined for two months to confirm their successors. Hayes's devotion to the cause undoubtedly won popular favor for civil-service reform and helped hasten its final accomplishment. He himself, however, did not always live up to his lofty ideals, for he provided berths for many of the Carpetbaggers whom the withdrawal of troops had left high and dry in the South.

Though Hayes's bitterest foes were in his own party, the Democrats took every occasion to remind the public of the circumstances of his entry into office, calling him "Old Eight-to-Seven" and the *"de facto* President." By keeping the issue alive, they hoped to sweep the country in 1880 in a dramatic campaign of vindication. In May, 1878, the Democratic House directed the so-called Potter committee to investigate Hayes's title to the presidency. After examining over two hundred witnesses concerning conditions in Florida and Louisiana in 1876, the committee by a strict party vote decided that Tilden had been rightfully elected. The edge of the findings was dulled, however, by the enterprise of a Republican Senate committee in unearthing a batch of cipher telegrams that had been sent, or received, by Democratic leaders during the heat of the campaign. These, when decoded, revealed efforts to bribe the Florida and South Carolina returning boards. Thanks to someone's foresight, Republican telegrams sent at the same time could nowhere be found. Most of the Democrats implicated by the "cipher despatches" did not deny the essential charges, justifying their course on the plea that they were merely trying to "ransom stolen property from thieves." Tilden himself was shown to be innocent of any complicity. It was clear that the garments of both parties were soiled, and the "political crime" as a Democratic campaign issue was robbed in advance of much of its effectiveness.

The Democrats also bestirred themselves to bring about a repeal of the force acts that had been passed in 1870–1871 during the Ku Klux troubles and which Supreme Court decisions had already enfeebled (see page 28). By holding up the army-appropriation bill the House in June, 1878, forced the Senate and President to accept a bill barring the use of troops at the polls. When the fall elections of that year put the Democrats in control of both branches, they tried to complete the process; but on eight different occasions Hayes's veto defeated their attempts. Though rendered harmless by disuse, these last vestiges of the old Reconstruction machinery survived until rescinded by a Democratic Congress and President in 1894.

The successful showing of the opposition party in the congressional elections of 1878 rendered it prudent for the Republicans to bury their differences as the presidential election drew near. Hayes was out of the running because he had solemnly pledged himself against a second term. This cleared the way for Conkling and his group to engineer a comeback for Grant who had recently returned from a triumphal tour of the world. The anti-Grant elements, thoroughly alarmed, organized No-Third-Term leagues, and even held a national Anti-Third-Term convention. Nevertheless, when the Republicans convened in Chicago on June 2, 1880, three hundred and six of the seven hundred and fifty-five delegates voted doggedly for Grant throughout the balloting. They succeeded in preventing the choice of Blaine, who stood second in the race, but the convention on the thirty-sixth ballot stampeded to a "dark horse," James A. Garfield of Ohio. An ex-soldier and moderate Halfbreed, Garfield had seen continuous service in Congress since 1863. As a peace offering to the "Grant Phalanx," the second place was given to Chester A. Arthur of New York, the recently dismissed customs collector. The platform blended self-laudation with disparagement of the Democrats, praised the protective-tariff system and, however reluctantly, indorsed Hayes's civil-service policy.

The Democrats were in a dilemma. Tilden was not available because of ill health and the powerful opposition of Tammany in his own state. Meeting at Cincinnati on June 22, the convention on the third ballot chose General Winfield S. Hancock of Pennsylvania, with William H. English, a wealthy Indiana banker, as his running mate. Hancock's nomination was an attempt to refute the customary Republican charge of disloyalty and, at the same time, to capitalize the popularity of a faithful war veteran. The platform, while demanding civil-service reform and a tariff for revenue only, proclaimed the "great fraud of 1876–77" as the issue that "precedes and dwarfs every other."

In the campaign, however, the "great fraud" excited little attention despite the fact that the Republican nominee had served on the electoral commission that seated Hayes. Nor did the efforts to discredit Garfield because of his connection with the Crédit Mobilier and other scandals yield any greater success. The Republicans, on their part, once more stirred the devil's brew of sectional animosities, and made the most of their candidate's rise from a barefoot canal boy in Ohio.[1] They scoffed at Hancock as "a good man weighing two hundred and fifty pounds." Schurz, Godkin and other independents supported Garfield though with little conviction. Hancock's chief campaign utterance was a repudiation of the Democratic tariff plank on the score that the tariff was necessarily a "local issue." The return of prosperity for the first time since 1872 greatly helped the Republicans, and Garfield won by an electoral majority of 214 to 155. The state of the public mind is better mirrored by the popular vote. Despite Hancock's ineffective leadership he polled 4,442,000 votes (48.23 per cent) to 4,449,000 (48.3 per cent) for his opponent.

SHACKLING THE SPOILS SYSTEM

The announcement of Garfield's cabinet reopened the Republican breach, which the common effort put forth during the campaign had temporarily closed. Roscoe Conkling deemed the choice of Blaine as Secretary of State a personal affront, while he found some of the other cabinet selections

[1] Appropriately enough, Horatio Alger, past master of the art of portraying the "success" theme in thrilling boys' books, presently produced *From Canal Boy to President, or the Boyhood and Manhood of James A. Garfield.*

scarcely more to his liking.[1] Even in making federal appointments in Conkling's state, Garfield went his own way,
ignoring the practice of "senatorial courtesy" which custom-
arily bound Presidents to rubberstamp the recommendations
of Senators of their own party. The circumstances indicate
that his purpose was not to improve standards of officeholding, but to humble Conkling and build up a Garfield-
Blaine machine in New York. "Lord Roscoe" determined to
make an issue of William H. Robertson's nomination as New
York customs collector. Not only was the office the most lu-
crative in the whole public service, but Robertson was Conkling's bitterest foe in the state. When it became clear that he
could not prevent confirmation by the Senate, Conkling and
his fellow Senator, Thomas C. Platt, resigned their seats and
appealed to the New York legislature for reëlection as vindication. Vice-President Arthur went to Albany to use his
influence on their behalf. To their mortification and the
country's amusement both were defeated after fifty-six ballots. Conkling retired permanently to private life, "Me Too"
Platt to temporary oblivion.

Meanwhile Thomas L. James, the new Postmaster-General, uncovered a nest of corruption in the postal service,
involving men of such prominence as Thomas W. Brady,
who since Grant's time had been an Assistant Postmaster-
General, and ex-Senator Stephen W. Dorsey of Arkansas, secretary of the Republican national committee. Brady attempted to block the investigation by threatening the President with unpleasant consequences. When Garfield remained
unmoved, he made public a letter—known to fame as the

[1] The other members were William Windom of Minnesota, Secretary of the
Treasury; Robert T. Lincoln of Illinois, Secretary of War; William H. Hunt
of Louisiana, Secretary of the Navy; Wayne McVeagh of Pennsylvania, Attorney-General; Thomas L. James of New York, Postmaster-General; and
Samuel J. Kirkwood of Iowa, Secretary of the Interior.

"My dear Hubbell" letter—in which Garfield as a presidential candidate had approved the practice of levying campaign assessments on officeholders. The trials of the conspirators in the Star Route frauds, as they were called, dragged on until 1884 when, on technical grounds, the chief culprits managed to escape prison. Some good resulted, however, for the ring was broken up, and public attention called anew to the need for better officials.

While still struggling with problems of patronage, President Garfield was shot in a Washington railway station by a crazed office seeker on July 2, 1881, only four months after his inauguration. At the time, the Vice-President was still at the New York capital lobbying for Conkling and Platt; and when Garfield after a gallant fight died on September 19, many people shared the dismay of the man who exclaimed, "Chet Arthur President of the United States! Good God!" Handsome, affable, debonair, the new President was best known to his countrymen as a machine politician. Yet the responsibilities of office revealed him in a new light. As chief executive he displayed unexpected courage and sagacity and, to the surprise of his former associates, he devoted himself earnestly to the task of reform. Arthur presently reorganized the cabinet, appointing Frederick T. Frelinghuysen of New Jersey as Blaine's successor in the State Department. Only Secretary of War Lincoln, son of the martyred President, stayed throughout the term.[1] But most of Garfield's other appointees remained undisturbed, including Robertson, whose selection as customs collector had prompted Conkling's resignation. Nor did Arthur's firmness of purpose end here. In 1882, when the Republican Congress voted $19,-

[1] The other new appointments were Charles J. Folger of New York, Secretary of the Treasury; William E. Chandler of New Hampshire, Secretary of the Navy; Benjamin H. Brewster of Pennsylvania, Attorney-General; Timothy O. Howe of Wisconsin, Postmaster-General; and Henry M. Teller of Colorado, Secretary of the Interior.

000,000 for river and harbor improvements in five hundred different localities, he rejected the bill as unwise and extravagant. This first of our modern "pork-barrel" measures had many friends in both parties, however, and his veto was quickly overridden. As will be seen, he also worked for tariff revision.

Most surprising of all was Arthur's interest in civil-service reform. In messages of 1881 and 1882 he urged upon Congress suitable legislation. Fifteen years of discussion had created a robust public opinion on the subject, and the President's efforts were reënforced by the agitation of state and national civil-service-reform associations as well as by countless articles in the *Nation, Harper's Weekly* and other journals. Revelations of a Senate investigating committee, showing that the Republicans had collected nearly a hundred thousand dollars from federal employees in the congressional elections of 1878, touched the public on the raw, as did likewise the knowledge, derived from the "My dear Hubbell" letter and other sources, that this practice had been repeated in 1880. Garfield's murder seemed an irrefutable answer to all objections to immediate action. Many thoughtful persons agreed with George W. Curtis in blaming the crime on "the ferocity and insanity of party spirit, bred by the spoils system of office patronage." But Congress was not to be hurried into a reform which would deprive the members of accustomed perquisites.

In the fall elections of 1882 the Democrats carried the new House as well as thirteen of the sixteen states in which governors were chosen. Though Republican factionalism helped bring about this result, the failure of the party to safeguard the public service was a prime contributing factor. In the important state of New York Grover Cleveland, a Democrat and ardent civil-service reformer, was elected governor by the unprecedented plurality of a hundred and ninety-two thousand. The outgoing Republican Congress, chastened by these reverses and fearing a more drastic law at the hands of the victorious Democrats, now hastened to enact the desired legislation while time permitted. The Pendleton act in January, 1883, drafted by Dorman B. Eaton of the National Civil Service Reform League, provided for a bipartisan commission which should set up and administer a system of competitive examinations as a test of fitness for appointment to federal office. It further forbade government officials to solicit campaign contributions from other officeholders and protected the latter from removal for failure to pay. The new plan went into effect at once only in the executive departments in Washington, the customhouses and the larger post offices (those employing fifty or more); and the President was authorized to extend the classified list, as it was called, to other groups of workers at his discretion.

The statute left much to be desired. The rules affected only future appointments and, at first, less than fourteen thousand positions, leaving nearly nine tenths of the total personnel still subject to partisan politics. Nevertheless, the Pendleton act has rightly been termed the "Magna Charta of civil-service reform," for, through the provision for enlarging the classified list, Arthur and his successors were enabled to extend the merit system to ever greater numbers of federal employees. While devotion to the public weal contributed to this progress, gross partisanship also played a part, for an outgoing administration oftentimes increased the classified list in order to protect its appointees from dismissal by the victors. This practice gave coinage to the saying, "To the vanquished belong the spoils." On the whole, few backward steps have been taken, the most rapid advances being made under Presidents Theodore Roosevelt, Taft and Wilson. Incidentally, the passage of the Pendleton act strengthened the hands of civil-service reformers in local politics, leading Massachusetts and New York within a year to apply the system to state offices and encouraging many municipalities to try similar measures. The Pendleton law failed principally in not putting an effective end to the practice of levying party assessments on officeholders.

THE EMERGENCE OF GROVER CLEVELAND

The victory for good government, signalized by the civil-service act, was followed in the campaign of 1884 by further evidence of popular revolt against low political standards. President Arthur desired the Republican nomination but in vain, for he had lost his former Stalwart support without wholly convincing the Halfbreeds that his conversion was real. The convention, meeting in Chicago on June 3, chose the perennial aspirant, James G. Blaine of Maine, on the fourth ballot, though over the protests of George W. Curtis and of younger delegates like Theodore Roosevelt and Henry Cabot Lodge. As his candidacy lacked the customary recommendation of war service, amends were made by completing the ticket with General John A. Logan of Illinois. To the reform wing of the party Blaine's nomination meant a negation of all the progress toward governmental purity that had been achieved since Grant left office. A conference of Independent Republicans denounced the convention's action and called upon the Democrats to offer better men. Convening in Chicago on July 8, the Democrats rose to the occasion, nominating Grover Cleveland on the second ballot. Thomas A. Hendricks of Indiana, Tilden's running mate in 1876, was given the second place in a feeble effort to resurrect the old "fraud" issue.

Cleveland's nomination admirably met the requirements of the situation. With none of the qualities of the dashing political cavalier or the wiles of the professional intriguer, he had strongly impressed himself upon the people, not only of his state but of the nation. As mayor of Buffalo in 1881, he had shown what an incorruptible official could do to stem the tide of municipal misrule and later, in the governor's chair, he had displayed a similar aggressive devotion to the public weal. In appearance Cleveland was rather unimpressive, his cheeks clean-shaven when most statesmen affected beards. What he lacked in height he made up in bulk, weighing over two hundred pounds. "We love him most for the enemies he has made," said General Edward S. Bragg in seconding his nomination. The Independents at a later meeting indorsed Cleveland as an exemplar "of political courage and honesty and of administrative reform," while stigmatizing Blaine as "a representative of men, methods, and conduct which the public conscience condemns."

The platforms of the two parties presented no real points of difference. Both pledged tariff revision without injury to domestic industries, both applauded civil-service reform, and both dangled pension promises before the old soldiers. Accordingly, the contest turned upon the pervasive influence of party loyalty and the personal fitness of the candidates. The Democrats played up Cleveland's precept, "Public office is a public trust," while the Republican bolters, contemptuously dubbed "Mugwumps" by the regulars and captained by men like Schurz, Curtis and Godkin, stumped the East and Midwest, urging official rectitude as the issue paramount to all others. To their assistance came additional Mulligan letters, giving fresh cogency to charges of Blaine's illicit financial relations with privilege-seeking corporations. The force of the attack seemed likely to be nullified, however, when Cleveland, accused of being the father of a seven-year-old illegitimate son, frankly admitted the truth. At once clergymen throughout the North carried the "moral issue" into the pulpit. A middle-class people, deeply imbued with rigid notions of chastity, faced the bitter choice between a candidate of loose private morals and one of loose public morals.

Meanwhile, Blaine—the first presidential nominee since Greeley in 1872 to tour the country—employed his magnificent oratorical powers in waving the bloody shirt. His campaign managers made heroic efforts to wean Irish Catholic voters from their traditional Democratic allegiance, Blaine's mother being of that faith. A convention of the Irish Land League at Boston was induced to announce that, if Blaine were elected, "Ireland would be free in thirty days." But the Democrats had the better of the argument when the Reverend Samuel D. Burchard, presiding at a New York ministers' gathering a few days before the election, introduced the Republican nominee as leader of the party opposed to "rum, Romanism and rebellion"—a remark which Democratic newspapers promptly attributed to Blaine himself. Both sides received generous subscriptions from industrial and financial interests, though the Republicans fared better because of their past performance on behalf of the business classes.

The contest proved so close that three days passed before the outcome was definitely known. Cleveland received 219 electoral votes to 182 for Blaine, and 48.9 per cent (4,911,000 votes) of the popular ballots to 48.3 per cent (4,848,000). The Democrats carried the usually doubtful states of New Jersey, Connecticut and Indiana by a few thousand each, and the pivotal state of New York by but 1149 out of a total popular vote of over a million. Had Cleveland lost New York with its 36 electoral votes, or had he lost New Jersey and either of the other two states, Blaine would have won a majority in the electoral college and hence the presidency. Many factors helped tip the scale for Cleveland: the lukewarmness of the Stalwarts toward Blaine, the deflection of

Republican votes into the Prohibition party, Burchard's injudicious remark, a brief business recession, and the participation of many new voters grown to manhood since the war. But, in last analysis, the major credit belonged to the Mugwumps, who wielded their greatest influence in those states where the Republicans could least afford losses.

Cleveland's election, the first Democratic triumph since Buchanan, indicated less the strength of his party than a popular rebuke to reactionary Republicanism. Indeed, countless voters who had confidence in the victorious candidate disliked and distrusted his heterogeneous following. For many years the Democrats, itching for power, had relied upon opportunism rather than principles. To Cleveland fell the choice—as once it had to Andrew Jackson—of letting the party continue undirected and adrift, or of seizing the helm and steering a bold course. The new President was happily situated for the latter alternative. A newcomer in national affairs, he was unhampered by political entanglements. Moreover, his temperament rendered him impervious either to flattery or to threats. Possessing little advance knowledge of national problems, he gave them unremitting study, and his conclusions, once formed, became his inflexible chart of conduct.

The key to his political thinking appeared in the statement in his inaugural address: "The people demand reform in the administration of the government and the application of business principles to public affairs." Like the progressive members of the Republican party, he was interested mainly in questions of administrative efficiency, being largely indifferent to those profound influences which were already breeding labor unrest and class friction. The opportunity of the Democrats either for good or ill was seriously limited, however, for the Senate remained Republican throughout Cleveland's term. The new policies, therefore, did not take the form of statutes, but were embodied in presidential recommendations, executive orders and veto messages.

Cleveland's cabinet, headed by Thomas F. Bayard of Delaware, compared favorably in ability with those of his Republican predecessors. The Solid South was recognized by the appointment of Augustus H. Garland of Arkansas and Lucius Q. C. Lamar of Mississippi respectively as Attorney-General and Secretary of the Interior.[1] In dealing with minor appointments the President's sincerity as a civil-service reformer was sorely tried. Old-time party spokesmen, like Arthur P. Gorman in the Senate and Samuel J. Randall in the House, openly flouted the "Goody Two-Shoes" reform, and even introduced bills to repeal or modify the Pendleton act. Almost alone in its advocacy in his party, Cleveland had to move cautiously to avert factional dissension which might defeat other policies he hoped to accomplish. As far as he could, he stilled the "everlasting clatter for offices" with places from the unclassified service, while quietly applying the merit system to twelve thousand more positions and extending the competitive principle to include promotions as well as first appointments. If he failed to realize the lofty ideals of the reformers, he alone knew, as he wrote Eaton in 1885, "the conditions which bound and qualify every struggle for a radical improvement in the affairs of government."

In his desire to apply efficient business standards to governmental operations, Cleveland made a determined effort to stamp out laxness and fraud in the granting of pensions. One of the worst abuses was Congress's habit of passing special acts to satisfy individuals whose applications had been,

[1] The other members were Daniel Manning of New York, Secretary of the Treasury; William C. Whitney of New York, Secretary of the Navy; William C. Endicott of Massachusetts, Secretary of War; and William F. Vilas of Wisconsin, Postmaster-General. Bayard, Garland and Lamar were all Senators at the time of their appointment to the cabinet.

or were likely to be, rejected by the Pension Bureau. After painstaking examination the President vetoed two hundred and thirty-three such bills. One applicant, who alleged "long and faithful service," was shown to have spent most of his time in prison for desertion. Another claimant, a veteran's widow, asked recompense for her husband's death at the hands of a neighbor who was trying to shoot an owl. In 1887 Congress sought to rebuke Cleveland by passing a general pension measure, based upon the novel principle of compensating ex-soldiers of ninety days' service who found themselves unable to make a living. This he successfully rejected on the ground that its loose phraseology would make the pension list a refuge for impostors instead of a "roll of honor." Followed shortly by an executive order (later revoked) for returning the captured Confederate battle flags, the veto was hailed by the old-soldier element as proof of the unpatriotic character of the party in power. "May God palsy the hand that wrote the order!" shouted the head of the chief veterans' organization, the Grand Army of the Republic. Senator John Sherman in a public address termed the Democratic party "the left wing of the new Confederate army." [1] Yet Cleveland signed far more private pension bills than he vetoed, and in his four years the annual appropriation for pensions grew from fifty-six million dollars to eighty-one.

Other acts also attested his stern determination to impose economy on public expenditures. In 1887 he vetoed an extravagant rivers-and-harbors bill and, as further evidence of his conception of duty, he rejected an appropriation of ten thousand dollars for distributing seed grain to drought-stricken Texas farmers. This latter action he justified on the

[1] It is worth noting that, when a Republican Congress ordered the return of the battle flags in 1905, the act was looked upon as "graceful" instead of "disgraceful"

ground that, "though the people support the government, the government should not support the people." Again, in 1888, he blocked a congressional bill for refunding to the states the direct tax of 1861 amounting to fifteen million dollars. In all his vetoes he was withstanding the demands of a House controlled by his own party as well as of a Republican Senate.

THE SURPLUS REVENUE AND THE TARIFF QUESTION

Cleveland's interest in "the application of business principles to public affairs" caused him to devote increasing attention to the tariff, a subject about which he knew little before entering office. Since 1881 a surplus had been piling up in the treasury at the rate of more than a hundred million dollars a year. This excess of revenue over normal expenditures meant that the people were paying needless taxes, and also that money desirable for business development was being kept out of circulation. Moreover, the brimming treasury tempted Congress to extravagant appropriations—"surplus financiering," as it was called. Some of the money went toward diminishing the national debt, but more characteristic were pork-barrel measures, such as Arthur and Cleveland vetoed, and the lavish outlays for pensions. By keeping the surplus expended, the Republicans hoped to avoid reducing the tariff of 1875, which was the mainspring of the difficulty. A growing popular demand, however, had caused President Arthur to urge action to relieve "industry and enterprise from the pressure of unnecessary taxation"; and in May, 1882, Congress, somewhat reluctantly, had provided for a special commission which, after studying the country's industrial needs, should propose a revision of the tariff "just to all interests."

The nine members of the tariff commission all held protectionist views. Four of the number, including the chairman, John L. Hayes of the National Association of Wool Manufacturers, were directly connected with great protected industries. Nevertheless, the commission ended its investigations by recommending reductions averaging from twenty to twenty-five per cent. At once lobbyists flooded the capital, among them Hayes himself who now, as spokesman for the wool manufacturers, set about to defeat the proposals which he as the commission's chairman had accepted. Leading Republicans, such as Justin S. Morrill of Vermont and Nelson W. Aldrich of Rhode Island in the Senate and William McKinley of Ohio and "Pig-Iron" Kelley in the House, supported such efforts. As finally enacted, the tariff of 1883 left the protective system virtually unchanged. While substantial cuts were made in internal-revenue duties, the decreases in import duties averaged less than five per cent, and these concerned manufactures little affected by foreign competition.

Though the Democrats had been the low-tariff party before the Civil War, their attitude in more recent years had been unsteady and confused. Indeed, some of the leaders, notably Samuel J. Randall of Pennsylvania who voted for the tariff of 1883, were ardent protectionists. Nor had the Democrats while in control of the House from 1875 to 1881 passed any bill to lessen duties. Nevertheless, a rising sentiment within the party among the members from the agricultural West and South favored tariff reform, and in the new House meeting in December, 1883, this element helped defeat Randall's candidacy for the speakership. Yet early the next year a bill fathered by William R. Morrison of Illinois, proposing a twenty-per-cent horizontal cut of most duties, failed of adoption, thanks to a coalition of forty-one Randall Democrats with the Republican minority. Even the platform on which Cleveland entered office reflected the protectionist influence, with the result that the party was pledged to tariff revision that would not "injure any domestic industries."

Cleveland was little given to abstract theories and at no time did he espouse that extreme form of tariff doctrine known as "free trade." Confronted, however, by a large annual surplus revenue, he studied the problem assiduously and resolved to attack the evil at its source. In this resolution he was stiffened by the continued success of the Randall Democrats in obstructing action by the House. From a rather vague indorsement of tariff reduction in his message of 1885, he grew more definite in 1886 and finally in December, 1887, defied all precedent and startled the country by devoting his entire annual message to the subject. Branding the tariff of 1883 as "the vicious, inequitable and illogical source of unnecessary taxation," he declared that the surplus revenue would inevitably breed business stagnation. He charged the system of high protection with enhancing the cost of living for the masses in order to give "immense profits" to an exclusive manufacturing class. As a remedy, he proposed a "readjustment" to eliminate the "hardships and dangers" of the present tariff without, however, "imperiling the existence of our manufacturing interests." He excluded theoretical considerations as irrelevant, for, he added in a phrase quick to catch the public ear, "It is a *condition* which confronts us, not a theory." Cleveland's thunderbolt cleared the air. The Mills bill, incorporating his ideas, passed the House in July, 1888, with only four Democrats dissenting. Since the Senate was Republican, further action awaited the outcome of the presidential election.

Cleveland had already been renominated by acclamation at the Democratic convention in St. Louis the month before, with Allen G. Thurman of Ohio as his running mate. The platform devoted most space to commending the President's tariff program. The Republicans lacked an outstanding candidate, for Blaine declined to allow his name to be considered. Meeting in Chicago on June 19, they finally chose on the eighth ballot ex-Senator Benjamin Harrison of Indiana, a war veteran, strong protectionist and grandson of William Henry Harrison. Levi P. Morton of New York was associated with him. The platform resounded with praise of the "American system of protection," besides promising additional pensions from an "overflowing treasury" and declaring that the surplus should be wiped out by repealing internal-revenue taxes.

The campaign was the first in American history to turn mainly on the tariff. Though the Democrats advocated merely lower duties, not a tariff for revenue only, Republican spellbinders shouted from every stump that their opponents were "free traders," while the Philadelphia merchant, John Wanamaker, who had had wide experience in raising money for the Y. M. C. A., appealed to the protected manufacturers for financial aid. "If you were confronted with from one to three years of general depression by a change in our revenue and protective methods," he asked them, "what would you pay to be insured for a better year?" The Republican campaign hymn was:

> Protection, oh Protection, the joyful sound proclaim
> Till each remotest nation has heard the Tariff's name.

Funds rolled in to the extent of three million dollars, the largest sum hitherto expended by a political party in a presidential contest.

Neither side, however, forgot the influence of the Irish vote in the election of 1884, and both platforms feelingly, if prematurely, congratulated the Irish Americans upon the approach of "home rule" in the Emerald Isle. This time the advantage lay with the Republicans, for Democratic tariff reform might be represented as a surrender to British manufacturing interests. A campaign poster displayed the names of the Democratic nominees under the British flag and the Republican ticket under the Stars and Stripes, with the statement, falsely ascribed to the London *Times:* "The only time England can use an Irishman is when he emigrates to America and votes for free trade." [1] Next to the tariff, Cleveland's pension vetoes came in for unrestrained attacks. With great ingenuity Republican speakers combined the two issues by asserting that the "Solid South" had been "encouraged by English sympathy, as was the Confederacy in the dark days of our civil struggle." Moreover, Cleveland received only half-hearted backing from the professional politicians in his own party, and in New York there is reason to believe that Tammany threw its support to his opponent. Most of the Mugwumps of 1884, however, rallied again to the Democratic standard.

The Republican nominee, carrying the large states by small pluralities, secured an electoral majority of 233 to 168, though in the popular vote Cleveland was the favorite, polling nearly 48.7 per cent (5,538,000 votes) to 47.8 per cent (5,440,000) for Harrison. By losing New York's 36 electoral votes Cleveland lost the election. The buying of votes by Republicans in Indiana, Connecticut, West Virginia and certain other close states had been so bold and widespread as to make the campaign of 1888 probably the most corrupt in American history. An important incidental result was the great impetus given to the adoption of the so-called Australian ballot system, which required secret voting and the use of uniform, official ballots. Beginning early in the year with Kentucky and Massachusetts, all but four states of the Union adopted the reform in some form or other within a decade.

[1] In pursuance of the same purpose, the British Minister at Washington was tricked into writing a letter to a supposed former fellow countryman, in which he implied that Cleveland would be the better President for England. This correspondence was given wide publicity by the Republicans. Cleveland in much perturbation secured the Minister's dismissal.

THE TRIUMPH OF PROTECTIONISM

The new President's chief claim to distinction before taking office had consisted in long and faithful service to his party. A stocky, bearded man, gentle by nature, he shrank from leadership. His reserved manner tended to repel even his political friends, and gave point to the saying: "Harrison sweats ice-water." From the outset he leaned heavily upon men high up in the Republican organization: Blaine, who had helped to engineer his nomination; Speaker Thomas B. Reed of Maine, whose iron rule of the new House won him the nickname of "Czar"; and, for a time, large-state bosses like Senators Platt of New York and "Matt" Quay of Pennsylvania. Harrison put Blaine at the head of his cabinet, and rewarded Wanamaker with the office of Postmaster-General.[1]

In dispensing patronage he permitted the spoilsmen to have almost unobstructed sway in the unclassified service. J. S. Clarkson of Iowa, Assistant Postmaster-General, fairly won the title of "headsman" by changing thirty thousand officials in a single year before he himself was beheaded. Like Grant, Harrison gave many jobs to relatives by blood or marriage. On the other hand, after waiting two years, he extended the merit system to new classes of offices. His greatest service to the cause, however, was his appointment to the Civil Service Commission of Theodore Roosevelt, whose aggressive championship of the reform made his name a source of real terror to politicians in both parties during his six-year tenure.

Congress, now Republican in both branches, quickly set about to cope with the problem of excessive revenue. The

[1] The other members were William Windom of Minnesota, Secretary of the Treasury; Redfield Proctor of Vermont, Secretary of War; William H. H. Miller of Indiana, Attorney-General; Benjamin F. Tracy of New York, Secretary of the Navy; John W. Noble of Missouri, Secretary of the Interior; and Jeremiah M. Rusk of Wisconsin, Secretary of Agriculture (a cabinet office created in 1889).

platform allusion to the "overflowing treasury" was not forgotten, and James ("Corporal") Tanner of New York, upon becoming head of the Pension Bureau, is reputed to have cried, "God help the surplus revenue!" At any rate, in the six months he was allowed to remain, he drummed up new claimants, reopened cases formerly rejected, and increased allowances already granted. In June, 1890, the general pension bill, which Cleveland had vetoed, was repassed by Congress. During Harrison's term the annual outlay for pensions rose from $81,000,000 to $135,000,000. Congress in 1891 did away with $15,000,000 more of the surplus by repassing the bill to refund the direct tax to the states, which Cleveland had also rejected. Enlarged appropriations for the navy account for other expenditures.

The Republican leaders knew full well that such methods dealt with effects rather than causes, but they were resolved not to reduce the tariff unless they could do so without reducing protection. Under the guidance of William McKinley, head of the House ways-and-means committee, a solution was found. A son and grandson of iron manufacturers, McKinley had long held high protection in almost religious veneration. As he read the lesson of the country's growth, "We lead all nations in agriculture, we lead all nations in mining, and we lead all nations in manufacturing. These are the trophies which we bring after twenty-nine years of a protective tariff. Can any other system furnish such evidences of prosperity?" He also believed the customs wall to be the chief bulwark of steady employment as well as high wages.

The McKinley tariff of 1890 lifted the general level of duties from thirty-eight per cent to nearly fifty, yet, through ingenious arrangements, yielded a smaller financial return. Thus, removal of the duty on raw sugar lopped off fifty million dollars from the surplus revenue, while a compensatory bounty of two cents a pound to domestic sugar growers got rid of ten million dollars more. In other instances, such as cotton and woolen textiles and metal products, the rates were fixed so high as virtually to exclude importations. An additional cut in the surplus came from lowering the internal taxes on tobacco and alcohol.

In two further respects the McKinley tariff introduced novelties. Duties on imported farm products were substantially advanced in the hope of spreading the benefits of protection to the farmer as well as to the manufacturer. A second new feature, that of reciprocity, was introduced at the urgency of Secretary Blaine, who charged that the bill as originally drafted disregarded the interests of the growing export trade, and particularly the possibilities of commerce with Latin America. As a result, certain articles commonly imported from Latin American countries, such as molasses, tea, coffee and hides, were placed on the free list, with the proviso that the President might impose duties on them in the case of any nation which levied "unjust or unreasonable" duties on American products.[1]

The generally high rates prescribed by the new tariff were quickly reflected in retail prices, causing widespread dissatisfaction. The fall elections of 1890, coming about a month after the act went into effect, inflicted a stinging defeat on the Republicans, McKinley himself failing to regain his seat. In the new House the Democrats lacked but a few votes of a three-fourths majority. The law, however, met the expectations of its framers in drying up the source of superabundant revenue. The provisions for revenue reduction, together with Congress's lavish expenditures, rapidly wiped out the surplus, and in Harrison's last months a deficit appeared.

[1] Under this provision commercial agreements were effected with ten nations; and the President reimposed duties against three others. These agreements came to an end with the new Democratic tariff in 1894.

The new Democratic House, standing alone, could not hope to alter the tariff situation, but it passed a series of "popgun" bills, designed to fasten public attention on the worst spots in the McKinley act as the election of 1892 approached. In the circumstances Cleveland, who had been quietly practicing law in New York City since his retirement, was the logical Democratic nominee, though he was stubbornly opposed by the professional politicians, especially those connected with Tammany in his own state. After naming him on the first ballot, the convention, meeting in Chicago on June 21, added Adlai E. Stevenson of Illinois to the ticket. The platform, as presented to the convention, reiterated the pledge of 1888 for tariff reduction without injury to domestic industries; but the radical wing induced the delegates to substitute a declaration that any tariff, except for revenue only, was unconstitutional. Though Harrison's renomination was regarded without enthusiasm by the Republicans, the party, hardly daring to repudiate a President of its own choosing, selected him on the first vote at Minneapolis on June 7, along with the New York editor, Whitelaw Reid. On the foremost question of the day the platform contained a ringing reaffirmation of the "American doctrine of protection."

As four years before, the storm center of campaign oratory was the tariff. Cleveland quietly disposed of the doctrinaire utterance in the Democratic platform by declaring in his speech of acceptance, "We need not base our attack upon questions of constitutional permission." Once more the Republicans collected the sinews of war from the great industrialists, but a violent labor outbreak at the Carnegie steel works in Homestead, Pennsylvania (see page 150), helped turn public opinion against the party. The trouble stemmed from wage reductions and, since steel manufacturing enjoyed an unusual measure of protection, the vaunted connection between high pay and a high tariff seemed disproved.

Cleveland won a decisive victory, polling 277 votes in the electoral college to 145 for Harrison, and 46 per cent of the popular ballots (5,557,000 votes) as compared with less than 43 per cent (5,176,000). The remaining 22 electoral votes went to a third candidate, James B. Weaver of Iowa, nominee of the People's party. The spectacular rise of this party denoted the emergence of factors and forces with which the old parties had failed to reckon. The story of the Populists, however, can be better understood in connection with the later discussion of the rising demand for silver inflation (see pages 226-229).

Cleveland returned to the White House, heartened by the people's indorsement of tariff reform and their confidence in his own unflinching integrity. At last the way seemed clear for the party to enact its policies into law since, for the first time in nearly a third of a century, the Democrats controlled both Congress and the presidency. Appearances, however, proved deceptive. Cleveland's second term in office was cut across by currents and countercurrents in American political and social life—business depression, labor conflict, agrarian unrest (see pages 229-234). The multiplying difficulties aroused all the President's fighting qualities; but what had formerly been termed sturdiness of character now sometimes appeared to be mere stubbornness, while to many persons his independence of public opinion seemed indifference to the public welfare. Time, however, has softened such judgments and has revealed him, in spite of his limitations, as an honest, fearless and patriotic executive.

In express recognition of the low-tariff elements in the two parties, Cleveland made Walter Q. Gresham, an Illinois Republican, Secretary of State and John G. Carlisle, a Kentucky Democrat, head of the Treasury.[1] As in his first administration, he appeased the hunger for spoils with offices not yet in the classified list, but during the four years he more than doubled the number of positions under the merit system, bringing their total to about 32,000 out of 200,000-odd in the public service.

Work on a new tariff bill began under the leadership of William L. Wilson of West Virginia, chairman of the ways-and-means committee. A former president of West Virginia University, Wilson had long been active in Congress as a tariff reformer. In striking contrast to the object of the McKinley act, his purpose was to increase the revenue and decrease protection. The Wilson bill, adopted by the House in February, 1894, embodied certain principles which, broadly speaking, were to guide later Democratic efforts at tariff revision. Basic raw materials used in manufacturing and construction—wool, sugar, lumber, iron ore and the like—were placed on the free list. As this enabled industrialists to lessen costs of production, protective duties on manufactures were generally reduced. In order to offset losses in revenue, new internal duties were placed on domestic liquors, tobacco and other luxuries and, for the first time since Civil War days, an income tax was adopted. This last provision—a two-percent levy on incomes above $4000—was the price the Democrats paid for Populist support of the bill, and was championed as a means of shifting the tax burden to those best able to pay.

Once more lobbyists swooped down upon Washington,

[1] The other members were Daniel S. Lamont of New York, Secretary of War; Richard Olney of Massachusetts, Attorney-General; Wilson S. Bissell of New York, Postmaster-General; Hilary A. Herbert of Alabama, Secretary of the Navy; Hoke Smith of Georgia, Secretary of the Interior; and J. Sterling Morton of Nebraska, Secretary of Agriculture. On Gresham's death in June, 1895, Olney became Secretary of State.

determined to undo in the Senate the mischief wrought by the House. Their path was eased by the willingness of Democratic members from the industrial sections to join the Republicans in obtaining rates beneficial to their own states. The truth of Hancock's remark that the tariff was a "local issue" again found illustration. Outright corruption may also have played a part. Senator Quay, among others, admitted to an investigating committee that he had speculated in sugar stock for a rise when the sugar schedule was under consideration. "I do not feel that there is anything in my connection with the Senate," he asserted, "to interfere with my buying or selling the stock when I please; and I propose to do so." Under Senator Gorman's guidance six hundred and thirty-four amendments were attached to the House bill, altering it not only in detail but also in principle. The most important articles, including sugar, were taken from the free list, and protective duties generally advanced. Only the income tax and the internal-revenue duties remained without material change.

After stubborn opposition in the House, the Gorman version was finally accepted; and in August, 1894, the President, bitterly assailing the Senate's action as "party perfidy and party dishonor," allowed the measure to become a law without his signature. The Wilson-Gorman act lowered the general scale of duties to only about forty per cent. Another blow was yet to fall. In 1895 the Supreme Court by a vote of five to four knocked out the income-tax provision, thereby reversing an earlier decision of 1881. The majority held that a tax on incomes was a "direct" tax and thus subject to the constitutional limitation of being apportioned among the states according to population.[1]

[1] Pollock *v.* Farmers' Loan and Trust Company. All later income taxation by the federal government had to await the adoption of the Sixteenth Amendment in 1913 because, of course, the distribution of population is no index of the relative concentration of wealth.

This series of mishaps, along with the hard times continuing from the Panic of 1893, helped discredit the Wilson-Gorman act with the public. Though the tariff was only a minor issue in the next election, President McKinley when he entered office in March, 1897, summoned Congress in special session to revise the tariff according to the Republican pattern. The outcome was the Dingley act of 1897, a thoroughgoing protective measure which raised the customs wall to the highest point it had yet reached, an average of fifty-seven per cent. The principle of reciprocity, abandoned by the Democrats, was restored, though in so complicated a form as to be virtually unworkable. After a decade of almost ceaseless controversy victory thus rested with the ultraprotectionists. The remarkable prosperity which shortly burst upon the country was hailed by the Republicans as vindicating their most extravagant claims for the protective system. For ten years the tariff disappeared as a public issue.

SELECT BIBLIOGRAPHY

Old Issues and New Attitudes, 1877–1897. The general surveys of the period include Oberholtzer, *History,* IV-V; Rhodes, *History,* VIII; Sparks, *National Development, 1877–1885;* Dewey, *National Problems, 1885–1897;* Josephson, *Politicos;* and Peck, *Twenty Years of the Republic* (from 1885). Significant public figures are treated in Williams, *Hayes;* Smith, *Garfield;* Howe, *Arthur;* Nevins, *Cleveland;* Olcott, *McKinley;* Chidsey, *Gentleman from New York* (Conkling); Dyer, *Evarts;* Burton, *John Sherman;* Barnes, *John G. Carlisle;* Robinson, *Thomas B. Reed;* Fuess, *Schurz;* Cary, *George William Curtis;* and Ogden, *Godkin.* Stanwood, *History of the Presidency,* I, emphasizes the presidential elections, while Ostrogorski, *Democracy and the Party System,* traces the Independent movement. Thomas, *Return of the Democratic Party to Power in 1884,* is more comprehensive than the title indicates.

For the spoils system the best works are Fish, *Civil Service and the Patronage;* Stewart, *National Civil Service Reform League;*

and Sageser, *First Two Decades of the Pendleton Act.* Oliver, *History of Civil War Pensions,* and Glasson, *Federal Military Pensions,* are standard references. For the evolution of tariff legislation and the triumph of protection, see the writings by Taussig, Stanwood and Tarbell cited at the end of Chapter III.

Chapter V

EMBATTLED INDUSTRY, 1865–1900

THE TREND TOWARD BIG BUSINESS

AS THE tariff wall rose higher and higher, manufacturers benefited increasingly from the cutting off of foreign competition, and fresh capital poured into mills and mines. Meanwhile, the expanding network of rails facilitated the shipment of merchandise to distant points, and high-pressure methods of advertising educated the public to new needs. The amount spent on newspaper advertising alone grew from about forty million dollars in 1880 to nearly ninety-six in 1900. These totals, of course, did not include the cost of traveling salesmen or of outdoor signs and bill-boards. "America is daubed from one end of the country to the other with huge white-paint notices of favorite articles of manufacture," wrote one observer. Jacques Offenbach, the European operatic composer, spoke of advertising in the United States as "playing upon the brain of man like a musician does upon a piano."

To meet the waxing domestic demand for goods as well as the growing export trade, business leaders turned more and more to large-scale methods of production. Industry conducted with limited capital in a restricted area began to give way to operation with unstinted capital for far-flung markets. Whether in manufacturing or transportation, the drift set strongly toward the merging of smaller into larger units, with a consequent reduction of competition and a corresponding concentration of control. By the 1880's organization on a nation-wide basis became a distinguishing feature of the economic world.

The advantages of combination and consolidation were many. Through its ampler command of capital a large business concern could employ more efficient managers, install improved machinery, buy raw materials more cheaply, effect economies in marketing and finance, and withstand more easily the demands of employees for higher pay and better working conditions. To the extent that the business was monopolistic, the owners were in a position to reduce production and raise prices. A big plant could also make profitable use of wastes and by-products that smaller establishments had to discard. As the newspaper humorist, "Mr. Dooley" (Finley Peter Dunne), said of one of the mammoth Chicago packing houses, "A cow goes lowin' softly in to Armours an' comes out glue, gelatine, fertylizer, celooloid, joolry, sofy cushions, hair restorer, washin' sody, soap, lithrachoor an' bed springs so quick that while aft she's still cow, for'ard she may be anything fr'm buttons to pannyma hats." [1] With such advantages captains of industry could appease the clamor of investors for bigger returns and, when they wished to do so, satisfy the public's demand for cheaper prices.

In order to command the financial support needful for huge undertakings, the type of business organization known as the corporation rapidly supplanted individual ownership and the partnership, the forms commonly employed before the Economic Revolution. Through the sale of stock a wide reservoir of capital could be tapped. Besides the expectation of unusual profits, the investor was attracted by the fact that he was liable only to the extent of his stock in case of business failure, whereas in a partnership each member could be

---

[1] Actually, Mr. Dooley's fiction hardly exceeded the fact, for the by-products included glue, gelatine, fertilizer, soap, leather, felt, knife handles, combs, buttons, brushes, pepsin, albumen, oils, oleomargarine, candles, glycerine, isinglass, lard, tennis strings, hairpins, umbrella handles, dice, perfume-bottle caps and artificial teeth.

held for the firm's full indebtedness. The corporation enjoyed the further advantage of being able to plan its activities without reference to the lifetime of particular individuals. Moreover, if it wished to hide excessive profits from
the public, it could "water" its stock, that is, grant additional
shares to its stockholders and so disguise the rate of dividend.
Thus, a corporation earning twelve per cent might, by doubling the stock held by each individual, cut the nominal rate
of return to six per cent without denying each stockholder
his full profits. In such case the board of directors could,
with a specious show of sincerity, combat the demands both
of consumers for lower prices and of wage-earners for better
pay. Watering was also a regular practice of unprincipled
financiers who seized the opportunity to sell stock to gullible
investors without warning them of its diminished value. One
expert estimated in 1883 that more than a quarter of the
railroad capitalization represented water.

The actual process of absorption and consolidation was
directed by business leaders who, because of their boldness,
creative energy and relentless driving power, embodied many
of the mythical elements of folk heroes. By common consent
they were termed "steel kings," "coal barons," "railway magnates," "Napoleons of finance." Foremost among them were
Cornelius and William H. Vanderbilt, J. Edgar Thomson,
Jay Gould, James J. Hill and Edward H. Harriman in railroad organization; John D. Rockefeller, Henry H. Rogers
and Henry M. Flagler in the oil industry; Andrew Carnegie,
Henry C. Frick and Charles M. Schwab in steel; Philip D.
Armour, Nelson Morris and Gustavus F. Swift in meat packing; and Jay Cooke and J. Pierpont Morgan in the financial
field. Arising in most cases from obscure origins, and unhindered by moral scruples, they were fired by a passionate
will to succeed. They conceived of themselves as above the
law though always willing to hide behind it. "Law!" roared

Cornelius Vanderbilt. "What do I care about the law? Hain't I got the power?" Some of these men were builders with far-reaching plans; others were wreckers with no plans at all. The story of their activities is a singular blend of the heroic and splendid with the sordid and sinister.

For the most part, they were free to carry out their schemes without let or hindrance from the government, for the American people traditionally held to the gospel of individualism or laissez faire, that is, the right of citizens to be let alone in their economic pursuits. Yet the captains of the new order proclaimed the doctrine with tongue in cheek, for, while they opposed governmental intervention to their detriment, they constantly advocated interference with the free play of economic forces through tariffs, subsidies and the gift of natural resources. The country's belief in individualism was an inheritance from pioneer days when the doors of opportunity swung wide for all; only gradually did the public come to realize that, under modern conditions, unbridled freedom for the few threatened economic servitude for the many. The philosophy of the new leadership was a primitive one. It may be summed up in the phrase, "Everyone for himself," or, in the terse expression attributed to William H. Vanderbilt, "The public be damned!" Yet, with all their cynicism, the best of these men were spurred by the conviction that they were laying the foundations of a new America, that the accumulation of colossal wealth by a select class would indirectly benefit all ranks of society.

The tendency toward combination in the United States resembled a similar development abroad, for everywhere the advantage lay with large-scale economic enterprises. In Great Britain, an older industrial country than America, the process of railway amalgamation started sooner. As a result, the government began to regulate the roads as early as the 1840's and in 1873 set up a commission to safeguard the interests of the public. In Germany the railroad problem was solved in most instances by government ownership, but the trend toward industrial consolidation was more marked than in England. The reason was that the Germans, like the Americans, had hitherto lagged far behind in manufacturing and were trying to catch up. As one means of stimulating industry, Germany paralleled the course of the United States in increasing her tariff duties in 1879, 1885 and 1887. In Europe, however, the combinations did not attain the gigantic size of those in America, for the countries were smaller and many of the other favorable conditions were absent.

RAILROAD CONSOLIDATION

Though occasional mergers of railroads had earlier taken place in the United States, the close of the Civil War ushered in the era of rapid and extensive amalgamation. Cornelius Vanderbilt was one of the first to vision the possibilities. Already past middle age, the possessor of riches amassed in steamboat traffic, he sold his vessels in 1865 in order to give his whole attention to developing a continuous rail route from the Atlantic Seaboard to the heart of the Midwest. Starting with a line joining New York City with Albany, he acquired the New York Central in 1867, making possible uninterrupted traffic from New York to Buffalo. In 1873 he extended the road to Chicago by leasing the Lake Shore and Michigan Southern. When he embarked on his railway career, Vanderbilt's wealth amounted to about ten million dollars; when he died twelve years later at eighty-three, he left nearly a hundred and five million, the first great modern fortune. Much of it came from unscrupulous manipulation of railway stocks and from methods of competition akin to the ethics of the jungle.

Meanwhile the Pennsylvania Railroad under J. Edgar Thomson's leadership outgrew its line from Philadelphia

to Pittsburgh, gaining entry to Chicago and St. Louis in
1869 and establishing connections with New York City two
years later. Its business methods, however, formed a welcome
contrast to Vanderbilt's. By 1875 three other trunk lines had
been completed between the Atlantic and Lake Michigan: the
Erie, the Baltimore and Ohio, and the Grand Trunk. Similar mergers took place in the Mississippi Valley. Three
through lines linked Chicago and St. Louis by 1870, and
others were later established. In the South, also, comparable
tendencies were at work.

It is doubtful whether enough business existed as yet to
support all these roads. At any rate, the rival companies engaged in furious strife for traffic between major shipping
points. Certain practices resulted that harmed both the railways and the public. Thus in 1869, and again in the years
from 1874 to 1876, the trunk lines between Chicago and the
seaboard waged relentless rate wars. A standard freight
charge of $1.88 per hundred pounds in 1868 was slashed to
twenty-five cents in 1869; sometimes the rates did not pay
the expense of operating the trains. Such contests proved too
costly to the railroads, however, to continue long at a time.

Another scheme was to charge higher rates between some
places than between others without regard to distance. Intent on taking business from their rivals, the companies held
down freight charges between cities having several rail connections, while exacting excessive rates between points on
their roads served by but a single line. As a result, it cost less
to ship goods from Chicago to New York than to places a few
hundred miles east of Chicago. The "long-and-short-haul"
device aroused popular indignation, especially among rural
inhabitants, who were the chief sufferers; but the practice
enabled the roads to offset losses elsewhere. Equally objectionable was the policy of discriminating against small
shippers by granting secret rebates to dealers in the same

area who provided the lines with a larger freight traffic. When, as sometimes happened, the railroads themselves conducted other businesses, such as coal mining, they had a special incentive to employ unfair methods in order to put competitors in such fields at a disadvantage. At the same time, the rail companies sought to influence legislation and public opinion by bestowing free passes on governors, legislators, judges, politicians, newspaper editors and preachers.

To escape the evils of cutthroat competition, the railroads from time to time tried various schemes of joint action. Rate agreements were entered into for fixing uniform charges, only to break down sooner or later for want of mutual confidence. Pooling, a somewhat similar device, proved more successful. By this plan the rival companies divided the freight business according to some prearranged ratio, or placed the total earnings in a common fund for like distribution. The first notable pool, that formed in 1870 by the roads connecting Chicago and Omaha—the Northwestern, the Rock Island and the Burlington—lasted fourteen years. Each line retained about half its earnings on the through traffic, leaving the balance to be shared equally among them. Meanwhile, railroads elsewhere made similar arrangements, their duration determined usually by the willingness of former competitors to trust one another.

Popular resentment at railroad practices deepened as the years rolled by. While the movement for state regulation culminating in the Granger laws (see page 87) had a good effect, the transportation problem was, by its very nature, interstate or national in character, calling for action by Congress. As early as 1874 a Senate committee, headed by William Windom of Minnesota, proposed that the government build and operate a double-track freight line from the seaboard to the Mississippi as a means of keeping down the charges of private companies. In 1874 and 1878 the House,

under Western pressure, passed bills for the federal regulation of railroads, and in 1885 both branches acted, though
without being able to agree on a common measure.

Final action was hastened by the decision of the Supreme
Court in 1886 in the case of Wabash, St. Louis & Pacific
Railway *v.* Illinois. The tribunal, reversing its view of nine
years before in the Peik case (see page 88), forbade individual states to fix rates on shipments passing beyond their
borders. At the time, about three fourths of the country's rail
traffic was of this character. The Wabash decision declared,
in effect, that this ever increasing volume of interstate business could be regulated only by the federal government. The
upshot was the interstate-commerce act which Cleveland
somewhat reluctantly signed on February 4, 1887. It forbade
unreasonable charges, special rates, pools, rebates and the
long-and-short-haul discrimination, and provided for an Interstate Commerce Commission of five members to guard
against violations. This body, however, could not fix traffic
rates or enforce its own decisions. If a railroad refused to
comply, the Commission must bring suit in a federal court.
The law, being based upon the interstate-commerce clause,
did not apply to traffic wholly within a single state.

This first experiment in the national supervision of transportation proved, in most respects, a disappointment. In
cases of appeal the Supreme Court was more apt to uphold
the companies than the Commission. Repeated decisions restricted its powers within the narrowest bounds. According
to Mr. Justice Samuel F. Miller's explanation of the laissez
faire attitude of most of his colleagues on the high court, "It
is vain to contend with judges who have been at the bar the
advocates for forty years of railroad companies, and all the
forms of associated capital, when they are called upon to decide cases where such interests are in contest. All their train-

ing, all their feelings are from the start in favor of those who need no such influence."

Accordingly, the railways were, for the most part, able to continue their evil ways, though they had to pay greater regard to external appearances than before. For example, since pooling was banned, the companies attained much the same result through traffic associations, which regulated rates and punished disobedient members. The Interstate Commerce Commission after a decade of experience declared the situation "intolerable both from the standpoint of the public and the commission." When the Supreme Court in 1897 by a vote of five to four held that traffic associations were illegal, a new consolidating movement began, which led to the merging of many hitherto independent lines.[1]

Despite the steady expansion of mileage in the later years of the century, the number of railroads declined from 1500 in 1880 to about 800 in 1900. At the latter date more than half the nation's trackage belonged to six major financial groups, the Vanderbilt, Morgan, Harriman and Pennsylvania interests owning approximately 20,000 miles each, the Gould group 16,000 and the Hill interests 5000. From this centralizing movement came benefits as well as abuses. Thanks to the economies inherent in large-scale undertakings, freight rates, which in 1860 had rarely fallen below two cents per ton-mile, averaged three quarters of a cent in 1900. Though the interstate-commerce act had largely missed its aim, nevertheless the principle of national regulation was established, and for such regulation official machinery existed which Congress might strengthen and enlarge whenever public opinion should demand.

[1] In this case, involving the Trans-Missouri Freight Association, the court held that the association was a combination in restraint of trade and hence that it contravened the Sherman antitrust act of 1890 (see page 139).

CONCENTRATION IN MANUFACTURING

The movement for the consolidation of manufacturing resembled that of railroad combination. Following the Civil War, industrial establishments, unhindered by legal barriers, waxed rapidly in size and, like the rail companies, waged desperate war with their competitors in the effort to absorb or destroy them. This phase in turn gave way to widespread attempts by the bigger concerns to stabilize particular industries through price agreements, pools and other devices for restricting output and lifting prices. Finally, with public opinion at full tilt against Big Business, both states and nation intervened with restraining laws. The unifying trend, while stronger in some branches than others, left untouched few industries of basic importance.

The career of the Standard Oil Company, one of the earliest and strongest industrial combinations, illustrates the process of concentration in other fields. In 1865 John D. Rockefeller, then a young man of twenty-six who had made a small fortune from army contracts during the Civil War, was the guiding spirit in a commission house in Cleveland, Ohio, a concern capitalized at $100,000. Joining hands with powerful capitalists there and in New York, he expanded his operations, absorbed rival establishments and in 1870 organized the million-dollar Standard Oil Company of Ohio, which controlled four per cent of all the oil refined in the United States. Now began a career of conquest that was Napoleonic in its daring, scope and execution. By 1872 the Standard owned twenty of the twenty-five independent plants in Cleveland. In the ensuing three years Rockefeller and his associates acquired the biggest refineries in New York, Philadelphia and Baltimore. The Standard next obtained control of the refining business of western Pennsylvania. Thus, within a decade, ninety per cent of all the refineries in the land had passed into its hands.

Many elements, good and evil, made possible this brilliant campaign. Not least was the remarkable group of men who gathered about Rockefeller—Henry M. Flagler, Henry H. Rogers, John D. Archbold and others—who strained every nerve to plan, plot and fight for the Standard and exacted an equal measure of devotion from their subordinates. Another factor was the superior efficiency attained through large-scale operation. The Standard not only set up factories to make its own barrels and produce its own acids, but it acquired tank cars and built great underground mains, or pipe lines, for the transportation of crude oil. It also created selling agencies and, instead of paying high storage charges, erected large tanks at strategic points. In addition to its main product, kerosene or coal oil, it utilized and popularized many by-products, such as lubricating oils, gasoline, paraffin and vaseline.

Its success was further assured by unfair methods of competition, ranging all the way from secret rebates on its rail shipments (a favor which it enjoyed for thirty years or more) to the bribery and blackmail of public officials. In 1872 the Standard, joining certain Pittsburgh refining concerns in the South Improvement Company, induced the railroads to agree to grant them secret rebates not only on their own oil but also on their competitors' shipments. The scheme was discovered before the arrangement went into effect and, in the face of a mighty popular wrath, all parties to the agreement disowned it. Before the public exposure, however, agents of the Standard used its existence as a club to force the sale of rival refineries. The Standard's favorite method of crushing competitors was through ruinous price-cutting campaigns, followed by proportionate increases once the object was attained.

By 1882 the Rockefeller group owned fourteen companies outright, besides a majority interest in twenty-six others. Price agreements and pooling arrangements had helped secure harmony of operation in earlier years, but now, with so vast a system to manage, the Standard undertook a novel form of organization: the industrial trust. It was an old device fitted to new conditions. Adopted in 1879 and revised in 1882, the plan provided for a secret union of the several companies under nine trustees to whom was confided all the stock of the individual companies and who thus exercised centralized direction. The original holders, in return for their stock, received "trust certificates" which entitled them to their due share of the earnings of the whole. Operating without a charter, the trust could do pretty much as it pleased. So successful did the scheme prove that between 1884 and 1887 it prompted the formation of trusts in other fields, notably the American Cottonseed Oil Trust, the National Linseed Oil Trust, the National Lead Trust, the Distillers' and Cattle Feeders' Trust (popularly termed the whisky trust), the Sugar Refineries Company (the sugar trust) and the National Cordage Association.

Meanwhile, the popular outcry against Big Business was reaching a climax. The gains to the public from the improved quality and generally lower prices of commodities were obscured by the brutal practices of muzzling competition, corrupting government officials, extorting excessive profits, watering stock and opposing labor welfare. The idea of monopolies had always been abhorrent to the American mind. Now, under the reign of laissez faire, not only the comforts but the very necessities of life—"from meat to tombstones," declared Henry Demarest Lloyd in his book *Wealth against Commonwealth*—were drifting into the maw of "soulless corporations." As he put it, "We now have Captains of Industry . . . rearranging from office-chairs this or that industry, by mere contrivances of wit compelling the fruits of the labor of tens of thousands of their fellows, who never saw them . . . ; sitting calm through all the hubbub raised in courts, legislatures, and public places, and by dictating letters and whispering words remaining the master magicians of the scene."

As an indication of the mounting tide of public protest, an Anti-Monopoly party appeared in the campaign of 1884, though with little success. President Cleveland took note of the situation in his tariff message of 1887 when he remarked that competition among businessmen "is too often strangled by combinations . . . which have for their object the regulation of the supply and price of commodities. . . . The people can hardly hope for any consideration in the operation of these selfish schemes." In the election of the next year the two old parties, for the first time, condemned trusts and monopolies. That they took this stand was due to pressure from the farming regions, where the aroused people were urging similar action on their state legislatures. In 1889 and 1890 fifteen commonwealths, mostly in the West and South, passed measures to ban conspiracies or agreements in restraint of free competition. Before the movement spent its force, all but New Jersey, Delaware and West Virginia followed suit. Unfortunately, remissness on the part of some states proved fatal because a corporation chartered in one of them could trade unmolested across state lines. With this in mind, Congress in July, 1890, adopted a national prohibitory law known as the Sherman antitrust act. It declared illegal "every contract, combination in the form of trust or otherwise, or conspiracy, in restraint of trade or commerce among the several States, or with foreign nations."

Passed in response to an imperious popular demand, the statute was drafted in such haste that the purport of its apparently simple and direct language was, for many years, the subject of impassioned controversy. The words might mean that all extensive business enterprises were illegal since, by their superior efficiency, they tended to be in restraint of competitive trade. If this were the true interpretation, then the law aimed to prevent the benefits of large-scale operation as well as its evils. But it was contended by others that, inasmuch as the terms used in the statute had been employed since ancient times in the common law, they had acquired a special technical meaning. If this were so, acts in restraint of trade, when reasonable and fair, were not intended to be affected. Other obscurities lurked in the statute. Were railway combinations forbidden as well as other kinds? Were labor organizations prohibited along with capitalistic combinations? These and similar questions had to be decided eventually by the judiciary.

The Supreme Court in these early years leaned toward an interpretation which made the antitrust act apply equally to reasonable and unreasonable restraints of trade.[1] On the other hand, the judges seriously crippled the law's effectiveness by defining the term "trade" as narrowly as possible. When the government sought to dissolve the sugar trust, the tribunal held in the case of United States v. E. C. Knight Company (1895) that the control of ninety-five per cent of the sugar refining of the country did not in itself constitute an act in restraint of trade. In other words, Congress could legislate concerning the distribution of products, but it lacked power to deal with industrial concentration as such. In the circumstances the executive department put little energy into trying to enforce the statute. Only seven suits were instituted under Harrison, eight under Cleveland and three under McKinley; and some of these were directed against labor combinations. It was left for later administrations to discover

[1] The court reversed this view in 1911 in the case of Standard Oil Company v. United States (see page 327).

means of rendering the Sherman act an effective instrument against Big Business.

With the antitrust act hardly more than an empty threat, it is not surprising that the centralizing trend in business proceeded with increased momentum. In the thirty years before 1890 twenty-four industrial combinations had been effected with an aggregate nominal capital of $436,000,000, but in the last decade of the century one hundred and fifty-seven came into being with a total capital of $3,150,000,000. The years 1898–1901 were particularly prolific, ushering in an era of superconsolidation signalized by the formation of the United States Steel Corporation (1901), the first billion-dollar amalgamation. This leviathan combined under one management two hundred and twenty-eight companies located in a hundred and twenty-seven towns and cities in eighteen states.

By this time, however, the particular type of organization known technically as the trust was a thing of the past. Two decisions in state courts were responsible, one in New York in 1890 against a unit of the Sugar Refineries Company, and another in Ohio two years later against the Standard Oil Trust.[1] But the word itself continued, in popular parlance, to denote any form of Big Business that in size approached a monopoly. In deference to these decisions the great capitalistic organizations now assumed a different legal framework. Some changed into single huge corporations. Others took the form of holding companies, organized to secure control of corporations in the same branch of industry through the purchase of stock. To many people the holding company seemed the old trust doing business under a different name and with better legal protection. Indeed, the changes in

[1] The New York decision held that the combination partook of the nature of a partnership of corporations and hence violated the common law. In the Ohio case, the decision rested explicitly on the contention that the object was to form a monopoly.

structure had no perceptible effect on efficiency of operation or on earnings. As a trust from 1882 to 1891 the Standard, for example, never made less than $8,000,000 a year; under a system of interlocking directorates from 1892 to 1896 the individual companies totaled from $19,000,000 to $34,000,-000; and as a holding company the annual profits from 1899 to 1905 ranged from $34,000,000 to $57,000,000.

The centripetal tendency in manufacturing and transportation was symptomatic of a similar movement in almost every other important sphere of economic activity. As the century drew to a close, the telephone, telegraph and express businesses gravitated into the hands of a few corporations. The Amalgamated Copper Company, formed in 1899, controlled sixty per cent of all the copper produced in the land; and a few years later the United States Steel Corporation controlled about seventy per cent of the iron and steel production. In the field of banking and finance the Morgan and Rockefeller groups had by 1900 acquired such immense power that it was virtually impossible to launch a large business undertaking without their participation or approval. In many instances their representatives exercised the directing power in industrial corporations, life-insurance companies, railroads, public-utility companies and the like. Thus the country was confronted with the spectacle of combinations and monopolies forming on nearly every hand. Thoughtful people began to wonder how long democratic institutions could withstand the strain.

THE RISE OF ORGANIZED LABOR

If the public at large awoke only slowly to a realization of the peril, the wage-earners had long since taken up the gage of battle with the new economic overlords. As industry changed over to large-scale methods and impersonal corporate control, the rift between those who worked for pay and those who paid for work steadily widened. More and more, workingmen lost the sense of being self-respecting craftsmen or masters of their own tiny shops, and became mere tenders of machines, their conditions of labor dictated by managers representing absentee owners. When stockholders clamored for bigger dividends or employers engaged in price-cutting competition, the wage-earners' pay was the first to suffer. They toiled in gloomy, ill-ventilated structures amidst dangerous unguarded machinery, and the workday, which in many branches had been cut to ten hours during the short-lived labor movement of the 1830's, tended to grow longer rather than shorter. The employers' rapacious demand for cheap labor drew increasing numbers of women and children into the mills and factories, while the plight of native workingmen was further aggravated by competition with the hordes of immigrant laborers.

Meanwhile, the number of wage-earners vastly increased, marking the first appearance of a genuine proletarian class in America. In 1860 only about one and a third million worked in factories, mines and rail transportation; thirty years later the total reached four and a quarter million, a rate of growth far exceeding that of the population in general. An aggrieved class in the United States usually turns to political action for relief, but for the workingmen the prospect was not encouraging in an era when government and people were enchained by the doctrine of laissez faire. Though some optimistic souls did from time to time try to launch labor parties, the shrewder labor leaders, mindful of the successes attained by capital through joint economic effort, devoted their energies to promoting similar combinations among the toilers. The factory system packed workingmen densely in cities where, mingling with their fellows and exchanging ideas, they responded readily to appeals to unite against the enemy.

War-time prosperity had caused a rebirth of the earlier labor movement, with the result that local unions were formed in many crafts, city trade assemblies were set up for more general action, and ten or more national unions came into being. In the flush years preceding the Panic of 1873 the movement continued to grow. Under the leadership of William H. Sylvis of the Iron Molders' Union, a promising attempt was made in 1866 to federate the country's labor organizations into an all-inclusive association called the National Labor Union. Its constitution declared: "Heretofore the highest form labor associations have taken is the national union of some of the trades. Between these organizations, however, there was no sympathy or systematic connection, no coöperative effort, no working for the attainment of a common end, the want of which has been experienced by every craft and calling." The new body also included groups espousing various political reforms.

The National Labor Union advocated the eight-hour day, better pay, arbitration as a substitute for strikes and, with particular emphasis, coöperative shops in which the workers should supply the capital and share the profits. Such coöperatives as were tried, however, including the iron foundries conducted by Sylvis's own union, failed either from mismanagement, inadequate capital or unfair competition. The National Labor Union held seven annual congresses, the last one for the purpose of launching a labor party. But internal dissension rent the organization, and the crash of 1873 administered the finishing blow.

In the somber years that ensued, the labor movement reached a low ebb, most of the local and national groups dissolving or maintaining a bare existence. The total number of union members fell from over three hundred thousand in 1873 to less than fifty thousand in 1878. One of the organizations that managed to keep alive served as the channel for a second and more successful effort to combine the varied forces of labor on a nation-wide basis. This was the Noble Order of the Knights of Labor, founded in 1869 at Philadelphia by Uriah S. Stephens and six other garment cutters. Unlike the National Labor Union, it aimed to unite all workers, skilled and unskilled, in one big union without regard to trade or vocation. The Knights of Labor held that the mechanization of industry was steadily erasing craft distinctions and thus putting all wage-earners on the same level, and that only through consolidated action could labor defend its rights against concentrated capital. Though differing in the basis of membership, the Knights championed many of the same demands as the National Labor Union—the eight-hour day, fairer wages, industrial arbitration, the establishment of coöperatives, the abolition of child labor and similar reforms.

For ten years the Knights grew but slowly. In order to protect members from persecution by employers, complete secrecy cloaked their doings, even the order's name being withheld from the public. With the return of prosperity in 1879 and the open use of the order's name two years later, the membership shot upward until in 1886 it reached seven hundred thousand, drawn chiefly from the ranks of unskilled labor. As a peaceable way of improving conditions for the workers, Terence V. Powderly, who headed the Knights from 1879 to 1893, encouraged the formation of coöperatives. More than a hundred and thirty-five were set up, principally in the mining, cooperage and shoe industries, where wages were exceptionally low; but these enterprises encountered the same difficulties as those of the National Labor Union and enjoyed no greater success. Meanwhile, the sudden expansion of membership drew into the order many socialists, radicals and other jangling elements. In spite of their avowed attachment to arbitration, the Knights became embroiled in an increasing number of strikes, boycotts and other disturbances. The disastrous failure of some important railway strikes in 1886 cast further discredit on the order, precipitating it into a decline as rapid as its rise.

Another reason for its collapse was the advent of a rival labor group based upon a wholly different principle of organization. Started in 1881 by disgruntled members of the Knights of Labor, this body adopted its present name, the American Federation of Labor, when it reorganized on a broader basis in 1886. Discarding the idea of one big union, the American Federation, like the British Trades Union Congress upon which it was modeled, was a confederation of self-governing labor bodies, supervised by a central board of officials. Its core consisted of national unions, but it also included city trade assemblies, state federations of labor and local unions lacking national affiliations. Thus, the new organization, comprising only skilled workers, made allowance for the special interests of particular groups among them. The central officials confined their activities to strengthening and extending the union movement, acting in an advisory capacity during industrial conflicts, and lobbying for favorable legislation. The Federation shunned coöperatives, but in other respects its program resembled that of the Knights, including the eight-hour day, legislative prohibition of child labor and the improvement of working conditions in factories and mines.

From the outset the dominant figure in the A. F. of L. was Samuel Gompers, born of Jewish parentage in a London tenement. As a member of the Cigarmakers' Union in New York, he had breathed into it a militant spirit which enabled it to issue from the depression years stronger than when it entered. President of the American Federation almost continuously until his death in 1924, he stamped it with his vigorous personality. Distrustful of intellectuals and theorists, he stood firm against all efforts to commit it either to a socialist program or to the experiment of a labor party. The membership of the affiliated bodies grew from 150,000 in 1886 to 200,000 in 1890 and to 550,000 in 1900. One important group of unions, the four Railway Brotherhoods (engineers, conductors, firemen and brakemen), did not join, feeling that, because of their strategic position in American economic life, they had everything to lose and nothing to gain from casting in their lot with the Federation. Moreover, the great bulk of unorganized and unskilled workers, perhaps ninety per cent of the whole, remained outside its ranks. The Federation's success rested on its effectiveness as an alert and compact minority.

INDUSTRIAL CONFLICT AND EFFORTS AT ADJUSTMENT

With the ranks of both labor and capital mobilized for defense and aggression, the stage was set for a trial of strength between the opposing forces. The antagonism usually turned on questions of wages, the length of the workday or the right of employees to form unions; but behind such specific issues lay a fundamental difference in point of view. Labor asserted its inalienable right to have a voice in determining working conditions, to share more amply in the profits of industry, to raise its standard of living through better homes and more leisure. In short, labor's spokesmen insisted that the lot of the toilers keep pace with the increase of the wealth they helped create. Employers, on the other hand, viewed labor as but one of many factors in industry, its rate of pay to be governed by the "iron law" of supply and demand, not by humanitarian considerations or notions of fancied right. Indeed, the rôle of the wage-earner seemed to them of small moment as compared with the indispensable part played by financial resources, inventive ability, machinery, managerial talent and business enterprise.

With two such irreconcilable attitudes, protracted industrial warfare was inevitable, particularly in view of what even President Cleveland called the "grasping and heedless exactions of employers." Yet neither side was wholly blameless in these encounters, for, in varying degrees, both were actuated by irresponsibility, greed and criminality.[1] Nor did either party envisage such contests as other than purely private affairs, of no concern to the public. It was many years before the American people came to realize that, whichever combatant won a strike, the community was the loser, thanks to business paralysis, enhanced prices and the added costs of police protection and of charity.

The first great struggle stemmed from a series of wage reductions on the Pennsylvania, New York Central and Baltimore & Ohio lines during the lean years after the Panic of 1873. In the latter half of July, 1877, rioting and lawlessness convulsed rail centers all the way from Baltimore to St. Louis and San Francisco. On appeal of the governors, President Hayes sent troops to Maryland, Pennsylvania, West Virginia and Illinois. At Pittsburgh the contest resembled a pitched battle. State guardsmen in the neighborhood, called to arms, fraternized with the men. When a militia detachment from Philadelphia killed nearly twenty strikers, a raging mob besieged the soldiers for twelve hours in a roundhouse. Order was finally restored by patrols of citizens. Meanwhile, about sixteen hundred cars, a hundred and twenty-six locomotives and most of the railway shops and supplies had been destroyed, a loss estimated at five million dollars. Here as elsewhere the strike failed. In the end the men went back to work at the reduced pay.

If the return of prosperity in 1879 did not lessen the ten-

[1] The extreme of labor lawlessness is illustrated by the Molly Maguires, a secret organization of Pennsylvania anthracite miners, whose career of terrorism and assassination was finally ended in 1876 by the punishment of the ringleaders.

sion between capital and labor, strikers generally found it easier to win their demands, for in boom times industrialists could offset added costs by raising prices to the consumers. According to the federal Bureau of Labor, nearly 24,000 strikes and lockouts took place in the score of years from 1881 to 1900, involving about 128,000 establishments and over 6,600,000 wage-earners, at a total loss to employers and employees of $450,000,000 and an incalculable cost to the public at large. The business recession of 1884–1885 yielded a startling harvest of industrial conflicts—strikes, sympathetic strikes, lockouts, nation-wide boycotts—causing the years 1885–1886 to be called the "Great Upheaval." Twice as many disorders occurred as in any previous two-year period.

Three of these disturbances involved the Gould railway system in the Southwest. The first, in March, 1885, resulted in the restoration of a ten-per-cent wage cut. Six months later a second strike, caused by discrimination against workers belonging to the Knights of Labor, also concluded triumphantly for the men. But the third and greatest of the outbreaks ended in their utter rout. Started in protest against the discharge of a foreman affiliated with the Knights, the conflagration raged during March and April, 1886, in all parts of the Gould domain, throwing nearly nine thousand employees out of work in five states and territories.

The same year signalized a country-wide movement for an eight-hour day, a demand given special point by the need of providing work for the jobless through a shortening of hours. Sponsored by the American Federation of Labor, the movement was backed by trade unions representing 340,000 members. Before May 1, the date set for a general strike, 150,000 wage-earners secured a shorter day (eight or nine hours) without a demonstration, whereas of those who actually struck only 42,000 won their point. In many cases, the gains were presently lost through the aggressive activities of employers' associations formed for the express purpose of fighting unionized labor. Yet the conception of an eight-hour day excited wide popular interest, and the public gradually came to accept it as a just demand.

The next historic strike took place in July, 1892, at Homestead, Pennsylvania, among the employees of the Carnegie Steel Company, who were confronted with wage reductions and a refusal to recognize their right to organize. The hiring of three hundred armed Pinkerton detectives to guard the plant precipitated a fierce battle, resulting in ten deaths and the injury of over sixty. Reënforced by eight thousand militia, the company gradually resumed operations with nonunion men. The strike dragged to a close in November, and the defeat prevented organized labor for many years from unionizing the steel industry. Meanwhile, far to the west, repeated wage cuts due to the falling price of silver ore goaded the miners of the Cœur d'Alene district in Idaho to bloody measures. In order to combat strike breakers imported by the management, the men seized the property and harried the "scabs" out of the district. But, at the governor's request, President Harrison sent in troops, martial law was declared, and the strike failed. This affair, however, proved the forerunner of intermittent disorders that ravaged Cœur d'Alene for years.

The widespread unemployment and distress bred by the Panic of 1893 plunged the labor world into another welter of struggles which, because of their destructive character, made thoughtful men fear for the stability of the social order. The number of wage-earners involved in strikes during 1894 reached six hundred and ninety thousand, surpassing the mark set in 1886. The gravest disturbance took place in Chicago as the outgrowth of drastic wage cuts by the Pullman Palace Car Company. The reductions did not apply to the highly paid officers and managers, and it was well known that the company had on hand a surplus of over four million dollars. The employees' cause was promptly championed by the American Railway Union, a new organization formed by Eugene V. Debs in the hope of combining all rail workers in a single body. It was the precursor of the vertical or industrial union, which was to constitute the basic idea of the CIO in the 1930's. After demanding vainly that the company submit the dispute to arbitration, the American Railway Union ordered its hundred and fifty thousand members to cease handling Pullman cars on all roads. In the last week of June the strike spread to twenty-three lines, affecting traffic operations in twenty-seven states and territories.

The vortex of the storm, however, was Chicago. There, until the United States government took a hand, the principal antagonists were the General Managers' Association, representing the rail companies, and the American Railway Union. Lawless mobs and gangs of hoboes and criminals, always present on such occasions, terrorized the community, burning, looting and killing. The damages, direct and indirect, inflicted on the property and business of the country were later estimated at eighty million dollars. Despite Governor John P. Altgeld's refusal to ask for federal troops, President Cleveland intervened on his own authority. On July 2 the government secured from the federal circuit court a "blanket injunction" which forbade Debs, his fellow strike leaders and "all other persons whomsoever" to interfere in any manner, direct or indirect, with the operation of the railways. The next day two thousand soldiers were dispatched to Chicago under General Nelson A. Miles. Though the Constitution specifies that the governor or legislature should apply for federal protection against "domestic violence," Cleveland found warrant for his unprecedented course in the obligation to safeguard the mails, protect interstate commerce and uphold the processes of the federal courts. On July 10 Debs was arrested on the charge of conspiracy in restraint of trade under the Sherman antitrust act. Released on bail, he was rearrested a week later on a new charge, contempt of court, that is, violation of the judicial injunction of July 2. The government's vigorous action broke the back of the disturbance, causing its complete collapse a few weeks later.

Other than as a great labor insurrection, the strike of 1894 is epochal because of the new legal conceptions and practices which issued from it. The employment of United States troops without consent of the state authorities marked a novel and impressive development of national power. The application of the Sherman antitrust act to labor combinations—later upheld by the courts—threw unexpected light on that law. Perhaps most significant of all was the part played by the judiciary in using the injunction as a weapon in industrial warfare. Though this was not the first time it had been so used, the sweeping character of the injunction in the Pullman strike caused profound concern among the friends of labor. It was denounced as "judicial tyranny"—unjust because it seemed to range the might of the government on the side of the employers, illegal because those violating the court order were sentenced without trial by jury and subjected to penalties not prescribed by statute. Opposition to "government by injunction" became a cardinal issue of the American Federation of Labor, resulting finally in action by Congress under President Wilson intended to restrict its operation (see page 339).

The tumult and lawlessness attending this thirty years' war should not be allowed to divert attention from the constructive forces which, quietly but surely, were breeding saner relations between labor and capital. As trade unions grew in strength and improved in leadership, they were slower to resort to methods of coercion and violence. Amidst the "confused alarms of struggle and flight" they slowly learned lessons of self-control and responsible action in the economic sphere, not unlike the lessons in political self-government which the early colonists had learned through the town meeting and the provincial assembly. Enlightened employers, for their part, betrayed a greater readiness to meet their demands. In the words of the federal Anthracite Coal Strike Commission of 1902, "Experience shows that the more full the recognition given to a trades union, the more businesslike and responsible it becomes. Through dealing with business men in business matters, its more intelligent, conservative, and responsible members come to the front and gain general control and direction of its affairs." In the more strongly organized occupations the practice gradually developed of settling differences through joint conferences instead of the ordeal by battle, the arrangements being embodied in trade agreements. If adjustment by common consent proved impossible, the alternative still remained of peaceful arbitration by disinterested parties.

Some employers sought to improve the relations between capital and labor by removing the sources of friction before trouble arose. Such efforts were generally modeled on similar schemes in the leading industrial countries abroad. Thus, in 1880, the Baltimore and Ohio Railroad with the help of its employees instituted a fund for paying disability and death benefits, and four years later inaugurated an old-age-pension plan. A different device was to allow the workers to participate in a company's earnings over and above their regular wages. The Pillsbury Flour Mills in Minneapolis, which adopted profit sharing in 1882, was the largest establishment in the world using the plan at the time. By 1893 more than a hundred American concerns were doing so. By these and kindred measures it was hoped to spur the employee to greater endeavors and make him feel more genuinely a part of the business.

Some companies also founded "model towns" in order to take the men and their families out of the slums. From the standpoint of organized labor, however, this expedient smacked of feudal paternalism; and perhaps in most instances the employer's real motive was to head off the formation of trade unions. The company-owned towns frequently proved a means of exploiting the workmen through high charges for rent, food, water and light. Dissatisfaction with conditions in the town of Pullman, just south of Chicago, contributed to the ill feeling which produced the great railroad strike of 1894.

More acceptable to the labor elements were the gains accruing from legislation. These years beheld a growing tendency on the part of the states to depart from a rigorous laissez faire attitude. Such concessions, though falling far short of the thoroughgoing measures adopted in Great Britain and Germany, attested the ever greater effectiveness of the lobbying activities of organized labor. Before 1879 various legislatures had adopted acts for shortening the workday, but for one reason or another these statutes failed of their purpose, being unenforced or unenforceable.[1] In that year, however, Massachusetts set an example for other commonwealths by putting teeth into her earlier ten-hour law in regard to children and women in factories. Other industrial states followed, and the evil of child labor declined a third during the eighties, only to thrive again in the next decade as cotton mills multiplied in the South. During the eighties, too, acts began to be passed for guarding dangerous ma-

---

[1] In 1868 Congress took an advanced stand by specifying an eight-hour day for workmen employed by the federal government, but for nearly twenty years the law was ineffectively administered when not wholly disregarded.

chinery, assuring better sanitary conditions in factories, and providing for government inspection.

The ominous proportions of the Great Upheaval elicited in 1886 the first presidential message devoted solely to the labor problem. Tacitly recognizing the right of workers to organize, Cleveland proposed a national commission to assist in settling industrial controversies of an interstate character. Congress responded in 1888 with a law for arbitrating differences between interstate railways and their employees on condition that both parties should consent and neither be bound by the outcome. Not until ten years later did the Erdman act specify that, once a dispute was submitted to arbitration, the decision should be final. Meantime, fifteen states had enacted legislation for voluntary arbitration and nonenforceable decisions in cases falling within their jurisdictions. These as well as many of the other measures for labor welfare left much to be desired, while even adequate laws were seldom adequately enforced.

Least progress of all greeted the legislative efforts to secure a shorter workday for men. When such acts were adopted, the courts invariably held them unconstitutional, save in especially hazardous occupations, on the ground that they interfered with the individual's freedom of contract. As late as 1900 seventy per cent of the industrial wage-earners still labored ten hours or more each day. In particular fields the conditions were appalling. The steel industry generally maintained a twelve-hour day for seven days a week; trainmen commonly worked seventy hours a week; and the hours in the textile mills varied from sixty to eighty-four.

SELECT BIBLIOGRAPHY

The Trend toward Big Business. The process of consolidation receives attention in the textbooks of American economic history by Faulkner, Kirkland and Shannon, and is the special concern of Edwards, *Evolution of Finance Capitalism,* and Tarbell, *Nationalizing of Business.* Informing chapters can be found in Sparks, *National Development;* Dewey, *National Problems;* and Oberholtzer, *History.* For the rôle of advertising, Presbrey, *History and Development of Advertising,* is useful. Outstanding figures in the centralizing movement are portrayed in Nevins, *Rockefeller;* Burr, *Portrait of a Banker: James Stillman;* Harvey, *Frick;* Hendrick, *Carnegie;* Hovey, *Morgan;* Hutchinson, *Cyrus H. McCormick: Harvest;* Kennan, *Harriman;* Leech and Carroll, *Armour and His Times;* Pyle, *James J. Hill;* Tarbell, *Elbert H. Gary;* and Winkler, *Du Pont Dynasty.* For a less favorable view of the overlords of business, consult Josephson, *Robber Barons,* and Myers, *History of Great American Fortunes.* Material bearing on the Supreme Court's attitude toward consolidation appears in Warren, *Supreme Court in United States History,* II; Fairman, *Mr. Justice Miller and the Supreme Court;* and Swisher, *Stephen J. Field.*

Railroad Consolidation. Riegel, *Story of the Western Railways,* and Moody, *Railroad Builders,* sketch the history of leading roads. For the legislative background of the interstate-commerce act, Haney, *Congressional History of Railways,* is important. Technical aspects are emphasized in Jones, *Principles of Railway Transportation;* Ripley, *Railroads: Rates and Regulation;* and Daggett, *Railroad Reorganization.*

Concentration in Manufacturing. Hendrick, *Age of Big Business,* and Moody, *Masters of Capital,* offer excellent popular accounts. Moody, *Truth about the Trusts,* is a statistical survey of capitalized industry and finance as it existed at the apex of the consolidation movement. For particular industries, see Berglund, *United States Steel Corporation;* Clemen, *American Livestock and Meat Industry;* Coon, *American Tel. & Tel.;* Copeland, *Cotton Manufacturing Industry;* Jones, *Anthracite Coal Combination;* Kuhlman, *Development of the Flour Milling Industry;* Mussey, *Combination in the Mining Industry;* Tarbell, *History of the Standard Oil Company;* and Thornton, *History of the Quaker Oats Company.*

Organized Labor and Industrial Conflict. The fullest treatment is in Commons and others, *History of Labour,* II. Shorter accounts include Perlman, *History of Trade Unionism;* Harris, *American Labor;* and Ware, *Labor Movement.* Among the important special studies of organized groups are Lorwin, *American Federation of Labor;* Robbins, *Railway Conductors;* McCaleb, *History of the Brotherhood of Railroad Trainmen;* and Robinson, *Amalgamated Association of Iron, Steel and Tin Workers.* Wolman, *Growth of American Trade Unions,* and Peterson, *Strikes in the United States,* are primarily statistical. Yellen, *American Labor Struggles,* describes the major conflicts, while Coleman, *Labor Disturbances in Pennsylvania,* is concerned with the Molly Maguires, and Browne, *Altgeld,* is helpful for the Pullman strike. The following works deal with varied aspects of labor's status: Cahill, *Shorter Hours;* Berman, *Labor and the Sherman Act;* and the same author, *Labor Disputes and the President.*

Chapter VI

HUMANITARIAN STRIVING,
1865–1900

ECONOMIC PANACEAS

THE rank and file of the urban workers were wage-conscious, not class-conscious. They shared Henry George's opinion in *Progress and Poverty* (1879) that "squalor and misery, and the vices and crimes that spring from them, everywhere increase as the village grows to the city, and the march of development brings the advantages of the improved methods of production and exchange." Like George, they saw that "in factories where labor-saving machinery has reached its most wonderful development, little children are at work; wherever the new forces are anything like fully utilized, large classes are maintained by charity or live on the verge of recourse to it; amid the greatest accumulations of wealth, men die of starvation."

But they wanted no radical remaking of the economic order. While they rejected the current notion that it was the duty of the government to take care of the rich and the rich would take care of the poor, they also rejected the opposite doctrine of a class war on capitalism. With the discontented farmers, they desired a more generous share in the fruits of the capitalist system, not its overthrow. Their philosophy was well summed up by Adolph Strasser, president of the Cigarmakers' Union, before a Senate committee in 1885: "We have no ultimate ends. We are going on from day to day. We are fighting only for immediate objects—objects that can be realized in a few years. . . . We are all practical men." It was this attitude that gave point to the saying that the American wage-earner was a capitalist without money.

This psychology pervaded not only trade unions, but also the labor parties which sprang up from election to election to enjoy a brief moment of life. However roundly they might condemn the existing economic system as the "prolific womb" which spawned "the two great classes, tramps and millionaires," they offered no sweeping program of change. What they demanded was the reform of specific abuses, such as the long workday, bad factory conditions, the exactions of monopolies, the dearth of money and the inroads of immigrant competition.[1] Polling but a handful of votes, they nevertheless, through their incessant agitation, did something to educate the public to the need for remedial action.

Though the bulk of the workingmen were, in Strasser's phrase, "practical men," various minority groups preached more drastic schemes of reorganizing society. Through the labor world stalked Marxian socialists from Germany, French refugees who had taken part in the Paris Commune of 1871, and Russian nihilists. Rankling from Old World wrongs and scornful of the bourgeois aspirations of American labor, they saw in the startling extremes of wealth and want confirmation of their belief that America was going the way of Europe. The first socialist parties appeared in New York, Philadelphia, Chicago, St. Louis and other large cities shortly after the Civil War, making their chief bid to citizens of German stock. In 1877, under goad of the depression, the various local groups combined in the Socialist Labor party. Its purpose was not to reform but to revolutionize the basis of the nation's industrial life. Attributing the plight of the masses to the concentration of economic power in the irresponsible hands of a few, the new party proposed to abolish

[1] Of this type were the Labor Reform party (1872), an outgrowth of the National Labor Union; the Greenback-Labor party (1880 and 1884), which sought to combine the interests of rural and urban labor; the Anti-Monopoly party (1884); and the Union Labor party (1888).

the right of private property in the fields of transportation and communication as well as in other public utilities and large-scale industries. Instead, they urged that these basic enterprises be conducted on democratic principles, that is, that the people collectively own them and, in a sort of partnership with the employees concerned, operate them for the benefit of all.

For a dozen or so years the Socialist Laborites shunned ordinary political activities, seeking rather to worm their way into control of the Knights of Labor or the American Federation. At last presenting a presidential ticket in 1892, they mustered but 22,000 votes and, in the next election, only 34,000. The party was too foreign in its make-up, too aloof from American ways, to gain wide support. The result was the formation of a rival organization, called at first the Social Democratic party, then simply the Socialist party, which in 1900 won for its candidate, Eugene V. Debs, nearly 95,000 votes. Debs well represented the new influence in the movement. Born in Indiana, a friend of the poet James Whitcomb Riley, and American to the core, he had imbibed his belief in socialism from reading tracts while jailed for his activities during the Pullman strike. Four times more he was to be the standard bearer, but neither his party nor the older socialist organization ever succeeded in garnering an electoral vote.

During the eighties another foreign ideology contended for radical favor, one that was even more idealistic than socialism. Anarchism proposed to replace the political state with loosely federated groups, each owning its means of production and exchanging its products with the others. All activity should be voluntary and the power of coercion exist nowhere. As a means of attaining this benign social order, however, most of the leaders advocated the use of terrorism and violence. This fact repelled many who might otherwise have been attracted, and the cause never gained more than five or six thousand adherents, chiefly among the Chicago Germans.

In 1883 the leaders, including Albert R. Parsons, an ex-Confederate veteran who was about to found the fiery anarchist sheet *The Alarm,* gathered at Pittsburgh and issued a "manifesto" vociferating revolution and confiscation. But the public generally remained ignorant of the movement until May 4, 1886, when during a mass meeting at Haymarket Square, Chicago, where some anarchists spoke in protest against the shooting of strikers by the police, an unknown hand hurled a bomb that killed one policeman and wounded many others. The fighting that ensued caused ten more deaths, including six policemen. In a burst of popular rage Parsons and seven other anarchist leaders (six of them foreign-born) were promptly haled to trial. Although no trace of the bomb thrower could be discovered, nor the fact established that he had been incited by the accused, the jury found all eight guilty.[1] However unjust the conviction, anarchism received a blow from which it did not recover. The attempt of the Russian-born Alexander Berkman during the Homestead strike of 1892 to kill Henry C. Frick, head of the Carnegie Steel Company, intensified the popular aversion, and President McKinley's assassination at the hands of another anarchist brought about a law of 1903 banning anarchists from further admission to the country.

Meanwhile, the philosophy of discontent had been blossoming in native proposals for a perfect society. Between 1884 and 1900 over two-score American novelists indulged in such

[1] Parsons and three others were hanged, one took his own life and the remaining three were committed to prison. In a public statement at the time the usually mild William Dean Howells vigorously denounced the "principle" of killing men because of "their frantic opinions, for a crime which they were not shown to have committed." In 1893 Governor Altgeld braved the fury of mob hysteria by liberating those who had been imprisoned.

utopian fancies, expounding their views in volumes significant less as good literature than as an expression of the popular yearning to escape the chaos and injustices which the Economic Revolution had fostered. One of these books, Edward Bellamy's *Looking Backward, 2000–1887,* published in 1888, created a veritable sensation. The author had started out to picture a "cloud-palace for an ideal humanity," but in the course of writing he had become convinced of the practicability of his social scheme. He visioned a society in which the gigantic trust development of the later nineteenth century had culminated in one all-embracing trust, owned and operated by the people in their own interest. Under a system of universal service everyone must work, hence everyone had leisure. All workers were paid the same, not because they did equal amounts but because they put forth the same effort. Poverty was unknown; hospitals served in the place of prisons; and the creative energies of mankind were released for unparalleled cultural and technological achievement. Among other inventions Bellamy foretold the coming of the radio.

Within ten years four hundred thousand copies were sold in the United States alone; and the proposed system of "Nationalism" proved so alluring that in 1891 a hundred and sixty-three Nationalist Clubs were active in twenty-seven states. No political party was formed to advance the idea, however. Neither Bellamy nor any of his fellow utopian novelists used the terms "socialism" or "communism," a fact which suggests the purely American inspiration of their thinking. All agreed, too, that the changes must come through education and the ballot, not violence. They made their special appeal to the middle class of small business and professional men.

Less sweeping in its scope, but quite as unacceptable to the bulk of the people, was another native solution, embodied in Henry George's *Progress and Poverty*. George was a self-taught economist, unaware of other thinkers who had advanced somewhat similar ideas. While living in California he had been struck by the evils flowing from the concentration of land ownership, and a visit to New York City had shown him the same evils in exaggerated form. He believed that human beings were entitled to their fair share of land just as they were of air and water, and he held that a system which denied them this right was undemocratic.

George therefore proposed a tax on land so adjusted as to take away the gain ("unearned increment") arising from advantages of location and the growth of the community. It was wrong to tax values resulting from the owner's exertions, he declared, because that was "a fine upon improvement." His plan, he argued, would make it unprofitable to let real estate lie idle; it would tend to reduce the size of large individual holdings, thus multiplying the number of landholders; it would "abolish poverty, give remunerative employment to whoever wishes it, afford free scope to human powers . . . and carry civilization to yet nobler heights." So considerable would be the revenue yield that the government could dispense with all other taxes, to the great advantage of business enterprise. Moreover, the government, possessing abundant funds, could take over the railroads and telegraphs, and embark on a vast variety of social services such as public baths, playgrounds and theaters.

The single tax, as it was called, excited wide interest, winning George a surprising vote in his unsuccessful race for mayor of New York in 1886, and forming the cornerstone of the United Labor party, which offered candidates two years later in the presidential election. Over two million copies of *Progress and Poverty* had been sold by 1905. In England, and notably in Australia, the idea exerted a deeper influence than in the United States, where its chief importance, in the long run, lay in directing attention to more rational methods of local taxation.

The more extreme projects of social redemption presumed a condition of human misery and despair in America which, save at certain times and in certain places, did not actually exist. Though the rich were growing richer and the poor had never before been so numerous, the middle class was increasing by leaps and bounds, constantly receiving additions from below and serving as a balance wheel in the social structure. Hence the new ideologies made relatively few converts. On the other hand, the ferment of radical ideas helped to leaven the thinking of many who had grown too complacent, or too acquiescent in things as they were. Their point of view, surprisingly enough, found expression in President Cleveland's declaration to Congress in December, 1888: "Communism is a hateful thing and a menace to peace and organized government; but the communism of combined wealth and capital, the outgrowth of overweening cupidity and selfishness, which insidiously undermines the justice and integrity of free institutions, is not less dangerous than the communism of oppressed poverty and toil, which, exasperated by injustice and discontent, attacks with wild disorder the citadel of rule." Not a few leaders of the progressive movement in the early twentieth century received their initial impulse from youthful reading of Bellamy, the socialist writers or Henry George.

SOCIAL BETTERMENT IN THE CITIES

The typical social reformer in the years after the Civil War believed that his proper business was to correct present abuses rather than to draw up blueprints of a future society. Though he generally wanted to strengthen the labor movement, his primary concern was in making life more tolerable for underprivileged groups through the intervention of the state and municipal governments. The zeal for improving conditions betokened, in part, a resumption of reform energies which the sectional struggle had, for a time, driven into a single channel. Ex-abolitionists and ex-workers in the Sanitary Commission, spurning the notion that to the victor belongs repose, now turned briskly to fresh tasks of uplift. Thus, William Lloyd Garrison, having discontinued the *Liberator* in 1865 after the ratification of the Thirteenth Amendment, joined Wendell Phillips in furthering such causes as woman suffrage, Indian welfare, Negro education and prohibition. Phillips in 1870 ran for governor of Massachusetts on the Labor Reform ticket. The thinning ranks of these old-time crusaders were swelled by a host of new recruits, young men and women of the middle class whose consciences revolted at man's inhumanity to man as exhibited in the congested cities. To their hands fell the dynamic leadership in the new movements for social amelioration. In coping with problems of urban maladjustment they usually modeled their efforts on those rendered familiar by the experience of European humanitarians.

For many years before the Civil War the state and even some local governments had provided almshouses, orphanages, homes for inebriates, insane asylums and institutions for the deaf, dumb and blind. Most cities possessed, in addition, a considerable array of private benevolent societies. The difficulty was that these institutions, whether public or private, were too often run by incompetents; and in so far as they dealt with the problem of poverty, they contented themselves with methods of indiscriminate almsgiving, which tended to foster a condition of permanent pauperism. They did not see that their real function should be to enable the needy to make a fresh start in life.

In 1864 Massachusetts pointed the way toward a more constructive program by setting up a state board of charities to supervise and coördinate the work of the tax-supported relief institutions. Before the end of the century over half the Union had taken like action. Meanwhile, in 1877, the Reverend S. Humphreys Gurteen, who before coming to America had been active in the London Charity Organization Society, persuaded the private philanthropic agencies in Buffalo to join in a similar body. The plan involved not only a coördination of activities, but also methods of rehabilitating poor families. Other places fell into line until the century's close saw kindred federations, under various names, flourishing in a hundred and thirty-eight cities. Henceforth the system of "associated charities" became the normal provision of all sizable towns.

Even more significant perhaps was the migration of resident colonies of social workers into the slum districts. There, amidst conditions of squalor and vice, they offered opportunities for instruction and recreation to all ages—kindergartens, boys' clubs, gymnasiums, classes in arts and crafts, and the like—on the principle that a fence at the top of a precipice is better than an ambulance at the bottom. The movement was deeply indebted to the example of Toynbee Hall in London, which many of the pioneer American settlement workers had visited; and the effort appealed particularly to the idealism of young college men and women. From 1886 to 1900 more than a hundred social settlements were planted in American cities, the most famous being Hull-House, founded in Chicago in 1889 by Jane Addams and Ellen G. Starr. Among the other early leaders were Lillian D. Wald at the Henry Street Settlement and Stanton Coit at the Neighborhood Guild, both in New York; Robert A. Woods at the South End Settlement, Boston; and Mary E. McDowell at the University of Chicago Settlement.

Closely related to the problem of helping the poor was the question of decent housing. The tenement population of

New York City grew from twenty-one thousand in 1879 to one and a half million in 1900. In these dilapidated, ill-ventilated, filth-soaked structures, crowded together in solid blocks, the death rate was sixty-two per thousand as compared with twenty for the city in general. Over half the fires took place in the slum districts though they contained less than a third of the city's buildings. Jacob A. Riis, a reporter on the *New York Sun,* played a leading part in agitating for more humane housing requirements. His book, *How the Other Half Lives* (1890), vividly portrayed the horrors of slum life, the conditions making for disease, vice and crime, and awakened many persons to facts they had not suspected or had not wanted to know. Between 1865 and 1900 the New York legislature made four different attempts to regulate the building of tenements; but, thanks to the greed of landlords, faulty laws and lax enforcement, the situation only grew steadily worse. Nor was the state of affairs much better in Philadelphia, Boston, Cincinnati and other big cities.

Directly or indirectly, all such efforts had a vital bearing upon the welfare of the growing generation. As cities walled in an ever larger proportion of America's future citizens, society for the first time felt obliged to give energetic attention to what Kate Douglas Wiggin called "children's rights." The steps taken at first were halting, but grew firmer as the years passed. When a mother was haled before a New York municipal judge in 1874 for beating and starving her nine-year-old stepdaughter, the prosecution was undertaken by the Society for the Prevention of Cruelty to Animals, for as yet the law protected dumb brutes but not human offspring. In that dingy courtroom was born the Society for the Prevention of Cruelty to Children, the first of its kind in the world. It quickly developed branches in other communities, and everywhere the members strove for more humane laws and better opportunities for the young. The crop of child-labor legislation in the North during the eighties (see page 154) owed much to their agitation.

Meanwhile, an awakened public conscience sought to restore to childhood a part of its heritage of outdoor play. In 1877 a minister at Sherman, Pennsylvania, devised the scheme of "country week" for city waifs during the stifling hot season, a plan eagerly taken up by charitable agencies in leading towns and supported by the "fresh-air funds" of enterprising newspapers. A little later, in 1885, a Boston society tried the experiment of providing sand gardens for poor children. From this small beginning rose the playground movement, which spread to twenty-one communities by 1900 and was in after years to prevail in nearly all cities.

Attempts were also made to cope more intelligently with juvenile delinquency, a problem whose gravity stemmed from the fact that one out of every twenty persons in prison in 1880 was under twenty-one years of age. Deeply influenced by European example and notably by the Irish prison system of Sir Walter Crofton, reformers such as Enoch C. Wines and Zebulon R. Brockway maintained that the primary purpose of penal discipline should be to regenerate rather than to punish the offender. Make him good, they said in effect, and make him good for something. In 1877 the New York state reformatory, opening at Elmira under Brockway's direction, tried out the new conception on young men from fifteen to thirty years old. The inmates, freed from the usual association with confirmed criminals, were encouraged to shorten their stay through good conduct and an earnest application to means of self-improvement; then, conditionally released, they continued under supervision long enough to show evidence of the sincerity of their reformation. These two principles—the indeterminate sentence and the parole system—worked so successfully that other Northern and

Western states introduced the Elmira plan and, before the end of the century, even applied some of its features to older prisoners.

Urban congestion obliged public authorities to deal increasingly with the problem of contagious diseases. Since colonial times recurrent epidemics had taken their toll of townsfolk, but never before had these scourges had such dense populations on which to feed. Under spur of the peril Louisiana and Massachusetts set up state boards of health in 1867 and 1869, and thirteen other states did likewise before 1878. Then came the terrible yellow-fever pestilence of 1878–1879, which blazed a trail of death through the South, nearly depopulating Memphis. Twelve more commonwealths wheeled into line before 1882, with the rest presently following.

To the aid of these state boards of health and their municipal counterparts came certain timely medical discoveries of momentous import. In the 1870's and 1880's Louis Pasteur, Robert Koch and other European scientists laid bare the germ theory of disease, and somewhat later Theobald Smith, an American, showed by his studies of Texas fever among cattle that germs might be carried by insects. In the words of Austin Flint, a medical authority writing in 1888, "What has been accomplished within the past ten years as regards knowledge of the causes, prevention, and treatment of disease far transcends what would have been regarded a quarter of a century ago as the wildest and most impossible speculation."

This new knowledge provided, for the first time, an intelligent basis for the science of preventive medicine. Health officers could now make early and definite diagnosis of communicable maladies and devise more effective means of control. Quarantine was extended to other ills than the traditional ones of smallpox and yellow fever; and port cities were barred against imported plagues like cholera and typhus. Progress was made also in providing special hospitals for the isolation and treatment of contagious cases. At the same time, municipal enterprise in constructing waterworks and drainage systems (see page 69) formed an important ally in the public-health campaign.

The results, if not as far-reaching as later when the principles of public hygiene became more fully developed, were nevertheless profound, particularly in populous centers. The average expectation of life at birth is estimated to have been less than forty in 1855; it had reached forty-eight by 1900. In the last decade of the century, despite the increased herding of immigrants in the worst quarters of the cities, the death rate for the nation fell almost ten per cent. This improvement was due largely to diminishing mortality from tuberculosis, diphtheria and children's diseases. It was fortunate for America that, when the urban age dawned, medical advance made it possible to protect huddled populations from the dire scourges which for so many centuries had ravaged the cities of the Old World.

THE FIGHT AGAINST THE LIQUOR TRAFFIC

Urban growth also attracted acute attention to the liquor problem. The impressive gains for state-wide prohibition in the 1850's had been mostly lost during the Civil War. Army service gave the drink habit a new popularity, while the United States government itself lent the traffic a certain respectability by turning to it, for the first time, as a productive source of revenue. When the war closed, only Maine and Massachusetts remained "dry," and the latter soon fell by the wayside. In the years that followed, liquor manufacturing became one of the country's major businesses. The capital investment rose from $29,000,000 in 1860 to $67,000,000 in 1870 and to $269,000,000 in 1890.

With so vast a financial stake, producers and retailers entered politics both to advance their interests and to resist attempts at adverse legislation, whether heavier taxation or prohibition. As early as 1867 the United States Brewers' Association resolved to "sustain no candidate, of whatever party, in any election, who is in any way disposed toward the total abstinence cause." It has already been seen how, during Grant's sway, the whisky distillers were able to reach corrupt hands into the very precincts of the White House. The major parties avoided taking a national stand on the temperance question, fearing either to risk a new and uncertain issue with the voters or to lose campaign funds from the liquor magnates.

In the cities were the principal battlements of the "wet" interests. There the traffic in alcoholic beverages employed countless persons at every stage of manufacture, distribution and sale; there the teeming immigrants saw no reason to forgo cherished folk customs in a land of freedom; there, too, the saloon with its free lunch and rough sociability served as a sort of poor man's club. New York in 1890 possessed seventy-five hundred saloons, or one to every two hundred persons, while smaller cities like Albany, Cincinnati and San Francisco had an even higher number proportionately. By contrast, dry sentiment predominated in the farming regions, as had been the case at earlier periods. The churches most deeply rooted in rural villages and towns—the Methodist, Baptist and Presbyterian—crusaded tirelessly against "King Alcohol" and lent driving power to such bodies as the Prohibition party, founded in 1869, and the Women's Christian Temperance Union, which arose five years later.

The Prohibitionists demanded legal suppression of the traffic and advocated woman suffrage as the swiftest means to that end. Though they never won an electoral vote, they outrivaled other minor parties by managing at least to keep alive and, in the course of doing so, they carried on a continuing agitation for the cause. Of greater importance was the W. C. T. U. which, under Frances E. Willard's leadership, became the most militant force in the movement. It waged relentless war against the foe on every front, inducing legislatures to require "scientific temperance instruction" in the schools, and fighting everywhere for the restriction or destruction of the liquor business. Even in the cities the temperance forces gained adherents, notably among persons who, unmoved by the usual emotional appeals, turned against the saloon power as the invariable ally of corruption, criminality and political reaction. Here and there, too, large employers were beginning to see the advantages of a sober laboring force, especially on the railroads, while the Catholic Church, influential with immigrant wage-earners, encouraged habits of moderation or of total abstinence. In 1895 a new and aggressive body, the Anti-Saloon League of America, was formed to coördinate the various organized efforts aiming at prohibition.

The actual tide of battle swept back and forth, with the saloonless area expanding or contracting as victory perched on one side or the other, and with the temperance cause enjoying its principal successes in the rural sections. Thus, during the eighties, the question of state-wide prohibition was submitted to popular vote in at least sixteen commonwealths, but at the end of that time a net total of only three states—Iowa and the Dakotas—had been added to the four states of Maine, New Hampshire, Vermont and Kansas which were dry when the decade began. Other methods of combating the liquor traffic proved more successful, though they were less spectacular. On the principle of divide-and-conquer, the drys managed to advance their cause, notably in the rural districts of the Midwest and the South, through local option, that is, local prohibitory enactments adopted by popular vote. Elsewhere, in the hope of lessening their number, saloons were required to operate under high licenses costing from five hundred to a thousand dollars a year. One state, South Carolina, from 1893 to 1907 even tried the experiment of exclusive government stores for dispensing intoxicants. The purpose was to eliminate the private-profit motive from the sale of drinks.

But, whatever the system of restriction, enforcement of the regulations always proved a stumblingblock. Where alcoholic beverages could not be legally sold, "bootleggers" were apt to ply a brisk trade. Even in Maine, oldest of the dry states, the federal authorities collected internal-revenue taxes from a hundred and sixty-one Portland liquor dealers in 1893. Because of lax administration the measures of repression often failed of the desired effect. Partly as a result, the per-capita consumption of intoxicants for the country at large nearly trebled from 1860 to 1900. The most optimistic drys hardly dreamed that within the span of another generation their cause would find lodgment, temporarily at least, in the federal Constitution.

THE ADVANCE OF WOMEN

The leadership assumed by women in the temperance cause, the social-settlement movement and certain other reform enterprises attested their changing rôle in society. The impact of events had jarred them loose from the traditional seclusion of the home, obliging them whether they would or not to take an increasing part in the world beyond their domestic walls. Thus, the Economic Revolution forced more and more women to find jobs as factory hands, sweatshop workers, telephone operators, typists, clerks and helpers in offices and shops. Between 1870 and 1900 the total number of female breadwinners over sixteen years old leaped from 1,800,000 to 5,300,000.

Meanwhile, the portals of higher education swung open for an ever larger number of middle-class girls. Starting with

Vassar in 1865 and Wellesley and Smith a decade later, women's colleges began to offer instruction equal to that of the better men's institutions. More typical of the West was coeducation, which, though dating from before the war, now enlisted the widespread support of the state universities. In many quarters, however, opposition to the practice continued strong. In the opinion of Dr. Edward H. Clarke, author of *Sex in Education* (1873), "Identical education of the two sexes is a crime before God and humanity, that physiology protests against, and that experience weeps over."

Nevertheless, between 1865 and 1874 at least fourteen state universities, all but three of them in the Middle or Far West, opened their courses to both sexes. Their number included Michigan, which in 1870 admitted girls after having declined to do so for nearly three decades. The president of the university, at the end of ten years of the new system, solemnly assured an inquiring Englishwoman that "none of the ladies had found the curriculum too heavy for their physical endurance." By 1880 the number of mixed colleges had grown from twenty-odd at the close of the war to a hundred and fifty-four. In another twenty years over seventy per cent of all colleges and universities were coeducational.

As higher education reached an ever widening circle of women, they began to push into the professions. The displacement of men as schoolteachers occurred so rapidly that in 1900 two out of every three were women. They moved swiftly also into the professions of social work and nursing. In law, medicine and theology, however, their path proved thornier because of the reluctance of professional schools to afford them training. Yet by 1879 they were allowed to plead before the Supreme Court, and the close of the century saw over a thousand women lawyers in the nation, besides nearly as many dentists, more than three thousand ministers, and almost seventy-five hundred doctors and surgeons. As authors and journalists they occupied an increasingly important place and in Emily Dickinson provided the most talented writer of poetry.

Meanwhile, middle-class housewives in the cities, finding time for broader interests as a result of the rapid introduction of household conveniences, took an active part in the development of women's clubs. From the first two organizations in 1868—the Sorosis in New York and the New England Women's Club in Boston—the number grew so quickly and spread so far that in 1889 they joined in a nation-wide league called the General Federation of Women's Clubs. Such groups, as the years wore on, gave less attention to art, literature and cultural subjects and more to civic and social problems, some becoming centers of agitation for women's rights and equal suffrage.

As a result of the inexorable drift of events, the old common-law discriminations against married women, already beginning to crumble before the Civil War, continued to fall in state after state. Throughout most of the Union the legislatures gave wives the right to own and control their property, retain their earnings, make contracts, sue and be sued. In 1900 only a handful of commonwealths—Georgia, Louisiana, New Mexico, the Dakotas and California—still expressly designated the husband as head of the family and the wife subject to him. So generally was the principle of civil equality recognized that it was clear the remaining disabilities would presently be wiped out.

The progress toward political equality was slower. The desire for universal suffrage encountered the inertia, prejudice and active hostility not only of most men but also of a majority of the women themselves. The opponents protested that woman would lose her charm, that sex equality would cause the loosening of family ties, and that the feminine intellect was unfit to cope with problems of state. In the excited words of Horace Bushnell, author of *Women's Suffrage; the Reform against Nature* (1869), the proposal involved "an attempt to make trumpets out of flutes, and sun-flowers out of violets."

On the other side of the question were arrayed such forceful figures as Elizabeth Cady Stanton, Susan B. Anthony, Lucy Stone (who refused to take her husband's name of Blackwell), Anna Howard Shaw and Carrie Chapman Catt. They held that each sex had a distinctive contribution to make to public affairs, and that failure to accept the logic of woman's altered status in society was an effort to "put the bird back into the egg." As Wendell Phillips expressed it, "One of two things is true: either woman is like man—and if she is, then a ballot based on brains belongs to her as well as to him; or she is different, and then man does not know how to vote for her as well as she herself does."

As in the case of temperance, the earlier interest in equal suffrage had been shoved into the background by the Civil War. When peace came, the feminist leaders, arguing from the vantage ground of the unstinted war services of their sex, flooded Congress with petitions to obtain the ballot along with the freedmen. Their hopes were dashed, however, and in 1869 they proceeded, with some difference of opinion, to organize two woman-suffrage associations: the National, which under Mrs. Stanton's leadership strove for the ballot through state action, and the American, which struck boldly for a federal amendment.[1] Besides the Brooklyn clergyman Henry Ward Beecher, who headed the latter body, and Wendell Phillips, other prominent men lent their pens and voices to the cause, among them George W. Curtis, Senator George F. Hoar and John Greenleaf Whittier. The Knights

[1] Eventually, in 1890, they united forces in the National American Woman Suffrage Association.

of Labor and the American Federation of Labor also rallied
to the standard.

But if the outstanding suffragists hailed from the East,
the chief gains were made in the democratic West. Campaign
after campaign was fought in behalf of the reform. The initial steps, as in Great Britain and the Scandinavian countries
during these same years, took the form of the right to vote
on particular questions in local elections. Though Kansas's
example in 1861 of bestowing the ballot in school elections
went unheeded for a time, sixteen commonwealths, representing all parts of the country but the old Confederacy, fell
into line between 1875 and 1895. In addition, several states
—Kansas and Montana in 1887, Iowa in 1894 and Louisiana
in 1898—permitted women to vote on local bond issues, taxation questions and the like.

But full equality, the cherished goal of the feminists, was
not attained in any state until Wyoming, which as a territory had practiced it since 1869, entered the Union in 1890.
Colorado followed in 1893, Utah and Idaho in 1896. Meanwhile, determined efforts had been made to secure favorable
action from the federal government. The great political parties ignored the question, while the Prohibitionists may have
hurt it by linking it with their unpopular cause. Nevertheless, between 1878 and 1896, committees of the Senate reported five times in favor of a constitutional amendment,
and House committees twice. But action went no further.
For some years to come most Americans were to regard universal suffrage as merely an aberration of the wild and woolly
West.

THE REORIENTATION OF RELIGION

As with other aspects of American life, organized religion
was confronted with formidable problems of readjustment
after the Civil War. The sectional controversy itself was in

part responsible. As early as 1844 the Methodists and Baptists had each split into Northern and Southern branches over the slavery question; and the outbreak of the war had occasioned similar divisions among the Presbyterians and in most of the other large denominations. The zeal of Northern missionaries in following the advancing armies and seizing the property of the Southern churches widened the breach, and rendered it impossible to bridge the differences when peace returned. Indeed, the bitterness was deepened by the attitude of clerics like Bishop Gilbert Haven of the Northern Methodist Church who acclaimed the Carpetbaggers as the "true knight-errantry of the age" and favored racial intermarriage. Thus, without laying the ghosts of the past, American Christianity faced the even more difficult tasks which lay ahead.

The most challenging problem grew out of the new social and economic conditions in the cities. American Protestantism, traditionally rural and of the comfortable middle class, was ill adapted to serve the spiritual needs of hordes of laborers and newly arrived immigrants; and many congregations were frankly indifferent. During the years from 1868 to 1888, when two hundred thousand more people crowded into lower New York south of Fourteenth Street, seventeen Protestant churches moved out, and only two Catholic edifices and one Jewish were added. At the time Jane Addams founded Hull-House in Chicago, the neighborhood contained nine churches and missions and two hundred and fifty-five saloons. In the poorer quarters of these and other cities saloons and dens of vice sometimes outnumbered houses of worship a hundredfold.

The Y. M. C. A. and the Y. W. C. A., both dating from mid-century, provided countless young men and women with decent lodgings, gymnastic facilities and Christian surroundings, but these agencies, too, were middle-class institutions, out of touch with the depressed masses. Even such spirited revivalists as Dwight L. Moody and Ira D. Sankey performed their chief work among laggard members of existing congregations, doing little to reach the many without church affiliations. The growing alienation of the working class was due partly also to the failure of organized religion to cry out against the abuses of Big Business, a silence that caused labor leaders to assail the clergy as hostile to the welfare of the plain people. The fact that wealthy Trinity Church in New York derived a part of its revenues from the ownership of slum properties lent weight to such charges.

The increasing secularization of the Sabbath flowed in part from this situation, but other factors contributed to the same end. In the cities six days of grinding toil caused the masses to seek pleasure on the seventh. There, too, the immigrant influence was strong—the Germans accustomed to their Continental Sabbath, the Irish and other aliens with their Catholic Sunday, the Jews with their religious observance of Saturday. In vain did the American Sabbath Union and other similar bodies try to stay the tide, though they proved somewhat more successful when they joined with the trade unions in resisting employers' demands for unnecessary Sunday labor.

Only gradually did the forces of Protestantism learn how to cope with the new conditions. The success of the Catholic and Jewish faiths in attracting and holding the vast number of their communicants pouring in from Europe proved both an object lesson and a spur to action. Shortly after the Civil War the larger denominations began actively to plant religious missions in the needy districts of the cities. In 1879 the Salvation Army, an English importation, commenced its evangelistic labors on the street corners, preaching to "rumdom, slumdom and bumdom" the exciting gospel of repentance and reform. Ten years later it branched out into social work, maintaining cheap lodgings, employment agencies and rescue homes. Meanwhile, the Protestant churches in many cities began to develop "institutional" features, that is, to conduct systematic philanthropic and educational work among the poor. For such purposes an increasing number of congregations in the 1880's provided reading rooms, day nurseries, recreational facilities and manual-training courses along with religious instruction. Leaps in membership quickly justified their course and by 1894 institutional churches had become numerous enough to form a nation-wide league.

In harmony with these new tendencies, clergymen here and there began to insist that Christianity no longer stand apart from life but become a part of life—that seething, unsettling life of which earlier America had offered no counterpart. Notable among these pioneers of the social gospel were Lyman Abbott, Beecher's successor both as editor of the *Christian Union* and as pastor in Brooklyn; Josiah Strong, general secretary of the Evangelical Alliance; and Washington Gladden, Congregational minister in Springfield, Mass., and later in Columbus, Ohio. Gladden, for example, not only expounded his views in widely read books such as *Applied Christianity* (1886) and *Tools and the Man: Property and Industry under the Christian Law* (1893), but he actively interested himself in industrial disturbances as a champion of "the right and necessity of labor organizations." His hoped-for solution was an "industrial partnership" in which the workers would receive "a fixed share in the profits of production." In line with his convictions, he scourged religious bodies for accepting gifts from possessors of bloated wealth, branding such contributions as "tainted money," defiling the recipient as well as the giver. Some Eastern clergymen went even further and, under the leadership of the Reverend William D. P. Bliss of Boston, formed the Society of Christian Socialists in 1889 "to awaken members of Christian churches to the fact that the teachings of Jesus Christ lead directly to some specific form or forms of Socialism."

Meanwhile, within the Catholic fold, Cardinal Gibbons fought for a more enlightened understanding of labor's rights. In 1886, by interceding at Rome, he saved the Knights of Labor from papal condemnation. Against opposition from within his own ranks he also upheld the right of Catholics to espouse Henry George's panacea of the single tax. His bold course received high sanction in 1891 when an encyclical of Leo XIII, though denouncing socialism, approved of trade unions and called for the application of Christian ethics to the relations of capital and labor. In all faiths such churchmen were the exception rather than the rule. Yet their advent marked a definite turning toward an increased social emphasis in religion. Later years would yield a fuller fruition of their teachings.

As if the problem of social adjustment were not enough, organized religion also faced an intellectual crisis. To defenders of the old-time theology the validity of the Bible itself seemed challenged by new findings of science and scholarship. Religion, in other words, was confronted by one of those recurrent conflicts between orthodoxy and heterodoxy, between fundamentalism and modernism, which historically have formed a law of its growth. Those who sought to socialize religious practice were usually also at the forefront of the effort to liberalize religious thought. One source of dissension was the theory of biological evolution, which gradually had won friends in America after its elucidation by Charles Darwin in *The Origin of Species* (1859). Since it apparently contradicted the Biblical account of creation, the Darwinian hypothesis was generally condemned by the clergy as materialistic and atheistic. A growing number of American scientists, however, accepted it (see page 203); and, following in their train, liberal ecclesiastics like Beecher,

Abbott and Gladden insisted that, at the most, the theory imperiled theology, not genuine religion. Indeed, they saw in evolution a new and grander revelation of the mysterious way God moves His wonders to perform. The process of acceptance, however, was slow, particularly in those denominations which stressed emotional above intellectual factors.

Another shock to orthodoxy resulted from the "higher criticism," an attitude derived from German scholars who had freshly studied the books of the Bible as historical and literary documents rather than as the unerring word of God. To make matters worse, an increasing knowledge of Buddhism and other Asiatic religious systems, popularized by James Freeman Clarke in his *Ten Great Religions* (1871), seemed to rob the Christian faith of its exclusive character. As a consequence of these various influences, sharp divisions occurred among both clergy and laity, concluding oftentimes in heresy trials and the expulsion of those upholding the new views. Yet, as the years went by, a spirit of tolerance began to make itself felt. If clerics could not always agree on points of theology, they learned that, in the interests of common spiritual service, they could at least agree quietly to disagree. Equally significant was the gradual admission into theological seminaries of courses on the higher criticism, comparative religion and the relations of science and religion.

Notwithstanding the many difficulties which beset religion, church membership grew both numerically and relatively. The Catholic, Lutheran and Jewish gains were particularly notable because of large immigrant accessions. Nor did the religious spirit spend itself on strictly church activities. On the contrary, it pervaded most of the philanthropic efforts of the time. A great majority of the social workers and other humanitarians were started on their careers as a result of spiritual impulses.

As though the religious landscape were not already sufficiently varied, a new sect appeared on the scene—Christian Science, which based its doctrines upon *Science and Health*, a book published by Mrs. Mary Baker G. Eddy in 1875. The latest of a long succession of New England-inspired cults, it rejected medicine as the science of health and substituted therefor a belief in the supremacy of mind over matter. According to Christian Science, "disease is caused by mind alone," and may be banished by applying Christ's teachings as interpreted by Mrs. Eddy. The new system appealed particularly to nerve-racked urban folk and spread rapidly from Boston to New York and the cities of the Midwest.

THE PROBLEM OF RACIAL MINORITIES

While most of the social maladjustments of the time stemmed from urban conditions, two major problems, both involving racial minorities, were largely rural in character. One, the Negro question, affected the South. The other, the problem of assimilating the Indians, concerned the Great West. Each had its roots far back in American history, and each had assumed a critical aspect because of recent developments.

President Hayes's withdrawal of the last Southern garrisons in 1877 (see page 29) marked the end of active federal intervention on behalf of the ex-slave. In effect, the North, having become increasingly absorbed in the problems of its emerging industrial order, turned the race question over to the South to solve in its own way. Even if the Republicans had felt differently, they would have been helpless because during the next twelve years the party at no time controlled both Congress and the presidency. The bulk of the Negroes continued to dwell in the section where slavery had planted them. Increasing from four million in 1860 to six in 1880, their number advanced to eight million in 1900, a relative growth considerably less than that of the whites about them.

Though the Negro birth rate was higher than that of the dominant race, this fact was offset by greater infant mortality and by the inroads of diseases which the paternalistic life of the prewar plantation had served to hold in check.

Deserted by their former Northern allies, the Negroes faced a long, harsh, unremitting struggle with ignorance and poverty. The statesman of this new emancipation was Booker T. Washington, himself a former slave, who in 1881 founded the Normal and Industrial Institute at Tuskegee, Alabama, in the heart of the Lower South. Believing that his people should perfect the mechanical skills for which they had shown an aptitude in slavery, he and his coworkers, aided by funds from the state legislature and Northern sources, provided training in the trades and occupations necessary for gaining a foothold in Southern economic life. Deploring the "agitation of questions of social equality," he constantly urged the race to "make itself so valuable to the community in which it lives that it will not merely be tolerated, like a poor relative, but rather welcomed and sought after." "The opportunity to earn a dollar in a factory," he declared, "just now is worth infinitely more than the opportunity to spend a dollar in an opera-house."

Washington's leadership influenced the course of Negro education everywhere. The rapid extension of schools was hampered by the postwar poverty of the South, and particularly by the policy of teaching the two races separately, a costly plan which commonly meant inferior instruction for the blacks. Northern philanthropy did something to relieve the situation, notably through the Peabody Fund established in 1867, the John F. Slater Fund in 1882 and Daniel Hand's generous gift to the American Missionary Association six years later. Despite deterrent conditions, Negro illiteracy declined from seventy per cent in 1880 to forty-four in 1900.

The mass of the people stayed on the land, raising cotton

or tobacco and earning a bare livelihood. Handicapped on the one hand by the shiftless habits learned in slavery and, on the other, by the vicious credit system (see page 31), only the most ambitious were able to progress toward the cherished goal of independent farm ownership. By 1890 the Southern Negroes owned nearly a fifth of their homes. Ten years later the total value of the land they tilled reached almost half a billion dollars. At that time about two hundred thousand owned their farms, while about half a million worked as tenants. This progress was a substantial testimonial to a people who had been virtually landless in 1860. Others were employed in domestic and personal service, mostly in the towns, where also a growing minority entered the skilled trades.

Generally speaking, the Negro was unmolested by his white neighbors provided he "knew his place." That place the dominant race defined with increasing precision as the years went by and as the Negro's memory of his former inferiority in slavery dimmed. The color line was drawn most rigidly at points where racial association implied social or political equality. Besides the legal requirement of separate schools, a universal ban was placed on intermarriage. In 1881 Tennessee carried the principle of segregation further by adopting the first of the so-called Jim Crow laws, requiring Negroes to use different coaches or compartments on trains. Other states followed, and presently colored persons throughout the South found themselves compelled, by law or custom, to accept separate and usually poorer accommodations in public conveyances, hotels, restaurants and amusement places, when admitted at all.

Acts of social discrimination seemed to violate a law which Congress had passed in 1875 to assure Negroes full and equal rights; but the Supreme Court came to the aid of the Southern whites in the Civil Rights Cases (1883) by declaring the federal statute unconstitutional. The court held that the Fourteenth Amendment did not invest Congress with power to legislate on subjects which lay within the proper domain of state action. This decision afforded fresh evidence of the hands-off attitude of the rest of the nation. Violent racial antipathy sometimes broke out in the mob murder of individual Negroes. Between 1882 and 1903 inclusive, 1985 lynchings occurred in the Southern states, with Mississippi, Georgia and Louisiana as the worst offenders. Such lawless proceedings generally involved the worst elements of the two peoples. They tended to obscure the fact that in most respects race relations were peaceable.

Meanwhile, the whites proceeded to steal away the political gains which the Reconstruction constitutions had guaranteed the freedmen. Intimidation, violence and fraud gradually fell into disuse as the ruling class invented legal means of minimizing the colored vote. Through ingenious methods of redistricting (gerrymandering), they reduced Negro representation in the legislatures; and by imposing the poll-tax requirement, they lessened the number of Negro voters. For the same purpose they devised adroit regulations like that of South Carolina in 1882, which bewildered the illiterate black by requiring the voter to place each of his many ballots correctly in the eight or more boxes before him. In the next decade the dominant race went even further. The growth of agrarian unrest in the late eighties had divided the white electorate into two factions, with the result that the potential balance of power often lay with the Negroes. To allay this threat to white supremacy, steps were taken to alter the suffrage provisions in the state constitutions, though care had to be exercised not to infringe the letter of the Fifteenth Amendment (see page 24).

The three commonwealths in which Negroes outnumbered the whites were the first to act. Mississippi set the pace in

1890 by limiting the ballot to paid-up taxpayers who were able to read a passage from the state constitution, or understand it when read to them, or give "a reasonable interpretation thereof." These alternatives were avowedly designed to enable election officials to disfranchise illiterate blacks without disfranchising illiterate whites. Five years later South Carolina adopted a somewhat similar provision. Then, in 1898, Louisiana found a means of exempting whites from the property and educational tests through the so-called grandfather clause: over a period of several months she admitted permanently to the voting list all male applicants whose fathers or grandfathers had possessed the vote before 1867. Other states presently devised variants of these restrictions.[1] Under the new arrangements the proportion of colored voters continued to fall. Torn from his giddy heights of Reconstruction times, the Negro became a negligible factor in Southern politics.

The Indian problem was of a different character, though hardly less perplexing. These aboriginal Americans numbered about two hundred and sixty thousand in the mid-eighties. Reduced to a subject people after a quarter-century of conflict, the vast majority lived the traditional tribal life within the narrow bounds of government reservations, their health impaired by the white man's diseases and their self-reliance sapped by annuities and rations supplied by the "Great White Father" in Washington. Many of the government agents to whose care they were confided proved corrupt or incompetent, while the licensed white traders with

[1] In Williams v. Mississippi (1898) the Supreme Court declined to find the Mississippi suffrage provision contrary to the Fifteenth Amendment, for the complainants had failed to prove actual instances of race discrimination. In 1915, however, the court held the grandfather clauses in Oklahoma and Maryland to be in conflict with the amendment (Guinn v. United States, and Myers v. Anderson). This action probably reduced the number of illiterate white voters, but it did not change the status of the Negro voter.

whom they dealt generally overcharged and otherwise cheated them. Even their reservations were subject to encroachment by greedy whites, and the Washington authorities could not always be counted on to prevent such depredations.

Signs of a more responsible attitude on the part of the government appeared in the early 1870's when Congress, after aiding missionary schools among the tribesmen for over half a century, began gradually to assume the responsibility of providing educational facilities under direct federal auspices. By 1881 the annual appropriation for education amounted to more than $200,000, and by 1887 it had risen to $1,225,000. The purpose was to train the young Indians in agriculture, home economics and other practical pursuits in order to fit them for the white man's way of life. In 1887 over fourteen thousand children were attending two hundred and twenty-seven schools. Unhappily, the teachers were usually political appointees and the instruction was inferior. Moreover, whatever benefit the pupils derived disappeared when they returned to the enervating life of the reservation with its tribal ownership of land and dependence on government doles. For many years, however, Congress resisted repeated recommendations by Presidents, Secretaries of the Interior and Indian Commissioners to terminate the communal system of ownership and introduce the right of private property.

Two influences finally brought about the desired change. One was a strong protest by Eastern humanitarians, who were outraged by the wrongs inflicted on the once proud race. This sentiment, first finding passionate expression in Helen Hunt Jackson's book *A Century of Dishonor* (1881), led in the next two years to the formation of the Indian Rights Association and the annual Lake Mohonk Conference of Friends of the Indians. The other factor was the growing Western demand, as free homesteads grew scarcer, that the reservations be broken up in order to provide additional tracts for the whites. The Easterners sought rights for the Indians, the Westerners lands for themselves. President Cleveland, whose sympathies had been deeply stirred by Mrs. Jackson's pathetic portrayal, actively interested himself in the problem. The upshot was the passage in 1887 of a general allotment law, sponsored by Senator Henry L. Dawes of Massachusetts.

The Dawes severalty act authorized the President to end the tribal government in any reservation whenever time and circumstances seemed appropriate, and to allot the land to individual owners according to certain fixed amounts.[1] To protect such owners from white avarice, they were denied the right to sell or mortgage their holdings for twenty-five years or, at the President's discretion, for a longer period. In all other respects they should enjoy the same rights as white citizens, including that of voting. The land remaining after allotments were made might be bought by the government, the money to be held as a trust fund for educating and civilizing the Indians concerned.

The new law was widely hailed as the "Emancipation Act of the Indians." In the first twenty years over twenty-one million acres passed into the hands of a hundred and fifty thousand red men, while the government acquired some fifty-three million acres for sale to settlers or for use as forest reserves. But experience revealed unexpected flaws in the plan. The reformers had supposed that the parceling of land would cause the owner to acquire a sense of responsibility, build a home and accumulate more possessions. They forgot

[1] The first plan was to give 160 acres to each head of family with lesser allotments for others, the amounts to be doubled in the case of grazing lands. Because this arrangement discriminated against the younger and more educable tribesmen, a supplementary law of 1891 fixed a uniform size of 80 acres. The principles of the Dawes act were not applied to the Five Civilized Tribes in Indian Territory until 1898.

that the institution of private property ran counter to Indian tradition; and unfortunately the government neglected to provide adequate instruction in the efficient use of the allotments. Some individuals, of course, surmounted these difficulties, but the greater number found themselves at the end of the twenty-five-year period sadly unprepared for successful competition with their white neighbors. As voters, moreover, the Indians were often preyed upon by corrupt white politicians, and for many of them citizenship meant a license to drink to excess. To check the increase of drunkenness and crime, a supplementary statute in 1897 banned the liquor traffic during the probationary period. When the Supreme Court annulled this law in 1905 as a denial of the equal rights of citizens, Congress proceeded to revise the Dawes act.

The Burke law, passed in 1906, annulled the twenty-five-year provision and instructed the executive branch henceforth to bestow full property title upon deserving individuals whenever satisfied of their fitness. At the same time it postponed citizenship until full ownership was attained, thereby rendering illegal the drink traffic and helping to safeguard the sanctity of the ballot. But the Burke act did not cure all the evils, for it proved difficult to know when particular Indians were ready to become independent landholders, and many allotments were made prematurely. Moreover, as before, the government did little to teach the red men how to make a living from the land. The majority of them on acquiring full ownership of their tracts promptly sold them and squandered the proceeds. As a result, they became social derelicts, cut off from their former tribal ties and forced to eke out an existence as best they could. As the twentieth century grew older, it became increasingly clear that the well-intentioned scheme fathered by the humanitarians of the 1880's had gone awry. A new direction of Indian policy awaited the coming of the second Roosevelt to office.

SELECT BIBLIOGRAPHY

Economic Panaceas. The general account of labor parties and social programs contained in Commons and others, *History of Labour*, II, should be supplemented by Fine, *Labor and Farmer Parties;* Haynes, *Social Politics;* and Tarbell, *Nationalizing of Business*. For more detailed studies, see Hillquit, *History of Socialism;* Schuster, *Native American Anarchism;* David, *History of the Haymarket Affair;* and Young, *Single Tax Movement*.

Social Betterment in the Cities. Nevins, *Emergence of Modern America*, and Schlesinger, *Rise of the City*, treat urban social problems as well as other subjects in this chapter. The special works on scientific methods of charity include Watson, *Charity Organization Movement;* Warner, *American Charities;* and Woods and Kennedy, *Settlement Horizon*. For the living quarters of the poor the fullest treatment is Ford and others, *Slums and Housing*. Child welfare is the particular concern of Rainwater, *Play Movement*. Outstanding reformers are portrayed in Wise, *Jane Addams;* Wilson, *Mary McDowell;* Ware, *Jacob A. Riis;* and Woods, *Robert A. Woods*. The best study of penal methods is McKelvey, *American Prisons*. For preventive medicine, consult Ravenel, ed., *Half Century of Public Health;* De Kruif, *Microbe Hunters;* and Sigerist, *American Medicine*.

The Fight against the Liquor Traffic. The chief phases are treated in Cherrington, *Evolution of Prohibition*, and Colvin, *Prohibition*, both written with a temperance bias.

The Advance of Women. Bruce, *Woman in the Making of America*, and Irwin, *Angels and Amazons*, are popular sketches. For women as breadwinners, Abbott, *Women in Industry*, and Calhoun, *Social History of the American Family*, III, are helpful. Woody, *History of Women's Education*, treats all levels. The rise of woman's clubs is traced in Croly, *History of the Woman's Club Movement*. The contest for legal and political equality may be followed in Wilson, *Legal and Political Status of Women*, or, biographically, in Harper, *Susan B. Anthony;* Blackwell, *Lucy Stone;* and Lutz, *Created Equal*, a life of Mrs. Stanton.

The Reorientation of Religion. Sweet, *Story of Religions*, contains a factual survey, while Rowe, *History of Religion*, is an interpretation of tendencies. Garrison, *March of Faith*, treats religious development after 1865. Vander Velde, *Presbyterian Churches and the Federal Union,* shows the effects of the Civil War on one religious group, while Farish, *Circuit Rider Dismounts,* traces the social history of the Southern Methodists to the end of the century. Emotional aspects of American religion are set forth in Beardsley, *History of American Revivals,* and Loud, *Evangelized America.* Among biographies of important figures are Will, *Cardinal Gibbons;* Hibben, *Beecher;* Bates and Dittemore, *Mary Baker Eddy;* and Powell, *Mary Baker Eddy.*

The Problem of Racial Minorities. The changing status of the Negro is treated by members of the race in Brawley, *Social History of the American Negro;* Woodson, *Negro in Our History;* Nowlin, *Negro in American National Politics;* and Wesley, *Negro Labor.* Other general accounts include Evans, *Black and White in the Southern States,* and Thompson, *New South.* Lewinson, *Race, Class, & Party,* deals with Negro disfranchisement, and Cutler, *Lynch-Law,* with mob murder. The standard life of the foremost Negro leader is Scott and Stowe, *Booker T. Washington,* written by his secretary in collaboration with the grandson of Harriet Beecher Stowe. Besides the works on Indian history cited at the close of Chapter II, see Moorehead, *American Indian,* and Schmeckebier, *Office of Indian Affairs.*

Chapter VII

THE CULTURAL RENEWAL, 1865–1900

THE DIFFUSION OF KNOWLEDGE

IF THE city begot grave problems of social maladjustment, it also served as the dynamo of an active cultural life. As Josiah Strong wrote in 1887, "The city is the great center of influence, both good and bad. It contains that which is fairest and foulest in our civilization." The concentration of taxable wealth rendered possible an ampler financial support than rural communities could afford for schools, libraries and the like, while benefactions of the well-to-do supplemented governmental efforts. Moreover, the presence of a dense population provided the necessary patronage for the increasing array of cultural agencies. As a result, the urban communities contained the best schools, the best churches, the best newspapers and virtually all the bookstores, circulating libraries, art galleries, museums, theaters, concert halls and opera houses. In such an environment gifted individuals turned naturally to creative work in letters and the arts. Fortunately, they could always find others of kindred interests and, in an atmosphere of mutual encouragement and stimulating criticism, ripen their powers to the fullest. At the same time, the proximity of publishers, art dealers and wealthy patrons afforded an opportunity to sell the products of their talent. It is not surprising that the great cultural advances came out of the city or that its influence penetrated to the farthest countryside.

Never before had private riches contributed so greatly toward elevating the general level of education and taste. From

1871 to the close of the century no less than a third of a billion dollars was given for such purposes, half of it going to colleges and universities. Critics of the economic order cynically attributed this generosity to a love of ostentation, an eagerness for public approbation or, as Dr. Gladden would have said, a desire to drug an uneasy conscience. That there was also developing a sense of *richesse oblige* Andrew Carnegie made clear in an article in the *North American Review* in 1889, in which he asserted that a successful capitalist's career should consist of two periods, first, that of acquiring wealth and, second, that of distributing it for the public good. Whatever motives stirred the princely givers, the urban dwellers, who reaped most of the benefit, profited greatly in their cultural life.

The postwar years witnessed an educational renaissance like that of the 1830's and 1840's. In the North, where tax-supported elementary schools were already the rule, expansion and development occurred in every part of the educational system. Among the innovations was the kindergarten, a device for persuading youngsters through play activities to take the first steps in learning. Though Mrs. Carl Schurz, a pupil of Froebel, had conducted a private kindergarten for German children at her home in Watertown, Wisconsin, as early as 1855, the plan did not become attached to the regular school system until St. Louis set the example in 1873. By 1900 there were nearly three thousand public kindergartens in the nation.

At the upper educational levels methods of instruction showed constant improvement, partly through the introduction of better textbooks, and even more because an increasing number of commonwealths accepted the responsibility of teacher-training by establishing tax-supported normal schools. At the same time the North made school attendance compulsory, thus registering its conviction that education was not merely an opportunity for the individual child but a civic obligation. Meanwhile, free public high schools multiplied, growing from about five hundred in 1870 to six thousand in 1900. As home economics, manual training and other new subjects suited to the times crept into the course of study, the typical secondary school lengthened its term from three to four years. In this fashion twelve years of schooling came to be established as the standard period of preparation for college. *Ed. advance greatly*

Urban America recorded the greatest gains. The thinly populated country districts trailed behind the towns and cities and, by the same token, the South lagged behind the North. Rural schools, even in the East, generally remained ungraded, the terms short, and the teachers ill trained and wretchedly paid. As a section predominantly rural, Dixie was further handicapped by postwar poverty and by the heavy expense of maintaining separate schools for the two races, a burden borne chiefly by the whites. Moreover, having been little affected by the educational awakening of Horace Mann's time, the people had to build their system from the ground up. Despite such obstacles, most of the Southern states made adequate provision for elementary instruction before the century ended. The South at last formed a part of the national educational order. The principle of obligatory attendance was not applied, however, and the real development of high schools had to await the twentieth century.

In the nation as a whole, the school enrollment rose from about seven million in 1870 to fifteen and a half in 1900, a rate of increase one fifth greater than that of the population. Although the lion's share of the benefit fell to urban dwellers, yet nearly everywhere children who received any education at all were getting more than their parents had obtained. This fact is disclosed by the decline of illiteracy in the three decades from twenty per cent to less than eleven. The record would have been far brighter but for the thronging in of millions of immigrants. Further evidence of improvement appears in the fact that the total amount of schooling received by the average person in his whole lifetime increased from about three and a third years in 1870 to a little more than five at the century's close. On a positive basis, however, this showing left much to be desired. Public education still faced gigantic labors in order to perform its proper rôle in a democratic society.

Though the older generation stood outside the orbit of the school system, it nevertheless discovered its own means of offsetting the deficiencies of youthful training. Of these informal agencies of education none evinced so strikingly the popular zeal for knowledge as the Chautauqua movement. Beginning in the summer of 1874 on the wooded shores of Lake Chautauqua, New York, great annual gatherings listened to prominent authorities lecture on literary, scientific and political subjects, and a large number of those who attended were inspired to undertake a four-year plan of home reading and study. Many of their friends also took advantage of the opportunity, and by 1892 a total of a hundred thousand were enrolled in the Chautauqua Literary and Scientific Circle. Meanwhile, many parts of the country began to blossom with local Chautauquas, modest copies of the original, meeting usually under a tent for a week or two during the hot season. In every community they served as a stimulus to local intellectual activity.

In a different fashion the spread of public libraries served the same purpose. Though circulating libraries for the use of subscribers had existed since Benjamin Franklin's time, the legislatures of New Hampshire, Massachusetts, Vermont and Maine in the mid-nineteenth century were the first to empower local communities to set up free tax-supported libraries. In the last year of the Civil War other common-wealths began to follow until the entire Union had fallen into line. Soon free libraries became a normal provision of municipalities. The number of such institutions possessing a thousand or more volumes increased from two thousand in 1875 to nearly fifty-four hundred in 1900. Conspicuous among the private philanthropists who aided the cause was the ironmaster Carnegie, who in 1881 began the practice of presenting library buildings to towns that provided sites and pledged adequate maintenance through taxation. For this purpose he gave away ten million dollars by the end of 1900 and fifty million more before his death in 1919. Professional leadership in the movement fell to the American Library Association, formed in 1876, which promoted the adoption of progressive methods of service to the public and helped make American libraries the most efficient in the world.

The majority of people, however, kept abreast the changing world by reading newspapers and magazines. American journalism entered a new era. The war had accustomed newspaper owners to lavish outlays of money and had aroused in the public an appetite for exciting news. In the ensuing years the fast tempo and high tension of city life reënforced the popular demand for a lively, colorful treatment of the day's happenings. As a result, editors began to fill their columns with items selected not because of their intrinsic importance but because of their human interest or sensational qualities.

Charles A. Dana on becoming editor of the *New York Sun* in 1868 set the new pattern, but his efforts were surpassed by Joseph Pulitzer, a journalist of Hungarian birth, who took over the *St. Louis Post-Dispatch* in 1878 and five years later purchased the *New York World*. Pulitzer frankly directed his appeal to the increasing number of wage-earners—the least literate section of the population—shrewdly tailoring the form and content of his paper to their mental capacity and tastes. Most of the elements of present-day journalism developed under his hand: flaring headlines, political cartoons, thrilling "stories" of scandal and crime, separate departments for sports, amusements and the interests of women, and, last but not least, the bulky Sunday edition, divided into many sections for the convenience of the family group and featuring pictures, special articles and colored comics.

Within a few years the *World* became the most profitable and most widely imitated paper in the land. Pulitzer's example was responsible for bringing into the arena a young Californian, William Randolph Hearst, who acquired the *New York Morning Journal* in 1895 and quickly bested Pulitzer at his own game. The battle between these two masters of the craft—involving in part the publication rights of "The Yellow Kid," a daily colored cartoon—gave rise to the term yellow journalism, by which their brand of sensationalism has ever since been known. Yet the influence of the yellow press was not wholly bad. Such newspapers often attacked flagrant political and social abuses in their communities and waged battles for their removal. James Bryce held the opinion that in the war against political corruption "the newspapers of New York, Boston, Philadelphia, and Chicago have been among the most effective battalions." It should also be remembered that journals of the new type reached untold numbers who in earlier times had read nothing at all.

A different trend was indicated by the transformation of many of the great metropolitan dailies into mammoth business enterprises. Only rarely was a paper the external embodiment of a dominant personality as in Horace Greeley's time. The heavier cost of operation caused these undertakings to pass into the hands of newspaper corporations and to be conducted with a main eye to profit. With the enormous growth of retail stores and nation-wide merchandising, revenue from such sources exceeded the receipts from sales, and newspapers tended increasingly to become advertising sheets with a secondary attention to news. Gradually the control of policy shifted from the editorial sanctum to the office of the business manager, with a corresponding loss to the independence of the press. In William Dean Howells's *A Modern Instance* (1881) a newspaper owner loudly asserts, "The press is a great moral engine," but quickly adds, "It ought to be run in the interest of the engineer."

The growing dependence of the average American upon his daily paper is shown by the increase of such journals from less than six hundred in 1870 to nearly twenty-five hundred in 1900, and by the leap in their total daily sales from two and a half million to more than fifteen. To meet the huge jumps in circulation, new mechanical devices and more efficient processes were introduced, such as larger and faster presses and cheaper methods of making print paper. In 1885 the setting of type was converted into a machine process when Ottmar Mergenthaler invented the linotype, a mechanical marvel by means of which a skilled operator could cast from molten lead solid lines of type ready for printing. To the aid of the reporter came the typewriter, devised in 1868 chiefly by Christopher L. Sholes of Milwaukee and later improved, and also the first practicable fountain pen, invented in 1884 by Lewis E. Waterman. At the same time newspapers, in the interest of economy and efficiency, began to coöperate in gathering and distributing news. While the original Associated Press dated from before 1860, in the years after the war numerous competing news associations sprang up and contested the field with one another. In the last decade of the century the Western Associated Press, headed by Melville E. Stone of Chicago, gained the position of dominance, and in 1900 it was reorganized as the present-day Associated Press.

Though less widely read than newspapers, magazines also came to occupy a larger place in American life, with New York City as the chief publication center. From 1860 to 1900 the number of monthlies grew from two hundred and eighty to over eighteen hundred. Never before had they reached so high a plane of general excellence, or represented so well the diversified interests of the public. Periodicals such as the *Atlantic,* dating from 1857, the *Century* (reorganized under that name in 1881) and *Scribner's Magazine* (1887) welcomed to their pages the new generation of authors and provided them with their principal means of income. Among the journals appealing to special audiences were *St. Nicholas* (1873) for children, *Outing* (1882) for sport lovers, the *Ladies' Home Journal* (1883) for women, and the *Dial* (1880) in the field of literary criticism.

It was particularly fortunate that, in a period of the waning independence of the newspaper press, certain weekly magazines were at hand to prick complacency and perform the function of fearless public criticism. Of the free-lance editors perhaps the most significant was the Irish American, Edwin L. Godkin, who directed the *Nation* from 1865 to 1899 and deeply influenced the thinking of the educated minority. In the columns of *Harper's Weekly* the German-born Thomas Nast, whose cartoons had helped to expose the Tweed Ring and other frauds, laid the foundations of modern American political caricature by devising the familiar figures of the Republican elephant, the Democratic donkey and the Tammany tiger. The humorous possibilities of the American scene were more fully exploited by *Puck, Judge* and *Life,* three comic illustrated weeklies founded between 1877 and 1883. The nineties brought the culminating development: the advent of a group of monthlies—*McClure's,*

Munsey's and others—which, without sacrificing good standards, sold for ten or fifteen cents a copy instead of the traditional twenty-five or thirty-five. Cheaper manufacturing processes, large-scale production and greater reliance on advertising revenues made these new ventures possible. The result was a vast expansion of the number of magazine readers.

THE PROGRESS OF KNOWLEDGE

Not only did the general level of information and culture improve, but an ever increasing proportion of American youth attended the colleges and universities and a growing number of the graduates made notable contributions to knowledge. Between 1860 and 1900 over two hundred and sixty new institutions of higher learning were founded. Many of them, such as Vanderbilt (1873), Johns Hopkins (1876), Leland Stanford (1885), Clark (1889), the University of Chicago (1892) and the Armour Institute of Technology (1893), were the creation of private philanthropists, while others stemmed from denominational zeal. Under spur of the Morrill act of 1862 (see page 57) twenty more state universities opened before 1900, mostly in the Middle and Far West. Everywhere the cause of higher education was quickened. The need of the expanding industries and railways for technologists and the interest in social and economic problems created by the increasing complexity of American life turned the attention of educators to new fields of instruction, and outmoded the limited curriculum of earlier days. To give depth and direction to the modern trends in education there came to the fore a remarkable group of university presidents, including Andrew D. White of Cornell, James McCosh of Princeton, Charles W. Eliot of Harvard, James B. Angell of Michigan, Noah Porter of Yale, Daniel Coit Gilman of Johns Hopkins and William Rainey Harper of Chicago.

Under the leadership of men of this caliber the traditional college curriculum, besides being enriched with many new courses, was extended upward to include training for research and the granting of higher degrees. Since the 1860's increasing numbers of American college graduates had been frequenting German university centers, where they drank deep of the learning of some of the world's greatest scholars and scientists. In the 1880's, when the exodus reached flood tide, over two thousand were so engaged. Imbibing the Teutonic ideal of painstaking specialization, these eager young pilgrims returned home and, as President Eliot said, set about, each in his particular field, "to pierce, with his own little search-light, if only by a hand's-breadth, the mysterious gloom which surrounds on every side the area of ascertained truth."

Johns Hopkins University, established primarily to carry on graduate work, numbered among its faculty scarcely a professor who had not had German training. Under its tonic influence other institutions rapidly expanded their advanced instruction, the total number of nonprofessional graduate students increasing from about four hundred in 1875 to nearly fifty-seven hundred in 1900. By the latter date a dozen universities offered as rich opportunities for specialized training as could be found anywhere in the world. It is worth noting that, in a supposedly materialistic age, a larger percentage of young Americans than ever before consecrated themselves to careers in which the financial rewards were meager.

The zest for extending the bounds of knowledge reminded James Bryce of "the scholars of the Renaissance flinging themselves into the study of rediscovered philology." For the first time, American research workers began to hold their own with the scientists and scholars of the Old World. In order to keep in touch with fellow investigators. specialists in the different fields banded together in great nation-wide associations like the American Chemical Society (1876), the Modern Language Association (1883) and the American Economic Association (1885). The general government, too, turned actively to the promotion of research, not only by means of the agricultural experiment stations (see page 57), but also through such agencies as the federal Geological Survey and the Bureau of Ethnology, both established in 1879.

In nearly every line of investigation the evolutionary hypothesis, because of its emphasis on continuity, growth and interrelationships, cleared the way for new and significant findings. Though some of the older scientists like Louis Agassiz at Harvard sided with leading theologians against the theory, far more typical was the course of two of his colleagues: Asa Gray, who eagerly lent it the great weight of his reputation as a botanist, and John Fiske, who, reaching a wider audience through his popular lectures and writings, taught that the evolutionary process explained man's social as well as his physical development.[1] While the Darwinian concept proved most important in the biological sciences, it also exerted a fructifying influence on such branches of study as economics, history, philosophy and philology. G. Stanley Hall, himself a contributor to the new subject of experimental psychology, called it "the greatest intellectual stimulus of the modern age."

The advance of knowledge was the joint product of the minute investigations of myriad workers, but certain names stand out as of special note. Among such men in the natural sciences were Albert A. Michelson, who in 1879 began his epoch-making experiments in measuring the velocity of

---

[1] Fiske formulated his views most completely in *Outlines of Cosmic Philosophy* (1874). Though deeply indebted to the contemporary English social philosopher Herbert Spencer, he differed from his master in insisting that evolution implied the working out of a divine plan for the betterment of mankind.

light; Othniel C. Marsh and Edward D. Cope, whose excavations of vast fossil beds of prehistoric beasts in the American West enriched the world's knowledge of paleontology; and Simon Newcomb, famed for his recomputation of the elements of the solar system. In the opinion of a fellow scientist, "The sun and moon and planets have been weighed as exactly as sugar and tea at the grocer's and their paths measured as precisely as silks and woolens at the draper's." Greater than any of these, however, was J. Willard Gibbs, who laid the foundations for a new branch of research, physical chemistry, and is generally accounted the foremost scientist America has yet produced.

In the social sciences as well, towering figures appeared, such as Francis A. Walker and Richard T. Ely in economics; Lester F. Ward in sociology; Lewis H. Morgan in anthropology; John W. Burgess and Woodrow Wilson in political science; and John Bach McMaster, James Ford Rhodes, Henry Adams and Henry C. Lea in history. In 1893 Frederick J. Turner, a member of this last group, founded a new school of historical interpretation by pointing out the profound influence that the frontier, then rapidly vanishing, had exerted upon American development from the earliest days of settlement. In psychology William James was a dominant factor, as he also was in philosophy, where he developed the theory of method known as pragmatism. These men and their kind were as truly discoverers, explorers, pioneers, in the intellectual realm as were their forebears who had hewn a path through the physical wilderness of forest and mountain.

In their disinterested pursuit of truth, however, they sometimes offended the long-held opinions of the society about them. Professors in denominational colleges who taught the doctrine of evolution were apt to occupy uneasy seats, while even in the bigger universities scholars who dared to condemn the ethics and practices of Big Business ran the danger of dismissal. In 1894, when critics tried to oust Professor Ely from the University of Wisconsin for alleged radical views, the board of regents responded by declaring: "We cannot for a moment believe that knowledge has reached its final goal, or that the present condition of society is perfect. We must therefore welcome from our teachers such discussions as shall suggest the means and prepare the way by which knowledge may be extended, present evils be removed and others prevented. . . . In all lines of academic investigation it is of the utmost importance that the investigator should be absolutely free to follow the indications of truth wherever they may lead." Although many institutions did not attain this ideal, it was only through freedom of inquiry that American scholars and scientists were able to contribute so notably to the world's intellectual enlightenment.

THE LITERARY REVIVAL

No less fruitful were the forces at work in letters and the fine arts. In 1871 the poet Walt Whitman published his most noteworthy prose work *Democratic Vistas*. Boldly he called for a literary culture springing from the common life, one begot of the people, by the people and for the people. His challenge to the new era was what Ralph Waldo Emerson's *The American Scholar* had been to the generation of the thirties and forties. But where the Concord sage had pleaded for an aristocracy of literature—for the lone man thinking his own thoughts—Whitman pleaded for a democracy of literature, one "permeating the whole mass of American mentality, taste, belief, breathing into it a new breath of life." Know you not, he asked, "that the people of our land may all know how to read and write, and may all possess the right to vote, and yet the main things may be entirely lacking?"

Whitman exemplified his own teachings. Beginning as early as *Leaves of Grass* (1855), he had shown how the poet, bursting the fetters of rhyme, meter and conventional imagery, might trumpet the glories of common folk and common things in an authentic American manner.

As if summoned by his clarion call, there trooped forth from every corner of the land young writers eager to record their varied impressions of a traditional rural civilization fast disappearing before the standardizing blows of urbanism and industrialism. Impatient with the bookishness and fastidious diction of their predecessors, they told their stories simply, often with unconscious idealization, and always with careful attention to dialect and local color. Never before had American fiction so completely mirrored the regional diversities that characterized the national life. Edward Eggleston in *The Hoosier School-Master* (1871) and later novels depicted mid-century conditions in rural Indiana. "Mark Twain" (Samuel L. Clemens), drawing upon his own earlier experiences, offered a broadly humorous account of life along the Mississippi, producing his masterpiece in *The Adventures of Huckleberry Finn* (1884). With Bret Harte and the poet Joaquin Miller, he also helped make memorable the picturesque life of the Far West, while Helen Hunt Jackson in *Ramona* (1884) recalled the romance and drama of the passing of the old Spanish order in California.

Nor were other sections of the country less ably represented. There was a literary New South as well as a political and economic one. In delicately wrought sketches George W. Cable, Grace King and Kate Chopin introduced a wondering America to the exotic, orange-scented atmosphere of Creole life in Louisiana, while the chivalry of the old Virginia gentry lived again in the pages of Thomas Nelson Page and F. Hopkinson Smith. By contrast, "Charles Egbert Craddock" (Mary Noailles Murfree) in such stories as *In the Tennessee*

Mountains (1884) pictured the humble folk dwelling amidst the grandeur of the interior highlands, and Joel Chandler Harris immortalized the whimsical tales of Negro folklore through the mouth of Uncle Remus. In authors like Sarah Orne Jewett and Mary E. Wilkins (Freeman), New England had its regional spokesmen, but they were concerned not with a colorful past but with the drab hues of the present giving sympathetic portrayals of narrow, introspective lives in the era of New England's rural decline.

Still other writers found their themes in the main stream rather than the backwaters of American life. In a series of novels distinguished by such works as *The Rise of Silas Lapham* (1884) and *A Hazard of New Fortunes* (1889), William Dean Howells dealt with the trials and foibles of middle-class urban people, with ever sharpening emphasis upon the "economic chance-world" which governed human destinies under modern conditions. Henry James, residing abroad and writing with intricate precision, discovered rich literary ore in the psychological impact of Old World culture upon leisure-class Americans in Europe. Both men strove for realism, and, though they were influenced by the contemporary realists in France and Russia, they revealed their innate Americanism by dwelling upon the normal rather than the abnormal in human nature. As a wit remarked, "The present realism in fiction is in France a discovery of the unclean, and in America a discovery of the unimportant." A grimmer temper, however, displayed itself in a younger group of writers, notably Hamlin Garland, who in *Main-Travelled Roads* (1891) stressed the repellent aspects of Midwestern rural life, and Stephen Crane, whose *Maggie, a Girl of the Streets* (1892), exposed one of the tragic failures of the vaunted urban civilization. Their work foreshadowed the active concern with social and economic injustice which was to characterize the novelists of the early twentieth century.

The 1880's marked the full bloom of the new literary growths, with a greater number of good novels published than in any previous American decade. Yet the epoch was even more distinctive for its profusion of short stories, "literature in small parcels," a form which the writers of this generation molded into a finished work of art. It was peculiarly adapted to the taste of the hurrying, scurrying people who inhabited the cities. Through the short story America has made perhaps her greatest contribution to world literature.

The public, of course, did not confine its reading to American authors, or even to writers whose artistic merits were acclaimed by literary critics. Of the works of fiction published in the years 1875–1899, the following eventually sold a million or more copies: Mark Twain's *Tom Sawyer* (1875) and *Huckleberry Finn* (1884); Anna Sewell's *Black Beauty* (1877); Lew Wallace's *Ben Hur, a Tale of the Christ* (1880); Margaret Sidney's *Five Little Peppers* (1881); Robert Louis Stevenson's *Treasure Island* (1884); George Du Maurier's *Trilby* (1894); and Charles M. Sheldon's *In His Steps: "What Would Jesus Do?"* (1899). Three of the seven authors —Sewell, Stevenson and Du Maurier—were Englishmen. Judged by the number of juvenile books among the best sellers, children were the most voracious readers, while the taste of their elders ran toward religious fiction. Unfortunately, comparable figures for the circulation of library books are lacking.

Until the last decade of the century professional writers labored under a serious handicap because publishers could reprint foreign works without payment of royalty and could therefore sell them for less than the price of competing volumes of native composition. The rule naturally worked both ways; and as American publishers in the 1870's and 1880's saw more and more of their own books being "pirated" in England and Canada, they decided that the practice was working to their disadvantage. Joining hands with the authors, they induced Congress in 1891 to adopt the international-copyright act for protecting the rights of native authors in other lands and of foreign writers in the United States. Henceforth American practitioners of letters could pursue their profession without unfair competition from European productions and, at the same time, safeguard the profits of their sales abroad.

CREATIVE WORK IN THE ARTS

Equally as significant as the literary revival was the renaissance in the arts of line, color and form. Just as young American scholars and scientists were flocking to the German universities, so fledgling painters, sculptors and architects were invading the studios of Paris, the world's art center. During the seventies, as they returned home in ever increasing numbers, their advent was like a fresh wind on a sultry day, clearing the atmosphere of muggy traditions and introducing breadth, freedom and vigor.

In the domain of painting the clash of schools was so sharp as to cause the "Younger Men" in 1877 to form the Society of American Artists in opposition to the long-established National Academy of Design. Into their ranks they drew some of the more progressive older men like George Inness and John La Farge. The years that followed brought an epoch of creative achievement such as the nation had never before known. A few names will illustrate both the quality and variety of the productions. In George Inness America discovered perhaps her greatest landscape painter, an artist with a poet's insight into Nature's vagrant moods. By contrast Winslow Homer painted boldly colored canvases of the sea, while Thomas Eakins's work exemplified a matter-of-fact realism that led him to portray President Hayes in his shirt sleeves. James A. McNeill Whistler's genius appeared best in his nocturnes, which conveyed inimitably the hue and mystery and quiet of night. His well-known picture, "The Artist's Portrait of His Mother," a study in grays, was bought in 1891 by the French government. Albert P. Ryder devoted his brush to legendary and poetic subjects, which he interpreted with great imaginative power. La Farge transformed American mural painting into a fine art and, through his invention of opalescent glass, helped revive the ancient splendor of medieval stained-glass work.

In response to the new interest in painting, art schools increased from less than forty in 1880 to nearly a hundred and twenty at the century's close. The establishment of great art museums at Washington, New York and Boston in the postwar decade helped to foster a constant improvement in popular taste, and caused other large cities presently to make similar provision. In a less obvious way, the waxing popularity of the camera, especially after the simplifications introduced in the eighties by George Eastman of Rochester, helped to awaken in many a latent æsthetic sense.

In sculpture, gifted men like Daniel Chester French, Frederick W. MacMonnies and George Grey Barnard pushed to the front and exerted a profound influence for higher standards. The foremost practitioner, however, was the Irish-born Augustus Saint-Gaudens, whose statue of Admiral Farragut (1881) in Madison Square Garden, New York, first revealed his genius to the public. His symbolic figure, "The Peace of God," erected at the tomb of Mrs. Henry Adams in Washington in 1891, is generally considered the greatest sculpture America has yet produced. In no other branch of art had the national traditions been so poor. These men and their like raised the native product to a plane comparable with the best work in contemporary Europe.

The new influences made slower headway in architecture,

partly because of the enormous construction of new buildings required to accommodate the needs of the swift-growing cities, partly also because people did not know how to discriminate between ostentation and good taste. Even men of wealth and note oftentimes lived in houses disfigured with towers, turrets, Moorish arches and fantastic jigsaw work in wood and iron. It was Henry Hobson Richardson who ushered in a better day. Employing the heavy Romanesque style of southern France, he taught the superiority of sturdiness, unity and restraint as elements of design. His crowning achievement was Trinity Church, Boston, in 1877, for which John La Farge provided the murals and much of the stained-glass work.

Before Richardson died in 1886, many fellow craftsmen had risen up to foster the better standards; and from plans published in magazines like the *Ladies' Home Journal* even the ordinary person could learn how to build a well-designed, inexpensive house. The younger men wrought characteristically in the classic mode or some of its Renaissance derivatives. The Chicago World's Fair of 1893—largely the artistic creation of Daniel H. Burnham, Charles B. Atwood, Richard M. Hunt and the firm of McKim, Mead and White—marked the supreme attainment of the classic style. The effect was a poignant dream of loveliness reminiscent of the chaste perfection of late eighteenth and early nineteenth-century architecture in America.

A special problem was presented by the necessity of economizing ground space in the congested business quarters of big cities. The obvious solution was a lofty perpendicular structure, whose use the recent introduction of fast elevators rendered practicable. Masonry construction, however, required supporting piers so huge as to devour much of the desirable space in the lower floors. The outcome was the invention of the skyscraper, a building riveted securely in a metal frame and employing brick or stone merely to afford privacy and screen off the weather.

Less trammeled by tradition than the Eastern centers, Chicago first ventured upon the new departure, the original skyscraper being the Home Insurance Building (1885), which rose to what then seemed the dizzy height of ten stories. The most notable contributor to the new architecture was Louis Sullivan, who sought to break with the musty traditions of his craft and establish the principle: "Form follows function." His influence proved greatest, however, on the next generation of skyscraper designers. Meanwhile Chicago and New York, generally employing decorations in the Roman mode, pushed their commercial buildings higher and higher until in 1898 the Ivins Syndicate Building in the latter city achieved twenty-nine floors, a mere hint of what awaited in the next century. These "proud structures, defiant in their altitude," fittingly symbolized the titanic energy, the willingness to experiment, the superb engineering competence, that characterized the age. Since historical research has denied to Americans the credit of devising the log cabin, the skyscraper stands as the nation's unique architectural gift to the world.

If progress in musical composition was less brilliant, still the nation began in a modest way to repay its debt for the rich stores of melody it had long derived from Europe. The principal composers had all received their training in Germany. John Knowles Paine, George W. Chadwick and Horatio Parker won a transatlantic reputation for their orchestral and choral scores, while Edward A. MacDowell composed piano selections distinguished by originality and haunting beauty. Perhaps more significant was the heartening growth of musical appreciation. Conservatories of music sprang up in the more important cities; artists' recitals enjoyed a profitable patronage; choral societies flourished, particularly in German centers; and the founding of the New York Symphony Orchestra in 1878 and of the Boston Symphony Orchestra three years later signalized a new era in that branch. More than any other one person, Theodore Thomas, who had come as a youth from Germany in 1845, promoted an intelligent popular interest in music, organizing great music festivals, founding and conducting orchestras in various cities, and training his players to standards of performance never before known in his adopted country. Grand opera, too, secured a firmer footing with the opening in 1883 of the Metropolitan Opera House in New York. Such evidences of public support and improving taste augured well for future musical attainments.

THE PURSUIT OF LEISURE

All classes in the cities faced the problem of using wisely the increasing leisure at their disposal. Even the wage earners had more time than formerly, thanks to the gradual reduction of the workday. Life under pioneer conditions had taught the American people how to work but not how to relax. They therefore turned to pleasure with the same fierce energy that they devoted to money-making. In Bryce's contemporary phrase, they "make amusement into a business." Society life in the greater cities became characterized by frantic display, especially on the part of the newly rich eager to vault into the ranks of the exclusive. Though it was said the menfolk knew no masters, not even the Old Masters, they meekly left to their wives and daughters the strategy of advancing the family socially. Ways and means lay at hand. Palatial mansions and lavish entertaining hid the rise from humble origins; liberal patronage of fashionable charities smoothed the path; proper "ancestors" were always procurable from the right genealogists. But the supreme goal was a brilliant international marriage. So successful were ambitious mothers in this quest that toward the end of the century it was estimated that over $200,000,000 had been exported to replenish the coffers of impoverished European nobility.

The average person was little affected by such matters, but other leisure-time interests demanded his attention. None made a greater appeal than the opportunity to join one or more of the secret fraternal orders that sprang up as if by spontaneous generation. A product of urban conditions, these lodges not only provided a substitute for the neighborliness of rural communities, but, through their elaborate ceremonialism, enabled members to recover a sense of self-importance lost in the solitude of crowds. A further attraction appeared in the sickness and death benefits usually provided. Between 1880 and 1901 no less than four hundred and ninety different fraternal organizations were founded. A writer in the *Century Magazine* characterized this development as the "great American safety-valve." In 1890 Boston, Chicago and St. Louis had three times as many lodges as churches. As the century closed, the United States had firmly established its title of a "nation of joiners," with over six million names on the rosters of its secret societies.

At the same time, the multiplication of city dwellers rendered possible a vast expansion of popular entertainment. Between 1880 and 1900 the number of actors trebled. The serious drama probably has never been better presented than by such native performers as Edwin Booth, Clara Morris and Lawrence Barrett and by such foreign visitors as Sarah Bernhardt and Helena Modjeska. Bronson Howard, the principal dramatist, wrote plays that held the boards for from one hundred and fifty to four hundred nights. More characteristic of the times, however, was the enthusiastic patronage accorded the minstrel show and the circus, while blood-curdling melodramas pleased a public taste whetted by the dime novel and the sensational press. Yet no form of stage entertainment so well suited the restless urban spirit as vaudeville, which Tony Pastor, B. F. Keith and others made into a great success. Vaudeville, observed a contemporary, "belongs to the era of the department store and the short story." By the 1890's it accounted for the attendance of perhaps half the theatergoers.

Comic opera also made its appearance, floated into general favor on the wave of popularity that greeted "Pinafore" and other delightful concoctions of the Britons, Gilbert and Sullivan. Americans such as Reginald de Koven and Victor Herbert entered the field. The former in 1890 composed "Robin Hood," one of the most popular and melodious operas in the history of the American theater. The tunes from these performances swiftly became known from one end of the country to the other, thanks to the invention of the talking machine or phonograph. Devised by Edison in 1877–1878, the first crude instrument, consisting of a tin-foil cylinder record turned by hand, was presently improved by Edison and others through the adoption of flat waxlike disks and the use of spring or electric motors. The phonograph promoted a rage for popular songs which was without precedent in any earlier period. In the single year 1900 nearly three million phonograph records were sold.

These years also saw the rise of organized sport. As rural life steadily receded into the background, as normal outlets for physical exertion grew less, as more and more people slaved long hours in office and factory, some form of outdoor diversion became indispensable. Unhappily, softened muscles did not encourage active personal participation. Most people therefore were content to pay others to take their exercise for them, a tendency zealously abetted by sport promoters, who coveted the gate receipts which professional contests made possible. The "audience habit," nurtured by the theater, thus came to infect sport lovers as well. Many of the new games were imported from Great Britain, where an athletic revival had been proceeding since the mid-century. In the United States, however, they were deemed not a special perquisite of the upper classes, but a boon to be enjoyed by everyone. In the case of basketball, invented in 1891, Americans contributed a game all their own.

Of the older sports, thoroughbred racing enjoyed an era of unparalleled prosperity. Prize fighting, though still viewed askance by the respectable elements, brought to the fore a succession of world's heavyweight champions in John L. Sullivan (1882), James J. Corbett (1892), "Bob" Fitzsimmons (1897) and James J. Jeffries (1899). Baseball, long a favorite amateur pastime, began to assume its aspect of America's national game when the Cincinnati Red Stockings in 1869 turned themselves into a professional team. Soon professional baseball overspread the land, leading to the formation of intercity leagues and, in 1884, to the first "World Series" between the pennant-winning teams of the two major leagues. Football, an American version of the English game Rugby, developed somewhat more slowly, being closely associated with the growth of college athletics. The first intercollegiate contest occurred between Princeton and Rutgers in 1869, with twenty-five men on each team. Seven years later the American Intercollegiate Football Association was formed by Columbia, Harvard, Princeton and Yale; and in the next score of years the game, under constantly changing rules, spread to nearly all the colleges and most of the high schools of the land. At Connecticut Wesleyan, Professor Woodrow Wilson in his spare time helped to coach a team which in 1889 defeated Pennsylvania, Amherst, Williams, Rutgers and Trinity.

Of the newer sports, lawn tennis, golf and polo found their

way from Britain to America in the 1870's. Skiing was a contribution of the Norwegian Americans in Minnesota early in
the next decade. In these and other games, differences as to
rules caused the formation of national associations to establish
uniform regulations and often also to conduct annual tour-
naments. In some manner or other, all classes took part in
this new play life of the nation. The well-to-do signified their
approval by the establishment of athletic clubs, country
clubs and yacht clubs. Amidst his political activities Theodore Roosevelt took time to box, wrestle, fish, hunt and play
polo, exemplifying in these early years his championship of
the "strenuous life." President Hayes found relaxation in
shooting at a mark in Rock Creek Park, and his successors,
Arthur and Cleveland, were among the country's most expert fishermen. The attitude of the general public is reflected in the fact that, when John Greenleaf Whittier died
in the autumn of 1892, a leading New York newspaper devoted one column to that event and nearly a dozen to the
Corbett-Sullivan prize fight.

No sport, however, attracted so many participants as bicycling. Before the 1880's this form of exercise had been confined to riders whose courage was undaunted by an occasional fall from the lofty perch over the high front wheel.
But the introduction in 1884 of the "safety" bicycle—possessing two medium-sized wheels of equal height—and the later
substitution of pneumatic tires for solid rubber ones produced a cycling craze that ramified to every part of the nation. By 1893 a million bicycles were in use. Spurred by the
League of American Wheelmen, over half the states enacted
laws for improving their highways, a movement later to be
accelerated by the advent of the automobile. For untold
thousands cycling renewed the forgotten pleasures of open
road and countryside. It was recommended by physicians
and it also helped bring about more rational fashions for

women. "It is safe to say," declared an expert of the Census Bureau in 1900, "that few articles ever used by man have created so great a revolution in social conditions as the bicycle." This generation little dreamed that the rattling, snorting "horseless carriage," with which inventors in the nineties were hopefully beginning to tinker, would presently spell the doom of the universally popular "bike."

SELECT BIBLIOGRAPHY

The Diffusion and Progress of Knowledge. Nevins, *Emergence of Modern America,* and Schlesinger, *Rise of the City,* treat the subject matter of this and also the succeeding sections. Such works as Cubberley, *Public Education in the United States,* Reisner, *Evolution of the Common School,* and Knight, *Public Education in the South,* sketch the expansion of the public school system, while Curti, *Social Ideas of American Educators,* relates educational conceptions to the social and intellectual background of the age. Hurlbut, *Story of Chautauqua,* describes the new agency of adult education. Bleyer, *Main Currents in the History of American Journalism,* should be supplemented by individual newspaper biographies, such as Davis, *History of the New York Times;* Chamberlin, *Boston Transcript;* and Andrews, *Pittsburgh's Post-Gazette.* The fathers of the yellow press are treated in Seitz, *Pulitzer,* and Winkler, *Hearst,* and another phase of journalism forms the theme of Rosewater, *History of Coöperative News-Gathering.* Mott, *History of American Magazines,* carries the story to 1885 in the third volume and displaces all earlier discussions of the subject. On major trends in higher education, see Butts, *The College Charts Its Course;* Thwing, *The American and the German University;* and Ryan, *Early Graduate Education.* Outstanding contributors to the advancement of knowledge are considered in Jordan, ed., *Leading American Men of Science,* and Odum, ed., *American Masters of Social Science.* In many instances, individual biographies are available.

Literature and the Arts. Of the many surveys of American letters, Pattee, *American Literature since 1870,* and Parrington, *Beginnings of Critical Realism,* are particularly useful. Shove, *Cheap Book Production,* and Lehmann-Haupt and others, *Book* *in America,* deal with publishing. Isham, *History of American Painting,* Taft, *History of American Sculpture,* Tallmadge, *Story of American Architecture,* and Howard, *Our American Music,* are standard treatments. Weitenkampf, *American Graphic Art,* and Murrell, *History of American Graphic Humor,* treat illustrative art. The student will want to consult the excellent pictorial representations in Mather and others, *American Spirit in Art,* and Hamlin, *American Spirit in Architecture.*

The Pursuit of Leisure. Wecter, *Saga of American Society,* deals with social climbing. Dulles, *America Learns to Play,* covers many aspects of popular recreation. The stage is the particular concern of Hornblow, *History of the Theatre,* and Mayorga, *Short History of the American Drama.* Krout, *Annals of American Sport,* is an excellent general guide, while Weyand, *American Football,* and Spalding, *America's National Game* (baseball), trace the history of two major sports.

Chapter VIII

THE FARMERS TAKE THEIR STAND,
1880–1900

THE REVIVAL OF RURAL UNREST

A S THE eighties wore on, rural life lagged ever farther behind the van of urban progress. The Economic Revolution, which rained benefits on the city, worked to the detriment of the countryside. From their urban ramparts, as has been seen, the captains of industry and masters of capital directed the course of economic conquest, heedless of how rural welfare might be affected. Moreover, the husbandman reaped little or no advantage from the new mechanical inventions, such as the telephone, the electric light and the swifter means of transit. To make matters worse, he secured a rapidly dwindling share in the increasing national wealth. Whereas in 1880 the value of farms just equaled that of urban real estate, ten years later city real estate had advanced to double the value of farm land. The difference was even greater if other forms of property were included. A contemporary economist estimated that in 1890 the average wealth of rural families did not exceed $3250, while that of urban families surpassed $9000.

This disparity in worldly goods and economic progress was thrown into sharper relief by the many social opportunities which the city alone afforded. Not the least of these advantages was that of seeing and being with other people. In contrast with the European grouping of farmers in villages with their fields lying round about, American farm homes were widely scattered with no more than four to the square mile under the homestead law of 1862. In the circumstances isolation and loneliness were the almost inescapable conditions of existence in the newer West, a fact that proved a special hardship for womenfolk and the younger generation. They also lacked other benefits of the city—opportunities for choosing from among a variety of careers, for working shorter hours, for educational and cultural development, for amusement and recreation. Hamlin Garland called his fictional indictment of rural life *Main-Travelled Roads* (see page 207) because, as he said, the main road "is long and wearyful and has a dull town at one end and a home of toil at the other." Though many tillers of the soil continued to prefer their traditional occupation, the phenomenal migration from country to city suggests how greatly their neighbors and sons were affected by comparisons with a different manner of living. "The farm youth sees only the dazzling, gaudy side of city life," lamented one student of conditions. "He sees not that for every success there are scores, nay hundreds, who sink into darkness and misery."

This growing sense of rural inferiority, this deepening conviction that the husbandman was losing his ancient heritage of economic independence and equal opportunity, needed only specific bread-and-butter grievances to precipitate organized movements for farm relief. Such grievances the eighties provided in abundance. The return of prosperity in 1879 after six years of depression chiefly benefited the urban and industrial sections. Because of the enormous expansion of Western agriculture and of stiffer competition in the world's markets with the wheat-growing regions of Russia, Australia, Canada and the Argentine, crop prices fell disastrously during the decade. The farmer who received eighty cents a bushel for his wheat in the years 1882–1885 did well to get seventy-one cents in 1890. In Kansas at the latter date a bushel of corn sold for as little as ten cents and was commonly burned for fuel.

The farmer, toiling "from daybreak to back-break," blamed his ills not on overproduction but on other circumstances: the undue profits of the middlemen, the high transportation charges imposed by the railroads, and the heavy interest rates that his creditors (mostly Easterners) exacted. "There are three great crops raised in Nebraska," wrote one embittered agricultural editor. "One is a crop of corn, one a crop of freight rates, and one a crop of interest. One is produced by farmers who by sweat and toil farm the land. The other two are produced by men who sit in their offices and behind their bank counters and farm the farmers." As if the situation was not bad enough, an almost uninterrupted decade of drought, beginning in 1887 and attended by infestations of chinch bugs, destroyed the plantings of countless settlers who had taken up homesteads in the subhumid zone embracing the western halves of Kansas, Nebraska and the Dakotas. It seemed as though the hand of both man and Nature was raised against the husbandman. By 1890 mortgages averaged one for every two persons in Kansas and North Dakota, one for every three in Nebraska, South Dakota and Minnesota. In some counties ninety per cent or more of the land was saddled with debt.

Meanwhile, the Southern agriculturist complained of similar woes: low farm prices, high charges for what he bought, excessive transportation costs, heavy taxes, grinding debts. The market price of cotton, the principal staple, averaged less than nine cents a pound during the 1880's as compared with eleven cents in the mid-seventies. The crop-lien system, by which the farmer mortgaged his growing crop at high interest rates, enmeshed perhaps eighty or ninety per cent of the cotton growers, reducing them to a condition of "debt-peonage." Everywhere in the South, land tended to gravitate into the hands of money lenders, loan companies and a few of the financially stronger farmers. In the nation as a whole the mortgage indebtedness of farm lands grew from $343,-000,000 in 1880 to $586,000,000 in 1890.

As the decade of the eighties advanced, evidences of agrarian unrest multiplied. Farmers' groups, variously called clubs, associations, unions, wheels and alliances, sprang up in the South and West to consider common grievances and propose remedies. In this manner two great organizations developed in the cotton belt: the National Farmers' Alliance, started in 1879, and the Agricultural Wheel three years later. In 1889 they joined to form a body with over a million members, known popularly as the Southern Farmers' Alliance. Meanwhile a Northern Farmers' Alliance, founded in 1880, rose to a dominant position among the agricultural associations of the trans-Mississippi West. At first the organized farmers pinned their faith to nonpolitical measures. Taking a leaf from the experience of the Grangers (see page 87), they tried to cultivate a pleasanter rural life through picnics, lodge meetings and other social gatherings of one sort or another. Like the Grangers, too, local groups launched coöperatives, setting up stores, cotton yards, grain elevators, creameries, insurance companies and the like. But when these undertakings collapsed, as most of them did because of poor business direction or the cutthroat competition of regular merchants, the farmers began to seek legislative cures for their ills.

In various parts of the South new leaders "fresh from the soil," like "Ben" Tillman in South Carolina and "Jim" Hogg in Texas, leaped into prominence. Rousing the rural masses against the leadership of the upper classes and the towns, they captured the Democratic party in their states. In the strongly Republican commonwealths of the West the agrarian elements usually formed independent parties, sometimes through fusion with the Democrats. Such successes, however, promised only limited relief. The ultimate goal was the control of Congress, for from the national government the agrarians hoped to secure their chief means of salvation: currency inflation, a graduated income tax and the public ownership of railroads. Contemptuously termed "hayseed socialists" by Easterners, the farmers had no thought of overturning the capitalist system. Most of them owned land or expected to, and they aimed merely to insure better opportunities for themselves and their children. Like the urban wage-earners, they were capitalists on the make.

Of the several demands, the one for money inflation held first place. Although the greenback notion still lingered fondly in the minds of some, the circumstances of the time directed chief attention to "free silver." Until 1873 the country had been on a bimetallic standard, that is, the government had stood ready to coin into dollars all the gold and silver that might be brought to the mint. Congress in that year reorganized the monetary system and, among other things, omitted the standard silver dollar from the list of domestic coins. The act excited little attention at the moment because, thanks to the scarcity of silver metal, the amount of bullion required for a silver dollar exceeded its legal value, and hence none had actually been in circulation for forty years.

But almost at once a change occurred. The law, which had been passed by default, gained an ugly repute as the "Crime of 1873," and in the political discussions of the next quarter-century the demonetization of silver was ascribed to a sinister and corrupt plot of Big Business and Wall Street. This shift of attitude was due partly to an enormous and unexpected leap in the world's supply of silver ore as a result of the fabulous finds in the Far West. At about the same time several European governments, deciding to adopt the gold

standard, melted their larger silver coins and thus further increased the available supply.[1]

With the nation wallowing in the depression of the seventies, agrarian spokesmen, abetted by labor groups in the industrial centers, demanded a return to free silver; in other
words, a resumption of the unlimited coinage of the standard
silver dollar as in the years before 1873. Holding that a shortage of circulating medium had caused their woes, they cited
not only the "Crime of 1873," but also the fact that the
world's annual production of gold was virtually stationary.
By enlarging the volume of money in use, the silverites believed the government would indirectly help them get
higher prices for farm crops and better wages in industry,
and make it easier for them to pay their debts. But they reckoned without the waxing strength of the Eastern business
classes, which shrank from any measure that might diminish
the purchasing power of their incomes and enable debtors
to discharge their obligations in "cheap money."

To the aid of the inflationists, however, came the small
but energetic group of silver-mine owners, who saw the
market price of the bullion content of the old dollar drop
from $1.02 in 1872 to ninety-six cents in 1875, and to eighty-
two in 1885, with the downward trend unchecked. If the
government could again be induced to buy all the ore
brought to the mint for coinage, they reasoned that the
market price of the metal and the profits of silver production
would rise in response to the unlimited demand. The money
question did not become an issue between the parties for
many years. Within each party, however, it produced jangling discord, the members from the rural West and South
generally opposing those from the moneyed East and the
manufacturing sections of the Midwest.

[1] Germany demonetized silver in 1871, Denmark, Sweden and Norway in
1873, and in the latter year the Latin Union, composed of France, Italy, Belgium, Switzerland and Greece, limited silver coinage.

The first trial of strength came in November, 1877, when a free-silver bill passed the House of Representatives with Western and Southern support. Its father was "Silver Dick" (Richard P.) Bland of Missouri, whose advocacy stemmed from his youthful experiences in the Western mining country as well as from sympathy with his debt-ridden farmer constituents. Unwilling to go so far, the Senate at the instance of William B. Allison of Iowa altered the bill by directing the Treasury Department to buy only from two to four million dollars of silver bullion each month for coinage. President Hayes rejected the measure on the ground that, in the case of money borrowed earlier, it involved a virtual scaling down of debts and hence a breach of contract. But the bill was easily carried over his veto in February, 1878. As a compromise settlement, the Bland-Allison act had the effect of allaying further agitation for several years, though both Arthur and Cleveland recommended its repeal. The least amount of bullion permitted by the statute was purchased and coined each month, adding about $31,000,000 annually to the circulating medium.

Toward the end of the eighties the free-silver movement sprang to life again. The reasons were various. For one thing, the government, bent on reducing the surplus revenue (see page 113), was actively engaged in retiring the war bonds; and since the volume of national bank notes varied with the amount of federal bonds, this course of action caused these notes to shrink from a total of $359,000,000 in 1882 to $186,-000,000 in 1890. At the same time that this money was being taken out of circulation, the admission of six new plains and mountain states in 1889 and 1890 (see page 58) strengthened the hand of the silver forces, particularly in the Senate. Besides, the Farmers' Alliances now loomed big on the national political horizon. Party politicians were scarcely surprised when the fall elections of 1890 placed fifty-three "Alliance men" in Congress.

When the question of a new monetary law was taken up early in that year, it appeared that, contrary to their previous attitudes, the Senate now favored free silver while the House was opposed. The silverites in the House, however, finally forced the majority to make concessions by threatening to vote against the McKinley tariff bill, then in course of passage. In July, 1890, the Sherman silver-purchase act went into effect. Though not providing for free silver, it required the Treasury Department to buy four and a half million ounces of bullion each month (nearly twice as much as had been coined before), and to issue in payment therefor treasury notes of full legal-tender character, redeemable in either gold or silver at the government's option. William McKinley, who had cast his vote for Bland's free-silver bill in 1877, supported the new law as the next best thing to unlimited coinage.

POPULISM AND THE PANIC OF 1893

Unlike the Bland-Allison act, the new law failed to hush the outcry for free silver. Almost at once another downward plunge began in the prices of cotton, grain and livestock. An investigation made by the Department of Agriculture in 1893 showed that the cost of raising wheat and corn exceeded the prices received. In the single year 1891 no less than eighteen thousand covered wagons crossed from Nebraska to the Iowa bank of the Missouri River in full flight before the scorpion-whips of affliction. Between 1889 and 1893 more than eleven thousand mortgages were foreclosed in Kansas alone. Meanwhile, despite the greater absorption of silver by the mint, the bullion value of the dollar fell from eighty-one cents in 1890 to sixty in 1893.

A wave of despair swept over the West and South. Hamlin

Garland, who viewed the phenomenon at first hand, wrote many years later, "As ten-cent corn and ten per cent interest were troubling Kansas, so six-cent cotton was inflaming Georgia—and both were frankly sympathetic with Montana and Colorado whose miners were suffering from a drop in the price of silver." The new spirit was exemplified by Mrs. Mary E. Lease of Kansas, who, exhorting the farmers to "raise less corn and more hell," shouted to huge audiences, "The great common people of this country are slaves . . . . The West and South are bound and prostrate before the manufacturing East. . . . Our laws are the output of a system which clothes rascals in robes and honesty in rags." The effect on conservative Easterners was reflected in the New York *Evening Post's* caustic comment: "We don't want any more states until we can civilize Kansas."

Flushed by their successes in the November elections of 1890, the Farmers' Alliances laid plans to bring the urban wage-earners into the movement, and thereby enable the manual workers of the nation to present a united front. In May, 1891, over fourteen hundred representatives of agrarian, labor and reform groups, meeting in Cincinnati, resolved to form the People's party; and in July, 1892, a second convention, held in Omaha, made preparations for the presidential campaign. The platform promised that the Populists would restore the government "to the hands of the plain people" and, to that end, pledged such measures as free silver, greenbacks, a graduated income tax, government ownership of railways and telegraphs, a shorter workday for urban laborers and the popular election of United States Senators. When the platform was adopted, an onlooker reported that a tornado of cheers and yells "raged without cessation for thirty-four minutes, during which women shrieked and wept, men embraced and kissed . . . and leaped upon tables and chairs in the ecstasy of their delirium." James B.

Weaver of Iowa, veteran inflationist, who had headed the Greenback ticket in 1880, was named for President, with James G. Field of Virginia as his running mate. In the ensuing election the new party amazed old-party leaders by polling twenty-two electoral votes, all in the plains and mountain states, and more than a million popular votes. For the first time since the birth of the Republican party, a minor party won a place in the electoral college.

Nevertheless, as has been seen, Grover Cleveland, the Democratic nominee, easily captured the election on the tariff issue and, should economic conditions improve, it seemed likely that the political stream would subside once more into its usual channel. But such did not prove to be the case. No sooner did the new President enter office than a disastrous panic crashed upon the country. The catastrophe was bred of a complication of causes. Overinvestment in railways and industrial combinations, including too many of a highly speculative character, was a prime factor. Widespread depression in Europe since 1889, involving leading nations like Great Britain, Germany and France, aggravated the situation by causing a withdrawal of part of the gold which foreign capitalists had invested in American enterprises. An added, if not decisive, influence was the growing fear of the business classes that the flood of silver inflation freed by the Sherman act would sweep the government off a gold basis and force a suspension of gold payments.

Though the Sherman law permitted the government to redeem the new treasury notes in either gold or silver, gold was a popular symbol of the nation's financial integrity, and refusal to pay in the more precious metal would have destroyed public confidence. Yet no provision had been made in the act for enlarging the gold reserve. Hence, the fund of $100,000,000, established in 1875 to protect the value of the greenbacks (see page 90), must now serve, in addition, to back up the treasury notes that were increasing at a rate of $50,000,000 a year.[1] Indeed, since the gold reserve was not held separate from other public funds, there was the further danger that, under pressure of need, the government might use some of it for current operating expenses. Such an emergency confronted Cleveland when he took office. Because of lavish appropriations by Harrison's outgoing Congress and the meager revenue produced by the McKinley tariff, the gold reserve within six weeks fell below the $100,000,000 mark, greatly to the alarm of the business and financial classes. People everywhere rushed to get their treasury notes and greenbacks redeemed in gold, while foreign investors redoubled their efforts to secure prompt settlement of their American accounts in the only metal used in international trade.

Even a sounder economic structure might not have withstood this shock to public confidence. As it was, a paralysis of terror gripped the business world. More than eight thousand commercial concerns failed between April 1 and October 1, 1893, with liabilities of nearly $285,000,000. Many banks also toppled, particularly in the West and South, and a hundred and fifty-six railways went into receivership, including the Erie, the Northern Pacific and the Union Pacific. In the urban centers the problem of unemployment became acute, challenging all the resources of the new profession of social workers. The number of jobless was variously reckoned at from one million to four and a half million, the latter estimate being based upon trade-union figures. As in 1873, private benevolence came to the aid of the needy, and many cities appropriated public funds both for direct relief and for emergency projects, such as the paving of streets and

[1] Greenbacks to the amount of nearly $347,000,000 were in circulation. The 378,000,000 silver dollars issued under the Bland-Allison act were not, by law, redeemable in gold.

the building of sewers. Meanwhile, the farmers sank deeper into the abyss of adversity, with wheat selling for but forty-nine cents a bushel in 1894.

Cleveland, viewing the situation in strictly monetary terms, resolved at all hazards to maintain the gold standard. A sound-money man by conviction, he was stiffened in his purpose by unremitting pressure from Wall Street. He set about to accomplish his aim through two courses of action. In order to stop additional silver purchases and thus ease the strain upon the already overburdened gold reserve, he induced the House in August, 1893, to adopt a bill repealing the Sherman act. The upper chamber was in a more recalcitrant mood. Utilizing their opportunity of unlimited debate, the silver Senators indulged in filibustering tactics. On one occasion William V. Allen, the Nebraska Populist, held the floor for fourteen hours. Another persistent opponent was Henry M. Teller, a Colorado Republican. Finally, however, the President by applying the whip of patronage worked his will; and on the first day of November the repeal bill became law.

As a second move, Cleveland proposed to borrow gold faster than it was drained from the treasury for redemption. In this way he hoped to avoid a suspension of gold payments. Unhappily, paper currency presented for redemption had to be paid out again to defray the government's running expenses, and this money the recipients promptly exchanged for gold. Under the operation of what the President called "an endless chain," the gold fund dwindled from $95,000,-000 at the end of June, 1893, to $65,000,000 a year later. Congress, inspired in part by silver arguments, refused to authorize bond issues to maintain the reserve. Nevertheless Cleveland, discovering authority in an earlier statute, twice sold $50,000,000 worth of bonds to the public during 1894. Only temporary improvement resulted, however, for the bonds were bought, in large part, with gold that had been drawn out of the treasury by the presentation of paper currency.

In the quest for more substantial relief, the administration in February, 1895, arranged with J. Pierpont Morgan and a financial syndicate for a loan of $65,000,000 worth of gold in return for government bonds. The special condition was affixed that at least half the metal be procured from abroad, and that the bankers exert their influence to protect the gold reserve against further depletion. As a result, the strain on the government relaxed for the next four or five months, though the Populists and radical Democrats, embittered against capitalistic greed, charged Cleveland with allowing the Wall Street group to make an excessive profit on the transaction. The peak of the financial crisis was now passed. Normal conditions, however, did not return until the next year, when they were assisted by a fourth bond sale—this time directly to the public—of $100,000,000 in January, 1896, and also by a widespread improvement of business.

THE CLIMAX OF THE SILVER CRUSADE

When the bill repealing the Sherman law passed the House, "Silver Dick" Bland proclaimed that the struggle had but begun, and that it would end only in the establishment of free coinage. The events of the next few years made this prediction seem anything but an idle boast. Conditions continued to grow worse. In the late summer of 1894 torrid winds blew over the Midwestern corn belt, ravaging the fields and reducing the crop to a quarter of the previous year. As the farmers were plunged deeper into despair, more urban workers lost their jobs or suffered disastrous cuts in pay. Among the several million unemployed the social contagion spread rapidly. The labor outbreak centering in the

Pullman strike (see pages 150-152) was but the most portentous of such disturbances.

In the hope of mitigating their lot, organized bands of the jobless began a march on Washington. Through the issue of fiat money or otherwise, they wanted Congress to inaugurate a system of general work relief involving the extension of good roads and the construction of public buildings and municipal improvements. These "petitions in boots" moved slowly across the country, afoot and on horseback, sometimes stealing trains for faster transit. They came from many points of the compass—Los Angeles, San Francisco, Seattle, St. Louis, Chicago, as well as from towns along the way and places in New England. The "army" led by "General" Jacob S. Coxey of Massillon, Ohio, though by no means the largest, excited the most attention. After losing many of their number about twelve hundred men straggled into Washington from May to July, 1894. There they were able to accomplish nothing. Although their central idea was to be taken over by the New Deal during the Great Depression following 1929, at this earlier time Senators roundly denounced federal work relief as "socialism and populism and paternalism run riot." Coxey himself was arrested on the technical charge of trespassing on the Capitol grounds, and his footsore comrades, facing starvation and harassed by the police, presently scattered for parts unknown. The failure of the movement, however, did not heal the conditions that had given it rise.

The public's suspicion of the overweening power of Big Business increased as a result of the Senate's betrayal of President Cleveland's tariff policy in the Wilson-Gorman act (see pages 123-124); and the popular attitude seemed further confirmed by the Supreme Court's annulment of the income tax in 1895. This decision, reversing an earlier one, provoked the greatest outburst of wrath against that tribunal since the Dred Scott decision. As Mr. Justice Harlan, a member of the court, recalled many years later, "There was everywhere, among the people generally, a deep feeling of unrest. The Nation had been rid of human slavery . . . but the conviction was universal that the country was in real danger from another kind of slavery, . . . the slavery that would result from aggregations of capital in the hands of a few."

In the circumstances the battle over free silver took on the semblance of a holy war, arraying the West and South against the East, the debtor class against the creditor class, the countryside against the city. As a writer in the *Arena* magazine put it, the real meaning of the contest "lies far deeper than any question of one metal or two for a monetary base. It is a question of entrusting Federal power to men in hearty sympathy with the great common people or to men in sympathy with Wall Street." The growing enthusiasm for unlimited coinage displayed many of the elements of a mighty religious revival, and in 1894 appeared the Bible of the new faith—a cheaply printed, paper-bound book entitled *Coin's Financial School,* written by William H. Harvey. This little volume, enlivened with caricatures and addressed to the simplest understanding, set forth cogently the main silver arguments, and skillfully played upon the prejudices of the poor against the rich. Attaining a sale in 1895 of more than a hundred thousand copies a month, it made numberless converts. In ten thousand schoolhouses throughout the West and the South the people assembled to debate the absorbing question—not only the politician and the farmer, but the small merchant and the workingman, the preacher and the schoolteacher. Organized labor rallied to the cause, the American Federation of Labor warmly indorsing free silver.

The old parties were badly frightened, but knew not what

to do. In their state conventions before the autumn elections of 1894, the platforms of both Republicans and Democrats varied from ambiguous generalities to forthright declarations for unlimited coinage. A significant demonstration among Western Democrats took place in June at Omaha where, under the leadership of William Jennings Bryan of Nebraska, a mammoth convention demanded the immediate adoption of free silver. Handicapped by Cleveland's unpopularity, the Democrats suffered severe losses at the polls. The Republicans were the chief gainers, but the Populists elected six Senators and increased their popular vote over that of 1892 by nearly half.

On the heels of the election the silver Democrats redoubled their exertions to cast off Eastern control. During 1895 numerous conferences were held, organizations formed, speeches made, pamphlets circulated. When the national convention assembled at Chicago on July 7, 1896, triumph was assured. The platform acclaimed free silver as the question "paramount to all others," assailed the income-tax decision and, in an allusion to Cleveland's action in the Pullman strike, denounced federal interference in labor conflicts. The presentation of the platform precipitated one of the most exciting debates ever held in a party convention. Senator David B. Hill of New York stanchly championed the cause of gold and the East, ending his address with an appeal not "to drive old Democrats out of the party who have grown gray in the service, to make room for a lot of Republicans and Populists, and political nondescripts." After other speakers had entered the lists, the debate reached a dramatic climax in the concluding address of William Jennings Bryan.

Speaking with a full-toned, richly modulated eloquence unmatched in his generation, Bryan presented the free-coinage question as "a cause as holy as the cause of humanity."

Turning to those who opposed the silver plank, he thundered: "You tell us that the great cities are in favor of the gold standard; we reply that the great cities rest upon our broad and fertile prairies. Burn down your cities and leave our farms, and your cities will spring up again as if by magic; but destroy our farms and the grass will grow in the streets of every city in the country." His closing defiance to the gold adherents brought the vast audience in a frenzy to its feet: "You shall not press down upon the brow of labor this crown of thorns; you shall not crucify mankind upon a cross of gold." The "Boy Orator of the Platte"—he was thirty-six at the time—had made himself the man of the hour. Without strength before the convention met, he won the nomination on the fifth ballot, the second place going to Arthur Sewall, a Maine banker who shared Bryan's financial views. Most of the Eastern delegates abstained from voting.

When the Republicans convened at St. Louis on June 16, their ranks were divided among advocates of the gold standard, those who preferred the customary policy of evasion, and a resolute minority from the Far West bent upon a free-silver plank. William McKinley of Ohio, known to the public chiefly as an ardent protectionist, was the leading candidate, thanks to the tireless endeavors of his friend Marcus A. Hanna. The latter, a Cleveland capitalist, had long been active in state politics as a means of furthering his interests in mines, banking and street railways, but later he became enamored of the political game for its own sake. Hanna's efforts and money had facilitated McKinley's election as governor in 1891, and when two years later McKinley became involved in heavy financial obligations, Hanna joined with Carnegie, Frick and others in supplying the hundred and thirty thousand dollars that saved him from bankruptcy. In preparing the way for his fellow Ohioan's presidential nomination, Hanna spent not less than a hundred thousand dollars in a campaign of publicity and personal canvass among the delegates.

The question of a monetary standard involved serious difficulties for McKinley. An advocate of free silver as recently as 1890, he began to shift ground in his gubernatorial campaign the next year by asserting that the Sherman silver-purchase act was preferable to unlimited coinage. Partly because of his earlier record, partly because of his conciliatory temperament, and partly because of his fear that a gold pronouncement would "divide the party at the Mississippi River," he wanted the convention to straddle the issue and focus all attention on the tariff. Hanna, sinking the businessman in the politician, assented to the scheme, but not so the powerful leaders from the industrial regions, who made a gold declaration the price of their support. The outcome of many secret conferences between the factions was a shrewdly devised plank, which read in part: "We are . . . opposed to the free coinage of silver except by international agreement . . . which we pledge ourselves to promote, and until such agreement can be obtained the existing gold standard must be preserved."

Taken literally, the platform declared for international free silver, but since international conferences in 1878, 1881 and 1892 had demonstrated the unwillingness of European countries to depart from the gold standard, the plank was rightly construed by the silverites as a repudiation of free coinage. Thirty-four delegates, with Senator Teller of Colorado at their head, withdrew from the convention in protest. In the completed platform the money plank occupied an inconspicuous place in the middle, the first nine paragraphs being devoted to disparaging the Democrats and praising the protective system. McKinley was named on the first ballot, with Garret A. Hobart of New Jersey as his running mate.

The decision of the major parties led to a disruption of party loyalties comparable only to the effect of the slavery issue on the voters of 1860. A convention of old-school Democrats, acting with Cleveland's approval, reaffirmed the gold standard, and put up General John M. Palmer of Illinois and Simon B. Buckner of Kentucky as their candidates. Had the Republican platform been less emphatic on the tariff question, McKinley might have received their support. The Republican irreconcilables, calling themselves the National Silver party, indorsed Bryan and Sewall. As was to be expected, the People's party also backed Bryan, though for Vice-President they nominated one of their own group in preference to the Maine capitalist. Even the Prohibitionists were affected by the all-absorbing issue, and broke into two parties with different platforms and candidates.

The contest was unique and sensational to the end. Fearful of further defections from their ranks, Republican orators at first avoided the money question, placing all stress upon "Bill McKinley and the McKinley Bill." But it was Bryan who set the pace for the campaign when he undertook a remarkable stumping tour of eighteen thousand miles, addressing nearly five million people in twenty-nine states in fourteen weeks, and everywhere preaching free silver and the doctrine of discontent. Gompers and other leaders of organized labor exerted themselves on his behalf. Of no little influence were Homer Davenport's cartoons in Hearst's *New York Journal,* which showed Hanna, an ogre-like figure checkered with dollar signs, leading the child McKinley by a string. For campaign funds the Democrats leaned heavily upon the silver-mine owners, somewhat over a half-million dollars being subscribed in all.

To checkmate the efforts of the opposition, Hanna as head of the Republican national committee collected from the great banking and business interests an election fund of unknown amount, probably about four million dollars. The Standard Oil group alone contributed two hundred and fifty thousand dollars. With this money Hanna conducted a vast campaign of popular education. A small army was organized to address rallies, send out literature in ten different languages, and distribute campaign buttons. Of the more than five hundred posters that were prepared, the most popular was a lithograph picturing McKinley as "The Advance Agent of Prosperity." Most, though not all, of the leading economists and financiers opposed Bryan on the money question, and the president of the National Education Association declared against him. The country also witnessed the singular spectacle of all the members of Cleveland's cabinet repudiating their party's nominee. McKinley remained quietly at home, delivering from his front porch in Canton, Ohio, dignified addresses to visiting delegations.

As the campaign drew to a close, the excitement of the country became intense. Manufacturers made contracts contingent upon McKinley's election, and wage-earners were told that the factories would close in the event of Democratic success. By such newspapers as the *New York Tribune* Bryan was reviled as a "demagogue," an "anarchist" and a "madman." One Republican spellbinder, commending the designation "Boy Orator of the Platte," asserted that that river was "six inches deep and six miles wide at the mouth." Even so sober an organ as the New York *Evening Post* characterized the contest as one between "the great civilizing forces of the republic" and "the still surviving barbarism bred by slavery in the South and the reckless spirit of adventure in the mining camps of the West." Fortunately for the Republicans, crop failures in Russia, the Argentine and elsewhere lifted the price of wheat at Chicago from fifty-three cents a bushel in August to ninety-four in the week of the election, and thus greatly eased the farmers' distress.

The outcome was decisive. McKinley received 51 per cent of the popular ballots (7,112,000 votes) to less than 47 per cent (6,733,000) for his opponent, the largest majority since Grant's victory over Greeley. His preponderance in the electoral college was far greater: 271 to 176. In general, the industrial and older grain-growing states supported McKinley as against the cotton, prairie and silver-mining states. As was to be expected, Bryan polled a considerably smaller proportion of the votes of the cities than he did of the rural sections; and, for the first time, the Republicans carried New York City.[1] The farmers' attempt to beat back the new urban and industrial civilization had turned to rout. Yet the future was to disclose that the campaign marked the entry of novel and dynamic social forces into American political life.

THE AFTERMATH

The new President went into office with both branches of Congress safely Republican. A man of quiet dignity, with deep-set eyes under a Websterian brow, McKinley brought to public affairs qualities that sharply set him off from his Democratic predecessor: affability, tact, patience and a desire to keep in step with his party. To further his friend Hanna's ambitions, he appointed Senator John Sherman to the office of Secretary of State, so that Hanna might succeed to the vacant seat.[2] Advanced years and mental impairment pres-

[1] In commenting on the outcome, E. L. Godkin declared in the *Nation* that "the cities having the largest population and the largest percentages of foreign-born citizens cast the heaviest majorities in support of sound money and social order." He made no allowance, however, for the effect of employers' coercion and of the manipulation of election returns in producing this result.

[2] Other than Sherman, the members of the original cabinet were Lyman J. Gage of Illinois, Secretary of the Treasury; Russell A. Alger of Michigan, Secretary of War; Joseph McKenna of California, Attorney-General; James A. Gary of Maryland, Postmaster-General; John D. Long of Massachusetts, Secretary of the Navy; Cornelius N. Bliss of New York, Secretary of the Interior; and James Wilson of Iowa, Secretary of Agriculture.

ently caused Sherman to be replaced with William R. Day, another Ohioan; and the latter in turn retired in August, 1898, to make way for John Hay, also of Ohio, a much abler man than either of the others.

In spite of an apparently clear popular verdict against silver, McKinley chose to interpret his victory as primarily a mandate for tariff protection (see page 125). The fact was that the party remained divided notwithstanding the united front displayed at the election. Therefore it seemed to Mc-Kinley and his advisers the part of wisdom to let well enough alone in regard to the money question. However, in defer-ence to the platform pledge, an official commission was dis-patched to France and Great Britain in 1897 to explore the possibility of establishing free silver by international agree-ment. The anticipated refusal of Great Britain, followed presently by the distracting effects of the Spanish-American War, eased the path for the gold advocates.

Other events also worked in their behalf. An enormous in-crease occurred in the gold supply as a result of the cyanide process of extracting the metal from low-content ores and the discovery of fresh deposits in Alaska, Australia and South Africa. The world's annual production, which had averaged between five and six million ounces from 1860 to 1890, reached nearly eleven and a half million in 1897 and twenty-two in 1910. Paper currency also grew in volume, thanks to the purchase by national banks of the new government bonds issued during the war with Spain and to a liberaliza-tion of the national banking act. With all reasonable fear of the scarcity of money removed, the argument for silver infla-tion collapsed.

Meanwhile, prosperity returned to the farm, and some of the psychological drawbacks of rural life were lessened. A recurrence of foreign crop failures in 1897 sent the price of American wheat even higher than in the preceding season.

The value of grain exports increased by no less than $122,-000,000. As the farmers recovered a sense of material well-being, the introduction of free mail delivery at their homes, the spread of mutual telephone companies in rural communities after the expiration of the basic Bell patents in 1893, the advent of interurban electric railways and the extension of the good-roads movement brought to the countryside advantages which earlier had belonged only to the city.[1] These new conveniences of living—a mere earnest of what the future held in store—helped to dispel some of the loneliness of existence and appease the feeling of rural inferiority.

Emboldened by these favoring circumstances, Congress in March, 1900, adopted the gold-standard act. The statute declared other forms of money redeemable in gold on demand, and enlarged the gold redemption fund to $150,000,000. In order to avoid the difficulties that had vexed the Cleveland administration, the law made the gold reserve a separate and distinct fund, not to be drawn upon to meet current deficiencies in the revenue, and it provided further that, when paper notes were offered for redemption, they should not be paid out again except for gold. Thus the war of the standards closed, leaving the next generation to solve certain knotty problems arising from other imperfections of the circulating medium, notably its inelastic character.

SELECT BIBLIOGRAPHY

The Farmers Take Their Stand, 1880–1900. Among the general works dealing with the period, Josephson, *Politicos,* Oberholtzer, *History,* V, Peck, *Twenty Years of the Republic,* Schlesinger, *Rise of the City,* and Tarbell, *Nationalizing of Business,* contribute to an understanding of the farmers' difficulties. Hicks, *Populist Revolt,* traces with impartial hand the history of the Farmers' Alliances and the People's party, while such mono-

[1] Begun in 1896, rural-free-delivery routes lengthened from 1800 miles in 1897 to nearly 29,000 in 1900 and 950,000 in 1916.

graphs as Arnett, *Populist Movement in Georgia,* and Simkins, *Tillman Movement in South Carolina,* treat the situation in particular states. An insight into rural social life can be gleaned from Dick, *Sod-House Frontier,* and Garland's autobiographical *Son of the Middle Border.* On the silver controversy, Laughlin, *History of Bimetallism,* and Noyes, *Forty Years of American Finance,* should be supplemented by Hütter, *La Question de la monnai d'argent.* The business breakdown is studied from different angles in Lauck, *Causes of the Panic of 1893,* Weberg, *Background of the Panic of 1893,* and Feder, *Unemployment Relief.* In *Coxey's Army* McMurry presents a graphic account of the march of the jobless on Washington. Leading figures in the struggle over free silver are portrayed in Nevins, *Cleveland;* Barnes, *Carlisle;* Werner, *Bryan;* Croly, *Hanna;* Corey, *House of Morgan;* Haynes, *Weaver;* Woodward, *Tom Watson;* and Olcott, *McKinley.*

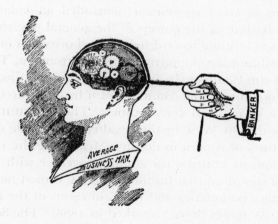

Chapter IX

THE STRENGTHENING OF NATION-ALITY, 1865–1900

THE DRIFT TOWARD CENTRALIZATION

THE presidential campaign of 1896 attested the firm texture of the Union that had come into being since the Civil War. Though the farmers' grievances were no less real than had been those of the slaveholders, there was no talk of nullification or secession, no John C. Calhoun or Jefferson Davis sounding the tocsin of state sovereignty. On the contrary, the agrarian spokesmen demanded an enlargement, not a limitation, of the powers of the general government.

This new attitude toward federal authority was one of the most significant developments of the postwar era. The overthrow of the Confederacy in 1865 had not only insured the geographic unity of the country, but it had also strengthened the sense of national consciousness. The adventure of settling the distant West further exalted the people's faith in the greatness of American destiny. Meanwhile the Economic Revolution, by knitting the country together with bonds of steel and ties of mutual business interest, caused men to disregard state boundaries and think in terms of the nation as a whole. As James Bryce remarked in 1888, "The South and the West need capital for their development, and are daily in closer business relations with the East. The produce of the West finds its way to the Atlantic through the ports of the East. Every produce market, every share market, vibrates in response to the Produce Exchange and Stock Exchange of New York."

Other influences—the increasing urbanization and standardization of American life, the extension of the public school system to all parts of the land, the universal appeal of the new literature, the country-wide absorption in athletic sport—yielded a similar result. As the republic reached the centenary of its birth, the heightened pride of nationality exulted in a series of patriotic celebrations, beginning with the anniversary of Concord and Lexington in 1875 and the Centennial Exhibition at Philadelphia in 1876, and continuing year after year until the setting up of the Supreme Court was commemorated in 1890 with due acclaim. Responsive to the nationalizing trend, a bewildering number of large-scale voluntary organizations sprang up—not only of capital and labor, but also, it will be recalled, of scholars, scientists, artists, social and political reformers, sport lovers and secret-society "joiners." Andrew Carnegie, paying grateful tribute to his adopted country in *Triumphant Democracy* (1886), remarked, "Groups of men with allied interests invariably have an organization to watch over the common weal." He attributed this trait to the natural instincts of a "people trained to govern itself." Whatever the cause, the effect in erasing local attachments and substituting larger loyalties was incalculable.

It is little wonder that Edward A. Freeman, the English historian, visiting America in 1882, noted that "where the word 'federal' used to be used up to the time of the civil war or later, the word 'national' is now used all but invariably. It used to be 'federal capital,' 'federal army,' 'federal revenue,' and so forth. Now the word 'national' is almost always used instead." A profound change had taken place since 1863 when Freeman had published the first volume of his *History of Federal Government from the Foundation of the Achaian League to the Disruption of the United States*.

No part of the country gave clearer evidence of the new gravitational pull than the South. Nearly every year yielded fresh proof that the Southern people accepted their defeat in good faith and that an ever larger number of them rejoiced that the "Lost Cause" was irretrievably lost. Even Jefferson Davis, writing in 1881 without apology for the past, expressed the earnest hope that "there may be written on the arch of the Union, *Esto perpetua.*" In that year, veterans' organizations of the blue and gray hosts began occasionally to hold joint reunions in order to compare war-time experiences in a spirit of amity and mutual respect. The Virginian, John S. Wise, probably voiced the thought of most of his former comrades-in-arms when he wrote a few years later: "Through our tears, and without disloyalty to the dead, in the possession of freedom and union and liberty, true Confederates, viewing it all in the clearer light of to-day, ought to thank God that slavery died at Appomattox."

Behind this transformation of attitude lay a multitude of reasons, notably the recovery of white rule in the South, the cessation of Northern intrusion in its race relations, the mingling of the two peoples as a result of freer intermigration, the increasing identification of the South with the national economic order and, not of least importance, the healing balm of time and the oncoming of a new generation. Southern contributions to local-color fiction (see page 206) did much to restore sectional self-esteem, while at the same time they gave Northerners a mellow and romantic picture of Southern life and ideals to offset the abolitionist exaggerations of bygone years. All these tendencies reached a climax in the Spanish war of 1898. For the first time, the former foemen were called upon to face a common enemy. The jubilant response stilled the last faint notes of ancient discord.[1] None could doubt that the Union had become one in spirit as well as in name.

---

[1] It was at this time that Congress removed the remaining disabilities imposed upon ex-Confederate leaders by the Fourteenth Amendment.

In national politics the centripetal tide swept parties and leaders before it. Republicans welcomed it, Democrats deplored it; but even the latter, when in power, yielded ground to it. Whether men sought to speed or to check the mighty forces remaking the economic order, they turned to Washington, not to their legislatures, for effective action. The Republicans abetted federal consolidation not only through the Thirteenth, Fourteenth and Fifteenth amendments, but also through national supervision of state elections, extreme tariff protection and lavish grants for railroad, river and harbor development. A Democratic House initiated and a Democratic President signed the interstate-commerce act, which embodied a startling new assertion of governmental authority.

A few years later, when Cleveland defied the state-rights view of the Constitution by sending troops to Chicago during the Pullman strike (see page 151), Governor Altgeld of Illinois felt obliged to remind the President that "the principle of local self-government is just as fundamental in our institutions as is that of Federal supremacy." Yet there was no time when Altgeld and other men of progressive or radical opinions would not gladly have used federal authority to implement policies which they themselves deemed desirable. Bryce acutely pointed out that the state, once a "self-sufficing commonwealth," had become "merely a part of a far grander whole, which seems to be slowly absorbing its functions and stunting its growth, as the great tree stunts the shrubs over which its spreading boughs have begun to cast their shade." The twentieth century was to bring an even greater expansion of national power, notably under Woodrow Wilson and Franklin D. Roosevelt.

The Supreme Court yielded more slowly to the temper of the times. The "convenient vagueness" of the first section of the Fourteenth Amendment admitted of a variety of interpretations, but the court's early decisions looked backward rather than forward. "No State," reads the amendment, "shall make or enforce any law that shall abridge the privileges or immunities of citizens of the United States; nor shall any State deprive any person of life, liberty, or property, without due process of law; nor deny to any person within its jurisdiction the equal protection of the laws." In the Slaughterhouse cases (1873), certain butchers of New Orleans appealed to the Supreme Court to annul the monopoly rights which the corrupt Carpetbag legislature had granted to a local slaughterhouse company. They alleged that the law in question abridged the privileges and immunities of "citizens of the United States" and that, further, it deprived them as "persons" of property without due process of law and denied them the equal protection of the laws. By a majority of five to four, the judges held that there was a difference between state citizenship and national citizenship and that, since the privileges and immunities in dispute belonged to state citizenship, the complainants must look for relief to Louisiana, not to the federal government. The court dismissed the other contentions by denying that the Louisiana law involved a taking of property without due process of law, and by asserting that the provision for equal protection was intended to apply to Negroes. The "one pervading purpose" of the framers of the Fourteenth Amendment, they said, had been to protect the rights of the ex-slave.

Four years later, as has already been seen (page 88), the tribunal took a somewhat similar stand in the Granger cases, declaring Illinois's untrammeled right under her police power to fix rates for businesses "clothed with a public interest," and denying that the complainants had been deprived of property without due process of law. The court displayed an equally resistant attitude in 1882 in the case of San Mateo County v. Southern Pacific Railroad Company by affirming that a corporation was not a "person" whose actions fell within the purview of the Fourteenth Amendment. In other words, the drift of the decisions was to restrain the federal authority from interfering with the activities of the states.

Later in the 1880's, however, the judiciary shifted its position and began to assert a boldly national point of view. This changed outlook was hastened by the appointment in 1881-1882 of much younger men to replace three older judges. One of the veteran members, referring to the new trend of the bench, lamented, "What was in 1862 called the 'medicine of the Constitution' has become its daily bread." The high tribunal, reversing its judgment of only four years before, now declared in the case of Santa Clara County v. Southern Pacific Railroad Company (1886) that a corporation was a "person" and hence entitled to the protection of the amendment. The same year it held in the Wabash case (see page 134), contrary to its view in the Granger cases, that states could not regulate rates that affected interstate commerce.

In the Minnesota Rate Case (Chicago, Milwaukee and St. Paul Railway v. Minnesota, 1890) the judges went even further and denied the state's uncontrolled right to fix rates of any kind, declaring in effect that, under the due-process clause, the court was the final authority as to the reasonableness of rates. In these and other later decisions the judiciary arrogated to itself the power of reviewing most state and local legislation affecting the rights of private property. That its influence generally favored the great corporate interests is less important in the present connection than the fact that the court, sensitive at last to the centralizing impulse, assumed the high function of arbiter and censor of the national economic order.

The centripetal trend in America accorded with a movement that was enveloping Europe at the same time. After the creation of the national states of Italy, Austria-Hungary, the French Republic and the German Empire in the 1860's and early 1870's, the tendency everywhere was to strengthen the hands of government and tighten its control over economic and social life. As in the United States, many factors, political, economic and psychological, were responsible. Bismarck in Germany, Crispi in Italy and Witte in Russia typify the statesmen who gave form and direction to the new tendencies. Thus America, though moved by her own inner compulsions, shared in a world stream of development.

THE CHANGING ATTITUDE TOWARD IMMIGRATION

The heightened sense of American nationality led also to a different attitude toward unrestricted immigration. Since colonial times migrants from across the sea had flocked to America without let or hindrance. The majority of them consisted of farmers and workingmen from the British Isles, Germany and, more recently, the Scandinavian countries. Of the 6,680,000 foreigners living in the United States in 1880, the Germans numbered about two million, the Irish 1,855,-000, the Canadians 717,000, the English 664,000 and the Scandinavians 440,000. Predominantly the newcomers took up farming, and in 1880 a higher proportion of immigrants dwelt in the upper Mississippi Valley than in any other section of the country. These folk were easily assimilated, for they represented the stocks from which the Anglo-Saxon people had originally sprung. So greatly were they desired that the newer commonwealths maintained official bureaus to encourage their coming. The railroads also helped, in some instances arranging to teach the new arrivals prairie agriculture and to build schoolhouses and churches for them. With plenty of land for settlement, their addition to the population caused no shock to the economic structure.

America's hospitality to the distressed of other lands was fittingly commemorated by the lines of Emma Lazarus in-

scribed on the Statue of Liberty, erected in 1886 at the entrance of New York Harbor as a gift of the French people:

> From her beacon-hand
> Glows world-wide welcome; her mild eyes command
> The air-bridged harbor that twin cities frame.
> "Keep, ancient lands, your storied pomp!" cries she
> With silent lips. "Give me your tired, your poor,
> Your huddled masses yearning to breathe free,
> The wretched refuse of your teeming shore.
> Send those, the homeless, tempest-tost to me.
> I lift my lamp beside the golden door."

But while the great monument was still in process of construction, events were foreshadowing a less cordial attitude.
The turning point came in 1882. In that year the influx
from Western and Northern Europe reached its crest, arrivals
began to appear in noticeable numbers from Eastern and
Southern Europe, and Congress enacted the first important
restrictive law. The hosts from Russia, Austria-Hungary,
Italy and other Mediterranean countries increased as time
went on until in 1896 they outnumbered those of the older
type. Many influences account for the "new immigration,"
notably, overcrowded conditions in the home countries,
anti-Semitic persecution in Russia beginning about 1881,
the opening of direct steamship connections between Mediterranean ports and the United States, and the attractions of
employment in the new mines and factories. Steamship companies stimulated the inflow to the extent of their advertising ability, while agents representing American corporations
offered to prepay the passage of laborers agreeing in advance
to work in their plants.

The new immigrants did not fade quickly into the American population as had the old. Impoverished and hiving in
the industrial centers, they formed self-contained communities that tended to perpetuate the peculiar institutions, folk

EUROPEAN SOURCES OF AMERICAN IMMIGRATION IN THE LATE
NINETEENTH AND EARLY TWENTIETH CENTURIES

customs and foreign-language newspapers of the homeland.
Unused to the American standard of living, they vastly complicated the problems of sanitation, health and housing for
the municipal authorities. For the same reason they gladly
toiled for wages and upon terms which native workingmen
scorned; and since one out of every three planned to go back
home after laying aside a little money, many remained indifferent, when not actually hostile, to the efforts of organized labor to improve conditions. Poorly educated, if educated at all, most of them also lacked familiarity with
democratic institutions and ideals. Though they were widely

charged with responsibility for municipal misrule, this could hardly be maintained when "American" cities like Philadelphia and Portland, Oregon, were as badly governed as New York and Chicago with their far higher proportion of foreign-born voters. Individuals among the recent comers proved equal to the best that the older strains produced, while the bulk of these Slavs, Magyars, Poles, Russians, Italians, Greeks and others provided the heavy labor upon which rested the remarkable development of mill and mine during these years.

The swelling tide of immigration from Eastern and Southern Europe hastened the adoption of a new national policy toward incoming aliens. The conviction was growing that, with the dwindling of free homesteads in the West and the formidable problems raised by the herding of immigrants in cities, national self-protection called for some measure of selective immigration. Organized labor urged the same course as a means of safeguarding native workers against unfair competition, while persons whose patriotism had been fired by the recurrent centennials of early American history joined in out of pride of ancestry. "Who shall respect a people who do not respect their own blood?" cried one of them. Congress responded to these various influences with legislation of increasing severity. The act of 1882 excluded lunatics, convicted criminals and persons likely to become public charges. Three years later the alien-labor-contract law forbade employers to import foreign workingmen under previous contract. Every few years saw the adoption of additional restrictions until by 1903 the prohibited classes embraced physical, mental and moral defectives of all kinds, professional beggars, assisted immigrants, polygamists and anarchists.

As a special device to discriminate against the new immigration without discriminating against the old, a strong sentiment developed in behalf of a literacy test, for over thirty-five per cent of the more recent comers were illiterate as compared with three per cent in the case of the older alien elements. But this scheme encountered vigorous opposition from persons who insisted that ability to read was a test of youthful opportunity, not of mental capacity or social usefulness. A bill for this purpose was vetoed by President Cleveland before he left office in 1897. He dismissed the charges as to the inferior character of the newer arrivals by saying, "The time is quite within recent memory when the same thing was said of immigrants who, with their descendants, are now numbered among our best citizens." Adoption of a literacy test had to await another twenty years.

The sheer magnitude of the immigration after 1865 is a source of amazement. In the period to 1900 no less than thirteen and a half million foreigners of all kinds entered the United States, a number exceeding by more than a million the total population in 1830; and the volume was to become bigger in the opening years of the present century. The mounting stream caused the social composition of certain sections to change in startling ways. As *Donahoe's Magazine* pointed out as early as 1889, "Boston is no longer the Boston of the Endicotts and the Winthrops, but the Boston of the Collinses and the O'Briens." In that year sixty-eight towns and cities of Massachusetts, including many of the largest, were governed by the Irish. Greater New York in 1890 was the world's chief center of immigrants, a veritable amalgam of nations, with half as many Italians as Naples, as many Germans as Hamburg, twice as many Irishmen as Dublin and two and a half times as many Jews as Warsaw. Chicago was hardly less cosmopolitan, having more Czechs, Poles and Canadians than New York, while the great agricultural empire to its northwest was rapidly turning into a new Scandinavia.

Yet everywhere, even in the dense population centers and among the new type of foreigners, the "melting pot" was performing its work. Sometimes, unusual success in business or the liberalizing effect of membership in a labor union hastened the process. More often, it was the democratic school system that brought the influences of the new land into the immigrant home. The American-born children were apt to intermarry with other national stocks, and accept American ways and ideals so zealously as wholly to forget their alien cultural heritage.

Though the government raised ever higher bars against undesirable individuals from Europe, it did not go so far as to exclude whole peoples. This more drastic course, however, it adopted to cope with the Oriental influx on the Pacific Coast. In the fifties and sixties, Chinese coolies in California had been in such demand as cheap labor that Leland Stanford and other captains of industry imported whole shiploads of them. By 1870 they numbered between fifty and sixty thousand, and ten years later over a hundred thousand. While the total was still relatively small, the United States made the Burlingame treaty of 1868 with China, which explicitly recognized the "inalienable right of man to change his home and allegiance, and also the mutual advantage of the free migration and emigration."

Almost at once local sentiment turned against the newcomers. White immigrant laborers, multiplying in California as the transcontinental railroads were completed, found themselves obliged to compete for jobs with a people whose low standard of living enabled them to work for a mere pittance. As Robert Louis Stevenson, who resided for a time in California, wrote, "Hungry Europe and hungry China, each pouring from their gates in search of provender, had here come face to face." Racial differences and a strong belief as to the unassimilability of the Orientals further sharpened the antagonism. In 1871 a riot in Los Angeles caused the death of twenty-one Asiatics, and for ten years the question was one of burning importance in state politics. A newly formed Workingman's party adopted the slogan, "The Chinese must go"; mob attacks took place upon the Chinese quarters of San Francisco and other places; and the legislature passed discriminatory laws, though most of these were set aside by the courts.

In time the violence of the agitation excited national attention. In 1879 the Democratic House of Representatives and the Republican Senate, vying with each other for the electoral vote of California, passed a bill revoking the Burlingame treaty and restricting Chinese immigration. President Hayes, disapproving the method but not the purpose, vetoed the measure and, instead, negotiated a new arrangement with China. The treaty of 1880 permitted the United States to "regulate, limit, or suspend," but "not absolutely prohibit," future coolie immigration. Under its terms Congress two years later adopted the first exclusion law, to remain in effect for ten years. Subsequent acts renewed the suspension from time to time, and in 1902 Congress made the prohibition indefinite. Though China in 1904 declined to give the practice further treaty sanction, the United States continued the exclusion upon its own authority.

THE CRUMBLING OF NATIONAL ISOLATION

With the enhanced nationalism at home came a new attitude in international relations. Though pledges of "isolation" and pronouncements against "entangling alliances" continued to punctuate the utterances of statesmen, the deep pull of events steadily loosened the nation from ancient moorings. As the Economic Revolution gained full momentum, industrialists found they needed to look elsewhere to market their growing surplus of goods, and capitalists began to scan the globe for opportunities to supplement their domestic investments. Between 1870 and 1900 foreign exports rose in value from less than $393,000,000 to nearly $1,395,-000,000, while American investments in other countries leaped from an unknown but trifling amount to $500,000,-000. The head of the Bureau of Foreign Commerce could rightly say in 1897, "The 'international isolation' of the United States so far as industry and commerce are concerned has, in fact, been made a thing of the past by the logic of the change in our economic requirements . . . now that we ourselves have become a competitor in the world-wide struggle for trade."

Other factors operated to the same end. Overseas missionary activity, particularly in the Pacific islands and the Orient, had long been a feature of American life, and the possibility of carrying the blessings of Christianity to the "benighted heathen" under protection of the Stars and Stripes touched a responsive chord in many hearts. In the case of some, this religious purpose was mingled with a deep conviction of the superiority of the Anglo-Saxon stock to all others. "This race of unequaled energy," declared the Reverend Josiah Strong in his widely read book *Our Country* (1885), "with all the majesty of numbers and the might of wealth behind it—the representative, let us hope, of the largest liberty, the purest Christianity, the highest civilization— . . . will move down upon Mexico, down upon Central and South America, out upon the islands of the sea." Such views and influences were strengthened by the fact that the national spirit of adventure and acquisition, thwarted by the occupation of the last continental frontier, sought fresh channels for expression. "In our infancy we bordered upon the Atlantic only," wrote Captain Alfred T. Mahan in 1893 in a plea for greater sea power, "our youth carried our boundary to the Gulf of Mexico; to-day maturity sees us upon the

Pacific. Have we no right or no call to progress farther in any direction?"

Sensitive to the broadening international outlook, heads of the Navy Department throughout the eighties pressed forward plans to enlarge and modernize the fleet. Other powers had gone over to steel warships, but the American navy remained upon a wooden basis. In 1883, during Arthur's administration, Congress made a start with four steel cruisers. Cleveland when he entered office vigorously lent his support to the "new navy," bringing about the construction of additional steel vessels, improvements in armament, the establishment of a naval ordnance plant and stronger coast defenses. Under Harrison the initial first-class battleships were built, and the total number of modern vessels in commission grew to twenty-two. The United States by 1893 had advanced from twelfth to fifth place as a sea power, and by 1900 to third.

Actuated by similar motives, the government departed increasingly from its hermitlike seclusion in world affairs. On the one hand, it united with other countries in a series of collective treaties dealing with such subjects as submarine cables, patents, weights and measures, and the suppression of the African slave trade. Without precedent in earlier American diplomacy, the United States signed fifteen such agreements between 1865 and 1900. In 1880 it also joined nine European powers in a pact defining and protecting the rights of foreigners in Morocco. Of the various treaties none aroused greater interest at home than the adherence of the Arthur administration in 1882 to the Geneva convention for establishing the International Red Cross Society. This agreement, formed originally by sixteen nations in 1864, provided that, in every country signing it, there should be set up a civilian organization to coöperate in time of war with the army medical corps in caring for the sick and wounded. Long indifferent to the matter, the American government was finally brought to action through the persistent advocacy of Clara Barton of Massachusetts, who had learned from her experiences as a nurse in the Franco-Prussian War (1870–1871) the superiority of the Red Cross to the United States Sanitary Commission in the Civil War. To her, too, belongs credit for the "American Amendment" to the Geneva convention in 1884, which extended the scope of the Red Cross to peace-time humanitarian work in connection with floods, earthquakes and other public disasters.

Besides joining with other countries in these matters of common concern, the Washington government struck out along its own lines in order to promote American foreign trade and investments. These efforts at economic penetration concerned two widely separate parts of the world, the Pacific area and Latin America, both rich in natural resources and both—to use the language of diplomacy—"backward regions." The steps were taken hesitantly and without a predetermined program, but they quickly carried the United States to the edge of the powerful current of imperialism that late in the seventies began to overspread Europe. Far more than America, these transatlantic powers felt the urge to capture new markets and sources of raw materials, to find fresh fields for the investment of capital, to acquire territories in which to colonize their surplus populations, and otherwise to enhance their national prestige. Before 1890 Great Britain, France and Germany had carved up most of Africa among them, with portions for Italy and Belgium.[1]

In the Pacific, as we shall see, the advancing outposts of Europe and America clashed, necessitating an accommodation of interests. In this rivalry the United States enjoyed

[1] From 1870 to 1900 the British Empire grew by about 5,000,000 square miles exclusive of spheres of influence, while France added 3,500,000 and Germany 1,000,000 to their possessions.

the advantage of being the only Occidental power with a front on the great ocean. In Latin America, on the other hand, Washington was able to play virtually a lone hand, thanks partly to the Monroe Doctrine, which held Europe at arm's length. Not only economic interest, but historical reasons and geographical proximity, impelled the United States to seek active leadership there.

EXPANSION IN THE PACIFIC

For many reasons the Hawaiian Islands were of special interest to America. They had long been a resort of traders and whalers. Lying in the mid-Pacific halfway between California and Asia, the little archipelago was well situated for a commercial coaling station, a naval base and a cable landing. Yankee missionaries had reduced the native language to writing and helped modernize the government; many of their children became landholders and sugar planters. In 1875 a treaty granted sugar and other Hawaiian products access free of duty to the United States and pledged the insular king not to dispose of any territory to another country. This was followed in 1884 by the lease of Pearl Harbor, near Honolulu, as a naval station. By 1890 American sugar plantations attained a value of twenty-five million dollars.

But the McKinley tariff of that year (see page 119) dealt the sugar producers a damaging blow. By putting all imported sugar on the free list the act leveled away Hawaii's favored position in that respect; and by providing bounties only for growers in the United States it further handicapped the planters. Annexation would, of course, cure the latter difficulty; and as a result sentiment for this step grew rapidly. In January, 1893, the crisis came. The native queen, who was ardently championing the policy of "Hawaii for the Hawaiians," was deposed by a revolt engineered by American residents and receiving moral support, at least,

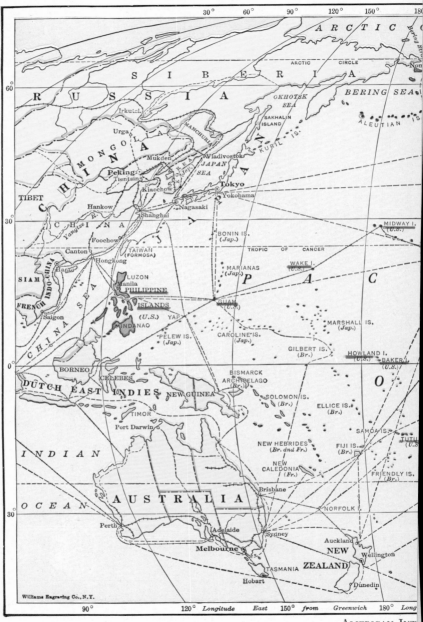

Williams Engraving Co., N.Y.

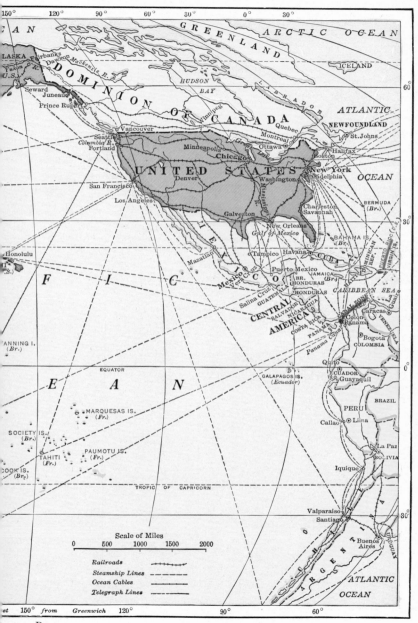

from the presence of United States marines landed at Honolulu for that purpose. The revolutionary government, headed by an American, promptly negotiated a treaty of annexation, but Harrison's term expired before the Senate could act.

President Cleveland, a stanch foe of imperialism, withdrew the treaty from the Senate until he might inquire into the circumstances. When an official investigation disclosed the complicity of the American Minister at Honolulu in the revolt, he roundly denounced the whole transaction. Yet his action only delayed the inevitable. American interest in Hawaii was increased by Japan's evident designs on the newly established republic; and when the Republicans returned to power and the Philippine operations of the Spanish-American War emphasized the naval advantages of ownership, Congress in July, 1898, acquired the islands by joint resolution.[1] "Annexation," declared McKinley, "is not a change. It is a consummation."

Meanwhile, another series of events was preparing a foothold for the United States far to the south. Four thousand miles from San Francisco, on the direct trade route to Sydney, Australia, lay the Samoan Islands. One of the group, Tutuila, possessed in Pago Pago the finest harbor of the South Pacific. In 1872 an American naval officer secured from a native chief permission to establish a coaling station there. Six years later this arrangement was embodied in a treaty and the United States, in return, pledged "its good offices" to adjust difficulties between the Samoan king and other nations. British and German commercial interests also made their appearance, and the islands soon became a tiny storm center of international intrigue and conflict.

[1] While the negotiations were in progress, Japan protested to the State Department that the transfer of ownership would "disturb the *status quo* in the Pacific."

In 1886, to block German designs, the American consul proclaimed a protectorate, an act promptly disavowed, however, by President Cleveland. Germany continuing aggressive, all three powers hurried warships to the scene in March, 1889. A destructive hurricane swept away hostile feeling for the moment, and led to an agreement of the powers to guarantee Samoan independence and neutrality under a tripartite protectorate. This arrangement, indubitably an "entangling alliance," did not work well. Finally, in 1899, the three countries agreed upon a division of the islands, the United States receiving Tutuila, Germany taking the rest, and Great Britain being compensated with other Pacific islands belonging to Germany.

Besides these more noteworthy accessions, the United States in the eighties and nineties asserted jurisdiction over more than fifty scattered small islands, mere specks on the surface of the Pacific. Among the largest were Canton, Enderbury, Wake, Gallego, Starbuck, Penrhyn, Midway, Palmyra, Howland, Baker, Jarvis, Gardner, Morell and Marcus. It was not clear what national advantage accrued from these annexations, but it was supposed that some of the islands might prove useful as relay cable stations. In the next century they acquired a new importance as possible air bases and radio stations.

TOWARD LEADERSHIP IN THE AMERICAS

In Latin America the United States sought leadership rather than dominion. Hitherto the government had stressed the negative aspect of the Monroe Doctrine: the obligation to prevent military or political interference by Europe in the affairs of the free nations of the Western Hemisphere. Now Washington adopted a more spirited policy, one that was designed both to insure America's political primacy among the New World republics and to forge closer commercial bonds.

To accomplish the first purpose, the State Department repeatedly tendered its good offices as mediator in controversies arising among the southern countries and between them and European powers. Thus in 1876 the United States arbitrated a boundary dispute between Argentina and Paraguay. In 1881 it interposed to induce a peaceful settlement of certain difficulties between Venezuela and France, urged Mexico to arbitrate a boundary dispute with Guatemala, and tried vainly to stop a war waged by Chile against Peru and Bolivia for possession of the nitrate district, Tacna and Arica.

In these efforts James G. Blaine, Secretary of State during Garfield's brief administration in 1881 and again under Harrison from 1889 to 1892, played an energetic part. His chief interest, however, lay in promoting economic relations with the southern republics. Though these countries sold vast quantities of raw materials to the United States, they bought the great bulk of their manufactured goods from Europe. Never large in amount, the export trade of the United States to Latin America actually decreased between 1860 and 1880. In answer to his tireless advocacy, the first Pan American Congress assembled at Washington in October, 1889, under Blaine as presiding officer. Among the subjects discussed were the formation of a customs union, a uniform system of trademarks and patents, improved railway and steamship connections, the creation of a monetary union and, finally, a comprehensive scheme of arbitration. The sole tangible results were the naming of a committee to report on an intercontinental railway, and the establishment in Washington, at the joint expense of the several countries, of the Bureau of American Republics (subsequently the Pan American Union) as a clearing house of commercial information.[1]

---

[1] Though the outcome proved disappointing, it will be recalled that Blaine accomplished a part of his purpose by inducing the United States Congress to add a reciprocity plan to the McKinley tariff of 1890 (see page 120).

Nevertheless, the discussion of common problems did something to dispel mutual jealousies and suspicions, and caused the congress to be the forerunner of a series of similar conferences in later years.

This tentative beginning of Pan American accord suffered a setback, however, as a result of the State Department's handling of certain difficulties arising out of the Chilean civil war of 1890–1891. The United States Minister in Chile, Patrick Egan, long conspicuous in America as a refugee agitator for Irish home rule, assumed an unfriendly attitude toward the victorious rebels, apparently because their success pleased the English in Chile. President Harrison, perhaps with an eye on the Irish-American vote in the next election, upheld him in this. Other incidents followed. Finally, on October 16, 1891, seamen from the United States ship *Baltimore* fell to quarreling with some Chileans in a saloon at Valparaiso. In the ensuing riot two Americans were killed and seventeen wounded. The Washington authorities, declining to regard the affair as a mere sailors' brawl, adopted a high-handed policy. The provisional government of Chile, equally defiant, refused to accord any sort of satisfaction. For a time the two countries teetered on the brink of war, but the election of a new government in Chile led to a more conciliatory attitude. Ample apologies and reparation followed.

The boldest assertion of American primacy in the New World came at the hands not of Republicans, but of President Cleveland. His pronouncement was the by-product of a long-standing dispute between Venezuela and British Guiana as to their common frontier. Like so many other South American boundaries, this one had never been accurately determined. After wearisome years of sterile controversy Venezuela began to insist that the matter be left to arbitration, a proposal which the United States warmly supported

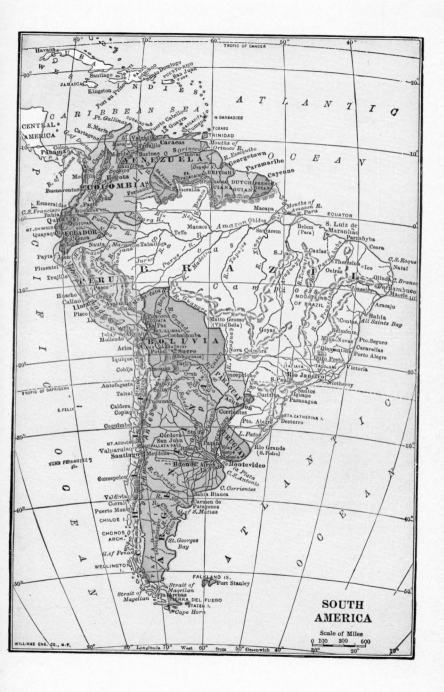

SOUTH
AMERICA

Scale of Miles

0 100   300   500

but which England rejected. The conviction gained ground in Washington that Britain by bullying tactics aimed to enlarge her borders at the expense of a weak and defenseless neighbor. With the discovery of gold in the disputed area in 1888, a settlement of the question became imperative. Hostile encounters took place during the next few years between English settlers and the Venezuelan police, and the appeals of Venezuela for protection grew increasingly insistent. These pleas were reënforced by American consular representatives who believed that action by the United States would assist trade relations.

Cleveland, whose acquaintance with the trouble dated from his first administration, decided in 1895 that the time had arrived for decisive measures. In a dispatch of July 20, drafted by Secretary of State Olney, he warned Great Britain that her failure to submit the dispute to arbitration would lead to grave consequences. Britain's conduct, he declared, looked like an attempt to encroach upon the territory of a free American nation and, accordingly, fell within the purview of the Monroe Doctrine. If, encouraged by America's silence, other powers should follow England's example, "it is not inconceivable that the struggle now going on for the acquisition of Africa might be transferred to South America." London was further told that "today the United States is practically sovereign on this continent" and, thanks to its "infinite resources combined with its isolated position," is "practically invulnerable against any or all other powers." This dispatch, blunt and provocative, elicited a long-delayed reply from Lord Salisbury, the British Foreign Minister, on November 26 to the effect that the Monroe Doctrine was not applicable to the controversy, and that the United States was wholly unwarranted in interfering.

Cleveland now took the question out of diplomatic channels. Announcing to Congress on December 17 that the Monroe Doctrine was in jeopardy, he asked for authority to appoint a boundary commission whose findings the United States should, if need be, enforce against any counterclaims of Great Britain. "In making these recommendations," he stated, "I am fully alive to the responsibility incurred and keenly realize all the consequences that may follow." Congress, promptly acceding to the President's wishes, unanimously voted funds for the commission's expenses.

To the general public in both nations, ignorant of the international crisis, Cleveland's peremptory message came like a bolt from the blue. Evidences soon appeared on every hand that the two English-speaking peoples were resolved to avert the war which the rashness of their rulers had brought near. Some of the leading American newspapers criticized the President's "jingoism." Business and financial groups were equally opposed. The New York Chamber of Commerce adopted resolutions condemning the "war craze," while J. P. Morgan expressed alarm at the "threatened disaster" to the "relations of confidence between the United States and the money markets of Europe." In England peace sentiment was equally vocal. Prominent public figures, including the Prince of Wales and the Archbishop of Canterbury, threw their influence on the side of conciliation, while thirteen hundred British authors addressed an appeal to their brethren in America to work for a friendly settlement.

Joseph Chamberlain, an influential member of the cabinet, voiced British official opinion when he declared in a speech at Birmingham in January, 1896, "We do not covet one single inch of American territory. War between the two nations would be an absurdity as well as a crime. . . . The two nations are allied and more closely allied in sentiment and in interest than any other nations on the face of the earth." Indeed, with Continental Europe already dividing into hostile alliances, British statesmen realized the folly of needlessly antagonizing the principal non-European power.[1] An impending clash with the Boers in South Africa served further to render imprudent a rupture with the United States. Accordingly, though the American boundary commission had already begun its work, Great Britain signified her willingness to submit the question to international arbitration. When a treaty for this purpose was drafted in February, 1897, the American commission ceased its labors. In 1899 the new tribunal, much to English satisfaction, awarded to British Guiana the larger part of the disputed area.

Despite this outcome, London's yielding did much to vindicate Washington's boastful claim of America's predominance in the Western Hemisphere. In foreign eyes the Monroe Doctrine gained new prestige. The incident is also significant as marking the adoption of a systematic policy on Britain's part to cultivate closer ties between the two English-speaking powers. The results became increasingly evident in the international developments of the years ahead.

SELECT BIBLIOGRAPHY

The Drift toward Centralization. Aspects of this trend are treated in Merriam, *American Political Ideas;* Malin, *Interpretation of Recent American History;* Schlesinger, *Rise of the City;* and Warren, *Supreme Court in United States History.* In the *Road to Reunion* Buck illuminates the diverse factors that operated to close the breach between the North and the South.

The Changing Attitude toward Immigration. Such works as Wittke, *We Who Built America,* Stephenson, *History of American Immigration,* and Garis, *Immigration Restriction,* deal with the inflow from Europe and Asia. Special studies of the newer immigrant elements include Foerster, *Italian Emigration;* Burgess, *Greeks in America;* Joseph, *Jewish Immigration;* Balch,

[1] The Triple Alliance, formed in 1882 by Germany, Austria and Italy, was renewed from time to time. Russia and France entered into the Dual Alliance in 1894. Great Britain, possessing interests apart from either coalition, held aloof until 1904 when she formed an Entente Cordiale with France and, three years later, with Russia.

Slavic Fellow Citizens; Coolidge, *Chinese Immigration;* and Sand-meyer, *Anti-Chinese Movement.*

The Crumbling of National Isolation. Coolidge, *United States as a World Power,* Faris, *Rise of Internationalism,* and Langer, *Diplomacy of Imperialism,* all help to clarify America's shifting position in world affairs. For the ideology of expansion and navalism in the United States, see Pratt, *Expansionists of 1898,* and Weinberg, *Manifest Destiny.* The development of the "new navy" is traced in Davis, *Navy Second to None,* and Sprouts, *Rise of American Naval Power.* Barton, *Clara Barton,* tells the story of the founder of the American Red Cross.

American Interests in the Pacific and Latin America. The large surveys of diplomatic history, such as those by Bailey and Bemis, deal with both areas. For the Pacific, Dulles, *America in the Pacific,* provides a general account, which should be supplemented by Ryden, *Foreign Policy of the United States in Relation to Samoa;* Masterman, *Origins of International Rivalry in Samoa;* and, in the case of Hawaii, Pratt, *Expansionists of 1898.* For Latin America, the comprehensive work is Robertson, *Hispanic-American Relations with the United States,* while Perkins, *Monroe Doctrine, 1867–1907,* is the standard treatment of that subject. Dennis, *Adventures in American Diplomacy,* and Henderson, *American Diplomatic Questions,* possess special value for the Venezuelan boundary dispute. Personal factors in diplomacy are stressed in Muzzey, *Blaine;* Tyler, *Foreign Policy of James G. Blaine;* Nevins, *Cleveland;* and James, *Olney.*

PART TWO

DEMOCRACY AND EMPIRE

Chapter X

AMERICA BECOMES A WORLD POWER, 1898–1903

THE CUBAN QUESTION

THE closing years of the nineteenth century brought to fruition the new tendencies in American foreign policy. The United States rose to the position of a world power, with insular possessions in two hemispheres and a potential voice in the affairs of Asia and Europe. The seething nationalism foamed over into imperialism. For this turn of events, unanticipated even by statesmen, American intervention in the revolt of Cuba against Spain was directly responsible. This fertile island, just about the size of Virginia, and occupied by a population of whom two thirds were white and the rest black or mixed, was, except for its smaller neighbor Puerto Rico, the sole remnant of Spain's once magnificent empire in the New World. Cuba had interested Americans even before Democratic politicians in the mid-century had urged its acquisition as additional slave territory. Its commanding position at the entrances of the Gulf of Mexico and the Caribbean Sea gave it a strategic naval importance, and its economic penetration by American capital in the period after the Civil War occasioned concern for the maintenance of orderly conditions there.

Spain, learning nothing from the revolt of her other colonies early in the century, continued her despotic rule in Cuba, exploiting the natives both politically and economically. From 1868 to 1878 civil strife harassed the island, marked by atrocities and irregular methods of warfare on both sides. Filibustering expeditions, clandestinely fitted out by Cuban agents, slipped away from American ports to lend help. When a Spanish gunboat captured one such vessel, the *Virginius,* outside Cuban waters in October, 1873, and eight Americans on board were shot, war was nearly precipitated between the two countries. The United States admitted the illegal nature of the expedition, but contended that, so long as the *Virginius* remained on the high seas, the American government alone might restrain the lawbreakers. After a time Spain offered an apology with suitable indemnity and reparation. In 1875 President Grant sounded European powers on the subject of American intervention in the struggle, but the proposal was not well received.

When the Ten Years' War dragged to a close three years later, the insurgents won some paper concessions for a small measure of self-government. As a matter of fact, however, the government continued to be a thinly veiled military autocracy. Meanwhile, the burden of taxation borne by the natives grew heavier, for they were saddled with the whole expense of their unsuccessful struggle. In February, 1895, their kindling wrath burst forth into a new war for independence.[1] The event was hastened by a severe depression of the sugar industry, occasioned by the repeal in 1894 of the McKinley tariff which had allowed Cuban sugar free entry into the United States (see page 124).

Great brutality and widespread destruction of sugar plantations and other property marked the progress of the hostilities. The plan of the insurgents was to avoid open battle, but to fight incessant skirmishes and devastate the country, with the purpose either of exhausting Spain or of bringing the United States into the conflict. Unable to distinguish

---

[1] In an effort to forestall the insurrection, Spain at the eleventh hour authorized a "council of administration" for the island. But since this body was to be advisory only, and would consist one half of Spanish appointees and the remainder of persons chosen under a severely restricted franchise, the only effect was to fortify the rebels in their resolution.

friend from foe, the Spaniards adopted the scheme of herding the rural inhabitants into *reconcentración* (concentration) camps, which quickly became pestholes filled with
starving and diseased unfortunates. In the province of Havana alone over fifty thousand perished.

The course of the uprising was watched in the United
States with growing concern. Apart from the people's traditional interest in Latin American struggles for independence, American investments in Cuban plantations, mines
and railways now amounted to no less than fifty million dollars, and trade with the island annually reached a hundred
million. These profitable relations were placed in jeopardy
by the civil strife. Moreover, American humanitarianism was
outraged by the cruel methods of warfare, particularly the
suffering inflicted on the *reconcentrados*. The yellow press,
led by the *New York World* and the *New York Journal,*
broke out in a rash of inch-high type, streamer headlines and
blood-curdling full-page illustrations playing up alleged
Spanish atrocities. "Blood on the roadsides, blood in the
fields, blood on the doorsteps, blood, blood, blood!" screamed
Pulitzer's *World*. "The old, the young, the weak, the crippled—all are butchered without mercy." In 1897 a party organized by Hearst's *Journal* actually effected the escape
from a Havana prison of Evangelina Cisneros, a Cuban girl
sentenced for treason. Such sheets ceaselessly churned the
public's emotions; and Hearst's organ erred merely in
claiming too much for one newspaper's enterprise when it
bragged to its readers after America's entry: "How do you
like the *Journal's* war?" Early in 1898 the American Red
Cross responded to the call of humanity by engaging in work
among the sick and starving *reconcentrados* near Havana.

Resolved not to be stampeded into war, President Cleveland as long as he remained in office put forth every effort to
preserve an attitude of impartiality. Official vigilance suc-

ceeded in stopping most, though not all, of the expeditions that Cuban agents fitted out in American ports. But in his last annual message to Congress (December, 1896), Cleveland declared that, should it presently appear that Spanish authority in Cuba had ceased "for all purposes of its rightful existence," America might feel compelled to intervene because of her "higher obligations" in the matter. The McKinley administration began to pursue the more aggressive policy foreshadowed by Cleveland. Partly in response to American protests, Spain modified somewhat the policy of *reconcentración* in October, 1897, and offered the natives a larger share of self-government, to become effective upon ratification by the Spanish parliament. Granted three years earlier, the concession might have assured a peaceful solution. After more than two years of relentless warfare, however, the revolutionists were unwilling to accept anything short of complete independence.

Now occurred two incidents which raised war sentiment in the United States to a fever pitch. Thanks to the exertions of the *New York Journal,* the American public on February 9, 1898, learned that Dupuy de Lôme, the Spanish Minister at Washington, had declared in a private letter that McKinley was a tricky politician and, further, had admitted his own duplicity in certain commercial negotiations then under way with the State Department. Spain refused to make a formal disavowal of the utterances and, instead of dismissing De Lôme, permitted him to resign. Of graver import was the destruction of the United States battleship *Maine* on February 15 while lying peacefully at anchor in Havana Harbor. The vessel was sunk and two hundred and sixty men were killed. An American court of naval experts ascribed the disaster to an external explosion, but a similar board appointed by Spain found the cause to be an explosion of one of the ship's forward magazines. Though the American findings were later confirmed when the vessel was raised in 1911, it remains unknown whether the destruction was due to an overzealous Spanish subordinate, to a Cuban patriot bent on precipitating intervention, or to an accident.

The outburst of patriotic feeling was unlike anything since 1861. Lashed by the sensational press, public gatherings throughout the land echoed the slogan: "Remember the *Maine!*" Congress seethed with bellicose spirit, while even the churches, hitherto the mainstay of the organized peace movement, hailed the prospect of a war "for humanity's sake." But President McKinley, who had asserted on taking office that "peace is preferable to war in almost every contingency," was resolved at this juncture to avert hostilities, if possible. Though his attitude provoked Roosevelt's impatient remark, "McKinley has no more backbone than a chocolate éclair," it accorded with the desires of the great financial and commercial interests. These men feared that war would disturb conditions and cause a setback to the prosperity which the country was enjoying after the long blight beginning in 1893. Only those businessmen who had an economic stake in Cuba beat the drums of war.

Seeking to compose the crisis by diplomatic means, McKinley on March 27 asked Spain immediately to abandon the policy of *reconcentración* and to conclude an armistice preliminary to peace negotiations to be conducted through himself. The first proposal was promptly accepted, but national pride and a deep-rooted habit of procrastination caused Spain to temporize in regard to the second. Nevertheless, the American Minister in Madrid cabled McKinley his conviction that the Spanish authorities and people sincerely desired peace. With a few months' delay, he promised, "I will get peace in Cuba, with justice to Cuba and protection to our great American interests." On April 7 the Washington representatives of Great Britain, Germany, France, Austria-

Hungary, Russia and Italy joined in an appeal to the President for a continuance of negotiations. Three days later Madrid informed him that, at the Pope's solicitation, the Spanish Queen had acceded to the request for an armistice.

By this time, however, McKinley had experienced a change of heart. Perhaps he doubted Spain's good faith in complying and felt that, after all, war was the only real solution. It seems more likely that he was frightened by the clamor of the war faction in Congress and feared a serious rupture in his own party. At all events, on April 11, he sent a message to Congress, in which, after scant mention of Spain's latest concession, he recommended armed intervention.[1] The grounds, he asserted, were the interests of common humanity, the need to protect the "commerce, trade, and business of our people" in the island, and the ending of a conflict which was "a constant menace to our peace." Eight days later Congress responded by authorizing the President to employ force for the establishment of Cuban independence. At the same time, on motion of Senator Teller, the lawmakers assured an incredulous world that the United States would claim no "sovereignty, jurisdiction, or control over said Island except for the pacification thereof," and, when that was accomplished, would "leave the government and control of the Island to its people."

European powers observed these developments with mixed feelings. In Germany, Austria-Hungary and France public opinion was frankly hostile to the United States, and talk

[1] "We may rest assured that if Mark Hanna had been President there would have been no war with Spain," says James Ford Rhodes, Hanna's brother-in-law, in his *McKinley and Roosevelt Administrations.* "To his dying day Mr. Cleveland never believed that the war with Spain was necessary," stated his personal friend George F. Parker in 1923. Joseph Pulitzer, who in 1898 demanded a "short and sharp" war, admitted in 1907, when deploring President Roosevelt's proposal to send battleships into the Pacific to impress Japan, that "Spain had granted to Cuba all that we had demanded, but passion in Spain and here forced the hands of the government."

was rife of a joint European intervention on behalf of Spain. British sentiment was mirrored in a widely quoted statement of the London *Spectator* on April 9, 1898: "If America were really attacked by a great Continental coalition, England would be at her side in twenty-four hours." In reality, all the powers observed an official neutrality toward the two belligerents, although at one juncture, shortly to be described, an impending clash seemed possible with the Germans in Far Eastern waters.

THE WAR WITH SPAIN AND ITS FRUITS

Blithely the American people entered upon a war that yielded quick dividends in martial glory for some, unexpected scandals for others, and new and heavy responsibilities for the government. Unlike most previous conflicts, sea power proved of paramount importance, with land operations subsidiary thereto. Those who had begun in the 1880's to nurse a new navy into being now won complete vindication. For the instant state of preparedness, however, credit was due largely to the foresight of Theodore Roosevelt, McKinley's energetic Assistant Secretary of the Navy. One squadron guarded the coasts of New York and New England, where fear existed of a Spanish bombardment of the great seaports. The main fleet had its headquarters at Key West in order to conduct operations in the Caribbean and to convoy troops to the theater of war. Throughout the short struggle the United States enjoyed the advantage of a considerable naval superiority.

In sad contrast was the condition of the army. The regular forces were enlarged from 28,000 to 62,000; and in April and May the President called for 200,000 volunteers, most of whom it was eventually unnecessary to send out of the country. Politics entered into the appointment of officers; and mismanagement, lack of plans and general confusion interfered seriously with the mobilization, feeding and transport of the troops. Moreover, the men were sent to fight in a tropical country outfitted in heavy winter uniforms, without due attention to the need of a hot-weather diet, and lacking proper hospital equipment. A picturesque feature of the

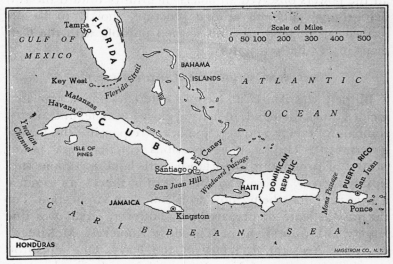

THE THEATER OF WARFARE IN THE WEST INDIES, 1898

volunteer cavalry was a regiment of "Rough Riders," recruited from cowboys, ranchers, Indians and college athletes by Roosevelt, who presently became their colonel.

The actual hostilities proved swift and decisive, lasting four months in all. The chief sphere of activity was the West Indies. Cuba was promptly placed under blockade in order to prevent the arrival of reënforcements and supplies from Spain. Nevertheless, on May 19 a fleet of seven vessels under Admiral Pasqual Cervera succeeded in reaching Santiago, which had rail connections with Havana, the capital. Santiago was at once placed under close blockade by Rear Admiral William T. Sampson and, in the ensuing weeks, troops under General William R. Shafter assembled for a land attack on the city. On July 1 they took El Caney and San Juan Hill, its outer defenses. Santiago now was doomed. In order to avoid capture, Cervera's fleet two days later made a gallant attempt to escape, but as the warships steamed out of the harbor, one by one they were engaged by the blockading vessels and either captured or destroyed. As Sampson was absent at the moment on an official errand, Commodore Winfield S. Schley was in actual command. The fall of Santiago followed on July 13. Shortly afterwards, an army under General Nelson A. Miles began the occupation of the nearby island of Puerto Rico.

Meanwhile, the Americans had successfully attacked the Spaniards in a different quarter of the globe. Immediately upon the outbreak of war Commodore George Dewey, then at Hong Kong, had proceeded with his squadron of six cruisers to the Philippine Islands, under orders to incapacitate the Spanish fleet there for operations in American waters. Though his nearest base was seven thousand miles away, Dewey, trained as a young man in the school of Farragut, executed his instructions with boldness and dispatch. Before dawn on May 1 he ran the batteries of Manila Bay, and by high noon he had destroyed the entire Spanish fleet of seven ill-equipped vessels without losing an American life. His main purpose accomplished, Dewey proceeded to blockade Manila and its environs preparatory to a combined attack upon the city when land forces should arrive.

As is usual on such occasions, men-of-war of neutral powers gathered on the scene to look after their national interests. The German force under Otto von Diederichs was actually stronger than the United States fleet, and its commander, differing with Dewey's interpretation of international law, failed to observe some of the American blockade regulations.

Time and again Dewey's patience was sorely tried, and on one occasion he heatedly told Diederichs, "If Germany wants war, all right, we are ready." By contrast, the attitude of Sir Edward Chichester, the British commander, toward the Americans was markedly friendly. Despite Dewey's suspicions and the sensational allegations in the home press, we know now that Diederichs's purpose was not to impede American effectiveness, but rather to strengthen Germany's position with reference to acquiring the Philippines in case the United States should decide not to take them in the peace treaty.

During July and early August the reënforcements from America arrived. The city was besieged with the aid of the Filipinos who, under the leadership of Emilio Aguinaldo, were fighting for independence. On August 13, after a joint sea and land attack, Manila capitulated. Meanwhile, in June, the cruiser *Charleston* had quietly secured the surrender of Guam and the other Ladrone Islands, tiny Spanish possessions lying fifteen hundred miles east of the Philippines.

The war proved tremendously popular with the American people, partly perhaps as an emotional escape from the economic distress that had so long burdened their spirits. A special bond issue of $200,000,000, offered in amounts as small as twenty dollars, was readily subscribed, while the government raised additional funds from a wide variety of internal taxes. The Red Cross amply demonstrated its wartime efficiency, extending its activities to all parts of Cuba as well as to the mobilization camps in southern United States and, eventually, to the Philippines and Puerto Rico. At home nearly two thousand branches were formed from coast to coast to coöperate in collecting money and supplies. By contrast, the almost criminal negligence of the War Department in safeguarding soldier health and welfare elicited sharp public criticism. Malaria and typhoid fever made their inroads on the unseasoned troops about Santiago, Shafter

reporting on August 3 that seventy-five per cent of his command were sick. After his general officers joined in insisting
that the troops be removed to the United States to avoid ex-
termination by that dread tropical scourge, yellow fever, the
government acquiesced.

Despite such conditions it is only fair to note that, thanks
to the progress of medicine in the intervening years, the proportion of deaths from disease was only about three fifths as
great as during the first year of the Civil War. An epochal
consequence of this initial contact of American science with
the tropics was the discovery in 1900 by an army medical
board under Major Walter Reed that yellow fever was transmitted by the female *Stegomyia* mosquito. In the words of
the Secretary of War, "The name of Dr. Jesse W. Lazear,
contract surgeon, who voluntarily permitted himself to be
inoculated with the yellow fever germ in order to furnish a
necessary experimental test . . . and who died of the disease,
should be written in the list of the martyrs who have died
in the cause of humanity." By means of this new knowledge,
the disease was soon banished from the island through the
efforts of Major Reed and Major William C. Gorgas, and the
way was opened for attacking the plague in other tropical
countries.

After hostilities had been under way about three months,
Spain asked France to ascertain peace terms from the United
States. An armistice, signed on August 12, 1898, foreshadowed
the provisions of the peace treaty, save in regard to the disposition of the Philippines, which was left undetermined. In
the final proceedings at Paris, William R. Day headed the
American delegation, which included three members of the
Senate. Since the United States was able to demand whatever
it wanted, the negotiations proved the simplest in which the
government had ever engaged. The treaty was signed on
December 10. Spain transferred Cuba to the United States

for temporary occupation preliminary to independence. It handed over Puerto Rico and Guam in lieu of war indemnity, and the Philippines on payment of $20,000,000. The civil and political rights of the native inhabitants of the ceded islands were to be determined by Congress.

The acquisition of Puerto Rico was a natural fruit of the war, while the annexation of Guam might be justified by its desirability as a coaling and cable station. But the taking of the Philippines marked a new and not wholly welcome innovation in American policy. These islands, aggregating an area as large as Arizona, not only formed a part of the coast line of Asia, but were inhabited by a people alien in race, language and institutions, who were not likely ever to achieve statehood. Moreover, the islands could not be expected to furnish room for the expanding American population, though it was hoped they might supply openings for trade and the export of capital and serve as a gateway to the markets of China. Before the peace conference McKinley had been undecided as to the wisdom of annexation, but strong pressure was brought to bear upon him by chambers of commerce and Protestant missionary bodies. There was, besides, a well-founded conviction that, if America did not take the islands, Germany, a dangerous trade rival in the Orient, would do so. As a matter of fact, Germany did purchase Spain's remaining possessions in the Pacific.

When the treaty came before the Senate for action, certain members violently attacked the Philippine feature of the settlement. George C. Vest, a Missouri Democrat, denied that constitutional authority existed "to acquire territory to be held and governed permanently as colonies." That sturdy Republican, George F. Hoar of Massachusetts, stressed the point that, since the Filipinos had declared their independence, annexation would occur without "the consent of the governed," and thus violate a precious American tradition,

The expansionists retorted with arguments about economic and strategic advantages, national prestige and the infamy of "hauling down the flag." A year later Senator Albert J. Beveridge of Indiana approvingly summed up their position in the words: "We will not repudiate our duty in the archipelago. We will not abandon our opportunity in the Orient. We will not renounce our part in the mission of our race, trustee, under God, of the civilization of the world." The opponents failed by two votes to block ratification. The Senate's action was accompanied by the McEnery resolution, which declared, in effect, that the treaty provision should not be deemed a final disposition of the Philippine question. Since the resolution received a mere majority vote, however, it did not count as an act of the treaty-making power.

In the light of earlier history the war was significant chiefly as marking the final expulsion of Spain from the Western Hemisphere. From a prospective point of view, however, it signalized a momentous departure in American policy. The United States, for the first time, became a colonial power in the New World and, through acquiring the Spanish holdings in the Pacific together with Hawaii and Tutuila, it became a Far Eastern power as well. Washington took under its wing nearly a million subjects of Spanish and Negro blood in Puerto Rico. It shouldered certain as yet undefined responsibilities in regard to Cuba. It was master and protector of seven and a half million people in the Philippines, ranging from the civilized Tagalogs of Manila to the primitive Moros of the Sulu Peninsula and the head-hunting Igorots of northern Luzon. Like the Great Powers of Europe, America had at last chosen the path of empire.

COMBATING THE POWERS IN CHINA

This fateful decision embroiled the United States almost at once in grave international rivalries on the Asiatic main-

land. Japan's success in wresting Formosa and other territorial concessions from China in the war of 1894–1895 had
served as an open invitation to Europe to join in the spoils.
In the next five years the various powers had busied themselves with acquiring naval bases, leased territories and spheres
of influence at China's expense. Through these devices they
secured not only monopolistic rights of trade, but usually
also exclusive privileges for the investment of capital by their
citizens in railway construction and mining development in
adjoining regions. Thus in 1898, a banner year, Germany
obtained control of the Shantung Peninsula in North China;
Russia secured the important harbor of Port Arthur, which
dominated the sea approaches to Peiping (then Peking);
Great Britain established its rights to Wei-hai-wei, lying
between the acquisitions of Germany and Russia; and France
took over Kwangchow Bay in southeastern China.

From the standpoint of the United States, newly intrenched
in the Philippines, this game of grab threatened to frustrate
hopes of a vigorous development of trade with China. American industrialists, notably the textile manufacturers, were
looking to the markets of North China and Manchuria, the
very regions most affected by German and Russian imperialism. American missionaries in China, numbering over a
thousand in 1899, also wanted their government to cut a
more important figure in Asia. In its earlier diplomatic relations with Oriental countries Washington had always insisted upon equality of commercial treatment for all nations.
If this principle were now to be preserved, a bold course was
necessary.

Great Britain was willing to lend support. That country
had by far the largest trade with China and it was to her interest to keep all the channels of commerce unobstructed.
Her sympathetic attitude toward America's acquisition of
the Philippines stemmed in part from a desire to entangle

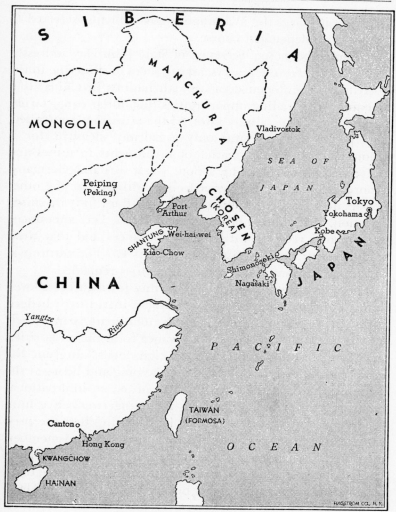

FOREIGN CONCESSIONS IN CHINA

the United States in Asiatic affairs. In 1898 she went so far as to suggest an Anglo-American alliance to preserve unrestricted trading rights. But, as in the instance of the Monroe

Doctrine in 1823, the Washington government preferred to pursue an independent course.

In September, 1899, Secretary of State John Hay addressed a circular note to the powers, asking them to subscribe to the doctrine of the "open door" for all nations in China, that is, equality of trading opportunities (including equal tariffs, harbor duties and railway rates) in the areas they controlled. The policy proposed was only a halfway measure, for it ignored the important matter of investments in mines and rail construction. To Hay's note Great Britain, Germany, France, Italy and Japan agreed on condition that the other powers do likewise, while Russia returned a thinly disguised rejection. In the hope of clinching matters, Hay announced that he had received satisfactory assurances and that these would be regarded "as final and definitive." The future was to disclose, however, that many difficulties remained.

The year 1900 furnished opportunity for a further development of American policy. The Chinese, increasingly hedged in by encroachments from without, took matters into their own hands and, with secret connivance from the authorities, struck out blindly against the "foreign devils." In June the insurgents, known as Boxers, seized Peiping and besieged the legations there. To deal with the situation, an international relief expedition was organized, including twenty-five hundred American troops. Secretary Hay, fearing that the presence of foreign armies would result in a naked dismemberment of China, promptly announced to the powers that the United States would oppose any disturbance of Chinese territorial or administrative rights or any violation of the Open Door.

Once the rebellion was quelled, however, it required all Hay's skill to carry through the American program, and to protect China from crushing indemnities. That he succeeded as well as he did was due to the distrustful attitude of the several countries toward one another. In October Great Britain and Germany signified their adherence to the Open Door and the preservation of Chinese independence, and the others presently followed. Two months later the powers announced the basic terms of their withdrawal: punishment of the rebel leaders, indemnities to foreign individuals and governments, and the adoption of measures to prevent future outbreaks. The details were embodied in a treaty of September, 1901.

Despite Hay's efforts, the total indemnity amounted to nearly twice as much as the American government deemed proper. Even the $25,000,000 awarded to the United States far exceeded the actual American losses. In 1907 nearly $11,000,000 was given back, and in 1924 an additional sum of $6,000,000 was remitted. This investment in international good will bore noble returns, for China set aside the money as a fund for sending students to American colleges. Russia's retention of troops in Manchuria, contrary to the peace treaty, made it clear that China still had perils to face, and caused Great Britain and Japan to form a defensive alliance in 1902 for the protection of their respective interests in Asia and the Pacific.

"IMPERIALISM" AND THE ELECTION OF 1900

Meanwhile, the presidential contest of 1900 gave the electorate a chance to pass judgment on the McKinley administration's program of foreign adventure and colonial aggrandisement. Meeting at Philadelphia on June 19, the Republicans expressed jubilation over the war with Spain, the insular accessions, the restoration of prosperity, and the effort to "obtain new markets" through "the policy of the open door." McKinley's renomination was a foregone conclusion, the second place going to Governor Theodore Roosevelt of New York, late of the Navy Department and hero of the Rough Riders. Roosevelt had not wanted the honor; but "Boss" Platt was determined to rid his state of an energetic and self-willed executive, and the genuine enthusiasm of the Western delegates made declination almost impossible.

The foes of overseas expansion rallied to the Democratic standard. The fact that since the previous February the Filipinos had been waging a war for independence against American rule affected public opinion at home, and placed the United States in the position of imposing its sway upon an unwilling people. At the same time, American tobacco and beet-sugar growers viewed with dislike the possibility of Philippine competition in the domestic market. When the Democratic convention assembled at Kansas City on July 4, the platform declared that "the paramount issue" was "imperialism," that is, "the seizing or purchasing of distant islands to be governed outside the Constitution and whose people can never become citizens." After affirming that "no nation can long endure half republic and half empire," the party also condemned America's entry into "so-called world politics, including the diplomacy of Europe and the intrigue and land grabbing in Asia." William Jennings Bryan was unanimously renominated and, at his behest, the platform included a perfunctory plank for free silver. Adlai E. Stevenson of Illinois, Cleveland's Vice-President, was chosen as Bryan's running mate.

As in 1896, Bryan's candidacy was indorsed by the Populists and the Silver Republicans, and reverberations of the silver question served to confuse the main issue. Mark Hanna, once more in charge of McKinley's campaign, ascribed the return of good times to Republican supremacy, and everywhere appeared electioneering emblems and posters of the "Full Dinner-Pail." Roosevelt rather than McKinley bore the brunt of the speechmaking, extolling America's new rôle as a world power, and shouting to vast audiences, "We are a nation of men, not a nation of weaklings." In spite of Bryan's eloquent condemnations of imperialism, the policy of overseas dominion seemed to strike most voters as a happy fulfillment of American destiny. In any event, the abounding prosperity would have assured Republican victory. Though fewer popular ballots were cast than in the preceding election, McKinley received a larger proportion of them: 51.6 per cent (7,200,000 votes) to 45.5 per cent (6,360,000) for Bryan. The electoral vote stood 292 to 155. The Republicans also increased their majorities in both branches of Congress.

LINKING THE ATLANTIC AND THE PACIFIC

McKinley did not live long to enjoy his triumph. On September 6, 1901, while attending an exposition at Buffalo held to symbolize Pan American unity, he was shot by an anarchist. Eight days later his gentle spirit took flight, and Theodore Roosevelt succeeded him. Impetuous, temperamental, pugnacious, "Teddy" was the most picturesque and dynamic figure to assume the reins since Andrew Jackson. His very appearance suggested divergence from the familiar type of President. His eyes were small and piercing behind thick glasses; his body was short and athletic; his voice rasping; and his prominent teeth were the delight of cartoonists. At forty-three he was the youngest man ever to occupy his high office.[1] Though he devoted his chief energies to domestic problems, it fell to him to perfect the nation's new imperial edifice with a waterway through Central America.

[1] Roosevelt retained McKinley's cabinet, composed at this time of John Hay, Secretary of State; Lyman J. Gage of Illinois, Secretary of the Treasury; Elihu Root of New York, Secretary of War; Philander C. Knox of Pennsylvania, Attorney-General; Charles E. Smith of Pennsylvania, Postmaster-General; John D. Long of Massachusetts, Secretary of the Navy; Ethan A. Hitchcock of Missouri, Secretary of the Interior; and James Wilson of Iowa, Secretary of Agriculture. In 1904 William Howard Taft of Ohio became Secretary of War and, upon Hay's death in 1905, Root succeeded to the State Department. Numerous other changes were made.

To accomplish this purpose a series of diplomatic obstacles had to be surmounted. The American government had long contemplated such a canal, either across the Isthmus of Panama, a Colombian possession, or through the Republic of Nicaragua. As early as 1846 a treaty with Colombia had granted American citizens "open and free" right of passage across the isthmus on condition that the United States "guarantee positively and efficaciously" the "perfect neutrality" of the isthmus and Colombia's "rights of sovereignty and property" there. Four years later the Clayton-Bulwer treaty between the United States and Great Britain evidenced a further definition of American policy. By its terms the two countries agreed that any canal which might be dug should be neutral, unfortified and under international guarantee. In a treaty of 1867 with Nicaragua concerning a possible route through its territory, Washington again assented to the principle of an international guarantee.

But the upsurge of nationalism in the years thereafter put a different face on affairs. In 1880 President Hayes informed Congress, "The policy of this country is a canal under American control. The United States cannot consent to the surrender of this control to any European power or to any combination of European powers." Despite persistent efforts, however, neither his administration nor the next could induce Britain to alter the Clayton-Bulwer treaty. Popular interest in constructing a waterway increased as a result of the economic development of the Pacific Coast states and the complaints of high freight charges by the transcontinental railroads. The desire for unfettered American control strengthened when it appeared that a French company, headed by Ferdinand de Lesseps, builder of the Suez Canal, might steal a march upon American enterprise.

Chartered in 1879, this company obtained the exclusive privilege of building a canal across Panama, the rights of the

United States under the treaty of 1846 remaining unimpaired. Though the French government was not officially involved, the project occasioned misgivings in the United States. De Lesseps from 1881 to 1889 spent $260,000,000 on the undertaking; but gross financial irregularities and unexpected engineering difficulties impeded operations, and forced the company into bankruptcy. Several interested Frenchmen then reorganized the company in order to keep alive its franchises and to salvage the canal equipment.

Meanwhile, stimulated by this competition, an American syndicate made plans to dig a rival waterway in Nicaragua. The Maritime Canal Company, chartered by Congress, began excavations at Greytown on the Atlantic side in 1890, only to have its work abruptly ended three years later by the Panic. Appeals to Congress for financial aid proved unavailing, for, though official commissions reported favorably on the Nicaragua route in 1895 and 1897, the government was unwilling to proceed further under the chafing Clayton-Bulwer restrictions.

Nevertheless, the acquisition of dependencies in two hemispheres during 1898–1899 made an interoceanic passage important not only for shortening trade routes, but also for the sake of naval defense. Both political parties demanded prompt steps to that end in the campaign of 1900, and fortunately the British government, true to her policy of cultivating American good will, was now well disposed. The Hay-Pauncefote treaty in 1901 expressly revoked the Clayton-Bulwer treaty, and granted the United States "exclusive" control over any canal that might be built. Though the "general principle of neutralization" received nominal recognition, the United States was authorized to maintain "military police" along the waterway adequate for its protection.

Further action now awaited the selection of a route. President Roosevelt strongly championed a Panama canal as both cheaper to build and shorter than the Nicaraguan alternative. Advocates of the latter, however, urged the superior advantages to be derived from using Lake Nicaragua and the San Juan River as connecting links. After considerable debate Congress in June, 1902, passed the Spooner act which instructed the President to proceed with the Panama route if, "within a reasonable time and upon reasonable terms," he could reach an agreement with the French company and also with Colombia; otherwise he should construct the waterway through Nicaragua. The moribund French company, whose sole remaining interest was to sell out its canal rights before they expired in 1904, promptly reduced its former exorbitant figure of $109,000,000 to the acceptable one of $40,000,000.

Roosevelt now held the key to the situation, but the key had to be fitted to the lock. Turning next to Colombia, the State Department in January, 1903, negotiated the Hay-Herrán treaty by which the United States was granted, on indefinite lease, a six-mile-wide belt of land across the isthmus in return for $10,000,000 and an annual rental of $250,000. But in August the Colombian senate, acting within its constitutional rights, unanimously rejected the treaty. The members felt that Colombia would surrender too much authority in the canal strip, and that, in any case, the compensation was too little as compared with the sum offered the French company. This action enraged Roosevelt. As he said later, "I did not intend that any set of bandits should hold up Uncle Sam." Others shared his indignation. The people in Panama saw their chance of standing at one of the great crossroads of the world's commerce blasted, and for the stockholders of the French company Colombia's decision involved an almost certain loss of $40,000,000. Here were the combustibles for a conflagration.

The rapid march of events in November, 1903, bears eloquent testimony to the unity of purpose which actuated the several interested parties. On November 2 the United States cruiser *Nashville* arrived in the harbor of Colón on the Atlantic side of the isthmus. The next evening occurred a bloodless revolution in the City of Panama on the Pacific side. On the fourth, marines from the *Nashville* prevented the rail transportation of five hundred Colombian troops from Colón to the seat of the trouble. Two days later Washington recognized the new Republic of Panama, and on November 18 a canal treaty was concluded. The United States was granted perpetual use and control of a zone ten miles wide across the isthmus, in return for the payments which Colombia had spurned and for an American guarantee of independence. Philippe Bunau-Varilla, former chief engineer of the French company, represented the isthmian government in these negotiations.

In a message to Congress Roosevelt later brilliantly defended the part he had played in the November transactions. Denying that the American government had fomented the revolution, he claimed justification on three grounds: "First, our treaty rights; second, our national interests and safety; and, third, the interests of collective civilization." By barring the use of the railway to Colombian troops, he asserted that the United States was merely executing its pledge of 1846 to protect the "perfect neutrality" of the right of passage. He disposed of the correlative treaty obligation—to protect Colombia's ownership of the isthmus—by insisting that this guarantee held only against external aggression. His further contentions—that transcendent interests of national and world import were involved in an interoceanic canal—no one could deny, but his critics did not fail to point out that a Nicaraguan waterway, the alternative proposed in the Spooner act, would have served these purposes equally well.

Three years later, in 1906, the War Department began excavating the canal. As an engineering feat, it was comparable in this new age to the transcontinental railway of four decades earlier. Eight years were required for completion, the cost reaching $194,000,000 in 1914. "It is," said James Bryce, "the greatest liberty man has ever taken with nature!" Yet the dearth of labor, questions of sanitation and the task of stamping out yellow fever and malaria offered difficulties nearly as great as the strictly engineering problems.

Meanwhile, Colombia's resentment over her high-handed treatment continued unabated. To allay this feeling, the Democrats when they came into power under Woodrow Wilson negotiated a treaty in 1914, which expressed America's "sincere regret that anything should have occurred" to cause ill will, and provided balm for Colombia in the sum of $25,000,000. In return that government agreed to recognize the independence of Panama. A militant Republican minority in the Senate prevented ratification, however. Finally, under President Harding, the expression of apology, though not the payment, was eliminated from the treaty, and in this modified form it went through in 1921.

SELECT BIBLIOGRAPHY

Democracy and Empire. No professional historian has yet done for the first decades of the twentieth century what Channing, McMaster and Schouler did for earlier periods. Volumes of the *American Nation,* the *Chronicles of America Series* and the *History of American Life* cover all or most of the years from 1900 to 1919. The only large-scale treatment is Sullivan, *Our Times: the United States, 1900–1925,* intended for popular consumption, but containing much of value to the student.

Cuba and the War with Spain. This and the other subjects in this chapter are dealt with in Oberholtzer, *History,* VIII, and Dennis, *Adventures in American Diplomacy,* as well as in the general surveys of foreign relations by Bailey and Bemis. Among the works devoted specifically to Cuban conditions and American intervention are Chadwick, *Relations of the United States and Spain;* Flack, *Spanish-American Diplomatic Relations;* Benton, *International Law and Diplomacy of the Spanish-American War;* and Millis, *Martial Spirit.* For the European background, consult Ferrara, *Last Spanish War;* Reuter, *Anglo-American Relations during the Spanish-American War;* and Keim, *Forty Years of German-American Political Relations.* Wisan, *Cuban Crisis as Reflected in the New York Press,* and Wilkerson, *Public Opinion and the Spanish-American War,* study the part played by American newspapers in generating hostile feeling, while Pratt, *Expansionists of 1898,* considers more broadly the various factors influencing popular sentiment.

Combating the Powers in China. Langer, *Diplomacy of Imperialism,* provides the international setting. America's rôle is set forth in Dennett, *Americans in Eastern Asia,* Griswold, *Far Eastern Policy of the United States,* and Treat, *Relations between the United States and Japan,* III. For this and the next section, Pringle, *Roosevelt,* and Dennett, *John Hay,* are useful.

Linking the Atlantic and the Pacific. The canal question is discussed from various angles in Arias, *Panama Canal;* Williams, *Anglo-American Isthmian Diplomacy;* Bennett, *History of the Panama Canal;* Perkins, *Monroe Doctrine, 1867–1907;* Hill, *Roosevelt and the Caribbean;* Parks, *Colombia and the United States;* and Miner, *Fight for the Panama Route.*

Chapter XI

THE RISE OF THE PROGRESSIVE
MOVEMENT, 1901–1908

THE ADVENT OF THE MUCKRAKERS

IN DOMESTIC as well as in international affairs President Roosevelt's accession heralded a new age in American political life. He was less the maker of an era than the beneficiary of a tide of unrest that welled up from nearly every village and community of the land. Since the early days of the Economic Revolution the farmers had been fighting a losing battle against the cities and the rising industrial class. Now the spirit of discontent and protest reached the cities, and aroused not only the wage-earners, who had long pitted their strength against their employers, but also members of the middle class, notably the white-collar workers and small businessmen. As a distinguished conservative (William Howard Taft) later admitted, "For thirty years we had [had] an enormous material expansion in this country, in which we all forgot ourselves in the enthusiasm of expanding our material resources and in making ourselves the richest nation on earth. We did this through the use of the principle of organization and combination, and through the development of our national resources. In the encouragement of the investment of capital we nearly transferred complete political power to those who controlled corporate wealth and we were in danger of a plutocracy."

To many thoughtful people the danger of which he spoke appeared an accomplished fact. It seemed as though America, in ironical perversion of Lincoln's words at Gettysburg, had become a government of the corporations, by the corporations and for the corporations. Organized wealth was active in municipal, state and national affairs, the laws to restrain railways and trusts were openly flouted, and a spirit of unbridled materialism infected every branch of business and society. Roosevelt reported Edward H. Harriman, the railroad magnate, as saying that "he could buy a sufficient number of Senators and Congressmen or State Legislators to protect his interests, and when necessary he could buy the Judiciary." The tocsin of revolt, sounded in 1896 against Wall Street and Big Business, had been hushed by the thronging of new and bewildering national interests as a result of the Spanish-American War, and in 1900 predatory capital was more firmly intrenched than ever before.

Indeed, the turn of the century saw Big Business take on Gargantuan proportions. In the single year 1899 ninety-two combinations were formed, including the Standard Oil Company of New Jersey, a holding corporation controlling the far-flung properties of the Standard group, and the Amalgamated Copper Company, a concern capitalized at $175,000,-000. Two years later there followed the billion-dollar United States Steel Corporation; the next year brought the International Harvester Company, which absorbed the five leading manufacturing businesses in its field; and similar huge monopolistic structures grew up in other branches of industry.

Invariably the guiding hand in such amalgamations was some dominant banking group, which thus imposed outside financial direction in place of management by the actual operators. "Finance capitalism" was rapidly usurping the rôle formerly played by the industrial capitalist who had founded and developed the business. To such an extent did the Morgan, Rockefeller and similar groups prompt, control and exploit the processes of consolidation that the Pujo committee of the House of Representatives in 1913, after a painstaking study, proclaimed the existence of a "money trust," that is, a "well-defined identity and community of interest between a few leaders of finance, which has been created and is held together through stock holdings, interlocking directorates, and other forms of domination over banks, trust companies, railroads, public-service, and industrial corporations, and which has resulted in a vast and growing concentration of control of money and credit in the hands of a comparatively few men." [1]

Toward this condition of affairs most people in the opening years of the century had a fatalistic attitude. They were oppressed with the hopelessness of battling against the evil. Only through bold and spectacular methods could the nation be aroused from its lethargy and the old, confident spirit of American democracy be revived. As someone has said, when people are deaf, you have to shout at them. To this mission a group of young journalists dedicated themselves. Newspapers and popular magazines led the van; fledgling novelists took up the hue and cry; and presently the crusade was given a practical turn by aspiring political reformers, including the new incumbent of the White House. The agitation eventually bred individuals who purveyed sensation for sensation's sake, and it was this fact that led President Roosevelt to liken such persons to the Man with the Muckrake in *Pilgrim's Progress,* whose absorption in the filth on the floor caused him to refuse a celestial crown. Though the term was unfair to most of the crusaders, they seized upon it as a badge of distinction.

The heyday of the Muckrakers extended from 1902 to

[1] The most powerful banking units, according to the committee, were J. P. Morgan and Company, the Morgan-controlled First National Bank and the Rockefeller-controlled National City Bank, with combined assets in New York City of over two billion dollars. Four allied financial institutions, it asserted, held three hundred and forty-one directorships in banks, transportation, insurance and public-utility companies, whose aggregate resources exceeded twenty-two billion.

1908. Of the countless exposures, one of the outstanding was Ida M. Tarbell's "History of the Standard Oil Company," based upon three years' study of government reports, court testimony and similar evidence. Beginning in *McClure's* late in 1902, the author month after month relentlessly unfolded the record of the Standard's methods toward independent producers, the public and the government. Thomas W. Lawson's trenchant series on "Frenzied Finance" in *Everybody's* in 1904–1905 dealt particularly with the Amalgamated Copper Company. The writer, a notorious Boston stock-market operator, purported to reveal, in realistic detail, the inner workings of the gigantic financial "System" which held the nation's economic and political life by the throat. In 1905 Upton Sinclair, using fiction as his medium, published a novel *The Jungle,* which exposed unsanitary conditions in the great Chicago packing houses and told of the grip of the beef trust on the nation's meat supply. The railways attracted their share of attention because of unfair manipulation of traffic rates, a notable series being Ray Stannard Baker's "The Railroads on Trial" in *McClure's* during 1905 and 1906. The fulminations against trust-controlled government reached their climax in David Graham Phillips's articles on "The Treason of the Senate" in the *Cosmopolitan* in 1906–1907. The members of that body were considered one by one, and the startling conclusion reached that seventy-five of the ninety served the railways, the beef and sugar trusts, the Standard Oil and the steel interests.

The activities of the Muckrakers also extended to other phases of American life. Lincoln Steffens contributed two series to *McClure's* under the titles, "The Shame of the Cities" and "Enemies of the Republic," which laid bare fetid conditions in municipal and state government. Samuel Hopkins Adams in *Collier's* gave aggressive attention to the fraudulent claims and injurious ingredients of patent medicines. In like fashion, articles were published to expose the unscrupulous practices of banking and insurance companies, the immoral traffic in women, the evils of food adulteration, the tragic effects of child labor, the appalling number of unnecessary industrial accidents. The Muckrakers did not fail to make their accusations specific and to name names. Hence light is thrown upon the substantial correctness of their charges by the fact that few of them were ever found guilty of libel. On the other hand, their disclosures of corruption and knavery led to court proceedings and legislative action to rectify some of the worst abuses.

The most beneficial effect of this "literature of exposure" was the moral awakening of the masses. The Muckrakers did not wish to abandon the capitalist system. By stressing its maladies they hoped to show the way to health. This more constructive aspect found persuasive expression in Herbert Croly's widely read volume *The Promise of American Life* (1909). Pointing out that continuous social improvement could no longer be left to "automatic fulfillment," Croly called on his fellow citizens to redeem the earlier promise of American life by transforming it into a "serious national purpose." Decrying "chaotic individualism" as the foe of genuine progress, he saw the cure in "regulation which will strike, not at the symptoms of the evil, but at its roots. . . . The American people, having achieved democratic institutions, have nothing to do but to turn them to good account." And he added, "The problem belongs to the American national democracy, and its solution must be attempted chiefly by means of official national action." This thoughtful indictment of laissez faire helped to energize tendencies already strongly at work. Together with the writings of the Muckrakers, it exerted a deep influence on the public and greatly strengthened the reform impulses in politics.

THE GROUND SWELL OF REFORM

The first battles for reform were waged in the cities and states. Thus the field of local government again demonstrated its utility as a laboratory of political and social experimentation. Conditions in the cities could hardly have been worse (see page 72). Whether one scanned the teeming immigrant centers of the Atlantic Seaboard or the newer municipalities in the West, corruption, inefficiency and boss rule nearly everywhere held sway. Yet, as the sequel showed, the civic conscience was dormant, not dead. Under the spur of mayors like "Golden Rule" (Samuel M.) Jones and Brand Whitlock in Toledo and Tom L. Johnson in Cleveland, the citizens turned on their oppressors, fought for municipal ownership of public utilities, and checked the power of the boss and the ring. Johnson, in Steffens's phrase, became the "best mayor of the best governed city in the United States." In a similar manner Joseph W. Folk, first as district attorney and then as governor, attacked corruption in St. Louis, and Judge Ben B. Lindsey of the Denver children's court warred against the machine domination of the Colorado capital. In Minneapolis, Hovey C. Clarke, foreman of a grand jury, uncovered the misdeeds of the Ames Ring in 1902 and freed the city from its toils. The election of Emil Seidel as Socialist mayor in 1910 began a new era for Milwaukee. Even New York secured a brief respite of honest government in 1901 by choosing to the mayoralty Seth Low, president of Columbia University.

Other influences tended in a like direction. As the result of a flood which destroyed nearly a third of Galveston in 1900, the citizens in their extremity reorganized their form of government and, departing radically from the conventional pattern, devised the commission plan in place of the more complicated mayor-and-council type. The advantages of this simpler arrangement excited emulation elsewhere, and presently led some communities to add the feature of a city manager employed by the commission to conduct the government. This break with the past implied a tardy recognition that the complex organism of a modern city more closely resembles a business corporation than it does a miniature state, as had been the earlier view. It also placed emphasis on training and expertness as prime requisites for the chief executive official. By 1912 the commission plan in some form or other had spread to over two hundred communities and was still growing in favor.

The rapid adoption of the new plan was facilitated by yet another reform: the introduction by various states of municipal home rule. By gaining the right to frame their own charters, cities were freed from legislative meddling, often corrupt in character, and were thereby enabled to deal more adequately with their own local problems. The number of state constitutions with home-rule provisions rose from four in 1900 to eleven in 1915, most of them in the Middle and Far West. The net effect of the civic renaissance was a heartening improvement in the standards of municipal administration. Much remained to be done, however, and the voters soon learned that even a model governmental system required eternal vigilance to save it from the designs of self-seeking politicians.

Meanwhile the billows of reform washed over into state politics. Riding into power on the mounting waters, young men like Joseph W. Folk of Missouri, Robert M. La Follette of Wisconsin, Albert B. Cummins of Iowa, Charles E. Hughes of New York and Hiram Johnson of California took up cudgels against the champions of intrenched privilege, the party bosses and all those whom Mark Hanna meant to compliment with the term "standpatters." As in municipal reform, the new spirit coursed most rapidly through the younger sections of the country. It affected both parties, and bred internal differences which in time divided each of them into progressive and conservative wings. In many a contest the progressives of the two parties fought shoulder to shoulder against the standpatters of the same parties—a fact which lent increasing unreality to the significance of party labels.

One crucial point of attack was the state nominating convention, another the legislature, for in these bodies the bosses and the special interests they represented held indomitable sway. In place of the convention method of naming candidates, the progressives advocated "direct nominations" by general vote of the party membership in advance of the regular election. Wisconsin enacted the first state-wide primary law in 1903; seven other commonwealths followed in 1907. From these beginnings the system spread through most of the Union. As a popular curb on the legislature, the reformers championed the initiative and referendum, a dual arrangement long used in democratic Switzerland.[1] After Oregon set the pace in 1902, the next decade saw fifteen other states introduce the system of "direct legislation" in some form or other, and presently half the Union had adopted the innovation.

As a further measure of democratic control, the progressives demanded that the voters enjoy the right to recall officials who no longer possessed the public's confidence. Oregon gave the plan state-wide application in 1908, and ten other commonwealths followed before the end of 1914, nearly all of them west of the Mississippi. The recall proved even more popular in the field of municipal government, where, too,

---

[1] The referendum is a device to enable the electorate to approve or reject, by popular vote, laws adopted by the legislature. The initiative allows the voters themselves to propose laws, either for action by the legislature or for submission to the people.

the initiative and referendum flourished. The legislatures also took action to restrain the lavish and corrupt expenditure of money in elections. By 1911 thirty-five commonwealths had passed laws for this purpose.

At the same time, the deep-seated distrust of the United States Senate as a "rich man's club" revived the old Populist demand that its members be chosen directly by the people, not by the legislatures, as the Constitution then provided. On several occasions the Senate blocked efforts of the House to secure an amendment to effect the change. But the democratic torrent could not be so easily stayed. Beginning with Nevada in 1899, various states passed laws which pledged candidates for the legislature to support for Senator the man who won indorsement in a state-wide primary election. By 1912 three fourths of the states had adopted some modification of this plan. It was only a question of time until the Senate should consent to its formal incorporation in the Constitution.

In spite of constant agitation by the women, the reformers were at first largely indifferent to the demand for equal suffrage. As it became increasingly clear, however, that the women might prove valuable allies in the political struggle, the cause sprang to life again. In 1910 and 1911 Washington and California gave them the franchise, and by the end of 1914 they enjoyed full voting rights in eleven states, all west of the Mississippi. Not much longer could the major parties afford to ignore their demand for universal enfranchisement.

At the inception of the progressive movement, the leaders fought primarily to democratize the mechanics of government. But, under the hammering blows of the Muckrakers, they came to concern themselves increasingly with laws to ameliorate the conditions under which the masses lived and worked. As a result, the states passed more social legislation in the first fifteen years of the century than in all previous American history. Laws in regard to child labor were strengthened; and new ones were adopted, raising the age limits, shortening the hours, restricting night work, closing dangerous trades to minors, and requiring better opportunities for school attendance. By 1912 such legislation existed in thirty-eight states, the South lagging behind the rest of the Union. In the same period twenty-eight commonwealths took steps to limit the number of hours a woman wage-earner might work; and a few states passed minimum-wage legislation for women and provided pensions for destitute mothers.

Progress was also made in shortening the workday for men. By 1912 most of the larger cities and more than half the states had established an eight-hour day for labor on public works. In certain especially hazardous employments, such as mining and rail transportation, the workday was likewise subjected to legislative regulation. Thus, in the single year 1907, as many as twenty-three states passed measures of this character. Hardly less important was the crop of employers' liability (or workingmen's compensation) laws. These acts, contrary to the old common-law doctrine, made employers legally responsible for injuries sustained by employees in the course of their work. Maryland led the way in 1902, and by 1917 all but ten legislatures had set up insurance systems, optional or compulsory, for administering the plan.

Meanwhile, the states sought to tighten their control over the corporations and railways operating within their boundaries. Beginning in Ohio in 1906, a wave of passenger-rate regulation overran the South and the Midwest, reaching its crest in 1907. Some of these acts were well designed to accomplish their purpose, but most of them overshot the mark. Oftentimes the fares were fixed so low as to hamper the roads in making needed repairs and extensions. New revenue laws were also enacted, which, by taxing in-

heritances, incomes and the property or earnings of corporations, aimed to place the burden of government on those best
able to pay.

This body of social and economic legislation ran counter
to the old laissez faire doctrine, which had usually guided
legislatures and courts in the past. Accordingly, the judiciary
at first wiped out many of the laws as contrary to the Fourteenth Amendment, alleging either that the employers were
being deprived of "property without due process of law," or
that the wage-earners were being denied the "liberty" to
work under any conditions they pleased. Much popular discontent resulted and criticism of the courts became rife.

In time, however, a more liberal view prevailed among
the judges. The bench began to sustain the legislation on
the ground that a state, under that vague authority known
as the police power, could act to promote the health, morality
and welfare of the people in opposition to special privilege.
The judicial conversion is strikingly shown in the instance
of the United States Supreme Court. In Lochner v. New
York in 1905, it annulled a New York ten-hour statute for
bakers, finding "no reasonable foundation for holding this
to be necessary or appropriate as a health law," but twelve
years later, in Bunting v. Oregon, it upheld an Oregon ten-
hour act for all factory workers as falling within a justifiable
exercise of the police power. This gradual yielding of the
laissez faire attitude to the doctrine of social responsibility
marked perhaps the most valuable advance made by the new
generation.

The American quest for social justice corresponded with a
similar but more vigorous trend abroad. William Jennings
Bryan on his return from a world trip in 1906 declared, "In
all the countries which I have visited there is a demand that
the government be brought nearer to the people." In Great
Britain during these years Parliament expanded its control

over industry, imposed minimum-wage requirements, set up health and unemployment insurance systems, provided old-age pensions for the needy, instituted slum clearance and better housing for the poor, and levied heavy taxes on incomes, inheritances and the unearned increment of land.[1] France took steps in the same direction, while Germany now rounded out the social legislation she had inaugurated in the 1880's. Thus it was in a world atmosphere of ferment and change that the American reformers carried on their crusade.

ROOSEVELT AND REFORM

Substantial as were the gains achieved through state and municipal action, Croly very properly pointed out in *The Promise of American Life* that the situation required effective interposition by the "American national democracy." Without backing from the federal government many of the reforms were rendered partial and of little avail. Industrial corporations and railways in their interstate activities could be regulated only by Congress. The same held true of the interstate sale of adulterated foods, the restriction of expenditures in national elections, and many other matters. But the general government was slower than the states to bend to public opinion. The great economic interests dominated Congress and the Republican organization, and had no intention of surrendering their cherished doctrine: to business belong the spoils.

To Theodore Roosevelt, President without the blessing of Wall Street, fell the task of changing the leopard's spots. Equipped by long experience in public life, he was a master politician. His past career had shown him, in turn, an opponent of Blaine's nomination in 1884 without becoming a

[1] These taxation measures were first proposed to Parliament in 1909 by David Lloyd George, who had been deeply influenced by Henry George's *Progress and Poverty* (see page 163).

Mugwump, an ardent civil-service reformer, an energetic police commissioner in New York City, a bitter foe of Populism,
a big-navy man, a Rough Rider, governor and Vice-President. Sensitive to new winds of popular sentiment, dog-
matically self-confident, he tended to view all questions as
moral issues, a fact which once led an associate playfully to
congratulate him on his "original discovery of the Ten Com-
mandments." More than any of his predecessors since Thomas
Jefferson, he was the scholar in politics, having won distinction in such varied fields as natural history, literature and
historical writing. Whatever this apostle of the "strenuous
life" did, he did with high emotional voltage. Above all else,
he possessed a flair for pungent utterances and an extraordinary gift for dramatizing his actions.

With the nation in a mood to swing to the left, Roosevelt
readily adopted the tenets of the progressive cause. Yet he
proved an enigma to many. Schooled in the old order of politics, a strict party man, he never flinched from working with
the bosses, and he seldom fought through a proposed reform
to its full attainment, being willing to accept something less
than the whole. Uncompromising fighters like Senator La
Follette saw his devotion to progressivism tinctured with opportunism and charlatanry. On the other hand, none of his
successors during the period faced such stubborn resistance
in Congress, and his leadership grew in decision and independence when in his second term he became President in
his own right.

Sending his first message to Congress in December, 1901,
Roosevelt took advantage of the occasion to expound his
views on the principal questions before the country. He
stressed the "serious social problems" growing out of the
"highly complex industrial development which went on
with ever accelerated rapidity during the latter half of the
nineteenth century." Acclaiming business concentration as a

natural and desirable evolution, he opposed the policy of trust prohibition, and demanded legislation to eliminate the abuses, while retaining the advantages, of large-scale enterprises. He also recommended broader powers for regulating railways, and directed attention to the need of conserving the nation's natural resources. Law-abiding labor unions received his approval, and he advocated protective legislation for women and children in all industries carried on directly or indirectly for the federal government.

The program elicited widespread popular approval, but it aroused no answering chord in Congress, where stolid conservatism reigned under Speaker Cannon's leadership in the House and that of Aldrich and Hanna in the Senate. During the summer and autumn of 1902 the President with characteristic vigor carried his message directly to the people, making speeches in New England and the Midwest. Everywhere he urged his policy of federal regulation, and demanded a "square deal" for all—for labor, for capital and for the public.

A great labor outbreak in the Pennsylvania anthracite fields called dramatic attention to corporate selfishness, and lent strength to the President's cause. For years the miners had been shamefully exploited and a storm had been brewing. A strike in 1900 had brought some slight concessions, and in May, 1902, the men again downed their tools. They asked a reduction of the ten-hour workday to nine hours for certain groups of workers and eight for others, also a twenty-per-cent wage increase and recognition of the union, the United Mine Workers. The mine owners declined either to negotiate or to submit the dispute to arbitration. The strike involved nearly a hundred and fifty thousand men and, ultimately, a loss to employers and employed of almost $100,-000,000.

As winter approached, the East faced a terrible coal famine. Roosevelt decided to intervene on behalf of the public whose interests, he held, transcended those of either of the contending parties. Though declaring privately that there was "literally nothing" which the federal government had "any power to do," early in October he urged the owners and the miners to submit their dispute to arbitration. When the former, denying his right to interfere, flatly refused, he let it be known that, if necessary, he would operate the mines with troops, and in the meantime appoint an arbitration board whose findings he expected Congress to support with appropriate legislation. J. P. Morgan and other New York financiers at once exerted strong pressure on the operators, and on October 23 the strike ended with an agreement that a board appointed by the President should arbitrate the controversy. After four months' investigation of the grievances, the board granted the men a ten-per-cent raise of pay and the shorter workday. Provision was also made for adjusting future difficulties by a board of conciliation representing equally the operators and the organized workers, with final appeal to the federal judge of the circuit. As a result, peace reigned in the anthracite fields until the days of general economic upheaval following the World War.

Goaded by an aroused public sentiment, Congress now made grudging concessions to Roosevelt's demands for extending government regulation. In February, 1903, it passed the Elkins act in an attempt to cure the rebate evil which the interstate-commerce law of 1887 had vainly tried to stop. The new statute forbade variations from the published rates and, in cases of violation, inflicted fines not only on the railroad and its officers but also on shippers who accepted special favors. The general power of rate-fixing, however, was left exclusively in the hands of the companies as hitherto, notwithstanding the strong popular feeling that charges were unreasonably high. A few days later Congress created the new Department of Commerce and Labor, including as one of its divisions a Bureau of Corporations empowered to investigate the affairs of large business aggregations.[1] Its function was not to prosecute offenders, but to provide data for the use of the Attorney-General and of Congress.

Meanwhile, the administration pressed for a stricter enforcement of the antitrust and interstate-commerce acts. Earlier judicial decisions, it will be recalled, had narrowed the scope of these laws and rendered difficult the conviction of offenders. In the case of the Northern Securities Company in 1904, which involved an attempt of the Morgan and Hill interests to unite the management of two transcontinental railways by means of a holding company, the Supreme Court by a bare majority vote dissolved the merger as a combination in restraint of trade. Encouraged by this friendlier attitude, the Attorney-General pushed other prosecutions. In January, 1905, the court rendered a decision against the beef trust. Altogether the Roosevelt administration in its seven and a half years secured twenty-five indictments.

By 1904 Teddy, as he was fondly called, had become the idol of the Republican rank and file. Even children in the nursery took to playing with "Teddy Bears." His striking personality, his flaming espousal of the "square deal," his "trust-busting" activities, his use of the "big stick" in taking the Canal Zone, captured the imagination of the man on the street. Nor did the machine politicians, left leaderless by Hanna's death early in 1904, dare refuse him a second term. The national convention in Chicago on June 21 named him by acclamation, with Senator Charles W. Fairbanks of Indiana for Vice-President. The influence of the standpatters, however, appeared in the platform, which was largely a eulogy of the party's historic achievements. On the trust ques-

[1] George B. Cortelyou of New York was appointed first Secretary of Commerce and Labor.

tion it declared simply that the combinations of capital and labor "are alike entitled to the protection of the laws . . . and neither can be permitted to break them."

For the first time since 1892, Democrats of the Cleveland stamp dominated the national convention of that party at its St. Louis meeting on July 6. In the preceding months William Randolph Hearst, now the owner of a chain of newspapers, had spent over a million dollars to capture the nomination; but on the first ballot the prize went to Judge Alton B. Parker, a conservative New York lawyer utterly unknown to the nation. Henry G. Davis of West Virginia was named for second place. The platform called for prohibition of capitalistic monopolies and for augmenting the powers of the Interstate Commerce Commission. Roosevelt was flayed for his "executive usurpation of legislative and judicial functions," and his whole course as President was condemned as "erratic, sensational, spectacular, and arbitrary."

"Rooseveltism," rather than any specific public question, proved the decisive factor in the campaign. Where the light is bright the shadows are deep; and like Andrew Jackson, Roosevelt had the faculty of exciting passionate enmity as well as fanatical devotion. Judge Parker represented, on the whole, the conservative elements, but the certainty of Roosevelt's success caused the great corporations to contribute to the Republican campaign chest as before. The *New York Sun,* phrasing the argument somewhat differently, said: "We prefer the impulsive candidate of the party of conservatism to the conservative candidate of the party which the business interests regard as permanently and dangerously impulsive." Progressive Democrats were drawn more to Roosevelt than to their own party candidate, though Bryan, who had opposed Parker's nomination in the convention, gave him a lukewarm support. The great prosperity of the country was another influence making for Republican victory.

The outcome was an extraordinary testimonial of public confidence in the President. He received 56.4 per cent of the popular ballots (7,629,000 votes) to 37.6 per cent (5,084,000) for Parker, and 336 electoral votes as compared with 140 for his opponent. Incidentally, the result was a vindication of the new-school Democrats, for in both 1896 and 1900 Bryan had polled over a million more votes than did the conservative Parker in 1904. When Roosevelt was notified of his victory, he announced to the press, "The wise custom which limits the President to two terms regards the substance and not the form, and under no circumstances will I be a candidate for or accept another nomination."

THE CONTEST RESUMED

Emboldened by his sweeping triumph, Roosevelt returned to office with fresh determination to advance the cause of reform. His first concern was a more drastic regulation of the railroads. Though the proposal met bitter opposition at every turn from the rail interests, who asserted that their charges were the cheapest in the world, the small shippers and the traveling public rallied to the President's standard. The House promptly passed a bill granting the Interstate Commerce Commission unrestricted power to fix interstate rates, but the standpatters in the Senate proved stubborn. In the end, a compromise was reached in the Hepburn act, adopted in June, 1906.

This law authorized the Commission to reduce unfair rates, its orders to become immediately effective unless challenged by the railroad before a federal court. Despite the disappointment of the progressives, the new law marked an advance over the act of 1887, for the burden of initiating litigation to test the validity of the Commission's orders now rested upon the railways, not upon the Commission as hitherto. The Hepburn act also extended the Commission's authority to express and sleeping-car companies and pipe lines. Free passes, long an insidious source of political corruption, were forbidden except under strict limitations. In addition, the tribunal was empowered to prescribe the methods of bookkeeping and accounting which the roads must follow, a regulation prompted in part by the practice of certain companies of concealing corrupt expenditures through manipulating book entries.

Other measures of Congress in 1906 carried the principle of federal control to new limits. As a result of Upton Sinclair's *The Jungle,* it passed an act requiring federal inspection of all concerns selling meats in interstate trade. In response to the Muckrakers' crusade against patent medicines and adulterated foods, the pure-food law prohibited the use of any "deleterious drug, chemical or preservative" in prepared medicines, preserved foods or liquors sold in interstate commerce. A third piece of social legislation made interstate transportation companies liable for injuries sustained by their employees. When the Supreme Court declared this act unconstitutional, one which met the court's objections was adopted in 1908. The question of the relationship of Big Business to politics was taken up in 1907, and a statute enacted forbidding corporations to make campaign contributions in federal elections. A sister bill providing for publicity of campaign funds and expenditures encountered defeat, however.

Meanwhile, the administration took active steps to assure enforcement of the regulatory laws. In 1907 it was discovered that the American Sugar Refining Company had defrauded the government out of a large amount of import duties. The resulting legal actions led to the recovery of over $4,000,000 and the conviction of several of the interested officials. In the same year the Standard Oil Company of Indiana, a subsidiary of the Standard of New Jersey, was indicted for receiving secret rebates on shipments over the Chicago and Alton Railroad. The changed temper of the times was reflected in the fine imposed by Judge Kenesaw M. Landis of the federal district court, amounting to $29,240,000 on fourteen hundred and sixty-two separate counts. To thoughtful people it seemed that the decision was actuated by a desire for vengeance rather than a spirit of justice, and the verdict was reversed by a higher court. Popular conviction as to the guilt of the defendants, however, remained unchanged; and Roosevelt's private comment on the higher court's action was: "There is altogether too much power in the bench."

Next to corporation control, President Roosevelt devoted chief attention to the conservation of the nation's natural resources. Because of the traditional policy of giving away land to all comers, the country now found itself confronted with unanticipated results. Timber had been ruthlessly destroyed, lands had been allowed to become eroded, soil fertility had been sapped, subsurface wealth had been wasted, all in the supposed interest of the individual owners. At the turn of the century it was reckoned that, at the current rate of use, the forests would last about thirty years longer, anthracite coal fifty years, bituminous perhaps a century. As another phase of the problem, there existed wide stretches of public domain which, though looked upon as worthless, needed only proper attention from the government to become fit for settlement. In the nineties Congress had adopted some preliminary measures looking toward the husbanding of natural resources. A statute of 1891 gave the President discretion to reserve from sale and settlement public lands bearing forests. Three years later the Carey act offered gifts of arid tracts to states agreeing to irrigate them and open them to settlers at reasonable prices.

Upon these beginnings Roosevelt greatly enlarged. Starting with his first annual message in 1901, he lost no occasion to preach the gospel of conservation until the masses came to understand the relationship between public-land policy and human welfare. In place of the chaos of the past he urged national planning. His program embraced four main objectives: forests, arid lands, minerals and inland waterways. Where his predecessors had set aside forty-seven million acres of unsold wooded land, Roosevelt increased the area by a hundred and forty-eight million and, through Gifford Pinchot, chief of the Division of Forestry, began systematic efforts to prevent forest fires and to retimber denuded tracts. The close of his presidency saw most of the great forests on the public lands in the Pacific and Rocky Mountain states set apart for perpetual use of the whole nation.

Hardly less noteworthy was the progress made in reclaiming unproductive agricultural tracts. Because the Carey act had accomplished little, the Newlands reclamation law in 1902 provided that the proceeds of public-land sales in sixteen semiarid Western states and territories should constitute a revolving fund to assist the construction of irrigation works. Soon one important project after another was undertaken, large dams and reservoirs were built, and great thirsty tracts supplied with water. A year after Roosevelt left office it was estimated that more than three million acres of farm land had been so improved as to yield an increased profit of $75,000,000 annually. Steps were also taken to reclaim swamp or overflowed lands of an interstate character. In order to safeguard mineral wealth, Roosevelt withheld from sale a total of eighty-five million acres containing oil, coal and other subsurface riches.

The interest in waterways resulted in part from the desirability of relieving the freight congestion of the railroads, and in part from the need of preventing recurrent destructive floods on the rivers, especially the Mississippi. In 1907 Roosevelt appointed an Inland Waterways Commission to

CONSERVATION AND RECLAMATION TO 1917

Forest Reserves
National Parks
National Monuments
Irrigation Projects
Reservoirs

study the problem from all angles; and on the basis of its report appropriations began to be made for a systematic development of the nation's rivers, lakes and canals. Realizing that the success of conservation required coöperation by the states, the President set a precedent by summoning the governors to a conference on the subject in 1908. Within eighteen months after its adjournment forty-one state conservation commissions were appointed and in active operation. Roosevelt's efforts had the effect of making conservation a major national responsibility. Only at their peril did his successors fail to give unstinted devotion to the cause.

As the campaign of 1908 drew near, the President was at the peak of his popularity. Unlike his predecessors, he had time and again taken his policies directly to the voters, winning their confidence and frightening laggard members of Congress into supporting his program. His great service to his country consisted less in specific additions to the statute book than in helping to give the people new faith in themselves. Furthermore, at a time when labor and capital were ready to leap at each other's throats, his voice declared with ringing emphasis, "The corporation has come to stay just as the trade union has come to stay," and, he unfailingly added, both must bow to the will of the public. Conservatives who thought him too radical and radicals who thought him too conservative failed to perceive that he sought to hold an even balance between the contending elements in modern society. Always deeply indebted to the pioneer efforts of the Muckrakers as well as to the progressive elements of both parties in Congress, he lent the prestige of his high office to the view that between the two extremes of unbridled individualism and paternalistic socialism lay the middle path of intelligent social control.

SELECT BIBLIOGRAPHY

The Advent of the Muckrakers.   Moody, *Truth about the Trusts,* Edwards, *Evolution of Finance Capitalism,* and Allen, *Lords of Creation,* show how Big Business grew bigger. Brandeis, *Other People's Money,* discusses the findings of the Pujo committee. Regier, *Era of the Muckrakers,* and Filler, *Crusaders for American Liberalism,* treat the "literature of exposure."

The Ground Swell of Reform.   For the improvement of conditions in municipal and state politics, see Faulkner, *Quest for Social Justice,* and DeWitt, *Progressive Movement,* which also deal with other topics in this chapter. Particular reforms are discussed in Munro, *Initiative, Referendum and Recall;* Carlton, *History and Problems of Organized Labor;* and Groat, *Attitude of American Courts in Labor Cases.*

Roosevelt's Reform Activities.   Ogg, *National Progress,* Rhodes, *McKinley and Roosevelt Administrations,* Dumond, *Roosevelt to Roosevelt,* and Sullivan, *Our Times,* I-III, treat the main facts. The relevant biographies include Pringle, *Roosevelt;* Jessup, *Root;* Croly, *Hanna;* Stephenson, *Aldrich;* Pringle, *Taft;* and Bowers, *Beveridge and the Progressive Era.* Conservation problems are viewed from various angles in Van Hise and Havemeyer, *Conservation of Our Natural Resources;* Teele, *Economics of Land Reclamation;* and Hibbard, *History of Public Land Policies.*

Chapter XII

PROGRESSIVISM AT FLOOD TIDE, 1908–1917

TAFT INHERITS THE PRESIDENCY

A S THE presidential election of 1908 approached, Roosevelt sternly repelled all suggestions of a "second elective term." Instead, he threw his support to William Howard Taft of Ohio, Secretary of War since 1904, who had consistently supported his policies in public and private and who knew the insular dependencies as no other American. "I think that of all the men in the country," Roosevelt wrote a friend, "Taft is the best fitted at this time to be president and to carry on the work upon which we have entered during the past six years." Despite this high sponsorship, the idea of Taft's nomination awakened little popular enthusiasm, and among progressive Republicans it excited positive distrust, for in his earlier career as federal judge he had displayed marked conservative tendencies. Nevertheless, they bowed to the judgment of their chief; and the latter, by adept use of the federal patronage and manipulation of the Southern delegates, won his point on the first roll call of the party convention at Chicago in the middle of June. James S. Sherman of New York was nominated for Vice-President. The platform praised Roosevelt's record in combating "the abuse of wealth and the tyranny of power," and called for ampler regulation of trusts. Recognition was accorded the growing demand for tariff reform by a pledge for "a revision of the tariff," to be based on the difference between "the cost of production at home and abroad, with a reasonable profit to American industries."

The stinging defeat suffered by the candidate of the conservative Democrats in 1904 brought the progressive wing
strongly to the fore. At its convention in Denver on July 7
the party on the first ballot gleefully named William Jennings Bryan for his third trial at the presidency, giving the
second place to John W. Kern of Indiana. "The overwhelming issue," declared the platform, is "Shall the people rule?"
—an issue forced on the nation by Roosevelt's dictation of his
successor, Speaker Cannon's "absolute domination" of the
House and the grip of the predatory interests on the party
in power. Stigmatizing the Republican tariff plank as belated
and insincere, the Democrats explicitly committed themselves
to "reduction." They also demanded the destruction of industrial monopolies and denounced the unfair use of injunctions in labor disputes.

In the ensuing campaign both nominees made long stumping tours, with Roosevelt vainly entreating the tranquil
Taft, "Hit them hard, old man!" As a consequence of the
administration's reform activities, Bryan found himself somewhat in the position of a soldier whose store of ammunition
had been depleted by the enemy. Partly for this reason, he
bore down heavily on the tariff question, and pressed Taft
so hard that the latter interpreted the Republican plank as
meaning revision downward. Organized labor, for the first
time, took part in a presidential contest when the American
Federation of Labor indorsed the Democrats because of their
stand on injunctions. In harmony with the new political
ethics, Bryan's followers during the campaign made public
all individual contributions received above a hundred dollars, and both parties issued postelection statements. The
Republican proved the victor, receiving 321 electoral votes
to 162 for Bryan, and 51.6 per cent of the popular ballots
(7,679,000 votes) to 43 per cent (6,409,000) for his opponent.
Taft's popular plurality was hardly a third of that polled by

Roosevelt in 1904, while Bryan exceeded Parker's vote by more than a million. Afterwards, in explaining his defeat, Bryan ruefully declared that the Republican party had enjoyed the unfair advantage of running two candidates: Taft the progressive who swept the West, and Taft the conservative who won the East. The Republicans also carried both branches of Congress.

While the campaign was under way, Roosevelt had written an English friend, "Always excepting Washington and Lincoln, I believe that Taft as President will rank with any other man who has ever been in the White House"; and he added, "He and I view questions exactly alike." Events quickly revealed that his judgment was mistaken. The new President, left to his own devices by Roosevelt's departure on an African hunting trip, speedily reverted to his naturally conservative outlook on public questions. It is likely that, without conscious disloyalty to his former chief, he believed the country needed time for recuperation and reflection after seven years of perpetual motion. Moreover, unlike Roosevelt, he was steeped in the law, and hence shaped his course with legalistic caution. It is significant of the bent of his mind that all his cabinet appointees, except two whom he took over from his predecessor, were lawyers.[1] If Teddy was essentially a man of action, "Big Bill" was essentially a man of deliberation. At any rate, the kindly nature and imperturbable good humor embodied in his three hundred and fifty pounds inclined him to conciliate the powerful party leaders whom his predecessor

[1] Taft's cabinet consisted of Philander C. Knox of Pennsylvania, Secretary of State; Franklin MacVeagh of Illinois, Secretary of the Treasury; Jacob M. Dickinson of Tennessee, Secretary of War; George W. Wickersham of New York, Attorney-General; Frank H. Hitchcock of Massachusetts, Postmaster-General; George von L. Meyer of Massachusetts, Secretary of the Navy; Richard A. Ballinger of Washington, Secretary of the Interior; James Wilson of Iowa, Secretary of Agriculture; and Charles Nagel of Missouri, Secretary of Commerce and Labor. Meyer and Wilson held over from Roosevelt's official family.

had antagonized. But progressive Republicans were soon convinced that he was an intentional traitor to the cause they cherished.

The most urgent problem confronting the administration was tariff revision, a question which Roosevelt had refrained from taking up. A growing number of people had come to believe that the Dingley act of 1897 had vastly accelerated the growth of business consolidation, and had thereby caused the upward trend of the cost of living, which was exciting popular dissatisfaction. The generating center of this sentiment was the Midwest, stronghold of the progressive movement. Summoned in special session to deal with the tariff, the House at the President's behest passed the Payne bill lowering the rates. But under Senator Aldrich's direction the upper chamber mangled the measure, adding eight hundred and forty-seven amendments, mostly increasing duties. The two houses ironed out their differences in the Payne-Aldrich act, signed by Taft in August, 1909.

As a result of the pulling and wrenching, the finished product actually imposed somewhat higher rates than the objectionable Dingley tariff. A flexible clause empowered the President to hoist duties by as much as twenty-five per cent in the case of countries which discriminated against American trade; and to aid in the administration of this provision, a bipartisan tariff board was created. At every step the increases had been fought by La Follette, Cummins, Beveridge and other Western Senators of the party, but to no avail. One novel feature of the act, however, was inserted as a sop to them: a one-per-cent tax on the net earnings of corporations above five thousand dollars. "Schedule K" proved a particular abomination to the progressives, for it left virtually unchanged the high duties on wool and woolens at a time when woolen manufacturers were declaring dividends up to fifty per cent. Even the President did not defend these duties, though in an address at Winona, Minnesota, he pronounced the tariff as a whole "the best the country ever had."

The Payne-Aldrich act was the first step in Taft's downfall. Hard on its heels came two other events that alienated Roosevelt's old followers. One appeared to involve the President's good faith toward the conservation of natural resources. In the summer of 1909 Gifford Pinchot, the chief forester, accused Secretary of the Interior Ballinger of lack of zeal in the protection of water-power sites and coal lands and of conniving with the interests which were seeking to plunder the public domain. Taft, convinced that the charges were unjust, sided with Ballinger and dismissed Pinchot for insubordination. There ensued a bitter newspaper controversy, heightened by the fact that Pinchot was a political and personal intimate of Roosevelt. In the end, Ballinger, hoping to relieve his chief of embarrassment, resigned.

Reform sentiment was further inflamed by the President's failure to aid the Western Republicans in their fight to unhorse Speaker Joseph G. Cannon. In the course of years the presiding officer of the House had come not only to appoint all committees, but also, through his domination of the rules committee, to limit debate and control the whole process of lawmaking. A confirmed standpatter, Cannon used his autocratic authority to thwart the purposes of the progressives. Consequently, on March 19, 1910, a group of Republican insurgents under the leadership of George W. Norris of Nebraska joined with the Democratic minority in a successful effort to curtail the Speaker's powers. Though permitted to retain his office, Cannon was shorn of the right to appoint the rules committee and to act as one of its members. When the Democrats came into control the next year, they went further and made all committees elective.

The revolution in the House foreshadowed a greater one in the fall elections. On the issues of tariff reform and

"Cannonism" the Democrats won decisive victories in all sections of the country, and turned a Republican majority of forty-seven in the House into a Democratic majority of sixty-three. Ex-President Roosevelt, once more in his native country, undertook a long speaking tour and, though not yet openly hostile to the administration, centered his efforts on the election of progressive Republicans. Even New Jersey, a boss-ridden Republican state hitherto the despair of reformers, placed in the governor's chair a progressive Democrat, Woodrow Wilson, recently president of Princeton University.

The lesson of the election was not lost upon Taft. In an effort to appease the low-tariff sentiment he proposed to Congress a reciprocity agreement with Canada, providing for the reduction or abolition of duties on many Canadian food products and raw materials in return for similar concessions on American farm implements and certain other commodities. This measure, which left untouched the principal Eastern manufactures, proved acceptable to the Republicans of that section; but it sowed a whirlwind of protest among the farming and lumbering interests of the Middle and Far West, which feared the consequences of Canadian competition. Under the astute leadership of Representative Oscar W. Underwood of Alabama, the Democrats took prompt advantage of this new breach in Republican ranks. Viewing Canadian reciprocity as an entering wedge for general tariff reduction, they helped Taft carry his scheme through Congress in July, 1911.[1] Then, to offset the displeasure of the progressive Republicans, the Democrats combined with them to pass a number of bills for lowering the tariff on Eastern manufactured articles. A "farmers' free-list bill" was enacted,

[1] Taft's victory, as it turned out, was short-lived because Canada rejected the terms. This result was due in part to an indiscreet utterance of Champ Clark, Democratic Speaker of the House, that he favored reciprocity because he hoped "to see the day when the American flag will float over every square foot of the British North American possessions clear to the North Pole."

the notorious "Schedule K" revised, and bills were carried to scale down the duties on cotton goods, chemicals, iron and steel. All these ran afoul the veto of the President, who thereby intensified his unpopularity both within and without the party.

Yet, despite Taft's inept leadership and the growing revolt against him, the administration had done much in a quiet, untheatrical way to further the cause of reform. In 1910 Congress put new teeth into the interstate-commerce law by passing the Mann-Elkins act, which extended the Commission's authority to telegraph and telephone companies, and amended the Hepburn act (see page 313) so as to make the Commission's orders for lower rates effective, even when a court investigation was being conducted into their reasona-bleness. In a similar fashion, Congress tackled the question of campaign contributions, adopting legislation in 1910 and 1911 limiting the amount of money a candidate might spend in running for the House or Senate and requiring that all receipts and expenditures be published before and after both primaries and elections.[1]

Moreover, the dust raised by the Ballinger-Pinchot affair obscured the fact that Congress in 1911, on President Taft's recommendation, enlarged the scope of conservation by pro-viding for the purchase of forest lands near the headwaters of navigable streams in the White Mountains and the south-ern Appalachians. In addition, steps were taken in 1910 to improve the public-land laws, a Bureau of Mines was estab-lished, and stricter provision was made for safety appliances on railways. Two years later a Children's Bureau was set up to study problems of child welfare and a parcels-post law was placed on the statute book. The last days of Taft's presi-

---

[1] In Newberry v. United States (1921), the Supreme Court held uncon-stitutional that part of the law of 1910 which sought to regulate the expendi-tures of senatorial candidates in primary elections.

dency saw the creation of a Department of Labor with membership in the cabinet.

Apart from this legislative record, the administration conducted nearly twice as many prosecutions against business consolidations as had Roosevelt's Attorney-General. In 1911 the Supreme Court ordered the dissolution of the Standard Oil Company of New Jersey and also of the American Tobacco Company. The immediate rise in the value of Standard stock, however, indicated of what little practical consequence was the decision. More important was the fact that the high tribunal in these two cases set its face against reckless attempts to break up large-scale enterprises. This appeared in a new construction of the Sherman antitrust act. Where that statute had outlawed "every" contract or combination "in restraint of trade" (see page 139), the court now interpreted the prohibition as applying only to undue or unreasonable restraints of trade.

Most noteworthy of all was the initiation of two new amendments to the Constitution. The controversy begun by the Supreme Court's judgment against the income tax in 1895 (see page 124) was solved, once and for all, when the Sixteenth Amendment was submitted to the states at Taft's suggestion in 1909. By its terms Congress was empowered to levy an income tax without the necessity of apportioning it among the states according to population. The Seventeenth Amendment, proposed by Congress in 1912, represented the climax of the popular demand for a reconstitution of the Senate. It provided that Senators should be elective by popular vote of the state instead of by the legislature. The first amendment was ratified by the state legislatures in 1913 shortly before Taft left office, and the second three months later. It was significant of the changed outlook of America that the Taft administration should clothe with constitutional sanction two reforms which the Populists had first brought to national notice.

THE POLITICAL UPHEAVAL OF 1912

Had Taft possessed his predecessor's qualities of showmanship, he might have capitalized these constructive achievements to political advantage. As it was, the progressive Republican leaders began to lay plans as early as January, 1911, to prevent his renomination. With some misgivings they fixed upon Senator Robert M. La Follette as their choice. "Fighting Bob's" lifelong battle for popular rights had placed him at the van of the progressive cause, but he had never made the same appeal to the popular imagination as the colorful Roosevelt, and the feeling grew that he lacked the vote-getting qualities necessary to unseat Taft in the convention. Such doubters cast longing eyes toward the ex-President who, with many professions of reluctance, finally yielded to their importunities in February, 1912.

Though La Follette stayed in the race, he was almost forgotten as the country beheld the distressing spectacle of the President and the ex-President, recently devoted friends, engaging in a campaign of caustic personal recrimination. Taft denounced Roosevelt's "explosive inconsistencies," and warned the people against "political emotionalists" certain to plunge the country "into a condition that would find no parallel except in the French Revolution." Roosevelt in his turn charged Taft with reaction and added bitterly, "It is a bad trait to bite the hand that feeds you." The advantage by no means lay wholly on Roosevelt's side. If he commanded a wider popular following, the President's supporters in most of the states dominated the party machinery for selecting delegates, while they absolutely controlled the South, where the delegates were usually federal officeholders. But in the thirteen states where preferential primaries prevailed, Roosevelt won two hundred and seventy-eight delegates, Taft sixty-eight and La Follette thirty-six. Elsewhere Taft was generally the favorite, though the number of contested seats was unusually large.

When the Republican convention assembled in Chicago on June 18, the administration-controlled national committee, employing what the progressives called steamroller tactics, awarded most of the disputed seats to Taft delegates, and constructed a majority which renominated Taft and Sherman on the first ballot. Three hundred and forty-four Roosevelt supporters, representing a third of the delegates, refused to vote, though critics unkindly pointed out that Roosevelt himself had jammed through Taft's nomination by similar methods four years before. The platform, while declaring for a "self-controlled representative democracy," carefully skirted questions provocative of factional bitterness. The chief planks called for a federal commission to regulate trusts, a "readjustment" of the tariff with the aid of a board of experts, and a reformation of the monetary system. The Roosevelt followers, unappeased, prepared to carry their case directly to the people.

The Republican schism lent unusual interest to the proceedings of the opposition party at Baltimore on June 25. For the first time in many years the Democrats felt confident of victory, and, emboldened by this circumstance, the conservative elements and professional politicians made a desperate effort to regain mastery of the party. Either Governor Judson Harmon of Ohio or Congressman Underwood would have been acceptable to them as a nominee, and they resolved at all costs to prevent the selection of Woodrow Wilson, who as governor of New Jersey had shown himself a militant progressive. A fourth aspirant, Speaker Champ Clark of Missouri, flirted with both factions, and on several ballots actually received a majority of the votes. That he failed of the requisite two thirds was due to the energy and skill of William Jennings Bryan who, sitting as a member of the Nebraska delegation, distrusted Clark's equivocal attitude. At every turn he fought the "predatory interests," meanwhile keeping the outside public constantly informed of his plans, with the result that thousands of approving telegrams poured in upon the delegates. The spirited contest concluded with Wilson's nomination on the forty-sixth ballot, Governor Thomas R. Marshall of Indiana being chosen to run with him. The platform blamed the high cost of living on the Republican tariff, pledged "immediate downward revision," repeated the injunction plank of 1908, promised to restore the Sherman act to its original vigor, and demanded revision of the banking and currency laws.

Meantime, the disappointed Roosevelt supporters had been organizing their forces and in Chicago on August 5 they launched the Progressive party. Amid scenes of feverish excitement, Roosevelt and Governor Hiram Johnson of California were named as the standard bearers. The platform was the most unusual yet to be framed by a party having reasonable hopes of victory. Its keynote was the pledge to "build a new and nobler commonwealth." To that end the platform favored not only such political devices as direct primaries, woman suffrage, the initiative, referendum and the recall, but also a referendum on court decisions that annulled state laws. As economic reforms, it advocated a federal commission to regulate combinations, tariff revision along protective lines through an expert commission, and an overhauling of the banking and currency laws. In addition, it indorsed a wide range of measures for "social and industrial justice," including the eight-hour day, a "living wage," prohibition of child labor, and safeguards against industrial accidents and occupational diseases.

In view of its dramatic prelude the campaign proved surprisingly quiet. Roosevelt was inevitably the central figure. His followers assumed the nickname of Bull Moosers from a chance expression dropped by their sportsman-leader. His opponents, digging up his declaration in 1904 against a third term, flayed him for his unseemly ambition and boundless egotism. The most startling incident was the attempt made on his life by an insane man in Milwaukee. Though the Progressive program was widely condemned as radical and socialistic, the ticket commanded warm support from certain well-known capitalists who saw in the elaborate provisions for government control of industrial conditions the promise of an efficient and contented labor force. It is significant that Samuel Gompers, as in 1908, called on organized labor to back the Democrats. Indeed, the Progressive platform nowhere definitely affirmed the wage-earner's right to organize and strike. Wilson's dignified and well-phrased utterances won growing favor with thoughtful people, who came to regard him as standing midway between candidates of extremist tendencies—"a progressive with the brakes on."

In any event, the divided opposition insured Democratic success. Wilson mustered 435 electoral votes, Roosevelt 88, Taft 8. But the distribution of popular ballots mirrored the situation more accurately, Wilson winning 41.8 per cent (6,286,000 votes), Roosevelt 27.4 per cent (4,126,000), and Taft 23.2 per cent (3,484,000). The victor received one and a third million less than the total polled by his two rivals, and fewer than Bryan had commanded in any of his three candidacies. The Democrats also gained both houses of Congress. Benefiting from the political confusion, the Socialist nominee, Eugene V. Debs, doubled his popular vote of 1908, reaching nearly a million. The remarkable showing made by the Progressive party promised to give it a permanent place in American politics if, indeed, its strength represented anything more than attachment to a brilliant chief.

WILSON'S TRIPLE ASSAULT ON PRIVILEGE

The new President embodied the finest traditions of the party that elected him. A Virginian by birth, he had spent his mature years in the North, serving from 1890 as professor and then as president of Princeton University. Like Jefferson, he was a student and philosopher of political institutions. His works on political science ushered in the modern study of that subject in America. Like Jackson, he was a militant believer in democracy, and possessed an intuitive understanding of the unspoken hopes of the plain people. His unvarying self-command and obstinate courage, derived perhaps from his Scotch Presbyterian ancestry, recalled still another Democratic predecessor, Grover Cleveland, whose neighbor he had been at Princeton. More than any of these men, however, he surveyed the world with singular mental detachment, with the eyes of a scholar accustomed to probe beneath the immediate flux of events and to seek for guiding principles.

Wilson's espousal of popular rights, it is not too much to say, sprang rather from his head than from his heart. By personal taste an aristocrat, he loved humanity in the abstract, not as anxious, striving individuals. He lacked the common touch of a Lincoln or a Roosevelt, the trait of being at home with all sorts and conditions of men; yet he evoked deep affection from his intimates. His high forehead, narrow, ascetic face and aggressive jaw suggested the special qualities that gave character and force to his leadership. His hold on the people rested more on their growing confidence in his disinterested and penetrating intelligence than on a devotion to his personality. Not the least of his gifts was a literary style that made of his public utterances a fine tapestry woven of noble and luminous phrases. His intellectual aloofness and stubborn independence proved a constant irritation to his political opponents, and often to his own party leaders, and in the end contributed to his defeat in the last great battle of his career, that for ratification of the League of Nations.

The election of 1912 was a victory for progressivism, if not for the Progressives. Wilson showed no disposition to evade or straddle any of the urgent questions of the time. He felt a solemn mission to commit the Democrats unalterably to reform and, by appointing Bryan Secretary of State, he served notice at the outset of his open alliance with the liberals of his party.[1] In any case, this course accorded with political wisdom, for thereby the President might hope to sap the strength of the Progressive party and win for his administration the majority support that had been wanting in the election.

Though the Democrats controlled both branches of Congress, the party, long out of power, lacked cohesion and responsible leaders. To Wilson this was no deterrent. As a professional student of government, he had for many years maintained that the chief executive should be not a mere presiding officer of the nation, but an active and aggressive director of public policy, bearing a relationship to his party and the people like that of the English Prime Minister. In his *Constitutional Government in the United States* (1907) he had written, "The President is at liberty, both in law and conscience, to be as big a man as he can. His capacity will set the limit." Accordingly, he frankly assumed the reins of leadership, revived the custom, abandoned by Jefferson, of

[1] The other members of the cabinet were William G. McAdoo of New York, Secretary of the Treasury; Lindley M. Garrison of New Jersey, Secretary of War; James C. McReynolds of Tennessee, Attorney-General; Albert S. Burleson of Texas, Postmaster-General; Josephus Daniels of North Carolina, Secretary of the Navy; Franklin K. Lane of California, Secretary of the Interior; David F. Houston of Missouri, Secretary of Agriculture; William C. Redfield of New York, Secretary of Commerce; and William B. Wilson of Pennsylvania, Secretary of Labor. The party's indebtedness to the Solid South was evidenced by the appointment of five members, including McAdoo, who were natives of ex-slave states.

reading his messages to Congress, and in other ways out-stripped even Roosevelt in enhancing the prestige of his office. In accounting for his legislative achievements, how-ever, it must always be remembered that his administration was the beneficiary of all the agitation for democratic reform that had occurred since the opening of the century.

Summoned in special session, the new Congress proceeded to carry through a legislative program which, in scope and importance, proved one of the most notable in American history. Its first task was tariff revision. "We must abolish everything," declared the President, "that bears even the semblance of special privilege or of any kind of artificial ad-vantage, and put our businessmen and producers under the stimulation of a constant necessity to be efficient, economical, and enterprising." To safeguard their vested interests, agents of the protected manufacturers followed their usual course of gathering from far and near to press their claims; but Wilson promptly put them to rout by calling in the newsmen and exposing "the extraordinary exertions" of "astute men" seeking "to create an artificial opinion and to overcome the interests of the public for their private profit."

The Underwood act, passed early in October, 1913, was the most revolutionary tariff since 1846. It provided sub-stantial reductions in the rates on important raw materials and foodstuffs, cotton and woolen goods, iron, steel and other commodities, and removed the duties from more than a hun-dred articles. Although the act retained many protective features, a real attempt had been made to lower the cost of living. In order to make up for the expected loss of revenue, advantage was taken of the recent Sixteenth Amendment to levy a graduated tax on the incomes of individuals and cor-porations. The actual fiscal effects of the Underwood act were never fairly tested, for the outbreak of the World War in 1914 caused a decline of dutiable imports and customs revenue. The law did not continue the tariff board, established in 1909, but agitation in favor of such a body presently became so strong that in 1916 Congress created a bipartisan commission of six to assist in tariff legislation.

The second item on the Democratic program was a reorganization of the banking and currency system. The act of 1900, while establishing the gold standard, had left unaltered another serious defect of the monetary system: its lack of elasticity. The currency—a jumble resulting from fortuitous historical conditions—was ill adapted to meet the normal ebb and flow of business needs.[1] There was no way to expand or contract its volume as dull times required more or busy times less. This and other faults had been dramatically projected on the public consciousness by a sharp financial panic in November, 1907.

That event had been preceded by several years of unhealthy speculation, notably in trust development, which had sent many industrial securities soaring far beyond their real value. Though the country's condition was fundamentally sound, confidence suddenly became impaired in the leading financial communities, and for a time business suffered a severe setback. Thirteen banks crashed in New York City alone. To afford relief, pay-roll checks and other substitutes for money were put into circulation, gold was imported from Europe, and the national treasury poured its surplus into banks of deposit. By the middle of January, 1908, normalcy returned. Other than overspeculation, the root of the trouble seemed to be the inability of national banks to enlarge the volume of their currency in a time of money stringency.

---

[1] The amount of greenbacks, treasury notes, and silver certificates was stationary, and the quantity of national bank notes, being based upon ownership of government bonds by the banks, showed little fluctuation. Though the volume of gold varied from time to time, its movements were governed by the demands of international trade and bore no relation to domestic economic needs.

Many business concerns with adequate resources failed because powerless to convert their assets into ready money. An important contributory cause was the fact that each bank had to meet the emergency substantially alone. Although few of the stronger institutions were without ample funds in their vaults, they hesitated to part with their cash for fear of being themselves left in the lurch. The difficulties were increased by the unscrupulous activities of certain big financiers in New York, the nation's money center. The crisis left a trail of indictments and suicides in high financial circles.

Shocked into action by the panic, Congress in 1908 passed the Aldrich-Vreeland law which, as a temporary expedient, made it possible for national banks in times of emergency to issue additional bank notes. These should be guaranteed by the government and be taxed on a graduated scale in order to insure their retirement as soon as the stringency ceased. The act further authorized the creation of a monetary commission to investigate the whole problem of currency and credit and to propose a permanent reformation of the system. In 1912 the commission submitted its report which, among other things, recommended a great central reserve bank, to be owned and controlled by private banking interests. To the Wilson administration, however, this proposal was unacceptable. Nevertheless the Democrats found the commission's investigations of great service in shaping their own solution.

This solution took the form of the federal reserve act, adopted in December, 1913. The law was designed to cure the three glaring flaws which experience had revealed in the system of money and credit: lack of coöperation among banks in crises; the inelasticity of the currency supply; and the concentration of power in the hands of a few financial magnates. Upon the existing banks the act superimposed a new framework. The country was divided into twelve districts or regions with a federal reserve bank in each. These regional institutions were to serve as depositories for the cash reserves of the national banks and of such state banks and trust companies as might join the system. Their primary function, in other words, was to act as a bank for banks.

In order to accomplish the first of the underlying purposes of the law, it was provided that, under strict regulations, the funds thus accumulated might be used to assist individual local banks at times of temporary embarrassment. To achieve the second object, provision was made for the issuance of federal reserve notes to meet business demands. Local banks might deposit with the federal reserve banks approved commercial paper (for example, promissory notes of reliable business concerns), receiving in exchange federal reserve notes for use during the period of need. Finally, to curb the unlimited control hitherto exercised by large private bankers, the delicate and complex machinery of the new banking plan was intrusted to the immediate oversight of the boards of the regional reserve banks and to the general supervision of a Federal Reserve Board, consisting of government representatives.[1]

The new scheme was a landmark in American banking history comparable to Hamilton's financial plan and the national banking system established during the Civil War. Though its passage had been energetically contested by the private banking interests, and though it went into effect under the abnormal conditions caused by the onset of the World War, it quickly demonstrated its utility. By the middle of November, 1914, the extensive financial machinery had

[1] The act discontinued the subtreasury system, a Democratic reform of the forties, by requiring the government to deposit its funds in the federal reserve banks. Provision was also made for the eventual replacement of national bank notes with federal reserve bank notes. The federal reserve banks were located in Boston, New York, Philadelphia, Richmond, Atlanta, Cleveland, Chicago, Minneapolis, St. Louis, Kansas City, Dallas and San Francisco.

been set up, and the system put into operation. The regional banks worked harmoniously with one another; currency demands were promptly met; crop-moving difficulties, notably in the South, were overcome; and progress was made toward unifying the basic banking resources of the nation. After America entered the conflict, the plan gave indispensable aid to the government itself. Without it far greater difficulty would have been experienced in financing the war. Yet, despite the notable forward step, many evils remained in the American banking system, as the Great Depression of 1929 was to disclose.

The next important task of the Democrats was trust regulation. Experience commended a system of control similar to that of the Interstate Commerce Commission over the railways, but it required Wilson's most vigorous efforts to secure appropriate action. The results were embodied in two laws. One, enacted in September, 1914, abolished the Bureau of Corporations, dating from 1903, and transferred its powers of investigating abuses to a new agency, the Federal Trade Commission. In the interests of greater effectiveness, the Commission was empowered to order businesses in interstate trade to cease "unfair methods of competition," and it was authorized to seek aid from the courts in instances of disobedience. The second act, passed in October, forbade many corporate practices that had thus far escaped specific condemnation by federal statute, such as interlocking directorates, the acquisition by one corporation of stock in like enterprises to the extent of substantially lessening competition or creating a monopoly, and the practice of price discriminations with a similar purpose in view.

This latter law, known popularly as the Clayton antitrust act, also extended important safeguards to labor. It exempted from antitrust prosecution all labor and agricultural organizations "lawfully carrying out the legitimate objects thereto."

It proclaimed that strikes, peaceful picketing and boycotting were not violations of any federal law. Finally, it prohibited injunctions in labor disputes growing out of the terms and conditions of employment "unless necessary to prevent irreparable injury to property," and required jury trial for contempt of court, except when the offense was committed in the judge's presence. The last provision harked back to troubles connected with the Pullman strike of 1894 (see page 152).

The public at large greeted the new trust legislation with high satisfaction. In labor circles the elation was unexampled. Decisions of the Supreme Court, however, tended to chip away many of the benefits of the labor clauses, and to rob the unions of immunities which they had believed theirs. In one notable case, that of Duplex Printing Press Company *v.* Deering (1921), the court upheld an injunction issued by a lower court to prevent the membership of a national union from boycotting an employer. The decision was based upon the view that the exemptions of the Clayton act applied only to the employees immediately and directly involved in a controversy, not to members of their union throughout the country who, by order of the national officers, joined in the boycott. Again, in the case of United Mine Workers *v.* Coronado Coal Company (1922), the court held that unions, although unincorporated, were in every other respect like corporations, and hence liable for damages, including triple damages under the Sherman antitrust act.

FILLING IN THE REFORM PROGRAM

The congressional elections of 1914 gave the voters a chance to pass judgment on the President's masterful course. At the same time, they had an opportunity to declare whether, upon sober second thought, they wished to abandon the historic Republican party for the new Progressive party. On both points the outcome was clear. The Progressives revealed startling weaknesses all along the line, polling less than half their strength of 1912. As a result of Republican gains, the Democratic majority in the House fell from a hundred and forty-seven to twenty-nine; but the administration had cause for rejoicing, for it had maintained its control of Congress in what was essentially a two-party contest. It was evident that large numbers of Progressives had gone over to the ranks of the President's followers.

Though foreign affairs, notably the great conflict in Europe, occupied increasing attention during the next two years, the Democrats nevertheless proceeded actively to the task of rounding out their program of economic and social legislation. These measures dealt with varied subjects. In 1915 a seamen's act, sponsored by Senator La Follette, required improvement of the living and working conditions of employees on ocean-going vessels and on lake and river craft. The federal workingmen's compensation act in 1916 authorized a government allowance to civil-service employees during periods of disability. In the same year a rural-credits law was enacted in order to give farmers credit facilities comparable to those extended by the federal reserve system to manufacturers and merchants. Under general administration of a Federal Farm Loan Board, named by the President, agriculturists were enabled to borrow from federal land banks on farm-mortgage security over long periods of time at a lower rate of interest than an ordinary commercial bank would charge.

Congress also attacked the thorny problem of child labor. Though most of the states had laws on the subject, the statutes were often poorly enforced, while in other states the evil flourished unchecked. The progressives of both parties, urged on by Jane Addams and her fellow social workers, called for action by the federal government. The Constitution, however, nowhere explicitly confers this authority on Congress, and for a number of years nothing was done. In 1916 the Democrats resolved to test the issue with the judiciary. Stretching to the utmost its power to regulate interstate commerce, Congress excluded from interstate transportation the products of establishments employing workers under fourteen years. While only about a hundred and fifty thousand children fell directly within the scope of the act, it was hoped that the example would indirectly benefit the two million beyond reach of the national authority. The Supreme Court, however, by a vote of five to four declared the law unconstitutional. In 1919, during Wilson's second administration, Congress tried a different expedient. Acting under its power "to lay and collect taxes," it imposed a ten-per-cent tax on the net profits of companies employing children under the age of fourteen. Again the judicial lightning struck [1] At once a demand developed for a child-labor amendment to the Constitution. By the time this movement came to a head, however, the country was in a far more conservative mood (see page 493).

SELECT BIBLIOGRAPHY

Progressivism at Flood Tide.   Besides the works of Faulkner, Ogg, Dumond and Sullivan cited at the close of the preceding chapter, the student should consult Paxson, *Pre-War Years,* which surveys Wilson's first administration. Among the studies dealing with special phases of governmental policy in the years 1908–1917 are Taussig, *Tariff History;* Knauth, *Policy of the United States toward Industrial Monopoly;* Jones, *Principles of Railway Transportation;* Willis, *Federal Reserve System;* Warburg, *Federal Reserve System;* Henderson, *Federal Trade Commission;* and Frankfurter and Greene, *Labor Injunction.* The biographies include Pringle, *Taft;* Bowers, *Beveridge and the Progressive Era;*

[1] The two cases were Hammer *v.* Dagenhart (1918) and Bailey *v.* Drexel Furniture Company (1922).

Stephenson, *Aldrich;* Bishop, *Roosevelt;* Pringle, *Roosevelt;* and Baker, *Wilson.* Two more recent political studies are Hechler, *Insurgency: Personalities and Politics of the Taft Era,* and Josephson, *President Makers.*

Chapter XIII

SOCIAL AND INTELLECTUAL
FERMENT, 1900–1917

THE MARCH OF LABOR

SOCIETY'S increasing willingness to give legislative protection to wage-earners accorded with the progressive spirit of the age. It also reflected the rapidly growing strength of organized labor. The American Federation of Labor rose from 550,000 members in 1900 to 1,562,000 in 1910 and topped 2,371,000 in 1917, exclusive of unaffiliated bodies such as the powerful Railway Brotherhoods. With the return of industrial prosperity after 1897, the unions demanded a restoration of the wage cuts made during the depression and a betterment of working conditions. More strikes took place in the years 1901–1905 than in the whole preceding decade, with victory usually perching on the side of the men, as in the anthracite-coal strike of 1902 (see page 310). Notwithstanding the opposition of the National Association of Manufacturers and other employers' organizations, wages advanced, and the workday shortened until eight hours prevailed in most skilled occupations. Ten hours continued to be the rule on the railroads, however, and the steel industry remained immune to unions. Progress also occurred in the spread of trade agreements. The acceptance of a joint partnership of labor and capital in fixing conditions of employment afforded heartening evidence of saner relations between the great contending forces.

In 1906 the American Federation of Labor made its first tentative plunge into partisan politics by backing candidates for Congress who were sympathetic with labor. Two years later, as has been seen, it inaugurated the practice of indorsing one of the major-party tickets in the presidential race. True to its earlier attitude, it flinched from launching a special party of its own, nor did it view with friendly eyes the waxing strength of the Socialists. That party increased its popular following from 95,000 in the election of 1900 to 897,000 in 1912.

How effective was the policy of "Reward your friends and punish your enemies" is problematical. The Democratic administration, however, bestirred itself to justify the Federation's support. The appointment of William B. Wilson, a founder of the United Mine Workers, to the new post of Secretary of Labor in 1913 was a first step in that direction. Congress's legislative program afforded even clearer evidence of the administration's attitude. Samuel Gompers, head of the Federation, went so far as to acclaim the Clayton act as "Labor's Magna Charta." In addition to its other activities on behalf of the working class, Congress in the Newlands law of 1913 set up a permanent board of mediation and conciliation to assist in settling railway labor controversies. Though the board lacked compulsory powers, the provision marked a decided advance over the Erdman act of 1898 (see page 155). Already by October, 1916, the new agency had helped to adjust sixty-one disputes.

Yet in March, 1916, when the four great Railway Brotherhoods demanded a basic eight-hour day, they declined to submit the matter to the board's adjudication. Instead, they threatened a country-wide strike unless the rail companies gave them the shorter day at the same pay as for ten hours, with a time-and-a-half rate for overtime. Labor in the saddle was no more disposed to resort to arbitration than employers who held the whip hand. To avert the disaster of a general tie-up of transportation, President Wilson went before Congress on August 29 and asked the immediate enactment of legislation granting ten hours' pay for the first eight hours of work, with a proportionate additional wage for overtime. In defending his unusual course, he declared that "the eight-hour day now undoubtedly has the sanction of the judgment of society in its favor." Within exactly one hundred hours the Adamson law embodying his proposals was passed. He had also urged that the Newlands act be so amended as to make it illegal to call a strike or lockout while a government investigation was pending; but Congress ignored this recommendation. Critics of the administration believed the government's "surrender" to be a precedent fraught with dangerous consequences for the future.

Though organized labor greatly extended its membership and strength, the American Federation ignored the bulk of ill-paid, unskilled, often foreign-speaking toilers in the mills and also the migratory workers in the Great West who followed the harvest and cut the timber. To look after their interests, a new organization, the Industrial Workers of the World, sprang up in 1905 under the leadership of "Big Bill" (William D.) Haywood, a fighter trained in the savage industrial warfare of the Cripple Creek mining district in Colorado. Like the old Knights of Labor, the I. W. W. proposed to unite all workingmen, skilled and unskilled, regardless of trade, in "one big union," but to this program it added two significant features. In the first place, it announced that the struggle must go on until the wage-earners "take possession of the earth and the machinery of production and abolish the wage system. . . . It is the historic mission of the working class to do away with capitalism." In addition, it advocated "direct action" (the general strike, the boycott and sabotage) as the way to victory.[1]

The I. W. W. was a catch-all for socialists, anarchists, op-

[1] Sabotage may be peaceable, such as loafing on the job, or it may involve violent methods like destroying property.

portunists, idealists and malcontents of many varieties. Probably at no time did the "Wobblies" exceed sixty thousand; but for nearly ten years they kept the Pacific Northwest in a state of turmoil, and in 1912 and 1913 they reached eastward to conduct desperate strikes among the sweated textile workers in Lawrence, Massachusetts, Paterson, New Jersey, and Little Falls, New York. Only the Lawrence effort proved victorious. Their violence frightened a public used to the more orderly methods of the old-line unions, and in some instances provoked communities to lawless or extralegal reprisals to rid themselves of the disturbing element. In 1917 the opposition of the I. W. W. to America's entry into the European war arrayed the government against it and hastened its collapse. Yet its brief and stormy career called attention to a grave failure of the older labor movement, and caused the American Federation to pay somewhat greater attention to unskilled and unorganized wage-earners.

DIFFICULTIES OF THE MELTING POT

The radical fringe of the labor movement consisted largely of workingmen of foreign birth. The American Federation's demand for raising higher bars against immigration rested less on this fact, however, than on the effect of the incoming horde in providing employers with cheap labor and holding down the standard of living. From 1900 to 1917 a total of nearly fourteen and a third million migrated to the United States. President Roosevelt, informing Congress in 1905 that over a million had arrived in twelve months, added: "In other words, in the single year that has just elapsed there came to this country a greater number of people than came here during the one hundred and sixty-nine years of our Colonial life which intervened between the first landing at Jamestown and the Declaration of Independence." Though so high an annual figure had never before been reached, it was exceeded on five later occasions during this period. The years 1915–1917 sharply reduced the inflow, however, because of the European war.

In considerable part, the huge influx was due to the arrivals from Southern and Eastern Europe. What had earlier been a trickle now became a flood. "Into the lower levels of the American community," wrote the Englishman H. G. Wells in *The Future in America* (1906), "there pours perpetually a vast torrent of strangers, speaking alien tongues, inspired by alien traditions, for the most part illiterate peasants and working-people." The number from Southern and Eastern Europe trebled from 1900 to 1914. Of the 1,218,500 immigrants in the latter year they furnished 921,000.

All the earlier fears as to the nation's power to digest them deepened, while organized labor became clamorous on the subject of unfair competition. In these circumstances the device of a literacy test, which Cleveland had blocked in 1897 (see page 254), revived in favor. Since the great bulk of the Southern and Eastern Europeans were uneducated, the requirement of a reading knowledge of English or some other language would separate them from the older type of immigrant. But when Congress sought to impose this test in 1913, President Taft rejected the bill, and two years later Wilson did likewise. Illiteracy, they asserted, implied not absence of natural capacity, but lack of youthful opportunity. In 1917, however, shortly before America entered the war, Congress passed the measure over Wilson's objections.

Meanwhile, the question of Oriental immigration had arisen in a fresh form. Though an effective curb had already been put upon Chinese arrivals, growing numbers of Japanese appeared in the early years of the century on the Pacific Coast. Thrifty, hard-working, inured to a bare subsistence, they began to displace white workers, notably in truck gardening. Talk soon became rife of a new "yellow peril," organized labor demanded Japanese exclusion, and the people of California gave hearty support. Yet California's fears looked to the future rather than to the present, for in 1910 the newcomers numbered only two per cent of its population. It was also true that a federal statute had long barred Japanese and other Asiatics from naturalization, though, of course, their American-born offspring acquired citizenship under the Fourteenth Amendment.

In 1906 the antagonism flared up in an order of the San Francisco board of education to restrict Japanese children to a separate building, this despite the fact that there were but ninety-three in the schools out of a total of twenty-five thousand pupils. The home government promptly protested the action as a violation of its treaty with the United States. Though the authorities in Washington had no jurisdiction whatsoever over school affairs in San Francisco, President Roosevelt induced the board to withdraw its decree and took steps to bring about an understanding between the two countries in regard to the larger issue. The upshot was the "Gentlemen's Agreement" in 1907 by which Japan engaged to take its own measures to prevent the future emigration of laborers to the United States.

Anti-Japanese feeling in California persisted, however, and in 1913 led the legislature, over President Wilson's protest, to adopt the Webb act, which forbade aliens ineligible to citizenship to own agricultural land in the state. The Japanese, however, found means of evasion by taking out the title in the name of their American-born children, or by leasing rather than buying the land. To plug up these and similar holes, the Asiatic land law, passed by California in 1920, expressly forbade such practices. Tokyo continued to remonstrate, but the American government, insisting that no actual treaty rights were denied, proposed to leave the question to the Supreme Court. In 1923 the court affirmed the constitutionality of the Webb act and of a similar statute of the state of Washington. In the following year, as we shall see, Congress gave statutory backing to the Gentlemen's Agreement by excluding all immigration from Japan. This needless offense to Japan's dignity became a disturbing factor in the future relations of the two powers.

THE ADVANCE OF SOCIAL REFORM

Meanwhile, in the urban centers, the pioneer work of the humanitarians in the 1880's and 1890's bore fruit in wide-flung efforts to relieve poverty and distress. The conservation of human resources, no less than of natural resources, became a watchword of the age, one ably sustained by the fast-growing profession of welfare workers. Charity-organization societies and social settlements multiplied, spreading to many of the smaller cities and extending westward and southward until the whole nation was covered. At the same time, the slum evil was attacked with fresh zeal. Prompted by the fact that no city in the world housed its poor as wretchedly as New York, the legislature in 1901 enacted a tenement-house code for the state which was, in most respects, a model of its kind. Unfortunately, however, the statute did not require slum clearance and thus left for continued occupancy in New York City sixty-four thousand of the filthy "old-law" tenements. Nevertheless, the legislation substantially improved conditions in all the larger centers of the state, and inspired Pennsylvania, New Jersey, Connecticut and other commonwealths, as well as many cities, to establish similar regulations. In 1916 New York City again proved a pacemaker by adopting zoning requirements in order "to prevent unwholesome and dangerous congestion both in living conditions and in street and transit traffic and to reduce the hazards of fire and peril to life."

All such measures, directly or indirectly, betrayed a renewed concern for children's rights. Further evidence appeared in municipal ordinances safeguarding the quality of the milk supply, in the setting up of separate courts for juvenile delinquents, and in the multiplication of community playgrounds. Rochester led the way in providing milk stations, and Milwaukee and Buffalo in establishing juvenile courts. The playground movement gathered such momentum that by 1910 a hundred and fifty cities had taken action. Only five years later the total had risen to well over four hundred and the number of playgrounds to nearly thirty-three hundred. By providing outlets for children's energies it was hoped, on the one hand, to promote their health and pleasure and, on the other, to lessen juvenile tendencies to crime. The introduction of the Boy Scouts from England in 1910 and the establishment two years later of the Girl Scouts and the Campfire Girls represented yet other efforts to turn the gang spirit natural to youth into constructive channels.

New gains also came to the temperance movement. The widening reach of the social settlements and the increase of urban recreational facilities steadily undermined the saloon as the "poor man's club"; and the pecuniary advantage of sober employees was driven home to industrialists by the spread of workingmen's compensation laws (see page 305). Though nearly every religious denomination had its temperance committee or teetotal society, the brunt of the attack was borne by the W. C. T. U., the Temperance Society of the Methodist Church and a relatively new and markedly militant body, the Anti-Saloon League. These groups left little undone to arouse public opinion against the liquor traffic and to agitate for restrictive measures.

As the century opened, only Kansas, North Dakota, Maine, New Hampshire and Vermont possessed state-wide prohibition, and the last two reverted to local option in 1903. In other directions, however, the increase of dry territory was startling. For the first time, the South, spurred by the desire to keep strong drink from the Negroes, took state-wide action; between 1907 and 1915 eight Southern commonwealths adopted prohibitory legislation. In 1915 and 1916 the movement swung into the Great West, scoring victories in Arizona, Oregon, Washington, Colorado and Idaho. Meanwhile Iowa joined the state-wide group, and local option had largely dried up other rural parts of America. Nearly everywhere, however, there were serious difficulties of enforcement; and in 1913 the temperance forces induced Congress to pass the Webb-Kenyon law to protect dry areas from liquor shipments from outside the state. The larger cities stubbornly resisted the trend. In order to bring them to heel, the prohibitionists determined to secure a federal constitutional amendment. As will be seen, the unusual conditions created by America's entrance into the war gave them their opportunity.

At all points, the quest for community betterment received support from persons affiliated with churches and, to an increasing extent, from the churches themselves. Building on the social gospel of the 1880's and 1890's, organized religion showed an ever greater disposition to further the progressive ideals in city, state and nation. During the first decade and a half of the century most of the great Protestant denominations set up social-service commissions and issued declarations of social purpose. Institutional churches broadened their scope and grew in number; ministers' conferences sent fraternal delegates to city trade assemblies; congregations established helpful relations with various types of welfare agencies. Not all religious groups advanced with equal pace, but few failed to devote greater attention to the social teachings of Jesus.

In 1908 the Federal Council of Churches, which had been formed by thirty-three evangelical sects to bring about closer coöperation with particular reference to applied Christianity, adopted a social creed which, in a sense, anticipated and outstripped the Progressive platform of 1912. It declared labor's right to organize, advocated a living wage, shorter hours, a six-day week and old-age insurance, denounced child labor and the sweating system and, in general, demanded "the application of Christian principles to the acquisition and use of property" as well as "the most equitable division of the product of industry that can ultimately be devised." The Federal Council's function, however, was not so much to accomplish results itself as to stimulate other religious bodies to greater activity and to correlate their efforts. To that end it diligently fostered the formation of state and local interchurch federations. Meanwhile the Catholic Church, strong in organization, alert to its opportunities, enlarged its welfare activities and employed its energies to conserve the gains that accrued from the mounting immigration from the Catholic countries of Europe.

The problem of rural communities also commanded increasing attention from religious leaders. Drained of much of their best blood by the exodus to the cities, such places were apt to be overstocked with Protestant churches whose listless spiritual life was galvanized occasionally by temporary revivals. Improvement began to appear, however, as the people forgot ancient doctrinal differences and joined in federated or union churches. Theological seminaries coöperated by providing special courses for the training of country ministers. As a result, better men were attracted into the service and rural religion took on new vitality.

LITERARY CURRENTS

In the newspapers and magazines the mass of the people found their mirror of the times. If the mirror sometimes seemed to give off a distorted reflection, it was due to the zeal of particular editors in joining hands with the Muck-rakers and the progressives in trying to make America a better place to live. Though the number of dailies rose only from 2190 to 2410 between 1900 and 1917, their circulation doubled. The business of coöperative news gathering grew in comprehensiveness and efficiency as rivals of the Associated Press appeared in the International News Service (1906) and the United Press (1907), the former sired by William Randolph Hearst. The tendency toward standardizing news presentation was further strengthened as a result of the formation of newspaper chains under a single control, an application to the journalistic field of a well-recognized principle in the business world. The Scripps-McRae (later Scripps-Howard) League, founded in 1895 with four dailies in the Midwest, had by 1910 acquired twenty-two papers in many parts of the land. By the latter date thirteen chains were active, with the number rapidly increasing.

As prodders of the public conscience, however, the low-priced magazines surpassed the newspapers. Never before had they been so widely or so attentively read. While Thomas W. Lawson's "Frenzied Finance" was running in *Everybody's,* the circulation leaped in a year from a hundred and fifty thousand to more than seven hundred and fifty. Such periodicals proved a training ground for some of the ablest writers of the period. For example, *McClure's* at various times commanded the services of Lincoln Steffens, Jack London, Theodore Dreiser, Ida M. Tarbell, Ray Stannard Baker and William Sydney Porter ("O. Henry"). Of the weeklies, the *Nation* after a temporary eclipse resumed its rôle as fearless critic, and in 1914 it was joined by the *New Republic,* founded by Herbert Croly and a group of progressive-minded associates. Yet the dinosaur among the weekly periodicals was of a different ilk, being less concerned with voicing social and economic criticism than with expressing the traditional ideals of the comfortable middle class. This was the *Saturday Evening Post,* for which Cyrus H. K. Curtis had paid a thousand dollars in 1897, and which within a decade mustered nearly a million weekly buyers. Through its stories and articles, and even its advertising columns, the *Post* appealed to such familiar middle-class traits as optimism, nationalistic feeling, the gospel of hustle, and glorification of material success. Some of the best fiction of the time appeared in its pages.

The restless spirit of the generation pervaded much of the literature that these years begot. Under the spell of the Spanish-American War there was a temporary flurry of interest in historical novels, and books like Paul Leicester Ford's *Janice Meredith* (1899), Mary Johnston's *To Have and To Hold* (1900), Winston Churchill's *The Crisis* (1901) and Owen Wister's *The Virginian* (1902) enjoyed an enormous vogue. As the rumblings of insurgency became louder, however, makers of fiction tended to desert the glamorous past for the grim present. Frank Norris in *The Octopus* (1901) pictured the struggle between the farmers and the rail magnates. The socialist Jack London, after writing adventure stories about the Arctic North, heralded an impending social revolution in *The War of the Classes* (1905) and *The Iron Heel* (1907). David Graham Phillips added *The Plum Tree* (1905), *Light-Fingered Gentry* (1907) and a host of other novels exposing the flaws and injustices of a money-mad society, and Theodore Dreiser portrayed the rise of an unscrupulous capitalist in *The Financier* (1912) and *The Titan* (1914). Churchill contributed *Coniston* (1906), a tale of the railroads in politics, while Upton Sinclair and many other writers brewed a similar mixture of love interest and social propaganda.

Though these offerings accurately represented the dominant social mood of the age, many readers sought relief in milder, or at least different, fare. Thus O. Henry's scintillating short stories of metropolitan life enjoyed a numerous following. But even his writings were not awarded the popular crown of a million or more sales. This distinction fell to Edward N. Westcott's *David Harum* (1900), Owen Wister's *The Virginian* (1902), Kate Douglas Wiggins's *Rebecca of Sunnybrook Farm* (1903), Jack London's *The Call of the Wild* (1903), John Fox's *The Little Shepherd of Kingdom Come* (1903), Harold Bell Wright's *The Winning of Barbara Worth* (1911), and Eleanor H. Porter's *Pollyanna* (1913) as well as to four novels by Gene Stratton Porter. Not many of these volumes, however, survived their temporary acclaim.

The legitimate drama went through somewhat the same cycle as fiction. Content at first with stage versions of successful historical novels and with the society plays of Clyde Fitch, Augustus Thomas and others, the public soon gave an enthusiastic patronage to shows that dealt trenchantly with contemporary problems. Among the more popular offerings were Charles Klein's "The Lion and the Mouse" (1906), inspired by Ida M. Tarbell's *History of the Standard Oil Company;* Charles Rann Kennedy's "The Servant in the House" (1908), which revealed how far the practice of Christianity might fall short of the theory; Charles Kenyon's "Kindling" (1911), a play depicting slum life; and Edward Sheldon's "The Boss" (1911), which dealt with the struggle between capital and labor. Players like Mrs. Minnie Maddern Fiske, John Drew, Richard Mansfield, Otis Skinner, Julia Marlowe and E. H. Sothern did much to sustain the high standards of acting inherited from the previous generation.

NEW IMPULSES IN EDUCATION AND THE ARTS

Meanwhile, the schools quietly carried on their work of banishing illiteracy and handing on the torch of knowledge. The task became ever greater as throngs of immigrant children stormed the doors; but public and private funds streamed into the educational system in unprecedented volume, and physical equipment and the quality of teaching reached a new high-water mark. The total expenditures rose over three times between 1900 and 1917 while the total enrollment grew from 15,500,000 to around 20,500,00, embracing a larger proportion of American youth than ever before.

Though the cities continued to set the pace, notable progress was made toward improving educational facilities in the country districts. Aided by the good-roads movement and the introduction of the motor bus, rural inhabitants began to abandon their scattered "little red schoolhouses" with their ungraded methods, and to pool their resources in a centrally located "consolidated" school, where better instruction, modern equipment and separate grades were provided. Especially striking was the advance in the South. Throughout the section compulsory-attendance laws were now enacted, public appropriations were greatly enlarged, and high schools were added to round out the system. The Negro schools, however, continued to be inferior to those for the whites. Despite the impressive gains nearly everywhere manifest in the nation, the total schooling which the average person received in his entire lifetime increased only from about five years in 1900 to six and a half in 1916. Much remained for the future to accomplish.

Sensitive to the democratic strivings of the day, outstanding educational leaders emphasized the function of the school in preparing young America for an intelligent part in a civilization growing ever more complex and dynamic. Professor John Dewey, the most outspoken critic of the older pedagogy, maintained that social utility, not mere knowledge, should be the goal of education. In such works as *The School and Society* (1899) and *Democracy and Education* (1916), he taught that "the primary business of the school is to train children in coöperative and mutually helpful living," and that the school should "reproduce on the child's level the typical doings and occupations of the larger, maturer society into which he is finally to go forth." In tune with his ideas, a committee of the National Education Association declared in 1918 that education should aim to "develop in each individual the knowledge, interests, ideals, habits, and powers whereby he will find his place and use that place to shape both himself and society toward ever nobler ideals." Dewey's conceptions served gradually to modify educational purposes and procedures not only in the United States, but in many other countries as well.

Though the public schools increasingly stressed preparation for life above preparation for college, university enrollments advanced by leaps and bounds. The chief divergence from earlier educational practice came in the development of the junior college, limited to the Freshman and Sophomore years. First successfully launched with public funds in 1902 at Joliet, Illinois, the innovation spread rapidly through the Middle and Far West. Sometimes the two years would be added to the regular school system; sometimes colleges with insufficient funds would eliminate the Junior and Senior years; sometimes junior colleges would be created independently. Whatever the procedure, the new institution usually afforded opportunity for advanced study nearer home, and also supplied a shorter unit of training for those who could not complete the full college course.

The din of the economic conflict echoed in academic halls, heightening the interest of undergraduates in the social sciences, and causing professors to play an increasing rôle as consultants on social and economic reforms in city, state and nation. "Fighting Bob" La Follette of Wisconsin worked closely with members of the state university faculty, and derived from them expert advice and constant encouragement in his labors for progressive principles. The universities steadily drifted more closely toward the main currents of American life. The nation did not hesitate to make Woodrow Wilson, a former college president, its chief magistrate, nor had it been surprised when his predecessor retired from the White House to a chair of law at Yale.

Even scholarly work showed the impress of the times. Roscoe Pound of the Harvard Law School taught the doctrine of "sociological jurisprudence" in an effort to gear legal principles to the current needs of society. Thorstein Veblen of Chicago, Leland Stanford and Missouri subjected orthodox economies to the razor of his intelligence, and exposed the antisocial effects of the profit system, absentee ownership and predatory business. In like fashion, Charles A. Beard injected a fresh realism into the study of history and political science, applying the economic interpretation to even so sacrosanct a subject as the making of the Constitution. His colleague at Columbia University, James Harvey Robinson, added to the illumination by calling for a "new history," a scrutiny of the past which should go beyond the traditional bounds of politics and diplomacy and embrace all of mankind's varied interests. Contributions of this character helped to give point and direction to a mass of scholarly production exceeding anything the nation had before known.

In a quite different way, science played an ever larger part in the daily life of society. Chemists manifested their wizardry by creating many new articles and by showing how familiar natural products might be concocted through artificial means. Coal tar, for example, was turned into commodities ranging all the way from coloring matter for cake frosting to high explosives. They also discovered a world of new knowledge in regard to food constituents, thereby causing the public to give greater attention to vitamins as an element of diet, and arming medical scientists for a fresh attack on scurvy, rickets and similar ills attributed to improper food.

Equally important advances were made in other phases of the healing art. Aside from American enterprise in ascertaining the transmitting source of yellow fever (see page 281), Dr. Howard T. Ricketts of the University of Chicago found that Rocky Mountain fever was a tick disease and, with Russell M. Wilder's collaboration, proved that typhus was carried by body lice. American ownership of Puerto Rico prompted a scientific inquiry under Major Bailey K. Ashford into the cause of anæmia, which held ninety per cent of the islanders in its grip. The discovery that a tiny intestinal parasite called the hookworm was responsible led to Dr. Charles W. Stiles's identification of the species as one which was also prevalent in the rural South, where its ravages helped to explain the backwardness of the poor-white class. Financed by John D. Rockefeller, a campaign was begun in 1908 to stamp out the malady. After nineteen years the International Health Board was able to report, "At the present time it is fair to say that hookworm disease has almost disappeared from the United States, and is rapidly coming under control in many parts of the world."

In these and like instances, new knowledge of the causation of disease equipped medical scientists with ampler means of prevention, control and cure, and greatly strengthened the effectiveness of the public-health agencies that had been growing up since the Civil War. Between 1900 and 1920 the expectation of life at birth increased from forty-eight years to a little over fifty-six. Decline in the death rate was particularly notable in such maladies as typhoid, diphtheria, croup, tuberculosis and scarlet fever. The enlarging American contribution to world science thrice won signal recognition during these years when the Nobel Prize was awarded in 1907 to the physicist, Professor Albert A. Michelson of the University of Chicago; in 1912 to the surgeon, Dr. Alexis Carrel of the Rockefeller Institute for Medical Research; and in 1914 to Professor Thomas W. Richards of Harvard for distinguished work in chemistry.

Progress in the fine arts stemmed from the beginnings made in the eighties and nineties. Many of the master figures of the earlier era now reached the full bloom of their powers, while younger men introduced fresh vigor and originality. In painting the bent toward realism, prefigured by the marine scenes of Winslow Homer, found a bolder expression in the work of Robert Henri, William J. Glackens, George W. Bellows and George Luks. In a special sense, Joseph Pennell's etchings of skyscrapers, the great locks of the Panama Canal and other miracles of the new technology tingled with the life of the age. The masses, however, derived their knowledge of art mainly from the popular magazines, in which illustrators like Charles Dana Gibson and Howard Chandler Christy portrayed idealized types of American girls and men which excited untold thousands in real life to eager imitation.

Meanwhile, the parks and public squares of the cities became studded with statuary fashioned by sculptors whose work ranked with the best of contemporary Europe. These compositions usually commemorated warriors and statesmen, but, more and more, themes typifying a broader national achievement crept in. Solon H. Borglum, drawing on his youthful experiences as a rancher, executed such works as "Burial on the Plains" and "The Blizzard." Among other notable productions were George Grey Barnard's "Hewer" (1902) at Cairo, Illinois; Charles H. Niehaus's "The Driller" (1902), erected by the Standard Oil Company at Titusville, Pennsylvania; and Lorado Taft's grand plan of sculptured decoration for Chicago, beginning with "The Spirit of the Lakes" (1913).

Like painting and sculpture, architecture derived its inspiration from what had gone before. It expressed itself most strikingly in impressive urban edifices: great apartment houses, which multiplied in number to accommodate the increasing army of "cliff dwellers"; monumental passenger terminals, such as the Union Station (1907) in Washington, the Pennsylvania Station (1910) in New York and the Kansas City Union Station (1914); and steel-framed office buildings which dwarfed the skyscrapers of the 1890's. The Singer and Woolworth buildings in New York, completed in 1908 and 1913, and soaring respectively forty-one and fifty-one stories, revealed possibilities of the majestic beauty which the future would further unfold. A new note was also struck in domestic architecture, notably by Louis Sullivan's pupil Frank Lloyd Wright who, scorning mere decorative convention, endeavored to develop the natural qualities of the materials and to set his structure in "the embrace of rock and tree and shrub."

For better or for worse, the traditional local types of architecture tended to fade rapidly away before the styles popularized by the cities. A hotel or schoolhouse or bank in Atlanta might just as well have been in Philadelphia or Minneapolis so far as externals went. Even in domestic architecture the contagious spread of the New England Georgian style and the Midwestern bungalow to all parts of America served to make residential and suburban districts everywhere look more or less alike. Yet, whatever its drawbacks, it is well to remember that the standardization of architecture usually meant better architectural standards.

CHANGING CONDITIONS OF LIVING AND LEISURE

Notwithstanding the advancing cost of living, the mass of the people, particularly in the cities, enjoyed numerous advantages and opportunities unknown to earlier generations. This was due in part to a host of mechanical inventions affecting many of the relations of life. It was due, further, to collectivist enterprises which taxpayers supported on an ever increasing scale, such as schools, parks, playgrounds, sewerage, public-health measures and good roads. Governmental undertakings of this character helped to diffuse more widely the gains of the rapid production of wealth. Equally striking was the voluntary diversion of a part of the huge private fortunes to broad social purposes, usually through the setting up of "foundations," managed by self-perpetuating boards of trustees, and staffed by experts charged with the responsibility of advising how the funds should be spent.

Between 1902 and 1911 Andrew Carnegie created five such bodies: the Carnegie Institution of Washington, designed to encourage "research and discovery, and the application of knowledge to the improvement of mankind"; the Carnegie Hero Fund Commission; the Carnegie Foundation for the Advancement of Teaching; the Carnegie Endowment for International Peace; and the Carnegie Corporation, whose assets of $125,000,000 should be devoted to causes which the trustees might deem most significant. Rockefeller's benefactions, amounting to $400,000,000 by 1921, went into four great foundations: the Rockefeller Institute for Medical Research (1901); the General Education Board (1903); the Rockefeller Foundation (1913), established "to promote the well-being of mankind throughout the world"; and the Laura Spelman Rockefeller Memorial Foundation (1918), similarly created for the advancement of human welfare. In addition, many lesser foundations made their appearance to give lift and drive to humanitarian enterprises, cultural development and scientific research. By 1920 there were over a hundred of these agencies, and by 1931 more than three hundred and fifty. Critics did not fail to flay an economic system that allowed the few to amass stupendous wealth and then dole it back to the many in the form of charity; but the fact remained that such private accumulations increasingly found their way into the channels of general usefulness.

More directly, the comfort of daily life was influenced by countless labor-saving gadgets that relieved housework of much of its drudgery and added to the pleasure of living. Many of these resulted from the application of electricity to the traditional tasks of the housewife. Applied science also invaded the field of amusement, scoring its greatest triumph during these years in the motion picture. Crude animated films had been projected on screens in the United States as early as the mid-nineties, but not till 1905, when Edison set up the first studio for indoor production, did they begin to attain a satisfactory standard of mechanical perfection.

To an even greater extent the movie's artistic development rested on the resourcefulness of David W. Griffith who in filming "The Birth of a Nation" (1915) went far toward freeing the screen from the restrictive methods of the stage. Griffith was the first director to move his cameras about, obtaining close-ups, distant views, fade-outs and angle shots, and he also introduced the device of the flashback. Where he led a host of others followed. Though the film was not yet wedded to the phonograph and the performances were all in pantomime, the movie quickly established itself as a major form of entertainment, reaching multitudes who seldom, if ever, attended the regular theater. Such performers as Charlie Chaplin and Mary Pickford ("America's Sweetheart") commanded a devoted following not only in the United States but in other countries as well.

The stage, however, showed as yet no signs of suffering from the competition. Particularly popular were the musical comedies, not delightfully satirical operas of the Gilbert and Sullivan type, but usually hodgepodges compounded of expensive scenery, an aimless plot, vaudeville stunts, a few high-paid principals and a large prancing chorus. A brilliant exception to the rule was the work of Victor Herbert, who provided the musical setting for such successful offerings as "Babes in Toyland" (1903), "The Red Mill" (1906) and "Naughty Marietta" (1910). Abetted by the ubiquitous phonograph, a kind of syncopated melody called ragtime laid its spell upon the masses, symbolizing as it did the increasing tempo and nervousness of American life. At the same time the more serious forms of music commanded a growing patronage. This interest, which came in part from the activities of the National Federation of Musical Clubs formed in 1898, fostered the organization of symphony orchestras, hitherto restricted to a few leading centers, in cities as far removed as Minneapolis, New Orleans and Seattle.

Meanwhile, outdoor recreation attained new proportions. The trend toward the professionalization of sports grew continually stronger, attracting tremendous crowds who were content to take their exercise visually instead of muscularly. In a similar fashion, college athletics, notably football, became so hedged about with highly paid coaches and so dominated by gate receipts as to render it more of a business than a pleasure, even for the participants. Signs of a reaction appeared in the increasing popularity of golf. Hitherto it had been a fad of the wealthy few. As late as the fall of 1908 President Roosevelt warned Taft, then making his first bid for the White House, against the aristocratic implications of the latter's addiction to the game: "I have received literally hundreds of letters from the West protesting about it." But in the older parts of the country golf was already becoming a sport for the multitude as inexpensive courses were laid out and even municipalities provided facilities for their citizens.

The chief transforming influence in the open-air life of the people, however, was a new mechanical marvel, the self-propelling motor vehicle. As far back as 1893 ingenious young mechanics—Charles E. Duryea at Chicopee, Massachusetts, Henry Ford in Detroit, Ransom E. Olds in Lansing—had devised crude gasoline-driven cars, but European inventors had anticipated them and, for over a decade, the French and English produced more and better cars than did Americans. As American manufacturers made progress in standardizing the processes, however, and resorted increasingly to mass production, the price fell until it was within reach of the average purse, and the automobile swung into a tremendous popularity. The number in use rose from 300 in 1895 to 78,000 in 1905 and to 3,513,000 in 1916. The motor car ceased being a luxury of the rich—of the "automobility," as a wag put it—and became a part of the normal equipment of American life.

The social effects were incalculable. Not only did the auto restore the forgotten delights of the open country to growing numbers of urban dwellers, not only did it help break down provincial barriers and mitigate rural isolation, but it begot a whole new brood of industries, providing employment for millions. It also speeded the good-roads movement, accelerated the growth of suburbs and, in countless ways, heightened the momentum of American civilization. The widespread introduction of the self-starting device in 1913 and 1914 insured that the future would see women rival men as drivers.

Even more spectacular was the progress in navigating the heavens. Long an aspiration of mankind, and vainly attempted by numberless inventors, flying in heavier-than-air machines was made practicable through the ingenuity of Orville and Wilbur Wright, two bicycle mechanics in Dayton, Ohio.[1] Familiar with what other experimenters had

---

[1] Samuel P. Langley, secretary of the Smithsonian Institution in Washington, had devised a small steam-propelled model that flew 3000 feet in 1896, but his later experiments with a man-carrying, gasoline-driven craft in 1903 proved unsuccessful because of difficulties in launching it.

done, and undaunted by a series of failures, they succeeded in contriving a gasoline-driven airplane which on December 17, 1903, remained aloft for a trial flight of eight hundred and fifty-two feet at Kitty Hawk, North Carolina. The secret of the eagle was now within grasp. In the years that followed, they and other inventors, notably in France, introduced changes and greatly improved the mechanism of flying; but aviation required the furnace heat of war to bring about its most notable development. Few people failed to appreciate the revolutionary import of the dramatic shortening of distances when the ninety-three-year-old Ezra Meeker, who had taken six months to cover the Oregon Trail to Washington by ox team in 1852, winged the distance in 1924 in twenty-four hours.

The multiplied uses of electricity—its increasing application to the work of home and factory, to lighting, heating, traction and communication—brought about a tremendous development of the sources of electric energy. The generating capacity of power companies grew nearly sixfold from 1902 to 1914; the number of customers from less than six hundred thousand to more than five million. Particularly noteworthy was the rapid spread of hydroelectric plants until one or more were to be found in every state. Water-power sites assumed an enormous importance, and were acquired by private corporations usually without adequate safeguards to assure good service and cheap rates for the public. As in other branches of industry, the desire for economical operation and the hope of bigger profits led to a consolidation of ownership and to the weaving of a network of transmitting cables over great areas. An ampler public regulation of power companies was one of the problems which this generation, hardly appreciating its importance, bequeathed to its successors.

Into every phase of life, power and the machine extended

their sway. Historically, Americans had always displayed mechanical ingenuity and a flair for tinkering; the twentieth century with its flowering of technology seemed the culmination of a long-cherished dream. The environment of the people became to a surprising degree made up of machines, much as the environment of wild animals is composed of fauna, flora and climate. No one could doubt the beneficial effects. Machinery freed mankind from an immeasurable amount of back-breaking toil. It pointed the way to shorter working hours without loss of productive capacity. It turned out more and cheaper goods. It conferred a degree of material comfort such as no nation had ever enjoyed. It widened horizons, created new pleasures for the many, enlarged the range of activity, and added color and variety to everyday life. Moreover, through curtailing distances, it linked all parts of the land in closer comradeship and forged stronger bonds of nationality.

As the century advanced, however, thoughtful persons began to ask whether these gains did not come at too high a price, in other words, whether man's servant was not usurping the rôle of master. The deadly monotony of machine tending in the mill, the tremendous speeding up of industry, the displacement of faithful workers by the introduction of machines, the wastage of natural resources through mass processes, the loss of individual craftsmanship in the making of standardized commodities, the growing dependence of people upon mechanical appliances for utilizing their leisure instead of relying upon their inner resources—all these bulked large on the debit side of the ledger. Yet no bold voice cried out for a return to a machineless age. The fault indeed lay not in machinery, but in man's attitude toward it. Sooner or later, if he would achieve a more wholesome life, he must learn how to conserve the benefits of his extraordinary mastery over Nature and to combat its evils.

SELECT BIBLIOGRAPHY

The March of Labor. Faulkner, *Quest for Social Justice,* is the best general treatment of this and the other topics in the chapter. Commons and others, *History of Labor,* III-IV, offers a detailed survey of the labor movement, while Perlman, *History of Trade Unionism,* and Harris, *American Labor,* include brief accounts. Wolman, *Growth of American Trade Unions,* is also helpful. Two contrasting labor organizations are described and interpreted in Lorwin, *American Federation of Labor,* and Brissenden, *I. W. W.*

Difficulties of the Melting Pot. Wittke, *We Who Built America,* and Garis, *Immigration Restriction,* present a general picture. Jenks and Lauck, *Immigration Problem,* is particularly valuable as a summary of the *Report* of the federal Immigration Commission in 1911. For the new Oriental influx, see Buell, *Japanese Immigration,* and Bailey, *Theodore Roosevelt and the Japanese-American Crises.*

The Advance of Social Reform. Watson, *Charity Organization Movement,* Woods and Kennedy, *Settlement Horizon,* and Rainwater, *Play Movement,* sketch leading phases of welfare work. Ford and others, *Slums and Housing,* deals principally with New York City. Cherrington, *Evolution of Prohibition,* should be supplemented by Odegard, *Pressure Politics,* and Steuart, *Wayne Wheeler, Dry Boss.* Main trends in religion are set forth in Rowe, *History of Religion;* Garrison, *March of Faith;* Smith, ed., *Religious Thought;* and Macfarland, *Progress of Church Federation.*

Intellectual and Cultural Life. For journalism, literature, the drama, education and creative achievement in science and the arts, many of the references cited at the close of Chapter VII are useful. In addition, attention is called to Pattee, *New American Literature;* Van Dorens, *American and British Literature since 1890;* Lee, *Daily Newspaper in America;* Meyer, *Development of Education;* Dorfman, *Veblen and His America;* Barnes, *New History and the Social Sciences;* Slosson, *Creative Chemistry;* Stieglitz, *Chemistry and Recent Progress in Medicine;* and Starrett, *Skyscrapers.*

Changing Conditions of Living and Leisure. Kaempffert, ed., *Popular History of American Invention,* discusses many of the new inventions. Particular ones are treated in Lubschez, *Story of the Motion Picture;* Epstein, *Automobile Industry;* Barber, *Story of the Automobile;* and Lougheed, *Vehicles of the Air.* For music, the theater and popular recreation, consult the references listed at the end of Chapter VII. Cohen, *Good Old Days,* portrays the period as seen through the pages of the Sears, Roebuck catalogues.

Chapter XIV

FORGING A COLONIAL EMPIRE,
1900–1917

ADAPTING THE CONSTITUTION TO AN IMPERIAL SYSTEM

THE political and social ferment of the early twentieth century caused many states to change their basic laws for the purpose of incorporating the new devices of government. Some commonwealths accomplished this by framing new constitutions; others attained the same result by the amending process. For example, Ohio in 1911 modernized its political system through the adoption of thirty-three amendments. The admission of three new states, all in the West, afforded opportunity for further progress along these lines. When Oklahoma (including within her borders Indian Territory) entered the Union in 1907, she frankly ranged herself on the side of progressive principles. Her constitution embraced virtually all the democratic reforms of the day.

Five years later the forty-seventh and forty-eighth states achieved the coveted goal. New Mexico territory, as created in the stormy days of the Compromise of 1850, had been subdivided into Arizona and New Mexico in 1863 at the time of the discovery of precious minerals. The population of the twin territories remained small, though a new era opened toward the close of the century with the progress of irrigation and of large-scale mining. As in the case of Oklahoma, their constitutions reflected the new political ideals, and the Arizona instrument went so far as to include a provision for the popular recall of judges. Congress, upon President Taft's recommendation, declined to complete the act of admission in the latter instance until this innovation should be removed. Arizona acceded, but only to restore it as soon as full statehood was achieved. The admission of New Mexico and Arizona completed, for the time at least, the process of state building and federal integration that had started with the natal days of the republic.

For a number of years, however, the United States—"in a fit of absent-mindedness," as Seeley once said of Great Britain —had been acquiring colonial holdings in distant parts of the globe. These lands contained peoples of diverse races and religions at every stage of cultural and political progress; their historical traditions and governmental usages were totally unlike those of the American stock. The nation therefore had to face the problem whether the usual large powers of self-government should be granted these dependencies as a preparation for eventual statehood, or whether they should be administered permanently as provinces. To this question publicists and statesmen gave anxious attention. Its solution was inextricably entangled with motives of political expediency as well as with considerations involving time-honored American ideals. In final analysis, it devolved upon the judiciary to say whether any departure from ancient practice was warranted by the Constitution.

In the so-called Insular cases, most of which arose in 1900 and 1901, the Supreme Court made its position clear.[1] In reply to the basic question, "Does the Constitution follow the flag?" it decided "yes," but with important and sweeping qualifications. The Constitution was held to consist of two classes of provisions, "fundamental" and "formal," only the former of which applied to the dependencies. The court intimated that, from time to time as specific cases arose, it would declare which provisions possessed this "fundamental"

[1] Downes *v.* Bidwell (1900), De Lima *v.* Bidwell (1900), Dooley *v.* United States (1901), Pepke *v.* United States (1901), Hawaii *v.* Mankichi (1901) and Dorr *v.* United States (1904).

character. The cases then under consideration enabled the judges, however, to settle at once some of the most important points involved.

In the light of this series of decisions, the inhabitants of these scattered possessions were not to be citizens of the United States unless and until Congress should expressly confer citizenship on them. The constitutional guarantees enjoyed by citizens, such as indictment by grand jury and trial by jury, did not belong to them unless and until Congress should so provide. As respects tariff laws, duties might be freely imposed on their commerce with the United States. In other words, Congress might, for all practical purposes, administer the acquisitions as it saw fit. Accordingly, the government was able, without hampering restrictions, to work out a colonial policy in which diversity, rather than uniformity, was the guiding principle. In each instance, an effort was made to legislate in accordance with the special needs of the dependency, and to suit the regulations to its stage of political and social progress.

As the system gradually rounded into shape, it came more and more to resemble the structure of the British Empire. Attached to the continental cluster of self-governing states were the outlying organized territories, inhabited by alien nationalities enjoying a large share of home rule. Whether or not these territories might expect eventual membership in the Union remained an unsettled question. On a plane below this group were the numerous insular possessions comparable to Britain's Crown Colonies. These were under direct tutelage of Washington with little or no rights of self-government. A few of the subject peoples, one notably, were held against their desires, and longed for independence; but nearly everywhere the extension of American sovereignty effected striking improvements in the living conditions of the masses. Nor did the resemblance to the British system end here. The imperial structure was given its final touch by the establishment of a fringe of political and economic protectorates in the Caribbean. Despite occasional outbursts of criticism from Democratic and liberal sources, the American people viewed the assumption of these new responsibilities with approval. Not till the Great Depression of 1929 did signs of a contrary attitude appear.

GOVERNING THE DEPENDENCIES

In line with earlier practice, territorial status was granted to dependencies as quickly as circumstances seemed to warrant. Between 1900 and 1917 this boon was conferred upon three widely separated possessions: Hawaii, Alaska and Puerto Rico. The Filipinos also received a large degree of autonomy, but, as we shall see, their situation differed in essential respects from that of the others.

In the case of Hawaii the organic act of 1900 granted American citizenship to the inhabitants, enfranchised all men who could read, write and speak either Hawaiian or English, and authorized an elective legislature with a governor appointed from Washington. Under American rule the new territory, half the size of Maryland, made steady progress as American capital stimulated the development of sugar production and the growing and canning of pineapples. Its yield of sugar cane per acre soon exceeded that of any other country. The rapidly increasing population, numbering a hundred and fifty-four thousand at the time of annexation, sprang from divers origins, over a third being Japanese, with strong infusions of Filipinos, Portuguese, Chinese and Americans. The pure native stock formed a dwindling minority, partly because of intermarriage with other strains. To offset this racial diversity, an excellent school system, capped by the tax-supported University of Hawaii, was established. The literacy qualification on the suffrage served to keep the political power largely in the hands of the English-speaking islanders.

Alaska, an American possession since 1867, and embracing an area over twice that of Texas, had for many years lived up to its reputation as "Seward's Ice-Box." Its chief springs of wealth were the fur-seal industry and the fisheries, but these had been developed by outsiders rather than by the native Eskimos and Indians. Though the treaty of purchase had bestowed all the rights of American citizenship on the inhabitants (the uncivilized tribes excepted), it was not till 1884 that Alaska was given a resident civil government, and then without any local popular control. In the ensuing years white penetration of the interior gradually laid bare its dowry of inland natural resources. The finding of gold on Klondike Creek in 1896, on the Canadian side of the border, precipitated a rush from all parts of the world, which soon led to the discovery of valuable deposits in American territory—along the Yukon, around the head of Cook Inlet, and near Nome. Before 1921 this treasure-trove yielded $320,000,-000 in gold from Alaskan sources alone. Few of the adventurers, however, became permanent settlers.

Increasing knowledge of Alaska's resources caused the question of safeguarding this reservoir of potential riches to loom large in Roosevelt's conservation program. The best timberlands were set aside as national preserves, and efforts were made to protect coal and other mineral beds from unlawful encroachment. With the gradual growth of a settled white population, Congress in 1912 granted Alaska territorial status with the usual provision for an elective legislature and an appointive governor. The first legislature extended the suffrage to women. Poor transportation facilities continued to hamper the territory's development; and, in default of other means, Congress in 1914 provided for the governmental construction and operation of a railroad, which eventually stretched some five hundred miles from Seward to Fairbanks. Never before had the United States essayed the rôle of railway owner and operator in time of peace. The population continued small, with the whites forming less than a majority. Despite many difficulties yet to overcome, there could be no doubt that under favorable conditions Alaska would turn out to be one of America's most profitable acquisitions.

Five years after Alaska received territorial status, Puerto Rico was given similar rights. This sunny island, half again as big as Delaware and occupied by a population largely white, had been relieved of military rule in April, 1900. Congress then authorized the male inhabitants to elect the lower house of the legislature, but it did not declare the Puerto Ricans American citizens, and it provided that the President should appoint both the governor and the upper house. American dominion brought vast improvements in social and economic life. In the score of years after 1899, the highways lengthened from four hundred and thirty miles to more than nineteen hundred, while the number of public school buildings increased from none at all to well over five hundred. Meanwhile illiteracy declined from eighty per cent to fifty-five. Public-health safeguards, including sewerage, quarantine regulations and hospitals, were introduced, and such scourges as yellow fever, smallpox and anæmia almost vanished. Economic progress was quite as marked, sugar-cane culture outstripping coffee growing as the chief occupation, with tobacco ranking third.

While the Puerto Ricans assisted whole-heartedly in these advances, they were discontented because they had not gained American citizenship or a larger measure of autonomy. In 1914 President Wilson reconstructed the upper house so as to give the natives a majority of the appointments, and three years later their demands were more nearly met by the Jones act, which granted them full citizenship and the right to elect the entire legislature. Nevertheless, restiveness continued among the islanders, partly because of the growing concentration of land in a relatively few hands and a corresponding increase of farm tenancy. A rising sentiment favored statehood, or some equivalent status, so that the people might enjoy greater freedom to deal with their problems in their own way.

Other parts of the overseas empire had to remain content with simpler and less democratic forms of government. In the Panama Canal Zone all political authority was vested in a resident official of the War Department, while Guam and Tutuila were similarly ruled by governors appointed by the Navy Department. As for the multitude of other Pacific islands—Midway, Wake, Howland, Baker and the rest—they contained few or no inhabitants and were given no local government at all.

The acquisition of the Danish West Indies or Virgin Islands in 1917, however, necessitated some type of political provision. These islands, situated sixty miles east of Puerto Rico, had their nucleus in St. Thomas, St. Croix and St. John. After Secretary Seward's abortive effort to purchase them in 1867 (see page 33), the project had languished until the progress of the isthmian-canal plans endowed them with strategic importance as outworks of defense. A treaty of annexation was approved by the Senate in 1902, but was rejected by the Danish upper chamber. Another attempt in 1916, however, resulted in the transfer of the islands to the United States the next year for $25,000,000. The acquisition was placed under a governor appointed directly by the President. The people, mostly Negroes, were allowed limited rights of local self-government, and in 1927 were declared citizens of the United States. Unlike most of the other possessions, the dependency made only halting economic and social progress.

AMERICA IN THE PHILIPPINES

The special position of the Philippines in the imperial system was due to the expectation, raised by the McEnery resolution at the time of annexation (see page 283), that the islands would eventually be set free. When America took them over, the Filipinos resumed against their new sovereign the war for independence they had been waging against Spain. The odds, however, were badly against the insurgents, who lacked not only military skill but also adequate weapons and ammunition. Repeatedly overcome in pitched engagements, they resorted to guerrilla tactics, laying waste fields, and surprising and massacring small troop detachments. The Americans, angered by the barbarous treatment of captive comrades, often inflicted reprisals in kind. Finally, in March, 1901, a small party under Brigadier General Frederick Funston captured Emilio Aguinaldo, the rebel chieftain, through a daring exploit, and the latter presently issued a proclamation to his followers to give up the fight. But it was not until July 4, 1902, that President Roosevelt officially declared the islands pacified. Even afterward, sporadic outbreaks occurred, notably among the Moros and other wild tribes. The cost of subduing the Philippines amounted to $170,000,000, more than eight times the purchase price.

Under American tutelage the islands advanced steadily toward the goal of political autonomy. In July, 1901, the military government gave way to an American civil commission of five, headed by William Howard Taft, the future President, and enlarged a few months later to include three appointed native members. Governor-General Taft and his fellow members promptly set about to reorganize the local governments; and, for this purpose, the suffrage was granted to all men of twenty-three and over who were taxpayers, or who could speak, read and write English or Spanish. After a year of this system Congress made more permanent provision for the islands in the organic act of July 1, 1902. It declared the inhabitants "citizens of the Philippine Islands, and as such entitled to the protection of the United States." Most of the constitutional guarantees of life, liberty and property were extended to them, except trial by jury, which could not easily be grafted onto the old Spanish legal system. Though the governor-general and the commission were continued in sole control for the time, the statute provided for the eventual creation of a legislature. In 1907 this pledge was fulfilled, the commission then becoming the upper house and the lower being chosen by the voters.

Meanwhile, the islands awakened from their long tropical sleep to a new interest in the bustling life of the modern world. One long-standing native grievance had been the economic and political power wielded by three Catholic orders which owned great tracts of fertile land. The Filipinos hated the friars so bitterly that, during the revolt, they had expelled them from the islands with great cruelty. When the establishment of American rule led the friars to reassert their legal rights, the natives generally continued to ignore them. As a way out of the difficulty, Governor-General Taft took up the matter in person with the papal authorities at Rome, and in 1903 the United States purchased the four hundred and ten thousand acres for $7,239,000. In addition, a currency system was instituted, and a comprehensive program of public works carried on, including highways, bridges, port improvements, lighthouses and irrigation projects. With the aid of American capital agriculture made rapid strides, notably in the growing of sugar, coconuts, hemp and tobacco. Public order was assured through an able native constabulary, and prison administration was reorganized. There remained, however, insufficient provision for public health, sanitation and hospitals.

Public education, which had been unknown under the Spanish, made astonishing progress. To get the system under way, hundreds of young American men and women went to the islands and taught Filipino children, and the normal school at Manila was greatly enlarged to speed the training of native teachers. With two hundred thousand pupils in the schools in 1902, the total more than trebled by 1917. In order to provide for the increasing number of high-school graduates, the tax-supported University of the Philippines was opened in 1909. English gradually supplanted the numerous native dialects and languages, much to the relief of the Filipinos themselves who, divided by speech barriers, saw in a common tongue a necessary basis for national solidarity. The population, which numbered less than seven million under Spain, exceeded ten in 1917.

In all the reforms that were undertaken the islanders warmly coöperated. Keenly aware of their own political inexperience, they sought to learn what they could from this intimate contact with a progressive Western people. In return, the American officials placed natives in positions of trust and responsibility as rapidly as conditions seemed to justify. The people never forgot their aspirations for national freedom, however. After the first few years every Philippine political party unfurled the banner of immediate independence. In America their cause was championed by the Democrats. President Wilson upon entering office insured full native control of the insular legislature by appointing Filipinos to a majority of the seats in the upper house. Three years later, in 1916, Congress adopted the Jones act, which granted the islands what was, in many respects, a territorial status. Both legislative houses were now made elective, with the governor-general appointive as hitherto. The provision for extending the suffrage to all men of twenty-one and over who could read and write a native dialect trebled the number

of voters in the first election. American citizenship was withheld, however, since the Philippines were not considered a
permanent possession.

The Jones act further stated Congress's purpose to recognize the independence of the islands "as soon as a stable
government can be established therein." Almost at once the
Filipinos were confronted with a severe test of their capacity
for self-rule, due to the financial and economic disturbances
attendant upon the World War. Hostile critics saw evidences
of governmental incompetence on every hand. Nevertheless,
President Wilson informed Congress in December, 1920, that
the people, having "succeeded in maintaining a stable government," were ready for independence. The accession of the
Republicans a few months later held up the expected action
for more than a decade, however. Added to their earlier
belief in the desirability of holding the Philippines was the
fear that, if America let go, Japan would seize the islands.
In this situation matters remained until the Great Depression forced a reconsideration of the problem.

THE CARIBBEAN SPHERE OF INFLUENCE

Meanwhile, events had caused Washington to establish a
chain of protectorates in the Caribbean. The first impulse in
this direction arose from the responsibilities which the government had assumed toward Cuba under the peace treaty of
1898. When the American military administration took
charge on January 1, 1899, the island was disorganized politically and economically, and two thirds of the people were
illiterate. Under the vigorous direction of Major General
John R. Brooke and later that of Major General Leonard
Wood, emergency relief was afforded the destitute, far-
reaching sanitary reforms were introduced, order was established, the legal system reorganized, and an extensive program of highway construction begun. Likewise, church and

state were separated, and the public educational system was revived and greatly extended.

On General Wood's initiative, a constitutional convention assembled at Havana in November, 1900, and drafted a basic law for the new republic modeled on that of the United States. Despite his urgent representations, the instrument was silent as to future relations with the United States. Congress met the situation in the Platt Amendment to the army-appropriation act of March, 1901, which instructed the President to prolong the military occupation until certain specified provisions should be inserted in the insular constitution. These conditions included Cuba's obligation to allow no foreign power to impair her independence and never to go into debt beyond the capacity of her ordinary revenues to pay, and also her express recognition of America's right to intervene to preserve the island's freedom or orderly government. In addition, Cuba must permit the United States to acquire naval bases within her borders.[1] Reluctantly the convention made the required concessions. Two years later, the stipulations were embodied in a "permanent" treaty.

In May, 1902, the government of independent Cuba was formally installed. Handicapped by a bad heritage, the people were slow to value the ballot over the bullet in settling public issues. Corruption was also developed into a fine art. At some presidential elections the total number of votes far exceeded the total number of voters. Civil disorders arising from the presidential election of 1906 led to the first application of the Platt Amendment, the military occupation lasting from September of that year to January, 1909. In a message to Congress President Roosevelt made it clear that, though the United States had no desire to annex Cuba, it was "absolutely out of the question" for the island to con-

---

[1] Naval stations were presently leased at Bahia Honda and Guantanamo, but the former was relinquished in 1913.

tinue independent should the "insurrectionary habit" become "confirmed." The warning, however, was soon forgotten. In 1912 marines were landed for several weeks near Santiago to protect American-owned mines and sugar plantations during a Negro uprising. Five years later a revolt, provoked by a disputed election of 1916, caused forces to be sent to Santiago, Camaguey and elsewhere for the preservation of order, the detachment at Camaguey remaining until 1922. To prevent a recurrence of such disturbances, a new electoral code, drafted with the help of General Enoch H. Crowder of the United States army, was adopted by the insular legislature in 1919. But Cuba had not yet mastered the lesson of self-government, and other troubles lay ahead. On no later occasion, however, did Washington resort to armed intervention.

From an economic point of view, Cuba as the century advanced became more and more a preserve of American capitalists. American investments grew from $80,000,000 in 1901 to $220,000,000 at the outbreak of the World War, by far the largest amount of United States money invested in any Latin American country except Mexico. Aided further by preferential tariffs in the United States, Cuba became the "sugar bowl of the world," sending the great bulk of her supply to the United States. Real estate, railways, government bonds, public utilities, mines, manufacturing and tobacco represented other significant ramifications of the economic penetration. Similarly, American financial houses extended their dominion, the National City Bank of New York establishing a number of branches in the island. To some Cubans it seemed that they had won independence from Spain only to turn over the country to Yankee business interests; but there could be no doubt that this economic relationship, plus the political balance wheel of the Platt Amendment, gave the island a measure of prosperity, and even of governmental stability, that it could not otherwise have attained.

Shortly after Cuba unwillingly accepted the Platt Amendment, a second protectorate came into being under circumstances quite as natural. The Panama revolution in 1903 (see page 293) put the infant republic in need of a defender against Colombia at a time when the United States sought a controlling hand in the territory bordering on the Canal Zone. As a result, the American government agreed in the treaty of November 18 to guarantee Panama's independence in return for the privilege of being allowed to use armed force whenever necessary "for the safety or protection of the Canal" or its auxiliary works. Under this arrangement the United States intervened in Panama five times between 1908 and 1921.

Even before this new protectorate was set up, a dramatic incident foreshadowed further and unexpected applications of the Platt Amendment principle. In December, 1902, Great Britain, Germany and Italy undertook a blockade of Venezuela, on the south shore of the Caribbean, in order to compel payment of long-standing debts to their subjects. Although the United States had been given advance notice of this action, the presence of a hostile European fleet boded ill for a weak Latin American country, and the State Department successfully bestirred itself to have the blockade lifted and the claims referred to arbitration.

To President Roosevelt the moral of the episode seemed clear. He informed Congress in December, 1904: "Chronic wrongdoing . . . may in America, as elsewhere, ultimately require intervention by some civilized nation, and in the Western Hemisphere, the adherence of the United States to the Monroe Doctrine may force the United States, however reluctantly, . . . to the exercise of an international police power." In other words, according to the "Roosevelt Corollary," the Monroe Doctrine imposed an obligation on the Washington government to safeguard defaulting republics against possible foreign intervention by itself assuming responsibility for their financial good faith. A doctrine of non-interference by Europe in the affairs of the New World thus became a doctrine of unmistakable interference by the United States.

If the Washington authorities originally entered upon the policy of protectorates somewhat blindly, the desire to prevent new European establishments within striking distance of the Panama Canal speeded the process. Still another factor was the inflow of American capital into the region. By 1913 these investments amounted to $269,000,000 and were rapidly increasing.[1] American capital was particularly active in the exploitation of sugar, fruit, coffee, public utilities, asphalt and oil. At the same time, commerce with the United States grew from $195,000,000 in 1900 to $272,000,000 in 1913. As a result of these varied influences, the circle of protectorates steadily widened, and the Caribbean Sea acquired its character of the "American Mediterranean."

The Dominican Republic, occupying the eastern part of the island of Santo Domingo, was the first country to which the Roosevelt Corollary was applied. In order to avert probable foreign intervention for the collection of debts long overdue, President Roosevelt in 1905, with the insular government's consent, placed an American financial expert in charge of its revenues, with power to arrange for the gradual payment of the foreign bondholders. Two years later, the

[1] According to Max Winkler, a leading authority, the total amount sixteen years later was about $1,745,000,000. American investments in the Dominican Republic rose from $4,000,000 in 1913 to $24,000,000 in 1929; in Haiti from $4,000,000 to $31,000,000; in Nicaragua from $3,000,000 to $24,000,000; in Cuba from $220,000,000 to $1,526,000,000; and in Panama from $5,000,000 to $36,000,000.

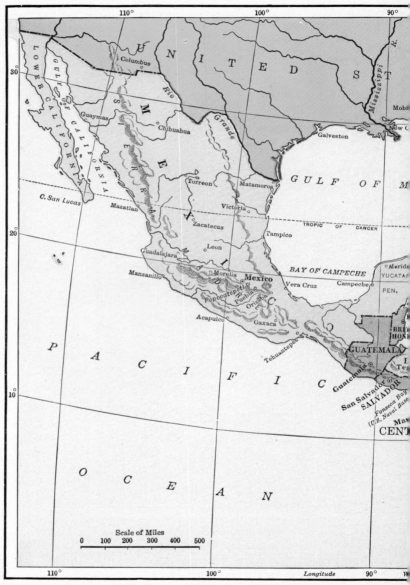

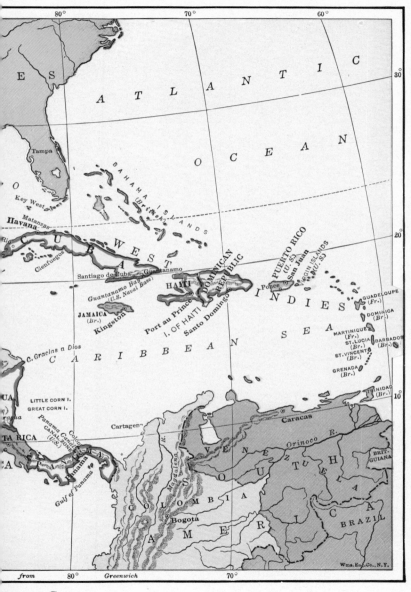

AND THE CANAL

stipulations were embodied in a treaty, the United States obtaining authority to accord "such protection" to the general receiver of customs and his staff as might "be requisite for the performance of their duties."

Under this elastic provision American representatives supervised the Dominican elections of 1913, and three years later marines landed for the purpose of quelling a revolt. The intervention quickly grew into a complete military occupation. The American administration restored peace to the country, enforced sanitary measures, reorganized and expanded the school system, and undertook an elaborate program of good roads and public works. Wrathy at outside intrusion in their affairs, the natives insisted again and again upon a termination of the occupation. In June, 1921, Washington announced that withdrawal would occur only when the insular government entered a treaty ratifying all the acts of the military régime and enlarging the powers of the general receiver of the customs. These terms, though deeply resented, were eventually accepted. American evacuation occurred in the summer of 1924, though the customs receivership continued.

Meanwhile, the adjacent republic of Haiti, inhabited by Negroes, was subjected to similar supervision. Following a revolutionary outbreak early in 1915, marines took possession of the chief towns. The outcome was a treaty in September, which established American management of Haitian finances, provided for a constabulary officered by Americans, and empowered the United States to intervene when necessary for the preservation of Haitian independence or an orderly government. The American administration, with characteristic efficiency, carried through extensive sanitary, fiscal and governmental reforms, and stabilized economic conditions. Bitter native antagonism, however, resulted from the revival in 1917–1918 of the *corvée* system of forced labor on the roads, and from alleged abuses of authority by the marine corps. A Senate committee, after visiting the island, recommended unanimously in 1922 that the military occupation be continued. As will be seen, the marines stayed on until 1934.

Efforts were also made to extend the protectorate policy to Central America. In 1911 President Taft, following in Roosevelt's footsteps, negotiated treaties for fiscal receiverships in Honduras and Nicaragua, but these were rejected by the Senate. Nevertheless, Nicaragua the same year, with the State Department's approval, put her customs in charge of an American financial expert as the price of securing a loan from certain New York banking houses. In August, 1912, marines were landed to allay civil disorder, and remained until 1925 as a legation guard at the capital. In the interval order was preserved at elections with the aid of American bayonets. A treaty of 1914 granted the United States exclusive and perpetual right to build a canal through Nicaragua, turned over to America certain naval bases, and stipulated a payment of three million dollars for these privileges. In December, 1926, the marines returned, and eventually stayed on until 1933, fighting rebels and bandits and supervising elections. Thus, without express treaty sanction, Nicaragua found herself in fact, if not in law, an American protectorate. In 1922 Salvador placed herself in a similar position, accepting an American customs receiver in order to secure a loan from New York bankers.

This whole line of policy was variously regarded in the United States as an altruistic assumption of what Rudyard Kipling had called the "white man's burden," as an ungrateful task imposed by considerations of national safety, and as an ugly manifestation of economic and financial imperialism. Doubtless all these elements entered into the program. Nothing more clearly evinced the limited objectives of the progressive movement than the failure of these crusaders for democracy at home to insist upon applying the democratic principle of self-determination to the Caribbean. Only in the case of Mexico, which will next be considered, did an American President attempt to do so.

RELATIONS WITH MEXICO

Though the United States made no move to establish protectorates beyond Central America and the Caribbean, the outward thrust of Yankee dominion created great uneasiness throughout the Latin American world. If, as Roosevelt asserted, the southward advance found its justification in the Monroe Doctrine, then it looked as though a policy originally forged as a defensive weapon had turned into an instrument of imperialistic aggrandizement. Resentment against "Monroeism" burned especially fiercely among the peoples of Argentina, Brazil and Chile, the so-called A. B. C. Powers, who felt that their political stability and cultural progress entitled them to freedom from alien tutelage. In such places a strong sentiment developed for a Pan American Doctrine which would substitute coöperative action by the New World republics for sole action by the United States in interpreting and enforcing the principles of the Monroe Doctrine. A Pan American Doctrine, of course, would operate as a curb on the "Colossus of the North" as well as on European powers.

To allay Latin American fears because of his cavalier treatment of Colombia during the Panama revolt, President Roosevelt solemnly avowed to Congress in December, 1905, that "under no circumstances will the United States use the Monroe Doctrine as a cloak for territorial aggression." To the Latin Americans, however, the difference between actually annexing territory and controlling it by means of a protectorate seemed immaterial. Hence his assurance and that of subsequent administrations did little to restore confidence. President Wilson's course during a prolonged reign of anarchy in Mexico served somewhat to clear the atmosphere, however. In 1911, when the troubles began, United States citizens held Mexican investments, mostly in oil fields, mines, railways and ranches, totaling a billion dollars. Fifty or sixty thousand of them carried on business there, and the bulk of Mexico's commerce lay with her northern neighbor. Notwithstanding these intimate economic relations, President Wilson made it clear from the outset that the administration's policy would not be controlled by selfish considerations. "We have seen material interests threaten constitutional freedom in the United States," he declared in a speech at Mobile in 1913. "Therefore we will now know how to sympathize with those in the rest of America who have to contend with such powers, not only within their borders but from outside their borders also." As his program assumed form, he took the unprecedented step of calling on Latin American nations to coöperate in the settlement of Mexican difficulties. Though his example was not emulated by any of his immediate successors in office, it prefigured the much fuller collaboration of New World republics achieved in the presidency of Franklin D. Roosevelt.

Since 1877 Mexico had been almost continuously under the iron rule of Porfirio Díaz, nominally president but actually dictator. Representative government existed in form only, and the agrarian masses, mostly of Indian blood, were tied to the soil by a system of peonage. But peace and order prevailed, foreign capital was welcomed, and the country experienced a wonderful material transformation. In time, however, native dissatisfaction increased to a dangerous pitch, and in 1910 the eighth "election" of Díaz proved the signal for a popular uprising headed by Francisco Madero, a sincere reformer. In 1911, when the aged Díaz fled to Europe, Madero became his successor. The tide of lawlessness, however, still ran strong. In February, 1913, General Victoriano Huerta, supported by the old Díaz faction, overturned the new government and, there is good reason to believe, instigated Madero's assassination. Once more Mexico plunged into anarchy, with Venustiano Carranza leading the insurgent bands as Madero's political heir.

Though European powers promptly recognized Huerta, President Wilson declined to follow suit, justifying his course on the novel ground that the régime rested on force and murder. "My ideal," he told a newsman, "is an orderly and righteous government in Mexico; but my passion is for the submerged eighty-five per cent of the people of that Republic who are now struggling toward liberty." Convinced that Huerta's authority would collapse without American recognition and financial aid, he notified Congress that his policy would be one of "watchful waiting." Meanwhile, the destruction of life and property continued, and American interests bent on armed intervention savagely denounced the President as an impractical idealist. Even Wilson found the game of waiting an arduous one. When Huerta failed to make suitable apology for arresting some American marines at Tampico, the President in April, 1914, ordered the seizure of Vera Cruz. He then accepted an offer of the A. B. C. governments to mediate the difficulties. This action, however, proved of little practical consequence, for Huerta, overwhelmed by his enemies, fled Mexico almost at once. Carranza, the chief insurgent leader, succeeded to his place, and in November the American forces evacuated Vera Cruz.

With the popular party once more in control, the situation assumed a new aspect, for the victors fell to quarreling among themselves. Francisco Villa, a former bandit chieftain, proved the main disturbing element, and so fierce was the ensuing strife that Mexico City thrice changed hands in a single month. His patience sorely taxed, Wilson once more turned to Latin America for counsel. A joint conference of Bolivia, Uruguay, Guatemala, the A. B. C. Powers and the United States decided in October, 1915, to recognize Carranza as the true head of Mexico. This action strengthened Carranza's hold, but Villa succeeded in prolonging his stormy career for over a year. In a spirit of pique against the United States, he raided across the border in March, 1916, killing seventeen persons in Columbus, New Mexico. A punitive expedition under General John J. Pershing went in pursuit. It dispersed many lawless bands, and although Villa himself managed to elude capture, he was forced to cease his activities. Meanwhile, Wilson called out a hundred and fifty thousand state militiamen to guard the international boundary. Not till January, 1917, were the forces recalled.

A few months later Mexico adopted a constitution embodying the reforms of the revolutionary era. Besides stipulations for improving the lot of industrial workers, the new instrument provided for breaking up the huge landed estates, and asserted national ownership of all oil and other mineral resources. The provision (Article 27) in regard to property rights vitally affected the security of American investments, and provoked sharp protests from Washington. Finally, Mexico in 1923 gave assurance that Article 27 would not be so applied as to work the confiscation of American mineral rights acquired under the previous constitution, and agreed further to compensate American citizens whose estates had been expropriated and partitioned. Other difficulties remained to be ironed out, but with Mexico now enjoying a state of peace and stability, their solution seemed assured through the normal channels of diplomacy.

THE PEACE MOVEMENT

The rising tide of democracy throughout the world, the new value placed upon the welfare of the common man, the incessant internationalist agitation of the socialists, the tightening network of financial and commercial ties among peoples, the staggering cost of national armaments—influences such as these smoothed the way for the growth of a powerful peace movement in the early twentieth century. To an increasing number of persons in all countries war seemed a relic of barbarism fated to disappear in the not distant future. In the hope of hastening that time the United States played an active part. Indeed, no other country had done more in the past to encourage the pacific settlement of international disputes. But it was at the suggestion of the Czar of Russia that twenty-six powers conferred at The Hague in 1899 on plans for promoting universal amity. This gathering drafted certain principles to govern the conduct of warfare on land and sea, and established a Permanent Court of Arbitration to sit at The Hague. In 1907 a second Hague conference of forty-four countries, held this time at the prompting of President Roosevelt, adopted additional rules to mitigate the horrors of war, reorganized the court, and indorsed the principle that the debts of one country to the citizens of another should not be collected by force.

In the ordinary sense, the Hague tribunal was not a court. It comprised a list of judges selected by the several countries, from which special courts might be composed with the consent of the governments directly concerned whenever specific disputes arose. Though the submission of cases was left optional and the machinery of adjustment proved somewhat cumbersome, the tribunal's establishment was an important move in the right direction. It settled seventeen controversies between 1902 and 1917. To four of these the United

States was a party. The most notable case involved the long-standing question of American rights in the fisheries off Newfoundland and Labrador. The decision, rendered in 1910, favored the United States.

Unofficial endeavors paralleled these official ones. Though the promising peace crusade of the early nineteenth century had been blasted by the Civil War, humanitarian and church groups had presently resumed the agitation. But it was not until the new century came and practical men of affairs lent their support that the movement assumed real consequence. Thanks to the benefactions of Andrew Carnegie, Edwin Ginn and others, foundations were set up to investigate the causes of war and suggest means of cure. In addition, Carnegie, who had made part of his fortune from the sale of armor plate, paid for the Pan American Union building in Washington as well as the "Palace of Peace" at The Hague. Peace agencies multiplied, their literature received wide distribution, and the larger universities aided by creating international exchange professorships.

These exertions did not go unopposed. Thus the Navy League, formed in 1903 and dominated by retired naval officers and manufacturers of war materials, kept up an incessant propaganda for bigger armaments. Nor did the increase of investments abroad always promote a pacific attitude. Not only did it foster undeclared wars in the Caribbean, but American bankers found it profitable to supply the financial sinews for other nations' conflicts. In 1900 and 1901, through J. P. Morgan and Company, the British government borrowed $223,000,000, one fifth of the cost of the Boer War. A few years later, loans floated in the United States assisted Japan, at Russia's cost, to extend her sway into southern Manchuria. By 1909 American investments in various parts of the globe had climbed to two billion dollars, and four years later to over two and a half billion, a seventh of which was in Europe itself.

Nevertheless, Roosevelt struck a responsive chord when he assumed leadership in an effort to supplement and enlarge the authority of the Hague court beyond the limits set. In 1904 he submitted to the Senate a group of treaties which, departing from the existing arrangement, *obligated* the United States and the signatory powers to submit all their disputes to the Hague tribunal save those involving vital interests, independence or national honor. An unhappy quarrel between the President and the Senate prevented ratification in a form acceptable to him, and the matter hung fire until 1908–1909 when the United States entered into twenty-two agreements of this kind. As a promoter of peace, however, Roosevelt did not subscribe to many of the tenets of the professional pacifists. Even his arbitration treaties, through their exclusion of certain large subjects, left the gate wide open for a resort to force. Ever an ardent nationalist, he held that heavy armaments were, after all, the best preventive of war.

At the same time he took the position that the United States was justified in plunging into the hurly-burly of international politics in the interests of world peace. In 1906, when war threatened in Europe because of a controversy between Germany and France over the latter's claims to Morocco, the United States joined with ten other governments in a conference at Algeciras in Spain for composing the differences. The Senate in ratifying the act of settlement cautiously disclaimed any "purpose to depart from the traditional American foreign policy which forbids participation . . . in the settlement of political questions which are entirely European in their scope." Meanwhile, in the Far East, a bloody conflict between Japan and Russia in 1904–1905 stirred Roosevelt to action. The President's sympathies, like those of the American public, lay with the smaller country; but he feared that a complete triumph by either would unsettle the balance of power in the Orient and menace the Open Door (see page 286). As Japan drew near the end of her resources, he persuaded the belligerents to join in a peace conference at Portsmouth, New Hampshire, from which Japan, the victorious combatant, issued with less than she wanted, but with considerable territorial gains, including Russia's lease of Port Arthur in China.

In the ensuing years, the gravest threat to American peace, Mexico excepted, proved to be the increasing friction with Japan. Roosevelt's pressure on Japan's delegates at Portsmouth not to insist upon extreme demands, coupled with the discriminations against her subjects on the Pacific Coast and America's increasing rôle in the Far East, steadily fed the flames of Japanese resentment. The United States on its part suspected the island empire of designs against China's freedom and the Open Door. As has been seen, the question of Japanese immigration was presently set at rest (see page 348); and in 1908 an endeavor was made to dispose of the more fundamental problem.

In the Root-Takahira agreement of that year the two powers, "uninfluenced by any aggressive tendencies," pledged themselves to respect each other's territorial possessions in the Pacific and to support "by all pacific means" Chinese independence and the Open Door. As now defined, the Open Door went beyond John Hay's original formulation, and included equal rights for all nations in industrial as well as commercial development. The commitments assumed the form of an executive understanding, not a treaty, and hence were not acted upon by the Senate. In 1917, in the Lansing-Ishii agreement, the two powers reaffirmed these assurances, with the imprudent admission by America that "territorial propinquity" gave Japan "special interests" in China. Innocently intended by Secretary of State Lansing, the phrase was construed by Japan to sanction new aggressions.

In the meantime President Taft had bent his efforts to create larger opportunities for the export of capital to China. From 1900 to 1914 American investments there grew from seventeen and a half million to forty-two. To accelerate the process, Taft's State Department encouraged American financial groups to unite with bankers of other countries in joint loans to the Chinese government for railway construction and similar purposes. A six-power consortium for lending $125,-000,000 to the new-fledged Chinese republic was thus being formed when President Wilson appeared on the scene in 1913. Disapproving certain of the terms and particularly the "implications" of governmental responsibility, he withdrew official support, with the result that the American syndicates dropped out. Several years later, however, he saw the problem from a different angle—as a means of checking Japan's economic advance into China. Hence American bankers, with the government's full blessing, took the lead in forming the four-power consortium of 1920.

The advent of the Democrats led to a notable extension of the arbitration principle beyond the scope of the Roosevelt treaties. Long before becoming Secretary of State, Bryan had advocated referring every sort of dispute, even those involving national honor or vital interest, to a commission of inquiry. In April, 1913, with Wilson's approval, he invited the governments of the world to sign treaties with the United States committing the parties to submit their controversies "of whatever kind" to an investigating commission, and to refrain from hostilities until after the commission had reported its findings. By allowing time for bellicose passions to subside he believed most wars could be averted. The plan was so well received that thirty countries agreed to enter "cooling-off" treaties, and twenty-one ratifications were eventually exchanged. A new era of international brotherhood seemed to be dawning when suddenly, almost without warning, the great European war of 1914 cast a deep black shadow over the world.

SELECT BIBLIOGRAPHY

Adapting the Constitution to an Imperial System. Dealey, *Growth of American State Constitutions,* describes the course of constitutional revision. For the development of colonial policy, consult two works by Willoughby: *Territories and Dependencies of the United States,* and *Constitutional Law of the United States;* and Reinsch, *Colonial Administration.*

Governing the Dependencies. Among the more useful studies dealing with particular areas are Kuykendall, *History of Hawaii;* Nichols, *Alaska;* White, *Puerto Rico and Its People;* Westergaard, *Danish West Indies;* and Tansill, *Purchase of the Danish West Indies.*

America in the Philippines. Most of the works on this subject are controversial, having been written by Americans for or against insular independence, or by Philippine patriots. Much enlightening information may be gleaned from Forbes, *Philippine Islands;* Worcester, *Philippines, Past and Present;* LeRoy, *Americans in the Philippines;* and Reyes, *Legislative History of America's Economic Policy toward the Philippines.*

The Caribbean Sphere of Influence. The summaries of diplomatic history by Bailey and Bemis are helpful for this and the two following sections. Munro, *United States and the Caribbean Area,* and Rippy, *Latin America in World Politics,* trace the American advance into the West Indies and Central America, while Perkins, *Monroe Doctrine, 1867–1907,* and Winkler, *Investments of United States Capital,* discuss certain aspects. For the Venezuelan incident, see Hill, *Roosevelt and the Caribbean,* which punctures a widely accepted earlier version. Particular protectorates receive detailed treatment in Chapman, *History of the Cuban Republic;* Jenks, *Our Cuban Colony;* Fitzgibbon, *Cuba and the United States;* Knight, *Americans in Santo Domingo* (the Dominican Republic); Millspaugh, *Haiti under American Control;* Montague, *Haiti and the United States;* and Cox, *Nicaragua and the United States.*

Relations with Mexico. Priestley, *Mexican Nation,* Gruening, *Mexico and Its Heritage,* and Callcott, *Liberalism in Mexico,* make clear that country's internal situation. For American relations Hackett, *Mexican Revolution and the United States,* Rippy, *United States and Mexico,* Callahan, *American Foreign Policy in Mexican Relations,* and Dunn, *Diplomatic Protection of Americans in Mexico,* are important.

The Peace Movement. Significant phases of the revived interest in universal peace are discussed in Curti, *Peace or War,* and his *Bryan and World Peace;* Beales, *History of Peace;* and Scott, *The Hague Peace Conferences.* See also the biographies of the several Presidents (cited in earlier chapters) and Jessup, *Elihu Root,* II. Far Eastern relations are treated in Griswold, *Far Eastern Policy of the United States;* Treat, *Japan and the United States;* Tupper and McReynolds, *Japan in American Public Opinion;* Dennett, *Roosevelt and the Russo-Japanese War;* and Norton, *China and the Powers.*

Chapter XV

AMERICA AND THE WORLD WAR, 1914–1918

THUNDER ACROSS THE SEA

THE seeds of the European war were sown as early as the Franco-Prussian War of 1870–1871 when the Germans inflicted a harsh peace on their vanquished foe. The soil was fertilized in the years thereafter by the intensified nationalisms, which, as we have seen, sent the European powers on a world-wide scramble for territory, spheres of influence, raw materials, markets and trade routes. Both from motives of aggression and from dread of one another, the rival governments undertook an exhausting competition in armaments, leading to ever bigger armies and navies. As part of the drift of events, there occurred an ominous division of Europe into two armed camps, each with its ambitions, fears, secret treaties and unrecorded commitments. Russia, France and Great Britain headed one coalition, Germany and Austria-Hungary the other. Both sides prepared for war while hoping somehow to avoid it.

By 1914 Europe had become a powder magazine which needed only a careless match to explode it. This spark fell on June 28 when the Austro-Hungarian heir-apparent was assassinated by a youth belonging to one of the many subject peoples composing the empire. With no more than suspicion of Serbia's complicity, Austria-Hungary charged that government with being a party to the crime and, after making certain of the German Kaiser's support, declared war on Serbia a month later. Though Austria-Hungary and her ally expected to keep the struggle a local affair, such was the tenseness of feeling and the obligation of alliances that all the Great Powers quickly plunged into the conflict, with the Central Empires—Germany and Austria-Hungary—captaining one set of belligerents, and the Entente Allies—Russia, France and Great Britain—the other.[1]

The outbreak of the World War took the peoples of all countries by surprise. No government had deliberately willed it and none had wanted it. Deep-lying forces had prepared the way, and the stupidity of statesmen had hastened the culmination. The earlier years of the century had been marked by social and material progress, by peaceful development and the promise of the abolition of war. Now suddenly all was changed. Mankind faced the most destructive struggle it had yet experienced. The World War, as the sequel was to show, ended an era of enlightenment and ushered in one of dislocation and disillusion.

In particular, the American people were stunned by the event. Notwithstanding the rapid advance of the United States as a world power since 1898, the progressive movement had largely chained public attention to domestic problems, leaving the nation blind to the forces that were driving Europe to disaster. On August 4, when five countries had taken up arms, President Wilson issued a proclamation of neutrality, which he repeated as successive nations joined the conflict. Later in August he made a special appeal to his countrymen to be "impartial in thought as well as action." The former step accorded with a century and a quarter of consistent practice. The latter, however desirable, was impossible of fulfillment.

[1] Between July 28 and November 5 Austria-Hungary, Germany and Turkey entered the war on the one side, Serbia, Russia, France, Belgium, Great Britain (including Canada, Australia, New Zealand and South Africa), Montenegro and Japan on the other. Italy, after carefully calculating the advantages, joined the Allies in May, 1915. Smaller European countries followed in 1916.

From the outset a predominant sentiment favored the Allies. Of the hundred million Americans nearly half were of British or Canadian lineage, and even the descendants of other nationalities had unconsciously imbibed Anglo-Saxon traditions and ideals from their surroundings. Through Shakespeare, Dickens, Scott, Tennyson and countless other masters of literature the people shared a common cultural heritage with England, and were further bound by ties of language, law and custom. This basic sympathy was strengthened by the attitude of the Eastern business classes, who had long enjoyed close financial relations with London and who disliked and feared German commercial methods. The Teutonic powers, of course, did not lack friends. A fifth of the American stock derived from Germany and Austria-Hungary, and many persons of this blood, especially the recent immigrants, instinctively sided with their ancestral homelands. From the Irish Americans, who generally joined with the Germans in hating England, came another source of support. Finally, the "ancient grudge" against Britain, nourished by school histories, rendered a goodly number of old-stock Americans doubtful of the righteousness of the Allied cause.

With still other European groups represented in the population, it is not surprising that, as the conflict developed, it deeply stirred emotions born of national attachments, family relationships and rekindled patriotisms. A foreign observer, impressed by the din of argument carried on by "hyphenated Americans," remarked, "America is no nation, just a collection of people who neutralize one another." Despite this clash of sympathies, however, most persons eagerly supported the President's position of official neutrality, viewing the European resort to bloodshed as something horrible and unclean. Of 367 editors polled by the *Literary Digest* in November, 1914, 105 favored the Allies, 20 the Central Empires, and 242 neutrality. The stronghold of isolationist feeling was the Midwest, hitherto the breeding ground of progressivism.

THE USES AND ABUSES OF NEUTRALITY

The European holocaust placed America in somewhat the same position she had occupied a century before during the Napoleonic wars. With German shipping swept from the seas and a large part of Britain's merchant marine devoted to war uses, the United States became the chief carrier of the world's trade. The derangement of European industry and agriculture and the insatiable demand for munitions, metal products, foodstuffs and raw materials poured a flood of gold into America, especially from the Allied countries, whose markets were easy of access. The value of explosives exported rose from $6,300,000 in 1914 to $803,000,000 in 1917; of chemicals, dyes, drugs and the like from $22,000,000 to $181,-000,000; of iron and steel from $252,000,000 to $1,134,000,-000; and of wheat from $88,000,000 to $298,000,000. As a Senate investigation conducted in 1934–1936 by Gerald P. Nye of North Dakota was to reveal, immense profits accrued to American bankers and manufacturers. The J. P. Morgan firm made $30,000,000 from acting as the financial agent of the British and French governments, the Du Pont munitions company reaped profits of over $265,000,000 between 1914 and 1918, and other large financial and industrial concerns came in for their proportionate share.

The country's shipping proved unequal to the rapidly increasing demand. In an effort to remedy the situation, Congress in August, 1914, facilitated the purchase of merchantmen built in neutral nations by a law admitting such ships to immediate registry without the customary five-year restriction. A few weeks later it instructed the government to set up a Bureau of War Risk Insurance for the purpose of keeping marine insurance charges within reasonable limits. These steps, however, failed to reach the heart of the difficulty: the need of constructing additional ships. To solve this problem, the administration proposed that the government itself engage in the business.

Congress, slow to act through fear of possible foreign complications as well as from dislike of government ownership, waited until September, 1916, when it set up the United States Shipping Board with authority to build, buy or lease merchantmen and to operate them until five years after the war. In addition, the Board was granted permanent powers to regulate private vessels engaged in interstate or foreign commerce. By this latter provision it attained a footing similar to that of the Interstate Commerce Commission and the Federal Trade Commission in their respective spheres. Unfortunately the law came too late to be of much use before America's entry into the war; but thereafter the Board was given virtual control of the entire shipbuilding resources of the nation and in that capacity performed indispensable service.

Although the initial impact of the conflict had disrupted normal trade relations and created fears of a deepening depression, the war boom soon ushered in an era of great prosperity whose benefits ramified to all classes. Since the abnormal expansion of industry occurred at a time of sharply declining immigration, organized labor was in a position to demand higher wages and other concessions which employers found it easy to pass on to the public in the form of higher prices. The war also stimulated an extraordinary export of capital to embattled Europe. At first the administration, at the prompting of Secretary Bryan, who held that loans to belligerents violated the "true spirit of neutrality," set its face against the practice; but late in 1914, under pressure from the banking interests, the President relaxed the policy and sanctioned the advancing of credits. When the United States finally joined the struggle, Americans had purchased nearly $2,300,000,000 of Allied securities and $27,000,000 of German.

As in Napoleon's time, along with the tide of material prosperity came grave perils to the maintenance of national security. Neither group of belligerents was willing to allow the interests of countries at peace to endanger its chances of victory. Accordingly, as the principal power not engaged in war, America was obliged once more to assume her historic rôle as champion of neutral rights. Great Britain's infringements, in large part, involved arbitrary and vexatious interruptions of American trade with the neutral countries bordering on Germany. She freely intercepted cargoes of contraband in order to prevent war materials from finding a backdoor into enemy territory. The United States, asserting the right of neutrals to absolute freedom in trading with other neutrals, denounced the interferences as illegal, but the seizures continued. Already before the end of 1914 the British had taken over thirty-one cargoes of copper to a value of $5,500,000.

Partly to obviate American objections, Britain in March, 1915, adopted a policy that amounted to a long-distance blockade of the German coast and near-by neutral ports. This move likewise evoked a protest from Washington emphasizing the point that under international law it was "illegal and indefensible" to blockade countries at peace. But the London authorities, again pleading the law of national self-preservation, declined to yield. The British government also expanded the list of contraband articles greatly beyond those tentatively agreed to at a ten-power conference at London in 1909. Early in 1915 it even forbade the shipment of foodstuffs to the civil population of Germany, contending that a recent German order nationalizing the food supply made it impossible to distinguish between provisions intended for non-combatants and those for the army.

Such practices, irritating and unlawful though they were, inflicted property losses merely. The troubles with the Central Empires cut more deeply because they involved, in addition, plots against American domestic tranquillity and the destruction of lives. Since German success required that the Allied shortage in munitions should not be replenished from outside sources, Teutonic agents in the United States launched a vigorous propaganda to induce Congress to place an embargo on military supplies. The government, however, was not to be persuaded. Not only was the munitions trade fully sanctioned by international law, but the Germans themselves had indulged in the traffic in previous wars. It was no fault of the United States that Germany found herself unable to buy in the American market.

Thwarted at this point, the Central Empires tried to accomplish their purpose through a campaign of terrorism. "It is my impression," boasted the Austro-Hungarian Ambassador, Dr. Constantin Dumba, to his government in August, 1915, "that we can disorganize and hold up for months, if not entirely prevent, the manufacture of munitions in Bethlehem and the Middle West." At the instigation of Teutonic agents and pro-German sympathizers, explosions and incendiary fires damaged or destroyed munition plants, bombs were concealed aboard vessels carrying cargoes to the Allies, and strikes were fomented among seamen and munition workers. The federal authorities apprehended most of the culprits, and soon managed to establish a linkage with the Teutonic embassies in Washington. In September, 1915, the President forced the recall of Dumba and, three months later, that of two German naval and military attachés.

Along the sea lanes the Central Empires engaged in an even more desperate attempt to prevent shipments to the

Allies. Outmatched by the British on the ocean's surface, Germany had developed undersea craft ("U-boats") to a point of perfection hitherto unknown. The use of submarines, though recognized by international law, was subject to severe regulations. A merchantman or passenger vessel must not be attacked unless, after being warned, it refused to allow visit and search, and it should not be destroyed without safeguarding the lives of those on board. From Germany's unwillingness to abide by these restrictions stemmed all the difficulties that arose over submarine warfare. In justification, she pleaded the inability of U-boats to carry additional passengers, and contended that, by rising to the surface to give warning, the frailty of the vessels exposed them to quick destruction from hostile gunfire. The United States, on its part, maintained that, if the weapon could not be used according to the long-established rules, then the weapon must be abandoned, not the rules.

Germany began her undersea operations with a proclamation that from February 18, 1915, she would destroy every enemy merchantman found in the waters about the British Isles without regard to the safety of passengers or crew, and that even neutral ships might, through accident, suffer like treatment. At once Wilson replied that, if this "unprecedented" action should cause the loss of American vessels or lives, he would hold Germany to a "strict accountability." Nevertheless, in March a United States citizen was drowned by the torpedoing of the British steamer *Falaba,* and on May 1 the *Gulflight,* an American tanker, was attacked. Six days later occurred the most shocking incident of all when the British transatlantic liner *Lusitania,* carrying military supplies, was sent unwarned to the bottom, with a loss of nearly twelve hundred persons, including a hundred and twenty-eight Americans.

The United States blazed with resentment. "It is a deed

for which a Hun would blush, a Turk be ashamed, and a Barbary pirate apologize," declared the New York *Nation;* and the writer added: "The torpedo that sank the *Lusitania* also sank Germany in the opinion of mankind." Had a less resolute friend of peace been in the White House, war might easily have resulted. Instead, Wilson in a series of diplomatic notes demanded that the German government disavow her lawless practices, take prompt steps to prevent their recurrence, and make all possible reparation for the damages already inflicted. Even this action of the President impressed Secretary Bryan as carrying the country dangerously near the brink of war. In discussions with his chief he took the position that citizens should travel on belligerent merchantmen at their own risk, and argued that, in any event, the difficulties with Germany could best be composed by resorting to the principle of the "cooling-off" treaties (see page 395). In June, he resigned in protest, making way for Robert Lansing of New York, an expert in international law who had been Bryan's chief legal adviser in the State Department.

Meanwhile, the submarine depredations continued, culminating on August 19 in the sinking of the British liner *Arabic* and the loss of two more American lives. Fearful of the consequences, Germany thirteen days later definitely pledged that "Liners will not be sunk by our submarines without warning and without safety of the lives of noncombatants." In October she offered apologies and indemnity for the *Arabic* disaster. Though Wilson had won a diplomatic victory, its edge was dulled by lack of confidence in Berlin's good faith. Thus in February, 1916, when Germany offered payment for the lives lost in the *Lusitania,* she refused to admit the illegality of the destruction.

On March 24, American lives were again placed in jeopardy by the torpedoing without warning of the French channel steamer *Sussex.* Since this constituted an outright violation of the *Arabic* pledge, the President rejected the German excuse that the U-boat commander had made an unfortunate mistake. In a note of April 18 he delivered an ultimatum to the effect that, unless unrestricted submarine attacks ceased, the United States would sever diplomatic relations. Berlin, convinced at last of the aroused state of American opinion, grudgingly made the concession. The crisis was over, at least for the time. For the next nine months relations between the two countries showed less tension than at any time since hostilities had begun.

FROM BYSTANDER TO BELLIGERENT

When the war opened in 1914, it had seemed remote from the ordinary concerns of American life. But successive incidents, such as British interferences with United States trade, German plots against American industry and the ruthless submarine operations, had gradually caused the people to think of the conflict as intimately affecting their own well-being and safety. Their initial pro-Ally leanings grew stronger, partly because of the greater enormity of the Teutonic infractions of American neutrality and partly because of Germany's violation of Belgium's neutrality at the start of the war. "As by a lightning flash," wrote the prominent peace advocate David Starr Jordan of the German armies sweeping through Belgium, "the issue was made clear: the issue of the sacredness of law; the rule of the soldier or the rule of the citizen." [1]

All such tendencies were reënforced by a well-organized propaganda conducted from London. The British had com-

[1] American concern for the plight of the Belgians was greatly stimulated by the fact that Herbert Hoover, an American mining engineer, organized relief measures for them. As head of the Commission for the Relief of Belgium, he secured widespread financial support in the United States, obtained much-needed food and, in spite of many hindrances, provided for effective distribution of the supplies.

plete control of the transatlantic cables and censored all messages that passed over them. Besides, as one of their number later divulged, they supplied newspapers with a weekly pro-Ally review of the war, formed connections with "eminent people of every profession in the United States, beginning with university and college presidents, professors and scientific men and running through all the ranges of the population," and also streamed their "documents and literature" into public libraries, clubs, Y. M. C. A. branches and newspaper offices. Through such channels were disseminated appalling, if oftentimes fanciful, tales of Teutonic war atrocities and barbarities. An increasing number of people came to fear a triumphant Germany as a positive menace to the United States itself.

As the Teutonic cause grew in unpopularity, its supporters, led by the widespread German-language press, waxed more and more strident in their efforts to stem the tide. The nation, as it were, turned into a vast and vociferous debating society, with the President a somewhat lonely figure bent on avoiding intervention save as a last resort. Increasingly he became a target for acrid criticism from hyphenated Americans—both pro-Germans, who accused him of dealing too gently with Great Britain, and pro-Allies, who charged him with weakness toward Germany. Wilson's ill-timed statement in a speech shortly after the *Lusitania* disaster that "There is such a thing as a man being too proud to fight" was interpreted, not as the expression of a lofty ideal, as he intended, but as a confession of the administration's willingness to truckle to German military might.

The President at first resisted outside pressure to expand the national armaments, for, like most of his countrymen, he attributed the agitation to hysteria. The demand arose principally from the National Security League, financed largely by munitions and armor-plate interests and international bankers, and having eloquent spokesmen in such figures as ex-President Roosevelt and General Leonard Wood. Convinced at last by the thickening dangers, Wilson advocated "preparedness" in his annual message of December, 1915, and toured the Midwest to educate public sentiment on the question. At his insistence Congress in June, 1916, passed the Hay act to strengthen the military forces. It provided for augmenting the regular army by five annual accretions, for enlarging the state militia and placing it under federal control, and for establishing civilian training camps and introducing military instruction into schools and colleges. Secretary of War Garrison, believing the bill too mild, resigned in protest and was replaced by Newton D. Baker of Ohio. In August Congress, turning its attention to the navy, adopted a three-year program for the construction of ten dreadnaughts, six cruisers and a hundred and forty minor war craft, and made provision for a government-owned armor-plate plant. At the same time, Congress authorized a Council of National Defense of six cabinet members, to serve as a board of strategy for industrial mobilization if war should come.

With Wilson preparedness for war represented a reluctant second thought. From the beginning of hostilities he had devoted his chief energies to meeting the international crisis through the healing methods of diplomacy. Nor had he been content to confine his efforts to safeguarding the rights of neutrals. On the contrary, he endeavored to attack the evil at its source by repeatedly offering his good offices to the belligerents to end the conflict. In these transactions his confidential agent was Colonel Edward M. House of Texas, a man of wide acquaintance abroad but without experience as a diplomat. The President made an even bolder gesture in February, 1916, while the opposing armies lay deadlocked on the western front. Through Colonel House he assured the

British government that he stood ready to call a peace conference at which he would act as mediator, and that, if Germany declined, the United States "would probably enter the war against Germany." [1] This offer the English leaders rejected, possibly because they hoped through continuing the struggle to secure better terms, possibly because Walter Hines Page, the pro-Ally American Ambassador at London, scoffed at the administration's sincerity, and perhaps also because the word "probably" did actually leave the way open for Wilson to recede from his position. At any rate, America's delay in entering the conflict, so bitterly criticized by Allied statesmen, may in some degree be laid at their own door.

But already the President was arriving at a new conception of peace terms. Deeply influenced by the League to Enforce Peace, an organization founded in 1915, he adopted as his own the notion of a world federation for the prevention of war. The idea also enlisted the support of ex-President Taft and of other public figures irrespective of party. As a means of getting the proposal before the belligerents, Wilson on December 18, 1916, requested them to state "their respective views as to the terms upon which the war might be concluded, and the arrangements which would be deemed satisfactory as a guarantee against its renewal." On January 22, 1917, he reported the results to the Senate in an address intended for the whole world to hear. The Central Empires, he said, had refused to define their purposes, while the Allies had indicated in general terms their aims and expectations. As a neutral whose rights the struggle had put "in constant jeopardy," he asserted America's vital interest in a righteous and enduring peace—not "a victor's terms imposed upon the

---

[1] According to a memorandum of Sir Edward Grey, countersigned by Wilson, the President had in mind as peace terms "the restoration of Belgium, the transfer of Alsace and Lorraine to France, and the acquisition by Russia of an outlet to the sea," with compensation to Germany for her territorial losses in "concessions to her in other places outside Europe."

vanquished" and hence provocative of future bloodshed, but "a peace without victory." The settlement must embrace such principles as the right of self-determination, freedom of the seas, limitation of armaments and a league to guarantee "the permanence of peace."

Through the President's efforts, the United States was rapidly attaining the moral leadership of the earth. At home, however, the address exposed him to fresh volleys of execration because of the expression "peace without victory," which to his critics meant a blindness to the immediate issues at stake. In reality, the conception underlying the phrase remained the essence of America's purpose even as a belligerent, though, in view of the altered circumstances and his certainty of direct participation in the peace negotiations, Wilson later changed the expression to a "peace of justice."

Before the President sent his note to the warring powers, the campaign of 1916 had taken place. On June 7 the Republicans and the Progressives held simultaneous conventions at Chicago in the hope that the two parties might unite on a single ticket. But the passions of four years before had not yet sufficiently cooled. The Republicans wanted to nominate Charles E. Hughes, who as a member of the Supreme Court since 1910 had kept free from partisan embroilments; but the Progressives, despite Hughes's earlier reform record in New York, would have none other than Theodore Roosevelt. In the end, each group named its own candidate, the Republican ticket being completed with Charles W. Fairbanks of Indiana for Vice-President. The Republicans stigmatized Wilson's foreign policy as one of "phrase-making" and "shifty expedients," indorsed thoroughgoing preparedness, and promised a "strict and honest neutrality between the belligerents."

Roosevelt, who had no liking for lost causes, waited until the Progressive convention had adjourned and then declined to run, urging his supporters to follow him back into the Republican fold. His running mate, John M. Parker of Louisiana, declared for Wilson, however. The Democrats, convening at St. Louis on June 14, renominated their ticket of 1912. For the first time in many years they could point to a record of actual achievement. After rehearsing the party's epoch-making economic and humanitarian measures, the platform condemned "hyphenism," pledged adequate preparedness, and vaunted the President's diplomatic victories in safeguarding neutrality.

The ensuing contest proved close and exciting. As the "Outs," the Republicans brought all their batteries to bear upon the shortcomings of the "Ins." The pro-Germans, incited by a group called the German-American Alliance, helped Hughes by bitterly denouncing Wilson, and until the last week of the campaign the Republican nominee avoided saying anything that might alienate their support. In the words, "He kept us out of war," Democratic orators found an effective vote-getting slogan, especially in the case of the women, who now possessed the franchise in eleven states. Wilson's own speeches, however, contained nothing to justify an expectation that peace would necessarily continue.

The American Federation of Labor advocated his reëlection and, as the campaign wore on, the independent voters began to turn to him, largely because of Hughes's lukewarm utterances regarding social and economic reforms. The outcome was in doubt for several days after the election. The President received 277 electoral votes to 254 for his opponent, and 49.2 per cent of the popular ballots (9,130,000 votes) to 46 per cent (8,538,000). The Democratic ticket swept the South and the Far West, including nearly all the woman-suffrage states. For the first time in almost fifty years, if the Hayes-Tilden contest be excepted, a candidate won without the electoral vote of New York.

The significance of the outcome was misunderstood in the Central Empires. "The Germans," later declared James W. Gerard, the American Ambassador at Berlin, "believed that President Wilson had been elected with a mandate to keep out of war at any cost, and that America could be insulted, flouted, and humiliated with impunity." Hence they redoubled the secret exertions already begun for the most extensive and destructive submarine campaign within their resources. On January 31, 1917, Germany abruptly informed the United States that henceforth, in disregard of the *Sussex* pledge, she would sink on sight all ships, neutral as well as belligerent, in certain waters about the British Isles and in the Mediterranean. At once Wilson, faithful to his ultimatum on the previous occasion, broke off diplomatic relations, and appealed, vainly, to all neutral countries to follow America's example so that the weight of world opinion might be thrown against Germany. Meanwhile, seeing a possibility of halting the Kaiser in his reckless course by drawing Austria-Hungary into a separate peace, he exerted pressure upon the Allies to make known to her their willingness to accept milder terms than they had hitherto contemplated. Though Britain met his wishes part way, Austria-Hungary proved obdurate.

On February 26 the chief executive, making another move in defense of time-honored American rights, asked Congress to authorize a policy of armed neutrality. The House promptly responded, but in the Senate a dozen Western and Southern members, including Robert M. La Follette and George W. Norris, managed to block action before the session ended a few days later. Nevertheless, the President, by authority of an almost forgotten statute, directed the arming of merchant ships.[1] Already Teutonic ruthlessness had begun to take its

[1] On the Attorney-General's advice, Wilson resorted to a law of 1819 which had specific reference to piratical vessels.

toll. From February 3 to April 1, eight American vessels were sent to the bottom with a loss of forty-eight lives. Armed neutrality was fast proving its futility when Wilson called a special session of Congress for April 2.

Before that date two events helped further to clarify the public's thinking in regard to the nature of the crisis. One was the so-called Zimmermann note, whose contents were made public on March 1 through the enterprise of the British Intelligence Service. This document, signed by the Kaiser's Foreign Minister on January 19, instructed the German Minister in Mexico to urge that government to attack the United States in case the latter declared war on Germany, and to offer as inducements "general financial support" and the opportunity to recover "the lost territory of New Mexico, Texas and Arizona." The American people, deeply shocked by the disclosure, found fresh reason to fear the menace of German militarism. The other event was the news of the Russian revolution and the setting up of a republican government. By the Czar's overthrow the principal European Allies all became exponents of popular government, leaving to the Teutonic powers and Turkey the dubious distinction of being the last strongholds of military autocracy.

When the special session assembled, President Wilson in words that profoundly stirred the nation asked Congress to recognize the existence of a state of war with Germany. Reciting the submarine depredations and the conspiracies against American security culminating in the Zimmermann note, he pictured these as the inevitable accompaniments of "autocratic governments backed by organized force which is controlled wholly by their will, not by the will of their people." The United States, he said, would battle for the rights of mankind, "for the ultimate peace of the world and for the liberation of its peoples, the German peoples included."

And he added, in a phrase that rang round the globe, "The world must be made safe for democracy."

The period of indecision was at an end. After three years of unexampled forbearance, Wilson led the nation into the conflict when the people were convinced that no alternative remained. Moreover, he made the fateful choice turn not on motives of revenge or of selfish national gain, but on the opportunity to extend traditional American ideals to oppressed peoples. On April 6 Congress by overwhelming majorities voted to sustain the President. A declaration of war against Austria-Hungary was withheld until December 7 in the hope that meanwhile she might still be weaned from her alliance with Germany.

Just what weight should be assigned the various factors that brought about American intervention it is difficult to say. From the beginning, public opinion leaned toward the Allies because of impalpable cultural bonds with England. Allied propaganda was another influence. This factor, however, can easily be exaggerated, for propaganda succeeds only when it falls upon minds already favorably inclined. At most, the British manipulation of news gave precision and effect to forces it could not have created. The creeping involvement of financial ties also played a part. In the view of Ray Stannard Baker, Woodrow Wilson's authorized biographer, "By the end of the year 1914 the traffic in war materials with the Allies had become deeply entrenched in America's economic organization, and the possibility of keeping out of war by the diplomacy of neutrality . . . had reached the vanishing point." On March 5, 1917, Ambassador Page cabled from London that, because of the British government's diminishing financial resources, "orders by all the Allied governments will be reduced to the lowest minimum"; and he added, "Perhaps our going to war is the only way in which our present prominent trade position can be maintained and a panic averted." But however greatly such considerations may have swayed certain persons, minute research has failed to disclose any evidence that the President himself was so influenced; and it was he who made the decision to fight. Both his personal temperament and his hostility to Big Business would seem to preclude the possibility that he was acting either as the agent or the dupe of Wall Street.

It is improbable that all these factors added together would have taken the nation into the conflagration. On the other hand, it is clear that, given the circumstances, Germany's action in launching unrestricted submarine operations rendered it impossible for the United States to stay out any longer. The Berlin authorities understood the situation, but believed they could smash their way to victory before America could mobilize her strength. President Wilson seized the occasion to appeal to American idealism, yet this was more than an afterthought. The public had gradually become persuaded by the course of events that the struggle involved opposing principles of government and that a world dominated by Germany would imperil democracy everywhere. Wilson merely clothed with memorable words what lay in people's minds. In 1919, after the war, he told a Senate committee that he believed this issue alone would have eventually caused America's intervention; but this conclusion seems doubtful in the absence of some specific violation of national rights.

America's entry set an example for many other neutral countries. The response of the republics of the Western Hemisphere was particularly significant because of the light it shed upon Pan American solidarity. Between April, 1917, and July, 1918, Panama, Cuba, Brazil, Guatemala, Nicaragua, Haiti and Honduras declared war, while most of the other countries, not wishing to go so far, severed diplomatic relations.

ACTIVITIES ON THE HOME FRONT

The World War was the fourth great European struggle in which the American people had become involved, not counting the century of conflict between the English and French colonists. The War of Independence, after France intervened in 1778, had widened into a general international contest; and the naval hostilities with France in 1798–1800 as well as the War of 1812–1815 had been American phases of the Anglo-French duel for predominance in the Old World. Every major European war involving operations in the Atlantic had, sooner or later, drawn America into it. When she unsheathed the sword against Germany, the war had been raging for two years and eight months. At the outset the Germans had tried for a speedy decision, but, after getting within fifty miles of Paris, they had been halted by the battle of the Marne. Since then, in spite of titanic Allied exertions, they had retained possession of most of Belgium and an important section of northeastern France. Besides fighting on the western front, the opposing forces struggled on the Russo-Austrian frontier and, after the spring of 1915, also on the Austro-Italian frontier. On land the advantage lay everywhere with the Central Empires. But their commerce had been swept from the seas, nearly all the German colonies had been captured, and the Allied blockade had steadily tightened its grip on essential supplies.

The war had developed unusual features. With millions of men engaged on the two sides, open-field fighting had given way to trench warfare on a vast scale. Moreover, inventions and discoveries which had been evolved in peace time to promote human welfare were now converted to purposes of human destruction. Chief among these were the motor car and the airplane. The former not only quickened the movement of men and materials but, in the form of armored tanks, became itself an engine of warfare. The latter, developed by the combatants to new perfection, rendered indispensable service in scouting, bombing and combat. Among other inventions, wireless telegraphy (devised in 1895 by Guglielmo Marconi, an Italian) proved valuable for keeping the many units of the gigantic armies in constant communication, while the beneficent peace-time discoveries of the world's chemists were utilized in the manufacture of hand grenades, explosive bombs and clouds of poison gas. The new machinery of warfare gave unexpected importance to petroleum or gasoline, which supplied motive power for conveyances on land, in the air and under the water, and was even displacing the use of coal on warships. "It is as necessary as blood in the battles of tomorrow," wrote Georges Clemenceau, the French Premier, to President Wilson.

America's entry placed at the disposal of the Allies not only an unplumbed reservoir of man power, but also unlimited quantities of money, foodstuffs, minerals, manufactures, shipyards and material resources of every kind. Perhaps equally significant was the fresh enthusiasm and ardent idealism that the United States brought to the struggle, for a spirit of exhaustion and defeatism lay heavily on the Allied peoples. Official missions, hastening to Washington, made clear the extent of Allied needs and urged the greatest possible speed in the sending of troops. While military preparations were getting under way, the United States before the close of 1917 lent the Allied governments $885,000,000, a mere earnest of the huge sums that were to follow. These loans were not advanced in gold, but in credits in American banks with which to purchase war supplies in the United States. Though resolved to coöperate to the fullest extent, the government did not forget that it had joined the war for American, not European, reasons. It refrained therefore from entering a formal alliance, preferring to regard the Allies officially as "Associates" in a common effort.

However remiss the administration may have been in fore-arming against war, it sought now to make up for lost time by organizing the nation with a thoroughness and on a scale unparalleled in American annals. Under Wilson's compelling leadership, and against fierce opposition from leaders of his own party, Congress on May 18, 1917, adopted the selective-service act. The President was empowered to conscript a million men from between the ages of twenty-one and thirty inclusive, with exemption or deferred classification for public officials, clergymen, members of religious sects opposed to war, persons engaged in employments essential to military success, men upon whom others were dependent, and physical and mental defectives. A year later the draft age was lowered to eighteen and raised to forty-five. No one was permitted to purchase exemption or hire a substitute, as in the Civil War. The President justified conscription on the democratic principle "that there is a universal obligation to serve and that a public authority should choose those upon whom the obligation of military service shall rest, and also in a sense choose those who shall do the rest of the nation's work."

Without loss of time the men of draft age were registered, and this, with the subsequent enrollment of youths later coming of age, made available more than ten million. The names of the first half million to be called to the colors were drawn on July 20, 1917. The operation of the draft occasioned local protests, but, unlike Civil War times, no serious disturbances. The act of May 18 also increased the regular army to two hundred and eighty-seven thousand, and incorporated the entire national guard in the federal service. With these additions, the total military strength at the end of 1917 attained one and a quarter million men and more than a hundred thousand officers.

The problem of assembling the elements of an army proved less difficult than that of fitting them for the grim business ahead. Sixteen great tent-camps in the South served as training quarters for the augmented national guard, while a similar number of cantonments in various parts of the country took care of the national or draft army. Swiftly constructed, these cantonments resembled full-fledged towns more than camps. Each comprised a thousand or more frame barracks and other buildings for about forty-eight thousand men, and each was equipped with sewers, running water, artificial light, camp newspapers, libraries, theaters, laundries and hospitals. Here, thanks to able direction and conscientious devotion to duty, the men completed their preparations in an average period of six months. Officers were supplied through special training camps, the best known being at Plattsburg, New York. The curse of political appointments, which had marred the conduct of earlier wars, was avoided by the adoption of a scientific rating system designed to recognize ability and experience. Even the colleges were formed into training schools, and ultimately about a hundred and seventy thousand youths in five hundred institutions joined the Students' Army Training Corps.

Simultaneously with the creation of an army, thoroughgoing steps were taken to mobilize the country's material resources. "Under modern conditions"—to quote Secretary of War Baker—"wars are not made by soldiers only, but by nations. . . . The army is merely the point of the sword." The Council of National Defense, authorized before America's entrance, assumed general charge, though much of the actual work was carried on through an advisory commission composed of seven men thoroughly familiar with the nation's industrial, professional and labor potentialities. Thus, Daniel

Willard, president of the Baltimore and Ohio Railroad, acted as expert in transportation, Julius Rosenwald, head of a Chicago mail-order concern, in clothing and similar supplies, and Samuel Gompers in labor matters. From this group as a generating center there developed from time to time, as need demanded, numerous subcommittees and special technical boards. This elaborate national organization was, in many of its features, paralleled by the states. Every state had its own council of defense, and some of them a network of local agencies as well. Everywhere the people showed that capacity for practical coöperation in face of an emergency which had distinguished them on many an earlier occasion.

Of the committees of the Council of National Defense, that on munitions attained such importance that in July, 1917, it was reorganized as the War Industries Board. Under the vigorous direction of Bernard M. Baruch it exercised dictatorial powers over the processes of manufacture. It regulated all businesses engaged in producing war materials, developed new industries and sources of supply, eliminated waste, enforced efficiency and fixed prices. It purchased for the Allies as well as for the American government and determined priorities of production and delivery. The making of some thirty thousand commodities came under its supervision, and that supervision was extraordinarily minute. At the war's close its efforts were estimated to have increased the nation's industrial output at least twenty per cent.

Notwithstanding these Herculean labors, the swift progress of events abroad did not allow time for rebuilding and equipping factories to produce certain military essentials. In many instances the very tools for fabricating the needed articles had first to be devised and manufactured. The worst failure involved the production of heavy artillery, machine guns and aircraft. For these the American army was forced to rely largely upon the French and British. In July, 1917, the

Washington authorities had launched an ambitious plan for making eleven thousand five hundred combat planes and a large number of training craft before the following summer. But the lack of manufacturing facilities, together with other difficulties and delays, some of them avoidable, held up the program, greatly to the public's exasperation. Not till well into the second year did substantial results begin to appear, but even when the armistice was signed, only about twelve thousand aircraft had been completed, a third of them service planes.

Another branch of the Council of National Defense, the Food Administration, derived its importance from a dangerous shortage of foodstuffs in the Allied countries and the need to collect huge supplies for the American forces. This agency, headed by Herbert Hoover, famed as the organizer of Belgian relief, at first lacked adequate authority, but in August, 1917, it received from Congress practically unlimited power to boost crop production and conserve food. To assist in the work, subordinate food administrators were appointed in the states and local subdivisions. The problem centered mainly in wheat, meat, sugar and fats. In order to increase output, every effort was exerted to expand the existing acreage. Farmers were stimulated to enlarge their normal plantings by the government's agreement to buy all wheat raised in 1918 at two dollars a bushel. Even city dwellers converted their yards and near-by vacant lots into "war gardens" and, by consuming their own produce, lessened the strain on the commercial supply.

In order to curtail domestic consumption, the Food Administration resorted both to official restriction of the sales of wholesalers and retailers and to the encouragement of voluntary coöperation by the public. The slogan, "Food Will Win the War," appeared on all the billboards of the country, and a new verb, "to hooverize," entered the American vocabulary. Housewives hung cards in their windows to proclaim their fidelity to the regulations, and showed patriotic zeal in the use of substitutes and the observance of "meatless meals" and "wheatless days." The results amply justified the Food Administration's efforts. In the four summer months of 1918 the American people through savings from their regular consumption sent abroad half a million tons of sugar. The autumn saw an increase of nearly a million tons of pork products over that available the preceding year. In general, during the crop year of 1918, America doubled the average amount of food exported to Europe immediately before the war. By such means the United States was able not only to feed the Allied armies, but also to save their peoples (and later much of Central and Southeastern Europe) from almost certain starvation.

The Food Administration hardly began its work before it was paralleled by the establishment of a Fuel Administration, authorized by the same law. As in the case of food, the coal problem involved both greater production and frugal use. Miners and operators zealously coöperated, while householders observed unwonted domestic economy. Difficulties of shipment were heightened by congested rail conditions, and by the cruelly cold winter of 1917–1918 which imprisoned coal barges in icebound harbors. At one juncture Harry A. Garfield, the fuel administrator, ordered a temporary shutdown of factories in the trans-Mississippi region in order that the coal might be diverted to more essential purposes. Attention was also given to increasing oil production. As its contribution to the cause, the motoring public reduced pleasure riding to a minimum and willingly heeded the request for "gasless Sundays."

As the fuel situation made evident, success in industrial mobilization required the most efficient use of rail facilities. The problem of troop movements was similarly involved.

Because the railways, burdened with an unprecedented volume of traffic and hampered by long-established habits of competition, could not rise to the emergency, the President in the closing days of 1917 put them in charge of Secretary of the Treasury McAdoo. Calling to his aid experienced rail executives, McAdoo as director-general operated the principal lines as a single system. He cut passenger trains to a minimum, subordinated ordinary freight to the carrying of war materials, used terminals and repair shops wherever they were found, and did everything possible to clear the rails for essential uses. In these respects his success was remarkable; but he found it necessary to raise wages by more than $600,-000,000 and also to increase freight and passenger rates. Despite the higher transportation charges, the greatly enhanced costs caused the railways to be operated at a deficit throughout the period of federal control. In July, 1918, the Postmaster-General, by direction of the President, took over the telephone and telegraph lines, and later extended his authority to cables. In a similar fashion the express business was placed under federal management in November. At the stern behest of Mars the government, for the time being, moved far in the direction of state socialism.

SELECT BIBLIOGRAPHY

America as a Neutral. These years are systematically surveyed in Paxson, *Pre-War Years*, which should be supplemented by the more informal treatment of Sullivan, *Our Times*, V. America's relations to the European conflict are discussed from various angles in Borchard and Lage, *Neutrality for the United States;* Millis, *Road to War;* Morrissey, *American Defense of Neutral Rights;* Notter, *Origins of the Foreign Policy of Woodrow Wilson;* Seymour, *American Diplomacy during the World War;* Tansill, *America Goes to War;* and James, *German Subs in Yankee Waters.* For propaganda and the activities of foreign emissaries in the United States, see Child, *German-*

Americans in Politics; Jones and Hollister, *German Secret Service in America;* Peterson, *Propaganda for War;* Squires, *British Propaganda;* and Wittke, *German-Americans and the World War.* Biographies, important for this and the next section, include Baker, *Wilson,* V-VII; Seymour, *Intimate Papers of Colonel House;* Pringle, *Roosevelt;* Palmer, *Baker;* Hendrick, *Life and Letters of Walter H. Page;* and Arnett, *Claude Kitchin and the Wilson War Policies.*

America in the War. Paxson, *America at War,* provides a general account, while Sullivan, *Our Times,* V, adds much local color. Activities on the home front are portrayed in Crowell and Wilson, *How America Went to War,* a comprehensive account devoted chiefly to economic mobilization; Willoughby, *Government Organization in War Time;* Van Hise, *Conservation and Regulation in the United States during the World War;* Hines, *War History of American Railroads;* Surface, *Grain Trade during the World War;* Powell, *Army behind the Army;* Clarkson, *Industrial America in the World War;* and Kolbe, *Colleges in War Time.* For the military mobilization, see references at the end of Chapter XVI.

Chapter XVI

THE PATH TO PEACE, 1917–1920

ARMED OPERATIONS OVERSEAS

THE navy was the first to begin operations. Its task was twofold: to help cripple German sea power in Europe, and to convoy the United States forces across three thousand miles of ocean. Within eighteen days after America's entry six destroyers started for the theater of war, where under Admiral William S. Sims they at once set about to aid the British in chasing and sinking submarines. Battleships and cruisers followed until, at the close of the war, five thousand naval officers and seventy thousand enlisted men were serving abroad. The three-year construction plan, adopted in 1916 as part of the preparedness program, was accelerated and expanded. In the first nine months of 1918 no less than eighty-three new destroyers were launched. The government also commandeered private craft and took over German ships that had been interned in American ports. During the war period the total number of vessels in commission increased from less than two hundred to more than two thousand.

Among other exploits, the navy, with British assistance, laid a great mine barrage, extending nearly two hundred and fifty miles from the Norwegian coast to the Orkney Islands, in the effort to prevent German U-boats from reaching the high seas. Also with British coöperation, it worked out a suc-cessful scheme of protecting troop ships from submarine raids while crossing the Atlantic. One notable American contribution to this type of warfare was the invention of an effective sound detector for indicating the approximate location of submerged U-boats. This device overcame the greatest obstacle to hunting them down. The results amply attested Anglo-American naval efficiency, for of the whole number of transports only six were torpedoed, and of these two managed to make port.

Shortly after the declaration of war General John J. Pershing, whose ability had been tested in the Philippines and in the punitive operations across the Mexican border, went to France to act as chief of the American Expeditionary Force (A. E. F.). At the urgent request of the French, a division of regulars followed in June and July as a visible symbol of the hosts which were to come later. These hosts, however, were still in course of training, and by the end of 1917 only a hundred and ninety-five thousand soldiers had reached France. But then their numbers increased rapidly. During the four months from May to August, 1918, more than a million made the overseas trip.

To look after their multifarious needs, the Services of Supply, an organization formed by Pershing in February, 1918, made colossal preparations. From its headquarters at Tours, the S. O. S. assumed responsibility for assembling and distributing all food, equipment and other materials required for the A. E. F. Besides building gigantic docks at the ports of arrival, it erected great hospitals and warehouses and constructed a thousand miles of railroad and more than a hundred thousand miles of telegraph and telephone. Stores of all kinds had to be brought from the United States— everything from bags of cement to monster locomotives ready to run from the vessel's hatch under their own steam. Before the armistice, over seven million tons of supplies, including more than seventeen thousand freight cars and nearly thirty-five thousand motor trucks, had thus been transported. The fighting forces as they arrived usually underwent further training for a month or so before going to the front and then, brigaded with French or British troops, they spent another month in a quiet part of the line. But in January, 1918, Pershing began to gather the scattered fragments of his command, though it was not until August that he established a distinct American army.

While the United States was organizing its strength, the enemy, fearful of the might of the western giant when fully aroused, tried to end the war with a series of terrific blows. In October, 1917, a crushing defeat at Caporetto at the hands of the Austrians demoralized Italy. In March, 1918, war-weary Russia, now dominated by the communists, concluded an inglorious peace with the Central Empires at Brest-Litovsk. Rumania, left in the lurch by Russia's defection, had little choice but to follow her example, which she did the same month. Free at last to concentrate their armies on the western front, the Central Empires under Erich von Ludendorff made gigantic preparations for a smashing drive. In March, 1918, as the offensive got under way, the Allies for the first time buried their national jealousies and gave supreme direction of the several armies to a single person, Marshal Ferdinand Foch of the French command.

Though the Americans had hitherto done little beyond joining in nocturnal raids and occasional attacks, now, inured to the novel conditions of warfare and eager to get into the fray on their own account, they played their full part, along with the seasoned Allied veterans, in resisting the German onslaughts. Of the American participation certain phases stand out. On May 28 the First Division took Cantigny. Three days later the Third Division helped the French check the Teutonic advance at Château-Thierry on the Marne River, only forty miles from Paris. Near by, enemy forces occupied a densely forested tract known as Belleau Wood. After six days of furious hostilities, marked by hand-to-hand

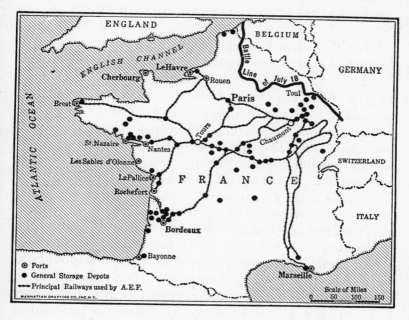

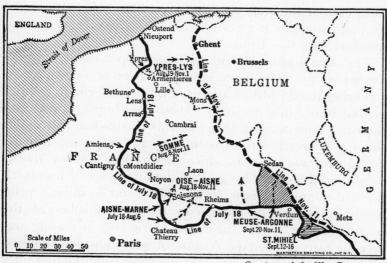

Courtesy of the War Department

THE A. E. F. IN FRANCE, 1918

fighting, the marines of the Second Division ejected them on June 11. A new assault by the Germans on July 14 brought the Third Division into action again, and on the next day a Franco-American charge drove the enemy back a mile and captured the villages of Chezy and Montlevon.

The Teutonic offensive, as the sequel proved, was a gambler's last throw. The enemy not only failed to win a decisive victory, but suffered irreplaceable losses in men, equipment and morale. Unexpectedly, in mid-July, Marshal Foch launched a mighty counteroffensive. Once more the Americans contributed to victory. On the eighteenth, in coöperation with picked French troops, they made a successful drive on Soissons. The following weeks found them repeatedly in action until, on August 3, they assumed sole responsibility for a section of the front, about eighty-five miles in length, lying to the southeast of the principal British and French forces. This position threatened vital German communications and, at the same time, permitted the concentration of men and supplies at a point behind the lines which did not interfere with the Allies.

The Americans now enlarged their operations. On September 12-15 they succeeded, against feeble resistance, in capturing the St. Mihiel salient, a triangle of enemy ground jutting into Allied territory. About five hundred and fifty thousand Americans engaged in this battle—five and a half times as many as in the Union army at Gettysburg. But the most important action in which they assisted was the Meuse-Argonne offensive. The goal of the attack was a four-track railroad running parallel to the front and forming a principal supply line of the enemy. From September 26 the battle proceeded with little abatement and increasing success for forty-seven days. A total of a million two hundred thousand American soldiers, besides eight hundred and forty airplanes and three hundred and twenty-four tanks, took part. At last, in the first week of November, a section of the coveted railway passed into the hands of the French and Americans. In General Pershing's words, "We had cut the enemy's main line of communications, and nothing but surrender or an armistice could save his army from complete disaster."

During the whole course of the war the Americans captured about forty-four thousand prisoners and fourteen hundred guns of all kinds, while Yankee aviators brought down seven hundred and fifty-five enemy planes, themselves losing nearly half that number. Though the military operations were confined chiefly to France, United States soldiers appeared on other fronts as well. At Italy's urgent request a regiment went to the Austro-Italian front in July, 1918. In October two divisions reënforced the French in Belgium. America also became involved in hostilities with Soviet Russia, although the two nations were officially at peace. The Allies refused to acknowledge the separate peace concluded with Germany at Brest-Litovsk and were further angered by Russia's cancellation of her foreign debt. Accordingly, they sent armed forces to assist anticommunist movements and to safeguard large stores of military supplies in northern Russia. About five thousand Americans joined an Allied expedition which fought minor engagements in the vicinity of Archangel and Murmansk from September, 1918, until May, 1919, when their withdrawal began. Another detachment of about ten thousand took part in an Allied expeditionary force to Vladivostok and eastern Siberia, where they remained until January, 1920.

Of every hundred American soldiers two died of wounds or disease during the period of active warfare. In the Union army during the Civil War, the comparable figure was about ten, and among other Great Powers in the World War between twenty and twenty-five. That the American fatalities in

AMERICA'S WAR EFFORT IN SUMMARY

Total number registered in draft	24,234,021
Total draft inductions	2,810,296
Graduates of officers' training schools	80,568
Total size of the army	4,000,000
Total armed forces, including army, navy, etc.	4,800,000
Men who went overseas	2,086,000
Men who fought in France	1,390,000
Greatest number sent in one month	306,000
Tons of supplies shipped to France	7,500,000
Battles fought by American troops	13
Months of American participation in the war	19
American casualties in Meuse-Argonne battle	120,000
American battle deaths in war	50,000
American deaths from disease	57,500
Total deaths in the army	115,000
Total deaths in the navy	10,000
Cost of army to April 30, 1919	$13,930,000,000
Cost of war to April 30, 1919	$21,850,000,000

battle were not greater was due largely to the fact that the heavy fighting lasted only two hundred days. For every man killed in action, six were wounded and, of these, five eventually returned to duty. Romance has always portrayed the soldier as shot through the heart, but in every earlier war of the United States many more had died from disease than from battle. Even in the World War more than half the losses in the army as a whole were from disease, but this resulted from a dreadful epidemic of influenza-pneumonia, which swept through the country during the fall and winter of 1918 and took its heaviest toll in the crowded camps and cantonments. More than twice as many men perished from this cause as from all other diseases.

Apart from this baffling plague, the health record was exceptional, thanks to the great advance of medical science as well as to the completeness of hospital facilities. Into the army medical corps were drawn over thirty-one thousand physicians and surgeons from civilian life, among them the foremost leaders of the profession. They not only facilitated the adoption of the latest methods of prevention and cure, but themselves made new discoveries of vast human benefit. The preventive measures included thorough camp sanitation, precautions as to drinking water and compulsory vaccination against typhoid fever. Intestinal disorders, such as dysentery, typhus, cholera and typhoid, which had ravaged armies in the past, were virtually banished as causes of death.

While war still raged on the several fronts, President Wilson renewed his efforts, begun as a neutral, to turn the greatest war yet known to mankind into an instrument for enduring peace. In his view, military victory was an opportunity not for vengeance, but for a "peace of justice," one that would deal fairly with all parties and foster lasting international good will. By tacit consent he became the spokesman of the powers fighting Germany. If they did not subscribe to all his passionate idealism, they at least believed his utterances might have the useful effect of weakening the hold of the military clique on the war-weary Teutonic peoples and thus shorten the struggle.

Addressing Congress on January 8, 1918, Wilson set forth Fourteen Points that embodied the most complete statement he had yet made of acceptable terms. The first group of five points struck at four of the deeper springs of the conflict: secret diplomacy, economic rivalry, militarism and imperialism. He demanded the abandonment of secret international understandings, a guarantee of freedom of the seas, the removal of economic barriers among nations, a reduction of national armaments, and an adjustment of colonial claims with due regard to the interests of the inhabitants affected. Next followed eight points, more specific in character but all concerned with assuring European nationalities rights of self-determination and unhampered economic development. The German-conquered sections of Belgium, France, Russia, Rumania, Serbia and Montenegro, he said, should be evacuated and restored; the oppressed nationalities of Austria-Hungary and Turkey must gain political autonomy; [1] an independent Poland should be created out of German, Austrian and Russian territory; and the Franco-German and Austro-Italian frontiers should be readjusted along lines of nationality. For his fourteenth point Wilson reserved the keystone of his arch of peace: the formation of an association of nations to afford "mutual guarantees of political independence and territorial integrity to great and small states alike." In closing his address he intimated that America and the Allies would be unwilling to make peace with a government which spoke for the military party rather than for the people of Germany.

But it required Foch's great offensive of the summer of 1918 to convince Germany that she faced unavoidable disaster. Her allies, hemmed in on every side, their morale shattered, were preparing to give up the fight with or without her consent. The German people were seething with revolution, and the Kaiser was about to abdicate and flee. On October 4 the government at Berlin asked Wilson to take steps toward peace on the basis of the Fourteen Points. After assuring himself that the appeal came from representatives of the people rather than of the military clique, the President referred it to the Allied leaders. The latter, reluctant to approve of the Fourteen Points, hesitated until Colonel House, acting as Wilson's representative, threatened that otherwise the President would be obliged to consult Congress as to the advisability of continuing the fight for their special objectives. Thereupon the Allies acceded, subject to reservations as to freedom of the seas and to an explicit admission of German obligation for all damages to civilian life and property. On this basis the armistice was concluded on November 11.

[1] Later, however, he altered the formula in the case of Austria-Hungary to one of political independence for the subject peoples.

THE WAR AND THE AMERICAN PUBLIC

In no previous conflict had the American people backed the government so whole-heartedly. Differences of opinion as to the relative merits of the European belligerents were drowned in a swelling tide of patriotism. Customary party lines vanished, though the Republicans reserved the right to insist on a more vigorous conduct of the war and grew increasingly restive under what they termed Wilson's "dictatorial" methods. Organized labor rallied strongly to the support of the government. Even citizens of Teutonic origin, almost without exception, made America's cause their own. In Congress the President found them among his most zealous adherents. The provost marshal general reported that "men of foreign and of native origin alike responded to the call to arms with a patriotic devotion that confounded the cynical plans of our archenemy and surpassed our own highest expectations."

As a force for unifying and invigorating popular opinion, the Committee on Public Information, created a few days after the declaration of war with the liberal journalist George Creel as chairman, played an important part. Creel proceeded to mobilize the mind of America just as Secretary Baker was mobilizing the man power and Bernard Baruch the industrial resources. The Committee supplied twenty thousand columns of news a week to the press, withholding such as might aid the enemy. It also carried on a mammoth campaign of popular education regarding America's objects in the war and the dangers of German imperialism. For these purposes it published a daily newspaper, issued seventy-five million circulars and pamphlets, produced many patriotic films, directed seventy-five thousand speakers in over five thousand communities, established press agencies in Allied and neutral countries, and showered down propaganda from the skies on the enemy countries.

Notwithstanding the unexampled upsurge of loyalty, of course unanimity did not exist. The farmers of the upper Mississippi Valley retained some of their earlier pacifism, and occasional individuals came into conflict with the law. But the chief dissent arose from the Socialists who, meeting in St. Louis on April 7, 1917, branded America's entry as a crime of the capitalist class against the people, and pledged a "continuous, active and public opposition to the war through demonstrations . . . and all other means within our power." Though their position was anticapitalist and antimilitarist rather than pro-German, the public generally refused to recognize the distinction. Many prominent Socialists, including Allan Benson, the presidential nominee in 1916, bolted the party in protest.

In order to cope with this and kindred situations, Congress in June adopted the espionage act. It provided stringent penalties for willful attempts to obstruct recruiting or to "cause insubordination, disloyalty . . . or refusal of duty" in the armed forces. It also instructed the Postmaster-General to exclude from the mails any matter deemed seditious or treasonable. A year later, in May, 1918, the law was strengthened by the sedition act, which amplified the list of crimes, including among them abusive utterances in regard to the government, the Constitution or the flag. A third statute in October empowered the Secretary of Labor to deport, without jury trial, aliens who "believe in or advocate" the forcible overthrow of government, or who sought the unlawful destruction of property, or who belonged to organizations holding such views.

All three measures, while in course of passage, were assailed as infringing the constitutional rights of free speech and free press and as exceeding the alien and sedition acts of 1798 in intolerance. As during the Civil War, however, the real or fancied rights of the individual were not suffered to hamper the majority will. Federal agents systematically prevented supposedly dangerous Socialist activities, censoring and suppressing their newspapers, raiding their meetings and prosecuting their speakers. Debs, four times Socialist candidate for President, was among those sent to prison. In all, over nineteen hundred judicial proceedings were brought against Socialists and other offenders up to July 1, 1919, and about half the cases resulted in convictions. In many instances the zeal of the authorities outran their judgment. Thus one Socialist speaker, Rose Pastor Stokes, received a ten-year sentence for saying, "I am for the people, and the government is for the profiteers." Men were even imprisoned for excited remarks made in the heat of private argument. Higher courts set aside a number of the decisions, including that involving Mrs. Stokes.

The national legislation against disloyalty was matched by similar and frequently more drastic statutes in many of the states. But even without resort to law, war hysteria inflicted distress and suffering on many individuals. Those suspected of lacking the expected degree of patriotism were likely to find yellow paint daubed on their doors; their places of business were boycotted; and oftentimes they were dismissed from teaching positions in schools and colleges. Senator La Follette, who had voted against the declaration of war, was censured by the Wisconsin legislature and became a nation-wide target for opprobrium despite the fact that he supported all the administration's measures for prosecuting the war.

In particular, anything bearing a Teutonic label evoked popular wrath. Many states through legislation erased German-language courses from the public schools, or attained the same result by local administrative action, while in the colleges students shunned the subject. Twenty years after the armistice German had not recovered its former position in the curriculum. Some wanted to go further and suppress public worship in the enemy tongue, though apparently only Missouri actually took the step. In the two war years the number of periodicals published in German fell from about five hundred to less than three hundred and fifty. Bands and orchestras played German music at their peril, and many families and even towns with Teutonic names hastened to anglicize them in order to avoid trouble or to advertise their loyalty.

Without an ardent public support of the war it would have been more difficult to raise the huge sums necessary for its prosecution. From the first of April, 1917, through April, 1919, the United States spent more than $1,000,000 an hour on the struggle, or a total of $21,850,000,000. In addition, loans to the Allies proceeded at the rate of nearly half a million an hour, amounting in the same period to $8,850,000,000. The war expenditures proved almost three times as great as the total outlay of the government for all purposes during the first century of its existence. In order to place as much of the burden as possible on the living generation, the administration saw to it that a third of the cost was raised by taxation—more than in any earlier war, or in other nations during the World War. An effort was also made to tax heavily those most able to pay. Income rates were increased at every level, rising finally to seventy-seven per cent for incomes of $1,000,000 and over. In like fashion, corporation profits in excess of normal prewar earnings were taxed on a progressive scale. Aside from these chief founts of revenue, levies were placed upon inheritances and postage rates raised, while internal-revenue duties were extended until they touched virtually all the luxuries and many of the necessities of life. The tariff, long the mainspring of government receipts, contributed less than a twentieth of the whole.

To facilitate the borrowing of money, Congress authorized

five great bond issues, the first four known as Liberty Loans and the last—floated after the armistice—as the Victory Loan. Campaigns of publicity such as had never been seen in America popularized the bonds, which could be bought in denominations as small as fifty dollars. In the fourth sale twenty-one million subscribers responded, nearly one for every family in the nation. Though the government aimed to tap every available source of revenue, almost equally important was the desire to give a maximum number of people a financial stake in the war. These purposes were further served by the sale of war-savings certificates in denominations of five dollars, and of "thrift stamps" as low as twenty-five cents. Local sales committees sometimes overshot the mark and coerced unwilling buyers, particularly if they possessed German names. In the end, hardly a man, woman or child in the entire population had failed to contribute a "silver bullet" toward victory.

At the same time Congress set a new standard in humane legislation for the soldiers and their dependents. An act of October, 1917, provided that fifteen dollars, or half the pay of a private, should be sent home each month as an "allotment," the government increasing the sum by an "allowance" which normally amounted to fifteen dollars or more, according to nearness of kin and the number of dependents. The maimed soldier was promised vocational training at national expense in case he should be unable to resume his former employment. In addition, the act included a war-risk insurance plan whereby the men, at low cost, could take out government insurance against death or disability. It was hoped by these provisions to prevent a repetition of the pension abuses that had followed the Civil War.

Meanwhile, voluntary organizations to befriend the soldiers and sustain the national morale appeared on every hand. Chief among these was the American Red Cross, which now scaled new heights of service to distressed mankind. Besides safeguarding the interests of needy soldiers' families at home, it took charge of sanitary conditions in the civil districts adjoining the camps, distributed comfort articles among the troops and aided civilian refugees fleeing the war zone. It also recruited ambulance companies, trained and directed vast numbers of nurses and organized great base hospitals. On March 1, 1919, Henry P. Davison, chairman of the Red Cross War Council, reported that in twenty-one months the American people had supplied $400,000,000 in cash and materials— "by far the largest voluntary gifts of money, of hand and heart, ever contributed purely for the relief of human suffering." Scarcely less important was the work of other civilian agencies, notably the Young Men's Christian Association, the Young Women's Christian Association, the National Catholic War Council, the Jewish Welfare Board, the Salvation Army, the American Library Association and the War Camp Community Service. These groups carried on their work without class, racial or sectarian bias and, as in the case of the Red Cross, the public supported their efforts with a lavish hand.

Such support was facilitated by the widespread and dazzling prosperity which had climaxed the economic revival of the era of neutrality. To the insistent call of the Allies for foodstuffs, manufactures and munitions was added the imperative need of the American government for these supplies. Heroic efforts were made to meet the demands. In order to stimulate production, the banks freely lent money and the government added the bait of high prices. Meanwhile, thanks to the abnormal trade relations with Europe, sales abroad vastly exceeded purchases, changing the position of the United States from a debtor to a creditor nation. As the passing months saw an increasing inflow of gold available for investment, every nerve of industry was energized. The farmer shared in the general well-being, receiving prices beyond his wildest dreams of a few years before. The chief benefits of the war-puffed prosperity, however, fell to businessmen, whose rapidly mounting profits permitted them to keep safely ahead of the climbing costs of operation. From 1917 to 1920 the ranks of American millionaires grew from sixteen thousand to twenty.

As prices swung upward, the cost of living sharply advanced. To meet their heavier expenses, wage-earners demanded higher pay. The government at Washington, unlike previous administrations, exerted constant pressure on employers to improve wages and working conditions. To this end the American Federation of Labor was given representation not only on the advisory commission of the Council of National Defense, but also on the War Industries Board and other important agencies. In May, 1918, President Wilson appointed a War Labor Policies Board, headed by Felix Frankfurter, which formulated a set of principles essential to a sound labor program, including recognition of the right to organize, the maintenance of factory codes, equal pay for women, a basic eight-hour day and a living wage. The years 1916 and 1917 had been unusually stormy ones in the labor world, with the latter witnessing 4450 strikes and lockouts; but in 1918, thanks to the new machinery for mediation and the rising pay of rail, shipyard and munition workers, the number fell to 3350. Before the war closed, real wages had reached a higher level than probably ever before in American history. Meanwhile, a half-million new members streamed into the American Federation, raising the total at the end of 1918 to 2,726,000.

One unexpected consequence of the abnormal demand for labor was the exodus of hordes of Negroes from the South to better paid jobs in Northern mills. It is reckoned that four hundred thousand migrated in the years 1916–1919, and an equal number from 1921 to 1923. To industrial centers like Chicago, East St. Louis, Cleveland and Detroit they resorted in dense colonies. As a result, Northern communities soon began to experience the problem of race relations at first hand.

WILSON AND THE PEACE SETTLEMENT

Though the American President had been acting as spokesman for the world, he had already begun to lose the right to speak for his own countrymen. The accumulating resentment of Wilson's political foes against his imperious leadership found unrestricted vent for the first time in the election of a new Congress in November, 1918. His appeal to the voters to name a Democratic majority fell on unheeding ears, and the Republicans captured both branches. Undeterred by this event, the President turned his attention to the approaching peace negotiations at Paris. As author of the Fourteen Points, he decided to shatter precedent by attending the conference in person, taking as fellow delegates Secretary of State Lansing, Henry White, a retired diplomat, Colonel House and General Tasker H. Bliss. The group as a whole was not a strong one. White, the only Republican, counted for little in the party counsels, and many felt that the Senate should have had representation, as in the negotiations concluding the Spanish-American War. To the delegation was added a host of legal, economic, historical, geographic and military experts who had been spending many months compiling an enormous mass of pertinent information under Colonel House's direction. The American Inquiry, as it was called, proved of great service to the President in applying his general principles to specific problems.

From the moment he reached France in mid-December till the peace conference began on January 12, 1919, Wilson enjoyed a triumphal progress through Western Europe such as no man had ever known. Everywhere the populace acclaimed him as the savior of humanity and showered him with gifts and honors. But when the veteran Allied statesmen sat down to deliberate peace terms, the atmosphere chilled. Though thirty-two nations nominally participated in the proceedings, all the major decisions fell to Great Britain, France, the United States, Italy and, in certain matters, Japan. The vanquished foemen were denied representation until summoned to learn what fate had been meted out to them.

From the outset Wilson strove tirelessly to secure an idealistic basis for the settlement—that "peace of justice" which he deemed essential to world stability. But his purpose quickly partook of the quixotic. The very air of Paris reeked with fear and hatred of Germany. In every country there represented, including his own, the vast bulk of the people held Germany responsible for the war and for the havoc it had wrought. They remembered, too, the bitter peace which Germany had inflicted on Russia and Rumania only nine months before, and believed that, if she had been equally successful on the western front, no better terms would have been granted.

Another stumbling block was that the broad principles enunciated in the Fourteen Points often lent themselves to differing, or even conflicting, interpretations when applied to particular situations, a fact which the President's antagonists promptly exploited to their own advantage.[1] Finally, despite Wilson's example and their own public professions, the victors were resolved, true to time-honored custom, on a division of the enemy spoils. Some countries, notably England, France, Italy, Japan and Rumania, had driven advance bargains through secret treaties, and every nation had its own special necessities, jealousies and aspirations. The President knew of the secret treaties, but, as he had told Colonel House

---

[1] Thus the Poles demanded the application of Point 13 promising them "a free and secure access to the sea," but, in order to accord this to them, it was necessary to create the Polish Corridor dividing Germany into two parts and placing a million or more Germans under alien sovereignty. This arrangement violated the spirit of the principle of self-determination that animated other of the Fourteen Points.

in July, 1917, he thought the powers concerned could be
forced to "our way of thinking" because at the war's close
"they will, among other things, be financially in our hands."
In reality, however, he did not play this trump card at Paris.

As the discussions proceeded behind closed doors, starvation spread over half the continent, communism was gaining
new adherents in Central Europe, and nearly a score of little
fires of war, left over from the great one, still burned fiercely.
The conferees were hard-driven by the lash of events. As
Prime Minister David Lloyd George later declared to the
House of Commons in a vivid figurative passage, "We had to
. . . work crowded hours, long and late, because, while we
were trying to build, we saw in many lands the foundations
of society crumbling into dust. . . . I am doubtful whether any
body of men with a difficult task have worked under greater
difficulties, with stones crackling on the roof and crashing
through the window, and sometimes wild men screaming
through the keyholes."

Wilson's chief adversary in the negotiations was the French
Premier, Georges Clemenceau, grim, grizzled and cynical—
an uncompromising representative of the old diplomacy.
Lloyd George, whose magnetic personality and mental agility
reminded Americans of their own Roosevelt, usually sided
with the President, but he could not be relied upon. Vittorio
Orlando of Italy counted for less, though at one juncture the
Italian claim to the Adriatic port of Fiume, at Yugoslavia's
expense, led to an open clash with Wilson. The Italian delegation actually left the conference temporarily, but subsequently negotiated a compromise. The Japanese, watchful
and assertive where their own interests were involved, took
little part in the strictly European settlements. As for the
smaller nations, each lifted a piping voice, and accepted such
crumbs as fell to its lot.

As the weeks went by and the President felt obliged to

make one concession after the other, many of the Fourteen Points crumbled.[1] Yet, notwithstanding the inconsistencies and injustices that found lodgment in the treaty, its terms would have been far more punitive and imperialistic but for Wilson's constant watchfulness. At one crisis, when the tide of greed ran unusually strong, he summoned the *George Washington* to take home the American delegation. This dramatic gesture effected an immediate toning down of demands. Among other things, the President prevented France from detaching the entire Rhineland from Germany and taking permanent possession of the Saar basin; he resisted the Polish demand for East Prussia; and he wrung from Japan a pledge not to retain indefinitely the German-leased territory of Shantung in China.

Against all attempts to tamper with Point 14 Wilson stood firm as a rock. In an "association of nations" he saw an opportunity to repair the mistakes and inequities of the treaty as well as to insure future world peace. "This is the central object of our meeting," he told the delegates. "Settlements may be temporary, but the actions of the nations in the interests of peace and justice must be permanent. We can set up permanent processes. We may not be able to set up permanent decisions." On February 14 the conference formally adopted a provisional covenant or constitution of a League of Nations, largely the handiwork of Lord Robert Cecil of England and General Jan Smuts of the South African Union.

Wilson sailed the next day for America in order to take

[1] For example, the Paris conference's own proceedings violated Point 1 ("open covenants of peace openly arrived at"); Point 4 (pledging an effective reduction of national armaments) was deferred for possible future action of the League of Nations; and Point 5 (regarding the disposition of colonies) was so interpreted as to give most of Germany's possessions to the British Empire under cover of the League's system of "mandatories." On the Continent itself the principle of national self-determination was ignored not only in the case of the Polish Corridor, but also in the transfer of enemy territory to other newly created countries.

counsel with leading Senators and with distinguished publicists like Charles E. Hughes, ex-President Taft and Elihu Root. Armed with their comments, he returned to Paris and succeeded in inserting in the document an explicit recognition of the Monroe Doctrine as well as certain other changes they had suggested. By these alterations he believed he had assured American adherence, though while he was yet in the United States thirty-nine Senators under the leadership of Henry Cabot Lodge, chairman of the foreign-relations committee, had declared their opposition to the proposed League.

In the form finally embodied in the treaty, the Covenant established an international organization at Geneva consisting of an Assembly, in which each League member should have an equal voice; a Council, composed of representatives of the five Great Powers and of a few lesser countries selected from time to time by the Assembly; and a permanent Secretariat or administrative division. The League's principal function was stated to be "to achieve international peace and security by the acceptance of obligations not to resort to war." For this purpose various safeguards were provided. Authority was vested in the Council to propose plans for reducing national armaments, secret treaties were outlawed, and a Permanent Court of International Justice was authorized (see page 475). It was further declared the "friendly right" of any League member to call attention to "any circumstance whatever" inimical to international peace. If war should threaten anywhere, the League was empowered to "take any action that may be deemed wise and effectual to safeguard the peace of nations." More specifically, the members agreed, in accordance with the principle of the Bryan "cooling-off" treaties, that when diplomatic means failed they would submit their differences to arbitration, and in no case declare war until three months after the decision was rendered. Violation of this provision subjected the offender to drastic international boycott. If armed coercion proved necessary, the Council was to "recommend" what forces each country should furnish.

Article X, framed by President Wilson as an additional guarantee of peace, pledged the members "to respect and pre-serve as against external aggression the territorial integrity and existing political independence of all members of the League. In case of any . . . danger of such aggression, the Council shall advise upon the means by which this obligation shall be fulfilled." Thanks also to the President's influence, as has been seen, the Covenant asserted that "regional understand-ings like the Monroe Doctrine" lay outside the scope of the League. By another provision the Geneva body was granted general supervision of the administration of the former enemy colonies, though these were confided directly to var-ious powers acting as trustees or "mandatories." Finally, the League was charged with promoting international coöperation in certain matters of humanitarian concern, such as humane conditions of labor and the traffic in opium and other dan-gerous drugs. No important decisions could be made with-out a unanimous vote of the Assembly and Council, and no amendment to the Covenant without the consent of all the nations represented in the Council.

On June 28, in the Hall of Mirrors of Louis XIV's famous palace at Versailles, representatives of the new German Re-public in great bitterness signed the treaty, which they de-nounced as contrary to the Fourteen Points and intolerably severe.[1] On July 10 President Wilson submitted it to the

[1] The treaty of Versailles, a document containing eighty thousand words, required Germany to admit her guilt for the war, restored Alsace-Lorraine to France and otherwise sheared down Germany's boundaries in Europe, im-posed military and naval disarmament on her, stripped her of her overseas empire, and saddled her with reparations of an indeterminate amount. To-gether with the peace terms imposed on the other enemy powers, the Ver-sailles settlement ushered into the world a group of new European sovereign-ties—Austria, Czechoslovakia, Hungary and Poland—and enlarged Serbia into Yugoslavia. United States representatives signed the treaties with Austria and Hungary respectively in September, 1919, and June, 1920.

EUROPE AND ASIA MINOR BEFORE AND AFTER THE WORLD WAR

Senate for ratification. At once a tempest of protest and denunciation, which had been gathering strength for several months, broke loose in the Senate and, only to a less degree, in the country at large. This hostility stemmed from a variety of sources. Part of it was due to Wilson's characteristic aloofness and self-assurance, which had become intensified under the stress of war-time exigencies. Part of it came from liberal spokesmen who, hitherto friendly to the President, now accused him of betraying his own ideals of a just peace. More important politically was the attitude of Republican leaders, who perceived a strong party advantage in advertising the treaty's flaws and their own efforts to "Americanize" it by means of amendments. To their aid came various hyphenate groups, notably the Irish Americans, who feared that Article X would block Irish aspirations for independence, and the German Americans, who disapproved the treaty's harshness and the initial exclusion of the German Republic from the League. Beneath these springs of opposition, however, lay a deep-rooted and sincere hesitation of many Americans to depart from what they believed to be the traditional national policy of abstention from European entanglements.

Out of the storm and confusion of controversy there gradually emerged definite groupings among the Senators: those who, like Wilson himself, urged ratification without material change; those who were willing to accept mild reservations; those who demanded amendments or strong reservations; and, lastly, the irreconcilables who opposed ratification in any form. The first two groups were predominantly Democratic in complexion, the latter two Republican. The two middle groups were led respectively by Gilbert M. Hitchcock, a Nebraska Democrat, and Henry Cabot Lodge, the veteran Massachusetts Republican. Though few in number, the irreconcilables were singularly fortunate in having as spokesmen such men as Hiram Johnson of California and

William E. Borah of Idaho, long known to the public as persistent champions of popular rights.

On September 10, 1919, Senator Lodge, acting for the foreign-relations committee, recommended ratification with forty-two amendments and reservations (subsequently reduced to fourteen). The principal changes concerned certain features of the League Covenant, notably Article X which in its existing form was alleged to guarantee the status quo and to obligate the United States, at the League's behest, to send troops to defend even unjust territorial settlements. The Lodge amendments expressly repudiated any such obligation except by specific vote of Congress when occasion should arise. In anticipation of the committee's attitude, the President had left Washington a week before on a Western stumping tour to arouse popular backing for unconditional ratification. But the effort proved too great for a physique worn by months of fearful strain and terrific responsibility. On September 26, while in Colorado, he suffered a paralytic stroke which ended the tour and confined him to the sick room for most of the remainder of his presidency. By this catastrophe the pro-League forces lost their commanding general, and the way was cleared for the ultimate triumph of the opposition.

The Senate discussions continued with increasing rancor through the succeeding weeks. When the treaty came up for vote on November 19, it failed to command a majority either with or without reservations. Had the spirit of acrimony been less intense or President Wilson more amenable, it is possible that the requisite two thirds might even then have been secured through compromise. Senator Hitchcock, on behalf of the Democrats, did indeed offer a series of reservations which differed from Lodge's chiefly in details of phraseology; but on the eve of a presidential election neither party was willing to yield to the other the credit for saving the peace.

On March 19, 1920, the treaty came up a second time, modified by fifteen Lodge reservations. Once more ratification failed though the vote stood 49 to 35 in favor. A switch of seven nays would have put America into the League. The minority consisted of a combination of the irreconcilables with those Democrats who stood squarely by the President. Pleading the impossibility of action through the treaty-making process, the Republicans set about to conclude a separate peace by a majority vote of the two houses. The Knox resolution, repealing the declarations of war, was passed on May 27, only to be vetoed by the President. The question of peace was at a deadlock so far as the American government was concerned. Further action awaited an expression of the popular will in the approaching election, which Wilson asked should take "the form of a great and solemn referendum."

SELECT BIBLIOGRAPHY

Armed Operations Overseas.   For this and the next section Paxson, *America at War,* and Sullivan, *Our Times,* V, are helpful. Spaulding, *United States Army,* and Davis, *Navy Second to None,* offer short accounts of the American war effort, while the following works go into greater detail: Harbord, *America in the World War;* Frothingham, *American Reinforcement in the World War;* Beamish and March, *America's Part in the World War;* Ayres, *War with Germany,* a statistical summary; Chambrun and Marenches, *American Army in the European Conflict,* a French view; Sims and Hendrick, *Victory at Sea;* Thomas, *History of the A.E.F.;* Marcosson, *S.O.S.;* Graves, *America's Siberian Adventure;* Baker, *Wilson,* VI-VII; and Palmer, *Newton D. Baker.*

The War and the American Public.   Slosson, *Great Crusade and After,* gives a vivid picture of war-time life in the United States. Particular phases receive attention in Mock and Larson,

Words That Won the War: the Story of the Committee on Public Information; Chafee, *Freedom of Speech;* Bates, *Land of Liberty;* Thomas, *Conscientious Objector;* Bogart, *War Costs and Their Financing;* Clark, *Costs of the World War;* Davison, *American Red Cross in the Great War;* Mayo, *"That Damn Y,"* dealing with the Y. M. C. A.; Bing, *War-Time Strikes;* Lorwin, *American Federation of Labor;* and Wesley, *Negro Labor.*

Wilson and the Peace Settlement. American participation in the peace conference is treated in Baker, *Woodrow Wilson and World Settlement;* Seymour, *American Diplomacy during the World War,* and *Intimate Papers of Colonel House;* Baruch, *Making of the Reparation and Economic Sections of the Treaty;* Nevins, *Henry White;* and Palmer, *Bliss, Peacemaker.* On the conflict over the treaty in America, the best work is Fleming, *United States and the League of Nations.*

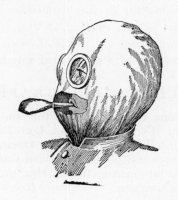

PART THREE
THE QUEST FOR SECURITY

Chapter XVII

THE REPUBLICANS AND THE WORLD SCENE, 1920–1932

POSTWAR READJUSTMENTS, SOCIAL AND ECONOMIC

THE bitterness displayed in the fight over the treaty reflected the spirit of intolerance and political bigotry that raged throughout the land. National sentiment had been effectively mobilized for war purposes; it now proved difficult to demobilize it. Though Germany lay prostrate, people looked nervously about for other threats to the American way of life. "Property was in an agony of fear," wrote an English observer later, "and the horrid name 'Radical' covered the most innocent departure from conventional thought with a suspicion of desperate purpose." In particular, many persons feared the effects of Russian Soviet propaganda on radical groups in the United States, and seemed to see their suspicions confirmed when the left-wing Socialists in 1919 broke away from their party and formed a new one, the Communist (or Workers') party. Responsive to the popular excitement, Attorney-General A. Mitchell Palmer and his assistants devoted their energies to the suppression of unorthodox political and social opinions, whether concerned with the war or not. Agitators suspected of communist leanings received special attention. In 1919 two hundred and forty-nine foreigners were put aboard the ship *Buford* and deported to Russia.

In many states the authorities, abetted by local feeling, were equally active. One incident bred of the hysteria eventually attracted international notice. In the spring of 1920 two Italian immigrants, Nicola Sacco and Bartolomeo Vanzetti, were charged with murdering a paymaster and his guard near Boston. Though the evidence of their complicity in the crime was flimsy and contradictory, the trial disclosed that they were draft dodgers, atheists and philosophical anarchists, and, as in the case of the Chicago Haymarket trial in 1886 (see page 161), these revelations unleashed the passions of those who thought "reds" ought to be strung up on general principles. Convicted of the murder charge, and unable to get their case retried in a higher Massachusetts court despite new evidence which rendered their guilt even more doubtful, the two men were finally executed in 1927. During the long seven-year wait people throughout the country and in many parts of the world came to take an intense interest in the affair—not only radicals of various brands, but also many conservatives who, though unsympathetic with the men's opinions, defended their right to a fair and impartial trial. Their death occurred to the accompaniment of demonstrations of protest all over the United States and in lands across the sea.[1]

While the red scare was still at its height, the New York legislature in April, 1920, went so far as to expel five of its members because they were Socialists. The incident chal-

[1] Another case almost as notorious grew out of the arrest of Thomas Mooney, a labor organizer and militant Socialist, on the charge of killing ten people in a bomb explosion during a preparedness parade in San Francisco in July, 1916. Condemned to death—the sentence later being commuted to life imprisonment—Mooney made persistent but vain attempts to secure a retrial. Responsible persons, including the trial judge, the state attorney-general and most of the jurors, subsequently asserted that perjured testimony had produced the conviction. Three federal commissions also declared he had been unjustly sentenced. Finally, in 1933, Mooney managed to get a trial on a related murder indictment that had stood against him since his conviction, and he was promptly acquitted; but the earlier judgment caused his return to prison. The case figured as an issue in the gubernatorial campaign of 1938; and one of the first official acts of the newly elected executive, Culbert L. Olson, in 1939 was to grant Mooney a full pardon. Thus Mooney regained his freedom after nearly twenty-three years. Later Governor Olson liberated Warren K. Billings, who had been sentenced in 1916 as an accomplice of Mooney.

lenged nation-wide attention. In a vigorous protest, former Justice Charles E. Hughes of the Supreme Court asserted, "This is not, in my judgment, American government. . . . I count it a most serious mistake to proceed, not against individuals charged with violation of law, but against masses of our citizens combined for political action, by denying them the only resource of peaceful government; that is, action by the ballot box and through duly elected representatives in legislative bodies." Though the ousted members were not restored to their seats, Hughes's ringing appeal for fair play may have deterred other legislatures from emulating New York's example.

Meanwhile, champions of intolerance banded together in a secret organized movement under the name of the Ku Klux Klan. Though patterned on the old Reconstruction organization in its method of operation, the new K. K. K. more nearly resembled mid-century Know Nothingism in its aims. Its slogan was "100 per-cent Americanism," which to the fanatical minds of the members meant the right of native white Protestants to have everything their own way. Founded five years before in Georgia, the Klan did not command a nation-wide membership until the peace-troubled year of 1920. To carry out its objects, the masked, white-robed members did not hesitate under cover of darkness to resort to threats, floggings, tar-and-feathering and even murder. Its following became so great, particularly in the South and Midwest, that in 1922 it entered politics, backing friendly candidates of the old parties, carrying a number of local and state elections and, as will be seen, wielding influence in the Democratic national convention of 1924. Part of its strength was doubtless due to the inability of many Americans to resist the temptation of joining another secret society. As time passed, the Klan became the foe not only of immigrants, Negroes, Catholics and Jews, but also of prohibition repeal, birth control, the League of Nations, pacifism and other evidences of minority opinion. Before entering on a decline, the order in 1925 attained a membership of between four and five million.

The cessation of hostilities also threw the labor world into turmoil. Industry, freed from war-time restraints as to conditions of employment, tried to recover lost ground, while the wage-earners, harried by the ever ascending cost of living, fought back on every front. During 1919 more than four million—nearly three and a half times as many as in 1918—took part in labor upheavals at a total cost to employees of over $800,000,000 and to employers of $1,300,000,000 or more. An ominous feature of the situation was the large number of "outlaw" strikes—undertaken against the wishes of the national unions—which engaged a quarter of the whole number of strikers. The biggest disturbances involved 125,000 men in the New York building trades in February, 250,000 railway shop workers in August, 367,000 iron and steel employees in September and 435,000 bituminous-coal miners in November.

The coal strike, greatest of all the walkouts, marked a reversal of the government's earlier sympathetic attitude toward labor. Attorney-General Palmer, taking advantage of the fact that the country was still technically at war with Germany, secured two court injunctions to prevent the United Mine Workers and "all persons whomsoever" from supporting the strike. Though bitterly protesting against this action, the union officials felt obliged to acquiesce. Through federal mediation the miners eventually secured a wage advance of twenty-seven per cent, but with no change in the hours or conditions of labor. During the year the membership of the American Federation of Labor greatly increased, reaching four million in 1920, twice the number in 1914.

The soaring prices indicated a continuance of the war-time business boom. With her industries still badly deranged, Europe continued in need of American exports, while at home the people, made gay by unwontedly fat purses and the sudden relaxing of the war strain, engaged in an orgy of extravagant buying and fast living. Overexpansion, speculation and swollen prices reached new extremes both in industry and agriculture. But during 1920 the foreign demand began to fall off, the products of mill, mine and farm soon glutted the domestic market, prices dropped, and a depression began that lasted somewhat over two years in the industrial regions and much longer among the farmers. About twenty thousand business firms failed in 1921, 4,750,000 workingmen were rendered idle, and wages generally declined. Thanks to the efficient working of the federal reserve system, however, bank failures were kept to a minimum, and the deflation, though severe, did not attain the proportions of a nation-wide panic.

As steps toward restoring normal conditions, Congress in 1920 enacted two important laws. One, the Esch-Cummins act in February, fixed the terms upon which the railways should be handed back to private ownership and management. Passed after much controversy, it embodied certain new principles growing out of the experience of government operation. The idea that competition must be enforced among the companies was abandoned. Pooling, hitherto forbidden, was legalized under supervision of the Interstate Commerce Commission, and plans were authorized for ultimately consolidating the lines into a limited number of systems. In addition, the Commission was empowered to set minimum as well as maximum rates, so that the roads would be assured a fair profit at the same time that they would be prevented from obtaining an excessive one. Other sections of the law provided for special tribunals to deal with railway labor difficulties.

The second piece of legislation, the merchant-marine act adopted in June, announced Congress's policy in regard to the fleet of fifteen hundred merchantmen which the United States Shipping Board (see page 402) had acquired during the war. The law ended further shipbuilding by the Board, but continued the experiment of government ownership and operation. The Board, at its discretion, was empowered to dispose of the vessels from time to time to American purchasers, and to accumulate out of its profits a fund from which loans might be made to private builders. By such means it was hoped—vainly, as the sequel was to show—that America might maintain her recently regained importance in the carrying trade.[1]

Meanwhile, the upheaval of war had brought about two changes in the nation's fundamental law. The first had to do with the long-agitated question of prohibition. By the time America entered the conflict thirty-two commonwealths had outlawed the liquor traffic, while much of the remaining territory was dry under local option. In all, over three fourths of the national area was saloonless. In most parts of the country only the large cities and mill towns remained wet, Chicago possessing more saloons than the whole group of Southern states. Aside from other factors, the increasing menace of drunken automobile drivers on the highways lent strength to the prohibition cause. War conditions prompted the federal government to add its efforts to those of the states and local authorities. In order to stimulate grain and coal conservation, Congress in August, 1917, forbade the use of food products in making distilled beverages, and gave the Presi-

[1] Disappointment with the results of this law led to the passage of the merchant-marine act of 1928, which enlarged the loan fund and also, through generous mail contracts, provided a substantial subsidy to private owners. In 1933 the Shipping Board was abolished, and its thirty-eight remaining vessels transferred to the Department of Commerce.

dent power, which he later exercised, to restrict the manufacture of beer.

Meantime, the ownership of so many breweries and distilleries by persons of German stock helped to sharpen public

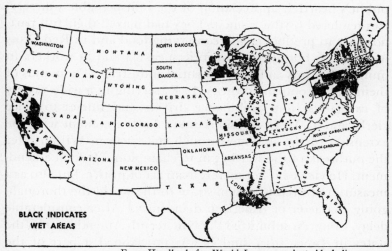

From Handbook for World League against Alcoholism, 1919.

DRY TERRITORY ON THE EVE OF NATIONAL PROHIBITION

resentment against the drink traffic and to prepare the way
for the adoption of the Eighteenth Amendment by Congress
in December, 1917. This amendment, the first to seek to
regulate a citizen's strictly personal habits, provided for prohibiting the manufacture, transportation and sale of intoxicants one year after its ratification. On January 16, 1919, it
became a part of the Constitution and before the wave of
popular enthusiasm subsided all but two states—Rhode Island
and Connecticut—passed resolutions of ratification. The
apparent finality of the decision is further indicated by the
fact that 78.5 per cent of the total vote cast by the lower

houses of the state legislatures was in favor, and about 85 per cent of the vote of the upper houses.

The other amendment, the Nineteenth, granted the long-sought boon of universal equal suffrage. Its adoption, inevitable in any event, was prompted at this time by the public's heartfelt appreciation of the indispensable war services rendered by the women. They had played their full part, not only in producing and conserving food and in Red Cross workrooms, but also as patriotic speakers and as workers in munition plants and other essential industries. Thousands of them had accompanied the A. E. F., serving in a wide variety of capacities from ambulance drivers and nurses to office clerks and Y. M. C. A. entertainers. Earlier content with the extension of the suffrage through state action, Wilson after the outbreak of the war began to champion a federal amendment. He viewed it not merely as an act of justice, but also as a measure required to demonstrate to the world the thorough-going character of American democracy.[1] After considerable delay, Congress submitted the Nineteenth Amendment to the states in June, 1919, and it was proclaimed a part of the Constitution on August 20, 1920, in time for the women to take part in the national election.

THE NATION TURNS REPUBLICAN

As the campaign of 1920 approached, the popular mood strongly favored a change of rulers. All over the world a tide of accumulating resentment due to the sacrifices and hardships of fighting had swept the war governments from office. In America the party in power labored under the further

[1] Though a pioneer in the movement, the United States had been outdistanced during the war period by other countries. In 1917 woman suffrage was granted in Russia and Mexico; in 1918 in Austria, Germany, Hungary, Poland, Czechoslovakia, England, Scotland, Wales, Ireland and Canada; and in 1919 in Belgium, Luxembourg, Sweden, Iceland, British East Africa and Rhodesia.

handicap of the President's stubborn stand on the League issue as well as of the blight which had fallen on the nation's economic life. When the Republicans met in Chicago on June 8, their proceedings were dominated by Henry Cabot Lodge and Wilson's other senatorial foes. These men blandly ignored a vigorous outside sentiment for Herbert Hoover, the only American in the war who had stirred the public's imagination; and when neither of the leading contenders, General Leonard Wood and Governor Frank O. Lowden of Illinois, could obtain a majority, they steered the nomination on the tenth ballot to one of their own number, Warren G. Harding of Ohio, a Lodge reservationist and safe organization man. The second place went to Governor Calvin Coolidge of Massachusetts, whose supposed part in quelling a police strike in Boston had attracted national notice. The platform, after assailing "executive autocracy," promised governmental economy, farm relief and the return of prosperity and, in language designed to satisfy all shades of opinion on the League question, declared "for agreement among the nations to preserve the peace of the world." [1]

In San Francisco on June 28 the Democrats nominated Governor James M. Cox of Ohio on the forty-fourth ballot after a hot three-cornered contest in which Attorney-General Palmer and Wilson's son-in-law, William G. McAdoo, were his chief rivals. Franklin D. Roosevelt of New York, Assistant Secretary of the Navy and a fifth cousin of the Republican "Teddy," was named for Vice-President. The platform lauded the administration's domestic and foreign policies, promised farm betterment, and declared for immediate

[1] This section of the platform was very long and involved a constant restatement of the Republican position on the League, the last one being: "We pledge . . . such agreements with the other nations . . . as shall meet the full duty of America to civilization and humanity . . . without surrendering the right of the American people to exercise its judgment and its power in favor of justice and peace."

ratification of the peace treaty without material reservations. As usual, minor parties entered the lists. The Socialists, for the fifth time, nominated Eugene V. Debs, although he was still behind the bars in the Atlanta prison. A new group, the Farmer-Labor party, offered candidates in the hope of crystallizing the growing discontent of the rural and industrial classes.

The nominee of neither of the major parties was a prominent national figure, and one of the liberal weeklies suggested that the choice lay "between Debs and dubs." But the outcome was clear from the start. The action of the American Federation of Labor in indorsing the Democratic ticket did little to help it. The electorate was in a captious mood and eager to lay all its troubles at the door of the party in power. As for the League question, the Republicans succeeded in befuddling the issue. Leading irreconcilables like Hiram Johnson maintained that Harding's election would mean the treaty's repudiation. On the other hand, thirty-one Republican notables, including Hughes, Root and Hoover, assured the public in a joint statement that "the true course to bring America into an effective league" was through a Republican victory. Harding's own speeches, if somewhat ambiguous, indicated a preference for "an association of nations," based possibly on a modification of the Covenant.

The election was a Republican landslide. The huge plurality of over seven million was due in part to the new women voters. In the electoral college the vote stood 404 to 127, while Harding received 60.3 per cent of the popular ballots (16,152,000 votes) to 34.2 per cent (9,147,000) for Cox. Even the Solid South was shaken, Tennessee deserting to the enemy for the first time since Carpetbag days. The Republicans also elected substantial majorities in both branches of Congress.

The new President had had a long but undistinguished

career in Ohio politics, where he had always lent himself to conservative views and purposes. A handsome man with heavy features and a large frame, he possessed the modesty and amiability of a Taft without the latter's brains or singleness of devotion to the public weal. He was better known for his gifts of good fellowship than for any evidences of states-manlike ability. As if to offset his own mediocre qualities of mind and character, he placed in his cabinet three men of conspicuous ability: Charles E. Hughes as head of the State Department, Andrew W. Mellon, a Pittsburgh millionaire, as Secretary of the Treasury, and Herbert Hoover as Secretary of Commerce. Some of his other and less happy choices stemmed from an undiscriminating personal friendship. Thus, ex-Senator Albert B. Fall of New Mexico, a resolute anticonservationist, was made Secretary of the Interior, and Harry M. Daugherty, an Ohio machine politician, Attorney-General.[1] Several months after entering office, Harding paid a graceful compliment to the only living Republican ex-President, William Howard Taft, by appointing him Chief Justice of the Supreme Court.

In dealing with the major issue of the campaign, the President yielded to the most vociferous element in his party and abandoned his own earlier attitude. The strong upswing of nationalism marking the postwar years indicated this as the safest course. Congress, summoned in special session, revived the Knox resolution which Wilson had vetoed (see page 451), and in July, 1921, repassed it in somewhat modified form. This act, after declaring the war at an end, reserved to the United States all the rights and advantages which it would have received as a signatory of the treaty of Versailles, and

[1] The remaining members of the cabinet were John W. Weeks of Massachusetts, Secretary of War; Will H. Hays of Indiana, Postmaster-General; Edwin Denby of Michigan, Secretary of the Navy; Henry C. Wallace of Iowa, Secretary of Agriculture; and James J. Davis of Pennsylvania, Secretary of Labor.

provided that all enemy property seized by the government during the war should be retained until Germany, Austria and Hungary agreed by treaty to satisfy America's war claims. The resolution, of course, involved repudiation of the League of Nations. In August treaties with the enemy powers expressed assent to these terms. One year later Germany and the United States provided for a mixed commission to determine the amount of American losses from submarine depredations and other sources, and similar tribunals were later arranged with Austria and Hungary.[1]

Harding's election introduced an era of Republican supremacy that was to last for twelve years. The tapering off of the depression in 1922 ushered in a boom period which continued year after year and on which the party claimed an exclusive patent. Neither Harding nor his successor, Coolidge, possessed reform inclinations or the itch for strong executive leadership. The economic policies fostered by Congress accorded with the desires of Big Business, and Mellon, one of the country's richest men, remained at the helm of the Treasury until 1932. Though at times sorely tried, the ordinary voter preferred to let well enough alone while he, too, nibbled at the fat ears of prosperity. The Democrats, on their part, seemed singularly lacking in leadership and cohesion, sacrificing through factional differences whatever chances they might have had for success in 1924 and 1928. As for the newly enfranchised women, the evidence indicates that those who bestirred themselves most actively came from communities and states with strong Republican leanings, and hence during these years their votes increased the preponderance of the majority party.

[1] As of 1928, the United States was awarded $231,000,000 from Germany, $370,000 from Austria and $173,000 from Hungary. Counterclaims against the United States were allowed as follows: $87,000,000 to Germany, $913,000 to Austria and $54,000 to Hungary.

But for these favoring conditions the Republican sway might not have outlasted the term for which President Harding was elected. Able and disinterested as were certain members of his cabinet, in domestic affairs he gave greater heed to the advice of a coterie of intimates, the so-called Ohio Gang, who had hastened to Washington to be near him when he entered the White House. The extent of the corruption in which they involved his administration was not revealed until after the President's unexpected demise in San Francisco on August 2, 1923, while returning from a trip to Alaska. Though ugly rumors long persisted as to the cause of his death, probably the true reason was a stroke of apoplexy induced by worry over his criminal failure to safeguard the public interest and the certainty that his negligence would become known. In a moment of self-revelation shortly before the end, Harding told his friend Nicholas Murray Butler, president of Columbia University, "I am not fit for this office and should never have been here." [1]

The disclosures of official rascality came as a result of a series of Senate investigations. The unsavory record surpassed anything known since President Grant's time. The first notable instance arose from Charles R. Forbes's activities as director of the Veterans' Bureau, an agency which had taken over the functions of the Bureau of War Risk Insurance. In his two years in office, the Senate committee found him guilty of "almost unparalleled waste, recklessness and misconduct" in the handling of construction contracts and the purchase of supplies and equipment. The losses sustained

[1] Hoover, who accompanied the President on the Alaska trip, declared in 1931 in a speech dedicating the Harding Memorial at Marion, Ohio, "We saw him gradually weaken not only from physical exhaustion but from mental anxiety. Warren Harding had a dim realization that he had been betrayed by a few of the men whom he had trusted. . . . It was later proved in the courts of the land that these men had betrayed not alone the friendship and trust of their staunch and loyal friend but they had betrayed their country."

by the government were estimated at more than $200,000,000. In 1924 Forbes was indicted for conspiracy and fraud and subsequently sent to Leavenworth prison.

Close on the heels of this exposure came spectacular revelations involving members of the President's official family. The evidence showed that in 1921 Secretary Denby of the Navy Department had, with Harding's approval, transferred to Secretary of the Interior Fall the administration of certain oil reserves which Taft and Wilson had set apart for exclusive use of the navy. In 1922 Fall, without seeking competitive bids, secretly leased Reserve No. 3 (Teapot Dome) near Casper, Wyoming, to Harry F. Sinclair, and another and larger reserve at Elk Hills, California, to Edward L. Doheny. Though the government reserved rights of royalty, these leases diverted the oil from its intended purpose to the enormous gain of private commercial interests. However unwise, the transactions bore no sinister aspect until a Senate committee, headed by Thomas J. Walsh of Montana, discovered that late in 1921 Doheny had lent Secretary Fall $100,000 without interest or security, and that, after Fall's retirement from the cabinet in March, 1923, Sinclair had similarly given him $25,000. Government suits ultimately brought about a cancellation of the leases and obtained a prison sentence for Fall for bribetaking.

While the oil scandal was still under investigation, another Senate committee brought to light shocking facts concerning Daugherty's actions as Attorney-General. The testimony, which was of a highly sensational character, indicated that he had been working hand in glove with the most disreputable members of the Ohio Gang and that important decisions of his department had been dictated by corrupt motives. He escaped court conviction, however.

It was on the eve of these revelations that Harding's death brought Calvin Coolidge to the helm. Thin-faced, tight-lipped, with a nasal twang reminiscent of his Vermont fore-bears, he was a conscientious, matter-of-fact man who, in Dryden's celebrated phrase, had mastered the art of "saying much in little and often in silence." Though Coolidge had a moral integrity lacking in his predecessor, so completely negative a person had probably never before occupied the White House. Little known outside his own state, he had shown himself a competent executive while governor of Massachusetts. He was the first native New Englander to reach the presidency since Chester A. Arthur's succession under similar circumstances. Faced with the exposures of graft in high places, he displayed an unruffled calm; but in February, 1924, yielding at last to the popular clamor, he accepted the resignation of Secretary Denby, whose chief fault had been negligence, and a month later he dismissed Daugherty. In the long run, his simplicity, Yankee caution and patent sincerity won him the firm confidence of a public unwilling in the midst of great prosperity to dwell long on the seamy aspects of governmental affairs. His sentiment, "The business of America is business," showed he was attuned to the times.

Hoping to capitalize the Harding scandals to their own advantage, the Democrats in high glee made preparations for the election of 1924. Their convention in New York City on June 24, however, turned into a pitched battle between two closely matched cohorts, the one led by Governor Alfred E. Smith of New York, a wet and a Catholic, the other by William G. McAdoo, now of California, a dry, a Protestant and the recipient of Ku Klux Klan support. When neither contestant could secure the prize, the tired, sweltering delegates stampeded on the hundred and third ballot to John W. Davis, an able New York corporation lawyer and former Ambassador to Great Britain. Governor Charles W. Bryan of Nebraska, brother of William Jennings Bryan, was added to dilute the conservatism of the ticket. The Democrats denounced Republican corruption and incapacity, promised legislation to restore rural prosperity, and favored a popular referendum on the League of Nations. Meanwhile, the Republicans had nominated Coolidge without opposition in Cleveland on June 10, giving the second place to Charles G. Dawes, a Chicago banker. The platform pointed with pride to Republican retrenchment and tax reduction, the nation's recovery from the depression, and the administration's success in promoting international peace without the entanglements of the League.

Discontented with the conservative outlook of both major nominees, some of the more radical trade unions and farmers' organizations met with various middle-class reform groups in Cleveland on July 4 to form a new Progressive party. Senator La Follette, veteran leader of the earlier progressive movement, was named for President on a platform assailing official corruption and private monopoly, and pledging farm relief, public ownership of water power and railroads, and a constitutional amendment to enable Congress to override Supreme Court decisions. To widen the party's appeal, Burton K. Wheeler, Democratic Senator from Montana, was nominated for Vice-President. The ticket was promptly indorsed by the Socialist party, the Farmer-Labor party, the American Federation of Labor and many national unions and state federations.

The new party evoked little response from the prosperity-drugged electorate, but Republican spellbinders took advantage of its existence to use it as a bogey. On every occasion they besought the public to "Keep Cool with Coolidge," and, in the President's words, maintained that the vital issue was "whether America will allow itself to be degraded into a Communistic and Socialistic state, or whether it will remain American." The wounds inflicted on Democratic unity by the convention rancors impaired the effectiveness of the efforts for Davis. A novel feature of the contest was the extensive use which the nominees made of the radio, a means of instant communication with the voters developed during the war. Assisted by an overflowing campaign chest, Coolidge scored a decisive victory, winning 382 electoral votes to 136 for Davis and 13 for La Follette—his own state of Wisconsin. Coolidge had behind him 54 per cent (15,725,000) of the popular ballots as compared with 28.7 per cent (8,386,000) and 16.5 per cent (4,823,000) respectively for his two rivals. The Republicans retained their control of both branches of Congress by large majorities.

Coolidge's good fortune attended him during his second administration.[1] As before, he favored the policies which business leaders favored and opposed those which they opposed; peace and plenty prevailed; and general contentment reigned. Had he been willing once more to bear aloft the Republican standard in a race for the presidency, his party would have rejoiced. But this he chose not to do. When the convention met in Kansas City on June 12, 1928, the nomination went on the first ballot to Secretary of Commerce Hoover, the ticket being completed with Senator Charles Curtis of Kansas. The Democrats meeting at Houston, Texas, on June 26 faced as easy a choice. Since 1924 "Al" Smith had gained steadily in popularity in the country at large as well as in New York, where he had been elected governor for the fourth time in 1926 by a plurality of nearly two hundred and fifty thousand. He too was named on the first ballot, with Senator Joseph T. Robinson of Arkansas as his running mate. Though the Progressive party had not survived its first baptism of fire, other minor parties offered

[1] In 1925 he made four changes in his cabinet, appointing Frank B. Kellogg of Minnesota, Secretary of State; Dwight F. Davis of Missouri, Secretary of War; John G. Sargent of Vermont, Attorney-General; and William M. Jardine of Kansas, Secretary of Agriculture.

candidates, the Socialists nominating Norman Thomas of New York and the Workers (Communists) William Z. Foster of Illinois.

The platforms of the two major parties offered few points of contrast, both promising agrarian relief, prohibition enforcement, reduction of armaments, protection to labor and care for the war veterans. The Republicans assured the country that "A continuation of this great public peace of mind now existing, which makes for our material well-being, is only possible by holding fast to the plans and principles which have marked Republican control," while the Democrats, abandoning their traditional hostility to protection, pledged a tariff based on the "actual difference between the cost of production at home and abroad, with adequate safeguard for the wage of the American laborer."

The Democratic nominee proved a colorful campaigner, whipping a laggard electorate into a new interest in governmental affairs, and flaying the administration for what he regarded as its veiled partnership with Big Business, particularly the public-utility interests. Departing from the party platform, he denounced the existing prohibition legislation (the Volstead act) as too stringent and pledged his efforts to secure a repeal of the Eighteenth Amendment with safeguards against the return of the saloon. But Governor Smith faced insuperable odds. Hoover, stigmatizing his opponent's utterances on farm relief, hydroelectric power and prohibition as "state socialism," dwelt fondly on the country's phenomenal prosperity under Republican rule, and heralded the speedy day "when poverty will be banished from this nation." The Democratic candidate, moreover, suffered from severe personal handicaps, especially in the rural South and West—his religious affiliations, his Tammany connections, his occasionally ungrammatical speech and his hostility to the temperance cause.

Prosperity, prohibition and prejudice carried the day, giving Hoover a smashing victory. Forty of the forty-eight states cast their electoral votes for him, a total of 444, leaving but 87 for Smith. The latter lost not only his own state, but every border state and five of the former Confederacy. The popular ballots, however, proved somewhat more evenly distrib uted, Hoover receiving 58 per cent (21,392,000 votes) and Smith 40.7 per cent (15,016,000). The Republicans also continued their control of the House and Senate. The Democrats derived what satisfaction they could from polling the largest popular support a nominee of their party had ever obtained.

The President entering office in these auspicious circumstances had a past career which seemed amply to justify the unstinted public confidence. A mining engineer of international reputation, Hoover had demonstrated during the war his unusual constructive abilities, first as head of Belgian relief and then as federal food administrator. Under his direction, too, the Department of Commerce had rapidly expanded its functions, showing industries how to cut costs through standardizing products and processes, and becoming, in the words of the *Republican Campaign Text-Book,* "the world's most formidable engine of foreign trade conquest." The purpose of government, Hoover held, should be to guide and foster, not to coerce and restrain, business and finance, thus insuring free play for what he termed "rugged individualism." His chubby face suggested geniality, but most of those who came in contact with him found his manner cold and indifferent. By promoting him to the White House the voters believed they had ended the Harding-Coolidge era of drift. Unhappily, however, Hoover despite his long public record had never held an elective office; he had dealt with subordinates, not with equals. It remained to be seen whether he was master of the difficult art of party leadership and political accommodation.[1] And not far ahead loomed the clouds of the Great Depression.

EFFORTS FOR COLLECTIVE SECURITY

Meanwhile, their uninterrupted lease of power had enabled the Republicans to develop a program for international peace as a substitute for that sponsored by Woodrow Wilson and the Democrats. In his inaugural address in 1921 President Harding had enunciated its guiding principles: "We seek no part in directing the destinies of the world. . . . We are ready to associate ourselves with the nations of the world, great and small, for conference and counsel, for the suggestion of plans of mediation, conciliation, and arbitration; but every commitment must be made in the exercise of our national sovereignty." The new formula thus became "coöperation without entangling alliances" or, as its critics said, "power without responsibility."

The League might be rejected, but it could not be ignored. Thriving without the sun of Washington's approval, the Geneva organization had speedily won the adhesion of fifty-four nations, including seventeen in the New World. Many of its activities and decisions involved matters in which the United States had a vital interest. After six months, during which Secretary of State Hughes did not so much as answer League communications, the administration began hesitantly to send "observers" to conferences where questions of concern to America were at stake. They were authorized to present the government's viewpoint, but not to vote in determining

[1] His original cabinet consisted of Henry L. Stimson of New York, Secretary of State; Andrew W. Mellon of Pennsylvania, Secretary of the Treasury; James W. Good of Iowa, Secretary of War; William D. Mitchell of Minnesota, Attorney-General; Walter F. Brown of Ohio, Postmaster-General; Charles F. Adams of Massachusetts, Secretary of the Navy; Ray L. Wilbur of California, Secretary of the Interior; Arthur M. Hyde of Missouri, Secretary of Agriculture; James J. Davis of Pennsylvania, Secretary of Labor; and Robert P. Lamont of Illinois, Secretary of Commerce.

the outcome.[1] Meantime, private coöperation went much farther, for American experts in law, medicine and finance in their individual capacites freely accepted important League appointments. Thus, Henry Morgenthau of New York headed the committee to provide an international loan to Greece, and Norman H. Davis of New York presided over the commission which settled a boundary dispute between Poland and Lithuania.

The ice having been broken, the government itself took a further step in 1924 by sending official delegates to participate fully in League conferences when the national interest seemed to warrant. By March, 1930, America had dispatched observers to over twenty such meetings and official delegates to twenty-two more. Before the end of another year she had adhered to a total of thirteen international agreements sired by the League, had five permanent officials stationed at Geneva and, under circumstances shortly to be related, even appointed a representative to sit with the League Council during the Manchurian crisis. Some people saw in this steady drift of events ultimate membership in the League; but Republican spokesmen continued to assert that the issue was "as dead as slavery."

Toward the World Court, President Harding and his successors took a bolder attitude, though ever fearful lest American adherence bear the appearance of a backdoor entrance into the League. This tribunal, officially called the Permanent Court of International Justice, and authorized by Article XIV of the Covenant, had been set up at The Hague in January, 1922, in conformity with a plan which Elihu Root had helped draft. On the original bench was another American, Professor John Bassett Moore of Columbia. Unlike the

[1] In this manner, for example, the United States attached observers to the League committees on health, the opium trade, communications and transit, and the traffic in women and children.

earlier Hague tribunal (see page 391), it was an actual court with a fixed personnel and was always to be open to litigants. The judges were selected by the League Council and Assembly from nominations made by the older Hague body. The new tribunal had jurisdiction over "any dispute of an international character which the parties thereto submit to it." In addition, it might issue advisory opinions on request of the Council or Assembly.

In February, 1923, Harding recommended American adherence on conditions which Coolidge later somewhat amplified. The irreconcilables blocked favorable action, however, until January, 1926, when the Senate voted to join with reservations along the lines that the chief executive had suggested. These included the right of the United States to participate in the choice of judges, an American veto over any amendment of the statute of the court, a similar veto over requests for advisory opinions touching any question "in which the United States has or claims an interest," and, finally, a disclaimer that membership in the World Court entailed any obligations under the League Covenant or the Versailles treaty.

In September the fifty-odd nations in the World Court, meeting at Geneva, agreed to all the reservations save the one on advisory opinions. The deadlock thus created was finally broken in 1929 when Elihu Root, at the League Council's invitation, devised a formula that proved acceptable to the State Department and to the other governments concerned. In essence, it provided that the judges should not, without America's consent, render an advisory opinion in any dispute to which she was a party; should cases arise in which she claimed merely "an interest," the Washington government might, if it thought proper, withdraw from the court "without any imputation of unfriendliness." There the matter rested. The Senate failed to take action, though both parties

in the next presidential election declared for American participation. The United States and Soviet Russia continued to
be the only important powers outside the court.

The American government meantime had launched a series of efforts to scale down national armaments. Now that
the trouble-breeding difficulties in Europe were apparently
solved by the Versailles treaty, the greatest threat to world
peace seemed to lie in the disturbed conditions and international rivalries in the Orient. With this in mind, President
Harding acting under spur of a congressional resolution
called a conference of nine nations—China, Belgium, the
Netherlands and Portugal in addition to the five Great
Powers—which met in Washington from November, 1921, to
February, 1922. On the opening day Secretary Hughes dramatically proposed a drastic reduction in navies, following
which the five Great Powers presently agreed to a limitation
of their respective strength in large battleships. The fleets of
the United States, the British Empire and Japan were fixed
respectively at a ratio of 5:5:3, with 1.75 each for France and
Italy; and the arrangement was to continue until the end of
1936, or even later unless one of the signatories should desire
to withdraw. By this treaty a new balance of sea power was
established, with the two English-speaking nations on an
equality and jointly overtopping the other three. The five
governments also agreed to limit their relative strength in
aircraft carriers, and they joined in a declaration condemning
unrestricted submarine warfare and the use of poisonous gas.

In the effort to remove Far Eastern incitements to war,
Great Britain, Japan, France and America pledged themselves to respect each other's possessions in the Pacific Ocean
and, if danger threatened from some outside source, to confer "as to the most efficient measures to be taken, jointly or
separately." This four-power guarantee involved the abrogation of the Anglo-Japanese alliance of 1902, which was un-

popular in the United States, and at the same time quieted American fears as to Japan's designs against the Philippines. The Open Door policy, which the Japanese had flouted during the war by imposing certain exclusive demands on China, attained full international sanction in the agreement of the nine powers to respect China's independence and maintain "the principle of equal opportunity for the commerce and industry of all nations." No country should seek "special rights or privileges which would abridge" those of the citizens of other countries.[1]

Important as were the gains for world peace, the American government had failed in its endeavor to apply the principle of restriction to minor naval craft such as cruisers, destroyers and submarines. Competition in these vessels, particularly in ten-thousand-ton cruisers, promptly began among the powers. To stop this new arms race, President Coolidge called a conference at Geneva in 1927; but only Great Britain and Japan accepted, and agreement proved impossible even among these three. In 1930 President Hoover made a fresh effort. With his backing, the English government assembled a five-power conference in London, at which the United States, Great Britain and Japan engaged to limit all their auxiliary armed vessels until the end of 1936, the two English-speaking nations on a basis of parity and Japan on a more favorable ratio than that fixed for battleships at the Washington conference. Franco-Italian jealousies prevented those governments from joining in the arrangement. In the case of both the Washington and London conferences America was allowed a larger navy than Congress was willing to build.

Encouraged by the substantial progress in curtailing sea power, the League of Nations called a world disarmament

[1] Other Far Eastern sources of irritation were dealt with. Thus, a nine-power treaty established the principle of China's control over her own tariff; and in 1923, a year after the conference, Secretary Hughes induced Japan to cancel the troublesome Lansing-Ishii agreement of 1917 (see page 394).

conference at Geneva in February, 1932, to consider plans for limiting the other two major branches of warfare, those of land and air. More than thirty nations took part, and many far-reaching proposals were offered, including America's to reduce all existing armaments by approximately one third. The sessions continued into 1933, but Japan's seizure of Manchuria and the threatening state of affairs elsewhere prevented any conclusions from being reached.

Meanwhile, the Coolidge administration had helped to organize a peace offensive of a different kind. When Premier Aristide Briand in 1927 suggested on behalf of France a treaty to outlaw war between the two powers, Secretary of State Kellogg countered with a proposal to widen the declaration to include all nations. The upshot was the pact of Paris in August, 1928, which bound the signatories to renounce war "as an instrument of national policy" and never to seek to settle their "conflicts of whatever nature . . . except by pacific means." By August, 1932, sixty-two of the sixty-four nations of the earth had signed. To many the Briand-Kellogg pact seemed a pious gesture or, as Senator James Reed of Missouri put it, "an international kiss." It provided no explicit means of enforcement, and the State Department had informed the signatories that the "right of self-defense"—a pretext which could easily be used to cloak aggression—was not affected. But others felt that this voluntary collective pledge was of profound import, that it haled the nations "not into a court of law, but into the forum of conscience." President Hoover went further in a joint statement with Ramsay MacDonald during the British Prime Minister's visit to America in October, 1929: "Both our Governments resolve to accept the Peace Pact not only as a declaration of good intentions, but as a positive obligation to direct national policy in accordance with its pledge."

Events in North China presently put the matter to a test.

The invasion of Manchuria by Japanese armed forces led the United States in October, 1931, to send a representative to sit with the League Council to consider a basis for common action under the pact of Paris. Japan, sternly reminded of her obligations to renounce war, nevertheless continued her career of conquest. In November, Stimson, Hoover's Secretary of State, further protested Japan's course as a violation of the nine-power treaty guaranteeing China's territorial integrity. Meanwhile the League bestirred itself in the attempt to restore peace, but it shrank from applying coercive measures (sanctions) because of the apathetic attitude of Britain, the chief European power in the Orient. This was an object lesson not lost on Mussolini and Hitler in the ensuing years.

When in spite of Washington's efforts Japan occupied all Manchuria, Secretary Stimson in January, 1932, formally notified that country and China that America would not "recognize any situation, treaty, or agreement which may be brought about by means contrary to the covenants and obligations of the Pact of Paris." Two months later the League Assembly (Japan and China not voting) unanimously indorsed this action. But Tokyo denied any culpability, advancing the plea of self-defense, and setting up the "independent" state of Manchukuo in February to prove that the Chinese in Manchuria remained free to exercise the right of self-determination. Smarting under the international condemnation, Japan gave the required two-year notice in 1933 that she would withdraw from the League.

WAR DEBTS AND THE PEACE PROBLEM

From the outset it had been apparent that the postwar structure of peace was conditioned by the dual question of debts and reparations. The former involved reimbursing the United States for the war-time borrowings of the Allied governments, and the latter involved Germany's paying the Allies her crushing war indemnity. Of the ten billion dollars due the United States, more than ninety per cent was owing from Great Britain, France and Italy. America early assured the debtor countries of her willingness to take into account their capacity to pay in arranging terms of settlement. Between June, 1923, and May, 1930, seventeen nations entered agreements, Russia, Nicaragua and Armenia alone failing to do so. Great Britain, for example, promised to repay over a period of sixty-two years at an interest rate averaging 3.3 per cent; Belgium similarly at 1.8 per cent; France at 1.6 per cent; and Italy at 0.4 per cent.

For the wherewithal to discharge these obligations the leading powers relied upon the reparation payments from Germany. This sum had not been fixed in the Versailles treaty, but in 1921 a special commission had set the figure at thirty-three billion dollars. The burden, however, proved too heavy for Germany; and the Dawes plan in 1924 and the Young plan in 1929—named respectively after Charles G. Dawes and Owen D. Young, two Americans who helped draw them up—in turn provided for smaller amounts and easier terms. The Young plan frankly coupled reparations and intergovernmental debts by arranging for a still further reduction of German payments to the extent that America might in the future relax her demands on the Allies. This provision flew in the face of Washington's contention that the two transactions had no relationship to each other. But when presently depression settled on the world and an overstrained Germany seemed on the point of financial collapse, President Hoover in June, 1931, announced a one-year moratorium, or postponement, of both debt and reparation payments. His action was widely interpreted as a tardy admission that the two financial operations were interlocked.

In the summer of 1932, as the moratorium drew to a close, a conference of European powers at Lausanne decided that if a "satisfactory" debt settlement could be reached with America, they would let Germany end further reparation payments with a lump sum of $714,000,000. The resolution, obviously squinting at cancellation by the United States, caused Washington promptly to affirm that its policy remained unchanged. As a matter of fact, the Germans made no further payments. Both at home and abroad the agitation, long under way, for canceling or drastically revising the debts reached new proportions. Some argued that the act would make amends for America's delay in entering the war, while others pointed out that the debtor countries, lacking gold, could not send goods in sufficient quantities because of the high American tariff walls. European bitterness was represented by newspapers that spoke of Uncle Sam as Uncle Shylock. The official attitude of the United States was compounded of the feeling that extremely generous terms had already been granted, and that one third of the sum was not a war debt at all but a postarmistice loan. In December, 1932, France, Belgium and four other governments defaulted and in the next year all the other countries but Finland followed suit.

Despite the growing irritation caused by the debt situation, the years from 1921 had beheld an impressive collective effort by the nations toward the goal of a warless world. The American government's contribution to this advance had been abetted by an eager public opinion. Once the war had ended, the various peace groups had resumed their activities with redoubled zeal, and new organizations joined their ranks. A noteworthy indication of revived interest in the cause was afforded by a nation-wide poll of Protestant clergymen in 1931. Of the more than nineteen thousand who responded, twelve thousand (sixty-two per cent) declared that the churches should go on record as refusing to approve or support any future war, while more than ten thousand (fifty-four per cent) stated that they personally would not sanction any future war or actively participate in it.

Though such sentiments were opposed by other elements in the population, notably by veterans' groups and hereditary patriotic societies, yet the most significant scheme to strike at the war evil through purely domestic action originated with the American Legion, the chief ex-soldiers' organization. At its prompting, Congress created a War Policies Commission including five cabinet officials. This body in 1932, after consulting with industrial and labor leaders, army officers and spokesmen for civilian groups, framed a plan to eliminate the profiteering motive as an incentive to war. It proposed a constitutional amendment giving the government unrestricted war-time power to fix prices, and recommended legislation which, when war should break out, would automatically subject individuals and corporations to a tax of ninety-five per cent on all income above the previous three-year average. But Congress took no action. At home its attention was rapidly becoming absorbed in problems created by the deepening depression, while abroad Japan's lunge against China and the rising war temperature in Europe suggested the desirability of moving circumspectly.

SELECT BIBLIOGRAPHY

The Quest for Security. Apart from Sullivan, *Our Times,* which continues through 1925, no large-scale history exists for the years since the First World War. Two coöperative works of great value are Committee on Recent Economic Changes, *Recent Economic Changes,* and President's Research Committee on Social Trends, *Recent Social Trends.* As aids in linking current events with recent history, the following annual compilations are useful: Lippmann and others, *United States in World Affairs;* the *American Year Book;* the *New International Year Book;* and the *Americana Annual.*

Postwar Readjustments. For this and other topics in the

chapter, see Malin, *United States after the World War;* Allen, *Only Yesterday;* and Dumond, *Roosevelt to Roosevelt.* Besides the general account of postwar hysteria in Slosson, *Great Crusade and After,* particular aspects are treated in Bates, *Land of Liberty;* Hays, *Let Freedom Ring;* Mechlin, *Ku Klux Klan;* Williams, *Shadow of the Pope;* and Musmanno, *After Twelve Years,* dealing with the Sacco-Vanzetti case. Commons and others, *History of Labor,* III-IV, discusses the impact of peace on the labor movement.

The Nation Turns Republican. In the absence of detailed political studies of the 1920's, the following biographies are helpful: Fuess, *Coolidge;* Corey, *Truth about Hoover;* Pringle, *Alfred E. Smith;* Johnson, *Borah;* Bryn-Jones, *Kellogg;* and Jessup, *Root.* For the Harding scandals, consult Adams, *Incredible Era,* and Werner, *Privileged Characters.*

Efforts for Collective Security. The general accounts include Fleming, *United States and World Organization;* Jessup, *International Security;* Williams, *United States and Disarmament;* and Rappard, *Quest for Peace.* More restricted in scope are Jessup, *United States and the World Court;* Buell, *Washington Conference;* and Myers, *Origin and Conclusion of the Paris Pact.* For the Manchurian crisis, see Griswold, *Far Eastern Policy;* Bisson, *American Policy in the Far East;* and Pan, *American Diplomacy Concerning Manchuria;* and for the debt question, Moulton and Pasvolsky, *War Debts and World Prosperity.*

Chapter XVIII

FROM PROGRESS TO POVERTY,
1920–1932

REPUBLICAN ECONOMICS

IN DOMESTIC as well as in foreign affairs the Republicans pursued an energetic course. Predominantly the party of business, with a succession of Presidents predisposed to the largest possible freedom for private capital, the Republicans adopted as the watchwords of their twelve-year sway: economy in government; a high-powered promotion of economic enterprise; and tax reduction. In considerable part the program found fulfillment. At the very outset President Harding, succeeding where his two predecessors had failed, induced Congress in June, 1921, to create a Budget Bureau in the Treasury Department, headed by a director buttressed with authority, under the President, to prepare estimates of revenue and to recommend expenditures. The new system marked a sharp break with the time-honored practice by which requests for appropriations, arising from the several executive departments and administrative agencies and from sundry committees of Congress, were voted by Congress without adequate attempt to coördinate outgo with income. Under Charles G. Dawes, the first director, the plan quickly demonstrated its utility.

As part of the program of stimulating business, Congress in the same session turned to the customary Republican task of raising the tariff. In an effort to ward off the competition of low-priced Canadian grain, it imposed high duties on wheat and corn, along with meat, wool, sugar and certain other farm products. In 1922 a general tariff revision followed in which the industrial interests shared. This piece of legislation, the Fordney-McCumber act, was the highest protective measure yet passed. The effect of the excessive rates, however, was intended to be tempered by the provision that, upon advice of the Tariff Commission, the President might lift or lower duties as much as fifty per cent in order to equalize the costs of production in the United States and competing foreign countries. But, though Harding and his successors made extensive use of the flexible clause, it was usually to enhance rates.

A majority of the Democrats in Congress condemned the Fordney-McCumber act. They viewed it as a tax extorted by the manufacturers from the people, and held that it was certain to discourage foreign imports at the very time when the huge debts due from Europe would have to be paid chiefly in commodities. But the country's abounding prosperity made the public indifferent to such criticisms. As the decade drew toward a close, however, the evil plight of the Western farmers caused the beneficence of the tariff law to be increasingly questioned. To the rising chorus of protest the Republican answer was the need of more protection, not less. When Congress reopened the subject in the spring of 1929, representatives of the manufacturing interests—lawyers, publicity experts, professional agents—packed the lobbies. Joseph R. Grundy, president of the Pennsylvania Manufacturers' Association, frankly declared before a congressional committee that industrialists had contributed funds to elect President Hoover and that the legislators should take full cognizance of the fact. In November Grundy was appointed to a vacancy in the Senate in time to aid powerfully in putting his ideas into effect.

After months of what the stanchly Republican *Boston Transcript* called "the unrestrained play of selfishness and of petty politics," the Hawley-Smoot bill finally emerged in

June, 1930. Contrary to President Hoover's desire to limit action to a few mainly agricultural schedules, the measure was a general revision which increased protection by an average of perhaps twenty per cent above the unprecedented rates of 1922. In the case of certain articles, notably automobiles, duties were retained when a majority of the manufacturers had no wish for them. A protest signed by over a thousand economists from a hundred and seventy-nine colleges and universities urged the President to veto the bill. They stressed the harmful effects of the extortionate rates on living costs, foreign trade and investments and the debt situation. But Hoover signed the law, believing he could remedy its worst features through the flexible clause that the bill retained. The most startling result of the act appeared in reprisals by foreign governments. By the spring of 1932 more than twenty countries had raised their tariffs, some explicitly avowing their purpose to retaliate against America.

That the foreign trade of the United States steadily grew from 1922 to 1929 despite the steep customs wall was due partly to the enormous sums that Americans loaned abroad, much of which was used to pay for American goods. Foreign investments by United States citizens rose from $8,500,000,000 in 1922 to over $12,000,000,000 in 1927.[1] In view of the size of these transactions, the State Department in 1921 began the practice of having banking houses get its approval before floating foreign loans in the United States. In order to make the Department of Commerce "the world's most formidable engine of foreign trade conquest," Herbert Hoover as its Secretary induced Congress in 1927 to supplement the regular consular officers with a world-wide network of hustling special agents working under his supervision to search out openings for American commerce and the export of capital. The

---

[1] In the same period, investments by foreigners in America increased from $2,800,000,000 to only $3,700,000,000.

Washington government's announcement of the moratorium in 1931 (see page 481) stemmed in considerable measure from fear lest Germany's bad financial situation imperil American holdings in that country of nearly $2,000,000,000.

The rapid rise of American investments abroad resulted partly from the establishment of American-owned industries there. The high tariff made it difficult for foreigners to buy goods in the United States because of the barriers against their own export trade. As James Harvey Rogers, the Yale economist, pointed out in 1929, "substantial portions of our most highly developed and most profitable industries" found it expedient to migrate to alien lands, "carrying with them not only American organization and methods but also American talent, with all the resultant loss of purchasing of American domestic products and of the stimulus to American business in general." Thus, American automobile plants sprang up in Canada, cork factories in Spain, glove works in France, burlap mills in India. This condition helped to account for the growing opposition of mercantile exporters to excessive protection.

Obedient to the Republican purpose of fostering industrial enterprise, both the Attorney-General's office and the Federal Trade Commission displayed a much friendlier attitude toward Big Business than in the days of militant progressivism. A new consolidating movement began, usually taking the form of holding companies. Because of the bewildering complexity of their internal structure, such supermergers lent themselves readily to stock watering, speculation and dishonest accounting practices. The full possibilities of the financial jugglery became known in 1932 with the collapse of the Insull group of public utilities, which furnished power, light and heat to nearly five thousand communities in thirty states. The crash inflicted a staggering loss of nearly seven hundred million dollars on the investing public. Samuel Insull, the architect of this glittering empire, promptly fled to Greece and, when finally forced to return, managed to escape punishment for lack of necessary evidence.

As the Insull affair indicates, these colossal undertakings enjoyed a fungus growth in the electric-power industry, where the courts had ruled that the holding companies were not themselves public utilities and hence were free from regulation by state utility commissions. Since American homes, factories and transportation lines used as much current as all the rest of the world combined, electric energy was assuming the importance of a major natural resource; and the conservation question raised its head in a new and acute guise. More than a tenth of the total output moved across state lines and therefore afforded an opportunity for federal regulation. Yet only in the matter of water power did Congress take action. In 1920 President Wilson had signed a law creating the Federal Power Commission, consisting of three cabinet officers, with authority to license hydroelectric projects on navigable waters and in public lands. In the next ten years it issued permits for nearly four hundred and fifty projects, chiefly in the West, but the licensed plants in 1930 generated only a sixteenth of the nation's total power.

Not content with this slow progress, certain members of Congress, led by the veteran Republican liberal, Senator George W. Norris of Nebraska, pressed for more decisive action by the national government. The principal dispute revolved about the question of the disposition of the federal properties on the Tennessee River at the foot of Muscle Shoals near Florence in northern Alabama. Authorized by Congress as a war-time measure, President Wilson in 1918 had caused factories to be built there to make nitrates for explosives and fertilizers, and he had also begun the construction of dams to generate electric power for operating the plants. The national expenditure at Muscle Shoals totaled

$145,000,000. The progressive elements in both parties demanded government ownership and operation of the nitrate works and the hydroelectric station, while the industrial East insisted on turning them over to private companies. After prolonged controversy, two bills framed to accomplish the purpose of the progressives—one in 1928 and the other in 1931—were killed by presidential vetoes. President Hoover, faithful to his creed of "rugged individualism," denounced the nation's entrance into economic competition with its own citizens, and maintained that regulation of power utilities belonged properly to the states.

Out of the welter of discussion and conflict emerged two concessions to the progressives. One was Congress's authorization in 1928 of the Boulder Canyon project for erecting a dam across the Colorado River at the Arizona-Nevada border. The purpose was to insure flood control, provide water for irrigation and furnish electric power to the seven states of the Southwest, preference being given to state and municipal agencies over private companies. The act provided for creating an artificial lake more than a hundred miles long, at a total cost of $165,000,000, to be repaid to the government over a period of fifty years by the users of water and power. Actual construction began two years later. Less important was the law of 1930, which reconstituted the Federal Power Commission with five members appointed by the President, but left the scope of its authority unaltered. A final disposition of the Muscle Shoals question awaited the coming of the New Deal.

Meanwhile, the Republicans had bent their energies toward scaling down the public debt and lowering the high war-time taxes. So successful was the Secretary of the Treasury in the first respect that the national indebtedness shrank from twenty-four billion dollars in 1920 to about sixteen in 1930, a decline of approximately one third. In tax reduction, too, Secretary Mellon made substantial progress, Congress usually accepting his recommendation to slash most heavily the rates on the biggest incomes (those in the "upper brackets"), with slighter cuts for the smaller ones.

The chief obstacle to the smooth working out of this double-barreled program was the ceaseless clamor of the ex-soldiers for further compensation. Through the Veterans' Bureau the government already provided medical and hospital care for totally disabled soldiers, furnished vocational training to partly disabled ones, granted allowances to their dependents, and administered a vast insurance business on behalf of the ex-service men. In addition, at the close of the World War a discharge bonus totaling $256,000,000 had been paid them. Yet the veterans, led by the American Legion, insisted that the government owed them a further bonus to help offset the high war-time wages they might have earned in civilian employments. A bonus bill passed in 1922 was stopped by Harding's veto, but another one, in 1924, was carried over Coolidge's.

This measure provided for the issuance of adjusted-service certificates in the form of paid-up insurance policies, with the stipulation that the government should pay the principal in 1945. Other acts from time to time liberalized the compensation allowed under earlier laws, and one in 1930 authorized grants for disabilities even though they had been suffered after the war. When the country began to feel the pinch of unemployment in 1930, the ex-soldiers started an agitation for immediate redemption of the adjusted-service certificates. Over President Hoover's ringing veto, Congress in February, 1931, conceded a part of the demand by increasing the loan value of the certificates from twenty-two to fifty per cent of their face value. Expenditures for World War veterans, which had cost the American people $402,000,000 in 1921, reached an annual total of over $860,000,000 in 1932.

LABOR AND THE IMMIGRATION QUESTION

While capital reaped the lush fruits of prosperity, labor issued from the dark years of the early 1920's into the sunlight of ampler pay and a better standard of living. As long as the depression lasted, however, wage cuts and unemployment marked the scene. In July, 1922, began a nation-wide strike of four hundred thousand railroad shopmen as a result of wage reductions ordered by the federal Railway Labor Board. After President Harding made several fruitless attempts to end the trouble through mediation, Attorney-General Daugherty on September 1, alleging the need of protecting the mails and interstate commerce, obtained a blanket injunction against the strikers. It was the most sweeping decree of the kind ever issued. Under its terms they could not even use peaceful argument or moral suasion to induce fellow employees to quit work. It was bitterly denounced as an infringement of labor's rights and of the Clayton anti-trust act. Though not the decisive factor, the government's move hastened the conclusive defeat of the men.

Yet 1922 and the return of good times ushered in an era unusually free from industrial upheavals. The number of strikes fell from 3400 in 1920 to 1100 in 1922, and dropped to as few as 600 in 1928. The number of wage-earners involved declined from nearly a million and a half in the first of these years to less than a third of a million in the last. Many factors helped to account for this trend. On the one hand, the unwonted peace owed much to the increasing use of injunctions against strikers as well as to the resolute drive of employers for the open or nonunion shop and their shrewdness in introducing company unions in place of unions affiliated with national labor organizations. By 1929 more than a million workers belonged to company unions. On the other hand, the employees were propitiated by better wages, profit-sharing plans, and employers' welfare programs involving such features as recreational facilities, sickness and death benefits and retirement pensions. As the profits of industry climbed ever upward, employers not only exerted themselves to insure a contented labor force, but many of them accepted the doctrine that high wages (and hence enhanced purchasing power) formed an essential element in the reigning prosperity. The membership of the American Federation of Labor fell from four million in 1920 to two million nine hundred thousand in 1929.

Though a declining force in the industrial world, the American Federation nevertheless left its mark on legislation. Many states were induced to strengthen the enforcement of their workmen's compensation acts, raise the scale of payments, and furnish ampler medical and hospital care. A new type of social legislation appeared in old-age pensions, modeled on European prototypes, for which seventeen commonwealths had made provision by 1930. Organized labor also pushed forward the battle against the hiring of children workers. After the Supreme Court in 1922 checkmated Congress's second attempt to diminish the evil (see page 341), the lawmakers in 1924 submitted to the states a constitutional amendment to grant Congress the "power to limit, regulate, and prohibit the labor of persons under eighteen years of age."

Had the proposal been made when the progressive movement was at its peak, it doubtless would have been speedily ratified. But coming in the period of postwar reaction, it excited little favor outside of labor and humanitarian circles; and Southern employers of children, Northern investors in Southern mills and conservatives generally united to arouse opinion against it. Only five states—none in the industrialized East—ratified before the crash of 1929, while twenty-four rejected it. The widespread unemployment thereafter reawakened interest in the amendment, however, for the abolition of child labor seemed one way of creating jobs for adults. Twenty-three legislatures, including New Jersey, Pennsylvania and Maine in the East, added their approval between 1931 and 1937. It remained to be seen whether the requisite eight more states would ratify.

The American Federation directed its principal efforts toward securing federal legislation which would restrict the use of court injunctions in industrial disturbances, and also protect workers from so-called yellow-dog contracts, a means by which employers bound their employees not to join outside labor organizations. The Federation's zeal increased as new Supreme Court decisions, notably the Bedford Cut Stone Company case (1927), further weakened the anti-injunction features of the Clayton act (see page 339). Finally, after extended controversy, Congress in February, 1932, passed a law, sponsored by Senator Norris and Congressman Fiorello La Guardia, which declared yellow-dog contracts unenforceable in the federal courts, and also explicitly exempted certain forms of activity in labor conflicts from injunctions. In general, the statute provided that "no persons participating in, or affected by, such disputes shall be enjoined from striking, or from striving for the success of the strike by customary labor union effort, short of fraud or violence." The immunity extended to all persons "in the same industry, trade, or occupation," thus considerably enlarging the benefits of the Clayton act, which the court had construed as applying only to the employees of the company immediately concerned.

Organized labor found it an easier matter to marshal popular support for tightening the clamps on immigration. The intense nationalism bred by the war, the dread of a deluge of low-grade newcomers from devastated Europe, the waxing power of the Ku Klux Klan—such influences impelled Congress to give ready ear to labor's fears of competition from hordes of destitute foreign workingmen. Prompt measures seemed called for by the arrival of over eight hundred thousand immigrants in the twelve months after July 1, 1920.

IMMIGRATION BEFORE AND AFTER THE QUOTA LAWS

	COUNTRIES OF NORTHERN AND WESTERN EUROPE	COUNTRIES OF SOUTHERN AND EASTERN EUROPE AND ASIA
Average annual number, 1907–1914	176,983	685,531
Quotas under act of 1921	198,082	158,367
Quotas under act of 1924	140,999	21,847
Quotas under national-origins provision of 1929	132,323	20,251

The result appeared in a series of measures of increasing severity. In 1921 Congress, without repealing any previous restrictions, limited the annual quota of persons from any European or African country to three per cent of the number of its immigrants in the United States in 1910. The law accomplished a dual purpose. It not only insured a reduction in the total number of arrivals, but also discriminated in favor of those from Northern and Western Europe. The door still stood too far open to satisfy public opinion, however. Hence Congress embarked on a more thoroughgoing scheme. The Johnson act of 1924 specified that, for the immediate future, the quota should be cut to two per cent, based on the number of foreign-born of each country in the United States in 1890, instead of 1910. The naming of the earlier census year involved even greater partiality for the older immigration. As a permanent arrangement, the statute provided that, as soon as the exceedingly difficult calculations could be completed, the annual number of arrivals should not exceed approximately a hundred and fifty thousand and that these should be so distributed among the various countries as not to alter the existing composition of the American people.

Native-born residents of Canada and Latin America were not included in these restrictions. The national-origins provision, as it was called, went into effect in 1929.

The Johnson act also dealt with Oriental immigration, which for many years had been on a different footing from European. In a clause especially aimed at Japan, the law provided that aliens ineligible to citizenship should be barred from the United States. The State Department had tried in vain to keep this clause out of the bill, for it involved abrogating the Gentlemen's Agreement of 1907, which Tokyo had observed in good faith. If the same restrictions had been applied to the Japanese as to the others, the number admitted would have been very small. In the circumstances Japan deemed Congress's action a gratuitous insult and entered a sharp protest against it.

This series of restraints, climaxed by the national-origins provision, attested the republic's unwillingness henceforth to let the melting pot simmer and seethe as it willed. Since the adoption of the Constitution profound changes had taken place in the make-up of the white American stock. If the statistical computations be assumed approximately correct, the proportion of British, Scotch-Irish and Canadian blood had declined from 77 per cent to 45.7, while the German strain had grown from 7.4 per cent to 16.3, the southern and central Irish from 4.4 to 11.2 and the Scandinavian from less than one to 4.3, with the Poles (4.1 per cent), the Italians (3.6), the Russians (1.8), the Czechs (1.8) and other groups emerging as new strains of importance. Resolved not to leave the future composition of the American people to chance, Congress now sought to stabilize it in accordance with the ancestry of the population in 1920. Among other things, this implied that the United States, reversing its historic policy, would no longer be a free refuge for the peoples of the Old World.

It could not be expected, however, that the balance of alien stocks in the population would remain wholly unaltered. The various countries would not always fill their quotas and, in any event, changes would result from the differing birth rates of the foreign groups in the United States. Another variable consisted in the exemption of the peoples of the Western Hemisphere, particularly the Mexicans, from quota limitations. Attracted by opportunities of unskilled work in the mines, construction camps, fruit groves, and cotton and beet fields of the trans-Mississippi West, the number of Mexicans residing in the United States rose from four hundred thousand in 1910 to nearly a million and a half in 1930. The older restrictions, however, applied to them as well as to European comers; and in 1929 the government actively began to check the inflow, principally by turning back persons who were likely to become public charges. As for the total immigration from all countries, the annual arrivals fell off from 805,000 in 1921 to 35,500 in 1931, hardly a quarter of those who might have entered in the latter year according to the quotas. For this drastic decline below the legal limits the Great Depression was responsible.

THE FARM PROBLEM

Though prosperity heavily blanketed the country in general during the 1920's, the farming sections had failed to recover from the postwar depression. While the World War continued, the reserve power of American agriculture had been brought into play. Under the stimulus of the highest prices the farmers had ever known, they had rapidly mechanized their operations, enlarged their holdings and vastly expanded their output. Between 1916 and 1919 the annual sales of tractors leaped from less than twenty-eight thousand to more than a hundred and thirty-six thousand.

The agrarians, determined to improve their status in other

ways as well, sought to modernize their methods of marketing. The Farmers' Nonpartisan League, centering in North Dakota, induced that commonwealth in 1919 to undertake a program of state-owned and operated flour mills, grain elevators and a bank. More typical was the widespread interest in coöperatives. From 1914 to 1919 the number of these organizations increased from less than three thousand to nearly six, most of them dealing in grain, dairy products, citrus fruits, vegetables and livestock. In the latter year over half a million persons in this manner sold products valued at $722,000,000, while more than three hundred thousand made purchases of $84,000,000 through a similar pooling of resources. Unlike earlier experiments, these coöperatives were conducted with businesslike efficiency, and bade fair to remain a permanent feature of farm operations. The war period also witnessed a revival of the more familiar type of agrarian organizations—groups like the Farmers' National Council, the United Farmers of America and, notably, the American Farm Bureau Federation—which acted as watchdogs over agricultural interests and well-being.

From the dizzy heights of boom times the postwar slump plunged the farmers into a slough of starvation prices, grinding debts, mortgage foreclosures and bankruptcies. A prime source of their affliction was the sharp falling off of the European demand for American foodstuffs, which left the agriculturists with unsalable surpluses on their hands. Prompt readjustment to a restricted world market was difficult, if not impossible. Their plight was aggravated by the greatly increased taxes, the steep freight rates continuing from the war, and the difficulty of borrowing money to tide over the bad times. Moreover, when conditions in the urban business world returned to normal, the position of the farmer remained as before, except that he was obliged to pay higher prices for the goods he needed. Data collected by the Department of Agriculture in 1922 showed that the cost of growing a bushel of wheat or oats exceeded the average selling price.

The Harding administration, partial to urban industrialists, at first displayed little interest in the agricultural situation. But at the prompting of the American Farm Bureau Federation with its million members, a bipartisan group in Congress, mostly Westerners, formed a so-called farm bloc in the spring of 1921 to secure remedial legislation. Holding the balance of power between the two major parties, they steered through Congress a series of laws designed, on the one hand, to improve rural credit facilities and, on the other, to curb the power of the middlemen.

To accomplish the first purpose, Congress in 1921 temporarily revived the War Finance Corporation, authorizing it to assist in financing the exportation of farm products. In the twelve months after December 1, 1921, $433,500,000 was advanced in this manner in thirty-seven states. Congress also increased the capacity of the federal land banks (see page 340) to lend on farm mortgages; and the intermediate-credits act in 1923 enabled agriculturists to borrow on livestock and crops on their way to the market.

A second group of measures aimed to reduce the great disparity between the small price paid the farmer and the high price charged the public. An act of 1921 granted the Secretary of Agriculture supervision of the packing houses, stockyards and commission merchants, with authority to correct price manipulations and other unfair practices. The grain-futures law several days later empowered the same official to prevent improper speculation upon the exchanges in regard to grain sold for future delivery.[1] In the Capper-Volstead act in 1922 Congress expressly exempted coöperative

[1] Held unconstitutional by the Supreme Court, this act was replaced in 1922 by a new one based on the interstate-commerce clause instead of the taxation clause.

associations in interstate commerce from antitrust prosecution and charged the Secretary of Agriculture to see that they did not become monopolies extorting unfair prices. Besides these statutes, the tariff acts of 1921 and 1922 threw sops to the agrarians.

Notwithstanding the helping hand extended by Congress, the total farm income dwindled from fifteen and a half billion dollars to five and a half between 1920 and 1932. Wheat selling for $1.82 a bushel in 1920 brought thirty-eight cents in 1932; corn fell from sixty-one cents to thirty-two; and cotton from sixteen a pound to six. The trouble was that the government's efforts ignored the heart of the difficulty: overproduction. So long as the agriculturists raised more products than could command a profitable market, prices could not attain a paying level. Moreover the farmers, widely scattered and traditionally individualistic, were not themselves in the position of an industrial combination which could regulate output in the interests of better prices.

As a way out, agrarian leaders proposed that the federal government should create a huge loan fund with which to buy up the crop surplus and send it abroad for sale. From 1924 on, this scheme became the subject of bitter controversy in Congress, the farm spokesmen insisting on their right to the same benevolent care that tariff protection had long accorded the industrialists. As embodied in the McNary-Haugen bill, the plan provided that through a federal farm board the government should purchase the annual surplus of certain crops, collecting from the growers of each an "equalization fee" to defray any losses to the government from an unfavorable difference between the domestic and foreign selling prices.

The bill passed Congress in 1927 and, in slightly modified form, again in 1928, each time to run afoul Coolidge's veto. With unwonted heat he denounced the scheme as price-fixing, a grant of special favors and an abuse of the taxing power as well as an incentive to overproduction. The question of farm relief figured in the election of 1928, as it had in the two preceding ones, and Hoover as President moved at once to put into execution the counterproposal he had offered during the campaign. The agricultural-marketing act in June, 1929, established a Federal Farm Board which should stimulate the formation of coöperatives, propagate the doctrine of crop limitation, and use its fund of $500,-000,000 to stabilize agricultural prices. In this last effort it bought up, through subsidiary agencies, 330,000,000 bushels of wheat and 1,320,000 bales of cotton, but these operations failed to stay the downward spiral of prices. The situation awaited a more fundamental solution.

PROHIBITION IN PRACTICE

While the country was occupied with such varied and far-reaching problems, the people had embarked upon one of the boldest social experiments of all time. Launched by an apparently overwhelming sentiment (see page 461), the attempt to change deep-rooted personal habits over a continent-wide area seemed at the outset almost certain of success. In the Volstead act, effective in January, 1920, Congress defined as intoxicating, and hence illegal, all beverages containing more than half of one per cent of alcohol. But it proved to be one thing to legislate and another to secure compliance. The federal government lacked both the experience and the prior organization to administer a law of this character; and as time went on and public opinion grew increasingly doubtful as to the wisdom of the war-time decision, difficulties of enforcement thickened.

A brisk smuggling trade along the Atlantic Coast and an overland traffic southward from Canada brought in much foreign liquor, while within the national borders illicit distilling and the illegal conversion of industrial alcohol to drinking purposes formed an even greater source of supply. Though Congress from time to time strengthened the supervisory machinery, the task of enforcement proved staggering because of the vastness of the territory, the frequent failure of state and local authorities to coöperate, and oftentimes the venality of the prohibition agents themselves. From 1920 to 1932 a grand total of nearly six hundred thousand cases was brought into the federal district courts, and the number of persons killed in the course of enforcement was two hundred and fifty-four, including seventy-nine government agents.

Compliance with the law was most nearly attained in the rural sections and small towns, where a strong dry sentiment had long prevailed. In the big cities, bribery of officials, "racketeering," "hijacking" and other forms of organized criminality thrived on the profits of making supplies available to "bootleggers," "speakeasies" and "roadhouses," which in turn dispensed the liquor, good or bad in quality, to consumers. Defiance of the Volstead act by otherwise law-abiding citizens became in many circles almost a matter of pride. Even President Harding did not feel called upon to sacrifice his personal inclinations to the constitutional mandate. Particularly alarming was the seeming demoralization of the young people, who found in carrying a hip flask the spice of adventure and sophistication. Imperfect statistics suggest that the total consumption of alcoholic stimulants fell off under the Eighteenth Amendment, but both wets and drys testified to a change from the earlier preference for beer and light wines to hard drinks like whisky, rum and brandy. Prohibitionists, however, hopefully claimed credit for the reduction of poverty, the increased savings deposits, the greater consumption of candy, milk and soft drinks, and the generally improved condition of the poor.

With characteristic timidity the major parties avoided making an issue of the question until "Al" Smith, true to his city upbringing and contrary to the spirit of the Democratic platform, boldly injected the demand for repeal of the Eighteenth Amendment into the campaign of 1928 (see page 472). The results of the election seemed hardly to warrant a repetition of such hardihood. Yet, as the future was to disclose, the "experiment, noble in purpose"—to use President Hoover's phrase—could hardly have been tried at a time less likely to attain success. Urban sentiment had always been the mainstay of the wet cause, and the decade from 1920 to 1930 saw the proportion of people living in cities of ten thousand and upward increase from a little over forty-two per cent to nearly forty-eight. Perhaps even more significant was the fact that the percentage dwelling in centers of twenty-five thousand or more rose from 35.8 to 40.2 and that, through the newspapers, magazines, movies and the radio, cosmopolitan notions and prejudices penetrated to the remotest corners of the land. Moreover, the trial was made at a period when the recoil from war-time self-sacrifice brought a relaxation of morals both in personal behavior and in public life, a tendency prolonged by the hectic living and easy-going standards of an era of extraordinary prosperity.

National prohibition lingered on until the Great Depression and a change of parties cleared the way for repeal. After the economic collapse of 1929 the abolition of the liquor traffic came in for redoubled criticism as a cause of unemployment and of withholding needed revenues from the government as well as a blow to the farmers who had lost a profitable outlet for their cereals and sugar. As will be seen, the Democrats in the campaign of 1932 promised repeal; but before their nominee, Franklin D. Roosevelt, entered office, the outgoing Congress in February, 1933, had taken the necessary constitutional step, with the proviso that the proposed Twenty-first Amendment, contrary to the invariable previous practice, should be approved by state conventions instead of by legislatures. On this issue delegates were chosen in every state of the Union. The Eighteenth Amendment had required thirteen months for adoption; the Twenty-first was ratified in less than ten. It became a part of the Constitution in December, 1933.

THE GREAT DEPRESSION BEGINS

In point of fact, the prosperity of the 1920's passed by not only agriculture, but also shipbuilding, the railway-equipment industry and the coal, textile and shoe trades. But in nearly every other respect the nation basked in the sunshine of unexampled opulence. A committee of economists, writing in 1929, noted with amazement the "outpouring of energy" which in seven years had "piled up skyscrapers in scores of cities; knit the 48 States together with 20,000 miles of airways; moved each year over railways and waterways more than a billion and a half tons of freight; thronged the highways with 25,000,000 motor cars; carried electricity to 17,-000,000 homes . . . and fed, clothed, housed, and amused the 120,000,000 persons who occupy our twentieth of the habitable area of the earth." In particular, the expansion of the radio, motion-picture, automobile, rayon, chemical, electrical and construction industries surpassed the fondest hopes of their sponsors. Responsible public men and business leaders spoke of a "New Economic Era"—a dream of good wages, high prices, inflated credits and fat profits from which there would be no awakening.

Little wonder that people became dizzy with great expectations. Real-estate booms overspread the country. A fever of installment buying infected untold millions, causing them to spend beyond their means. Shopgirls and washerwomen, lucky in the stock market, wore fur coats and drove to work in their own cars. At the same time expenditures by the state and municipal governments piled up beyond precedent. In 1928 and 1929 values in the stock market soared to heights out of all rational relationship to earnings, present or prospective. A craze for speculation akin to that of the South Sea Bubble in eighteenth-century England seized upon the country. Banking houses, which should have given their clients conservative advice, became high-pressure salesmen for investments, domestic and foreign, of which they knew no more than what the roseate prospectuses imparted. People withdrew lifelong savings and even mortgaged their homes in the hope of doubling and trebling their money through the financial legerdemain. In 1929 the daily volume of trading in the New York Stock Exchange averaged nearly four million shares. In vain did the Federal Reserve Board, by restricting bank credits, seek to stem the flood of speculation. In late October the crash came. Good securities and bad tumbled down like a house of cards. The Great Depression had begun.

Flashes and mutterings of the impending storm might have forewarned a people less befogged with the mirage of sudden wealth. Not only had the prosperity been unevenly distributed, but technological unemployment, due to the introduction of labor-saving machines, had rendered something like two million men jobless during the years 1920–1927. Even before the financial collapse, business, geared to an output exceeding any likely demand, showed signs of slowing down. The building boom ended late in 1928; automobile and steel production began to slacken in the summer of 1929. Moreover, the Washington government's postwar program of nursing foreign trade had largely ignored the interdependent character of world commerce. Economic nationalism as expressed most strikingly in the mounting tariff wall prompted other countries to similar measures; the intergovernmental debt situation operated to the detriment of American trade; and political and economic unrest in many lands endangered the unparalleled amount of American investments abroad. Added to these factors were certain others domestic in character: the reckless or fraudulent nature of many of the new business enterprises; the mountainous taxes levied by state and municipal governments; and the wasteful habits of living of all classes.

The United States had experienced protracted depressions before—in 1837, in 1873, in 1893—but on each occasion certain saving circumstances had facilitated recovery: the existence of Western lands free for the taking; the rise of new industries; the demand for goods created by a rapidly growing population; and the opportunities afforded by an expansible foreign trade. These favoring conditions were lacking as the nation faced the hard times inaugurated by the stock-market panic in 1929. The depression proved the worst America had ever known in either intensity or persistence. It spread ruin deep and wide through every part of the country and every section of the population. In other lands, too, the creeping paralysis of stagnation was at work, and in the summer of 1931 the débâcle definitely became worldwide.

The full extent of the catastrophe in America was apparent as the year 1930 advanced. Prices shrank; business fell off; factories and mines shut down; agriculture lay prostrate. Commercial and bank failures during the year totaled nearly twenty-eight thousand with liabilities of more than $1,522,-000,000. Among their number was the largest bank failure in all American history, that of the Bank of United States in New York City, which before the run on it began held deposits of $200,000,000 in the vaults of its sixty-two branches. Winter found men tramping the streets, bread lines forming in the industrial centers, charitable agencies straining to keep even with the widening circle of want and woe. In all, nearly five million men were thrown out of work during this first year. Summer brought further suffering, for a prolonged drought, the severest yet recorded in the nation's history, blighted the corn, hay and other crops in thirty states from Virginia to Montana and from Pennsylvania to Texas. In fifteen of them the average rainfall was about half the normal.

In the months following the stock-market crash Secretary Mellon and business executives generally viewed the situation with unquenched optimism. President Hoover read the portents quite as badly when he asserted in January, 1930, that the "trend of business" was "upward," and assured the people even as late as December that the nation had already weathered the worst of the storm. This faith in the recuperative powers of "rugged individualism" and the "New Economic Era" made the administration slow to undertake decisive measures to cope with the crisis. In November, 1929, the President called a conference of industrial and labor leaders, which declared against a policy of wage cuts, but already by March reductions of pay had begun. He also speeded up the government's construction program in order to provide jobs, and appointed a committee to stimulate and coördinate the relief activities of the states and local communities. At his recommendation, Congress lowered the income-tax rates as a boon to business enterprise—a curtailment of federal revenues soon to be repented. As late as March, 1931, he vetoed a bill, sponsored by Senator Robert F. Wagner of New York, for creating a national employment system which should help to finance and work with state employment agencies in the effort to improve conditions.

Meanwhile, certain new factors entered the situation and nerved the chief executive to bolder action. In Congress the progressives of both parties demanded with increasing vehemence direct federal subsidies for the relief of distress and favored other strong measures that enlisted a growing outside support. In November, 1930, popular discontent with the President's hesitant course elected a Democratic majority to the House and effected an almost even balance of parties in the Senate—the first Republican setback since Wilson's time. As 1930 drew to a close and the new year began, the depression instead of lifting grew steadily deeper. In May the Austrian *Kredit Anstalt* crashed; in June the German financial system collapsed; and England's abandonment of the gold standard in September served as a signal for thirteen other countries to follow before the year ended. In America during 1931 business failures amounted to nearly twenty-nine thousand with liabilities of $736,000,000, while about twenty-three hundred bank suspensions involved a further loss of $1,690,000,000. Foreign trade reached its lowest point since 1914; the jobless totaled over eight million; and the end of the fiscal year in June showed a deficit in the federal revenues of more than $900,000,000, with a larger one in prospect.

When Congress met in December, Hoover announced that "the time is ripe for forward action to expedite our recovery," and to that end he submitted a sheaf of far-reaching proposals. Unhappily, his relations with Congress, which had never been harmonious, grew constantly more rancorous as the weeks passed and his program ran the gantlet of searching criticism from his old progressive foes as well as from the newly victorious Democrats. From January to July, 1932, the measures were all enacted into law, though some were much modified at Congress's hands. The most important one provided for creating a Reconstruction Finance Corporation, empowered to use funds of two billion dollars for making emergency loans to banks, life-insurance companies, savings institutions, farm-mortgage associations, railroads and the like. Three other acts strengthened the federal land banks, enlarged the credit facilities of the federal reserve system, and set up a special home-loan banking system to assist building-and-loan associations and other concerns that disbursed money for residential construction.

These were moves to bolster up the top of the economic pyramid in the belief that the benefits would reach down to the common man who supported its base. The President had no wish to involve Congress in unemployment relief, maintaining that this responsibility rested on the state and local authorities and on private charity. In this attitude he was following an unbroken national tradition, for even in the worst depressions of the past the government at Washington had let the people fend for themselves. Yet though he had told Congress in December, "I am opposed to any direct or indirect Government dole," and had later vetoed one measure of the kind, he felt obliged in July, 1932, to accept another bill that authorized a total appropriation of $2,122,-000,000, of which $1,800,000,000 was to be loaned to states and municipalities for the relief of distress and for self-liquidating public works, and the remainder to be spent on federal construction projects.

A controversy almost as bitter took place over the question of new taxes to offset the deficit in revenues or, in the current phrase, to balance the budget. The act as finally passed increased the income tax all along the line, with rates on incomes above $1,000,000 reaching fifty-five per cent, and at the same time imposed a bewildering variety of excises. Since the levies fell short of Hoover's object, he next proposed economy measures to reduce the cost of government. Once more occurred a pitched battle, and the act as accepted, though effecting substantial savings, fell far short of wiping out the deficit. Meanwhile the system of government lending went into effect as quickly as circumstances permitted. By October 1 the Reconstruction Finance Corporation had advanced funds to nearly six thousand banks, other financial institutions and railroads, and had similarly made loans to thirty-seven states for public works and relief of the jobless.

THE REPUBLICAN ROUT OF 1932

While the federal machinery for fighting the depression got under way, the condition of the country continued to grow worse. More banks and business houses toppled; the federal deficit at the end of June, 1932, reached $2,942,000-000; while the decline of state and local revenues necessitated shorter school terms and the slashing of teachers' pay. Colleges and universities, suffering from diminished resources, joined commercial employers in cutting salaries and other expenses. With twelve and a half million wage-earners idle, many a city dump saw "depression villages" spring up overnight bearing such resentful names as Hooverville and Hoover Heights. In rural America wheat plumbed twenty-five cents, said to be the lowest level in over three hundred years; and farmers presently began to rally in armed bands to protect their homes from foreclosure sales. During midsummer more than ten thousand unemployed ex-soldiers gathered in Washington to urge immediate cash payment of their adjusted-service certificates. There the Bonus Expeditionary Force, as it was promptly dubbed, lingered to the annoyance of the police and the administration until the authorities at last drove it out, unresisting, with army tanks and gas bombs.

Despite occasional stirrings of unrest, the scene as a whole was singularly free from the industrial conflicts and social upheavals that had marked earlier prolonged depressions. Labor groups agitated for a six-hour day and a five-day week, and many employers accepted the new basis in order to keep more men on the pay roll and relieve privation. Proposals for unemployment insurance attracted wide notice after a Wisconsin law for this purpose was signed by Governor Philip F. La Follette, a son of the late Senator and brother of Robert

M., Jr., who had succeeded to his father's seat in 1925. More significant perhaps was the increasing attention which intellectuals and enlightened business leaders, fired by the example of Soviet Russia, gave to the subject of long-range economic planning. Through such means, either sponsored by the government or industrial groups or both, they saw the only sure cure for predatory individualism and perhaps the only certain bulwark against the deep-lying forces threatening the whole capitalist order.

As the party chieftains turned to preparations for the impending presidential election, one thing was undeniably true: the people were in a sullen mood, and disposed to ascribe all their troubles to the man in the White House, who they believed had failed them in foresight and leadership. In Chicago on June 14 the Republicans in a convention containing an unusually high proportion of officeholders renominated Hoover on the first ballot, with Vice-President Curtis as his running mate. The platform resounded with praise of the President's policies, and endeavored to compromise internal differences over prohibition by pledging the party to submit a repeal amendment while leaving individuals free to support or oppose ratification as they liked.

Meeting in the same hall on June 27, the Democrats on the fourth ballot named Franklin D. Roosevelt, the popular governor of New York—much to the chagrin of his erstwhile friend "Al" Smith, who went to the convention with few votes but with high hopes of a stampede in his own direction. John N. Garner of Texas, Speaker of the House of Representatives, was given the second place. The platform, the shortest ever framed, pictured the hard times as the evil and inevitable fruit of Republican postwar policies, and pledged a twenty-five-per-cent cut in government costs and thoroughgoing steps to lift the depression. Among these steps were an expansion of public works and the "extension of federal credit" to provide relief for the needy; shorter hours of labor; unemployment and old-age insurance; a "competitive tariff for revenue" coupled with reciprocal trade treaties; an "effective control of crop surpluses" and an easier financing of farm mortgages; federal regulation of security issues, stock exchanges and holding companies; an overhauling of the banking system; the "use of the nation's water power in the public interest"; and, in general, a "continuous responsibility of government for human welfare." As regards the Eighteenth Amendment, the party demanded immediate repeal.

Informed of his nomination, Governor Roosevelt violated precedent by flying to Chicago to deliver his speech of acceptance to the assembled delegates. In September he launched forth on an aggressive campaign of speechmaking that eventually carried him into thirty-seven of the forty-eight states. Everywhere he charged the Republicans with favoring Big Business to the detriment of the "forgotten man," denounced their impotence in face of the economic crisis, and promised that the Democrats would inaugurate a "new deal." His opponents derided his proposals for betterment as the superficial generalities of an "amiable man with many philanthropic impulses"; but other people found in the fundamentals of public policy that he set forth a tonic assurance of old-time Wilsonian liberalism.

Saddled with the blame for the depression, the Republicans faced a task rendered all the more hopeless by a bad split in their ranks, for most of the leading progressive Senators of the party—Bronson Cutting of New Mexico, Hiram Johnson of California, "Young Bob" La Follette of Wisconsin, Norris of Nebraska and others—openly declared for Roosevelt. Republican spellbinders rang the changes on the theme, "It might have been worse," while Hoover himself cited sixteen different remedies he had applied to heal the nation's wounds, and warned that under a Democratic tariff

"The grass will grow in the streets of a hundred cities, a thousand towns." To his aid came many large employers of labor, men like Henry Ford who posted bulletins in his wide-strewn plants announcing, "To prevent times from getting worse and to help them to get better President Hoover must be elected."

On election day Roosevelt carried the country in a landslide comparable to that on which Hoover had ridden into office. He won 472 electoral votes—every state in the Union but six—to 59 for his opponent, and received 57.4 per cent of the popular ballots (22,800,000 votes) to 39.7 per cent (15,760,000) for his opponent. The Democrats also swept both branches of Congress. Particularly surprising in view of the widespread discontent was the small popular support accorded the Socialists and Communists. Norman Thomas for the former polled but 880,000 votes and William Z. Foster for the latter slightly more than 100,000.

Before the victors took over the reins, the Twentieth Amendment became imbedded in the nation's fundamental law. Championed by Senator Norris since 1923, and seven times approved by the Senate before the House accepted it early in 1932, the amendment provided for doing away with the so-called lame-duck session of Congress—that session held by an outgoing Congress from December to March 4 after a new membership had been chosen. The advocates of the change contended that the old system was undemocratic and that, furthermore, the lame ducks, being no longer subject to popular control, often yielded to the temptation of passing legislation harmful to the public interest.

The amendment was ratified by the requisite number of states in February, 1933. It specified that, instead of March 4, Representatives and Senators should take office on January 3 following the election, and the President and Vice-President on January 20. Since the plan was to go into effect on October

15 following ratification, the transition to the new arrangement involved somewhat foreshortened terms for Roosevelt, Garner and the newly elected members of Congress. Other sections of the amendment provided for certain contingencies overlooked by the Constitution, for example, that Congress should have full power to deal with the situation should both the President-elect and Vice-President-elect die or be otherwise unable to qualify for the office. These latter provisions assumed an unexpected importance when President-elect Roosevelt narrowly escaped death at the hands of a mentally unbalanced person on February 15 while in Miami, Florida. One of the assailant's shots ended the life of a member of his party, Mayor Anton J. Cermak of Chicago.

SELECT BIBLIOGRAPHY

Republican Economics. For most of the topics in this chapter the following general accounts are helpful: Allen, *Only Yesterday;* Beards, *America in Midpassage;* Dumond, *Roosevelt to Roosevelt;* Hacker, *American Problems of Today;* Malin, *United States after the World War;* and Slosson, *Great Crusade and After.* The two composite works, *Recent Economic Changes* and *Recent Social Trends,* contain essential information, while special phases of economic development are discussed in Taussig, *Tariff History;* Jones, *Tariff Retaliation;* Dunn, *American Foreign Investments;* Williams, *Economic Foreign Policy;* Laidler, *Concentration of Control in American Industry;* Berle and Means, *Modern Corporation and Private Property;* Hardy, *Recent Growth of the Electric Light and Power Industry;* and Bonbright and Means, *Holding Company.*

Labor and the Immigration Question. Commons, ed., *History of Labor,* III-IV, Lorwin, *American Federation of Labor,* and Frankfurter and Greene, *Labor Injunction,* deal with the labor movement in the 1920's. The foreign influx receives attention in Garis, *Immigration Restriction,* and Gamio, *Mexican Immigration,* and, with reference to the Japanese, in Griswold, *Far Eastern Policy,* and Paul, *Abrogation of the Gentlemen's Agreement.*

The Farm Problem. Various aspects of the farmers' situation are canvassed in Fossum, *Agrarian Movement in North Dakota;* Wiest, *Agricultural Organization;* Williams, *Power on the Farm;* Forrester, *Large Scale Coöperative Marketing;* Capper, *Agricultural Bloc;* Nourse, *American Agriculture and the European Market;* and Black, *Agricultural Reform.*

Prohibition in Practice. Among the noteworthy studies of this "experiment, noble in purpose," are Feldman, *Prohibition, Its Economic and Industrial Aspects;* Bruère, *Does Prohibition Work?* and Merz, *Dry Decade.*

The Great Depression Begins. An account of the early stages of the economic slump may be found in Leonard, *Three Years Down;* Seldes, *Years of the Locust;* and Allen, *Since Yesterday.*

Chapter XIX

THE DEMOCRATS ATTACK THE DEPRESSION, 1933–1936

ROOSEVELT AND THE NEW DEAL

IN BOTH political experience and personality the new chief executive formed a striking contrast to the outgoing President. In many respects he resembled his famous kinsman and earlier predecessor in the White House, Theodore Roosevelt, whose niece Eleanor he had married. Each of the two men belonged to a well-to-do family of old colonial stock. Each served his political apprenticeship in the New York legislature. Each later became Assistant Secretary of the Navy. Each was nominated for Vice-President, though unsuccessfully in the younger man's case. Each was elected governor of New York, and for each this office proved a steppingstone to the presidency. The earlier Roosevelt defied tradition by running for a third term and, in time, the later one would also do that.

The one Roosevelt, however, sprang from Republican forebears and preferred to use that party as the instrument of reform. The other, born into a Democratic family, just as naturally employed his talents in the opposition party. Both symbolized the progressive idealism of their times; and the greater liberalism of the second Roosevelt may, in considerable degree, be ascribed to his later appearance on the stage and to the opportunity afforded by the economic crisis to accomplish change swiftly. Like his elder relative, Franklin Roosevelt's mind was agile rather than profound, synthetic rather than original. Each knew how to dramatize public issues and to summarize vague popular aspirations in an impelling phrase. The "square deal" of the earlier era readily became the "new deal" of the later. Both men knew the art of creating public opinion so that they might follow it; but Franklin Roosevelt possessed the incomparable advantage of the radio, which he used with consummate effect in keeping the electorate informed of his plans, difficulties, hopes and achievements. In personality he was more urbane, less combative, than the first Roosevelt, but his conciliatory manner, disarming to both friend and foe, was his way of yielding on small points in order eventually to attain greater ones.

A year after his spirited campaign for Vice-President in 1920, Franklin Roosevelt had been stricken with infantile paralysis, a dread disease which he patiently and gallantly fought until, crippled from the waist down, he returned to political life in time to present Alfred E. Smith's name to the Democratic convention in 1924. The President's broad shoulders, vibrant spirit and tireless energy made people forget his handicap. Indeed, he seemed to forget it himself, for before the end of 1936 he had traveled nearly a hundred thousand miles by land and sea, observing the country, mingling with his fellow citizens, addressing audiences and visiting Hawaii, the West Indies and South America. His example breathed new hope into all persons who had physical disabilities to overcome and brought about the development of a great sanatorium at Warm Springs, Georgia, for the treatment of victims of infantile paralysis.

In selecting his cabinet Roosevelt recognized the diverse elements which had made possible his overwhelming victory. Besides Cordell Hull of Tennessee, a sterling Democrat of the low-tariff school whom he named Secretary of State, he chose three former Republicans—William H. Woodin of New York, Secretary of the Treasury, Harold L. Ickes of Illinois, Secretary of the Interior, and Henry A. Wallace of Iowa, Secretary of Agriculture—and he set a precedent by including a woman, Secretary of Labor Frances Perkins, who had served him in a similar capacity in New York state.[1] For advice as to legislation, however, he usually relied upon a small group of private counselors, the so-called Brain Trust, which shifted in membership from time to time, and of which Raymond Moley, recruited from the Columbia faculty, at first bulked largest in the public eye. With their help he worked out the details of the New Deal, communicating his proposals to Congress in short crisp messages that the man on the street might read, and usually accompanying the messages with bills ready for passage. None of his predecessors had so nearly approached the ideal of responsible parliamentary leadership.

Roosevelt delivered his inaugural address on March 4, 1933, at a time of national despair. Thirteen million persons were out of work and a bank depositors' panic had shut the doors of nearly every financial house and stock exchange in the land. In ringing tones the President summoned his countrymen to face the future with confidence and courage. "The only thing we have to fear," he asserted, "is fear itself—nameless, unreasoning, unjustified terror which paralyzes needed efforts to convert retreat into advance." Nor did the Constitution stand in the way of the requisite measures, he said. In the past it had "met every stress of vast expansion of territory, of foreign wars, of bitter internal strife, of world relations," and now it would enable the government "to meet extraordinary needs by changes in emphasis and arrangements without loss of essential form. That is why our con-

[1] The remaining officers were George H. Dern of Utah, Secretary of War; Homer S. Cummings of Connecticut, Attorney-General; Claude A. Swanson of Virginia, Secretary of the Navy; James A. Farley of New York, Postmaster-General; and Daniel C. Roper of South Carolina, Secretary of Commerce. On Woodin's death late in 1933 Henry Morgenthau, Jr., succeeded to the Treasury. Other changes took place subsequently.

stitutional system has proved itself the most superbly enduring mechanism the modern world has ever seen."

His vigorous words were followed by equally vigorous action. Within thirty-six hours of taking office he issued two proclamations, one declaring an official bank holiday throughout the country and the other calling Congress at once to Washington. Meeting on March 9 for a session which lasted a hundred days, Congress under the President's spur enacted a series of epochal laws with breath-taking speed. To meet the banking emergency, it put all financial institutions under what was virtually a licensing system, permitting them to reopen only after satisfying the Treasury Department as to their soundness. Pursuant to this plan the great bulk of them quickly resumed operations. In an effort to balance the budget, Congress, on the one hand, imposed additional taxes and, on the other, empowered the President to effect drastic governmental economies. Under this warrant Roosevelt slashed $125,000,000 from the federal pay roll and, to the amazement of the old-time politicians, reduced the compensation of war veterans by more than $300,000,000.

Much more significant was the group of statutes which, in effect, made the administration director and coördinator of the nation's economic life. This body of legislation, assuming clear-cut form in the special session, was supplemented and elaborated in later sessions and by later Congresses as changing circumstances seemed to require. Roosevelt expressed its underlying spirit when he declared during his campaign for the presidency, "The country demands bold, persistent experimentation. It is common sense to take a method and try it. If it fails, admit it frankly and try another." The main legislative endeavors were foreshadowed by Roosevelt's own efforts while governor of New York on behalf of unemployment relief, farm betterment, reforestation and the governmental development and operation of hydroelectric facilities. They were even more clearly forecast by the platform on which he was elected in 1932.

Such immediate considerations apart, the New Deal may properly be regarded as a reassertion and extension of the ideals of the earlier progressive movement, which had suffered shipwreck when America entered the European conflict in 1917. In striving to give effect to these ideals, Roosevelt applied to the peace-time crisis many of the methods which the Wilson administration had used to mobilize the country's economic resources during the World War. It is significant that George W. Norris of Nebraska, a battle-scarred progressive of the older days, stood at the forefront of the President's supporters in the Senate, while among those outside Congress who helped in an official or private capacity to shape the "Roosevelt revolution" were Bernard M. Baruch, Hugh S. Johnson, and Professor Felix Frankfurter of the Harvard Law School, all of whom had taken active part in the war-time government. The President himself had been a Wilsonian liberal and in the Navy Department had participated in organizing the nation's war effort.

In another respect, the New Deal was an attempt to bring the government abreast the social and economic programs of European countries (see pages 306-307), in other words, to adapt comparable foreign experience to American conditions. Great Britain, Germany, the Scandinavian countries and others had adopted many of the New Deal reforms a generation before. In Italy nation-wide schemes of public works had been in operation for a full decade, while Soviet Russia had been working on central economic planning ever since the Revolution of 1917. Under the impact of the depression, moreover, many governments had resorted to a curtailment of agricultural production as a means of boosting prices. Thus, France had restricted her acreage of wheat, the Netherlands and Denmark had reduced their output of cattle and hogs, and in 1933 Brazil ordered the destruction of twelve million bags of coffee. Roosevelt and his counselors were well aware of these undertakings elsewhere. At one juncture the President sent an official commission to Sweden and England to study coöperatives, which had come to occupy an important place in the economic life of those and other lands. The New Deal in its initial phases differed from the emergency actions of European nations mainly in the fact that nowhere else were the cards dealt so fast and in so many directions.

Neither earlier nor later did the "Roosevelt revolution" aim to destroy the economic foundations of American society. The President and his advisers held that the trouble with the capitalist system was the capitalists, not the system. By expanding governmental control beyond any previous precedent Roosevelt hoped to prevent future abuses of power by financial and industrial interests, to enhance the position of labor and agriculture, and to insure the "forgotten man" a fuller, freer and securer existence. Knowing the direction in which he wished to go and believing in "persistent experimentation," he subscribed to no single school of economic thought, but stood ready to employ any or all means that promised results. Critics might, and did, accuse him of confusion of method, but always he labored in the spirit of Macaulay's dictum: "Reform in order to preserve."

Because he steered this middle course he was constantly assailed by zealots to his left, who urged him to move faster and farther, and by zealots to his right, who feared he was plunging the country into communism and chaos. After a time his bitter denunciations of industrial magnates provoked the wrath of Big Business; but from the plain people, whose mute hopes he so accurately voiced, he won an ever increasing measure of confidence. In particular, the President enjoyed the strong support of organized labor and of the agrarian groups. These two elements had formed contending interests in earlier administrations, but the Roosevelt program, made up in part of their own proposals, showed a whole-hearted concern for their common welfare.

The New Deal involved not only the greatest peace-time centralization of federal authority yet known in the United States, but also a vast extension of the power of the executive at the expense of the legislative. In many of the laws Congress merely laid down broad principles of action, leaving the President free to work out the details, to allocate the funds and oftentimes to set up such administrative tribunals as he saw fit. Soon a maze of commissions, boards and other agencies sprang up in Washington, many of them empowered to issue rules and regulations that bore the effect of law though Congress had not expressly passed upon them. Some of these bodies were limited to the emergency; others were permanent. Some resembled the Interstate Commerce Commission and the Federal Trade Commission in their powers; others exercised far greater authority. The public quickly learned to speak of all of them by their alphabetical abbreviations: NRA for the National Recovery Administration, SEC for the Securities and Exchange Commission, NLRB for the National Labor Relations Board, and the like.

The setting up of these administrative units caused a great augmentation of the federal civil service. In four years 241,-000 positions were added to the 583,000 already in existence. Of these new offices three out of every five belonged to the emergency agencies. Political foes denounced this "New Deal bureaucracy" for increasing government costs and "intruding with official sanction into the private business of citizens." Moreover, since the proportion of places outside the merit system was allowed to double in the four years after June, 1932—rising from one fifth to two fifths of the whole service —they pointed to the use of many of the offices as political spoils. This practice they branded as "Farleyism" after the Postmaster-General, the administration's principal dispenser of patronage. New Deal supporters, however, defended Roosevelt's apparent indifference to the examination system of appointment on the ground that the national emergency called for a recruitment of personnel admitting of no delay, and they took just pride in the fact that no earlier peace-time government at Washington had ever attracted into the public service, especially the higher ranks, so large a number of disinterested, high-minded and well-trained persons. Scarcely a college or university in the land failed to contribute one or more of its faculty for a longer or shorter time to some branch of the new régime. As will be seen, no effective steps were taken to meet the objections to "Farleyism" until Roosevelt's second term.

The task that faced the New Deal was threefold in character. The immediate need was to save the thirteen million unemployed from privation and despair. Beyond this, the government must help to set the wheels of economic life in motion again. Finally, it was pledged to seek permanent cures, if possible, for the deep-seated evils that had produced the industrial breakdown. In other words, the administration's aims were relief, recovery and reform. The business and conservative classes, though friendly to many of the steps for relief and recovery, angrily resisted the proposals for reform. The latter, they argued, if adopted at all, should be delayed until normal times. But Roosevelt, eager to make progress while the popular mood permitted, insisted on his full program. The "three R's" were not always sharply separable in the measures undertaken. Sometimes the purposes overlapped or even conflicted. Nevertheless, they serve clearly to illuminate the myriad activities which made up the New Deal.

RELIEF MEASURES

Contrary to the attitude of President Hoover, who had opposed direct succor of the needy by the Washington government (see page 509), Roosevelt proclaimed it a national responsibility to see that no one starved and, in line with that resolve, launched the most colossal program of relief ever undertaken anywhere. His policy involved outright gifts of federal funds, and thus indirectly imposed on the taxpayers of the wealthier states the burden of helping out the poorer ones. To meet the immediate demand, the government spent millions on direct material relief, supplying the jobless with food, clothing and fuel. But in the case of able-bodied recipients, it sought as quickly as possible to replace the dole with work relief, for it believed that labor for pay would better sustain their morale.

A variety of special agencies helped to administer the huge sums which Congress from time to time made available. In May, 1933, the Federal Emergency Relief Administration was set up under the direction of Harry L. Hopkins, who had supervised the state relief activities of New York when Roosevelt was governor. The FERA devoted chief attention to supplementing the depleted revenues of the states, leaving the local administrators free to use the money for direct or work relief as they preferred and to aid both the physically fit and unemployables. So great was the exhaustion of local funds that in thirteen commonwealths the federal grants totaled over ninety per cent of the entire relief expenditures. Only three states shouldered as much as fifty per cent of the cost. As an adjunct to the FERA, the Civil Works Administration was established in November, 1933, to provide additional work relief for the approaching winter. Though this agency was terminated on May 1, 1934, it spent nearly $845,-000,000 in financing civic projects that could be completed within a few months. Unlike the FERA, the CWA operated under centralized federal control. The FERA, which continued through 1935, eventually disbursed over three billion for relief.

A different attack on the unemployment problem was made through the United States Employment Service, which sought to discover available jobs rather than to create new ones. It had been set up under the Wagner act, which Hoover had vetoed but which the special session readopted with Roosevelt's approval. The Employment Service promoted the establishment of state and local employment exchanges and, by linking them in a nation-wide system, greatly improved their

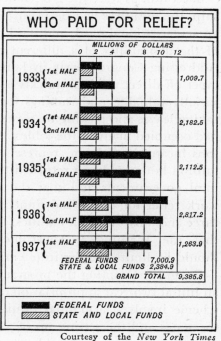

Courtesy of the *New York Times*

effectiveness. Though called into being by the emergency, the new agency was made a permanent bureau of the Department of Labor.

By the close of 1934 over five million households, representing twenty million men, women and children, were on relief. This was nearly five million more persons than in July, 1933. The average monthly payments to households had risen from $15.30 in July, 1933, to $28.40 in December, 1934. Various factors had enlarged the number of dependents, notably the depletion of family savings, the increased use by employers of labor-saving machinery, and the growing up of young people without opportunities of work.

Successful as were the government's efforts to relieve hardship, the measures had been hurriedly devised in the face of an acute national need, and the President became convinced of the desirability of a different and more efficient system. Addressing Congress early in January, 1935, he proposed to taper off direct relief as quickly as possible and to substitute socially valuable undertakings for the trivial tasks (such as raking leaves and picking up waste paper in the parks) which had occupied many of the jobless. He further urged that persons incapable of labor, representing about one and a half million households, be returned to the care of the state and local governments and that the federal authorities pledge work relief for one breadwinner in each of the remaining three and a half million families. In other words, he declared that the Washington government's future responsibility should be limited to destitute employables.

Congress, accepting the program, responded in April with an initial two-year appropriation of $4,880,000,000. The new scheme involved a gradual liquidation of FERA grants to the states and the setting up of a system under firm federal control. The states and local communities were, however, to share in the cost and responsibility of operation. The Works Progress Administration, promptly organized under the experienced Harry Hopkins, undertook at the President's direction a "coördinated execution of the work relief program as a whole." The total number of persons assisted by the WPA reached a peak of approximately 3,840,000 early in March, 1936, at an average monthly payment of $22.15. Three months later Congress voted an additional appropriation of $1,425,000,000.

From the first the government's relief exertions had encountered a running fire of criticism. Hopkins and his assistants not only faced a situation for which there was no prior experience, but they were further handicapped by the lack of an adequate, well-paid and efficient civil service. As a result, politics, waste and incompetence played an inevitable part. Administration foes quickly applied the term "boondoggling" to the inconsequential tasks to which some of the unemployed were assigned. But quite apart from the value of the work performed, the business classes tended to favor the dole rather than work relief as a cheaper way of caring for the idle. Labor's spokesmen, on the other hand, objected to the relatively low wages allowed relief workers on the ground that the government's course might encourage private employers to hold down pay. The Washington authorities made many modifications of the wage scale without, however, satisfying organized labor.

On the credit side of the ledger the gains were indubitable. Work relief not only saved people from starvation, but fostered their self-respect and enabled them to retain their occupational skills. Nor were manual and clerical workers the only ones helped, for as the program was expanded, notably under the WPA, it came to include many writers, artists, teachers, architects, musicians and actors as well as research experts in the natural and social sciences. Moreover, as hastily prepared projects gave way to more maturely conceived ones, public improvements of lasting value resulted in every part of the land.

Examples of some of the accomplishments will indicate the extent to which the expenditures for humanitarian purposes yielded long-time social and material benefits. By the summer of 1936 over six thousand schoolhouses had been erected or repaired; numerous playgrounds, parks, libraries, hospitals, bridges and airports had been constructed or improved; modernized sewerage had been installed in five thousand communities; and about a hundred and twenty-eight thousand miles of secondary roads had been built or repaired. Relief funds had also been used in the construction of twenty-three great irrigation projects in the West, including the initial work on the Grand Coulee Dam on the Columbia River. Among the white-collar projects, countless historical records were ferreted out of forgotten places and plans made for their preservation; the compilation of a series of comprehensive guidebooks for the various states and local communities was undertaken; and free concerts and inexpensive plays afforded entertainment and inner enrichment for vast numbers unaccustomed to such opportunities.[1]

Though the principal relief measures concerned older persons, the government also attacked the difficult problem created by young men and girls who were reaching working age during these dark years. The first days of Roosevelt's presidency had seen hordes of youths roaming the country in a vain search for employment—likely recruits for a career of crime. In order to throw a life belt to such unfortunates, the Civilian Conservation Corps was promptly instituted with a membership varying at different times from two hundred and fifty thousand to five hundred thousand, mostly young unmarried men chosen from destitute families. Scattered in twenty-six hundred camps, paid wages they were required to share with their families, given opportunities of schooling in their moments of leisure, they carried on an extensive work of protecting the nation's natural resources—draining marshlands, building bridges and erosion dams, planting trees, fighting forest fires, and combating the ravages of insects and

[1] Up to October 1, 1937, about 37 per cent of the total cost of WPA undertakings then in operation had gone into highways, roads and streets; nearly 11 per cent each into public buildings, into parks and other recreational facilities, and into white-collar projects; nearly 10 per cent into sewer systems; and around 5 per cent into conservation projects.

plant diseases. By the middle of 1936 over a million six hundred thousand men had received CCC training. Probably no other New Deal enterprise enjoyed such unqualified popular approval. On a smaller scale, beginning in 1934, the camp idea was applied to temporarily unemployed women and to girls looking for their first jobs. By mid-1936 over three thousand girls were enrolled in forty-seven camps, where they lived on a coöperative plan and studied problems of interest to women wage-earners.

In order to keep as many young folk as possible in school, the relief authorities assisted states whose educational revenues were insufficient and, starting in December, 1933, also made direct grants to needy college students in return for part-time employment. FERA funds enabled the rural schools in twenty-three states to remain open. The National Youth Administration, created by executive order as a branch of the WPA in June, 1935, enlarged the earlier program of student aid. During its first year it paid small stipends to over four hundred thousand youths in schools, colleges and graduate schools in compensation for work done after hours. In addition, it employed nearly two hundred thousand young men and women beyond the legal school age in special projects. The youth-relief program in its various ramifications not only counteracted the corroding effects of enforced idleness, but also equipped the rising generation more adequately for their life work and, by the same token, delayed their entrance into the already overcrowded labor market.

RECOVERY MEASURES IN BUSINESS AND INDUSTRY

Indirectly, the huge expenditures for relief also promoted recovery, the second of the New Deal's "three R's." The enhanced purchasing power of those on relief, together with the demand for materials created by the multitudinous work projects, helped to keep many a business afloat. But other of the administration's acts struck at the problem in a more fundamental way: they aimed to "prime the pump" of economic life so that it might function continuously on its own motion. Thus the business of relief was accompanied by efforts for the relief of business. These measures covered a broad front.

One of the earliest and most successful undertakings, the Reconstruction Finance Corporation, was an adopted New Deal agency. Set up originally by the Hoover administration in 1932 (see page 508), it had sought through government loans to enable financial institutions and railroads to survive the stringency. The Democratic Congress in 1934 extended its authority to industrial enterprises. By means of loans made on adequate security, and through the purchase of bonds and preferred stock in business and banking concerns, the RFC rendered an indispensable service in steadying the country's basic economic structure. It was also the channel through which funds for emergency purposes were disbursed to other federal agencies and to the states. From the beginning to October 1, 1936, it handled over eleven billion dollars, of which a considerable part was soon repaid by the beneficiaries.[1]

Of equal importance was the far-reaching scheme of public works—"internal improvements," to use the pre-Civil War phrase—which the general government undertook in conjunction with state and local authorities. To further this purpose the Public Works Administration was established in June, 1933, under Secretary Ickes of the Interior Department. The PWA proved slow in getting under way, partly because of Ickes's insistence that the government get full value for its money, and partly because local communities

[1] Of the six and a quarter billion advanced to commercial and financial concerns and railroads, approximately two thirds had been returned by the end of this time.

sometimes hesitated to incur additional indebtedness, or were legally restrained from doing so. By the summer of 1934, however, the program had gathered momentum.

Far more than the WPA and the other relief-dispensing agencies, the PWA concentrated on heavy construction projects, the work being performed under contract by private firms which were not required to hire relief labor. It sought, in other words, to restore the normal course of business by means of major undertakings of enduring public benefit. For every two workers on PWA projects it was estimated that five other persons received indirect employment. In so far as the enterprises partook of a local character, the federal government aided the states and municipalities through loans and also through gifts varying in amount from thirty to forty-five per cent of the total cost.

Thanks to Ickes's unceasing vigilance, few of the undertakings were marred by politics and graft, and the positive achievements proved impressive. By July 1, 1936, the PWA had carried out projects in all parts of the country costing nearly two and a half billion, thus giving a tremendous stimulus to many lines of business. These projects included about fifteen hundred waterworks and seventy municipal power plants, an investment of nearly half a billion dollars in over two hundred and fifty hospitals, high-school and college buildings, the erection of a great number of federal, state and municipal buildings, and an expenditure of eight million on public-health work and of more than a quarter of a billion on naval construction.

Since the building business occupied a position of central significance in the economic world, utilizing materials produced by myriad industries, the Roosevelt administration bent its energies to revive residential construction as well as to stimulate public works. The need was dire, for private building had shrunk ninety-five per cent from 1928 to March,

1933, and the impoverished owners of dwellings had neglected even essential repairs. At the latter date homes were being sacrificed under the sheriff's hammer at the rate of a thousand a day. Congress in June, 1933, created the Home Owners' Loan Corporation to enable persons to recover their properties, or to pay off outstanding mortgages, by means of government loans over a long period at moderate interest rates. With this assistance more than a million residences were saved to their owners in the next three years. In addition, the Federal Housing Administration, established in 1934, facilitated the repair and modernization of residential and business properties by guaranteeing, or insuring, the repayment of a certain part of the money lent for such purposes by private agencies.

Meanwhile the government through various instrumentalities encouraged new construction. Through the Federal Housing Administration it insured commercial loans to prospective builders up to as much as four fifths of their investment. But it directed its principal effort toward better housing for the poor, a field in which the demand was acute and which private capital feared to enter. To this end the Washington authorities (acting through the PWA) assisted local governments with both loans and gifts. By the summer of 1936 slum clearance had been undertaken in twenty-seven city districts, and forty-nine "demonstration units" of model tenements were under way in different places. Moreover, through the Resettlement Administration, created in 1935, the government constructed, near large population centers, three "greenbelt" suburban communities, where wage-earners living in rustic surroundings might eke out their earnings by means of subsistence gardening.

Measured by the high expectations, the results of these various endeavors for better housing proved disappointing. Though the volume of private residential construction somewhat increased, it lagged considerably behind the business revival in other lines. As for the government's own housing projects, from the outset the program encountered obstacles because of difficulties raised by the courts, the excessive prices that property owners asked for the land, or the bitter opposition of local real-estate interests. The United States Chamber of Commerce early in 1936 estimated that the country still lacked about two million housing units. Furthermore, the government's zeal to provide thoroughly sanitary, up-to-date living quarters enhanced the cost of construction and put the rentals beyond the reach of the very poor. Accordingly, the benefits accrued mainly to members of the middle class, about a hundred and thirty thousand in all.

Transportation was another nerve center of business which the New Deal sought to reinvigorate. Even before the crash of 1929 the railroads had felt the effects of the increasing competition with motor, water and air traffic. The depression years from 1929 to 1933 halved their revenues from passengers and freight, throwing nearly a third of the nation's total mileage into bankruptcy or receivership. In these same years motor carriers more than doubled their share of the nation's freight business. But for the timely financial aid extended by the Reconstruction Finance Corporation many of the roads would have suffered complete collapse, in which case they would have pulled down countless insurance companies and savings banks that had invested heavily in rail bonds. In order to put the lines on a more profitable basis, Congress in 1933 provided for a federal coördinator of transportation, who should recommend ways of reducing the huge wastes of competition and make proposals for modernizing the lines and effecting their financial reorganization.

Though the recommendations when formulated remained not much better than a paper plan, the railroads managed nevertheless to improve their position. In the effort to increase traffic, the Western companies cut their passenger fares from 3.2 to two cents a mile. When a fifty-per-cent gain of business ensued, the Interstate Commerce Commission in June, 1936, required all lines to adopt the new rate though over the protests of some of the Eastern ones. Aided by government loans, the roads also installed substantial improve-

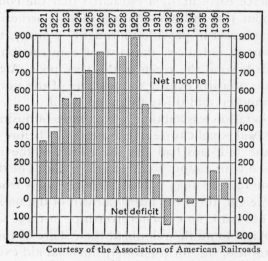

Courtesy of the Association of American Railroads

RAILROAD EARNINGS (IN MILLIONS OF DOLLARS)

ments of service, notably the introduction in some instances of motor-driven, air-conditioned, streamlined trains. These and other steps to check the encroachments of the newer modes of transportation promised a brighter day for the railroads. A law passed in August, 1936, further helped by vesting the Interstate Commerce Commission with power to regulate motor busses and trucks engaged in interstate trade. Thus the second of the twin giants of modern American transport was, for the first time, placed under centralized national control. It was not until 1939, however, that the regulation of water traffic was confided to the ICC; and in the meantime the government's huge expenditures for improved highways and waterways had the effect of bestowing special favors on the railroad's chief rivals. Other difficulties also confronted the lines: heavy debts, high taxes and, in some cases, problems presented by overcapitalization and top-heavy financial structures. Nevertheless the rail companies after four years of deficit began to show a profit in 1936; and despite all their handicaps they continued to carry two thirds of the nation's freight.

In the case of the railroads the New Deal aimed at recovery through a policy of increasing their income by means of lower rates. In other branches of economic life it sought to attain the same result by employing the opposite expedient, that of making business profitable through higher prices. This purpose bulked largest in the transactions regarding the currency and in the measures adopted for rehabilitating industry and agriculture. No other emergency actions broke so boldly with tradition or provoked such heated controversy.

In the effort to reduce the value of money and thus raise prices, the government in April, 1933, went off the gold standard; and in June Congress canceled the gold clauses in public and private contracts, making all debts payable in paper money and silver. Other steps to the same end included the purchase of all the available gold on the market at home and abroad at artificially advanced prices. It was hoped that by this means the value of the dollar would further be cheapened in terms of gold. Similar action was taken in respect to silver bullion, but here the motive, in part, was to aid the Western mining industry and thus check the political pressure for free silver. Congress had also empowered the President to establish unlimited coinage of silver, but he had no intention of using this discretionary authority.

Alarmed by the "currency tinkering," businessmen protested that the economic revival would be held up as long as uncertainty as to the circulating medium continued. Roosevelt in considerable degree satisfied such complaints in February, 1934, by acting with congressional authority to reduce the gold content of the dollar to fifty-nine per cent. In the older sense, this was not a return to the gold standard, for no resumption of gold coinage was provided; but the effect was much the same since Congress set up a special fund of two billion dollars for regulating and stabilizing the devalued dollar in relation to all other forms of currency. The Treasury at the time held over a third of the world's gold supply, an amount which by the summer of 1936 grew to nearly half.

Judged by its effects, the policy of monetary manipulation proved inconclusive. Prices rose in some measure, but the vast governmental expenditures and many other factors in the complex economic situation may have been responsible. Devaluation did, however, temporarily enlarge the export trade because the fall of the dollar in international exchange substantially lowered the price of American products to foreign purchasers.

The far-reaching New Deal plan for resuscitating industry and trade coupled higher prices with devices for increasing the buying power of wage-earners and for improving their working conditions. The National Recovery Administration, created in June, 1933, to carry out this program, was placed in charge of Hugh S. Johnson, an ex-army general who had had wide executive experience in both government and business. A dynamic personality addicted to picturesque and explosive speech, he speeded the process of code making authorized by the statute. In each industry a representative group framed a "code of fair competition," which upon the President's approval had the full force of law. A "code authority," controlled usually by the biggest employers, was then set up to administer the regulations. With time pressing, Roosevelt in July promulgated a blanket code which businessmen were asked to sign pending the formulation of special codes. Administrator Johnson used the press, the radio and the movies to rally popular enthusiasm behind these efforts; and by authorizing NRA employers to display the emblem of a Blue Eagle on their goods and in their places of business, he encouraged the public to single out all others for boycott.

Within less than two years seven hundred and fifty code authorities were in operation. Practically all the codes specified a minimum pay of from twelve to fifteen dollars a week, a work week of forty hours and the abolition of child labor under the age of sixteen. These regulations aimed not only to insure higher wages (increased purchasing power), but also to provide additional jobs and establish more humane working conditions. As a further safeguard for the wage-earners, Section 7a of the statute required the codes to grant employees "the right to organize and bargain collectively through representatives of their own choosing" without "the interference, restraint, or coercion of employers of labor, or their agents."

This drastic reconstruction of business encountered difficulties from the start, due to the complexity of American industry, its wide geographic distribution, the hurried character of the code making and, oftentimes, the selfish attitude of the industrialists affected. Moreover, though the NRA regulations were really intended for large employers of labor, undue zeal on the part of officials—prompted frequently by businessmen themselves—caused the plan to be extended to many small retailers, thus adding to the problems of administration.

Equally contrary to the spirit of the statute were the clauses inserted in over half the codes for uniform prices within an industry and, in many codes, for limiting production and assigning quotas to particular plants. Such monopolistic practices, however, were made possible by Congress's express exemption of NRA agreements from the antitrust laws. These stipulations often worked to the detriment of the smaller producers in an industry, and in frequent instances enabled employers to offset some of the benefits of higher pay by an even more rapid increase of prices. Moreover, the minimum-wage requirements favored highly mechanized factories at the expense of those employing a larger proportion of hand labor. Many small concerns survived only by disregarding the provisions of the codes.

In order to maintain the right of collective bargaining, the President on his own initiative created the National Labor Board in August, 1933, with Senator Wagner of New York as chairman. The NLB soon faced a barrage of difficulties. The big employers sought to turn Section 7a to their own advantage by forming company unions unconnected with national unions and therefore more amenable to control. The American Federation of Labor, on the other hand, insisted on the exclusive rights of its own unions. The Washington authorities, hesitant to side with organized labor because of the harm the great industrialists might do to the government's other recovery efforts, pursued a wavering course. The NLB itself declared the right of a majority of the employees to decide which type of union should prevail. But Roosevelt ignored this ruling in the spring of 1934 when a shutdown threatened in the important automobile industry. Instead, he permitted both company and A. F. of L. unions to exist with the stipulation that representation for purposes of collective bargaining should correspond with the proportionate strength of the two groups.

Notwithstanding these and other troubles, the NLB before its discontinuance settled four fifths of the 3755 disputes referred to it, mediated 1300 strikes and averted nearly 500 others. Efforts to secure a statute outlawing company unions came to nought, but Congress in June, 1934, made an important concession to labor by replacing the President's board with one of its own creation whose decisions he could not review. This new agency, the National Labor Relations Board, was, like the earlier one, limited to the duration of the NRA. It was expressly empowered to conduct elections to determine the representation of workers under Section 7a, and, to allay any possible doubt, Congress explicitly affirmed labor's right to strike.

To that right labor had increasingly turned as the first bright hopes of Section 7a began to dim. A mounting wave of industrial unrest swept over the country: 1700 strikes and lockouts in 1933 (over twice as many as the year before); 1860 in 1934; 2000 in 1935. Violence characterized many of these —destruction of property, affrays of the men with "scabs" (strikebreakers), intervention of the militia. One of the gravest outbreaks took place when twelve thousand longshoremen at San Francisco in May, 1934, set about to enforce recognition of their union. In July the contest developed into a general strike, crippling the business energies of the entire Bay district. The trouble was ended by the longshoremen agreeing to submit the issue to a special federal arbitration board. In September occurred an even more critical disturbance: a nation-wide tie-up of the cotton textile industry, precipitated by the refusal of the owners to grant a shorter work week and to recognize the union. Over four hundred thousand mill workers took part. As in the longshoremen's strike, peace returned when Roosevelt secured an agreement to refer the dispute to federal arbitration.

In May, 1935, the ambitious NRA experiment came to an end. The Supreme Court in the Schechter case destroyed the legal foundations on which it rested. The court held unanimously that Congress could not "delegate legislative power to the President to exercise an unfettered discretion" in the making of codes, and that, in any event, the interstate-commerce clause did not justify Congress in regulating the poultry business carried on locally in Brooklyn by the Schechter Brothers.[1] The court's action deeply angered Roosevelt. Two months before, he had asked Congress to change the basic statute so as to prevent price fixing and other monopolistic features of the NRA codes; but at the same time he had defended the law as having extended the practice of collective bargaining, eliminated cutthroat methods of competition and abolished child labor. In addition, he affirmed that the NRA had given jobs to four million persons and had raised the total annual wages by three billion dollars.

Anti-New Dealers, warmly approving the decision, hailed the judiciary as a modern St. George slaying the dragon of state socialism. The public at large, pleased with the progress of other recovery measures, displayed little interest one way or the other. Congress at the President's urging proceeded to salvage what it could from the wreckage. In July, by the Wagner act, it gave the National Labor Relations Board permanent status and strengthened the Board's authority. In August it passed the Guffey coal act applying a form of code control to the bituminous industry, where chaotic conditions had long been chronic. But the latter law fell before a six-to-three decision of the Supreme Court in May, 1936 (Carter *v.* Carter Coal Co.). Not until his second term, when the judiciary was more favorably disposed, did Roosevelt move to recover more of the ground that had been lost.

RECOVERY MEASURES IN AGRICULTURE

New Deal efforts to succor industry and trade were paralleled by equally elaborate plans to revive agriculture. The

---

[1] The court's action had been foreshadowed by its eight-to-one decision in January, invalidating a special section in the same law for controlling the interstate shipment of oil (Panama Refining Co. *v.* Ryan).

farmer had been in hard straits since the World War (see pages 498-501). Despite the exertions of the Harding, Coolidge and Hoover administrations, the value of agricultural holdings had fallen twenty billion dollars from 1920 to 1929, and plunged twenty-two billion more between 1929 and 1933. When Roosevelt entered office, two out of every five farms were under mortgage. Though the farmers themselves were the immediate sufferers, the inability of a quarter of the nation's inhabitants to buy needed supplies at a time of general business decline acted as a drag on recovery everywhere. Congress set about to restore the farmers' purchasing power through two sets of enactments, one designed to ease their crushing load of debt, the other to induce them by means of federal subsidies to undertake crop control.

For the first purpose, legislation in 1933 and 1934 authorized the federal land banks and other designated bodies—all acting under supervision of a new agency, the Farm Credit Administration—to refinance agricultural mortgages at substantially lower interest rates, and also to advance money for current operations and for buying back property that had already been foreclosed. The Frazier-Lemke act, passed in the latter year, went so far as to postpone the foreclosure of mortgages for six years if the farmers concerned meanwhile paid a rent deemed fair by a federal district judge. This law, however, the Supreme Court unanimously annulled in May, 1935, as violating the constitutional guarantee that private property shall not be taken without due process of law or just compensation (Louisville Joint Stock Bank Co. *v.* Radford). Congress in August replaced it with a second Frazier-Lemke act, which accomplished substantially the same purpose for a three-year period by means eventually acceptable to the Supreme Court.

As a special move to aid submarginal agriculturists, the Resettlement Administration purchased about seventeen thousand farms, mostly in Montana, South Dakota and ten Southern states, so that the impoverished owners might make a fresh start on better land. In order further to facilitate the purchase of new farms, the RA (renamed the Farm Security Administration in 1937) made long-time loans on easy terms, and in the case of a few thousand families established "subsistence-homestead" communities, such as those at Reedsville, West Virginia, Crossville, Tennessee, and Groveton, Texas.

Along with these efforts to lighten the debt burden, Congress at Roosevelt's behest ventured on what he called the "new and untrod path" of crop restriction. The agricultural adjustment act, passed in May, 1933, provided means whereby the growers of important staples could, under the Secretary of Agriculture's supervision, adjust the supply to the demand through voluntary collective action, as industrial combinations had long been accustomed to do by illegal means. Farmers who agreed to limit their output were to be paid for doing so out of money raised from taxing processors (meat packers, flour millers and others who prepared agricultural products for the market). On the financial side, the purpose of these benefit payments was to enhance the farmers' buying power immediately without waiting for the higher crop prices expected from controlled production. The original law confined the plan to cotton, wheat, corn, hogs, rice, tobacco and dairy products, but after a year's trial Congress, acting partly in response to political pressure, saw fit to extend the regulations to cattle, rye, barley, peanuts, flax, grain sorghums and sugar.

Under the Agricultural Adjustment Administration, set up for the purpose, the program made speedy headway. In order to curtail production already started, the AAA in the summer and fall of 1933 induced the cotton farmers by means of cash payments to plow under from a quarter to a half of their acreage, and also brought about the destruction of some of the tobacco crop as well as the slaughter of several million pigs. The butchered animals were converted into fertilizer and, in part, distributed as food to persons on relief. Looking to the next planting season, the AAA made over a million contracts with the cotton growers, which resulted in withdrawing ten million acres from cultivation, leaving about three fifths of the usual planting. Over half a million wheat farmers entered similar contracts for removing seven and a half million acres from tillage. Like agreements were concluded with the producers of certain other commodities.

Notwithstanding the reduction of cotton acreage thus attained, the new crop equaled that of the preceding year. This was due partly to more intensive cultivation and partly to unusually favorable weather. To prevent a similar outcome in the future, Congress in 1934 passed the Bankhead act which imposed a top limit on the total amount of cotton that might be raised. Somewhat similar restrictions were applied to tobacco a few months later.

Despite the refusal of some of the smaller producers to enter restriction agreements and occasional instances of evasion by farmers who did, the government's efforts were attended by a rapid rise of crop prices. But Nature was in part responsible, for a disastrous drought in 1934 parched the West and South and caused widespread dust storms the year following, with the result that agricultural production was further reduced. The farmers' cash earnings, thanks to higher prices and the AAA benefit payments, rose from four and a third billion dollars in 1932 to over seven in 1935. The market value of such commodities as wheat, corn, cotton and tobacco doubled or nearly did so.

City dwellers, viewing the situation with different eyes, kept up a steady murmur of complaint. The meat packers, flour millers and other processors, obliged to pay taxes to the

AAA for their raw materials, increased their prices to consumers, and this fact, coupled with the effects of crop curtailment, made the people pay more for their foodstuffs, thereby counteracting some of the advantages of higher wages. Behind such remonstrances, however, lay a deep-seated protest against an "economy of scarcity," involving an artificial shortage at a time when millions lacked sufficient nourishment. The President in some degree met this latter objection in October, 1933, by creating the Federal Surplus Commodities Corporation for buying excess farm products for distribution among the needy. It was through this channel, for example, that the pork and lard made from the swine slaughtered in 1933 reached persons on relief. Still other critics pointed with alarm to the fact that crop limitation in America stimulated the production of similar commodities in other countries, notably cotton in the case of Brazil, and thus caused a reduction of agricultural exports.

The Supreme Court, basing its disapproval on constitutional grounds, crippled the law in January, 1936, in a decision growing out of the refusal of the Hoosac Mills in Massachusetts to pay processing taxes (United States v. Butler). By a majority of six to three, the judges held that Congress had invaded the "reserved rights of the States" since "a statutory plan to regulate and control agricultural production" lies "beyond the powers delegated to the Federal Government." It therefore affirmed that processing taxes were a "means to an unconstitutional end." But the minority censured this "tortured construction of the Constitution," and agrarian leaders cried out in incredulous amazement.

By this pronouncement the court deprived the AAA of its basic means of operation: the legal power and financial sinews for enforcing crop restriction. Certain that the judiciary would also invalidate the special acts for cotton and tobacco control, Congress now repealed those laws and turned its attention to framing a statute that might in some other way yield advantages to the farmer. The outcome was the soil-conservation-and-domestic-allotment act of February, 1936. By this measure the government was authorized to make benefit payments to coöperating farmers for such objects as retiring worn-out land, shifting crops in the interest of soil enrichment, and taking effective measures against soil erosion. The Secretary of Agriculture, acting through the AAA, was given wide discretion in selecting the crops and settling other arrangements. Out of deference to the court's state-rights views, it was provided that after January 1, 1938, the program should be administered by state agencies operating in accordance with federal standards. The new law, however, contained no certain means of preventing farm surpluses. Not until two years later, after the bench had experienced a change of heart toward the New Deal, did Congress repair this defect.

REFORM MEASURES

Many of the recovery acts involved reform features, but these were usually incidental and not designed to outlast the depression. Some of the other recovery undertakings, such as the National Labor Relations Board and the Agricultural Adjustment Administration, began as temporary expedients, but under pressure of events were transformed into continuing agencies of the government. From the first, however, Roosevelt envisaged the New Deal not merely as a blade to cut through immediate difficulties, but one to destroy deep-rooted wrongs and inequalities. In this spirit, on taking the oath of office, he had declared "social values more noble than mere monetary profit," and had demanded "safeguards against a return of the evils of the old order"—those evils which even ex-President Hoover in 1937 called the "hidden abuses of the capitalistic system which exploded with the depression." The

New Deal's reform activities ranged widely, from a reconstruction of the nation's banking and credit system to far-reaching provisions for social uplift. Some of the measures were not pushed to enactment until Roosevelt's second term; but, whenever proposed, they met stubborn resistance from the business classes.

The collapse of the banks in the opening days of the administration dramatized the need and paved the way for substantial improvements of the banking system. From 1933 to 1936 Congress dealt repeatedly with the subject. It added industrial and savings banks to the federal reserve system and, as a further means of stabilizing business, enlarged the Federal Reserve Board's powers over credit regulation. For this latter purpose the Board, among other things, was given discretion to raise the legal reserve requirements of the member banks. Congress also reorganized the Board so as to make certain henceforth of unified action by the twelve regional reserve banks. In order to restore popular confidence in banking, it established a federal insurance system for the guarantee of bank deposits up to $5000. The Federal Deposit Insurance Corporation, set up in 1933, had extended the plan to over 14,000 of the 15,700 licensed banks by the end of 1936.[1] Finally, Congress forbade banks to engage in the investment business, a practice which in the past had often endangered depositors' accounts.

Other New Deal measures dealt more comprehensively with the problem of investments and speculation. The new principle, declared the President, was to "add to the ancient rule of *caveat emptor* the further doctrine, *Let the seller also beware.*" An act of 1933 imposed heavy penalties for failure to give the public full and accurate information concerning

[1] The capital of the FDIC is built up by subscriptions of the federal government, the federal reserve banks and all the other banks participating in the plan.

newly issued securities sent through the mails or the channels of interstate commerce. In 1934 Congress transferred the administration of this requirement from the Federal Trade Commission to a new agency, the Securities and Exchange Commission, and empowered the SEC to license stock exchanges and regulate their practices according to rules it might lay down. The Washington government thus, for the first time, exerted its authority to make stock exchanges less gambling resorts and more genuine market places.

With even greater boldness the Roosevelt administration grappled with the question of hydroelectric power. The New Dealers deemed electric energy a basic natural resource which, through governmental negligence, had been allowed to fall into the avaricious hands of private utility interests. To the excessive rates which consumers had to pay, they attributed the fact that only one in three American homes used electricity from central power plants, and of farm homes only three in twenty. The Tennessee River basin, where the government had built two nitrate plants and a power station at Muscle Shoals during the World War, gave the New Deal an opportunity to demonstrate the value of a more enlightened policy as well as to exhibit the advantages of regional planning. This turbulent stream, which ramifies into seven Southern states, drains an area nearly as large as England, one rich in undeveloped physical resources, and containing a rural population which had for generations failed to maintain a decent standard of living. Only a quarter of the people lived in cities.

The Tennessee Valley Authority, established by an act of May, 1933, launched a program of development on a scale surpassing the hopes even of Senator Norris, who had so long fought the battle of Muscle Shoals in Congress (see pages 489-490). It undertook to harness the river by means of a series of massive dams and reservoirs for the fourfold purpose of preventing floods, improving navigation, manufacturing nitrates and generating electric power. At the same time the TVA pushed forward plans for reforestation, scientific agriculture and the development of a rounded community life. It withdrew marginal lands from cultivation, resettled the farmers thus displaced, encouraged the wider use of fertilizers

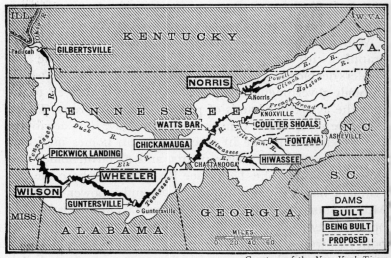

Courtesy of the *New York Times*

THE TENNESSEE VALLEY DAMS

and of safeguards against soil erosion, and promoted public health and recreational facilities. In addition, it built transmission lines and sold its surplus electricity to towns and coöperatives in the region and to private power companies at rates so attractive as to multiply the number of users.

By early 1938 it was distributing power through eighteen municipal plants and seventeen county coöperatives to nearly forty thousand homes and farms. As time passed, an increasing number of rural folk in the valley learned how to banish much of their age-old drudgery. They used electricity not merely to light their homes, but also to refrigerate their food-stuffs for the market and to perform household chores, such as heating water, cooking food and washing and ironing the family clothes. The government's investment in the Tennessee Valley amounted to over $170,000,000 by the middle of 1937, with anticipated expenditures estimated to bring the total eventually to nearly half a billion dollars. It was not expected that complete operation would begin until 1944. TVA experts predicted that the revenue from the sale of power would fully repay the government for its vast outlay within fifty years.

Looking beyond the immediate purpose, the TVA offered its rates as a "yardstick" to measure the charges of private utility companies in all parts of the country. The fairness of the comparison was challenged by the utility interests, which assailed the TVA's accounting methods and contended that its rates were not based on a proper distribution of costs among its several undertakings.[1] Whatever the merits of a dispute in which experts sharply disagreed, many private utilities quickly took steps to scale down their rates. In June, 1935, the annual saving to consumers was reckoned at nearly fifty million dollars. Yet as late as 1939 the average cost of TVA current for home use was 2.14 cents a kilowatt-hour as against 4.21 for the country as a whole.

Other New Deal measures struck more directly at the problem of cheap electricity for the nation. The PWA helped municipalities with gifts and loans to erect or modernize publicly owned power plants; and in May, 1935, the President

---

[1] The matter became one of the subjects of a congressional investigation in 1938–1939, with results which did little to dispose of the issue. The majority of the committee, "after considering the wealth of evidence on the subject," declared that the TVA provided a "legitimate, honest yardstick"; but the minority termed the accounting methods "indefensible" and the yardstick "deceptive, unfair and dishonest."

climaxed these efforts by setting up the Rural Electrification Administration to lend government money for building power plants and transmission lines in the farming regions. Within five years the REA had financed the building of a quarter-million miles of power lines and brought the boon of electricity to country dwellers in forty-three states. An even more ambitious undertaking was the construction, principally at the cost of the PWA, of the great Bonneville and Grand Coulee dams on the Columbia River, designed eventually to provide electricity as well as irrigation for millions of settlers in the Pacific Northwest. In the meantime Boulder Dam, built by the last Republican régime (see page 490), was already selling power to a considerable number of publicly owned plants in the Southwest.

The utility interests, representing a thirteen-billion-dollar industry, bitterly resented the government's competition. They branded it as unfair, unwarranted and unconstitutional, and tried through incessant litigation to delay or defeat the measures. Wendell L. Willkie, president of the Commonwealth and Southern Corporation, a holding company which owned operating concerns in Tennessee and ten other states, headed a vigorous campaign to arouse the fears of the business world, picturing the TVA as "the entering wedge" for the "government ownership of all essential industries." In the end, however, he abandoned the Tennessee field, selling his electrical properties there in 1939 to the TVA and a group of cities and rural coöperatives for $78,600,000.

Meanwhile Congress had proceeded to impose an additional curb on the utility magnates. The purpose was to cure the evils that had attended the formation of giant utility holding companies during the lush twenties. In many instances, these concerns mixed up the actual operating companies without regard to geography and without effecting economies of management. Moreover, holding companies had grown up on top of holding companies, rising sometimes to a pyramid of seven tiers, and affording irresistible opportunities for financial manipulation and the ruin of investors. With the Insull empire still fresh in people's minds (see page 488), Senator Norris pointed to the instance of the Cumberland County Power and Light Company of Portland, Maine, which was owned by the New England Finance and Investment Company, which was owned by the New England Public Service Company, which was owned by the Middle West Utilities Company (chartered in Delaware), which was owned by the Corporation Securities Company (chartered in Illinois), which in turn was controlled by the Corporation Utilities Company and the Insull Utilities Company.

To destroy such supergrowths, Congress in 1935 passed the Wheeler-Rayburn act requiring the Securities and Exchange Commission, as soon as practicable after January 1, 1938, to take steps for confining holding-company systems to natural regions, and to eliminate all companies which had more than one intervening holding company between them and the operating concerns. These restrictions applied to both electric and gas holding companies of an interstate character. The statute also authorized the SEC and the Federal Power Commission to regulate the financial practices of such companies in order to prevent abuses and afford greater protection for investors and consumers. While the act was in course of passage, the utility interests denounced it as a "death sentence" and vainly exerted tremendous pressure upon Congress against it.

Of all the New Deal reforms none dealt so comprehensively with the problem of the underprivileged as the social-security act, passed in 1935. In part, this law sought to make advance provision for persons whom future depressions might throw out of work, setting up an unemployment-insurance system for the purpose. Other sections, intended for normal as well as abnormal times, looked to the welfare of three groups of unemployables: the aged, the destitute blind and needy dependent children. In other words, the social-security act committed the nation to a permanent program of assisting the jobless and the impoverished through federal and state action. This step marked an advance beyond the conception of national responsibility for relief only in periods of emergency, though it did not preclude the latter. At the time the law was adopted, only seven states had ventured upon unemployment insurance, six of them in the half-year before, while pensions for the aged, a much older interest in the United States, prevailed in but thirty-five states. In both respects America lagged far behind Western Europe.

In order to aid people thrown out of work, the statute required employers of eight or more persons to pay a tax on their payrolls, rising to a maximum of three per cent in 1938 (later postponed to 1941). The fund so collected was to be administered by state insurance systems, the payments to the beneficiaries depending on the sum in hand. To assist employees who might retire at the age of sixty-five, provision was made for accumulating a fund in the United States treasury, derived from equal contributions by employers and employees and rising in each case to three per cent of the wages in 1949. These old-age insurance benefits, scheduled to begin in 1940, were to be not less than ten or more than eighty-five dollars a month. In neither instance, however, did the arrangements apply to public employees, farm laborers, domestic servants, casual workers and employees in religious, charitable and nonprofit educational institutions.[1]

In addition, the act provided federal pensions up to fifteen

---

[1] By a special measure Congress in 1934 had provided old-age insurance for railway workers on an employer-employee contributory plan. This act, falling before a five-to-four decision of the Supreme Court in May, 1935, as unwarranted by the interstate-commerce clause, was replaced in August by a more acceptably drawn statute.

(later increased to twenty) dollars a month for destitute persons already sixty-five years old on condition that the states in which they lived should contribute a like amount. Finally, the statute pledged annual grants to the states for aiding them to take care of dependent children and the blind, and provided for appropriations for public-health work, maternity and infant care, and vocational rehabilitation. General administration of the act was vested in a new federal agency, the Social Security Board.

Hailed by President Roosevelt as "a cornerstone in a structure which is being built," the law alarmed the business classes because of the new burdens saddled on industry. At the same time, radicals criticized the act for providing financial benefits that were both inadequate in amount and not extended to all classes of workers. Most people, however, believed that the government had ventured as far as it wisely could in embarking on an experiment of such magnitude and intricacy. In the next two years virtually all the states set up unemployment and old-age insurance systems to the satisfaction of the Social Security Board. By the end of 1937 nearly twenty-one million wage-earners were insured against unemployment, and over thirty-six million had joined the old-age retirement program. Besides, all but a handful of states had taken the required steps to entitle them to federal aid for looking after penniless children, the dependent blind and needy persons over sixty-five.

SELECT BIBLIOGRAPHY

The Democrats Attack the Depression. General accounts appear in Allen, *Since Yesterday;* Beards, *America in Midpassage;* Beard and Smith, *Old Deal and New;* Dumond, *Roosevelt to Roosevelt;* and Hacker, *American Problems of Today.* Pecora, *Wall Street under Oath,* presents the more important disclosures of the Senate committee which in 1933–1934 investigated the methods of American high finance. Sullivan, *Prelude to Panic,* tells the story of the bank holiday. For the government's fiscal measures Johnson, *The Treasury and Monetary Policy,* should be consulted. Special studies of relief efforts include Lane and Steegmuller, *America on Relief;* Burns and Williams, *Survey of Relief and Security Programs;* Whitman, *Bread and Circuses,* dealing with the Federal Theater; and Lindleys, *New Deal for Youth,* describing the activities of the NYA. Among the outstanding works on recovery measures and their effects are Roos, *NRA Economic Planning;* Dougherty, *Labor under the NRA;* Gayer, *Public Works in Prosperity and Depression;* and Nourse and others, *Three Years of the Agricultural Adjustment Administration.* Some of the principal New Deal reforms receive treatment in Hodge, *Tennessee Valley Authority,* and Whitman, *God's Valley,* dealing with the same subject; Douglas, *Social Security in the United States;* Straus and Wegg, *Housing Comes of Age;* and Aronovici, *Housing the Masses.* Crawford, *Pressure Boys,* throws light on lobbying activities in Washington.

Chapter XX

ROUNDING OUT THE NEW DEAL, 1936–1940

THE BALANCE SHEET IN 1936

MIDSUMMER of 1936 afforded a natural occasion for the electorate to take general stock of the "Roosevelt revolution." Behind the New Deal lay three years of trial, error and achievement; immediately ahead loomed the presidential campaign. What had the "three R's" so far accomplished? Though people differed violently in opinion, the vast majority, as the outcome of the election was to show, viewed the results with high approval.

As for relief, the administration's efforts, while costly and wasteful, had not only effected the primary purpose of feeding the hungry and sustaining their morale, but, by doing so, had restored the average man's confidence in democratic methods of government. He was reassured as to the will and capacity of a self-governing people to cope vigorously with the black forces of disaster. Consequently, no idle mobs congregated in city squares to brood over their injustices and indulge in rioting and bloodshed. Through work projects, moreover, states and municipalities had been enabled to carry on needed public improvements that would otherwise have gone by default.

The recovery remedies were more difficult to assess. Bewildering in their variety, expensive in operation, experimental and sometimes contradictory in their nature, some of the undertakings (such as the RFC, the PWA and the AAA) had helped materially to prime the economic pump, while others (notably the NRA) had created more difficulties than they had solved. But whatever the merit of particular features of the program, and however heavy the eventual cost to the tax-payers, these measures were attended by a great and general improvement of the nation's economic health. Climbing from the lowest point in March, 1933, business suffered temporary

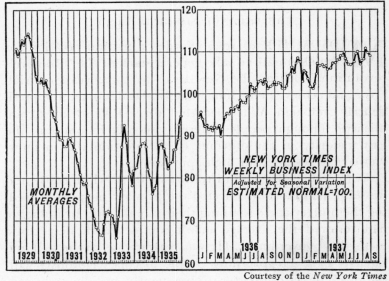

Courtesy of the *New York Times*

WEEKLY BUSINESS INDEX, 1929–1937

The index is made up of seven components: miscellaneous carload-ings, all other carloadings, steel-ingot production, electric-power output, automobile production, lumber production, and cotton-mill activity.

setbacks in the autumn of that year and again in the late sum-mer of 1934; but then the tide turned generally upward, as-suring a return of better times. Textiles, shoes and foodstuffs were among the first industries to revive.

The recovery, however, rested in part on an artificial basis: the continuance of federal spending. Trouble lay ahead if private business should not take up the slack as the government reduced its financial support. Moreover, the capital-goods industries—those engaged in making equipment for the use of other industries—had not shared proportionately in the upturn. This was partly because private construction of all kinds lagged conspicuously behind the general revival. It was also true that, though at a conservative estimate five and a half million persons had found work again, over eight million continued without regular jobs and about three and a half million remained on federal relief. Some of the unemployment was due to the half-million young people entering the labor market each year. Much of it was technological, for, thanks to improved machinery, industry could produce more goods with fewer workers than in 1929, and even at that prosperity peak it is believed that 1,800,000 were idle. Technological unemployment had always been the price of industrial progress in the past, but the number now involved was the biggest ever known, and it seemed possible that many of the victims would constitute a permanent burden on society.

The New Deal's reform undertakings probably made the deepest impression on the thoughtful voter and, because of their long-range character, will doubtless bulk largest in the eyes of posterity. No earlier administration had done so much to subordinate private business to the public weal, and none had so frankly devoted its energies to broad humanitarian purposes. Espousing the doctrine of federal responsibility for the general welfare, Roosevelt employed Hamiltonian means to achieve Jeffersonian ends. Conservatives denounced his program as socialism; but most liberals saw the New Deal not as socialism, but rather as an effort to prevent it by inoculation.

Though the President had repeatedly urged the need for national planning, few of the New Deal enactments fully realized the principle. Planning was best exemplified in the AAA scheme for rehabilitating agriculture, in the Tennessee

Valley and Columbia River projects, and in other far-flung measures for conservation. Never before had the country's natural resources been subjected to such thorough scrutiny, nor had such systematic provision been made to safeguard them in the public interest.

Of the many enterprises for this purpose, perhaps none excited greater popular interest than the program, launched in 1934, to redeem the nation's Dust Bowl, embracing over a hundred counties in Kansas, Colorado, New Mexico, Texas and Oklahoma. In order to increase soil moisture and establish an effective wind break, the United States Forest Service planted millions of trees in a shelter belt running along the eastern edge of the Great Plains region from the Canadian border to the Texas Panhandle. At the same time the Department of Agriculture taught the farmers better methods of protecting the land. Within four years the area subject to dust storms had been reduced from fifteen million acres to a million and a half. An unanticipated result was a vast increase of bird and wild life in many parts of the sheltered zone.

On the fiscal side, however, the government's masterful course had entailed an abandonment of the early economy drive and the efforts to balance the budget (see page 519). In 1934 Congress passed a bill over the President's veto restoring the salary cuts of federal employees and increasing veterans' payments. A more important element in enhancing government costs was Roosevelt's own program of lavish spending. And once the floodgates were opened, Congress embarked on outlays contrary to the White House's wishes. Thus in January, 1936, after a similar attempt had failed the preceding year, sufficient majorities were marshaled to override Roosevelt's veto of a bill for paying off the soldiers' bonus without awaiting the expiration date in 1945 (see page 491). The cost to the Treasury was nearly one and a half billion.

Though Congress increased the taxes from time to time and the proceeds in 1935–1936 were a billion dollars greater than in the fiscal year 1933–1934, the administration deliberately chose to finance the bulk of its expenditures through loans at low rates of interest. The President, unwilling to saddle a heavy burden of taxation on the people when they could least afford it, believed that the necessary fiscal measures should await the restoration of normal times. The inescapable immediate need, he declared, was "to balance the human budget."

A DECADE OF FEDERAL FINANCES

FISCAL YEAR	EXPENDITURES	DEFICIT
1930–1931	$4,901,598,000	$ 901,959,000
1931–1932	4,947,776,000	2,942,051,000
1932–1933	4,325,149,000	2,245,452,000
1933–1934	6,370,947,000	3,255,393,000
1934–1935	7,583,433,000	3,782,966,000
1935–1936	9,068,885,000	4,952,928,000
1936–1937	8,546,379,000	3,252,539,000
1937–1938	7,691,287,108	1,449,625,000
1938–1939	9,268,338,000	3,600,514,000
1939–1940	9,537,000,000	3,612,000,000

At the close of the World War the national debt amounted to $25,482,000,-000, or $246 per person as compared with $264 per person in 1936. As of July 1, 1933, Hoover had bequeathed Roosevelt a debt of $22,539,000,000. On July 1, 1937, it stood at $36,425,000,000, and three years later at $42,967,-000,000.

As a result, each year saw the recurrence of a big deficit, rising to the startling total of over thirteen billion dollars in the period from March 4, 1933, to July 1, 1936, and swelling the aggregate national debt to $33,779,000,000, the greatest up to that time in the country's history. Of this latter sum the deficits run by the Hoover administration accounted for $4,488,000,000; and of the remainder, four billion represented recoverable assets, that is, expenditures for which the government expected ultimately to be reimbursed. Foes of the New Deal pictured the country on the brink of bankruptcy, but its friends pointed out that, in relation to the national wealth and income, the public debt remained far below that of Great Britain or France.

THE VOTERS PASS JUDGMENT

The Republicans, demoralized by their disastrous rout in 1932, had little heart for contesting the New Deal program either in or out of Congress. Ex-President Coolidge, a high priest of the party, told an interviewer shortly after Roosevelt's election, "When I read of the new-fangled things that are now so popular, I realize that my time in public affairs is past. I wouldn't know how to handle them if I were called upon to do so." In so far as the bewildered leaders resisted the new trend of affairs, they found themselves wearing the castoff garments of the Democrats and standing forth as the champions of state rights and the enemies of federal centralization. The people at large, when given an opportunity to register their opinion of the administration in the fall elections of 1934, increased the already swollen Democratic majorities in both houses of Congress. Such concerted opposition as the New Deal encountered came from quarters outside the regular party organizations. Some of these bodies thundered at Roosevelt from the left, others from the right.

Of the various groups urging more radical action, each possessed its own panacea, carried on a colorful agitation and optimistically claimed millions of followers. The Share-Our-Wealth Society, captained by Senator Huey P. Long, political dictator of Louisiana, demanded a redistribution of wealth so that every family should have at least five thousand dollars and none possess more than three or four million. When Long was assassinated by a foe in his state in September, 1935, the mantle of his leadership fell on the Reverend Gerald L. K. Smith. Another organization, comprising six thousand local clubs, espoused the proposal of Dr. Francis E. Townsend, a sexagenarian California physician who had lost his savings in the depression. This plan called on the federal government to pay monthly pensions of two hundred dollars to all needy unemployed persons over sixty years of age who should agree to spend the money as rapidly as they received it. By this means it was hoped to stimulate business and at the same time make ampler provision for the aged. Of the other pressure groups the most important was the National Union for Social Justice, founded in 1935 by the Reverend Charles E. Coughlin of Detroit, a Catholic priest who had built up a vast radio following through his emphatic utterances on public affairs. At first a supporter of Roosevelt, he later came to class him with bankers and brokers as obstructing the true path to progress. Father Coughlin's organization advocated a somewhat vague program which centered in the demand that the government should own all the banks and natural resources and alone exercise the power to create currency and credit.

To the extreme right of these groups stood the American Liberty League, formed in 1934 to "combat radicalism, preserve property rights and uphold and preserve the Constitution." Heavily financed by the Du Ponts and other wealthy industrialists, it volleyed against the administration's course through all the avenues of publicity, spending over $900,000 for this purpose in 1935 and 1936. With John W. Davis and Alfred E. Smith, two former Democratic presidential nominees, on its board of directors, the League hoped to detach old-time Democrats from the President's support as well as to infuse new life into the moribund Republicans. Among its other activities, the League formed a committee of prominent corporation lawyers to pronounce on the constitutionality of New Deal laws before they reached the courts. This determined propaganda, however, suffered from the fact that the public distrusted it because of its sponsors.

More helpful to the conservative cause was the series of Supreme Court decisions handed down in 1935 and the early months of 1936. Of nine important New Deal acts the court threw out seven.[1] Opponents of the administration made the most of this turn of affairs, citing the bench's attitude as proof positive of the government's blatant disregard of the Constitution. Thoughtful observers, however, noted that two of the adverse judgments were rendered by bare majorities, and two others by six-to-three divisions. Furthermore, in all the split decisions Justices Brandeis, Stone and Cardozo sided consistently with the administration while four other judges as consistently opposed it, a fact which suggested that something more fundamental was involved than a logical application of the words of the Constitution. Many sober persons regarded the majority judges as cloistered old men, blindfolded by technicalities of their own devising and determined to return the republic to what Roosevelt called "horse-and-buggy days." Were the laws in question actually contrary to the Constitution, they asked, or merely contrary to the Supreme Court?

Even conservatives were shocked when the judiciary on June 1, 1936, struck down a New York statute establishing minimum wages for women and children in industry (Morehead v. New York ex rel. Tipaldo). At the time minimum-wage laws prevailed in seventeen states, some of which had been on the statute books for many years. Five out of the nine

[1] All seven decisions have been noted earlier except the judicial annulment of the municipal bankruptcy act, which had been passed in 1934 to enable insolvent cities to secure in a federal district court a readjustment of their assets and liabilities (Ashton v. Cameron County Water District, decided five to four in May, 1936). The two laws upheld were Congress's invalidation of the gold clause (five to four, Norman v. Baltimore & Ohio Railroad, February, 1935), and certain aspects of the TVA (eight to one, Ashwander v. TVA, February, 1936). In the latter case the court sustained the government's right to sell power from the Wilson Dam, a project of World War times at Muscle Shoals.

judges held that the act involved a deprivation of liberty and property without that due process of law guaranteed by the Fourteenth Amendment. Mr. Justice Stone, however, in his dissenting opinion doubted whether "any grounds, other than our personal economic predilections," explained the ruling. Steeped in the laissez faire philosophy, the majority declared, in effect, that neither the federal nor the state governments had the authority to fix minimum wages.

While the reverberations of the minimum-wage decision still rang through the land, the political clans gathered for the impending presidential election. In Cleveland on June 9 the Republicans, shelving their discredited older leaders, unanimously nominated Alfred M. Landon of Kansas and Frank Knox, a Chicago newspaper publisher. As governor of his state Landon was expected to attract Western voters, while as a colorless personality unknown to national politics he offered an acceptable rallying point for anti-New Deal sentiment everywhere. The platform, after charging the Democrats with usurpation of power, "frightful waste" and "prolonging the depression," promised a continuance of relief expenditures, a more adequate system of social security and generous subsides for the farmers. All this the party engaged to do while reducing government costs, balancing the budget and preserving the "American system of free enterprise." Ex-President Hoover some months after the election ruefully admitted that the platform was "a mixture of conflicting ideas and grab-bag offerings." Before accepting the nomination Governor Landon, with the Supreme Court's recent decision in mind, wired the convention that, if circumstances required, he would propose a constitutional amendment authorizing the states "to protect women and children in the matter of maximum hours, minimum wages and working conditions."

The Democrats, meeting in jubilant mood at Philadelphia on June 23, unanimously renominated Roosevelt and Garner,

and adopted a platform eulogizing the New Deal and pledging its further development. If this could not be done within
the limits set by the Supreme Court, they would amend the
Constitution to assure to the legislatures and to Congress
adequate power "to regulate commerce, protect public health
and safety and safeguard economic security." Before adjourn-
ing, the convention abolished the two-thirds rule for nominations which had been the unbroken Democratic practice for a
hundred and four years. The moment was propitious for this
reform since no candidate's interest was at stake. As four years
before, Roosevelt appeared in person to accept the nomination.

To the usual array of minor political groups was added a
newcomer, the Union party, an offshoot of the National
Union for Social Justice with its boasted membership of
nearly eight million. Naming Congressman William Lemke
of North Dakota and Thomas C. O'Brien of Massachusetts as
its candidates, the new party offered a patchwork platform
designed to attract the Coughlinites, Townsendites and the
Share-Our-Wealth adherents. Public attention, however, was
not to be diverted from the two principal contestants. Roosevelt, displaying his usual incomparable skill in radio appeals,
flayed "economic royalists," reviewed the achievements of the
New Deal, and asked the people to contrast their present well-
being with the heartbreaking days when he entered office. Of
any plans he may have had for reforming the Supreme Court
he said nothing, nor did the judiciary question in any other
shape figure in the campaign. Landon's successive speeches revealed a steady drift toward the reactionaries in his party,
while Republican spellbinders everywhere harped increasingly on the dangers of dictatorship, communism and ruin
in the event of Democratic victory.

As the issue sharpened, traditional party lines tended to

vanish. Alfred E. Smith, John W. Davis and other anti-New Deal Democrats, abetted by the American Liberty League, took the stump for Landon as self-styled Jeffersonian Democrats. In order to rally the independent vote for Roosevelt, Senators Norris and La Follette established the National Progressive League. Organized labor helped similarly through the widespread exertions of the newly formed Labor's Nonpartisan League, while the United Mine Workers contributed a total of more than $420,000 to assist New Deal candidates in various parts of the country. In New York state the American Labor party was founded to back the Democratic ticket. Determined to offset the adverse tide, the Republican national committee poured nearly nine million dollars into the campaign as compared with a Democratic expenditure of a little over five and a half million. The Landon forces also enjoyed the backing of a great majority of the nation's newspapers, including the Hearst press which lost no opportunity to castigate

> The Red New Deal with a Soviet seal
> Endorsed by a Moscow hand,
> The strange result of an alien cult
> In a liberty-loving land.

Despite the din and confusion of the contest the result stood at no time in serious doubt. With traditional partisan attachments badly blurred, the issue confronting the voters was less a choice between the two historic parties than between the New Deal and an ill-defined and ambiguous alternative. Undoubtedly the improvement in economic conditions worked in the President's behalf, but most important of all was the people's confidence in his exhilarating leadership and his devotion to the welfare of the underprivileged. Cynics attributed the outcome to the colossal expenditures for relief, but, as a matter of fact, the avalanche of ballots came from all classes of the people and from all sections of the country.[1]

Roosevelt swept every state but Maine and Vermont, winning 523 electoral votes to 8 for Landon and 60.7 per cent of the popular ballots (27,750,000 votes) to 36.4 per cent (16,680,000) for his rival. It was the greatest victory in the electoral college since Monroe's nearly unanimous election in 1820. The New Deal increased its strength over 1932 in the big cities and industrial centers and in the Northeast and Far West, suffering slight losses in the farming region between the Mississippi and the Rockies. The Union party, polling its principal support in Ohio, Massachusetts and Illinois, mustered only 892,000 votes. The even poorer showing of other parties—187,000 for Norman Thomas, the Socialist, and 80,000 for Earl Browder, the Communist—indicated that many of their followers had deserted to Roosevelt rather than risk the election of Landon. The Democrats also enlarged their majorities in Congress, capturing 334 seats out of 435 in the House and overtopping the Republicans in the Senate by 75 to 17.

LABOR IN TRANSITION

The enthusiastic support that organized labor accorded Roosevelt in the campaign reflected its gratitude for favors received. No previous administration had committed itself so fully to labor's rights. If the official exertions on behalf of collective bargaining had sometimes seemed half-hearted, the net effect was nevertheless to give a powerful impulse to the cause. From a maximum membership of four million in 1920 the American Federation of Labor had fallen to about

[1] According to a preëlection analysis of voter preferences made by the nonpartisan American Institute of Public Opinion, 47 per cent of the voters in the top income group favored Roosevelt to 53 for Landon, 67 per cent in the middle income group to 33 for Landon, and 75 per cent in the bottom income group to 25 for Landon.

two million in 1933. The first three years under the New Deal saw the number rise to upwards of three and a half million.

The National Labor Relations Board, set up with twenty-two regional boards in 1935 under the Wagner act (see page 540), conducted more than fourteen hundred elections in the next three years to determine the proper employee groups for collective bargaining, averted or settled nearly two thousand strikes and handled a total of more than sixteen thousand disputes. This progress was made in spite of the fact that, until the Supreme Court settled the point in 1937, doubts as to the NLRB's constitutionality hampered its effectiveness. Though the number of strikes in 1936 showed a slight increase over the preceding year, the number of men involved was thirty per cent fewer.

With the marked revival of the labor movement, however, came increasing internal discord. The principal clash occurred over the question of craft versus industrial unions, or, to put it differently, "horizontal" versus "vertical" unions. Historically, the American Federation had consisted predominantly of craft unions, the "aristocracy of labor," which included only about a tenth of all the wage-earners. Since the vast bulk of persons—mostly the unskilled and semi-skilled—were left outside, it proved impossible for the workers in a given industry to exert their united strength against a recalcitrant employer. As a result, the A. F. of L. unions often won gains at the expense of the unskilled and unorganized. Even some employers saw an advantage in dealing with a single large body of all the employees rather than with a host of petty groups urging their special and sometimes conflicting demands.

The foremost champion of the industrial-union idea in the American Federation was John L. Lewis, long a stormy petrel in the labor world. As president of the United Mine

Workers, he represented a union which took in all the common laborers and semiskilled workers about the coal mines together with the electricians, carpenters and other craftsmen. Lewis contended that mass-production industries could be effectively organized on no other basis. The ruling group in the A. F. of L., however, fearing lest the power of the existing craft unions be diminished, resolved to make as few concessions as possible. Though the Federation convention in 1934 unanimously empowered the executive council to charter industrial unions in the automobile, steel, cement, aluminum and other mass-production industries, the council during the next year actually authorized such organizations only in the automobile and rubber fields, and did not permit even these bodies to include employees already attached to craft unions. When the convention in October, 1935, approved this action, the representatives of seven industrial unions decided to go ahead along their own lines, and for this purpose set up a Committee for Industrial Organization with Lewis as chairman. President William Green, denouncing this "challenge to the supremacy of the A. F. of L.," called on the CIO to disband. The latter, declining, declared that its purpose was to bring the parent organization abreast the conditions of modern industry and thus to make it more powerful.

Increasing tension between the contending factions caused the executive council in August, 1936, to suspend the CIO unions for "insurrection." Thereupon open warfare broke out between the two camps, each invading the other's territory and seeking advantages at the other's expense. The NLRB, involved in the controversy because of its power to decide which employee group should act in a given instance for purposes of collective bargaining, found itself criticized by both sides, but with particular venom by the A. F. of L. By the autumn of 1937 the CIO claimed a membership of

3,700,000 (distributed in thirty-two national unions) as compared with the 3,600,000 then belonging to the rival organization. If the two groups had joined forces, they would have formed the mightiest labor aggregation in the country's history. Moderates in the opposing ranks deplored the internecine strife, but could find no way of patching up the differences. Finally, in November, 1938, the CIO adopted a constitution and set up as an independent body, changing its name from Committee for Industrial Organization to Congress of Industrial Organizations.

In carrying the gospel of industrial unionism to the workers, Lewis and his associates directed their first blow at the unorganized automobile industry. The initial strike, beginning in November, 1936, was waged against the General Motors Corporation. Though the storm center was Flint, Michigan, the disturbance threw a hundred and thirty-five thousand men out of work in fourteen states. The United Automobile Workers, a CIO union, demanded recognition as the sole bargaining agent for all General Motors employees; and in order to enforce compliance the men adopted the device of the sitdown strike, refusing to surrender possession of the plants while the dispute continued. The company officials vainly sought to dislodge them with court orders and appeals for the militia. Governor Frank Murphy of Michigan, where the most acute conditions prevailed, declined to employ the militia actively against the strikers, for he believed a resort to force would breed hatred, rather than respect, for law and order. In February, 1937, his negotiations resulted in securing for the men recognition of their union and a substantial improvement of conditions.

The same sitdown tactics were then used, with comparable success, against the Chrysler, Hudson and other companies. As the wave of sitdown strikes spread over the country, however, public sentiment became increasingly antagonized by what some of the state and lower federal courts termed unlawful seizures of property.[1] President Green of the A. F. of L. publicly declared that such strikes were illegal, though the contagion of example caused many of his own unions to indulge in them. The United States Senate also passed a resolution of condemnation. The President, however, maintained a hands-off policy.

In the steel industry the CIO made even greater progress without recourse to the sitdown weapon. The United States Steel Corporation, hitherto famed for its hatred of unions, astonished the public by accepting the CIO's terms in March, 1937, without a strike. This agreement carried with it a ten-per-cent raise of pay. Other steel companies followed suit until over two hundred and sixty concerns employing nearly three hundred and sixty thousand men had signed up. "Big Steel" had yielded with surprising ease; but the Bethlehem Corporation and "Little Steel"—the Republic, the Inland and the Youngstown Sheet and Tube companies—proved a tougher proposition. In order to bring them into line, a strike was undertaken in the late spring. Soon industrial turmoil ravaged the steel belt from Chicago to western Pennsylvania, causing the intervention of the militia in Ohio and Pennsylvania. In all, ninety thousand workers were involved. The violence reached a tragic climax on Memorial Day when Chicago police without apparent provocation fired into a crowd of prospective pickets near a Republic steel plant, killing or fatally wounding ten of them.

In the end, the Inland Company granted some of the men's demands, but the employees of the three other companies drifted back to work during the summer without any con-

[1] Two years later, in 1939, the Supreme Court took the same view in the case of NLRB v. Fansteel Metallurgical Corporation. Between September 1, 1936, and the following June sitdown strikes involved nearly half a million workers, not only in motors, but also in rubber, textiles, shipbuilding, shoes, oil-refining, newspaper publishing, baking and many other lines.

cessions being made. These latter companies, however, employed only about fifteen per cent of all the nation's steel workers. The NLRB in April, 1938, reviewing the methods of the Republic Steel Corporation before and during the troubles, found it guilty of violating civil liberties, terrorizing the workers, fomenting disorder and even murder, and generally of flouting the provisions of the Wagner act. The officers were required to reinstate about five thousand men who had engaged in the strike, and to "cease and desist" henceforth from interfering with the self-organization of employees.[1]

The new militancy of labor, characteristic of the A. F. of L. as well as the CIO, and prompted in most instances by a determination to reap the full benefits of the Wagner act, produced a total of 4740 strikes in 1937, more than twice as many as in 1936 and involving over twice as many men. The events of the next two years, however, indicated an approach to more normal conditions, with but 2770 strikes in 1938 and 2615 in 1939. The disturbances of 1938 affected less than 690,000 workers, only a third as many as in the preceding year, but the year 1939, despite the decrease of strikes, saw the aggregate number of persons concerned rise to 1,171,000.

Agricultural labor, traditionally unorganized, also felt the impact of New Deal policies. Since Reconstruction days farm

[1] Of the Republic's labor policy the NLRB said in part: "Its spies shadowed union organizers; its police attacked and beat them; its superintendent and foremen threatened, laid off and discharged employes for union activities; its officers fostered and supported a whole series of puppet labor organizations which the company manipulated to oppose the union; and its president, Tom M. Girdler, publicly vilified the union's leaders, purposes and policies under circumstances intended to throw the weight of his influence against his employes' efforts at self-organization." Because of possible technical objections by the Supreme Court to its procedure in conducting the inquiry, the Board later withdrew its order, reheard the case and in October reaffirmed its decision. Evidence of similar practices by other industrial concerns had been made public in December, 1937, by a Senate committee of which Robert M. La Follette was chairman.

tenancy had constituted a growing social cancer in the cotton states stretching from South Carolina to Arkansas and Texas (see page 31). In 1930 five or six farms out of every ten were run by tenants, many of them occupying a position little better than that of peons. At the bottom of the scale was the share-cropper who, toiling in the field with his wife and children, eked out a bare existence in perpetual debt to the owner of the land, with whom he was required to share his crop. The cotton-restriction program of the AAA gave the lion's share of the money to the landlords, with the result that a disproportionately small amount found its way to the tenants whose acreage, rather than that of the owners, was usually withdrawn from cultivation. Nearly a million of these wretched, undernourished folk were thrown on the relief rolls.

Driven to despair by the fierce drought of 1934, the share-croppers in July of that year formed the Southern Tenant Farmers' Union. Conservative Southern sentiment, alarmed by this extension of the labor movement to agricultural workers, took further offense because its membership included both Negroes and whites. The union organizers met with threats and acts of physical violence, but the movement steadily gained strength and, most important of all, it helped to arouse the nation to the need for remedial action. As a result, Congress in the Bankhead-Jones law, adopted in 1937, provided means by which the underprivileged farmers might climb to ownership. For this purpose it empowered the Farm Security Administration to lend government money to share-croppers and other tenants at low interest rates, with a possible period of forty years for repayment of the principal. Out of its funds of $75,000,000 the FSA in the first three years started nearly thirteen thousand families, mostly in the South, toward the cherished goal of farm proprietorship.

Closely related to the share-cropper problem was that of

migratory farm families. These were predominantly white and of native birth, with proportionately few Negroes or foreign immigrants among their number. Though most of them moved only short distances, over a hundred and fifty thousand families eventually found their way to the West Coast, where it was estimated that only one job existed for every four applicants. Some of these nomads had been set adrift by the introduction of tractors in the Southern cotton fields. Many others were refugees from the Dust Bowl. On an average they were able to earn only from two hundred to six hundred dollars a year with four or five months of employment.

Their desperate plight was brought vividly to general attention in 1939 by the publication of John Steinbeck's novel, *The Grapes of Wrath,* based on the state of affairs that confronted the "Okies" and "Arkies"—so named because of the throngs who hailed from Oklahoma and Arkansas—when they reached California. Their presence created an acute social problem. Many of the landed proprietors, taking advantage of their helplessness, treated them with great brutality, hiring them at starvation wages and denying them ordinary civil rights. As part of the system of exploitation, the farm owners tried to strangle all efforts at organization. In 1937, however, some of the workers formed a CIO union, which grew slowly and promised an eventual betterment of laboring conditions.

Meanwhile, the wanderers took root wherever they could, usually settling in trailer camps or private labor camps, or developing slums on the fringes of cities. "On many of these properties," declared the Kern County Health Department regarding the slum areas, "can be seen three stages of the owners' life in the Golden State. On the back of the lot may be the remains of the family car or truck with obsolete license plates from the state of origin; the chicken shed was once the pasteboard-and-refuse house of their squatter camp residence; and on the front of the lot is a crude house of good, used lumber, perhaps with one side partially stuccoed or otherwise finished, built piece by piece as the family income permits." The Farm Security Administration used every means in its power to alleviate conditions. By making small subsistence grants to several hundred thousand families in the Dust Bowl and the South, it prevented an increase of the influx. In order to reduce the hardships of those already in flight, it built its own camps on the Pacific Coast, which provided decent living accommodations for about thirty thousand families. This program it hoped to extend. The situation, however, remained far from satisfactory.

THE EXECUTIVE CHALLENGES THE JUDICIARY

As the first President to take office under the Twentieth Amendment, Roosevelt entered his second term on January 20, 1937, instead of March 4. His inaugural address stressed what the New Deal had yet to accomplish rather than what it had already accomplished. In his last speech before the election he had cried, "We have just begun to fight!" Now in a spirit of solemn dedication he asked, "Shall we . . . turn our back upon the road that lies ahead?" Stating that a third of the American people were "ill-housed, ill-clad, ill-nourished," he roundly declared, "The test of our progress is not whether we add more to the abundance of those who have much; it is whether we provide enough for those who have too little."

In the weeks and months that followed, Roosevelt placed before Congress the recommendations which formed the foundation stones of what some observers called the second New Deal. Actually, they represented a logical development of the principles that underlay his program from the start. The proposals included (1) ampler means of assisting the "ill-housed"; (2) a more comprehensive plan of agricultural recovery; (3)

government intervention to secure better conditions for "ill-clad" and "ill-nourished" wage-earners; (4) an application of the TVA idea to six other major regions; and (5) a reorganization of the federal judicial and executive departments. As for relief expenditures, he urged a reduction as rapidly as returning prosperity and humane considerations should permit.

In carrying out this ambitious program, however, the President met with unexpected obstacles, notably the temper of the newly elected Congress, the political storm aroused by his endeavor to infuse new blood into the Supreme Court and, somewhat later, an unforeseen downward turn in business conditions. Though backed by the biggest majorities in Congress that any party had ever possessed, Roosevelt now found it harder to bend the members to his will. With the economic situation greatly improved, the legislators no longer felt the same compulsion to act quickly and unitedly. Moreover, many Democrats of the President's own way of thinking had come for personal reasons to resent his driving leadership, while others, reluctant supporters of the New Deal in the past, welcomed the opportunity to oppose further reform ventures. To members of this latter group, composed in large part of Southern Democrats, the government's failure to deal drastically with the epidemic of sitdown strikes betrayed an unwillingness to uphold basic property rights. Even the magnitude of the Democratic majority proved a weakness, for the greatly expanded membership lacked cohesion and tended easily to break ranks.

The spark which ignited these combustibles was Roosevelt's plan to reorganize the federal judiciary. Though he had not raised the issue during the presidential campaign, he had informed Congress on January 6 that "means must be found to adapt our legal forms and our judicial interpretation to the actual present national needs of the largest progressive democracy in the modern world." Notwithstanding this warning, his scheme when submitted to Congress on February 5 took the country by surprise. He recommended enlarging the membership of the Supreme Court from nine to a maximum of fifteen if judges reaching the age of seventy declined to retire. He also advised certain less controversial changes in regard to the lower federal courts.

Behind the main proposal lay the fact that of the six judges over seventy years of age Mr. Justice Brandeis was the only confirmed liberal. If the President was to save the New Deal from continuing onslaughts by the court, he must either neutralize the conservative members or, better still, supersede them. The specification of an age limit was the indirect means he chose to employ. In view of Roosevelt's enlarged conception of federal powers he had been singularly unfortunate in being the first chief executive since Andrew Johnson who had filled no vacancies on the high bench, whereas Taft had appointed five members, Wilson three, Harding four and Hoover three.

The court scheme precipitated a protracted struggle, with the outcome long in doubt. Not only in the halls of Congress, but over the radio and in thousands of public gatherings, the subject excited resounding debate. The proposal was denounced as unconstitutional—which it was not—and as a reckless step toward greater centralization—on which opinions might well differ. When the President's foes accused him of wanting to "pack" the court, his supporters retorted that he sought only to "unpack" it. The Senate judiciary committee by a vote of ten to eight declared against the plan, alleging that "it would subjugate the courts to the will of Congress and the President, and thereby destroy the independence of the judiciary." Senator Wheeler of Montana, hitherto a zealous New Dealer but now the bellwether of the opposition forces, argued not that the court had behaved well, but that any changes should be made through a constitutional amendment.

Probably nothing did so much to undermine Roosevelt's cause as an amazing change of front by the Supreme Court itself. Though the judges' new attitude may have been influenced by the President's overwhelming reëlection, it became unmistakably apparent during the heat of the congressional battle. In a chain of decisions from March 29 to May 24, the bench upheld four outstanding New Deal reforms, including the National Labor Relations Board and the social-security system.[1] It even affirmed the constitutionality of a minimum-wage act of the state of Washington despite its throttling of a similar statute in the instance of New York only nine months before (see page 562). A cynical observer of the sudden about-face remarked, "A switch in time saves nine"; but to the public at large Roosevelt's chief complaint against the tribunal seemed to collapse. Two further blows were inflicted against the proposal when seventy-eight-year-old Justice Willis Van Devanter, one of the die-hard conservatives, announced his impending retirement from the bench, and when Senator Joseph Robinson, leader of the court-reorganization group in the upper house, suddenly died in mid-July.

Early in the course of the conflict Congress had passed a law permitting judges seventy years old to retire voluntarily on full salary after ten years' service; but, aside from this trifling concession, Roosevelt was obliged to accept a bill in August which ignored his cardinal purpose. The statute, however, introduced certain procedural changes into the lower

[1] The court unanimously sustained the second Frazier-Lemke farm-mortgage law and also a statute of 1936 conferring rights of collective bargaining on railway employees; by five to four it confirmed the NLRB and also the unemployment features of the social-security act; and by seven to two it sanctioned the old-age insurance provisions.

United States courts, notably a provision to enable the Attorney-General to defend the constitutionality of federal laws in cases between private individuals, and to secure a direct appeal of the question to the Supreme Court.

The President had suffered the worst defeat of his career and at the hands of his own party. Nevertheless he had secured the substance of what he sought, for the court, at least for the time being, was committed to the New Deal position. That this attachment was likely to be more than temporary became evident in the next two and a half years. Roosevelt named Senator Hugo L. Black of Alabama, an ardent New Dealer, to replace Mr. Justice Van Devanter; and a succession of later vacancies—including the voluntary retirement in 1939 of the life-long liberal, Louis D. Brandeis—enabled the President to bring in four other men of his own stamp: Stanley F. Reed, who as United States Solicitor-General had defended the constitutionality of New Deal legislation before the court; Professor Felix Frankfurter, long a confidential adviser of the administration; William O. Douglas, the forty-year-old chairman of the SEC; and ex-Governor Frank Murphy of Michigan, who was Attorney-General at the time of his appointment. The former minority was now the majority, and the only persistent objector was Mr. Justice James C. McReynolds, a holdover from the old membership. In some bitterness of spirit he exclaimed in one of his chronic dissents, "Generally speaking, at least, our decisions of yesterday ought to be the law of today."

In this new atmosphere the court handed down judgments sustaining the registration requirements of the holding-company act, permitting the PWA to continue to subsidize municipal power plants, and denying private power companies their claim for damages from competition with the TVA. In a significant decision in 1940 (the Madison oil case) the tribunal declined to follow the rule-of-reason pronouncement in the famous Standard Oil case in 1911 (see page 327), and declared unconstitutional the practice of certain companies in buying "distress gasoline" for the allegedly "reasonable" purpose of remedying competitive abuses. A legal writer, referring to these and other decisions, asserted, "Never before in history has the Court so extensively altered so many basic principles in so short a time as in the three years since February 1937. And the reconstruction is still in process." With considerable justice President Roosevelt could say that, though he had lost a battle, he had won the war.

THE BUSINESS RECESSION OF 1937–1938

Despite Roosevelt's eventual triumph, the court fight cost him heavily by delaying action by Congress on his other reform proposals. Another complicating factor was an unexpected resumption of the depression. This latter event forced attention again to the vexatious problems of relief and recovery. The new business slump, beginning in August, 1937, pursued an abrupt downward spiral until January, 1938, and then, after occasional upward turns, touched bottom in June of that year. Its course was attended by falling industrial activity, lagging retail business, declining stock markets and rising unemployment.

The major cause was probably the government's sharp retrenchment of expenditures during the period of reviving prosperity in 1936–1937 or, to turn the proposition around, the failure of private business to expand as rapidly as the federal outlays shrank. From 1934 through 1936 the New Deal had poured between three and four billion dollars annually into relief and recovery; but in 1937, under insistent pressure from Big Business for a balanced budget, Congress slashed its appropriations for these purposes to about a billion and a half. Among the contributory reasons for the disaster were the nervousness of industrialists because of labor's militant drive for higher wages; the overbuying of supplies by many concerns in anticipation of a continuing rise of prices; the fears of the utility interests due to the government's invasion of their domain; and the uneasiness as to the future felt by

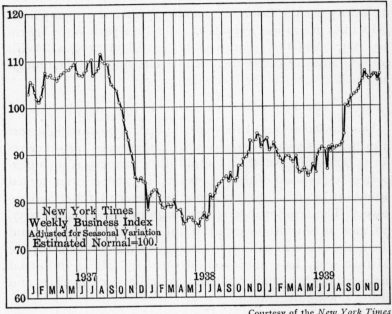

Courtesy of the *New York Times*

RECESSION AND REVIVAL, 1937–1939

the business world generally because of Roosevelt's new reform proposals as well as other possible moves he might make. According to the London *Economist,* the commercial community had worked itself up into such "a lather of hatred" for the President that its fury was "choking the whole industrial and financial machine."

Excited administration supporters blamed the recession on a "sitdown strike of capital," a deliberate plot of "economic royalists" to stop further New Deal undertakings. The conservative elements, ascribing the situation to purely political causes, called it the "Roosevelt depression." Whatever the merit of such contentions, the nation's economic structure was far better able to withstand the shock than in 1929, for the new downswing had not been preceded by a long period of reckless speculation and widespread overproduction. Moreover, the banking system was sound, credit was plentiful at low rates of interest, and the farmers were in a stronger position.

Yet, though the recession proved to be shorter and less severe than the earlier depression, it caused deep anxiety while it lasted. As soon as the President realized its gravity, he revoked the orders he had given the PWA and the RFC in the fall of 1937 to refrain from new commitments, and he directed the WPA to enlarge its relief activities once more. At his recommendation, Congress early in 1938 made a supplementary grant of $250,000,000 to the WPA, and authorized the RFC to devote an additional $1,500,000,000 to the relief of business. Roosevelt, convinced of the need of more vigorous action, induced Congress in May to adopt a spending and lending measure involving new outlays of $3,000,000,000 for the fiscal year beginning on July 1. Of this sum the PWA received nearly a billion for construction projects.

Meanwhile the country had begun to witness scenes reminiscent of the Great Depression. With factories and business houses curtailing the number of their employees or closing, it was estimated that well over ten million were out of work by the spring of 1938. Of these, perhaps five or six million had been idle since the previous emergency. As in the later years of the Great Depression, the federal authorities concentrated their efforts on helping the able-bodied unemployed. The RFC lent funds to tide over businesses in temporary difficulty. The WPA, which by September, 1937, had reduced its

relief rolls to less than a million and a half—the fewest since
the agency had been created—expanded its activities until by
the early fall of 1938 it was taking care of more than three
million. In addition, many of the jobless—nearly two million
in twenty-five states by May, 1938—were receiving unemployment compensation under the social-security act. Still others
obtained work, or were kept at work, through the program of
"pump priming" undertaken by private construction firms at
the joint cost of the PWA and local government units. By
October 1 nearly seven thousand PWA projects had been approved and were getting under way. Other agencies such as
the National Youth Administration, the Civilian Conservation Corps and the Rural Electrification Administration did
their part, and, as a few years before, the land began to
blossom with public improvements of lasting value to the
nation.

The principal departure from former relief methods was
the action of the WPA in purchasing fifteen million dollars'
worth of ready-made clothing from the factories for free distribution among the needy. Aside from the humane purpose,
this step was designed to stimulate business by clearing the
manufacturers' shelves of surplus stock. With a similar intent,
Congress in May, 1938, made it possible for the Federal
Surplus Commodities Corporation to enlarge its "buy-and-
give" program in relation to excess farm products. Since its
creation in 1933 the FSCC had spent at the rate of about
$20,000,000 a year; under the new authorization it made
purchases averaging nearly $200,000 a day. New Deal critics
objected to these practices as an encroachment on the proper
domain of middlemen and, if carried very far, as an incentive
to overproduction.

The railroads, already burdened with troubles, faced new
ones as a result of the general economic setback. In January,
1937, during the era of reviving prosperity, the Interstate

Commerce Commission had ordered a scaling down of freight charges in the belief that lower rates would beget a larger volume of business and greater aggregate profits; and in October the companies themselves had granted higher pay to their employees. But the rapid shrinkage of freight traffic attending the recession made many of the roads fear for their existence. Yielding to pressure, the Interstate Commerce Commission during the first half of 1938 authorized increases of freight and Pullman rates, and permitted the Eastern lines to raise their passenger fares from two to 2.5 cents a mile. The results proved disappointing, however, and a year later the roads voluntarily reduced their rates.

Meanwhile, in order to lessen operating costs, they announced a forthcoming fifteen-per-cent reduction of wages on October 1, 1938. When the Railroad Brotherhoods declared they would strike rather than accept the cut, President Roosevelt, acting under authority of the railway-labor act, secured a postponement of the crisis by appointing a special board to inquire into the merits of the dispute. This body, reporting on October 29, found the proposed wage decrease unwarranted, and surmised that the already improving traffic of the companies would enable them to solve their more urgent financial difficulties. Though the board's findings had no binding effect, the roads accepted the judgment rather than precipitate a calamitous nation-wide strike.

The advancing railroad revenues were merely one aspect of the general economic ascent which began in the summer of 1938. In most lines—automobiles, steel, lumber, residential construction, textiles, shoes and other manufactures—notable signs of renewed activity appeared. Moreover, farmers' incomes rose again in response to government subsidies; and foreign trade was on the upgrade, largely due to war preparations abroad. The General Motors and Chrysler companies alone rehired seventy thousand men between August 1 and

November 1; and in the country as a whole a million or more persons went back to work between June and November, cutting the total number of jobless to around 9,250,000. The WPA relief rolls continued at a high level, but the White House in October issued warning of a gradual reduction. In the next year, 1939, despite some ups and downs during the first six months, the march toward better times continued as the full force of the program of increased government spending for large-scale public works was felt.

The most sensational incident of the recession was the five-million-dollar failure in March, 1938, of Richard Whitney, a prominent Wall Street broker who from 1930 to 1935 had served as president of the New York Stock Exchange. Despite his commanding position in the financial community, he had engaged in irresponsible speculation to such an extent that for the last three and a half years his firm had, though not to the public's knowledge, been insolvent. "These enterprises," declared the Securities and Exchange Commission in its sifting of the facts, "carried him far afield from the brokerage business into the production and marketing of such unrelated products as applejack, peat humus and mineral colloids." In his desperate need for funds Whitney had used his official position as well as his business connections with J. P. Morgan and Company to borrow money without adequate collateral, had falsified his books of account, and resorted to misappropriation of his customers' securities.

Whitney's crash profoundly shocked the country, for he had long stood forth as a bitter foe of the New Deal's efforts to regulate security issues and exchange practices. His unscrupulous course, coupled with the New York Stock Exchange's reluctance to take disciplinary action, afforded a dramatic illustration, as the SEC pointed out, of the "attitude that the exchange was more of a private club than a public institution and that its responsibilities were to its members rather than to the nation of investors." Whitney was sentenced to five years' imprisonment for embezzlement; and the Stock Exchange, yielding to the popular outcry, installed a new management which proceeded at once to cooperate with the SEC in enforcing higher standards of financial integrity.

THE NEW DEAL EXTENDED

Though the business recession had obliged Congress to devote renewed attention to measures for relief and recovery, it indirectly helped the President's proposals for reform by throwing into bolder relief the economic maladjustments which he desired to correct. In vindication of his assertion when taking office for the second time that a third of the nation was "ill-housed, ill-clad, ill-nourished," an inquiry sponsored by the National Resources Committee produced a mass of evidence indicating that, even in the relatively prosperous period from the middle of 1935 to the middle of 1936, one third of the families of the United States had received an average income of but $471 a year, the next higher third only $1076, and the top third about $3000.[1] Over thirteen per cent of the total national income had gone to the less than one per cent of the families which enjoyed incomes of $10,000 and upward.

Though confronted with an unusually alert opposition both in and out of his party, Roosevelt in the first half of the year 1938 attained most of the reform objectives he had outlined at the beginning of his second term (see pages 574-575). He did not, however, risk a vote on the proposal to

[1] According to this report, *Consumer Incomes in the United States*, published in September, 1938, individual incomes in the bottom group ran up to $780, in the middle group to $1450, and in the highest group to more than $1,000,000. The estimates of income took into account home-grown food and other farm products used by families as well as cash receipts. The term, families, included single persons living alone.

extend the TVA principle to six other regions; nor did he then succeed in inducing the House to follow the Senate's example in adopting the plan for reorganizing the federal executive departments along more efficient lines. In the latter instance New Deal foes, still rankling from the President's efforts "to pack the Supreme Court," made the welkin ring with cries that the measure was a "dictatorship bill." As the sequel was to show, this defeat was merely victory deferred.

Congress began by taking steps to provide better housing for the underprivileged. The attempts during the Great Depression—the first ever made by the federal government—had failed badly because the costs of construction had boosted the rents beyond the reach of the poor. Even before the downturn of business had become evident, Congress in August, 1937, passed the Wagner-Steagall law, which was designed to repair this difficulty. The act set up a United States Housing Authority empowered to make loans, over a possible sixty-year period, to local public agencies for slum clearance and low-cost housing and also to grant subsidies for establishing the rents at a level which poor people could afford. This new body supplemented the Federal Housing Administration, which since 1934 had been engaged in stimulating private construction through a system of federal mortgage insurance designed to afford partial protection to lending institutions for any losses they might incur.

Under the shock of the recession, Congress early in 1938 increased the sum at the USHA's disposal from $500,000,000 to $800,000,000, and enabled the FHA to insure mortgages on easier terms. The USHA program was delayed for a time by the dearth of local housing agencies, but, once this hurdle was surmounted, results began to appear. By November 1 commitments of $576,000,000 had been made in a hundred and forty-two cities. Meanwhile, the more liberal terms offered by the FHA led to a marked speeding up of private construction. Partly because of these efforts, the year 1939 saw the number of urban dwelling units increase by a hundred and twenty-eight thousand, a gain of more than a third over 1938. Government-subsidized housing accounted for about ten per cent of all residential building. By the end of 1940 the USHA since its inception had helped to provide living quarters for about two hundred and forty thousand members of low-income families at rentals within their means.

Roosevelt's second reform purpose was accomplished when Congress in February, 1938, passed a new agricultural adjustment act, the most comprehensive yet adopted. The failure of the law of 1936 to provide effective means of crop curtailment (see page 545) had resulted in a recurrence of farm surpluses, and the consequent drop in prices had been speeded by the dwindling urban consumption due to the recession. In other words, the farmer was again threatened with that overwhelming plenty which had spelled poverty for him in the past. The new measure combined most of the essential features of earlier legislative remedies with much that was novel.[1] It was hailed by Secretary Wallace of the Department of Agriculture as a "complete charter of farm equality."

Basic to the statute was the plan to limit the size of the wheat, corn, cotton, tobacco and rice crops. The Secretary of Agriculture, acting through the AAA, was given power not only to fix the acreage to be planted each season, but, if unusually good weather should produce an unexpectedly large yield, to invoke "marketing quotas" for restricting the sales.

[1] Because of the Supreme Court's objections to the original AAA law, the statute included an advance plea for its own constitutionality, based mainly on the right of Congress to regulate interstate commence. The high court accepted this view in 1939 in a case involving the tobacco marketing quotas of the new act.

These quotas should become effective when approved by two thirds of the growers of the crop in a referendum. In bad seasons, on the other hand, the AAA was to make "parity payments" to the growers in order to offset the difference between the prevailing market prices and the purchasing power the products would have commanded before the World War. In addition, a system of permissive crop insurance was set up for wheat farmers, to begin with the 1939 harvest. Other parts of the act applied to all agriculturists. "Benefit payments" by the government were continued, though at a higher rate than before, for soil-conserving methods. Finally, through "commodity loans," provision was made for farmers to store crop surpluses in good harvest years for sale in lean ones. This last scheme—the "ever-normal-granary" plan—was designed to stabilize farm prices for the benefit of both the producer and the consumer.

The legislation was passed too late to have much effect in 1938, which turned out to be another year of teeming harvests. The AAA, however, brought its battery of devices into play as quickly as possible and did something to ameliorate conditions. With a fuller operation of the system in 1939 the results still fell short of the expectations. Agricultural production proved the second highest on record, though the continued low farm prices were offset by payments of over half a billion dollars from the federal treasury. The difficulties were due in part to overproduction in other countries as well as in the United States and to the many restrictions on international trade. In the effort to reduce the cotton and wheat surpluses the government inaugurated a system of export subsidies for these crops. Many obstacles remained to be surmounted before it would be clear that Secretary Wallace's "charter of farm equality" was a satisfactory solution of the agricultural situation.

The President won his third great victory with the adoption of the fair-labor-standards act in June, 1938. Ever since the Supreme Court's death blow to the NRA three years before, Roosevelt had resolved to find means of preserving the labor-welfare provisions which that experiment had embodied. His proposal for "a floor under wages and a ceiling over hours" passed the Senate in July, 1937, but for many months the bill was held back from a vote in the House by the rules committee, which reflected Southern fears lest higher labor requirements handicap Southern industry. When it eventually came up for consideration, Southern Congressmen tried vainly to obtain special and less rigorous regulations for their section. To this demand Representative Henry Ellenbogen of Pennsylvania replied in language reminiscent of the slavery controversy, "This nation cannot continue to exist half sweatshop and half decent shop. Either the standard of living of the North must come down to the lower level of the South, or the wages in the South must come up to those of the North."

The measure as finally passed, though differing in certain respects from the original Senate bill, retained the same fundamental objective of a forty-hour standard work week and a forty-cents-an-hour minimum pay in businesses of an interstate character. This goal was to be approached by gradual stages in order to allow small struggling concerns ample time for readjustment. For the year beginning in October, 1938, the statute fixed no more than forty-four hours nor less than twenty-five cents. In subsequent years it provided for further changes at specified intervals until the work week should reach forty hours by October, 1940, and the hourly wage forty cents in 1945. At every stage it was required that overtime should be paid at the rate of time and a half. Certain classes of workers such as farm laborers, employees of retail concerns, professional workers and seamen were, however, exempt from the regulations. The act struck at the evil of child labor by excluding from interstate commerce goods produced in establishments employing persons under the age of sixteen or, in especially hazardous occupations such as mining and manufacturing, under eighteen.

"From the economic standpoint," commented the conservative *Boston Herald,* "this is one of the most important acts ever passed in our history as a nation." It was equally important as a humanitarian measure. In both respects it enabled humane employers to maintain decent labor standards without fear of being undercut by unscrupulous competitors. Unlike the wage-and-hour laws prevailing in some states, the federal enactment affected men as well as women and minors; and it replaced the great variety of state labor requirements with a few simple uniform ones. The initial application of the law in the fall of 1938 resulted in higher compensation for 300,000 persons and reduced hours for 1,400,000, besides releasing 200,000 children from labor. A year later, when the minimum wage rose to thirty cents and the work week fell to forty-two hours, more than 650,000 wage-earners received pay increases and nearly 2,400,000 benefited from the shorter week. In 1940 the forty-hour limitation went into operation, affecting 12,600,000.

Along with the major New Deal successes went other reforms less central to the President's purpose. These provided in one way or another for further governmental control over the business classes. A statute of 1937 plugged up certain loopholes which wealthy persons had discovered in the income-tax law. The Lea-McCarran act in 1938 set up a Civil Aeronautics Authority to regulate and encourage commercial aviation. Another measure in 1938 established stricter governmental standards for foods, drugs, patent medicines and cosmetics. This last law marked a considerable advance over the act of 1906 (see page 314) by prohibiting under heavy penalties both the misbranding of products and the putting forward of false and misleading advertising claims. It was not evident, however, whether the enforcement provisions were adequate.

As the attention of the country turned to the congressional elections in the fall of 1938, the administration enjoyed the advantage not only of an impressive legislative record but also of greatly improved business conditions. In the campaign the Republicans generally expressed approval of the New Deal's objectives, but criticized its methods and personnel and accused the administration of misusing its relief funds to win backing for New Deal candidates. This charge was in part later substantiated by the revelations of a congressional investigating committee in regard to the activities of WPA employees in Pennsylvania, Kentucky and Tennessee. In a third of the states, mostly in the Middle and Far West, the Townsend old-age pension plan or some of its many variations provided a burning local issue, but the question cut across party lines and exerted little influence on the congressional outcome. The Democrats succeeded in maintaining their control of the national government, though with reduced majorities. They faced the next two years with 69 out of 96 members of the upper house and 262 out of 435 members of the lower. The Republican increase of 7 seats in the Senate and 80 in the House gave that party its first opportunity in six years to operate as an effective minority.

The administration's principal unfinished business when the new Congress assembled in January, 1939, was the plan for reorganizing the federal executive departments. Every President since the first Roosevelt had urged a simplification of what the second Roosevelt called the "higgledy-piggledy patchwork of duplicate responsibilities and overlapping powers." The multiplication of governmental activities under the New Deal made the matter one of imperative need. Though the preceding Congress had declined to follow the

White House's lead in this respect, it had passed a law in 1938 placing fifteen thousand postmasters of the first, second and third classes under the merit plan, and the President had accompanied this action with an executive order extending the system after January, 1939, to all federal employees except those expressly exempt by statute. Had this order gone fully into effect, eighty-one thousand additional positions would have been removed from politics, but the newly elected Congress prevented its application to the thirty-six thousand employees paid from emergency funds. Three hundred thousand posts still remained subject to spoils.

Despite this setback, Roosevelt was now successful in attaining his larger objective. Congress, viewing the reorganization plan with postelection calm, adopted it in March, 1939, in somewhat diluted form. The President was empowered to transfer, consolidate or abolish some sixty out of the more than one hundred executive boards and commissions; and his orders were to go automatically into effect unless revoked within sixty days by concurrent action of Congress. Under this authorization Roosevelt promptly regrouped twenty-three boards and departmental bureaus in three great units: the Federal Works Agency, the Federal Loan Agency and the Federal Security Agency. He believed that these and other changes which he effected would greatly promote efficiency and at the same time produce annual savings of twenty million dollars.

In July Congress dealt with a related subject, that of "pernicious political activities" such as had occurred in the recent election. The Hatch act forbade federal appointees (below the policy-making rank) to grant or withhold official favors in order to influence the outcome of a national election, or to solicit or accept contributions from recipients of relief, or to take "active part" in campaigns. A second Hatch act, in 1940, extended these regulations to the three hundred

TO THE WHITE HOUSE

THE BUDGET BUREAU (from Treasury)

Central Statistical Board (from independent status to Budget Bureau)
Central Statistical Committee (functions transferred to Budget Bureau)

also

National Resources Planning Board (combining independent National Resources Committee and Employment Stabilization office from Commerce)

One of six 'executive assistants' to serve as White House liaison agent on personnel

INTO A NEW FEDERAL SECURITY AGENCY

U.S. Employment Service (from Labor)
Office of Education (from Interior)
Public Health Service (from Treasury)
National Youth Administration (from WPA)
Social Security Board (independent)
Civilian Conservation Corps (independent)

TO A NEW FEDERAL LOAN AGENCY

These independent agencies:
Reconstruction Finance Corporation
Electric Home and Farm Authority
Disaster Loan Corporation
RFC Mortgage Company
Federal National Mortgage Association
Federal Home Loan Bank Board
Home Owners' Loan Corporation
Federal Savings and Loan Insurance Corporation
Federal Housing Administration
Export-Import Bank of Washington

TO A NEW FEDERAL WORKS AGENCY

WPA and PWA, (both independent)
Bureau of Public Roads (from Agriculture)
Public buildings branch of Treasury's Procurement division
Most of the Buildings branch of Nat'l Park Service (from Interior)
U.S. Housing Authority (from Interior)

TO DEPARTMENT OF AGRICULTURE

Farm Credit Administration
Federal Farm Mortgage Corporation
Commodity Credit Corporation
(all independent)

HAGSTROM CO., N.Y.

Courtesy of the *New York Times*

THE REORGANIZATION OF GOVERNMENT AGENCIES

thousand state and local employees who were paid partly or wholly from federal funds. In this supplementary enactment Congress took occasion also to confine the annual expenditures of each political party to three million dollars—a figure exceeded in 1936 as well as in some other campaign years—and restricted single contributions to not more than five thousand dollars. It remained to be seen whether politicians would not find ways and means of evading these cramping limitations.

The White House failed, however, to induce the new Congress to embark upon a lending program which, if adopted, would have involved an appropriation of $3,860,000,000 for a seven-year period. Though anti-New Deal partisanship contributed to this outcome, the President's defeat was due chiefly to a conviction that the substantial improvement of economic conditions rendered unnecessary huge and continuing outlays for public works and similar enterprises. On the other hand, the lawmakers in June, 1939, voted $1,775,-000,000 to aid the nearly ten million people without work. This sum, however, was much smaller than the preceding year's appropriation; and Congress further showed its teeth by abolishing the WPA theater project and placing restrictions on other white-collar undertakings. Work relief had employed as many as 3,335,000 persons in November, 1938; the new arrangement involved a reduction to a monthly average of 2,300,000. Incidentally, Congress now changed the name of the WPA from Works Progress Administration to Work Projects Administration. Though in these matters the legislators had loudly preached economy, in other respects they practiced extravagance. When Congress adjourned in August, 1939, the total appropriations exceeded $13,000,000,-000, a peace-time record. A good share of the money went into national defense and into the biggest amounts yet voted to help agriculture.

SELECT BIBLIOGRAPHY

Rounding Out the New Deal.   The general and special works cited at the close of Chapter XIX are, in most instances, also helpful for the later phases of the New Deal. For studies of the status and purposes of urban labor, see Harris, *American Labor,* and *Labor's Civil War;* Calkins, *Spy Overhead, the Story of Industrial Espionage;* Levinson, *Labor on the March;* Brooks, *Unions of Their Own Choosing;* and Rosenfarb, *National Labor Policy and How It Works.* The plight of rural labor is made clear in Wynne, *Five Years of Rural Relief;* Zimmerman and Whetten, *Rural Families on Relief;* Webb and Brown, *Migrant Families;* and McWilliams, *Factories in the Field.* For many topics in this chapter information can be found in scholarly journals such as the *Political Science Quarterly,* the *American Political Science Review,* the *American Journal of Sociology, Social Forces,* the *American Economic Review* and the *Quarterly Journal of Economics;* in monthly periodicals such as *Events, Current History* and the *Monthly Labor Review;* and in weeklies such as the *United States News, Time,* the *Pathfinder, Life,* the *New Republic* and the *Nation.*

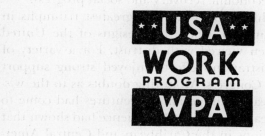

Chapter XXI

AMERICA'S FOREIGN RELATIONS, 1930–1940

THE REVULSION FROM IMPERIALISM

"IN THE field of world policy," Roosevelt had declared in his first inaugural, "I would dedicate this nation to the policy of the good neighbor—the neighbor who resolutely respects himself and, because he does so, respects the rights of others—the neighbor who respects his obligations and respects the sanctity of his agreements in and with a world of neighbors." Quite apart from an abiding desire for peace, the President realized that disturbances in other parts of the globe would affect his own country's welfare and that, if America herself should become embroiled in war, it would upset his plans for economic recovery and social progress.

The Good Neighbor policy won its greatest triumphs in respect to Latin America, where the designs of the United States had long been viewed with distrust. For a variety of reasons the administration's efforts enjoyed strong support both in and out of Congress. Mounting doubts as to the wisdom of America's earlier imperialistic ventures had come to a head with the Great Depression. Experience had shown that recurrent interventions in the Caribbean and Central America heightened the national tax load with resulting gains for no one save a few interested business and banking groups. Added to this, the intense concern with internal problems made the country flinch from unnecessary external responsibilities. The conviction crystallized that colonies and protectorates were a source of trouble and financial loss rather than of profit. It seemed evident, too, that the suspicion and ill will excited throughout Latin America by the "Colossus of the North" had impeded the development of a more advantageous trade. At the same time, the desire for improved relations was stimulated by fear of the aggressive designs of the European totalitarian powers, notably Nazi Germany, on the Western Hemisphere.

The retreat from imperialism began even before Roosevelt entered office. It scored its first signal success in the case of the Philippines, the former Spanish dependency off the Asiatic mainland. For years the feeling had been growing that the acquisition of these islands had been a mistake. The policy of the "white man's burden" had showered many blessings on the Filipinos; but it had failed to yield returns in dollars and cents to the United States, and it had saddled Washington with a difficult problem of naval and military defense. In 1916 Congress under President Wilson had promised the people eventual freedom (see page 380), and annually the insular legislature had reminded the world of this fact by unanimously resolving for immediate independence. In 1927 President Coolidge, after vetoing one of these resolutions, said that the best case for freedom was "not the argument that it would benefit the Filipinos"—which he denied—"but that it would be of advantage to the United States."

Domestic sugar growers had long objected to Philippine competition, and until 1913 had succeeded in maintaining restrictions on sugar imports from the islands into the United States. American dairy producers found coconut oil hurtful to the sale of their commodities. Organized labor became alarmed as low-priced Filipino workers multiplied on the West Coast, totaling forty-five thousand in 1930. The advent of the depression gave these disgruntled elements just the leverage they needed for swinging Congress into line to execute President Wilson's pledge. In January, 1933, a Republican Senate and Democratic House passed over President

Hoover's veto the Hawes-Cutting bill, which set forth specific terms of separation.

These conditions, subject to the insular legislature's assent, involved a ten-year transitional period during which the "Commonwealth of the Philippines" should enjoy almost complete self-government except in economic matters. Restrictions should be put upon the amounts of sugar, coconut oil and hemp products imported free of duty into the United States, and the Commonwealth government must levy increasing duties on exports to America. Emigration to the United States should be limited to an annual quota of fifty. Upon attaining independence the new republic should be outside American tariff walls, and the United States be permitted to retain certain military and naval stations. Though the economic provisions involved serious hardships for the islanders, the Philippine legislature rejected Congress's offer because of the military and naval clauses. To remove this objection, the Tydings-McDuffie act, approved by President Roosevelt in March, 1934, agreed to surrender all military bases and to leave the question of naval establishments to future discussion. On May 1, thirty-six years to a day after Dewey's memorable victory at Manila Bay, the legislature unanimously accepted the new terms. When Manuel Quezon was inaugurated as first president of the Philippine Commonwealth in November, 1935, he declared, "We are witnessing the final state of fulfillment of the noblest undertaking ever attempted by any nation in its dealings with a subject people." Troubles loomed ahead, however, before his country would achieve independence in 1946.[1]

A somewhat similar reversal of American sentiment manifested itself in regard to the Virgin Islands. Between 1917 and

[1] In 1939 President Roosevelt proposed to Congress that, in order to cushion the economic shock for the Philippines when they should attain freedom, certain trading privileges with the United States be continued until 1960. Congress has not yet acted on this recommendation.

1930 the population had fallen fifteen per cent, largely because of attractions of employment in the United States. After a visit in 1931, President Hoover called the colony "an effective poorhouse," adding, "Viewed from every point except remote naval contingencies, it was unfortunate that we ever acquired these islands." The possible naval need existed, however, and in any event the people had already been granted the status of American citizens. By congressional authorization in 1936 all who could read and write English received the right to vote, and a legislative assembly was installed.

More important from the standpoint of the New World republics was the course adopted by the Washington government to evince its nonaggressive attitude toward them. In 1930 President Hoover's State Department released a statement repudiating Theodore Roosevelt's claim (the "Roosevelt corollary") that the Monroe Doctrine justified the United States in intervening in Latin American countries in order to insure their responsible behavior toward European creditors (see page 384). In the same year Hoover started to withdraw from Haiti the marines who had been there since 1915. He planned to complete the process by 1936. In 1931 he refrained from intervening in a revolution in Panama. In January, 1933, he recalled the marines from Nicaragua, where they had been since 1926.

In support of the same line of action, President Roosevelt declared in a public address in December, 1933, "The definite policy of the United States from now on is one opposed to armed intervention." He added: "The maintenance of law and the orderly processes of government in this hemisphere is the concern of each individual nation within its own borders first of all. It is only if and when the failure of orderly processes affects the other nations of the continent that it becomes their joint concern; and the point to stress is that in such an event it becomes the joint concern of a whole continent in which we are all neighbors." Matching words with deeds, he not only hurried the last marines out of Haiti by August, 1934, but entered into a treaty with Cuba in May of that year abrogating the Platt Amendment and concluded another one with Panama in March, 1936, relinquishing the right of intervening in that country. In 1940 he ended the American customs receivership of the Dominican Republic, which had been in effect since 1905.

In a similar spirit the State Department resisted pressure in the United States to deal strongly with Mexico for having expropriated many million dollars' worth of American-owned property. Under the constitution of 1917 that government had undertaken a program of breaking up the great agricultural estates and of taking over foreign oil holdings. As a result, diplomatic relations with the United States from time to time experienced sharp strain. Washington did not deny Mexico's legal right to expropriate, but, in Secretary of State Hull's words, insisted on "prompt and just compensation" for the American owners. Finally, in 1938, the two countries agreed to let a joint commission decide the sum due for the agricultural lands taken since 1927. Under this arrangement Mexico in 1939 began paying the United States a million dollars a year. The oil claims remained to be settled.

Even clearer evidence of Roosevelt's Good Neighbor policy appeared in an epoch-making series of collective treaties consummated by the republics of the Western Hemisphere. The first of these, signed by six Latin American governments at Rio de Janeiro in 1933, condemned wars of aggression by any of them and obligated the adherents not to recognize territorial acquisitions gained by force. To this treaty Washington added its signature in 1934. Meanwhile, in December, 1933, the seventh Pan American Conference at Montevideo drew up a pact pledging the United States and the other countries not to intervene in the internal or external affairs of one another.

Early in 1936 President Roosevelt, desiring to clinch these agreements, called a special Inter-American Conference for the Maintenance of Peace at Buenos Aires on December 1, and he voyaged the twelve thousand miles to open the proceedings in person. The assembled delegates reaffirmed the earlier pledges and pronounced illegal the practice of collecting pecuniary obligations by armed force. Whenever war should threaten any of the countries from any source, they bound themselves by treaty to consult with one another on measures for maintaining peace. They rejected, however, Secretary Hull's proposal for a permanent consultative body, jealous apparently lest the United States dominate it. By another pact they agreed to consult together for the purpose of adopting a common course as neutrals should armed conflict break out between any two or more of them.

When the eighth Pan American Conference gathered at Lima in December, 1938, the governments found no need for further treaties, but in a series of resolutions reiterated their earlier commitments with two significant additions. Prompted by the aggressive course of Nazi Germany in Central Europe, they condemned racial and religious persecution in the American republics, and declared against the political activities of alien minorities in the interest of their native lands. The delegates also indorsed the principle of reciprocal trade treaties which Secretary Hull had been doing so much to foster in his own country.

The deeper import of these agreements and understandings lay in their bearing upon the Washington government's traditional policy toward Latin America. In effect, the United States after more than a century abdicated as sole interpreter and executor of the Monroe Doctrine. An historic cycle had come to a close. Henceforth the twenty-one nations of the

New World stood on a plane of equality and assumed common obligations. The Good Neighbor policy had rewritten the Monroe Doctrine into something like a Pan American doctrine of collective security. As the sequel was to show, this move for hemispheric collaboration came just in time to raise a shield against an Old World once more convulsed with war.

THE BREAKDOWN OF COLLECTIVE SECURITY

In contrast to his program toward Latin America, President Roosevelt encountered difficulty at home in winning support for his policies toward Europe. While the idea of collective security flowered in the Western Hemisphere, it rapidly withered elsewhere before the chill blasts of international distrust and mutual antagonisms. Congress furthered Secretary Hull's efforts to promote foreign trade, for it was expected that these would contribute to domestic betterment; but it stoutly resisted any steps which might possibly entangle the United States in the mesh of Old World hatreds. As early as June, 1934, Congress empowered the President at his discretion to raise or lower tariff duties by as much as fifty per cent in order to secure reciprocal concessions from other governments. The object was to stimulate America's external commerce and at the same time lessen the economic causes of war by promoting a freer flow of goods among nations.

Before the end of 1939 the State Department had negotiated executive agreements for this purpose with twenty-one countries, including Great Britain and Canada, America's two best customers.[1] On the list were over half the Latin American republics. Though the method involved a piecemeal reduction of the tariff, the act stipulated that the bene-

[1] Agreements were made—in the order of their signing—with Cuba, Belgium, Haiti, Sweden, Brazil, Canada, the Netherlands, Switzerland, Honduras, Colombia, Guatemala, France, Nicaragua, Finland, El Salvador, Costa Rica, Czechoslovakia, Ecuador, Great Britain, Turkey and Venezuela. Congress renewed the trade-agreements act in 1937 and again in 1940.

fits of each agreement should extend to all other countries that did not discriminate against the United States. This provision was in accordance with the unconditional most-favored-nation principle. The new policy excited criticism, notably from the farmers, but it produced a marked increase of trade. The chief gains were in the export of automobiles, machinery, office equipment and prepared foodstuffs and of certain agricultural products such as tobacco, fruits, vegetables, lard and wheat.

In a more direct pursuit of his quest for better world relations Roosevelt sought to enlarge on the efforts for collective security undertaken by his three Republican predecessors (see pages 474-480). A few days after first entering office, he announced he would ask Congress for authority to declare an embargo against aggressor nations when a foreign conflict was raging. At his behest Norman H. Davis went so far as to assure the world disarmament conference at Geneva in May, 1933, that, if an international gathering should take measures against any nation for waging war "in violation of its international obligations," America, if concurring in the judgment, would "refrain from any action tending to defeat such collective effort." The President, though forswearing any intention of placing the United States in the League of Nations, wished nevertheless to bring about the closest possible coöperation. As a kinsman of the first Roosevelt as well as the political heir of Woodrow Wilson, he desired to play a large rôle on the world stage, and, seeing farther ahead than most of his fellow countrymen, he sensed the grave perils that threatened the continuance of peace.

Since 1922 Benito Mussolini had been consolidating his position as dictator of Italy, stamping out democratic institutions, annulling traditional liberties and strengthening his military power. Beginning in 1933 Adolf Hitler pursued a similar course in Germany but with even greater vindictiveness. He destroyed the postwar republic, persecuted the Jews and Catholics, terrorized, killed or expelled political foes, and rearmed his people on a scale which boded ill for his less warlike neighbors. The "Rome-Berlin axis," formed in 1936, assured a common understanding by the Fascist and Nazi powers as regards external affairs. On the other side of the globe the Japanese, jubilant over their success in seizing Manchuria (see page 480) and encouraged by the passive attitude of Great Britain and France, nursed fresh and more ambitious designs against China.

In the face of these developments the pillars reared in the 1920's to support the structure of international peace began one by one to topple. The League's failure to halt Japan's invasion of North China in 1931 as well as Italy's conquest of Ethiopia in 1935 revealed the hollow pretensions of that body as a guarantor of peace. The Kellogg pact for outlawing war won ironic deference from aggressor nations by leading them to wage war without declaring it. Another landmark collapsed when the Japanese government refused to renew the Washington naval-limitation treaty of 1922, due to expire at the close of 1936 (see page 477). Hoping to save something from the wreckage, Great Britain, France and the United States signed a treaty in March, 1936, imposing uniform restrictions on the size of their naval vessels and the guns they carried, but placing no top limits on the fleets and leaving the signers free to ignore any or all the provisions if necessary to meet competition by other powers. Shortly before the signing, the British and American negotiators exchanged notes reaffirming the principle of Anglo-American naval equality. The three-power arrangement was virtually useless because of the abstention of Japan and Italy.

The American people observed the train of events with more distaste than alarm. It confirmed their feeling that the Old World was past reforming and that America's proper mission was to attend to her own affairs. Moreover, the sharp decline in immigration under the quota legislation of the 1920's had lessened the number of recent comers from Europe, and this fact, too, conduced to a cooler view of the situation. The descendants of earlier arrivals lacked the excitable interest of their forebears in the doings of their homelands.

Isolationist sentiment was intensified by doubts as to whether the country should have taken up arms in 1917. The people, haunted by fears of economic insecurity, were in a mood of disillusion; and writers who absolved Germany of the exaggerated charges of war guilt on the former occasion found a sympathetic and responsive audience. In 1934-1936 a Senate committee, headed by Gerald P. Nye of North Dakota, conducted an inquiry into the immense profits that American bankers, munition makers and other dealers in war supplies had reaped from the conflict. To thoughtful persons the disclosures (see page 401) fell far short of accounting for America's participation; but the effect on the popular mind was profound. When the American Institute of Public Opinion in April, 1937, just twenty years after the declaration of war, canvassed a typical cross-section of sentiment as to the wisdom of the nation's entry, seventy per cent pronounced it a mistake.

Resentment against America's former European comrades-at-arms was deepened by their continued failure to make payments on their war debts to the United States. Though this default stemmed largely from the high tariffs which the United States in the 1920's had erected against foreign imports, the ordinary person did not perceive the connection and noted only the ability of the governments concerned to spend money on armaments. Finland alone continued to live up to her obligations.

In view of these circumstances public opinion, obedient to President Roosevelt's desires in domestic matters, shied like a timorous horse at his proposal that the government be em-

powered to apply economic sanctions against aggressor powers. Congress, reflecting the belief that a policy of discrimination would embroil the United States in the hostilities,
ignored the White House's wishes, and embarked on a
course of action strongly isolationist in character. In the Vin-
son act, adopted with presidential support in 1934, the lawmakers provided for enlarging the fleet to the full strength
allowed by the Washington and London treaties (see pages
477-478), and in the next few years voted the largest peace-
time naval appropriations in the nation's history. On its own
initiative Congress in the same year passed the Johnson act,
which forbade the debt-defaulting nations to market their
securities in the United States while their obligations remained unmet. In January, 1935, it again took the bit in its
teeth when the Senate, despite Roosevelt's urging, declined
to place the United States in the World Court. America's
membership had been repeatedly pledged by both political
parties, but the Senate's favorable vote of fifty-two to thirty-
six fell seven short of the requisite two-thirds majority.

Isolationist sentiment reached its climax in a series of enactments reversing America's historic position as to neutral
rights. In 1812 and again in 1917 the nation had drawn the
sword in defense of freedom of the seas—the liberty of neutrals to trade in noncontraband goods with countries at war
—and President Wilson had championed the right as one of
his Fourteen Points. But in 1935–1937 Congress, excited by
the findings of the Nye committee, and willing to forgo trading profits and "national honor" for the sake of peace,
worked out a wholly different set of rules.

This legislation provided that, whenever the President
should proclaim the existence of a "state of war," trade with
the combatants should fall under three kinds of restraint.
First, an embargo should instantly stop all shipments of
arms, ammunition and implements of war. Secondly, the

President at his discretion might subject indirect war materials to the cash-and-carry provision, that is, the requirement that the purchaser must pay cash and carry them away himself. Thirdly, any commerce unaffected by these restrictions must conform to the cash but not the carry provision. The last two limitations were to lapse in May, 1939. In addition, Congress barred United States citizens from traveling on a belligerent merchant ship and prohibited loans by them to warring powers. In order not to hinder possible American aid in defense of the Monroe Doctrine it was expressly stipulated that hostilities between a Latin American republic and European or Asiatic countries were not included. The regulations, as originally framed, affected only international conflicts, but when the Spanish insurrection broke out in July, 1936, Congress took occasion early in 1937 to widen their scope to take in civil wars.

While the new neutrality code was under consideration, Roosevelt had repeatedly tried to obtain from Congress the right to apply the restrictions only against the belligerent nation which he should deem the aggressor. Invested with this discretionary authority, he could then join with other neutral powers in concerted efforts for world peace. Though he accepted the legislation without the desired concession, the outbreak of hostilities in the Far East was presently to show how far he was from surrendering his belief in collective action. Meanwhile, when Italy launched her thrust against Ethiopia in October, 1935, he proclaimed a "state of war" and invoked the neutrality regulations. In May, 1937, he took like action against the contending parties in the Spanish conflict. In that country the Loyalist government with some Russian support was fighting a losing fight against General Francisco Franco's rebel army, which was heavily reënforced by Italian and German soldiers and bombing planes. The withholding of munitions from the duly recognized Madrid government caused much criticism in American liberal circles because the Loyalists were regarded as upholding the cause of democracy.

The Japanese invasion of China in July, 1937, touched more vital nerves of American national interest and provoked a quite different course from the White House. Taking refuge in the fact that neither China nor Japan had formally declared war, Roosevelt declined to proclaim a "state of war" and thus deliberately prevented an application of the neutrality provisions. His motive was to avoid hampering ill-prepared China, America's long-time protégé, in a struggle that was viewed as transgressing the nine-power treaty as well as the Kellogg peace pact (see pages 478-479). The State Department took early steps to evacuate Americans who wished to leave the war-plagued areas; and in September the President, still without invoking the neutrality legislation, forbade government-owned merchantmen to carry arms to the combatants and warned private vessels that they would do so at their own risk.

As the fighting in China assumed ever bloodier proportions, Roosevelt's mind turned more and more to the desirability of collective international action for curbing Japan. Speaking in Chicago on October 5, he called on the "peace-loving nations" to unite in opposing "those violations of treaties and those ignorings of humane instincts" that were breeding a "state of international anarchy" against which "mere isolation or neutrality" stood helpless. "When an epidemic of physical disease starts to spread," he asserted by way of analogy, "the community approves and joins in a quarantine of the patients in order to protect the health of the community against the spread of the disease." On the next day the League of Nations formally pronounced Japan an aggressor and treaty breaker, and, acting with White House sanction, summoned a conference of powers to deliberate on appropriate measures. The representatives of America and eighteen other countries assembled at Brussels early in November. Japan was conspicuously absent. The only step on which the delegates could agree was a reassertion of Japan's guilt as a violator of solemn international engagements. A more decisive course was precluded both by President Roosevelt's vagueness as to how far the United States would cooperate in "quarantine" measures and by the unwillingness of England and France to let their energies be diverted from the lurking dangers in Europe.

As the Japanese, undeterred, continued on their career of conquest, Washington found increasing occasion for protest because of the infringement of American rights in China. Bombings with the loss of life and property, interferences with American trade, and treaty infractions occurred time and again. An air attack on the United States gunboat *Panay* near Nanking in December, 1937, was only one of the more flagrant incidents, and led Japan to apologize and pay an indemnity.

In November, 1938, Tokyo announced, in effect, that "the new situation fast developing in East Asia" would make Japan unable henceforth to recognize the Open Door principle of trade and industry; but the State Department emphatically denied her right to repudiate a policy to which she was committed by international pledge (see page 478). As a further mark of displeasure, the United States in July, 1939, gave the required six months' notice for abrogating the treaty of 1911 which guaranteed "reciprocal freedom of commerce" between the two nations. Since Japan relied largely on American sources for aviation gasoline, scrap iron and other war essentials, this move placed Washington in a position to cramp Japan's military effectiveness in China. But when the moment arrived the President delayed taking the expected action. In the meantime a much greater conflagration had flamed up across the Atlantic, and as a result America was confronted with more pressing problems. Japan, biding her time, hoped that Europe's misfortune might mean additional spoils for herself in the Orient.

WORLD WAR AGAIN

Roosevelt's Chicago speech in 1937, while aimed directly at Japan's aggression in China, referred unmistakably also to Hitler's menacing course in Europe. "The peace, the freedom and the security of ninety per cent of the world," the President said, "is being jeopardized by the remaining ten per cent, who are threatening a breakdown of all international order and law." Germany as well as Japan refrained from attending the Brussels conference; and in the next two years Hitler proceeded with the utmost ruthlessness to take advantage of the weakness of his neighbors. At first he announced the intention merely of bringing all Germans together in a common country, but soon the lust of conquest drove him to new extremes.

In March, 1938, the Nazi Fuehrer forcibly annexed Austria; and in September, with Britain and France assenting to what in any case they could not prevent, he seized Sudetenland, the German-inhabited section of Czechoslovakia. In March, 1939, he completed the rape of Czechoslovakia and intimidated Lithuania into surrendering the city of Memel. Five months later he negotiated a treaty of amity with Soviet Russia, thus eliminating that country as a possible enemy and revealing to an astonished world the spectacle of two totalitarian systems, supposedly representing antagonistic ideologies, in fraternal accord. With whetted appetite he turned upon Poland and demanded Danzig and the Corridor, Poland's outlet to the sea. This last action finally convinced the British and French governments that their policy of "appeasement"—of trying to placate Hitler through concessions

HITLER'S RISE TO POWER

1933

Jan. 30, Hitler is appointed Chancellor by President Paul von Hindenburg.

Feb. 27, a fire (attributed by many to the Nazis) burns the Reichstag building. A reign of terror against Communists, Jews and liberal political parties follows.

March 5, elections give Hitler an overwhelming majority in the Reichstag.

April 1, Hitler orders nation-wide boycott against the Jews.

Oct. 14, Hitler withdraws from the Geneva Disarmament Conference.

Oct. 21, Hitler takes Germany out of the League of Nations.

1934

Jan. 26, Hitler signs a ten-year amity agreement with Poland.

June 30, Hitler stages a "blood purge," executing many Nazis and anti-Nazis.

Aug. 2, President Hindenburg dies and Hitler combines the posts of Chancellor and President.

1935

Jan. 13, the Saar returns to Germany after a plebiscite.

March 16, Hitler denounces the Versailles treaty and reintroduces compulsory military service.

June 18, Hitler signs a naval treaty with Britain limiting the German fleet to 35 per cent of Britain's surface craft and to 45 per cent of her submarines.

1936

March 7, Hitler denounces the Locarno treaty. German troops enter the demilitarized Rhineland.

Oct. 23, the "Rome-Berlin axis" is formed.

Nov. 25, Germany and Japan sign an anti-Comintern pact.

1937

Oct. 13, Hitler pledges Germany to respect Belgian neutrality and territorial integrity.

Nov. 6, Italy joins the anti-Comintern pact.

1938

Feb. 20, Hitler in a speech demands the right of self-determination for the Germans of Austria and Czechoslovakia.

March 12, Hitler takes over Austria.

Sept. 15, Prime Minister Neville Chamberlain flies to Munich for the first of three meetings with Hitler during the Czechoslovakian crisis.

Sept. 30, Hitler wins the Sudeten area of Czechoslovakia at Munich. Prime Minister Chamberlain and Hitler announce the "desire of our two peoples never to go to war with one another again."

1939

March 14, Hitler takes over the rest of Czechoslovakia.

March 22, Lithuania surrenders Memel to Hitler.

April 28, Hitler denounces the Polish nonaggression pact and the British naval pact.

May 22, Hitler signs a ten-year military alliance with Italy.

Aug. 23, Hitler signs a nonaggression pact with Soviet Russia.

Sept. 1, Hitler orders the invasion of Poland.

—was a failure. On September 3, 1939, two days after the Nazi armies crossed the border into Poland, Great Britain and France declared war on Germany. Within a few weeks, before the Allies could get into action, Poland lay prostrate, and Germany divided the country with the Soviet Union, which had lent military assistance.

The onset of the Second World War found American opinion better informed than in 1914. By means of the radio, the news films and the press the people had followed Hitler's truculent career with horrified fascination. They had listened to him thunder over the air waves against the evils of liberalism and democracy and vaunt the virtues of his own despotic rule. They had sent money to bring to the United States many Jews and other refugees whom the Fuehrer's barbarous treatment had driven from the fatherland. As if to reassert the basic principles of the American political system against Nazi perversions of human liberty, in 1939 Georgia, Massachusetts and Connecticut—three of the thirteen original states which had neglected to ratify the bill of rights of the federal Constitution—commemorated the one hundred and fiftieth anniversary of the submission of these amendments by attaching their official approval. Equally with other citizens, the vast bulk of Americans of German stock viewed the totalitarian régime with abhorrence and alarm. Here and there knots of recent German or Italian immigrants defended the Axis powers in their newspapers and meetings; but they wielded little influence with the public at large, and tended to grow less assertive with the passage of time.

As the war had drawn closer, President Roosevelt repeatedly tried to stave it off by appeals to the Nazi and Fascist dictators against continued aggression. He saw the impending conflict as a disaster for all mankind, his own country as well as others. "When peace is broken anywhere," he declared, "it is threatened everywhere." At the time of the first Czechoslovakian crisis he informed Hitler, "I am persuaded that there is no problem so difficult or so pressing for solution that it cannot be justly solved by the resort to reason rather than by the resort to force." Such pleas, however, had no effect, and Roosevelt began to consider other ways of making America's influence count. As early as January, 1939, he told Congress, "There are many methods short of war, but stronger and more effective than mere words, of bringing home to aggressor governments the aggregate sentiments of our own people."

A poll taken the next month by the American Institute of Public Opinion indicated that sixty-nine per cent of the nation—more than two to one—favored supporting Britain and France by every means "short of war." Thus the opening of hostilities found the American public, from the chief executive down, committed emotionally to the cause of the two countries that were regarded as the chief bulwarks of democracy in the Old World. At the same time, however, the nation was firmly resolved to keep out of the struggle. What a majority of the citizens apparently wanted was to be as unneutral as possible without getting into the fray. It was an attitude pregnant with danger for America's future peace if the tide of battle abroad should turn decisively against the Allies.

The government's immediate steps were four: (1) to transport nearly a hundred thousand Americans home from the war zone as quickly as possible; (2) to give heed to the national defenses; (3) to adjust the neutrality regulations to the international situation; and (4) to enlist Latin America in joint measures against the possible spread of the holocaust to the Western Hemisphere. By speeding ships to Europe all United States citizens who cared to return were soon brought back. The President renewed his earlier appeals to Congress for more adequate preparedness, but for the time he accomplished little. Belief in the Allies' invincibility was strong among the members and they were reluctant to take action which might engender the war spirit at home.

Roosevelt proved more successful in getting the neutrality regulations revised. As required by law, he promptly applied the arms embargo against both the Allies and Germany; and in this as well as in other respects he deemed the state of affairs objectionable. The embargo cut England and France off from sorely needed munitions and implements of war which they alone possessed the sea power to transport. At the same time, owing to Congress's failure to readopt the cash-and-carry restrictions in May, 1939, United States citizens could now export in their own vessels all supplementary war materials. Administration leaders argued that this latter situation might lead to inflammatory incidents through the destruction of lives and property on the high seas, as in the First World War. Convening Congress in special session on September 21, the President met with stubborn and protracted resistance from the isolationists, who feared lest repeal of the embargo eventually draw America into the strife. The issue to some extent cut athwart party lines with an overwhelming majority of the Republican members lined up against Roosevelt. But a strong outside opinion made itself felt, on behalf of his wishes.

The act, as finally passed on November 3, abolished the arms embargo, and applied the cash-and-carry provision to all ocean commerce with combatants save in the case of their possessions and territories distant from the war zone. This exception, insisted on by American shipping interests, contained the safeguard that even in such instances exports of arms and munitions must be on a cash basis. The statute continued the prohibitions against United States citizens traveling on belligerent vessels and against their lending money to warring powers, and also barred American ships and travelers from zones of probable naval combat. It was further provided that the necessary announcement of a "state of war" might be made by either the President or Congress. As before, the regulations were not to apply to Latin American wars with Old World nations.

In the effort to keep the war out of the Western Hemisphere, Roosevelt brought about a conference of the twenty-one republics at Panama City, where the first Pan American congress had been attempted in 1826. The Good Neighbor policy now bore rich fruit. Assembling late in September, the delegates joined unanimously in creating a "safety belt" stretching from two hundred and fifty to twelve hundred and fifty miles out to sea and inclosing the two continents from the southern border of Canada to Cape Horn. Within this neutral zone the warring powers were warned to perform no hostile acts. The move was unprecedented in international law, and its effectiveness depended more on the belligerents' willingness to respect the collective pronouncement than on the ability of the American nations to enforce it. Within a few months several clashes occurred between Allied and German ships inside the zone. The New World governments, acting through the President of Panama, sent sharp diplomatic protests.

Economically, the first effect of the war was to lend impetus to the business recovery which had been proceeding in the United States since spring (see page 580). The stock market gained, production accelerated and prices rose. By the end of September, 1939, the number of unemployed had fallen to 8,800,000, and those on work relief had decreased to nearly two million. Events in the next few months, however, showed that the expected war boom had not materialized, or, rather, that its benefits were unevenly distributed. In the first half-year of the conflict American exports jumped one third over the corresponding period in 1938–1939, but the gains accrued to the producers of war materials, notably raw cotton, metals, aircraft, chemicals and metal-working machinery. Foreign orders for grains, fruits, tobacco and passenger cars, on the other hand, dropped sharply. It was not until some months later, when the United States began its own defense preparations, that business generally started to boom.

One reason for the restricted Anglo-French demand for American goods was the false sense of security felt by the Allies during the lull in the war following the Nazi *Blitzkrieg* against Poland. In the early winter of 1939–1940 Britain perfected her naval blockade in the hope of depriving the enemy of essential raw materials, and on the western front the contest seemed a deadlock, with the opposing armies resting behind massive fortified lines. Only Soviet Russia braved the winter by launching an unprovoked assault against the Finns, who presently succumbed after heroic resistance. Spring, however, brought a lightning change. Germany, outwitting the Allied high command, turned on her neutral neighbors and began smashing her way swiftly toward France.

For success Hitler relied upon "total warfare," first tried out on a smaller scale against the Poles. With coöperation from German "fifth columnists" in the country attacked, parachute troops seized the airfields and other key positions. Next, clouds of planes raining down bombs and bullets cleared a path for tanks and armored cars, which were in turn quickly followed by motorized infantry. All the operations were faultlessly timed, and rendered the bewildered defenders virtually helpless. In April, 1940, the Nazi hosts seized unresisting Denmark and conquered Norway. In May they overwhelmed the Netherlands, Luxembourg and Belgium and unleashed their fury against northern France. On June 10 Mussolini entered the fray in time to join Hitler in receiving the French capitulation a week later. England and its empire now stood alone against the serried Nazi might. German air raids on the island increased in intensity as the summer advanced and the autumn came; but the British government under Prime Minister Winston Churchill replied with similar, if less effective, thrusts against Nazi cities, and put up such stout resistance at home that Hitler did not venture on a mass invasion. Meanwhile, Italy proceeded to threaten the security of Britain's possessions in the Mediterranean and Red Sea areas.

AMERICA PREPARES

Hitler's conquering tread shook the entire globe. In the United States the people, hitherto anxious about the fate of the European democracies, turned to ways and means of defending their own system against dreaded Nazi aggression. With England in danger of annihilation, no safety remained except distance; and modern methods of warfare rendered even the broad Atlantic a doubtful protection. Roosevelt, when urging Congress in May to speed up defense measures, advised against any steps "which would in any way hamper or delay the delivery of American-made planes" to the Allies. Several weeks later, after Mussolini's declaration of war against France, he alluded in a speech at the University of Virginia to offers he had made to negotiate Italy's differences with the Allies, and added grimly, "The hand that held the dagger has struck it into the back of its neighbor."

An immediate concern of the government involved Hitler's intentions toward the colonies of the countries he had vanquished. Should the Nazi Fuehrer be allowed to take over the French, Dutch and, possibly, British possessions in the Western Hemisphere? And what should Washington's attitude be toward the Japanese or German seizure of the Dutch East Indies, whence America derived her principal supplies of rubber and tin, both vital to the nation's industry and defense?

In handling neither question did the administration hesitate. As early as 1938 Roosevelt had announced in a speech at Kingston, Ontario, "The people of the United States will not stand idly by if domination of Canadian soil is threatened by any other empire." With the collapse of France in June, 1940, Congress declared in a joint resolution that the United States "would not recognize any transfer, and would not acquiesce in any attempt to transfer, any geographic region of this hemisphere from one non-American power to another non-American power." [1] The President promptly served notice on Berlin and Rome, and simultaneously summoned a conference of the American republics to consider the situation.

Meeting at Havana in mid-July, the Latin American governments unanimously ranged themselves alongside the United States in opposition to any alienation of colonial ownership. The gathering resolved that territories whose status was openly or secretly threatened should be put under inter-American administration until they could safely revert to their previous relationship or until they should become independent. In addition, the delegates agreed to suppress fifth-column activities, a matter especially important in the A. B. C. countries, where the large population of German and Italian stock constituted an ever possible peril. With a view to mitigating the dislocation of Latin American trade resulting from the loss of the markets of Continental Europe, the conference authorized the preparation of plans for disposing of export surpluses through closer commercial relations within the New World. In September the United States Congress followed up these actions by authorizing loans to-

[1] Whether this matter was covered by President Monroe's phraseology in 1823 is perhaps an academic question, for the Monroe Doctrine has never been a static thing. In one part of the famous message he said, "With the existing colonies or dependencies of any European power we have not interfered and shall not interfere." More to the point is his statement that any attempt by European powers "to extend their system to any portion of this hemisphere" would be deemed "dangerous to our peace and safety."

taling $1,500,000,000 to Latin American countries for the acquisition of strategic materials and the expansion of defense industries.

At the same time President Roosevelt moved vigorously to seal the Western Hemisphere against attack at other points. In August he united with the Canadian Prime Minister in setting up a Permanent Joint Board to study the defense needs of the northern half of North America. This was followed in September by an even bolder step: a deal with England by which the United States obtained ninety-nine-year leases on eight naval and air bases scattered all the way from Newfoundland to British Guiana. In payment Roosevelt transferred fifty old destroyers, of which the British stood in dire need because of Nazi-inflicted losses. As part of the transaction the English government pledged that it would not surrender or sink its fleet should Germany win the war.

The President told Congress he deemed the acquisition of these "outposts of security" the "most important action in the reinforcement of our national defense that has been taken since the Louisiana Purchase." Though he had carried through the negotiations without asking leave of Congress and without the advance knowledge of the public, popular opinion accorded hearty approval. The State Department at once informed the twenty Latin American republics that the new facilities would be open to them "on the fullest coöperative basis." Late in October, when the Nazi-dominated French government seemed on the point of granting the use of Martinique, French Guiana and other Western Hemisphere bases to the Germans, Roosevelt served swift warning that such action would precipitate the seizure of these dependencies by the American republics in accordance with the Havana agreement.

In dealing with the situation across the Pacific the Washington government had to play pretty much a lone hand.

Though Japan was still far from mastering the Chinese after three years of fighting, she could not let slip the opportunity of profiting by Europe's affliction. Even before the Nazi invasion of the Netherlands the Tokyo authorities had expressed concern over the future status of the Dutch East Indies, with which, they said, their country was "economically bound by an intimate relationship." These islands, half the size of Europe and including Java, Sumatra, Borneo and New Guinea, had been conquered by the Dutch three centuries before and, because of their output of oil, rubber, tin, spices and other products, were regarded as the world's richest colonial estate.

The Japanese statement elicited from Secretary Hull on April 17 the blunt assertion that a change of ownership except by peaceful means would jeopardize the "stability, peace and security" of the entire Pacific area. Again in May, after the mother country's downfall, Japan raised the question; and again the State Department replied, reminding her of her pledge in the four-power treaty of 1922 not to disturb the colonial status quo (see page 477). The presence of the American fleet in the Pacific may have deterred Japan from more decisive action toward the orphaned islands, but it did not alter her purpose. Late in June her Foreign Minister announced what he chose to call a "Japanese Monroe Doctrine" for East Asia and the South Seas, declaring that this region should constitute a single economic sphere under Tokyo's "stabilizing power." Washington on the plea of defense needs now took the long-delayed step of placing restrictions on the shipment of high-grade aviation gasoline and certain kinds of scrap iron and steel outside the Western Hemisphere. Toward the end of September, as Japanese troops began moving into French Indo-China with the French government powerless to withhold assent, Roosevelt imposed a complete embargo, effective on October 16, on all scrap iron and steel going to Japan. The island empire had received ninety per cent of these vital military materials from America in 1939. As a further mark of disapproval, the United States lent $25,000,000 to China, bringing the total of such loans since 1938 to about $69,000,000.

The Tokyo authorities, deeply angered and fearing the consequences of being deprived of basic war supplies, struck back on September 27 by forming a ten-year alliance with Germany and Italy. The three governments expressly recognized the hegemony of the Axis powers in Europe and of Japan in "Greater East Asia," and agreed to come to the assistance of any of the partners which should be attacked by a country (other than Russia) not then a belligerent. Though Japan could not expect immediate help from her allies in the event of a war with the United States, she gambled on an early victory over Britain in Europe. Should this occur, America would find her hands tied in the Atlantic and the Japanese could do as they wished with the Far Eastern possessions of England, France and the Netherlands. The Axis powers, for their part, hoped that a bolder course by Japan would slow down American aid to Britain and isolate the United States fleet in the Pacific. The State Department promptly warned American citizens in Eastern Asia to return home with the least possible delay. Since hostilities in the Orient would endanger America's imports of rubber, tin and other military essentials, Washington proceeded to increase the stocks on hand and to try to develop new sources of supply in the United States and South America. Whether Japan was actually prepared to take on a war with a major power, only the future could disclose.

America's effectiveness against both Japan and the Axis powers depended upon her state of armed preparedness. During Hitler's total warfare in the Low Countries and France the administration by indirect sale had released to

the Allies substantial stores of weapons—rifles, heavy guns
and trench mortars—left over from the First World War. But,
looking ahead, the country needed greatly to increase and
modernize its own defenses. With as much dispatch as democratic methods and the magnitude of the task permitted,
the government moved toward this goal. In order to give the
effort a bipartisan character, President Roosevelt in June
brought into his official family two leading Republicans.
Henry L. Stimson of New York, who had served in the Taft
and Hoover cabinets, took over the War Department, and
Frank Knox of Illinois, Landon's running mate in 1936, became Secretary of the Navy. Both men were known as ardent
pro-Ally supporters.

Together with appropriations voted earlier in the year,
Congress between May and early November made nearly
eighteen billion dollars available for rearmament. It was
believed that a third of this sum would be spent by the middle of 1941, and the full benefit of the program could not be
expected until several years later. Though the fleet already
stood second only to England's, the threatening dangers in
Asia as well as Europe caused Congress to begin the construction of a two-ocean navy, one large enough to "meet any possible combination of hostile naval forces." The bulk of the
session's funds provided for equipping and raising an army
of a million two hundred thousand, for expanding the air
fleet to thirty-five thousand planes, for enlarging the number
of G-men to deal with fifth columnists, and for speeding up
the manufacture of war supplies.

In order to make sure of adequate man power, Congress in
August authorized the President to call out the national guard
for a year's intensive training, and in mid-September adopted
the Burke-Wadsworth bill for compulsory selective service,
though in the face of determined opposition from the Republican minority. The first conscription measure ever

adopted by the United States in time of peace, it provided for registering all men between the ages of twenty-one and thirty-five inclusive and for selecting annually by lot eight hundred thousand for a year's training. Somewhat as in the First World War, exemption or deferred classification was extended to public officials, ministers, conscientious objectors, the physically unfit, persons with dependents and those engaged in occupations "necessary to the national health, safety or interest." To protect the draftees against unnecessary economic loss, the government was directed to help them meet their insurance premiums, mortgage payments and similar dues while with the colors, and a legal obligation was placed on employers to rehire them after the year's service without reduction of wages or loss of seniority rights. The conscription law was to be in effect until 1945. On November 18 the first contingent of thirty thousand was inducted into service.

As a means of expediting industrial mobilization Roosevelt, acting under authority of Wilson's statute of 1916 (see page 409), created an Advisory Commission on National Defense consisting of seven persons familiar with the country's business, agricultural and labor resources. Congress endowed the government with power to finance, lease, commandeer or build plants engaged in the manufacture of war materials. These measures rendered possible a mobilization of the nation's defense industries on a scale rivaling that in Germany and Great Britain. In order to raise a barrier against profiteering on war contracts, Congress imposed a tax of from twenty-five to fifty per cent on excess corporate profits.

Meanwhile, on the humanitarian front, the American Red Cross took the lead in European relief activities. As the area of physical wreckage and human suffering spread from Poland to Finland and then swept from Norway through the Low Countries to France, the task became ever heavier. In the first eleven months of the war the Red Cross sent nearly eight million dollars in medical supplies, ambulances, clothing, food and the like to these countries and to England. The public contributed twenty million dollars to enlarge its efforts and Congress in July added fifty million. Other agencies created especially for the emergency, such as the American Jewish Joint Distribution Committee, the Allied Relief Fund, the American Friends of France, the Polish-American Council and Bundles for Britain, spent over five million in the same period. Especially noteworthy was the heartfelt interest in providing homes for English children whose parents wished to save them from the horrors of Nazi bombing attacks. In some respects, the most tragic refugees of all were the technical divisions of the League of Nations, which removed to America from war-girt Switzerland in the fall of 1940, most of them appropriately finding asylum at Princeton, the former home of Woodrow Wilson.

ROOSEVELT WINS A THIRD TERM

At this point matters stood when the voters assembled at the polls on November 5 to determine their government for the next four years. The preliminaries had presented some unusual features. The Republican convention at Philadelphia on June 24 could not make up its mind to nominate any of the three aspirants who had been indorsed in the state primaries: District Attorney Thomas E. Dewey of New York County, famed for his relentless pursuit of racketeers; Ohio's Senator Robert A. Taft, son of the former President and an ardent isolationist; and Senator Arthur H. Vandenberg of Michigan, also of the isolationist school. Instead, the prize went on the sixth ballot to Wendell L. Willkie of New York, president of the Commonwealth and Southern Corporation and archenemy of the various New Deal electrification projects as well as of the holding-company act. Willkie's frank preconvention utterances advocating all aid to England short of war had favorably impressed persons distrustful of the wiles of seasoned politicians; and his backers, working deftly from behind the scenes, had seen to it that the delegates at Philadelphia were deluged with telegrams in his behalf. To the galleries' rhythmic chant of "We Want Willkie" he was carried to success.

The choice violated political precedent, for the candidate was a Big Business magnate, a Wall Street lawyer and until two years before a registered member of the opposition party. Moreover, for the first time in American history, a major party offered a contender who had never held either an elective or an appointive governmental office. To disarm criticism of so unorthodox a selection, the ticket was completed with Senator Charles L. McNary of Oregon, a lifelong Republican who had consistently championed the New Deal's power program and who was an isolationist. It was expected that, because of his earlier connection with the McNary-Haugen farm plan (see page 500), he would make a particular appeal to the agricultural vote.

The Democrats also broke with tradition but in a different way. Though Roosevelt had kept mum as to his intentions, the Democratic primaries and state conventions generally had called for his renomination; and when the party convened in Chicago on July 15, he was named on the first ballot for a third consecutive term by a majority of 951 to 149. Addressing the delegates by radio from the White House, he justified his acceptance on the score that "In the face of the danger which confronts our time, no individual retains, or can hope to retain, the right of personal choice which free men enjoy in times of peace. He has a first obligation . . . to serve his country in whatever capacity his country finds him useful." At the President's behest the second place was given to Secretary of Agriculture Wallace, as forthright a New Dealer as his chief. In selecting their ticket the Democrats, unlike the Republicans, made no concessions to the dissidents in their ranks. Conservative Democrats were, in effect, invited to move out of the party.

Even more than in 1936, the rival platforms occupied common ground. Concerning foreign affairs, both declared for keeping America out of the European maelstrom, for giving Britain every assistance short of war, for defending Latin America against totalitarian aggression, and for building an impregnable national defense. On the home front, each pledged a continuance of relief for the unemployed and of benefit payments for the farmers, the maintenance of labor's right of collective bargaining, and an extension of the social-security act to more workers. But where the Democrats acclaimed the New Deal's success "in stopping the waste and exploitation of our human and natural resources, in restoring to the average man and woman a stake in the preservation of our democracy" and "in enlarging our national armaments," the Republicans condemned the party for piling up a stupendous debt, imposing a "régime of regimentation," paralyzing private enterprise, "fanning the flames of class hatred" and bungling national preparedness. Promising to deal more gently with business and to "confine government activity to essential public services," the Republicans said nothing specifically as to their intentions regarding hydroelectric power and the regulation of holding companies; but their attitude, asserted the Democratic platform, plainly appeared in their nomination of a utility executive. The Republicans concluded by proposing to amend the Constitution against a third presidential term.

The contest that ensued was the hardest fought in many years. The vocal warfare followed the lines laid down in the party creeds. Seeking to erase the stigma of his Big Business connections, Willkie delivered his address of acceptance in the simple surroundings of his boyhood at Elwood, Indiana. Between mid-September and election day he made nearly five hundred and fifty speeches in thirty-four states, exceeding Bryan's record in 1896. Everywhere he proclaimed his devotion to most of the New Deal reforms while denouncing the administration for leading the nation down a road "paved with good intentions" to the "destruction of our democratic way of life." He flailed the President for prolonging unemployment by his "persecution" of business, for incompetence in handling national defense, and for secretly planning to involve the country in war. A Republican campaign tract forecast a virtual cancellation of savings accounts and life-insurance policies if the administration stayed in power.

As the weeks passed, the Republican standard-bearer hammered increasingly on the dangers of a third term and predicted that, if the people upset the tradition, "our democratic system will not outlast another four years." His supporters observed October 23 as "No Third Term Day." Campaign buttons, banners and billboards in all parts of the land warned against the "doctrine of indispensability." One favorite poster read:

> IN RUSSIA
> *it's the Third International.*
>
> IN GERMANY
> *it's the Third Reich.*
>
> IN AMERICA
> *There Must Be*
> NO THIRD TERM.

Ex-President Hoover saw "national socialism" and "totalitarianism" ahead in the event of Republican defeat. The *Saturday Evening Post* in its last issue before the election solemnly assured its millions of readers that they would vote "on the fate of free government in this country."

The vigor of the Republican offensive caused Roosevelt in the closing weeks to abandon his rôle of an executive too busy with the international crisis to give much heed to politics. Stressing the great humanitarian achievements of the New Deal and the progress of the rearmament program, he reminded the public that the bulk of the Republicans in Congress had opposed both sets of measures. He derided their eleventh-hour repentance and saw dictatorship menacing America only if Big Business should regain its grip on the government. A host of other speakers defended his renomination because of the imperative need of an experienced hand to keep the country out of war, and in Lincoln's phrase they begged the voters not to "swap horses while crossing a stream." The President's defeat, they said, would disappoint all Latin America and delight the Axis powers. An effective campaign document was a special supplement of the *New Republic* charging subsidiaries of Willkie's holding company with anti-labor activities. Other writers recalled that the Republican nominee in 1935 had praised Samuel Insull (see page 488) as a "forceful, dynamic and attractive figure."

No presidential race had ever seen so extensive a crossing of party lines. Willkie, himself a recent Democrat, captained the Republican cohorts, while the Democratic vice-presidential nominee had been a Republican until the New Deal. "Al" Smith, as in 1936, campaigned against Roosevelt, with ardent support now from Hugh S. Johnson, former head of the NRA. On the other side, Gifford Pinchot, twice Republican governor of Pennsylvania and a conservation leader under Theodore Roosevelt, joined Senator Norris in painting the dangers of Willkie's election to public power development; and the columnist Dorothy Thompson, hostile to the New Deal in the past, indorsed the President because of his bold foreign policy. A variety of new allegiances was displayed in the mushrooming of such organizations as the Republicans-for-Roosevelt, the Democrats-for-Willkie, the Businessmen's League for Roosevelt and the No-Third-Term Democrats.

Though the Union party had not survived the 1936 campaign, Father Coughlin's group and Dr. Townsend supported Willkie's candidacy, as did also the Steuben Society, composed of German Americans. Through the Associated Willkie Clubs the Republicans tried to capture the independent vote, while Mayor La Guardia of New York and Senator Norris headed an organization to render a similar service for the President. Many persons usually inactive in politics—playwrights, movie stars, song writers, pugilists, college presidents and others—obeyed the urge to declare publicly for the one side or the other. To add to the confusion, John L. Lewis, head of the CIO, called on labor to oppose Roosevelt—an action promptly disowned by many CIO leaders and unions.

The bitterness and passion generated by the contest surpassed anything known since Bryan's silver crusade in 1896. In many places Willkie and those with him were greeted with eggs and other missiles. Each side accused the other of evading the Hatch legislation against "pernicious political activities," and to observers it seemed likely that both were right. In the general excitement the various minor parties were scarcely heard. The Communist nominee, Earl Browder, was barred from the ballot in fifteen states and the Socialist Norman Thomas in eleven, usually because these parties had cast an insufficient vote in previous elections. Four states, however, avowedly excluded the Communists on the ground that the party favored the forcible overthrow of the American government. Browder himself, awaiting appeal of a federal court sentence for a passport fraud, was not allowed to speak outside southern New York.

The outcome of the campaign was a sweeping victory for the President, though with reduced majorities. He won the 449 electoral votes of thirty-eight states, leaving Willkie with

82 electoral votes from ten states. Of the popular ballots Roosevelt received 27,242,000 to his opponent's 22,327,000. The Democrats also carried both branches of Congress, slightly increasing their membership in the House. The effort to take the New Deal away from the New Dealers had failed. With the international situation overshadowing all other questions, the majority of voters saw in the President a man who they believed could be trusted to master the crisis without needless sacrifice of peace-time social gains. Roosevelt was a known quantity; Willkie, a newcomer in politics, was necessarily a question mark.

Though the third-term issue had been debated as never before and many Roosevelt adherents had hesitated to violate the tradition, the people in general yielded to George Washington's prophetic view in 1788: "I can see no propriety in precluding ourselves from the services of any man, who on some great emergency shall be deemed universally most capable of serving the public." John L. Lewis's diversion on behalf of Willkie had little perceptible effect. On the other hand, a substantial economic upturn, due largely to armament orders, aided the President's cause. Six hundred and fifty thousand men had secured jobs in private employment in September alone; and by election day factory rolls approached the peak of 1929. Steel was producing at capacity; construction was booming; and other industries hummed with activity.

Despite the rancors of the campaign both nominees had agreed on the fundamentals of foreign policy. Both had backed the party declarations pledging the full might of America against totalitarian aggression. Both had gone beyond their platforms in indorsing peace-time conscription. Republican criticism had concerned details rather than substance. Whatever hopes the dictator governments may have cherished of an embittered and divided nation, the people issued from the battle of ballots more firmly resolved than ever to defend their system of government against the anti-democratic forces of the Old World.

SELECT BIBLIOGRAPHY

America's Foreign Relations, 1930–1940. Most of the general accounts listed at the close of Chapter XIX also treat American diplomatic interests. For more recent developments, consult the periodicals cited at the end of Chapter XX, to which should be added *Foreign Affairs,* the *American Journal of International Law* and the annual surveys: *United States in World Affairs* (edited in different years by Lippmann, Scroggs, Shepardson and others), *American Year Book, Americana Annual* and *New International Year Book.* Stuart, *Latin America and the United States,* develops the Good Neighbor policy. Tasca, *Reciprocal Trade Policy,* and Sayre, *Way Forward,* review the efforts to lower international commercial barriers. Light is thrown on the collapse of collective security by Jackson, *Short History of the World since 1918;* Rappard, *Quest for Peace;* and Griswold, *Far Eastern Policy.* America's reaction to the darkening war clouds is considered in Borchard and Lage, *Neutrality for the United States,* and Davis, *Navy Second to None.* Lavine and Wechsler, *War Propaganda and the United States,* deals with the tides and currents of American opinion regarding the belligerents in the early stages of the conflict.

Chapter XXII

SOCIAL AND CULTURAL
FACTORS, 1917–1940

THE OLD ORDER CHANGETH

IN THE twenty years or so following America's entry into the First World War the quest for security became, for the first time, a conscious national purpose. As has been seen, this purpose assumed a dual form: security against both outer and inner threats to the country's well-being. Once, the republic had been able to go about its affairs with only incidental attention to dangers from without and in the expectation that its citizens would possess a decent standard of living. America had enjoyed a geographic isolation remote from the principal centers of world conflict, and her relatively sparse population and undeveloped resources had allowed the people every opportunity for self-betterment. But even before the close of the nineteenth century these fundamental conditions had begun to change. It was a dawning realization of this fact that animated the progressive movement for domestic reform early in the twentieth century and which caused some of the progressives to espouse joint action with other countries to promote world stability. In a peaceful international community they saw the best hope of safeguarding and improving America's own way of life.

After the war of 1917–1918 this double goal assumed paramount importance. Initially, the government sought through a series of collective treaties to discourage the resort to armed strife. Despite the Senate's rejection of the League of Nations, the decade of the twenties evidenced Washington's unceasing concern for building up a system of mutual guarantees of peace. Though the structure unhappily proved frail, the effort was nevertheless memorable. In the next decade statesmen came to differ as to whether national safety lay in a continuance of such measures or in a return to isolationism; but the circumstances of the time directed chief attention to considerations of internal material welfare. As a result, the thirties marked the greatest strides ever taken in the United States to protect the "forgotten man" against economic calamities not of his own making. As the conservative *New York Times* remarked in 1940 on the fifth anniversary of the social-security act, "We have come a long way from the days when it was considered socially demoralizing to make provision against even some of the worst economic hazards that the individual encounters. Today millions of men and women are no longer haunted by the specter of poverty in old age, and even unemployment has lost much of its former terrors."

The people whose interests were thus being consulted had increased from 106,000,000 in 1920 to 131,670,000 in 1940. Americans had hitherto taken a rapid gain of population for granted. Now they were confronted with some arresting facts as to the speed of growth and as to its character. The rate was conspicuously slowing, being less than half as great in 1930–1940 as in 1920–1930. Moreover, thanks to higher health standards and better living conditions, the average expectancy of life at birth had lengthened from fifty-six years in 1920 to sixty-two in 1938. Accordingly, the proportion of elderly persons was mounting, a tendency accelerated by a decline in the birth rate. In 1900 only four in every hundred persons had been as old as sixty-five, in 1930 the number was between five and six in every hundred, and it was believed that in 1980 it would be at least fifteen. On the other hand, there were fewer children under the age of five in 1940 than in 1920. Thus, as more people grew older, the ranks of youth were being thinned. If the trend should continue, statisticians reckoned that the number of young people under nineteen would drop from about forty-eight million in 1930 to twenty-eight in 1980, while persons of sixty-five and older would increase from six and a half million to twenty-two. Furthermore, because of the sharply falling birth rate and curtailed immigration, America faced a time—somewhere near 1980— when her population would be at a standstill or would actually begin to lessen. This was a disturbing outlook for a people who as late as 1890 had been expanding by at least twenty-five per cent each decade.

Already, coming events were casting their shadows before. Some economists attributed the delay of business recovery after 1929 to the slowing down of population growth and the ebbing demand for consumer goods. Organized groups of the aged, rallying to the standard of Dr. Townsend and other persuasive captains, unsettled the political balance of power in many states and, as has been seen, prodded Congress into passing the social-security act in 1935. The diminishing enrollment in the elementary schools in the 1930's was another sign of the times, involving a redirecting of educational effort and the employment of fewer teachers. Looking ahead, the nation must prepare for many other adjustments. The burden of the elderly destitute both on the government and on private charity was certain to grow heavier. Changes might occur in political and voting habits as more and more old people lined up at the polls. Industry must gear itself to a shrinking supply of young labor and at the same time suit its product to an altered demand. In order to offset the dwindling growth of population, business must work to expand foreign sales and to raise domestic standards of consumption and buying power. There were also military implications if the country should long continue the system of training a large peacetime conscript army.

The part that immigration played in retarding population advance appeared in the decreasing number of foreign-born. As a result of deaths and of the successive governmental restrictions imposed in the 1920's (see pages 495-496), the total during the decade grew only from 13,921,000 to 14,204,000. In the next decade the Great Depression exerted a further restraining effect. Fewer immigrants arrived in the 1930's than in any decade since the 1830's, and in some years more left than entered. By 1940 the foreign-born in America numbered only about 11,500,000. The figure would have been smaller but for the flight of Jews and other expatriates from the Axis countries. Yet many who wished to depart were prevented by the American quota limitations. In Nazi Germany the United States consulates in June, 1939, had enough applications to fill the German quota for eleven years. In Czechoslovakia the registrations would have required nearly eighteen years for exhaustion. Though the government thus barred out many who would have made valuable citizens, public opinion seemed to approve, while it actively rejoiced that a growing proportion of the resident aliens were becoming naturalized. Those failing to take this step decreased from 7,430,000 in 1920 to 4,842,000 in 1940. The undigested immigrant no longer imperiled the nation's powers of assimilation.

Meanwhile, the urban trend increased in momentum, thrusting ever greater throngs of both foreign and native-born into the towns and cities. With a third of the people living in communities of eight thousand and upward in 1900, approximately half did so in 1930. During each of the three decades forty per cent or more of all the nation's counties actually lost in rural population, though there was a net gain in the thirty years of about eleven and a half million country dwellers. This growth, however, was dwarfed by the leap of over thirty-five million in the number of urban inhabitants. By 1930 nearly a third of the nation resided in centers of a

MOVEMENT TO AND FROM FARMS, 1920–1937

YEAR	PERSONS ARRIVING AT FARMS FROM CITIES, TOWNS, AND VILLAGES	PERSONS LEAVING FARMS FOR CITIES, TOWNS, AND VILLAGES	NET MOVEMENT FROM	
			CITIES, TOWNS, AND VILLAGES TO FARMS	FARMS TO CITIES, TOWNS, AND VILLAGES
1920	560,000	896,000	—	336,000
1921	759,000	1,323,000	—	564,000
1922	1,115,000	2,252,000	—	1,137,000
1923	1,355,000	2,162,000	—	807,000
1924	1,581,000	2,068,000	—	487,000
1925	1,336,000	2,038,000	—	702,000
1926	1,427,000	2,334,000	—	907,000
1927	1,705,000	2,162,000	—	457,000
1928	1,698,000	2,120,000	—	422,000
1929	1,604,000	2,081,000	—	477,000
1930	1,611,000	1,823,000	—	212,000
1931	1,546,000	1,566,000	—	20,000
1932	1,777,000	1,511,000	266,000	—
1933	944,000	1,225,000	—	281,000
1934	700,000	1,051,000	—	351,000
1935	825,000	1,211,000	—	386,000
1936	719,000	1,166,000	—	447,000
1937	872,000	1,160,000	—	288,000
1920–1924	5,370,000	8,701,000	—	3,331,000
1925–1929	7,770,000	10,735,000	—	2,965,000
1930–1937	8,994,000	10,713,000	—	1,985,000

hundred thousand or more. The Great Depression somewhat slackened the rate of urban advance in the 1930's; and 1932, the worst year, generated a back-to-the-farm movement which temporarily exceeded the countercurrent. Nevertheless, by 1940 a larger proportion of the people dwelt in towns and cities than when the decade began.

Urban preponderance revealed itself even more impressively in the rise of great metropolitan regions. These "city states" had begun to form in the nineteenth century as swifter means of transportation and communication flung the population outward into the suburbs. But it was the coming of the automobile and the motor truck and the extension of

electricity and other urban utilities into the surrounding territory that gave these supercommunities their enormous size.
Increasingly the bedrooms of American cities were to be
found in the outlying settlements, and many small retail businesses and factories obeyed the same impulse.

By 1930 ninety-six metropolitan districts had emerged,
each composed of one or more central cities with dependent
towns and rural areas, and each embracing a region united by
similar social and economic interests. The metropolitan district dominated by New York City extended into three other
states and contained two hundred and seventy-two towns and
cities. Greater Chicago consisted of a hundred and fifteen and
greater San Francisco of thirty-eight. Within the metropolitan regions the less congested and more lightly taxed urban
fringes tended to draw residents away from the core cities. So
large was this centrifugal migration in the 1930's that certain
cities such as Philadelphia, St. Louis and Pittsburgh had
fewer people within their corporate limits in 1940 than ten
years before.

The metropolitan districts, having arisen out of deep-felt
regional needs, usually possessed greater economic and cultural solidarity than the states in which they happened to lie.
But in governing themselves the people of any area were
hampered by the fact that they were fenced off into separate
municipalities and oftentimes divided by state lines as well.
Twenty-two of the metropolitan regions straddled two or
more states. One of the thorniest problems of local government was to discover means of surmounting these barriers
and administering the entire district's affairs according to a
mutually beneficial plan. A new strain was placed upon a
political system erected in the eighteenth century for a rural
people.

Notwithstanding such difficulties, cities generally showed
a reassuring improvement in governmental efficiency and

honesty. Capitalizing on what their predecessors had achieved earlier in the century (see pages 301-302), municipal reformers won new successes. The city-manager plan, existing nowhere in America in 1900, had spread by 1940 to more than four hundred and fifty communities, including places as large as Cincinnati, Rochester and Dallas. At the same time there occurred a widespread adoption of the nonpartisan ballot, an extension of the merit system of appointment to four fifths of the nation's city employees, and a steady increase in the number of municipally owned waterworks and other public utilities. The old-fashioned urban political boss, robbed of most of his traditional props of power, found the problem of survival increasingly difficult.

Along with these changes came the first sustained efforts at city planning. The new purpose was to substitute foresight for drift and confusion in order to make the community a more convenient, sanitary and attractive place in which to live. Beginning in 1905 at Columbia, South Carolina, and San Francisco, the city-planning movement at first developed slowly, but the hundred and eighty-five towns and cities with planning boards in 1922 increased to over eleven hundred by 1940. Even municipalities that did not go the whole length tried by means of zoning ordinances and building codes to safeguard the health, pleasure and general welfare of their citizens. As a result, urban life assumed an increasingly rural aspect. Parks, tree-lined boulevards and recreation centers multiplied far out of proportion to the piling up of population, and the municipal authorities, notably with New Deal help, devoted serious attention to slum clearance and better housing for the poor.

Caught between the rise of metropolitan regions and the expanding power of the federal government, the political entities known as states lost more and more of their importance.

In one respect, however, the Great Depression revived some of their energies with results injurious to the country as a whole. In the scramble for self-preservation the states resorted to legislation to protect home products and offset their failing revenues. By 1940 over a thousand regulations and practices of this kind had been adopted to discriminate against persons and commodities from sister commonwealths. For example, a five-ton truck traveling from Alabama to South Carolina had to pay a $400 tax in Alabama, $400 in Georgia and $300 in South Carolina. In Michigan the tax on wine from home-grown grapes was four cents a gallon as against fifty on wine from elsewhere. Under the guise of sanitary precautions some states practically excluded milk, eggs, livestock and other farm products originating beyond their borders. Thirty legislatures gave legal preference to local industries in purchasing supplies and construction materials for public purposes. California went so far as to declare that all school textbooks must be written by Californians.

"Isolationist" state laws saddled an unhealthy burden on that freedom of interstate commerce which the framers of the Constitution had intended. As time went on and action by one legislature led to reprisals by others, discrimination was seen to be a two-edged weapon. Thoughtful citizens were reminded of conditions under the Articles of Confederation. In 1938 a conference of governors took a strong stand against trade restrictions, and other groups joined in the agitation. Some relief arose from special agreements between states. There was also a slowing up in the imposition of additional barriers. In 1940 the Supreme Court intervened in an Arkansas case involving the special taxation of out-of-state gasoline carried in motor busses. The tribunal knocked out the law as interfering unduly with interstate commerce, and the minority opinion hinted that Congress should act to clear "the channels of trade between the States." With public opinion increasingly aroused, the prospect of a freer economic intercourse within the Union appeared brighter.

NEW DIRECTIONS OF HUMANITARIAN REFORM

A significant by-product of the changed social attitude attendant on the "Roosevelt revolution" was the assumption by the government of welfare activities hitherto left to private agencies. The most conspicuous development was Washington's leadership in this field, but a large majority of the states increasingly took on new responsibilities, oftentimes with the assistance of federal subsidies. Thus, such enterprises as old-age pensions, public-health measures and the care of needy children and the blind (see pages 551-553) were joint undertakings of the state and national authorities. Notwithstanding that these added functions involved heavier taxes, the public generally approved of a system which distributed the burden widely instead of putting it all on philanthropic-minded individuals.

Though the Great Depression sapped the resources of private charities, these organizations continued to play an important rôle, if only to supplement the work of governmental agencies. In the 1920's they had prospered with the times, greatly expanding their activities and more closely coördinating their programs. The ampler financial support was due in part to the device of raising funds through uniting in "community chests." Though Cleveland had initiated the scheme in 1913, it was the success of the joint money-raising drives of civilian relief agencies during the World War that led to its widespread adoption. From twelve chests in 1919 the number grew to three hundred and twenty-nine in 1929. With the economic blight other cities adopted the plan, for the dwindling contributions for charity fell sadly short of meeting the rapidly increasing need. By 1938 the total stood at four hundred and seventy-one. Two thirds of the urban inhabitants then lived in communities served by chests.

One social problem entered a new phase as a result of the repeal of national prohibition in 1933 (see page 503). The effect of the Twenty-first Amendment was to return the liquor question to the states. Either because the people had suffered an overdose of virtue, or because the temperance forces were too disorganized to be effective, the legislatures showed little disposition to resume their former restraints against intoxicants. Of the twenty-nine commonwealths which had banned the traffic before universal prohibition, all but five—Alabama, Mississippi, Tennessee, Oklahoma and Kansas—rescinded their enactments before 1936, and Alabama and Tennessee fell by the wayside in the next three years. Eighteen states containing a third of the nation's inhabitants followed the example of the Canadian provinces in making liquor selling a government monopoly, while the other commonwealths adopted various types of licensing regulations. In 1935 there were over two thousand state dispensaries with annual sales of close to $161,000,000. Nearly everywhere the restrictions discriminated between beer and stronger beverages. Even the so-called prohibition states permitted certain grades of beer to be sold.

With the relaxation of repressive measures the practice of drinking became more general though the amount of drunkenness apparently did not increase. The availability of legal liquor drove the bootlegger out of business and thus removed a fecund source of urban crime. Temperance advocates, forced to start again from scratch, made use of local-option laws, which existed in the great majority of the states. As in earlier times, dry victories were won most easily in the rural towns and farming regions. Even many wets deemed the restrictions against liquor inadequate or poorly enforced. But no reversal of popular sentiment toward national prohibition seemed in prospect. When the American Institute of Public Opinion took a poll on the subject in 1940, the vote stood two to one in favor of the system of state regulation.

A reconsideration of the Indian question brought about another change of social policy. Though the reformers of the 1880's believed they had started the tribesman on the road to civilization, the plan involved too sharp a break with his traditional way of life. Bred to a system of collective ownership, the red man failed to develop a sense of private property, with the result that he was easily swindled out of his holdings. Moreover, he drifted away from his own people and lost the cultural values that formed his natural heritage. He became a stranger in his own land, a man without a country. Rootless, poverty-stricken, oftentimes diseased, the "first American" constituted a problem of increasing gravity.

In 1924 Congress conferred citizenship on all members of the race, but this was a legal formality which left their social and economic status unaltered. It was not till President Roosevelt entered office that the government proposed a New Deal for the red man as well as for the white. By that time the Dawes severalty act of 1887 (see page 189) had resulted in whittling down the hundred and thirty-nine million acres of Indian domain to forty-seven million, much of it infertile. The Wheeler-Howard act of 1934 forbade further allotments to individuals, provided means of placing landless persons back on the soil, authorized a large measure of tribal self-government, affirmed both the Indians' cultural and civil rights, and offered government aid for conserving timber, grass and similar natural advantages as well as for other economic undertakings.

Under John Collier, an ardent champion of Indian rights whom Roosevelt appointed Commissioner of Indian Affairs, the system made rapid headway. Though acceptance of the plan was wholly optional, a hundred and eighty-nine tribes out of two hundred and sixty-six voted to come under it. As instances of awakened enterprise, the Northern Cheyenne developed a livestock coöperative, the Chippewa conducted a tourist camp and the Swinomish in Washington undertook a tribal fishing business. Educational effort was directed toward equipping Indian youth for responsible living in their own reservation communities, with emphasis placed on safeguarding physical resources and reviving native arts and culture. In 1936 Congress established an Indian Arts and Crafts Board for advising as to standards of quality and methods of marketing. In working out their new destiny the tribesmen have been hampered by the moral and economic disintegration from which they had long suffered. As one observer has put it, the experiment is "hopeful and unfinished." Its importance lies in the fact that, thanks to better medical care, the once "vanishing Indian" has recently been multiplying at a faster rate than any other racial minority. After declining from 266,000 in 1910 to 244,500 in 1920, the number rose in the next decade to 332,000 and in 1940 to more than 352,000.

In most of the reform enterprises of the time women were active. This, of course, was a familiar rôle for them to play, but now, armed with the ballot in every state, they were able to impress their views more effectively on the government authorities. As soon as the Nineteenth Amendment was ratified in 1920, the suffrage leaders had founded the League of Women Voters with branches throughout the Union. The organization proceeded to study local and national problems in a nonpartisan spirit and to formulate solutions. In this manner they helped to mold public opinion on such subjects as child welfare, housing, education and the protection of consumers against injurious foods and medicines.

Many women took a more direct part in government. There was a constant influx into appointive offices and a steady increase of those who held elective ones. On the twentieth anniversary of universal suffrage Secretary Frances Perkins noted that at the higher political levels three women had served as federal judges and twenty-eight as members of Congress. Two had also been ministers abroad and two others governors of states. The new importance of the sex was evidenced in the wife of President Roosevelt. Deeply interested in welfare work before entering the White House, Eleanor Roosevelt broadened her horizon to include all efforts to aid distressed mankind. Reaching a nation-wide audience through her travels, daily syndicated column and radio broadcasts, she translated complex social abstractions into simple human terms and inspired people to a fresh determination to correct conditions.

Another important factor in stirring the popular conscience was the activity of the churches. In harmony with the dictates of the social gospel (see pages 351-352), religious leaders sought to keep abreast the changing needs of postwar times. According to a pastoral letter of the Methodist bishops in 1919, "If Christianity is a driving force making for democracy, we cannot put a limit upon the extension of democracy; we must recognize the inevitability of the application of democracy to industry. While we rejoice in the adoption of such ameliorative measures as better housing and various forms of social insurance, we call for the more thoroughgoing emphasis on human freedom." The General Assembly of the Presbyterian Church likewise indorsed a "genuine democratization of industry," while the National Catholic War Council declared that the majority of wage-earners "must somehow become owners, at least in part, of the instruments of production."

Other religious bodies issued similar pronouncements and, despite inertia and opposition within their folds, sought to give reality to their professions. The National Catholic Welfare Conference, which replaced the National Catholic War Council in 1919, set about to promote and coördinate Catholic "works of education, social welfare, immigrant aid and other activities." In 1927 it joined with the Federal Council of Churches and the General Conference of Rabbis in investigating a strike on the Western Maryland Railroad, and four years later the three organizations united in a Conference on the Permanent Preventives of Unemployment.

As churchmen concerned themselves more and more with the world about them, the ancient theological differences of Protestantism grew fainter. Mergers of local congregations occurred with ever greater frequency. Much more significant were the mergers of entire sects. Between 1916 and 1926 eighteen groups took this step, including three Lutheran bodies which combined to form the United Lutheran Church. Later years saw other amalgamations, notably the Christian Church and the Congregationalists in 1929; two Northern Methodist denominations and the Methodist Episcopal Church, South, in 1939; and the Reformed Church and the Evangelical Synod of North America in 1940. In 1939 the Presbyterians and Episcopalians laid plans to emulate their example. On nearly every hand the portents indicated a determination to reduce the wastefulness of denominational rivalries.

As doctrinal dissensions subsided, so also did the former fears of the menace of science to Christianity. Occasional rumblings, however, could be heard of the earlier controversy over Darwinism, especially in quarters where the intellectual aspects of religion were subordinated to the emotional. The "fundamentalists" succeeded in inducing three Southern legislatures to outlaw the teaching of evolution in tax-supported schools. The movement reached a climax in 1925 when a young Tennessee high-school teacher was found guilty of disobedience. The state supreme court later reversed the decision, but affirmed the constitutionality of the statute. Subsequently the law fell quietly into disuse.

Despite the increasing distractions of modern life and the reduced church revenues resulting from the depression, religious membership lagged only a little behind the advance of population. From 1916 to 1936 the number of communicants rose from 42,000,000 to 55,800,000. Though the Catholics formed the largest single group, the combined Protestants outnumbered them more than two to one. Religion continued to be a potent force in American life.

INTELLECTUAL MAINSPRINGS

Never before had the American people found it so easy to keep informed about current affairs. Though the daily newspapers decreased from 2410 in 1917 to 2228 in 1937, their total circulation jumped by more than half—a rate exceeding the growth of population. The decline in the number of dailies stemmed in part from the increasing costs of newspaper production and in part from the competition of the radio and movie. Among the New York papers affected were the *Herald* and the *Tribune,* which were united in 1924, and the *World* and the *Telegram,* which were combined in 1931. As a result of consolidations, cities which had hitherto possessed five or more journals found themselves forced to rely upon one or two, perhaps under identical ownership. Chicagoans, who during the World War could choose among four morning papers, had only one to read twenty years later. Newspaper chains acquired a new importance as the number grew from thirty-one in 1923 controlling a hundred and fifty-three dailies to fifty-nine in 1935 controlling three hundred and twenty-nine papers. At the latter date they furnished over a third of the country's daily circulation.

Everywhere the tendency was toward greater uniformity

of presenting both news and views. The chain system, the news-gathering agencies and the syndication of "features" helped to make newspapers more or less alike the country over. On the other hand, readers gained the benefit of a better coverage of the world's events than would otherwise have been possible. Generally, the papers pursued a policy of pleasing all and offending as few as possible; but dependent as they were for advertising and other support upon corporate business, they usually took a strong stand in defense of economic orthodoxy during political campaigns. Since the vast bulk of the press opposed Franklin D. Roosevelt in each of his presidential runs, the evidence indicates that the newspapers had lost the public's confidence as political guides.

Largely as a gesture toward greater journalistic independence, they opened their pages during the 1930's to high-salaried columnists such as Walter Lippmann, Dorothy Thompson and Heywood Broun, who commented on national and international affairs in widely syndicated articles. Individual journals printing these discussions could disclaim responsibility for the opinions expressed. It usually happened, however, that the political coloration of the columnist harmonized with that of the newspaper.

The radio became a rival of the newspaper shortly after the first broadcasting station, KDKA, opened at Pittsburgh in 1920 in time to announce the returns of the Harding-Cox election. Broadcasting stations soon multiplied while the owners of radios increased at an even more rapid rate. The annual sales of sets leaped from a hundred thousand in 1922 to two million in 1925 and, despite the depression, to eight million in 1937. By the last date there were nearly seven hundred broadcasting stations, and the thirty-three million receiving instruments in American homes, offices, automobiles and schools outnumbered the nation's bathtubs. In twenty years the radio had nearly reached the goal toward which print had been working for five hundred: to extend its audience to include the whole population.

In 1926 the National Broadcasting Company, first of the great radio networks, was organized, to be followed in 1927 by the Columbia and presently by others. Broadcasting did not become a government monopoly as in most other countries; and stations vied with one another in making the largest possible popular appeal in order to strengthen their claims as advertising mediums. As the programs improved in quality and scope, the listener could tune in on current news, political discussions, sermons, shopping information, stock-market reports, sporting events, humorous skits, educational talks, domestic hints, musical performances, bedtime stories, etc. The radio became a talking newspaper with features that the printed page could not hope to emulate. In its advertising function it cut deeply into revenues on which the newspaper had long counted. While the older generation continued to read the daily press to confirm what they had first heard over the air, the younger generation tended more and more to rely solely on their auditory senses.

The radio not only brought people into closer communion but reached outward to all corners of the globe. In 1929 the nation listened eagerly to Commander Richard E. Byrd's announcement from the Antarctic of his flight over the South Pole. Another momentous event was Edward VIII's speech to a world-wide audience in 1936 following his abdication as King of England. With the outbreak of the Second World War expert commentators in European capitals gave Americans a dramatic sense of the meaning of total warfare and kept them better informed of the developing hostilities than were the peoples of the belligerent powers. Progress was also made in television. As early as 1924 the Radio Corporation of America transmitted photographs across the Atlantic, and by the 1930's the art had reached sufficient perfection for newspapers to avail themselves of it. Television in the home was slower in coming. The future was plainly mirrored, however, when the proceedings of the Republican national convention of 1940 were telecast to some fifty thousand persons.

As the radio was acquiring sight, so the movie long since had acquired a voice. The change came in 1927 when the producers Warner Brothers and William Fox began using synchronized sound effects. "The Jazz Singer" featuring Al Jolson, a singing comedian, convincingly demonstrated the possibilities and helped soon to sweep silent films into the discard. No longer bound by the restrictions of pantomime, a new galaxy of stars rose in Hollywood and the screen art made a fresh start. Though the motion picture was primarily an agency for entertainment, it also encroached on the domain of the newspaper in its newsreels and in special presentations such as "The March of Time." After the early years, however, it did not seek to compete as an advertising medium, for the box-office receipts rendered unnecessary this supplementary source of revenue.

By 1938 there were nearly sixteen thousand picture houses with a seating capacity of ten million. The weekly attendance was estimated at eighty-eight million. As in the instance of the radio, the industry tended to gravitate into the hands of a few major producing companies, which also owned many of the theaters. Apart from its commercial uses, the movie proved an important handmaid to education, especially in the teaching of science. Every up-to-date school and college felt it needful to possess one or more projecting machines.

Startled by the enormous popularity of the radio and the movie, some persons feared that the people were becoming all ears and eyes and no mind—the helpless victims of mass suggestibility. This alarm sprang in part from a failure to discriminate between the beneficial and harmful features of the new instrumentalities and in part from the growing prominence of organized propaganda in American life. Propaganda, that is, the deliberate manipulation of opinion either for good or ill, had always existed. What was new was its high-powered character, an inheritance from war days when men had "sold" patriotism according to the efficient methods of selling industrial products. By means of the air waves and the screen millions of minds could be now bombarded with an intensity of impact never before known; and, of course, the older channels for influencing public attitudes also continued to be used.

Fortunately, freedom existed not merely for one but for all kinds of propaganda; and this fact, coupled with official exposures of some of the more insidious efforts, soon made the nation acutely propaganda-conscious. Though the newspapers generally opposed Roosevelt in his various presidential campaigns, he easily overcame the handicap by use of the radio. To cite a different example, the utilities industry faced an aroused popular sentiment when the Federal Trade Commission in 1934 reported the results of its investigation in the Senate document: *Efforts by Associations and Agencies of Electric and Gas Utilities to Influence Public Opinion.*[1] Sometimes the line between purposeful propaganda and unbiased news was difficult to draw. Thus, the extensive efforts of the New Deal to publicize its multifarious and expanding activities through "information directors" and "specialists in visual information" seemed to its opponents sheer Democratic partisanship at the taxpayers' expense.

Beside the more vigorous engines of opinion, the periodical press wielded relatively little influence. Magazines, long

---

[1] "Barring, possibly, Government drives during war time," declared the FTC, "it is doubtful whether any publicity campaign ever approached this in variety, extent, comprehensiveness, minute thoroughness of planning and execution, and amount of expenditures involved."

since drained of their muckraking fervor (see page 299), were now generally content to instruct and amuse their readers. During the booming 1920's their total sales climbed skyward, but the hard times reduced the number of buyers from two hundred million in 1929 to a hundred and seventy-six million in 1935. From this ill wind, however, certain weeklies profited, thanks to their low selling price. The *Saturday Evening Post, Collier's* and *Liberty,* devoted mainly to fiction, amassed circulations of from two and a half to three million.

The principal new developments in the periodical world were represented by *Reader's Digest* (1922), which ably summarized outstanding magazine articles for the busy reader; *Time* (1923), which condensed and spiced the week's news; the *New Yorker* (1925), whose quips and cartoons set a new style of sophisticated humor; and *Life* (1936), *Look* (1937) and other pictorial weeklies, which exploited the new visual-mindedness of the public. Like the newspaper press and for much the same reason, most magazines of wide circulation leaned to the conservative side of public questions, if they expressed any views at all.

The novelists and poets did more to jolt complacency than the journalists and magazine writers. The period between the two World Wars had its share of romantic effusions, for authors living off their pens could not, if they would, ignore the popular demand for effortless reading. Some handled their themes with artistic merit, as Thornton Wilder in *The Bridge of San Luis Rey* (1928) and James Branch Cabell in a succession of novels. But more important was the work of a group of writers who viewed the American scene in a mood of postwar disillusion, a disillusion bred of a bitter sense of the moral wastes of war as well as a disgust with the vulgar standards that afflicted the nation in the 1920's. Often experimental in their literary techniques, they further defied

convention by treating sex with a frankness hitherto unknown in American letters. In the words of a contemporary
critic, they accomplished the "repeal of reticence."

John Dos Passos's *Three Soldiers* (1921), E. E. Cummings's
The Enormous Room (1922), William Faulkner's *Soldiers'
Pay* (1926) and Ernest Hemingway's *A Farewell to Arms*
(1929) stood out among the books which dwelt on the un-
heroic character of war. Works like these did much to feed
the isolationist sentiment of the public. In attacking cultural
values the writers, unlike their predecessors earlier in the
century (see page 354), were less concerned with muckraking Big Business than with exposing the shabby ideals and
misdirected energies of the host of middle-class Americans.
In such novels as *Main Street* (1920), *Babbitt* (1922) and
Arrowsmith (1925) Sinclair Lewis satirized the cant and
show that usually passed for successful achievement. Sherwood
Anderson told in *Winesburg, Ohio* (1919) and *The Triumph
of the Egg* (1921) of the cramping restrictions of small-town
life. With ponderous realism Theodore Dreiser in *An American Tragedy* (1925) unraveled the story of a weakling demoralized by the false standards of a commercial civilization.
Standing somewhat apart from these and their like, Willa
Cather in *O Pioneers!* (1918) and *Death Comes for the Archbishop* (1927) wrote with warmth and insight of quiet hero-
ism on the Nebraska prairies and in early New Mexico.

The Great Depression redirected fiction toward underlying economic realities. No longer criticizing their countrymen for living by bread alone, the novelists of the 1930's
concentrated on their fellow Americans who lacked bread.
On every hand they discovered evidences of the "ill-housed,
ill-clad, ill-nourished." Some of their books professed to be
"class-conscious" and "proletarian," but most of them belonged to the older tradition of social protest. Typical of the
torrential flood were William Faulkner's *As I Lay Dying*

(1930), Erskine Caldwell's *Tobacco Road* (1932), James T. Farrell's trilogy *Studs Lonigan* (1932-1935), Albert Halper's *Union Square* (1933), Jack Conroy's *The Disinherited* (1933), Robert Cantwell's *Land of Plenty* (1934), and John Steinbeck's *Of Mice and Men* (1937) and *The Grapes of Wrath* (1939).

As if to remind a disheartened public of its heritage of courage, there was also a resurgence of historical fiction. Neglecting the spectacular and the merely picturesque, Walter D. Edmonds, Kenneth Roberts, James Boyd and others peopled the American past with believable men and women who succeeded in overcoming stubborn odds in spite of their human frailties. Margaret Mitchell's *Gone with the Wind,* a novel of the Civil War and Reconstruction, was the publishing sensation of 1936.

Many of the writers of the 1920's and 1930's commanded an audience abroad. Two of them—Sinclair Lewis and Pearl S. Buck, the latter a delineator of Chinese peasant life in *The Good Earth* (1931) and other novels—won the accolade of the Nobel Prize in 1930 and 1938. With the playwright Eugene O'Neill, who attained the distinction in 1936, they were the first American authors to be so honored.

Poetry, which since Walt Whitman's time had been the poor relation of American letters, also came into its own. Such productions as Edgar Lee Masters's *Spoon River Anthology* (1915), Carl Sandburg's *Chicago Poems* (1916), Robert Frost's *New Hampshire* (1923) and Edwin Arlington Robinson's *Tristram* (1927) exhibited both the variety and the authentic American character of the achievement. Though the poets were superficially unlike, each writing in his own idiom, none was content with mere pretty phrases or with skimming the surface of experience. Some of them, like Masters, Sandburg and to a less extent Vachel Lindsay, cried out passionately against social wrongs. The new poetry, though often crude, was metal fresh from the mine, not coins smoothed and defaced by repeated use.

The general economic collapse hurt book publishing even more than magazine publishing. The total sales of books shrank by half between 1929 and 1933, the bleakest years of the depression. On the other hand, the number of volumes borrowed from public libraries rose from a quarter to a half. Moreover, the increase of enforced leisure was reflected in a greater circulation of books for adults than ever before recorded. Much discussion occurred as to the effect of the radio on reading. Contrary to a general impression, several investigations indicated that it enlarged the total amount by stimulating curiosity as to matters outside the listener's habitual orbit of interest. The movies may have exerted a similar influence. At any rate, surveys of the American Institute of Public Opinion in 1937–1939 revealed a concentration of interest on books which had previously been screened at Hollywood.

In the domain of formal education the 1920's witnessed a large increase of students, teachers and physical facilities. Public school enrollment grew from 20,500,000 in 1917 to 25,680,000 in 1930, while the total expenditures more than trebled. Educators, influenced by the individualism rampant in other phases of American life, experimented widely with "progressive" methods and "child-centered" instruction, much to the dismay of those parents who preferred to have the schools instill a sense of discipline in their children. John Dewey (see page 356) was the principal inspiration of the new educational practices, but the master must often have winced at the excesses of his disciples.

By curious contrast many legislatures, apparently distrusting the instrument of their own creation, imposed increasing restrictions on the liberty of teaching in the form of flag-saluting exercises, special oaths of loyalty for teachers, and the like. Postwar hysteria was initially responsible, but the movement persisted because of the fear that school children might develop a critical attitude toward established institutions. Governor Alfred E. Smith of New York in vetoing a teachers' oath bill in 1920 acutely pointed out, "If this law had been in force prior to the abolition of slavery, opposition to that institution which was protected by the Constitution and its laws would have been just cause for the disqualification of a teacher." Nevertheless, by the end of 1935 twenty-one commonwealths, including New York, possessed such legislation.

But for the active intervention of the New Deal the economic crisis would have paralyzed countless school systems for lack of local financial support. Though teachers' pay suffered, the PWA between 1933 and 1940 contributed $481,-500,000 toward constructing and improving nearly thirteen thousand educational buildings, including those of colleges. The NYA, as has been seen, did its part by helping needy students at the various stages to keep on. Accordingly, the total number in the public schools continued to mount, reaching 30,660,000 in 1940.

The slowing rate of increase was due to a new factor in the situation: the falling birth rate. Nearly two million fewer pupils attended the elementary grades at the end of the decade than at the beginning. Though this loss was more than offset by gains at the high-school level, it was estimated that in another ten years high-school enrollments would also begin to drop. Like the country's merchants and manufacturers, educators faced the necessity of adjusting their product to a waning demand. Opportunity for expansion lay obviously in two directions: a more adequate provision for rural children, especially in the South; and an extension of adult education to meet the leisure-time needs of the steadily aging population.

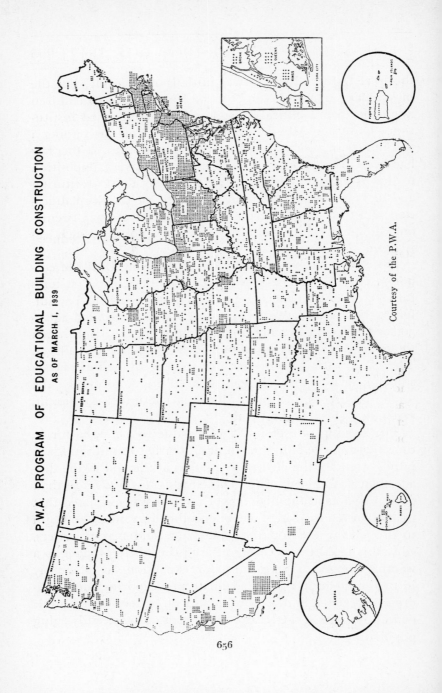

P.W.A. PROGRAM OF EDUCATIONAL BUILDING CONSTRUCTION

AS OF MARCH 1, 1939

Courtesy of the P.W.A.

Like the schools, the colleges and universities passed from the sunshine of the 1920's into the shadow of the 1930's. The number of students, which had been short of 115,000 in 1900, rose to nearly 438,000 in 1921 and topped 1,425,000 in 1940. By the last date one out of every six or seven of college age was in college, a record unequaled elsewhere in the world or earlier in the United States. After the crash of 1929 troubles accumulated for university administrators as legislative appropriations, private gifts and interest rates dwindled. Teaching efficiency suffered because of salary cuts, reduced staffs and diminished support for libraries and laboratories.

It is hardly surprising that in the circumstances higher education revealed a sharper awareness of the churning forces of the nation's life. Ivory towers offered fragile shelter from the dynamite blasts of economic disaster. President Roosevelt's so-called Brain Trust was only a conspicuous example of the greater participation of college professors and college-trained men in public affairs as speakers, technical advisers and frequently as officeholders. Undergraduates crowded the classes in economics, political science and sociology, and university authorities provided systematic courses for training young men for the public service.

At the Harvard Tercentenary in 1936 President James Bryant Conant reasserted the cherished right of scholars to "absolutely unmolested inquiry." "The origin of the Constitution, for example, the functioning of the three branches of the Federal Government, the forces of modern capitalism," he said, "must be dissected as fearlessly as the geologist examines the origin of rocks." In a similar spirit Professor Edwin G. Conklin of Princeton, speaking as president of the American Association for the Advancement of Science, declared in 1937, "Free thought, free speech and free criticism are the life of science." But in many localities conservative trustees, prospective donors and business groups, viewing professors even more distrustfully than they did schoolmen, did not accept this principle. The teachers' oath laws commonly affected university instructors as well as other teachers; legislative investigations had an intimidating effect; and according to a survey in 1936 of conditions since the World War, "More college professors have been dismissed or disciplined because of their views than in any other similar period in our history." Unwittingly, the repressive elements were seeking to enforce conformity of opinion by methods which the European dictators had developed to savage efficiency in their countries.

CREATIVE EFFORT AND THE USES OF LEISURE

Despite such obstacles the timeless search for truth continued as a major function of higher education. The aggregate product defies detailed summary or analysis. According to an authority writing in 1940, American scientists, compared with the rest of the world, had attained preëminence in astronomy, dentistry and neurosurgery and perhaps also in anatomy, physiology and certain branches of medicine. As further evidence of scientific leadership, the coveted Nobel Prize was bestowed after 1917 on eleven American investigators in chemistry, physics, physiology and medicine. In the humanities and the social sciences a series of large collaborative works, notably the *Dictionary of American Biography* (1928–1936), the *Encyclopaedia of the Social Sciences* (1930– 1934) and the *History of American Life* (1927–   ), served to crystallize the new points of view and stimulate students to fresh discoveries.

Cutting across all subjects was a growing belief that minute specialization, notwithstanding its manifest advantages, was often causing investigators to view their problems too narrowly, to lose sight of the larger implications and interrelations. Research of the traditional kind was breeding technicians and fact-finders who, as the popular saying ran, were engaged in learning "more and more about less and less." In order to reverse the trend, the National Research Council, the American Council of Learned Societies and the Social Science Research Council were formed between 1916 and 1923. Recruiting the nation's foremost scientists and scholars, these agencies set about to redirect intellectual energies along more fruitful channels and particularly to cultivate the borderlands between well-worked fields The undertakings frequently involved the banding together of experts in different branches for the purpose of prosecuting collective inquiries. The new emphasis was on the interdependence of human knowledge.

Not all research contributions emanated from academic centers. In the two decades after the war the number of research workers employed by private industry grew fivefold, with upwards of $200,000,000 spent on technological investigation in the single year 1940. The state and national governments gave increased attention to basic inquiries into matters affecting the public weal. The great educational foundations poured millions into exploring the unknown in many fields.

American research effectiveness further benefited from the arrival of distinguished minds from Europe, driven out of their own lands by totalitarian oppression. The first influx from Soviet Russia shortly after the war was followed by a second from Fascist Italy in the mid-twenties and by a third and larger one from Nazi Germany in the next decade. In this manner, for example, Michael Rostovtzeff of Russia became professor of ancient history at Wisconsin and later at Yale; the Italian literary scholar, Giuseppe A. Borgese, joined the faculty of Smith College and then of Chicago; and Albert Einstein of Germany, Nobel Prize winner in physics, was enabled to resume his scientific labors at the Institute of Advanced Study in Princeton. This flight of brains inflicted an incalculable loss on the countries involved.[1] America's gain was correspondingly great.

Among the refugees were also many painters, sculptors, musicians and the like who, each in his own line, helped to fertilize the nation's cultural soil. Such influences aside, American art, now as earlier, reflected the modes and methods emanating from the outside world. Yet none could doubt that the principal inspiration sprang from native sources. In every branch—painting, architecture, sculpture and the rest—artists strove to free themselves from threadbare conventions, to experiment with fresh ways and to impregnate their work with the meanings of contemporary American life. Laymen accustomed to the old sometimes stood aghast at the new; but as time dulled the edge of unfamiliarity, they viewed the accomplishments with increasing favor. A keener æsthetic sense even penetrated the domain of industry as popular taste demanded that articles be beautiful as well as useful. The result appeared in a wide variety of wares— from motor cars, bathtubs and kitchen stoves to phonographs, book bindings and coffins. As another sign of the times, the General Federation of Women's Clubs in 1927 persuaded a hundred and forty-one national advertisers to cease the practice of defacing the landscape with billboards.

The prosperous twenties encouraged a lavish patronage of the arts. The sales of statuary and other art objects doubled between 1919 and 1929 while the value of similar importations from abroad leaped more than threefold. Though the Great Depression changed the situation in this respect, the New Deal placed a protective wing over creative workers as well as factory employees and ditch diggers (see page 527).

---

[1] In 1940 New York City and its environs contained the greatest concentration of Nobel Prize winners ever known. Apart from American recipients, the list embraced the authors Maurice Maeterlinck from Belgium, Sigrid Undset from Norway and Thomas Mann from Germany as well as the German physicists Albert Einstein and James Franck.

The construction activities of the PWA and WPA incidentally afforded employment to thousands of architects, sculptors and mural painters; and the Federal Arts Project, established in 1935, expressly extended the work-relief program to include musicians, actors and others. Accordingly, creative expression, instead of withering, blossomed in new ground with the accomplishments widely distributed for all to see. Some fifteen hundred murals and thirty-five hundred sculptures were produced by WPA workers alone. The effect on popular taste proved far-reaching. The average man, even in remote rural towns, became aware of different and better æsthetic standards.

In the separate branches of art the practitioners were legion. The names of individuals seem less important than in earlier eras when men of distinguished talent were fewer. The World War produced a wave of memorial sculptures which in their chaste dignity and pictorial effectiveness made the "soldiers' monuments" of the Civil War appear stiff and repellent. In painting a significant new source of support came from commercial concerns, which now employed leading artists to decorate their walls as if to demonstrate that business had a soul above material gain. These murals, as in the Chicago Merchandise Market and the Groos Bank at San Antonio, portrayed historical events culminating in recent economic progress.

But the trends in painting were many. Under European influence a predilection for primitivism gripped some of the workers, who sought to reach behind externals of appearance to the essences of mass, color and design. Still others, revolting against "postimpressionism" and "abstract art," chose to delineate their American surroundings with fidelity to simple everyday fact, whether in the technological studies of Charles Sheeler, the rural scenes of Thomas H. Benton or William Gropper's pictures of lynchers. In particular, the art work fostered by the Federal Arts Survey unfolded the native scene, displaying its contrasts and emphasizing the wretchedness of the dispossessed in whose lot the painters themselves would have shared but for Washington's helping hand. Benton spoke for this large and growing school when he said, "American art can be found only in the life of the American people." He called upon his fellow painters to come out of their "cultural enclosures" and produce "goods which have meaning for the American people."

In architecture perhaps the principal new departure was the fashioning of the skyscraper into an object of impressive beauty and the application of the style to other than commercial structures. The new mode resulted, by accident as it were, from a New York municipal ordinance of 1916 which was intended to save the streets from perpetual twilight by requiring tall buildings to be constructed in tiers receding successively from the lot line as greater heights were reached. The "setback" design quickly revealed artistic possibilities that caused other cities to copy it. The new edifices assumed a terraced or steplike effect, exhibiting mass upon mass in a manner strangely reminiscent of Mayan architecture.

Hardly less significant was the adaptation of the skyscraper idea to college buildings, as in the instance of the Cathedral of Learning of the University of Pittsburgh, and also to state capitols, notably those of Nebraska and Louisiana. Ironically enough, the highest structure of all—the Empire State Building in New York, scaling a hundred and two stories—was completed in 1931 as the economic system was rapidly crumbling. The shift of population away from congested urban areas in the 1930's suggests that this noble edifice may be the last monument of its kind to American business optimism.

If musical composition lagged behind the other arts, musical appreciation attained dimensions hitherto unknown. This was due partly to the steady improvement of taste in earlier years (see page 364), partly to free municipal concerts which greatly increased in the 1920's, partly to WPA sponsorship during the depression and, most of all, to the influence of the radio. Though the radio at first purveyed only the latest popular tunes, the broadcasting companies soon discovered an appetite for compositions of recognized quality. As early as 1926 the New York Symphony Orchestra occasionally went on the air; and its Sunday afternoon concerts, begun in 1930, reached millions of listeners who seldom, if ever, had heard music of high merit. In 1931 the NBC took a further plunge by broadcasting the Metropolitan Grand Opera Company each week. So genuine was the response that in 1940, when the Metropolitan needed a million dollars to keep going, the unseen audience contributed a third of the amount.

In the first years the radio threatened the phonograph with virtual extinction; but as the popular education in music proceeded, the public responded increasingly to the phonograph advertisers' appeal of hearing "what you want when you want it." The sale of records of the biggest company multiplied six times between 1933 and 1938. The widespread interest in classical music helped to swell the demand. To this end the WPA also contributed. Through the Federal Music Project, initiated in 1935, it organized unemployed musicians in instrumental and vocal groups for public performances which featured Beethoven, Wagner, Tchaikovsky and other European masters along with native composers. Among its other activities it supported a hundred and sixty-two symphony and concert orchestras.

Most of the music issuing from the microphone and phonograph was of a more ephemeral sort. Soon after the war the earlier popular addiction to ragtime gave way to jazz—which Paul Whiteman, one of its ablest exponents, termed the "folk music of the machine age"—and when jazz tended to lose its spontaneity, it was succeeded by a madder form of improvisation known as swing. If the extreme examples fell on older ears like a deafening, dissonant blare, the younger generation found in these innovations a release for their inhibitions, while the musicianly possibilities were developed in such serious compositions as George Gershwin's "Rhapsody in Blue" and William G. Still's "Afro-American Symphony."

Light opera also exhibited fresh vitality; and in Irving Berlin, Jerome Kern, Cole Porter and Sigmund Romberg, not to mention others, the age found worthy successors of Reginald de Koven and Victor Herbert. Though musical comedies were of many kinds, the popular mood in the 1930's took particular delight in those that satirized the state of the nation. "Of Thee I Sing" (1931), composed by Gershwin, and Richard Rodgers's "I'd Rather Be Right" (1937) directed mocking shafts at Congressmen, cabinet officers, Supreme Court justices and other worthies. In the latter production President Roosevelt himself was supposedly the central character—greatly to his amusement, it was reported, when he witnessed a performance. Of similar vintage, though more specifically aimed against economic injustice, was Harold J. Rome's "Pins and Needles" (1938), a revue produced by the International Ladies' Garment Workers Union.

The legitimate stage in the 1920's had to learn how to live with its two lusty rivals: the screen and the radio. The number of road companies fell off and theatrical performances tended more and more to be confined to metropolitan centers. The players, however, like the dramatists, often found themselves in greater demand than before, for if Hollywood did not want them, the radio was likely to provide a market for their talents. The same situation applied as well to musical composers and performers. Though comedians were the chief beneficiaries, some of the best actors of the time, including Helen Hayes, James Cagney and Paul Muni, took advantage of the triple opportunity. Katharine Cornell was one of the few who retained an undivided loyalty to the stage. Even more than the films, the radio presented special problems for both playwright and performer. The poet Archibald Mac-Leish took the lead in trying to evolve a new drama form suitable for the ether, notably in his moving indictment of dictators, "The Fall of the City" (1937).

Closely paralleling the trends in fiction, the more significant theatrical productions provided a critical commentary on the times. In the 1920's the aversion to war found expression in such dramas as Laurence Stallings and Maxwell Anderson's "What Price Glory?" (1924), while a throng of plays, including Marc Connelly and George Kaufman's "To the Ladies" (1922), Sidney Howard's "They Knew What They Wanted" (1924) and George Kelly's "Craig's Wife" (1925), sniped away at smug conventions and the gospel of success. Displaying a more individual bent, Eugene O'Neill ceaselessly experimented with dramatic forms and technical devices and usually built his plots about primitive or repressed personalities. Though his reach often exceeded his grasp, "The Emperor Jones" (1920), "Anna Christie" (1921), "Desire under the Elms" (1924) and other of his efforts were accounted among the best plays of the decade.

A grimmer spirit pervaded the stage in the 1930's, however. Like the politicians, novelists and others, the dramatist thrust his searchlight into the sunless crevices of society, reporting his results in such plays as Elmer Rice's "Street Scene" (1929), John Howard Lawson's "Success Story" (1932), Clifford Odets's "Waiting for Lefty" (1935) and Maxwell Anderson's "Winterset" (1935). "Tobacco Road" (1933), dramatized by Jack Kirkland from Caldwell's novel of a depraved Southern tenant family, achieved the longest consecutive run in the annals of the American theater.

As in literature, and doubtless for the same reason, history also had its innings. Maxwell Anderson's "Valley Forge" (1934) and Robert Sherwood's "Abe Lincoln in Illinois" (1938) were notable among the dramas that recalled the valiant days of the past. By means of the Federal Theater Project, the WPA provided work for thousands of performers in stock companies, historical pageants, vaudeville units, circuses and puppet shows traveling through every state. Between 1935 and 1939, when Congress discontinued it, the Federal Theater presented over a thousand different plays to a total audience of nearly forty million and helped to develop actors and dramatists who later made good in the commercial theater.

In so far as motion pictures dealt with serious themes, they tended to follow the drifts of interest evidenced in the theater. This was not so apparent in the 1920's when the Hollywood magnates lavished millions on gaudy shows emphasizing crime and sex. The movies had to grow up before they could settle down. But even in that gilded age film plays like "What Price Glory?" (an adaptation from the stage) mirrored the unsentimental attitude toward war, while a host of other productions such as "The Covered Wagon" and "The Iron Horse" afforded veracious glimpses of bygone frontier episodes.

In the next decade, with the depression darkening over the country, Hollywood turned increasingly to contemporary social and economic problems, treating them often in a realistic spirit. Prison abuses, lynching, miscarriages of justice, political knavery and the violation of civil liberties counted heavily among the new subjects. Many of the offerings were picturized from novels and stage plays; and it may be surmised that the screen versions of "Cabin in the Cotton," "Winterset," "The Grapes of Wrath" and the like stimulated the social consciousness of countless persons who were neither book readers nor theatergoers. The emphasis in historical films shifted from incidents to personalities, with the Great Emancipator scoring three times in the "Abraham Lincoln" of Walter Huston (1930), the "Young Mr. Lincoln" of Henry Fonda (1939) and the "Abe Lincoln in Illinois" of Raymond Massey (1939).

As an art form the motion picture steadily grew in stature. The principal innovation was Walt Disney's imaginative achievement in endowing animated cartoons with the semblance of life. Mickey Mouse, Donald Duck and his other creations vied with flesh-and-blood stars for public favor. "Snow White and the Seven Dwarfs," produced in 1938, won critical acclaim as well as showings in forty-one countries. The Metropolitan Art Museum in New York exhibited some of the original water colors, while Harvard, Yale and the University of Southern California accorded their tribute by conferring honorary degrees on the artist.

Physical recreation also intrenched itself more firmly in American life. Though professional baseball and similar games continued to attract immense crowds, more significant was the far greater participation of the rank and file in outdoor sports. In many parts of the land municipalities now provided athletic fields, golf courses, bathing beaches and other facilities for their citizens; and an increasing number of communities employed trained persons to plan and direct recreational activities. The Great Depression vastly expanded the nation's equipment for play since, at a time when more people were idle than ever before, the New Deal spent millions on parks, beaches, tennis courts, baseball diamonds, swimming pools and the like. As never before, the country awakened to the value of sport, for sport itself was becoming democratized.

THE REDISCOVERY OF AMERICA

Amid the currents and countercurrents that marked American life in the twenty years after the First World War, the people were gaining a new appreciation of their country—its spaciousness, its variety, its traditions, its material and spiritual wealth and potentialities. Many influences were responsible, notably the greater ease of travel, the physical reconstruction of the nation undertaken by the New Deal, the widespread interest in natural parks and historic shrines, the increasing concern of writers, scholars and artists with native themes, and a rekindled faith in the American way of life prompted by aggressive totalitarianism abroad.

As the automobile grew progressively inexpensive and easier to operate, it achieved a universality unapproached in any other land. The number of vehicles in use rose from three and a half million in 1916 to ten and a half million in 1921 and to twenty-nine and a half in 1938. At the end of this period the American people owned ten million more motor cars than telephones. To meet the increasing demand for long-distance travel, the general government helped the states to build better highways. The motorist no longer had to fear getting stuck in the mud or to figure out how to avoid "taking the dust" of the driver in front of him, for under the federal aid program the surfaced roads lengthened from three hundred thousand miles in 1916 to a million two hundred thousand in 1940. As further conveniences of travel, service stations, eating places, overnight cabins and tourist camps sprang up in profusion.

At any time after 1925 the whole population might have piled into cars and started off for parts unknown. Five out of every six automobiles were for passenger use. The Americans had always been a migratory folk, and the auto permitted a freedom of movement and independence of choice as well as a cheapness of locomotion which the railroad had greatly restricted. If a person did not have his own car, public busses afforded an acceptable substitute; and if he lacked bus fare, he could join the army of hitchhikers who, in spite of discouraging legislation, freely "thumbed" rides to destinations far and near. Though in the earlier years vacation motoring had been confined to the warmer seasons, the use of closed cars and automobile heaters and the snow-removal activities of state and local communities tended to make it a year-round diversion. In the mid-thirties trailers began to appear on the road. These "homes on wheels," often having no permanent resting place, presently numbered a hundred thousand.

As a consequence of this amazing mobility the people learned about their homeland in a new and vivid way. The country became a vast schoolhouse in which the motor car instead of books served as the instrument of education. The endless ribbons of highway led past pleasant villages and densely packed cities out into the wooded prairies, treeless plains and huge rock-girt mountains. The traveler saw, and perhaps talked with, sheepherders, cotton pickers, cattlemen, miners, strikers, farmers, lumbermen, clam diggers, fruit growers—the myriad folk who made up an America he had scarcely known except by hearsay. He saw people sodden in misery, people drudging at unwelcome tasks, people abounding with ambition and confident in achievement. He perceived that American life was not encompassed by the *Saturday Evening Post,* nor was it fully reflected in the pages of the left-wing weeklies. In the depression years he observed the land and forests being restored by relief workers; electricity carried for the first time to farm homes; bridges, consolidated schools, libraries, hospitals and recreation centers springing up everywhere. By going to Grand Coulee Dam on the Columbia River he beheld the most massive structure ever reared by man and gained a lively sense of the far-reaching human benefits inherent in wise national planning.

Thanks to the enterprise of governmental authorities, historical societies and private philanthropists, the motorist was able to explore the past as well as the present. Perhaps he chose the prehistoric past as recorded in the geological wonders of national parks like Yosemite in California and Mammoth Cave in Kentucky. More often he chose scenes commemorating the trials and triumphs of earlier Americans. After the World War and notably during the New Deal such opportunities multiplied. Famous houses, battlefield sites, ruined forts and similar memorials of bygone days were restored and opened to the public, while historical museums increased many times.

In the Black Hills of South Dakota natural and human history met in Gutzon Borglum's colossal project, begun in 1927, of sculpturing the heads of Washington, Jefferson, Lincoln and Theodore Roosevelt on the granite front of Mt. Rushmore. Notable among purely private undertakings was the rebuilding of Virginia's ancient capital of Williamsburg by John D. Rockefeller, Jr. These visual lessons in American history were eagerly scanned by the people. Between 1933 and 1940 the number annually visiting the nationally maintained parks and shrines alone grew from three million to nearly seventeen.

Even more than the automobile, the airplane abbreviated distances, but as yet relatively few persons owned private machines and those who flew usually did so to reach their destinations in the shortest possible time. Commercial aviation on definite schedules began in the mid-1920's. With less than six thousand passengers in 1926 the number exceeded a million and a half in 1939. Before 1940 regular flying connections had been established with South America, Europe and

Asia. Though the traveler viewed the country only from afar, the swift panorama afforded a new sense of the diversity and interdependence of the nation's life. The airplane also served broader human needs by carrying mail, fighting forest fires, scattering insecticides, locating shipwrecks and performing kindred services.

Just as more and more people were viewing the United States at firsthand, so also they were discovering it anew through the eyes of their artists. As has been seen, novelists, poets, painters, playwrights and even movie writers drew sustenance from the life about them, probing into its many-sidedness and seeking to recapture its historical inheritance. Their temper might be critical or warmly sympathetic, but they rendered the nation and its problems important and meaningful to countless persons who had never cared to look beyond their own doors. New scholarly biographies, notably of Washington, Jackson and Lincoln, found eager readers, while such works as the Beards' *Rise of American Civilization* (1927) and James Truslow Adams's *Epic of America* (1931) attained the best-seller class.

At the same time, scholars in all parts of the country undertook elaborate investigations of American folklore, folk songs and folk speech, whether of cowboys, mountaineers, lumbermen or sailors; and the interest in colonial furniture became a passion, stripping old dwellings of their belongings and making the manufacture of "modern antiques" a thriving business. On the radio, portrayals of scenes of early bravery proved increasingly popular, while advertisers, catching the spirit of the times, garnished their offerings with historical pictures and allusions. In 1935 the United States government made up for past negligence by establishing the National Archives in Washington as a general depository for its historical records, and a few years later the Post Office Depart-

ment added its contribution in a series of stamps commemorating "Famous Americans" in nonpolitical fields of
achievement.[1] The average citizen was becoming conscious of
his homeland as never before: its past struggles, its accomplishments, its frustrations and its hopes for the future.

All such tendencies were strengthened and sharpened by
the rise of dictatorships abroad and the onset of the Second
World War. As the totalitarian powers snuffed out freedom
in one country after another, the American people reëxam-
ined their heritage and found it precious beyond price. The
"infant republic," as orators used to call it, had survived
three French republics. Empires had perished and bloody
revolutions been fought in many lands while the political institutions of the United States, maturing through a hundred
and sixty years, had adapted themselves to successive shocks
of war, internal dissension and social change. If democracy
at work had not always lived up to its promise, it was clear
that the fault lay not with the system, but with those who
operated and controlled it. In a spirit of fresh dedication to
American ideals the people realized that they need never despair of achieving their fondest dreams so long as men retained the liberty to think, to express themselves as they saw
fit and to apply their energies for the common good.

[1] Probably few citizens could identify all the persons selected, but this in
itself proved an incentive to a greater knowledge of the country's past. The
"Famous Americans" were Washington Irving, James Fenimore Cooper, Ralph
Waldo Emerson, Louisa May Alcott and Mark Twain in prose; Henry Wads-
worth Longfellow, John Greenleaf Whittier, James Russell Lowell, Walt
Whitman and James Whitcomb Riley in poetry; Horace Mann, Mark Hop-
kins, Charles W. Eliot, Frances E. Willard and Booker T. Washington in edu-
cation; John James Audubon, Crawford W. Long, Luther Burbank, Walter
Reed and Jane Addams in science; Stephen Collins Foster, John Philip Sousa,
Victor Herbert, Edward A. MacDowell and Ethelbert Nevin in music; Gilbert
Stuart, James A. McNeill Whistler, Frederic Remington, Augustus Saint-
Gaudens and Daniel Chester French in fine arts; and Eli Whitney, Samuel
F. B. Morse, Cyrus H. McCormick, Elias Howe and Alexander Graham Bell
in invention.

SELECT BIBLIOGRAPHY

The Old Order Changeth. Thompson and Whelpton, *Population Trends*, Committee on Population Problems, *Problems of a Changing Population*, and Odum and Moore, *American Regionalism*, are general surveys. The rôle of the city is further clarified in Urbanism Committee, *Our Cities;* McKenzie, *Metropolitan Community;* Lively and Taeuber, *Rural Migration;* and Vreeland and Fitzgerald, *Farm-City Migration.* For changes in municipal administration Stone and others, *City Manager Government*, and Adams, *Outline of Town and City Planning*, are helpful.

New Directions of Humanitarian Reform. For a conspectus of public and private welfare activities, see President's Research Committee, *Recent Social Trends.* Harrison and Laine, *After Repeal*, summarizes state and local regulations of the liquor traffic. The changing attitude toward Indian relations may be followed in Meriam and others, *Problem of Indian Administration;* Schmeckebier, *Office of Indian Affairs;* Kinney, *Continent Lost;* and La Farge and Post, *As Long as the Grass Shall Grow.* Sweet, *Story of Religions*, and Shipley, *War on Modern Science*, touch on recent religious conditions.

Intellectual, Artistic and Leisure-Time Interests. Information on these matters may be gained from *Recent Social Trends;* Allen, *Only Yesterday*, and *Since Yesterday;* Beards, *America in Midpassage;* Slosson, *Great Crusade and After;* and Sullivan, *Our Times*, VI. For the agencies of mass communication and amusement, consult Lee, *Daily Newspaper in America;* Goldsmith and Lescarboura, *This Thing Called Broadcasting;* Schubert, *Electric Word: the Rise of Radio;* Jacobs, *Rise of the American film;* and Thorp, *America at the Movies.* Varied aspects of the new rôle of propaganda are considered in Sellin and Young, eds., *Pressure Groups and Propaganda.*

Recent literary developments are examined in Van Doren, *American Novel;* Hartwick, *Foreground of American Fiction;* and Cowley, ed., *After the Genteel Tradition.* A different approach concerns Waples, *Social Aspects of Reading in the Depression.* Higher education and productive scholarship are treated in Butts, *The College Charts Its Course*, and Ogg, *Research in the Humanistic and Social Sciences.* The cultural contribution of the enforced migration from Europe is suggested in Fields, *Refugee in the United States.* The following works deal more specifically with the arts and their social implications: Duffus and Keppel, *Arts in American Life;* Cheney, *Modern Art in America;* Zanzig, *Music in American Life;* Grant and Hettinger, *America's Symphony Orchestras;* Krutch, *American Drama since 1918;* Overmyer, *Government and the Arts;* Whitman, *Bread and Circuses,* concerned with the Federal Theater; and Baker, *Government Aid during the Depression to Professional, Technical and Other Service Workers.* Dulles, *America Learns to Play,* is helpful for sports and amusements.

APPENDIX

APPENDIX

CONSTITUTION OF THE UNITED STATES

We The People of the United States, in Order to form a more perfect Union, establish Justice, insure domestic Tranquillity, provide for the common defence, promote the general Welfare, and secure the Blessings of Liberty to ourselves and our Posterity, do ordain and establish this CONSTITUTION for the United States of America.

ARTICLE I

Section 1. All legislative Powers herein granted shall be vested in a Congress of the United States, which shall consist of a Senate and a House of Representatives.

Section 2. The House of Representatives shall be composed of Members chosen every second Year by the People of the several States, and the Electors in each State shall have the Qualifications requisite for Electors of the most numerous Branch of the State Legislature.

No Person shall be a Representative who shall not have attained to the Age of twenty-five Years, and been seven Years a Citizen of the United States, and who shall not, when elected, be an Inhabitant of that State in which he shall be chosen.

Representatives and direct Taxes shall be apportioned among the several States which may be included within this Union, according to their respective Numbers, which shall be determined by adding to the whole Number of free Persons, including those bound to Service for a Term of Years, and excluding Indians not taxed, three fifths of all other Persons. The actual Enumeration shall be made within three Years after the first Meeting of the Congress of the United States, and within every subsequent Term of ten Years, in such Manner as they shall by Law direct. The Number of Representatives shall not exceed one for every thirty Thousand, but each State shall have at Least one Representative; and until such enumeration shall be made, the State of New Hampshire shall be entitled to chuse three, Massachusetts eight, Rhode-Island and Providence Plantations one, Connecticut five, New-York six, New Jersey four, Pennsylvania eight, Delaware one, Maryland six, Virginia ten, North Carolina five, South Carolina five, and Georgia three.

When vacancies happen in the Representation from any State, the Executive Authority thereof shall issue Writs of Election to fill such Vacancies.

The House of Representatives shall chuse their Speaker and other Officers; and shall have the sole Power of Impeachment.

Section 3. The Senate of the United States shall be composed of two Senators from each State, chosen by the Legislature thereof, for six Years, and each Senator shall have one Vote.

Immediately after they shall be assembled in Consequence of the first Election, they shall be divided as equally as may be into three Classes. The Seats of the Senators of the first Class shall be vacated at the Expiration of the second Year, of the second Class at the Expiration of the fourth Year, and of the third Class at the Expiration of the sixth Year, so that one-third may be chosen every second Year; and if Vacancies happen by Resignation, or otherwise, during the Recess of the Legislature of any State, the Executive thereof may make temporary Appointments until the next Meeting of the Legislature, which shall then fill such Vacancies.

No Person shall be a Senator who shall not have attained to the Age of thirty Years, and been nine Years a Citizen of the United States, and who shall not, when elected, be an Inhabitant of that State for which he shall be chosen.

The Vice President of the United States shall be President of the Senate, but shall have no Vote, unless they be equally divided.

The Senate shall chuse their other Officers, and also a President pro tempore, in the Absence of the Vice President, or when he shall exercise the Office of President of the United States.

The Senate shall have the sole Power to try all Impeachments. When sitting for that Purpose, they shall be on Oath or Affirmation. When the President of the United States is tried, the Chief

Justice shall preside: And no Person shall be convicted without the Concurrence of two thirds of the Members present.

Judgment in Cases of Impeachment shall not extend further than to removal from Office, and disqualification to hold and enjoy any Office of honor, Trust or Profit under the United States: but the Party convicted shall nevertheless be liable and subject to Indictment, Trial, Judgment and Punishment, according to Law.

Section 4. The Times, Places and Manner of holding Elections for Senators and Representatives, shall be prescribed in each State by the Legislature thereof; but the Congress may at any time by Law make or alter such Regulations, except as to the Places of chusing Senators.

The Congress shall assemble at least once in every Year, and such Meeting shall be on the first Monday in December, unless they shall by Law appoint a different Day.

Section 5. Each House shall be the Judge of the Elections, Returns and Qualifications of its own Members, and a Majority of each shall constitute a Quorum to do Business; but a smaller Number may adjourn from day to day, and may be authorized to compel the Attendance of absent Members, in such Manner, and under such Penalties as each House may provide.

Each House may determine the Rules of its Proceedings, punish its Members for disorderly Behavior, and, with the Concurrence of two thirds, expel a Member.

Each House shall keep a Journal of its Proceedings, and from time to time publish the same, excepting such Parts as may in their Judgment require Secrecy; and the Yeas and Nays of the Members of either House on any question shall, at the Desire of one fifth of those present, be entered on the Journal.

Neither House, during the Session of Congress, shall, without the Consent of the other, adjourn for more than three days, nor to any other Place than that in which the two Houses shall be sitting.

Section 6. The Senators and Representatives shall receive a Compensation for their Services, to be ascertained by Law, and paid out of the Treasury of the United States. They shall in all Cases, except Treason, Felony and Breach of the Peace, be privileged from Arrest during their Attendance at the Session of their respective Houses, and in going to and returning from the same; and for any Speech or Debate in either House, they shall not be questioned in any other Place.

No Senator or Representative shall, during the Time for which he was elected, be appointed to any civil Office under the Authority of the United States, which shall have been created, or the Emoluments whereof shall have been encreased during such time; and no Person holding any Office under the United States, shall be a Member of either House during his Continuance in Office.

Section 7. All Bills for raising Revenue shall originate in the House of Representatives; but the Senate may propose or concur with Amendments as on other Bills.

Every Bill which shall have passed the House of Representatives and the Senate, shall, before it become a Law, be presented to the President of the United States; If he approve he shall sign it, but if not he shall return it, with his Objections to that House in which it shall have originated, who shall enter the Objections at large on their Journal, and proceed to reconsider it. If after such Reconsideration two thirds of that House shall agree to pass the Bill, it shall be sent, together with the Objections, to the other House, by which it shall likewise be reconsidered, and if approved by two thirds of that House, it shall become a Law. But in all such Cases the Votes of both Houses shall be determined by Yeas and Nays, and the Names of the Persons voting for and against the Bill shall be entered on the Journal of each House respectively. If any Bill shall not be returned by the President within ten Days (Sundays excepted) after it shall have been presented to him, the Same shall be a Law, in like Manner as if he had signed it, unless the Congress by their Adjournment prevent its Return, in which Case it shall not be a Law.

Every Order, Resolution, or Vote to which the Concurrence of the Senate and House of Representatives may be necessary (except on a question of Adjournment) shall be presented to the President of the United States; and before the Same shall take Effect, shall be approved by him, or being disapproved by him, shall be repassed by two thirds of the Senate and House of Representatives, according to the Rules and Limitations prescribed in the Case of a Bill.

Section 8. The Congress shall have Power To lay and collect Taxes, Duties, Imposts and Excises, to pay the Debts and provide for the common Defence and general Welfare of the United States; but all Duties, Imposts and Excises shall be uniform throughout the United States;

To borrow Money on the credit of the United States;

To regulate Commerce with foreign Nations, and among the several States, and with the Indian Tribes;

To establish an uniform Rule of Naturalization, and uniform Laws on the subject of Bankruptcies throughout the United States;

To coin Money, regulate the Value thereof, and of foreign Coin, and fix the Standard of Weights and Measures;

To provide for the Punishment of counterfeiting the Securities and current Coin of the United States;

To establish Post Offices and post Roads;

To promote the Progress of Science and useful Arts, by securing for limited Times to Authors and Inventors the exclusive Right to their respective Writings and Discoveries;

To constitute Tribunals inferior to the supreme Court;

To define and punish Piracies and Felonies committed on the high Seas, and Offences against the Law of Nations;

To declare War, grant Letters of Marque and Reprisal, and make Rules concerning Captures on Land and Water;

To raise and support Armies, but no Appropriation of Money to that Use shall be for a longer Term than two Years;

To provide and maintain a Navy;

To make Rules for the Government and Regulation of the land and naval Forces;

To provide for calling forth the Militia to execute the Laws of the Union, suppress Insurrections and repel Invasions;

To provide for organizing, arming, and disciplining the Militia, and for governing such Part of them as may be employed in the Service of the United States, reserving to the States respectively, the Appointment of the Officers, and the Authority of training the Militia according to the discipline prescribed by Congress;

To exercise exclusive Legislation in all Cases whatsoever, over such District (not exceeding ten Miles square) as may, by Cession of particular States, and the Acceptance of Congress, become the Seat of the Government of the United States, and to exercise like Authority over all Places purchased by the Consent of the Legislature of the State in which the Same shall be, for the Erection

of Forts, Magazines, Arsenals, dock-Yards, and other needful
Buildings;—And

To make all Laws which shall be necessary and proper for
carrying into Execution the foregoing Powers, and all other
Powers vested by this Constitution in the Government of the
United States, or in any Department or Officer thereof.

Section 9. The Migration or Importation of such Persons as
any of the States now existing shall think proper to admit, shall
not be prohibited by the Congress prior to the Year one thousand
eight hundred and eight, but a Tax or duty may be imposed on
such Importation, not exceeding ten dollars for each Person.

The Privilege of the Writ of Habeas Corpus shall not be sus-
pended, unless when in Cases of Rebellion or Invasion the public
Safety may require it.

No Bill of Attainder or ex post facto Law shall be passed.

No Capitation, or other direct, tax shall be laid, unless in
Proportion to the Census or Enumeration herein before directed
to be taken.

No Tax or Duty shall be laid on Articles exported from any
State.

No Preference shall be given by any Regulation of Commerce
or Revenue to the Ports of one State over those of another: nor
shall Vessels bound to, or from, one State, be obliged to enter,
clear, or pay Duties in another.

No Money shall be drawn from the Treasury, but in Consequence of Appropriations made by Law; and a regular Statement
and Account of the Receipts and Expenditures of all public
Money shall be published from time to time.

No Title of Nobility shall be granted by the United States:
And no Person holding any Office of Profit or Trust under them,
shall, without the Consent of the Congress, accept of any present,
Emolument, Office, or Title, of any kind whatever, from any
King, Prince, or foreign State.

Section 10. No State shall enter into any Treaty, Alliance, or
Confederation; grant Letters of Marque and Reprisal; coin
Money; emit Bills of Credit; make any Thing but gold and sil-
ver Coin a Tender in Payment of Debts; pass any Bill of At-
tainder, ex post facto Law, or Law impairing the Obligation of
Contracts, or grant any Title of Nobility.

No State shall, without the Consent of the Congress, lay any

Imposts or Duties on Imports or Exports, except what may be absolutely necessary for executing it's inspection Laws: and the net Produce of all Duties and Imposts, laid by any State on Imports or Exports, shall be for the Use of the Treasury of the United States; and all such Laws shall be subject to the Revision and Control of the Congress.

No State shall, without the Consent of Congress, lay any Duty of Tonnage, keep Troops, or Ships of War in time of Peace, enter into any Agreement or Compact with another State, or with a foreign Power, or engage in War, unless actually invaded, or in such imminent Danger as will not admit of delay.

ARTICLE II

Section 1. The executive Power shall be vested in a President of the United States of America. He shall hold his Office during the Term of four Years, and, together with the Vice President, chosen for the same Term, be elected, as follows

Each State shall appoint, in such Manner as the Legislature thereof may direct, a Number of Electors, equal to the whole Number of Senators and Representatives to which the State may be entitled in the Congress: but no Senator or Representative, or Person holding an Office of Trust or Profit under the United States, shall be appointed an Elector.

The electors shall meet in their respective States, and vote by ballot for two Persons, of whom one at least shall not be an Inhabitant of the same State with themselves. And they shall make a List of all the Persons voted for, and of the Number of Votes for each; which List they shall sign and certify, and transmit sealed to the Seat of the Government of the United States, directed to the President of the Senate. The President of the Senate shall, in the Presence of the Senate and House of Representatives, open all the Certificates, and the Votes shall then be counted. The Person having the greatest Number of Votes shall be the President, if such Number be a Majority of the whole Number of Electors appointed; and if there be more than one who have such Majority, and have an equal Number of Votes, then the House of Representatives shall immediately chuse by Ballot one of them for President; and if no Person have a Majority, then from the five highest on the List the said House shall in like Manner chuse the President. But in chusing the President, the Votes shall be taken by States, the Representation from each State having one Vote; A quorum for this Purpose shall consist of a Member or Members from two-thirds of the States, and a Majority of all the States shall be necessary to a Choice. In every Case, after the Choice of the President, the Person having the greatest Number of Votes of the Electors shall be the Vice President. But if there should remain two or more who have equal Votes, the Senate shall chuse from them by Ballot the Vice-President.

The Congress may determine the Time of chusing the Electors, and the Day on which they shall give their Votes; which Day shall be the same throughout the United States.

No Person except a natural born Citizen, or a Citizen of the United States, at the time of the Adoption of this Constitution, shall be eligible to the Office of President; neither shall any Person be eligible to that Office who shall not have attained to the Age of thirty five Years, and been fourteen Years a Resident within the United States.

In Case of the Removal of the President from Office, or of his Death, Resignation or Inability to discharge the Powers and Duties of the said Office, the same shall devolve on the Vice President, and the Congress may by Law provide for the Case of Removal, Death, Resignation or Inability, both of the President and Vice President, declaring what Officer shall then act as President, and such Officer shall act accordingly, until the Disability be removed, or a President shall be elected.

The President shall, at stated Times, receive for his Services, a Compensation, which shall neither be encreased nor diminished during the Period for which he shall have been elected, and he shall not receive within that Period any other Emolument from the United States, or any of them.

Before he enter on the Execution of his Office, he shall take the following Oath or Affirmation:—"I do solemnly swear (or affirm) that I will faithfully execute the Office of President of the United States, and will to the best of my Ability, preserve, protect and defend the Constitution of the United States."

Section 2. The President shall be Commander in Chief of the Army and Navy of the United States, and of the Militia of the several States, when called into the actual Service of the United

States; he may require the Opinion, in writing, of the principal Officer in each of the executive Departments, upon any Subject relating to the Duties of their respective Offices, and he shall have Power to grant Reprieves and Pardons for Offences against the United States, except in Cases of Impeachment.

He shall have Power, by and with the Advice and Consent of the Senate, to make Treaties, provided two thirds of the Senators present concur; and he shall nominate, and by and with the Advice and Consent of the Senate, shall appoint Ambassadors, other public Ministers and Consuls, Judges of the supreme Court, and all other Officers of the United States, whose Appointments are not herein otherwise provided for, and which shall be established by Law: but the Congress may by Law vest the Appointment of such inferior Officers, as they think proper, in the President alone, in the Courts of Law, or in the Heads of Departments.

The President shall have Power to fill up all Vacancies that may happen during the Recess of the Senate, by granting Commissions which shall expire at the End of their next Session.

Section 3. He shall from time to time give to the Congress Information of the State of the Union, and recommend to their Consideration such Measures as he shall judge necessary and expedient; he may, on extraordinary Occasions, convene both Houses, or either of them, and, in Case of Disagreement between them, with Respect to the Time of Adjournment, he may adjourn them to such Time as he shall think proper; he shall receive Ambassadors and other public Ministers; he shall take Care that the Laws be faithfully executed, and shall Commission all the Officers of the United States.

Section 4. The President, Vice President and all civil Officers of the United States, shall be removed from Office on Impeachment for, and Conviction of, Treason, Bribery, or other high Crimes and Misdemeanors.

ARTICLE III

Section 1. The judicial Power of the United States, shall be vested in one supreme Court, and in such inferior Courts as the Congress may from time to time ordain and establish. The Judges, both of the supreme and inferior Courts, shall hold their Offices during good Behavior. and shall, at stated Times, receive for their Services, a Compensation, which shall not be diminished during their Continuance in Office.

Section 2. The judicial Power shall extend to all Cases, in Law and Equity, arising under this Constitution, the Laws of the United States, and Treaties made, or which shall be made, under their Authority;—to all Cases affecting Ambassadors, other public Ministers and Consuls;—to all Cases of admiralty and maritime Jurisdiction;—to Controversies to which the United States shall be a Party;—to Controversies between two or more States;—between a State and Citizens of another State;—between Citizens of different States,—between Citizens of the same State claiming Lands under Grants of different States, and between a State, or the Citizens thereof, and foreign States, Citizens or Subjects.

In all Cases affecting Ambassadors, other public Ministers and Consuls, and those in which a State shall be Party, the supreme Court shall have original Jurisdiction. In all the other Cases before mentioned, the supreme Court shall have appellate Jurisdiction, both as to Law and Fact, with such Exceptions, and under such Regulations as the Congress shall make.

The Trial of all Crimes, except in Cases of Impeachment, shall be by Jury; and such Trial shall be held in the State where the said Crimes shall have been committed; but when not committed within any State, the Trial shall be at such Place or Places as the Congress may by Law have directed.

Section 3. Treason against the United States, shall consist only in levying War against them, or in adhering to their Enemies, giving them Aid and Comfort. No Person shall be convicted of Treason unless on the Testimony of two Witnesses to the same overt Act, or on Confession in open Court.

The Congress shall have Power to declare the Punishment of Treason, but no Attainder of Treason shall work Corruption of Blood, or Forfeiture except during the Life of the Person attainted.

ARTICLE IV

Section 1. Full Faith and Credit shall be given in each State to the public Acts, Records, and judicial Proceedings of every other State. And the Congress may by general Laws prescribe the Manner in which such Acts, Records and Proceedings shall be proved, and the Effect thereof.

Section 2. The Citizens of each State shall be entitled to all Privileges and Immunities of Citizens in the several States.

A person charged in any State with Treason, Felony, or other Crime, who shall flee from Justice, and be found in another State, shall on Demand of the executive Authority of the State from which he fled, be delivered up to be removed to the State having Jurisdiction of the Crime.

No Person held to Service or Labour in one State, under the Laws thereof, escaping into another, shall, in Consequence of any Law or Regulation therein, be discharged from such Service or Labour, but shall be delivered up on Claim of the Party to whom such Service or Labour may be due.

Section 3. New States may be admitted by the Congress into this Union; but no new State shall be formed or erected within the Jurisdiction of any other State; nor any State be formed by the Junction of two or more States, or Parts of States, without the Consent of the Legislatures of the States concerned as well as of the Congress.

The Congress shall have Power to dispose of and make all needful Rules and Regulations respecting the Territory or other Property belonging to the United States; and nothing in this Constitution shall be so construed as to Prejudice any Claims of the United States, or of any particular State.

Section 4. The United States shall guarantee to every State in this Union a Republican Form of Government, and shall protect each of them against Invasion; and on Application of the Legislature, or of the Executive (when the Legislature cannot be convened) against domestic Violence.

ARTICLE V

The Congress, whenever two thirds of both Houses shall deem it necessary, shall propose Amendments to this Constitution, or, on the Application of the Legislatures of two thirds of the several States, shall call a Convention for proposing Amendments, which, in either Case, shall be valid to all Intents and Purposes, as Part of this Constitution, when ratified by the Legislatures of three fourths of the several States, or by Conventions in three fourths thereof, as the one or the other Mode of Ratification may be proposed by the Congress; Provided that no Amendment which may be made prior to the Year One thousand eight hundred and eight shall in any Manner affect the first and fourth Clauses in the Ninth Section of the first Article; and that no State, without its Consent, shall be deprived of its equal Suffrage in the Senate.

ARTICLE VI

All Debts contracted and Engagements entered into, before the Adoption of this Constitution, shall be as valid against the United States under this Constitution, as under the Confederation.

This Constitution, and the Laws of the United States which shall be made in Pursuance thereof; and all Treaties made, or which shall be made, under the Authority of the United States, shall be the supreme Law of the Land; and the Judges in every State shall be bound thereby, any Thing in the Constitution or Laws of any State to the Contrary notwithstanding.

The Senators and Representatives before mentioned, and the Members of the several State Legislatures, and all executive and judicial Officers, both of the United States and of the several States, shall be bound by Oath or Affirmation, to support this Constitution; but no religious Test shall ever be required as a Qualification to any Office or public Trust under the United States.

ARTICLE VII

The Ratification of the Conventions of nine States, shall be sufficient for the Establishment of this Constitution between the States so ratifying the Same.

DONE in Convention by the Unanimous Consent of the States present the Seventeenth Day of September in the Year of our Lord one thousand seven hundred and Eighty seven, and of the Independence of the United States of America the Twelfth.

ARTICLES IN ADDITION TO, AND AMENDMENT OF, THE CONSTITUTION OF THE UNITED STATES OF AMERICA, PROPOSED BY CONGRESS, AND RATIFIED BY THE LEGISLATURES OF THE SEVERAL STATES PURSUANT TO THE FIFTH ARTICLE OF THE ORIGINAL CONSTITUTION.

ARTICLE I

(The first ten Articles declared in force December 15, 1791)

Congress shall make no law respecting an establishment of religion, or prohibiting the free exercise thereof; or abridging the freedom of speech, or of the press; or the right of the people peaceably to assemble, and to petition the Government for a redress of grievances.

ARTICLE II

A well regulated Militia, being necessary to the security of a free State, the right of the people to keep and bear Arms, shall not be infringed.

ARTICLE III

No Soldier shall, in time of peace, be quartered in any house, without the consent of the Owner, nor in time of war, but in a manner to be prescribed by law.

ARTICLE IV

The right of the people to be secure in their persons, houses, papers, and effects, against unreasonable searches and seizures, shall not be violated, and no Warrants shall issue, but upon probable cause, supported by Oath or affirmation, and particularly describing the place to be searched, and the persons or things to be seized.

ARTICLE V

No person shall be held to answer for a capital, or otherwise infamous crime, unless on a presentment or indictment of a Grand Jury, except in cases arising in the land or naval forces, or in the Militia, when in actual service in time of War or public danger; nor shall any person be subject for the same offence to be twice put in jeopardy of life or limb; nor shall be compelled in any Criminal Case to be a witness against himself, nor be deprived of life, liberty, or property, without due process of law; nor shall private property be taken for public use, without just compensation.

ARTICLE VI

In all criminal prosecutions, the accused shall enjoy the right to a speedy and public trial, by an impartial jury of the State and district wherein the crime shall have been committed, which district shall have been previously ascertained by law, and to be informed of the nature and cause of the accusation; to be confronted with the witnesses against him; to have compulsory process for obtaining Witnesses in his favor, and to have the Assistance of Counsel for his defence.

ARTICLE VII

In suits at common law, where the value in controversy shall exceed twenty dollars, the right of trial by jury shall be preserved, and no fact tried by a jury shall be otherwise re-examined in any Court of the United States, than according to the rules of the common law.

ARTICLE VIII

Excessive bail shall not be required, nor excessive fines imposed, nor cruel and unusual punishments inflicted.

ARTICLE IX

The enumeration in the Constitution, of certain rights, shall not be construed to deny or disparage others retained by the people.

ARTICLE X

The powers not delegated to the United States by the Constitution, nor prohibited by it to the States, are reserved to the States respectively, or to the people.

ARTICLE XI

(*January 8, 1798*)

The Judicial power of the United States shall not be construed to extend to any suit in law or equity, commenced or prosecuted against one of the United States by Citizens of another State, or by Citizens or Subjects of any Foreign State.

ARTICLE XII

(*September 25, 1804*)

The Electors shall meet in their respective states, and vote by ballot for President and Vice-President, one of whom, at least, shall not be an inhabitant of the same state with themselves; they shall name in their ballots the person voted for as President, and in distinct ballots the person voted for as Vice-President, and they shall make distinct lists of all persons voted for as President, and of all persons voted for as Vice-President, and of the number of votes for each, which lists they shall sign and certify, and transmit sealed to the seat of the Government of the United States, directed to the President of the Senate;—The President of the Senate shall, in the presence of the Senate and House of Representatives, open all the certificates and the votes shall then be counted;—The person having the greatest number of votes for President, shall be the President, if such number be a majority of the whole number of Electors appointed; and if no person have such majority, then from the persons having the highest numbers not exceeding three on the list of those voted for as President, the House of Representatives shall choose immediately, by ballot, the President. But in choosing the President, the votes shall be taken by states, the representation from each state having one vote; a quorum for this purpose shall consist of a member or members from two-thirds of the states, and a majority of all the states shall be necessary to a choice. And if the House of Representatives shall not choose a President whenever the right of choice shall devolve upon them, before the fourth day of March next following, then the Vice-President shall act as President, as in the case of the death or other constitutional disability of the President. The person having the greatest number of votes as Vice-President, shall be the Vice-President, if such number be a majority of the whole number of Electors appointed, and if no person have a majority, then from the two highest numbers on the list, the Senate shall choose the Vice-President; a quorum for the purpose shall consist of two-thirds of the whole number of Senators, and a majority of whole number shall be necessary to a choice. But no person constitutionally ineligible to the office of President shall be eligible to that of Vice-President of the United States.

ARTICLE XIII

(*December 18, 1865*)

Section 1. Neither slavery nor involuntary servitude, except as a punishment for crime whereof the party shall have been duly convicted, shall exist within the United States, or any place subject to their jurisdiction.

Section 2. Congress shall have power to enforce this article by appropriate legislation.

ARTICLE XIV

(*July 23, 1868*)

Section 1. All persons born or naturalized in the United States, and subject to the jurisdiction thereof, are citizens of the United States and of the State wherein they reside. No State shall make or enforce any law which shall abridge the privileges or immunities of citizens of the United States; nor shall any State deprive any person of life, liberty, or property, without due process of law; nor deny to any person within its jurisdiction the equal protection of the laws.

Section 2. Representatives shall be apportioned among the several States according to their respective numbers, counting the whole number of persons in each State, excluding Indians not taxed. But when the right to vote at any election for the choice of electors for President and Vice President of the United States, Representatives in Congress, the Executive and Judicial officers of a State, or the members of the Legislature thereof, is denied to any of the male inhabitants of such State, being twenty-one years of age, and citizens of the United States, or in any way abridged, except for participation in rebellion, or other crime, the basis of representation therein shall be reduced in the proportion which the number of such male citizens shall bear to the whole number of male citizens twenty-one years of age in such State.

Section 3. No person shall be a Senator or Representative in Congress, or elector of President and Vice President, or hold any office, civil, or military, under the United States, or under any State, who, having previously taken an oath, as a member of Congress, or as an officer of the United States, or as a member of any State legislature, or as an executive or judicial officer of any State, to support the Constitution of the United States, shall have engaged in insurrection or rebellion against the same, or given aid or comfort to the enemies thereof. But Congress may by a vote of two-thirds of each House, remove such disability.

Section 4. The validity of the public debt of the United States, authorized by law, including debts incurred for payment of pensions and bounties for services in suppressing insurrection or rebellion, shall not be questioned. But neither the United States nor any State shall assume or pay any debt or obligation incurred in aid of insurrection or rebellion against the United States, or any claim for the loss or emancipation of any slave; but all such debts, obligations and claims shall be held illegal and void.

Section 5. The Congress shall have power to enforce, by appropriate legislation, the provisions of this article.

ARTICLE XV

(March 30, 1870)

Section 1. The right of citizens of the United States to vote shall not be denied or abridged by the United States or by any State on account of race, color, or previous condition of servitude.

Section 2. The Congress shall have power to enforce this article by appropriate legislation.

ARTICLE XVI

(February 25, 1913)

The Congress shall have power to lay and collect taxes on incomes, from whatever source derived, without apportionment among the several States, and without regard to any census or enumeration.

ARTICLE XVII

(May 31, 1913)

The Senate of the United States shall be composed of two senators from each State, elected by the people thereof, for six years; and each Senator shall have one vote. The electors in each State shall have the qualifications requisite for electors of the most numerous branch of the State legislature.

When vacancies happen in the representation of any State in the Senate, the executive authority of such State shall issue writs of election to fill such vacancies: *Provided,* That the legislature of any State may empower the executive thereof to make temporary appointments until the people fill the vacancies by election as the legislature may direct.

This amendment shall not be so construed as to affect the election or term of any senator chosen before it becomes valid as part of the Constitution.

ARTICLE XVIII

(January 16, 1920)

After one year from the ratification of this article, the manufacture, sale, or transportation of intoxicating liquors within, the importation thereof into, or the exportation thereof from the United States and all territory subject to the jurisdiction thereof for beverage purposes is hereby prohibited.

The Congress and the several States shall have concurrent power to enforce this article by appropriate legislation.

This article shall be inoperative unless it shall have been ratified as an amendment to the Constitution by the legislatures of the several States, as provided in the Constitution, within seven years from the date of the submission hereof to the States by Congress.

ARTICLE XIX

(August 26, 1920)

The right of citizens of the United States to vote shall not be denied or abridged by the United States or by any States on account of sex.

The Congress shall have power by appropriate legislation to enforce the provisions of this article.

ARTICLE XX

(February 6, 1933)

Section 1. The terms of the President and Vice-President shall end at noon on the twentieth day of January, and the terms of Senators and Representatives at noon on the third day of January, of the years in which such terms would have ended if this article had not been ratified; and the terms of their successors shall then begin.

Section 2. The Congress shall assemble at least once in every year, and such meeting shall begin at noon on the third day of January, unless they shall by law appoint a different day.

Section 3. If, at the time fixed for the beginning of the term of the President, the President-elect shall have died, the Vice-President-elect shall become President. If a President shall not have been chosen before the time fixed for the beginning of his term, or if the President-elect shall have failed to qualify, then the Vice-President-elect shall act as President until a President shall have qualified; and the Congress may by law provide for the case wherein neither a President-elect nor a Vice-President-elect shall have qualified, declaring who shall then act as President, or the manner in which one who is to act shall be selected, and such person shall act accordingly until a President or Vice-President shall have qualified.

Section 4. The Congress may by law provide for the case of the death of any of the persons from whom the House of Representatives may choose a President whenever the right of choice shall have devolved upon them, and for the case of the death of any of the persons from whom the Senate may choose a Vice-President whenever the right of choice shall have devolved upon them.

Section 5. Sections 1 and 2 shall take effect on the 15th day of October following the ratification of this article.

Section 6. This article shall be inoperative unless it shall have been ratified as an amendment to the Constitution by the legislatures of three-fourths of the several States within seven years from the date of its submission.

ARTICLE XXI

(December 5, 1933)

Section 1. The eighteenth article of amendment to the Constitution of the United States is hereby repealed.

Section 2. The transportation or importation into any State, Territory or possession of the United States for delivery or use therein of intoxicating liquors, in violation of the laws thereof, is hereby prohibited.

Section 3. This article shall be inoperative unless it shall have been ratified as an amendment to the Constitution by convention in the several States, as provided in the Constitution, within seven years from the date of the submission hereof to the States by the Congress.

LIST OF BOOKS CITED

Abbott, Edith, *Women in Industry*. New York, 1910.

Adams, S. H., *Incredible Era, the Life and Times of Warren Gamaliel Harding*. Boston, 1939.

Adams, Thomas, *Outline of Town and City Planning*. New York, 1935.

Allen, F. J., *The Shoe Industry*. New York, 1916.

Allen, F. L., *The Lords of Creation*. New York, 1935.

——, *Only Yesterday*. New York, 1931.

——, *Since Yesterday*. New York, 1940.

American Crisis Biographies. See Oberholtzer, E. P., ed.

American Nation, The. See Hart, A. B., ed.

American Political Leaders. See Nevins, Allan, ed.

American Statesmen. See Morse, J. T., Jr., ed.

——, 2d ser. 7 v. Boston, 1905–1916.

Andrews, J. C., *Pittsburgh's Post-Gazette*. Boston, 1936.

Arias, Harmodio, *The Panama Canal*. London, 1911.

Armes, Ethel M., *The Story of Coal and Iron in Alabama*. Birmingham, 1910.

Arnett, A. M., *Claude Kitchin and the Wilson War Policies*. Boston, 1937.

——, *The Populist Movement in Georgia* (Columbia University, *Studies*, CIV, no. 1). New York, 1922.

Aronovici, Carol, *Housing the Masses*. New York, 1939.

Ayres, L. P., *The War with Germany*. Washington, 1919.

Bailey, T. A., *A Diplomatic History of the American People*. New York, 1940.

——, *Theodore Roosevelt and the Japanese-American Crises*. Stanford University, 1934.

Baker, Jacob, *Government Aid during the Depression to Professional, Technical and Other Service Workers*. Washington, 1936.

Baker, R. S., *Woodrow Wilson*. 8 v. Garden City, 1927–1939.

Baker, R. S., *Woodrow Wilson and World Settlement.* 3 v. Garden City, 1922.

Balch, Emily G., *Our Slavic Fellow Citizens.* New York, 1910

Barber, H. L., *The Story of the Automobile.* Chicago, 1927.

Barclay, T. S., *The Liberal Republican Movement in Missouri, 1865–1871.* Columbia, 1926.

Barnard, Harry, *"Eagle Forgotten"; the Life of John Peter Altgeld.* Indianapolis, 1938.

Barnes, H. E., *The New History and the Social Studies.* New York, 1925.

Barnes, J. A., *John G. Carlisle (American Political Leaders).* New York, 1931.

Barrett, D. C., *The Greenbacks and Resumption of Specie Payments, 1862–1879 (Harvard Economic Studies, XXXVI).* Cambridge, 1931.

Barton, W. E., *The Life of Clara Barton.* 2 v. Boston, 1922.

Baruch, B. M., *The Making of the Reparation and Economic Sections of the Treaty.* New York, 1920.

Bates, E. S., *This Land of Liberty.* New York, 1930.

——, and Dittemore, J. V., *Mary Baker Eddy.* New York. 1932.

Beale, H. K., *The Critical Year.* New York, 1930.

Beales, A. C. F., *The History of Peace.* New York, 1931.

Beamish, R. J., and March, F. A., *America's Part in the World War.* Philadelphia, 1919.

Beard, C. A. and Mary R., *America in Midpassage (The Rise of American Civilization, III).* New York, 1939.

Beard, C. A., and Smith, G. H. E., *The Old Deal and the New.* New York, 1940.

Beardsley, F. G., *A History of American Revivals.* New York, 1912.

Bemis, S. F., *A Diplomatic History of the United States.* New York, 1936.

Bennett, I. E., *History of the Panama Canal.* Washington, 1915.

Benton, E. J., *International Law and Diplomacy of the Spanish-American War.* Baltimore, 1908.

Berglund, Abraham, *The United States Steel Corporation* (Columbia University, *Studies*, XXVII, no. 2). New York, 1907.

Berle, A. A., Jr., and Means, G. C., *The Modern Corporation and Private Property*. New York, 1933.

Berman, Edward, *Labor and the Sherman Act*. New York, 1931.

——, *Labor Disputes and the President of the United States* (Columbia University, *Studies*, CXI, no. 2). New York, 1924.

Bing, Alexander, *War-Time Strikes and Their Adjustment*. New York, 1921.

Bishop, J. B., *Theodore Roosevelt and His Time*. 2 v. New York, 1920.

Bisson, T. A., *American Policy in the Far East, 1931–1940* (Institute of Pacific Relations, *Inquiry Series*). New York, 1940.

Black, J. D., *Agricultural Reform in the United States*. New York, 1929.

Blackwell, Alice Stone, *Lucy Stone*. Boston, 1930.

Bleyer, W. G., *Main Currents in the History of American Journalism*. Boston, 1927.

Bogart, E. L., *War Costs and Their Financing*. New York, 1921.

Bonbright, J. C., and Means, G. C., *The Holding Company*. New York, 1932.

Borchard, Edwin, and Lage, W. P., *Neutrality for the United States*. Rev. edn. New Haven, 1940.

Bowers, C. G., *Beveridge and the Progressive Era*. Boston, 1932.

Branch, E. D., *The Cowboy and His Interpreters*. New York, 1926.

——, *The Hunting of the Buffalo*. New York, 1929.

Brandeis, L. D., *Other People's Money*. New York, 1914.

Brawley, B. G., *A Social History of the American Negro*. Rev. edn. New York, 1939.

Briggs, H. E., *Frontiers of the Northwest*. New York, 1940.

Brissenden, P. F., *The I. W. W.: a Study of American Syndicalism* (Columbia University, *Studies*, LXXXIII). New York, 1919.

Brooks, R. P., *The Agrarian Revolution in Georgia, 1865–1912* (University of Wisconsin, *Bulletin* no. 639). Madison, 1914.

Brooks, R. R. R., *Unions of Their Own Choosing*. New Haven, 1939.

Browne, W. R., *Altgeld of Illinois*. New York, 1924.

Bruce, H. A., *Woman in the Making of America*. Rev. edn. Boston, 1928.

Bruce, P. A., *The Rise of the New South* (*The History of North America*, XVII). Philadelphia, 1905.

Bruère, Martha B., *Does Prohibition Work?* New York, 1927.

Bryn-Jones, David, *Frank B. Kellogg*. New York, 1937.

Buck, P. H., *The Road to Reunion, 1865–1900*. Boston, 1937.

Buck, S. J., *The Agrarian Crusade* (*The Chronicles of America Series*, XLV). New Haven, 1920.

——, *The Granger Movement* (*Harvard Historical Studies*, XIX). Cambridge, 1913.

Buell, R. L., *Japanese Immigration* (World Peace Foundation, *Pamphlets*, VII, nos. 5-6). Boston, 1924.

——, *The Washington Conference*. New York, 1922.

Burgess, Thomas, *Greeks in America*. Boston, 1913.

Burlingame, Roger, *Engines of Democracy*. New York, 1940.

Burns, A. E., and Williams, E. A., *A Survey of Relief and Security Programs*. Washington, 1938.

Burr, Anna R., *The Portrait of a Banker: James Stillman*. New York, 1927.

Burton, T. E., *Financial Crises and Periods of Industrial and Commercial Depression*. New York, 1902.

——, *John Sherman*. Boston, 1906.

Butts, R. F., *The College Charts Its Course*. New York, 1939.

Byrn, E. W., *The Progress of Invention in the Nineteenth Century*. New York, 1900.

Cahill, M. C., *Shorter Hours: a Study of the Movement since the Civil War*. New York, 1932.

Calhoun, A. W., *A Social History of the American Family*. 3 v. Cleveland, 1917–1919.

Calkins, Clinch, *Spy Overhead, the Story of Industrial Espionage*. New York, 1937.

Callahan, J. M., *American Foreign Policy in Canadian Relations.* New York, 1937.

——, *American Foreign Policy in Mexican Relations.* New York, 1932.

Callcott, W. H., *Liberalism in Mexico, 1857–1929.* Stanford University, 1931.

Capper, Arthur, *The Agricultural Bloc.* New York, 1922.

Carlton, F. T., *The History and Problems of Organized Labor.* Rev. edn. Boston, 1920.

Cary, Edward, *George William Curtis* (C. D. Warner, ed., *American Men of Letters*). Boston, 1894.

Casson, H. N., *The History of the Telephone.* Chicago, 1910.

Chadwick, F. E., *The Relations of the United States and Spain.* 3 v. New York, 1909–1911.

Chafee, Zechariah, Jr., *Freedom of Speech.* New York, 1920.

Chamberlin, J. E., *The Boston Transcript.* Boston, 1930.

Chambrun, Colonel de, and Marenches, Captain de, *The American Army in the European Conflict.* New York, 1919.

Chandler, J. A. C., and others, *The South in the Building of the Nation.* 12 v. Richmond, 1909–1910.

Chapman, C. E., *A History of the Cuban Republic.* New York, 1927.

Cheney, Martha C., *Modern Art in America.* New York, 1939.

Cherrington, E. H., *The Evolution of Prohibition in the United States of America.* Westerville, 1920.

Chidsey, D. B., *The Gentleman from New York: a Life of Roscoe Conkling.* New Haven, 1935.

Child, C. J., *The German-Americans in Politics, 1914–1917.* Madison, 1939.

Chronicles of America Series, The. See Johnson, Allen, ed.

Clark, D. E., *The West in American History.* New York, 1937.

Clark, G. T., *Leland Stanford.* Stanford University, 1931.

Clark, J. M., *The Costs of the World War to the American People* (J. T. Shotwell, ed., *Economic and Social History of the World War*). New Haven, 1931.

Clark, V. S., *History of Manufactures in the United States* (Carnegie Institution, *Contributions to American Economic History*). Rev. edn. 3 v. New York, 1929.

Clarkson, G. B., *Industrial America in the World War*. Boston, 1923.

Clemen, R. A., *The American Livestock and Meat Industry*. New York, 1923.

Cohen, D. F., *The Good Old Days. A History of American Morals and Manners as Seen through the Sears, Roebuck Catalogues, 1905 to the Present*. New York, 1940.

Cole, A. H., *The American Wool Manufacture*. 2 v. Cambridge, 1926.

Coleman, C. H., *The Election of 1868* (Columbia University, *Studies*, CCCXCII). New York, 1933.

Coleman, J. W., *Labor Disturbances in Pennsylvania, 1850–1880*. Washington, 1936.

Colvin, D. L., *Prohibition in the United States*. New York, 1926.

Committee on Population Problems of the National Resources Committee, *The Problems of a Changing Population*. Washington, 1938.

Committee on Recent Economic Changes, *Recent Economic Changes in the United States*. 2 v. New York, 1929.

Commons, J. R., and others, *History of Labour [Labor] in the United States*. 4 v. New York, 1918–1935.

Coolidge, A. C., *The United States as a World Power*. New York, 1908.

Coolidge, Mary R., *Chinese Immigration*. New York, 1909.

Coon, Horace, *American Tel. & Tel. The Story of a Great Monopoly*. New York, 1939.

Copeland, M. T., *The Cotton Manufacturing Industry of the United States* (*Harvard Economic Studies*, VIII). Cambridge, 1912.

Corey, Herbert, *The Truth about Hoover*. Boston, 1932.

Corey, Lewis, *The House of Morgan*. New York, 1930.

Coulter, E. M., *William G. Brownlow*. Chapel Hill, 1937.

Cowley, Malcolm, ed., *After the Genteel Tradition*. New York, 1937.

Cox, I. J., *Nicaragua and the United States, 1909–1927* (World Peace Foundation, *Pamphlets*, X, no. 7). Boston, 1927.

Crawford, K. G., *The Pressure Boys*. New York, 1939.

Croly, Herbert, *Marcus Alonzo Hanna*. New York, 1912.

Croly, Jane C., *The History of the Woman's Club Movement in America*. New York, 1898.

Crowell, Benedict, and Wilson, R. F., *How America Went to War*. 6 v. New Haven, 1921.

Cubberley, E. P., *Public Education in the United States*. Rev. edn. Boston, 1934.

Curti, M. E., *Bryan and World Peace* (Smith College, *Studies*, XVI, nos. 3-4). Northampton, 1931.

——, *Peace or War; the American Struggle, 1636–1936*. New York, 1936.

——, *The Social Ideas of American Educators* (Commission on the Social Studies, *Report*, X). New York, 1935.

Cutler, J. E., *Lynch-Law*. New York, 1905.

Daggett, Stuart, *Railroad Reorganization* (*Harvard Economic Studies*, IV). Cambridge, 1908.

Dale, E. E., *The Range Cattle Industry*. Norman, 1930.

David, Henry, *The History of the Haymarket Affair*. New York, 1936.

Davis, Elmer, *History of the New York Times*. New York, 1921.

Davis, G. T., *A Navy Second to None*. New York, 1940.

Davison, H. P., *The American Red Cross in the Great War*. New York, 1919.

Dealey, J. Q., *Growth of American State Constitutions*. Boston, 1915.

Dennett, Tyler, *Americans in Eastern Asia*. New York, 1922.

——, *John Hay* (*American Political Leaders*). New York, 1933.

——, *Theodore Roosevelt and the Russo-Japanese War*. Garden City, 1925.

Dennis, A. L. P., *Adventures in American Diplomacy, 1896–1906*. New York, 1928.

DeVoto, Bernard, *Mark Twain's America*. Boston, 1932.

Dewey, D. R., *Financial History of the United States* (A. B. Hart, ed., *American Citizen Series*). Rev. edn. New York, 1931.

——, *National Problems* (*The American Nation*, XXIV). New York, 1907.

DeWitt, B. P., *The Progressive Movement*. New York, 1915.

DeWitt, D. M., *The Impeachment and Trial of Andrew Johnson*. New York, 1903.

Dick, Everett, *The Sod-House Frontier, 1854–1890*. New York, 1937.

Dorfman, Joseph, *Thorstein Veblen and His America*. New York, 1934.

Dougherty, C. R., *Labor under the NRA*. Boston, 1934.

Douglas, P. H., *Social Security in the United States*. Rev. edn. New York, 1939.

Du Bois, W. E. B., *Black Reconstruction*. New York, 1935.

Duffus, R. L., and Keppel, F. P., *The Arts in American Life*. New York, 1932.

Dulles, F. R., *America in the Pacific*. Boston, 1932.

——, *America Learns to Play, a History of Popular Recreation, 1607–1940*. New York, 1940.

Dumond, D. L., *Roosevelt to Roosevelt*. Boston, 1937.

Dunn, F. S., *The Diplomatic Protection of Americans in Mexico*. New York, 1933.

Dunn, R. W., *American Foreign Investments*. New York, 1926.

Dunning, W. A., *Reconstruction Political and Economic* (*The American Nation*, XXII). New York, 1907.

Dyer, Brainerd, *The Public Career of William M. Evarts* (University of California at Los Angeles, *Publications*, II). Berkeley, 1933.

Dyer, F. L., and Martin, T. C., *Edison*. Rev. edn. 2 v. New York, 1929.

Edwards, G. W., *The Evolution of Finance Capitalism*. New York, 1938.

Eisenschiml, Otto, *Why Was Lincoln Murdered?* Boston, 1937.

Epstein, R. C., *The Automobile Industry*. Chicago, 1928.

Evans, M. S., *Black and White in the Southern States*. New York, 1915.

Fairman, Charles, *Mr. Justice Miller and the Supreme Court, 1862–1890*. Cambridge, 1939.

Faris, J. C., *The Rise of Internationalism*. New York, 1915.

Farish, H. D., *The Circuit Rider Dismounts, a Social History of Southern Methodism, 1865–1900*. Richmond, 1938.

Farrar, V. J., *The Annexation of Russian America to the United States*. Washington, 1937.

Faulkner, H. U., *American Economic History* (G. S. Ford, ed., *Harper's Historical Series*). Rev. edn. New York, 1935.

——, *The Quest for Social Justice* (*A History of American Life*, XI). New York, 1931.

Feder, Leah H., *Unemployment Relief in Periods of Depression*. New York, 1936.

Feldman, Herman, *Prohibition, Its Economic and Industrial Aspects*. New York, 1927.

Ferrara, Orestes, *The Last Spanish War* (W. E. Shea, tr.). New York, 1937.

Fields, Harold, *The Refugee Problem in the United States*. New York, 1938.

Filler, Louis, *Crusaders for American Liberalism*. New York, 1939.

Fine, Nathan, *Labor and Farmer Parties in the United States, 1828–1928*. New York, 1928.

Fish, C. R., *The Civil Service and the Patronage* (*Harvard Historical Studies*, XI). Cambridge, 1905.

Fitzgibbon, R. H., *Cuba and the United States, 1900–1935*. Menasha, 1935.

Flack, H. E., *The Adoption of the Fourteenth Amendment*. Baltimore, 1908.

——, *Spanish-American Diplomatic Relations Preceding the War of 1898* (Johns Hopkins University, *Studies*, XXIV, nos. 1-2). Baltimore, 1906.

Fleming, D. F., *The United States and the League of Nations*. New York, 1932.

Fleming, D. F., *The United States and World Organization, 1920–1933.* New York, 1938.

Fleming, W. L., *The Sequel of Appomattox (The Chronicles of America Series,* XXXII). New Haven, 1919.

Flick, A. C., *Samuel Jones Tilden (American Political Leaders).* New York, 1939.

Foerster, R. F., *The Italian Emigration of Our Times (Harvard Economic Studies,* XX). Cambridge, 1919.

Forbes, W. C., *The Philippine Islands.* 2 v. Boston, 1928.

Ford, James, and others, *Slums and Housing with Special Reference to New York City.* 2 v. Cambridge, 1936.

Forrester, R. B., *Report on Large Scale Coöperative Marketing in the United States.* London, 1925.

Fossum, P. R., *The Agrarian Movement in North Dakota* (Johns Hopkins University, *Studies,* XLIII, no. 1). Baltimore, 1925.

Frankfurter, Felix, and Greene, Nathan, *The Labor Injunction.* New York, 1930.

Frothingham, T. G., *The American Reinforcement in the World War.* Garden City, 1927.

Fuess, C. M., *Calvin Coolidge.* Boston, 1940.

——, *Carl Schurz (American Political Leaders).* New York, 1932.

Gabriel, R. H., ed., *The Pageant of America.* 15 v. New Haven, 1925–1929.

Gamio, Manuel, *Mexican Immigration to the United States.* Chicago, 1930.

Garis, R. L., *Immigration Restriction.* New York, 1927.

Garland, Hamlin, *A Son of the Middle Border.* New York, 1917.

Garrison, W. E., *The March of Faith.* New York, 1933.

Gayer, A. D., *Public Works in Prosperity and Depression.* New York, 1935.

Giddens, P. H., *The Birth of the Oil Industry.* New York, 1938.

Gittinger, Roy, *The Formation of the State of Oklahoma, 1803–1906.* Rev. edn. Norman, 1939.

Glasson, W. H., *Federal Military Pensions in the United States.* New York, 1918.

Goldsmith, A. N., and Lescarboura, A. C., *This Thing Called Broadcasting.* New York, 1930.

Goodenough, E. R., *The Rise of the Social Gospel in American Protestantism, 1865–1915.* New Haven, 1940.

Grant, Margaret, and Hettinger, H. S., *America's Symphony Orchestras and How They Are Supported.* New York, 1940.

Graves, W. S., *America's Siberian Adventure, 1918–1920.* New York, 1931.

Griswold, A. W., *The Far Eastern Policy of the United States, 1898–1938.* New York, 1938.

Groat, G. G., *Attitude of American Courts in Labor Cases* (Columbia University, *Studies,* XLII). New York, 1911.

Gruening, E. H., *Mexico and Its Heritage.* New York, 1928.

Haas, W. H., ed., *The American Empire.* Chicago, 1940.

Hacker, L. M., *American Problems of Today.* New York, 1938.

——, Modley, Rudolf, and Taylor, G. R., *The United States, a Graphic History* (L. M. Hacker, ed., *The Modern World Series,* no. 1). New York, 1937.

Hackett, C. W., *The Mexican Revolution and the United States* (World Peace Foundation, *Pamphlets,* IX, no. 5). Boston, 1926.

Hamilton, J. G. de R., *Reconstruction in North Carolina* (Columbia University, *Studies,* LVIII). New York, 1914.

Hamlin, T. F., *The American Spirit in Architecture* (*The Pageant of America,* XIII). New Haven, 1926.

Hammond, M. B., *The Cotton Industry* (American Economic Association, *Publications,* n.s., no. 1). New York, 1897.

Haney, L. H., *A Congressional History of Railways in the United States, 1850–1887* (University of Wisconsin, *Bulletin,* no. 342). Madison, 1910.

Harbord, J. G., *America in the World War.* Boston, 1933.

Hardy, C. O., *Recent Growth of the Electric Light and Power Industry* (Brookings Institution, *Pamphlet Series,* I, no. 1). Washington, 1929.

Harper, Ida H., *The Life and Work of Susan B. Anthony.* 3 v. Indianapolis, 1898–1908.

Harris, Herbert, *American Labor*. New Haven, 1938.

——, *Labor's Civil War*. New York, 1940.

Harrison, L. V., and Laine, Elizabeth, *After Repeal*. New York, 1936.

Hart, A. B., ed., *The American Nation: a History*. 28 v. New York, 1904–1918.

Hartwick, Harry, *The Foreground of American Literature*. New York, 1934.

Harvey, George, *Henry Clay Frick*. New York, 1928.

Haworth, P. L., *The Hayes-Tilden Disputed Presidential Election of 1876*. Cleveland, 1906.

Haynes, F. E., *James Baird Weaver (Iowa Biographical Series)*. Iowa City, 1919.

——, *Social Politics in the United States*. Boston, 1924.

——, *Third Party Movements since the Civil War*. Iowa City, 1916.

Haynes, G. H., *Charles Sumner (American Crisis Biographies)*. Philadelphia, 1909.

Hays, A. G., *Let Freedom Ring*. Rev. edn. New York, 1937.

Hechler, K. W., *Insurgency: Personalities and Politics of the Taft Era*. New York, 1940.

Hedges, J. B., *Henry Villard and the Railways of the Northwest*. New York, 1930.

Henderson, G. C., *The Federal Trade Commission*. New Haven, 1924.

Henderson, J. B., *American Diplomatic Questions*. New York, 1901.

Hendrick, B. J., *The Age of Big Business (The Chronicles of America Series, XXXIX)*. New Haven, 1919.

——, *The Life and Letters of Walter H. Page*. 3 v. Garden City, 1922–1925.

——, *The Life of Andrew Carnegie*. 2 v. Garden City, 1932.

Henry, R. S., *The Story of Reconstruction*. Indianapolis, 1938.

Hesseltine, W. B., *Ulysses S. Grant (American Political Leaders)*. New York, 1935.

Hibbard, B. H., *A History of the Public Land Policies* (R. T. Ely, ed., *Land Economic Series*). New York, 1924.

Hibben, Paxton, *Henry Ward Beecher*. New York, 1927.

Hicks, J. D., *The Populist Revolt*. Minneapolis, 1931.

Hill, H. C., *Roosevelt and the Caribbean*. Chicago, 1927.

Hill, L. F., *The Confederate Exodus to Latin America*. N. p., 1936.

Hillquit, Morris, *History of Socialism in the United States*. Rev. edn. New York, 1910.

Hines, W. D., *War History of American Railroads* (J. T. Shotwell, ed., *Economic and Social History of the World War*). New Haven, 1928.

History of American Life, A. See Schlesinger, A. M., and Fox, D. R., eds.

History of North America, The. See Lee, G. C., and Thorpe, F. N., eds.

Hockett, H. C., *The Constitutional History of the United States*. 2 v. New York, 1939, in progress.

Hodge, C. L., *The Tennessee Valley Authority*. Washington, 1938.

Holbrook, S. H., *Iron Brew, a Century of American Ore and Steel*. New York, 1939.

Horn, S. F., *Invisible Empire; the Story of the Ku Klux Klan, 1866–1871*. Boston, 1939.

Hornblow, Arthur, *A History of the Theatre in America*. 2 v. Philadelphia, 1919.

Hovey, Carl. *The Life Story of J. Pierpont Morgan*. New York, 1911.

Howard, J. T., *Our American Music: Three Hundred Years of It*. New York, 1931.

Howe, G. F., *Chester A. Arthur (American Political Leaders)*. New York, 1934.

Hurlbut, J. L., *The Story of Chautauqua*. New York, 1921.

Husband, Joseph, *The Story of the Pullman Car*. Chicago, 1917.

Hutchinson, W. T., *Cyrus H. McCormick: Harvest, 1856–1884*. New York, 1935.

Hütter, J. P., *La question de la monnai d'argent aux États-Unis des origines à 1900.* Paris, 1938.

Hyde, G. E., *Red Cloud's Folk.* Norman, 1937.

Irwin, Inez H., *Angels and Amazons.* New York, 1933.

Isham, Samuel, *The History of American Painting* (J. C. Van Dyke, ed., *The History of American Art,* III). Rev. edn. New York, 1927.

Jackson, J. H., *A Short History of the World since 1918.* Rev. edn. Boston, 1939.

Jacobs, Lewis, *The Rise of the American Film.* New York, 1939.

James, H. J., *German Subs in Yankee Waters.* New York, 1940.

James, Henry, *Richard Olney and His Public Service.* Boston, 1923.

Jenkins, J. W., *James B. Duke.* New York, 1927.

Jenks, J. W., and Lauck, W. J., *The Immigration Problem.* 6th edn. New York, 1926.

Jessup, P. C., *Elihu Root.* 2 v. New York, 1938.

——, *International Security, the American Rôle in Collective Action for Peace.* New York, 1935.

——, *The United States and the World Court* (World Peace Foundation, *Pamphlets,* XII, no. 4). Boston, 1929.

Johnson, Allen, ed., *The Chronicles of America Series.* 50 v. New Haven, 1918–1921.

——, and Malone, Dumas, eds., *Dictionary of American Biography.* 20 v. New York, 1928–1936.

Johnson, C. O., *Borah of Idaho.* New York, 1936.

Johnson, G. G., *The Treasury and Monetary Policy, 1933–1938* (*Harvard Political Studies*). Cambridge, 1939.

Jones, Eliot, *The Anthracite Coal Combination in the United States* (*Harvard Economic Studies,* XI). Cambridge, 1914.

——, *Principles of Railway Transportation.* New York, 1924.

Jones, J. M., Jr., *Tariff Retaliation.* Philadelphia, 1934.

Jones, J. P., and Hollister, P. M., *The German Secret Service in America.* Boston, 1918.

Jordan, D. S., ed., *Leading American Men of Science* (W. P. Trent, ed., *Biographies of Leading Americans*). New York, 1910.

Joseph, Samuel, *Jewish Immigration to the United States* (Columbia University, *Studies*, LIX, no. 4). New York, 1914.

Josephson, Matthew, *The Politicos, 1865–1900.* New York, 1938.

——, *The President Makers.* New York, 1940.

——, *The Robber Barons.* New York, 1935.

Kaempffert, Waldemar, ed., *A Popular History of American Invention.* 2 v. New York, 1924.

Keim, Jeannette, *Forty Years of German-American Political Relations.* Philadelphia, 1919.

Kendrick, B. B., *The Journal of the Joint Committee of Fifteen on Reconstruction* (Columbia University, *Studies*, LXII). New York, 1914.

Kennan, George, *E. H. Harriman.* 2 v. Boston, 1922.

Kinney, J. P., *A Continent Lost—a Civilization Won. Indian Land Tenure in America.* Baltimore, 1937.

Kirkland, E. C., *A History of American Economic Life.* Rev. edn. New York, 1939.

Knauth, O. W., *The Policy of the United States toward Industrial Monopoly* (Columbia University, *Studies*, LVI, no. 2). New York, 1914.

Knight, E. W., *The Influence of Reconstruction on Education in the South* (Teachers College, *Contributions to Education*, no. 60). New York, 1913.

Knight, M. M., *The Americans in Santo Domingo.* New York, 1928.

Kolbe, P. R., *The Colleges in War Time and After.* New York, 1919.

Krout, J. A., *Annals of American Sport* (*The Pageant of America*, XV). New Haven, 1929.

Kruif, Paul de, *Microbe Hunters.* New York, 1926.

Krutch, J. W., *The American Drama since 1918.* New York, 1940.

Kuhlmann, C. B., *The Development of the Flour-Milling Industry in the United States.* Boston, 1929.

Kuykendall, R. S., *A History of Hawaii*. New York, 1926.

La Farge, Oliver, and Post, Helen M., *As Long as the Grass Shall Grow*. New York, 1940.

Laidler, H. W., *Concentration of Control in American Industry*. New York, 1931.

Lane, Marie D., and Steegmuller, Francis, *America on Relief*. New York, 1938.

Langer, W. L., *The Diplomacy of Imperialism, 1890–1902*. 2 v. New York, 1935.

Larson, Henrietta M., *Jay Cooke, Private Banker*. Cambridge, 1936.

Lauck, W. J., *The Causes of the Panic of 1893*. Boston, 1907.

Laughlin, J. L., *The History of Bimetallism in the United States*. Rev. edn. New York, 1910.

Lavine, Harold, and Wechsler, James, *War Propaganda and the United States*. New Haven, 1940.

Lawrence, A. A., *Petroleum Comes of Age*. Tulsa, 1938.

Lee, A. M., *The Daily Newspaper in America*. New York, 1937.

Lee, G. C., and Thorpe, F. N., eds., *The History of North America*. 20 v. Philadelphia, 1903–1907.

Leech, Harper, and Carroll, J. C., *Armour and His Times*. New York, 1938.

Lehmann-Haupt, Hellmut, and others, *The Book in America*. New York, 1939.

Leonard, J. N., *Three Years Down*. New York, 1939.

LeRoy, J. A., *The Americans in the Philippines*. 2 v. Boston, 1914.

Levinson, Edward, *Labor on the March*. New York, 1938.

Lewinson, Paul, *Race, Class, & Party*. London, 1932.

Lewis, E. R., *A History of American Political Thought from the Civil War to the World War*. New York, 1937.

Lewis, Oscar, *The Big Four: the Story of Huntington, Stanford, Hopkins, and Crocker, and of the Building of the Central Pacific*. New York, 1938.

Lindley, Betty and E. K., *A New Deal for Youth*. New York, 1938.

Linn, W. A., *Horace Greeley (Appleton's Historic Lives Series)*. New York, 1903.

Lippmann, Walter, and others, *The United States in World Affairs*. New York, 1931, in progress.

Lively, C. E., and Taeuber, Conrad, *Rural Migration in the United States* (WPA, *Research Monographs*, XIX). Washington, 1939.

Lonn, Ella, *Reconstruction in Louisiana after 1868*. New York, 1918.

Lorwin, L. L., *The American Federation of Labor; History, Policies and Prospects*. Washington, 1933.

Loud, G. C., *Evangelized America*. New York, 1928.

Lougheed, Victor, *Vehicles of the Air*. Chicago, 1919.

Lubschez, B. J., *The Story of the Motion Picture*. New York, 1920.

Lutz, Alma, *Created Equal, a Biography of Elizabeth Cady Stanton, 1815–1902*. New York, 1940.

McCaleb, W. F., *History of the Brotherhood of Railroad Trainmen*. New York, 1936.

Macfarland, C. S., *The Progress of Church Federation*. New York, 1917.

McKelvey, Blake, *American Prisons* (University of Chicago, *Social Service Series*). Chicago, 1936.

Mackenzie, Catherine, *Alexander Graham Bell*. Boston, 1928.

McKenzie, R. D., *The Metropolitan Community (Recent Social Trends Monographs)*. New York, 1933.

McLaughlin, A. C., *A Constitutional History of the United States*. New York, 1935.

Macleod, W. C., *The American Indian Frontier* (C. K. Ogden, ed., *The History of Civilization*). New York, 1928.

McMurry, D. L., *Coxey's Army*. Boston, 1929.

McWilliams, Carey, *Factories in the Field*. Boston, 1939.

Malin, J. C., *An Interpretation of Recent American History*. New York, 1926.

——, *The United States after the World War*. Boston, 1930.

Marcosson, I. F., *S. O. S.* New York, 1919.

Martin, T. C., and Coles, S. L., eds., *The Story of Electricity*. 2 v. New York, 1919–1922.

Masterman, Sylvia, *The Origins of International Rivalry in Samoa, 1845–1884*. London, 1934.

Mather, F. J., and others, *The American Spirit in Art (The Pageant of America, XII)*. New Haven, 1927.

Mayo, Katherine, *"That Damn Y."* Boston, 1920.

Mayorga, Margaret G., *A Short History of the American Drama*. New York, 1932.

Mechlin, J. M., *The Ku Klux Klan*. New York, 1924.

Meriam, Lewis, and others, *The Problem of Indian Administration* (Institute for Government Research, Brookings Institution, *Publications*). Baltimore, 1928.

Merriam, C. E., *American Political Ideas, 1865–1917*. New York, 1920.

Merz, Charles, *The Dry Decade*. New York, 1931.

Meyer, A. E., *The Development of Education in the Twentieth Century*. New York, 1940.

Millis, Walter, *The Martial Spirit*. Boston, 1931.

——, *Road to War: America, 1914–1917*. Boston, 1935.

Millspaugh, A. C., *Haiti under American Control, 1915–1930*. Boston, 1931.

Milton, G. F., *The Age of Hate*. New York, 1930.

Miner, D. C., *The Fight for the Panama Route*. New York, 1940.

Mitchell, Broadus, *The Rise of Cotton Mills in the South* (Johns Hopkins University, *Studies*, XXXIX, no. 2). Baltimore, 1921.

Mitchell, Stewart, *Horatio Seymour of New York*. Cambridge, 1938.

Mitchell, W. C., *A History of the Greenbacks* (Chicago University, *Decennial Publications*, 2d ser., IX). Chicago, 1903.

Mock, J. R., and Larson, Cedric, *Words That Won the War; the Story of the Committee on Public Information, 1917–1919*. Princeton, 1939.

Montague, L. L., *Haiti and the United States, 1714–1938*. Durham, 1940.

Moody, John, *The Masters of Capital* (*The Chronicles of America Series*, XLI). New Haven, 1919.

——, *The Railroad Builders* (*The Chronicles of America Series*, XXXVIII). New Haven, 1919.

——, *The Truth about the Trusts*. New York, 1904.

Moorehead, W. K., *The American Indian in the United States*. Andover, Mass., 1914.

Morrissey, Alice M., *The American Defense of Neutral Rights, 1914–1917*. Cambridge, 1939.

Morse, J. T., Jr., ed., *American Statesmen*. Rev. edn. 32 v. Boston, 1898–1900.

Mott, F. L., *A History of American Magazines*. 3 v. New York and Cambridge, 1930–1938.

Moulton, H. G., and Pasvolsky, Leo, *War Debts and World Prosperity*. New York, 1932.

Munro, D. G., *The United States and the Caribbean Area*. Boston, 1934.

Munro, W. B., *The Initiative, Referendum and Recall*. New York, 1912.

Murrell, William, *A History of American Graphic Humor, 1865–1938*. New York, 1938.

Musmanno, M. A., *After Twelve Years*. New York, 1939.

Mussey, H. R., *Combination in the Mining Industry* (Columbia University, *Studies*, XXIII, no. 3). New York, 1905.

Muzzey, D. S., *James G. Blaine* (*American Political Leaders*). New York, 1934.

Myers, D. P., *Origin and Conclusion of the Paris Pact* (World Peace Foundation, *Pamphlets*, XII, no. 2). Boston, 1929.

Myers, Gustavus, *History of the Great American Fortunes*. Rev. edn. New York, 1936.

Nevins, Allan, *Abram S. Hewitt*. New York, 1935.

——, ed., *American Political Leaders*. New York, 1930, in progress.

——, *The Emergence of Modern America* (*A History of American Life*, VIII). New York, 1927.

——, *Grover Cleveland* (*American Political Leaders*). New York, 1932.

Nevins, Allan, *Hamilton Fish (American Political Leaders)*. New York, 1936.

——, *Henry White: Thirty Years of American Diplomacy*. New York, 1930.

——, *John D. Rockefeller*. 2 v. New York, 1940.

Norton, H. K., *China and the Powers*. New York, 1927.

Notter, Harley, *The Origins of the Foreign Policy of Woodrow Wilson*. Baltimore, 1937.

Nourse, E. G., and others, *Three Years of the Agricultural Adjustment Administration*. Washington, 1937.

Nowlin, W. F., *The Negro in American National Politics since 1868*. Boston, 1931.

Oberholtzer, E. P., ed., *American Crisis Biographies*. 14 v. Philadelphia, 1905–1915.

——, *A History of the United States since the Civil War*. 5 v. New York, 1917–1937.

——, *Jay Cooke, Financier of the Civil War*. 2 v. Philadelphia, 1907.

Odegard, P. H., *Pressure Politics*. New York, 1928.

Odum, H. W., ed., *American Masters of Social Science* (same ed., *American Social Science Series*). New York, 1927.

——, and Moore, H. E., *American Regionalism*. New York, 1938.

Ogden, Rollo, *Life and Letters of Edwin Lawrence Godkin*. 2 v. New York, 1907.

Ogg, F. A., *National Progress (The American Nation, XXVII)*. New York, 1918.

——, *Research in the Humanistic and Social Sciences*. New York, 1928.

Olcott, C. S., *The Life of William McKinley*. 2 v. (*American Statesmen*, 2d ser., VII). Boston, 1916.

Oliver, J. W., *History of the Civil War Military Pensions, 1861–1885* (University of Wisconsin, *Bulletin*, no. 844). Madison, 1917.

Osgood, E. S., *The Day of the Cattleman*. Minneapolis, 1929.

Ostrogorski, M., *Democracy and the Party System in the United States*. New York, 1910.

Overmyer, Grace, *Government and the Arts*. New York, 1939.

Pageant of America, The. See Gabriel, R. H., ed.

Paine, A. B., *Th. Nast, His Period and His Pictures*. New York, 1904.

Palmer, Frederick, *Bliss, Peacemaker*. New York, 1934.

——, *Newton D. Baker*. 2 v. New York, 1931.

Pan, S. C. Y., *American Diplomacy Concerning Manchuria*. Providence, 1938.

Parks, E. T., *Colombia and the United States, 1765–1934*. Durham, 1935.

Parrington, V. L., *The Beginnings of Critical Realism in America* (*Main Currents in American Thought*, III). New York, 1930.

Pattee, F. L., *A History of American Literature since 1870*. New York, 1915.

——, *The New American Literature*. New York, 1930.

Patton, J. W., *Unionism and Reconstruction in Tennessee*. Chapel Hill, 1934.

Paul, R. W., *The Abrogation of the Gentlemen's Agreement*. Cambridge, 1936.

Paullin, C. O., *Atlas of the Historical Geography of the United States* (J. K. Wright, ed., Carnegie Institution, *Publications*, no. 401). Washington, 1932.

Paxson, F. L., *America at War, 1917–1918* (*American Democracy and the World War*, II). Boston, 1939.

——, *History of the American Frontier, 1763–1893*. Boston, 1924.

——, *The Last American Frontier*. New York, 1910.

——, *Pre-War Years, 1913–1917* (*American Democracy and the World War*, I). Boston, 1936.

Peck, H. T., *Twenty Years of the Republic, 1885–1905*. New York, 1906.

Pecora, Ferdinand, *Wall Street under Oath*. New York, 1939.

Peirce, P. S., *The Freedmen's Bureau* (University of Iowa, *Studies*, III, no. 1). Iowa City, 1904.

Pelzer, Louis, *The Cattlemen's Frontier, 1850–1890*. Glendale, 1936.

Perkins, Dexter, *The Monroe Doctrine, 1867–1907.* Baltimore, 1937.

Perlman, Selig, *A History of Trade Unionism in the United States* (R. T. Ely, ed., *Social Science Text-Books*). New York, 1922.

Peterson, Florence, *Strikes in the United States, 1880–1936* (United States Department of Labor, *Bulletin,* no. 651). Washington, 1938.

Peterson, H. C., *Propaganda for War: the Campaign against American Neutrality, 1914–1917.* Norman, 1939.

Powell, E. A., *The Army behind the Army.* New York, 1919.

Powell, L. P., *Mary Baker Eddy.* New York, 1930.

Pratt, J. W., *Expansionists of 1898.* Baltimore, 1936.

Presbrey, Frank, *The History and Development of Advertising.* Garden City, 1929.

President's Research Committee on Social Trends, *Recent Social Trends in the United States.* 2 v. New York, 1933.

Priestley, H. I., *The Mexican Nation.* New York, 1923.

Pringle, H. F., *Alfred E. Smith.* New York, 1927.

——, *The Life and Times of William Howard Taft.* 2 v. New York, 1939.

——, *Theodore Roosevelt.* New York, 1931.

Prout, H. G., *A Life of George Westinghouse.* New York, 1921.

Pyle, J. G., *The Life of James J. Hill.* 2 v. Garden City, 1917.

Quiett, G. C., *Pay Dirt.* New York, 1934.

Rainwater, C. E., *The Play Movement in the United States.* Chicago, 1921.

Ramsdell, C. W., *Reconstruction in Texas* (Columbia University, *Studies,* XXXVI, no. 1). New York, 1901.

Randall, J. G., *The Civil War and Reconstruction.* Boston, 1937.

Rappard, W. E., *The Quest for Peace.* Cambridge, 1940.

Ravenel, M. P., ed., *A Half Century of Public Health.* New York, 1921.

Regier, C. C., *The Era of the Muckrakers.* Chapel Hill, 1932.

Reinsch, P. S., *Colonial Administration.* New York, 1905.

Reisner, E. H., *The Evolution of the Common School.* New York, 1932.

Reuter, Bertha A., *Anglo-American Relations during the Spanish-American War.* New York, 1924.

Reyes, J. S., *Legislative History of America's Economic Policy toward the Philippines* (Columbia University, *Studies,* CVI, no. 2). New York, 1923.

Rhodes, J. F., *History of the United States from the Compromise of 1850 to the McKinley-Bryan Campaign of 1896.* 8 v. New York, 1892–1919.

——, *The McKinley and Roosevelt Administrations.* New York, 1922.

Rickard, T. A., *A History of American Mining.* New York, 1932.

Riegel, R. E., *America Moves West.* New York, 1930.

Ripley, W. Z., *Railroads: Rates and Regulation.* New York, 1912.

Rippy, J. F., *Latin America in World Politics.* Rev. edn. New York, 1938.

——, *The United States and Mexico.* Rev. edn. New York, 1931.

Rister, C. C., *Southern Plainsmen.* Norman, 1938.

——, *The Southwestern Frontier, 1865–1881.* Cleveland, 1928.

Robbins, E. C., *Railway Conductors: a Study in Organized Labor* (Columbia University, *Studies,* LXI, no. 1). New York, 1914.

Robertson, W. S., *Hispanic-American Relations with the United States (Carnegie Endowment Publications).* New York, 1923.

Robinson, J. S., *The Amalgamated Association of Iron, Steel and Tin Workers* (Johns Hopkins University, *Studies,* XXXVIII, no. 2). Baltimore, 1920.

Robinson, W. A., *Thomas B. Reed: Parliamentarian.* New York, 1930.

Roos, C. F., *NRA Economic Planning.* Bloomington, 1937.

Rosenfarb, Joseph, *The National Labor Policy and How It Works.* New York, 1940.

Rosewater, Victor, *History of Coöperative News-Gathering in the United States.* New York, 1930.

Ross, E. D., *The Liberal Republican Movement.* New York, 1919.

Rowe, H. K., *The History of Religion in the United States*. New York, 1924.

Ryan, W. C., *Studies in Early Graduate Education* (Carnegie Foundation for the Advancement of Teaching, *Bulletin*, no. 30). New York, 1930.

Ryden, G. H., *The Foreign Policy of the United States in Relation to Samoa*. New Haven, 1933.

Sabin, E. L., *Building the Pacific Railway*. Philadelphia, 1919.

Sageser, A. B., *The First Two Decades of the Pendleton Act* (University of Nebraska, *Studies*, XXXIV-XXXV). Lincoln, 1935.

Sandmeyer, E. C., *The Anti-Chinese Movement in California* (University of Illinois, *Studies*, XXIV, no. 3). Urbana, 1939.

Sayre, F. B., *The Way Forward*. New York, 1939.

Schlesinger, A. M., *The Rise of the City* (*A History of American Life*, X). New York, 1933.

——, and Fox, D. R., eds., *A History of American Life*. 12 v. New York, 1927, in progress.

Schmeckebier, L. F., *The Office of Indian Affairs* (Institute for Government Research, *Service Monographs*, no. 48). Washington, 1927.

Schmidt, L. B., and Ross, E. D., eds., *Readings in the Economic History of American Agriculture*. New York, 1925.

Schouler, James, *History of the United States of America, under the Constitution*. Rev. edn. 7 v. New York, 1894–1913.

Schubert, Paul, *The Electric Word: the Rise of Radio*. New York, 1928.

Schuster, Eunice M., *Native American Anarchism* (Smith College, *Studies*, XVII). Northampton, 1931–1932.

Schuyler, Hamilton, *The Roeblings*. Princeton, 1931.

Scott, E. J., and Stowe, L. B., *Booker T. Washington*. Garden City, 1916.

Scott, J. B., *The Hague Peace Conference of 1899 and 1907*. 2 v. Baltimore, 1909.

Scott, W. A., *The Repudiation of State Debts*. New York, 1893.

Seitz, D. C., *Joseph Pulitzer*. New York, 1924.

Seldes, Gilbert, *The Years of the Locust*. Boston, 1933.

Sellin, Thorsten, and Young, Donald, eds., *Pressure Groups and Propaganda* (American Academy of Political and Social Science, *Annals*, CLXXIX, May, 1935). Philadelphia, 1935.

Seymour, Charles, *American Diplomacy during the World War*. Baltimore, 1934.

——, *The Intimate Papers of Colonel House*. 4 v. Boston, 1926–1928.

Shannon, F. A., *America's Economic Growth*. New York, 1940.

Shipley, Maynard, *The War on Modern Science*. New York, 1927.

Shippee, L. B., *Canadian-American Relations, 1849–1874* (J. T. Shotwell, gen. ed., *The Relations of Canada and the United States*). New Haven, 1939.

Shove, R. H., *Cheap Book Production in the United States, 1870 to 1891*. Urbana, 1937.

Shugg, R. W., *Origins of Class Struggle in Louisiana: a Social History of White Farmers and Laborers during Slavery and after, 1840–1875*. Baton Rouge, 1939.

Sigerist, H. E., *American Medicine* (Hildegard Nagel, tr.). New York, 1934.

Simkins, F. B., *The Tillman Movement in South Carolina* (Duke University, *Publications*). Durham, 1926.

——, and Woody, R. H., *South Carolina during Reconstruction*. Chapel Hill, 1932.

Sims, W. S., and Hendrick, B. J., *The Victory at Sea*. Garden City, 1920.

Slosson, E. E., *Creative Chemistry*. New York, 1919.

Slosson, P. W., *The Great Crusade and After (A History of American Life, XII)*. New York, 1930.

Smalley, E. V., *History of the Northern Pacific Railroad*. New York, 1883.

Smith, G. B., ed., *Religious Thought in the Last Quarter Century*. Chicago, 1927.

Smith, J. P., *The Republican Expansionists of the Early Reconstruction Era*. Chicago, 1933.

Smith, J. R., *The Story of Iron and Steel* (*The Library of Useful Stories*). New York, 1908.

Smith, T. C., *The Life and Letters of James Abram Garfield*. 2 v. New Haven, 1925.

Spalding, A. G., *America's National Game*. New York, 1911.

Sparks, E. E., *National Development* (*The American Nation*, XXIII). New York, 1907.

Spaulding, O. L., *The United States Army in War and Peace*. New York, 1937.

Sprout, Harold and Margaret, *The Rise of American Naval Power*. Princeton, 1939.

Squires, J. D., *British Propaganda at Home and in the United States from 1914 to 1917* (*Harvard Historical Monographs*, VI). Cambridge, 1935.

Stanwood, Edward, *American Tariff Controversies in the Nineteenth Century*. 2 v. Boston, 1903.

——, *A History of the Presidency*. 2 v. Boston, 1916.

Starrett, W. A., *Skyscrapers and the Men Who Build Them*. New York, 1928.

Stephenson, G. M., *A History of American Immigration*. Boston, 1926.

Stephenson, N. W., *Nelson W. Aldrich*. New York, 1930.

Steuart, Justin, *Wayne Wheeler, Dry Boss*. New York, 1928.

Stewart, F. M., *The National Civil Service Reform League*. Austin, 1929.

Stieglitz, Julius, *Chemistry and Recent Progress in Medicine*. Baltimore, 1924.

Stone, H. A., Price, D. K., and Stone, Kathryn H., *City Manager Government in the United States*. Chicago, 1940.

Straus, M. W., and Wegg, Talbot, *Housing Comes of Age*. New York, 1938.

Streeter, F. B., *Prairie Trails & Cow Towns*. Boston, 1936.

Stuart, G. H., *Latin America and the United States*. Rev. edn. New York, 1938.

Sullivan, Lawrence, *Prelude to Panic; the Story of the Bank Holiday*. Washington, 1936.

Sullivan, Mark, *Our Times: the United States, 1900–1925.* 6 v. New York, 1926–1935.

Surface, F. M., *The Grain Trade during the World War.* New York, 1928.

Sweet, W. W., *The Story of Religions in America.* New York, 1930.

Swisher, C. B., *Stephen J. Field, Craftsman of the Law.* Washington, 1930.

Taft, Lorado, *The History of American Sculpture* (J. C. Van Dyke, ed., *The History of American Art,* I). Rev. edn. New York, 1924.

Tallmadge, T. E., *The Story of American Architecture.* New York, 1927.

Tansill, C. C., *America Goes to War.* Boston, 1938.

——, *The Purchase of the Danish West Indies.* Baltimore, 1932.

——, *The United States and Santo Domingo, 1798–1873.* Baltimore, 1938.

Tarbell, Ida M., *The History of the Standard Oil Company.* 2 v. New York, 1904.

——, *The Life of Elbert H. Gary.* New York, 1925.

——, *The Nationalizing of Business, 1878–1898* (*A History of American Life,* IX). New York, 1936.

——, *The Tariff in Our Times.* New York, 1911.

Tasca, H. J., *The Reciprocal Trade Policy of the United States.* Philadelphia, 1938.

Taussig, F. W., *The Tariff History of the United States.* Rev. edn. New York, 1931.

Taylor, A. A., *The Negro in South Carolina during Reconstruction.* Washington, 1924.

——, *The Negro in the Reconstruction of Virginia.* Washington, 1926.

Teele, R. P., *The Economics of Land Reclamation in the United States.* Chicago, 1927.

Thomas, H. C., *The Return of the Democratic Party to Power in 1884* (Columbia University, *Studies,* LXXXIX, no. 2). New York, 1919.

Thomas, N. M., *The Conscientious Objector in America.* New York, 1923.

Thomas, Shipley, *The History of the A. E. F.* New York, 1920.

Thompson, C. Mildred, *Reconstruction in Georgia* (Columbia University, *Studies*, LXIV, no. 1). New York, 1915.

Thompson, Holland, *The New South* (*The Chronicles of America Series*, XLII). New Haven, 1919.

Thompson, W. S., and Whelpton, P. K., *Population Trends in the United States* (*Recent Social Trends Monographs*). New York, 1933.

Thornton, H. J., *The History of the Quaker Oats Company.* Chicago, 1933.

Thorp, Margaret, *America at the Movies.* New York, 1940.

Thwing, C. F., *The American and the German University.* New York, 1928.

Treat, P. J., *Diplomatic Relations between the United States and Japan, 1853–1905.* 3 v. Stanford University, 1932–1938.

——, *Japan and the United States, 1853–1928.* Stanford University, 1928.

Trimble, W. J., *The Mining Advance into the Inland Empire* (University of Wisconsin, *Bulletin,* no. 638). Madison, 1914.

Tupper, Eleanor, and McReynolds, G. E., *Japan in American Public Opinion.* New York, 1937.

Tyler, Alice F., *The Foreign Policy of James G. Blaine.* Minneapolis, 1927.

Urbanism Committee of the National Resources Committee, *Our Cities; Their Role in the National Economy.* Washington, 1937.

Vander Velde, L. G., *The Presbyterian Churches and the Federal Union, 1861–1869* (*Harvard Historical Studies,* XXXIII). Cambridge, 1932.

Van Doren, Carl, *The American Novel, 1789–1939.* Rev. edn. New York, 1940.

—— and Mark, *American and British Literature since 1890.* New York, 1925.

Van Hise, C. R., *Conservation and Regulation in the United States during the World War.* Washington, 1917.

Van Hise, C. R., and Havemeyer, Loomis, *The Conservation of Our Natural Resources.* New York, 1930.

Vestal, Stanley, *Sitting Bull, Champion of the Sioux.* Boston, 1932.

Vreeland, F. M., and Fitzgerald, E. J., *Farm-City Migration and Industry's Labor Reserve* (WPA, *National Research Projects,* no. L-7). Philadelphia, 1937.

Waples, Douglas, *Research Memorandum on Social Aspects of Reading in the Depression* (Social Science Research Council, *Bulletin,* XXXVII). New York, 1937.

Warburg, P. M., *The Federal Reserve System.* 2 v. New York, 1930.

Ware, Louise, *Jacob A. Riis.* New York, 1938.

Ware, N. J., *The Labor Movement in the United States, 1860–1895.* New York, 1929.

Warner, A. G., *American Charities.* Rev. edn. New York, 1922.

Warren, Charles, *The Supreme Court in United States History.* Rev. edn. 2 v. Boston, 1926.

Watson, F. D., *The Charity Organization Movement in the United States.* New York, 1922.

Webb, J. N., and Brown, Malcolm, *Migrant Families* (WPA, *Research Monographs,* XVIII). Washington, 1938.

Webb, W. P., *The Great Plains.* Boston, 1931.

Weber, A. F., *The Growth of Cities in the Nineteenth Century* (Columbia University, *Studies,* XI). New York, 1899.

Weberg, F. P., *The Background of the Panic of 1893.* Washington, 1929.

Wecter, Dixon, *The Saga of American Society.* New York, 1937.

Weinberg, A. K., *Manifest Destiny.* Baltimore, 1935.

Weitenkampf, Frank, *American Graphic Art.* Rev. edn. New York, 1924.

Wellman, P. I., *Death in the Desert.* New York, 1935.

——, *Death on the Prairie: the Thirty Years' Struggle for the Western Plains.* New York, 1934.

——, *The Trampling Herd.* New York, 1939.

Werner, M. R., *Bryan.* New York, 1929.

Werner, M. R., *Privileged Characters*. New York, 1935.

Wesley, C. H., *Negro Labor in the United States, 1850–1925*. New York, 1927.

Westergaard, W. C., *The Danish West Indies*. New York, 1917.

Weyand, A. M., *American Football*. New York, 1926.

White, Trumbull, *Puerto Rico and Its People*. New York, 1938.

Whitman, Willson, *Bread and Circuses*. New York, 1937.

——, *God's Valley*. New York, 1939.

Wiest, Edward, *Agricultural Organization in the United States* (University of Kentucky, *Studies in Economics and Sociology*, II). Lexington, 1923.

Wilkerson, M. M., *Public Opinion and the Spanish-American War* (Louisiana State University, *Studies*, no. 8). Baton Rouge, 1932.

Will, A. S., *Life of Cardinal Gibbons*. 2 v. New York, 1922.

Williams, Arthur, *Power on the Farm*. New York, 1927.

Williams, B. H., *Economic Foreign Policy of the United States*. New York, 1929.

——, *The United States and Disarmament*. New York, 1931.

Williams, C. R., *The Life of Rutherford Birchard Hayes*. 2 v. Boston, 1914.

Williams, Mary W., *Anglo-American Isthmian Diplomacy, 1815–1915*. Washington, 1916.

Williams, Michael, *The Shadow of the Pope*. New York, 1932.

Willis, H. P., *The Federal Reserve System*. New York, 1923.

Willoughby, W. F., *The Constitutional Law of the United States*. 2 v. New York, 1910.

——, *Government Organization in War Time and After*. New York, 1919.

——, *Territories and Dependencies of the United States*. New York, 1905.

Wilson, H. E., *Mary McDowell, Neighbor*. Chicago, 1928.

Wilson, H. F., *The Hill Country of Northern New England, Its Social and Economic History, 1790–1930* (Columbia University, *Studies in the History of American Agriculture*, III). New York, 1936.

Wilson, Jennie L., *The Legal and Political Status of Women in the United States.* Cedar Rapids, 1912.

Wilson, N. C., *Silver Stampede.* New York, 1937.

Winkler, J. K., *The Du Pont Dynasty.* New York, 1935.

——, *W. R. Hearst.* New York, 1928.

Winkler, Max, *Investments of United States Capital in Latin America* (World Peace Foundation, *Pamphlets,* XI, no. 6). Boston, 1928.

Winston, G. T., *A Builder of the New South.* Garden City, 1920.

Winston, R. W., *Andrew Johnson.* New York, 1928.

Wisan, J. E., *The Cuban Crisis as Reflected in the New York Press, 1895–1898* (Columbia University, *Studies,* no. 403). New York, 1934.

Wise, Winifred E., *Jane Addams of Hull-House.* New York, 1935.

Wittke, Carl, *German-Americans and the World War* (*Ohio Historical Collections,* V). Columbus, 1936.

——, *We Who Built America.* New York, 1939.

Wolman, Leo, *The Growth of American Trade Unions, 1880–1923.* New York, 1924.

Woodburn, J. A., *The Life of Thaddeus Stevens.* Indianapolis, 1913.

Woods, Eleanor H., *Robert A. Woods.* Boston, 1929.

Woods, R. A., and Kennedy, A. J., *The Settlement Horizon.* New York, 1922.

Woodson, C. G., *The Negro in Our History.* Rev. edn. Washington, 1931.

Woodward, C. V., *Tom Watson, Agrarian Rebel.* New York, 1938.

Woodworth, J. V., *American Tool Making and Interchangeable Manufacturing.* New York, 1911.

Woody, Thomas, *A History of Women's Education in the United States* (J. M. Cattell, ed., *Science and Education,* IV). 2 v. New York, 1929.

Worcester, D. C., *The Philippines, Past and Present.* 2 v. New York, 1914.

Wright, R. M., *Dodge City, the Cowboy Capital.* Wichita, 1913.

Wynne, Waller, Jr., *Five Years of Rural Relief* (WPA, *Special Report*). Washington, 1938.

Yellen, Samuel, *American Labor Struggles.* New York, 1936.

Young, A. N., *The Single Tax Movement in the United States* Princeton, 1916.

Zanzig, A. D., *Music in American Life.* New York, 1932.

Zimmerman, C. C., and Whetten, N. L., *Rural Families on Relief* (WPA, *Research Monographs*, XVII). Washington, 1938.

INDEX

AAA. *See* Agricultural Adjustment Administration.
A. B. C. Powers, and Monroe Doctrine, 387; and Mexican imbroglio, 389, 390; and Second World War, 618.
A. E. F. *See* American Expeditionary Force.
Abbott, Lyman, and social gospel, 180; and evolution, 181-182.
Academic freedom, upheld, 205, 657; restricted, 654-655, 657-658.
Actors and actresses, 19th-century, 214; early 20th-century, 355, 363; of 1920's and '30's, 664-665, 667.
Adams, Henry, on Grant's administration, 77; historian, 204.
Adams, J. T., historian, 671.
Adams, S. H., exposes patent medicines, 299-300.
Adamson law, passed, 345.
Addams, Jane, founds Hull-House, 166, 178; urges child-labor legislation, 340-341.
Advertising, billboard, 127, 660; newspaper, 127, 199; immigration, 251; New Deal forbids misleading, 590-591; radio, 648; movie, 649; phonograph, 663.
Advisory Commission on National Defense, created, 623.
Africa, struggle for, 259; Boer War in, 267, 392.
Agassiz, Louis, against evolution, 203.
Agricultural adjustment act, provisions of, 542; new, 587-588.
Agricultural Adjustment Administration, curtails production, 542-543; protest against, 543-544; Supreme Court decision regarding, 544; made continuing agency, 545; hurts sharecroppers, 572; under new agricultural adjustment act, 587-588.
Agricultural-marketing act, provisions of, 501.
Agricultural Wheel, formed, 223.
Agriculture, postwar Southern, 6, 31-32; compared in 1860, 1880, 1890, 43; Economic Revolution in, 56-57; growth of scientific, 57, 59, 203, 497; depression in, 68, 83; and tariff, 114, 120; in Philippines, 378; during World War, 497-498; postwar depression in, 459, 497, 498-499; federal legislation for (1920's), 499-501; overproduction in, 500-501; Great Depression affects, 506; under the New Deal, 540-545, 571-574, 587-588. *See also* Crop limitation, Farmers.
Aguinaldo, Emilio, and Spanish-American War, 280; captured, 377.
Airplane. *See* Aviation.
Alabama, Negro in, 19, 184; reconstructed, 20; postwar taxes, 26; redeemed, 29; manufacturing, 61-62; prohibition, 641.
Alabama claims, 34-35.
Alarm, The, anarchist paper, 161.
Alaska, purchased, 34; gold, 241, 374; as American possession, 374-375.
Aldrich, N. W., and tariff, 114, 323; as conservative, 309.
Aldrich-Vreeland act, passed, 336.
Alger, Horatio, biographer, 102 *n.*
Alien act of 1918, 436-437.
Alien-labor-contract law, passed, 253.
Allied Relief Fund, created, 624.
Allies. *See* First World War, Second World War.

729

GOVERNMENT BY THE PEOPLE

IMPEACHMENT TRIAL OF PRESIDENT JOHNSON

COMPLETION OF THE PACIFIC RAILROAD, 1869

Photograph by Brown Brothers

BROOKLYN BRIDGE, 1883

TWO GREAT ENGINEERING ACHIEVEMENTS

ART GALLERY, PHILADELPHIA CENTENNIAL, 1876

Photograph by Brown Brothers

PALACE OF FINE ARTS, CHICAGO WORLD'S FAIR, 1893

ARCHITECTURAL ADVANCE

CAPTAIN CLEVELAND HAS TROUBLE WITH HIS CREW

THE TRUST PROBLEM ACCORDING TO THOMAS NAST

BURNING THE PITTSBURGH ROUNDHOUSE, 1877

MOBBING PINKERTON DETECTIVES AT HOMESTEAD, 1892

EMBATTLED INDUSTRY

STUDENT LIFE AT VASSAR, 1885

THE ADAMS MEMORIAL (1891) BY AUGUSTUS SAINT-GAUDENS

PLAYING CROQUET, 1869

BICYCLING ON RIVERSIDE DRIVE, NEW YORK, 1895

A PERILOUS SITUATION.

THE PRODUCERS OF THE COUNTRY IN DANGER FROM SILVER DEMAGOGUES AND POPULISTS.

AN EASTERN VIEW OF FREE SILVER

CASTLE GARDEN, IMMIGRANT RECEIVING STATION

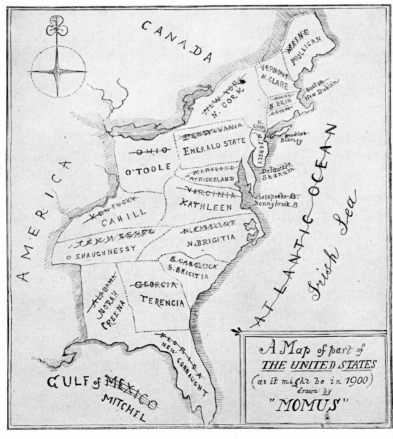

A HUMOROUS PREDICTION OF MIDCENTURY

THE TIRELESS TEDDY

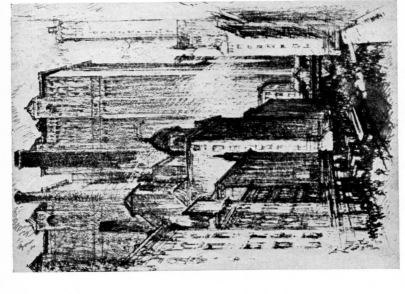

CORTLANDT STREET, NEW YORK

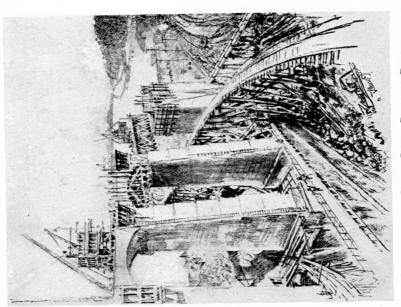

APPROACHES TO GATUN LOCK, PANAMA CANAL

TWO ETCHINGS BY JOSEPH PENNELL

REMAKING HIGHWAYS IN THE PHILIPPINES

SLUM CLEARANCE IN PUERTO RICO

PRESIDENT WILSON ENTERING PARIS WITH PRESIDENT POINCARÉ

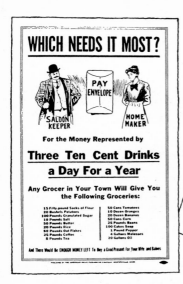

WORKING UP DRY SENTIMENT

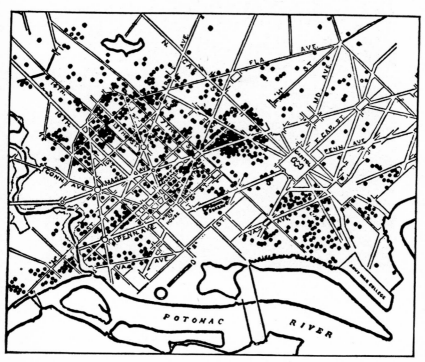

A "SPEAKEASY" MAP OF WASHINGTON, D. C., 1930

PWA AND WPA PROJECTS

British Refugee Children Arriving in America, July, 1940

TWO OF THE RESTORED BUILDINGS OF COLONIAL WILLIAMSBURG, VIRGINIA

THE WILLIAMSBURG HOUSING PROJECT IN BROOKLYN

AMERICA PONDERS TWO WILLIAMSBURGS

ARCTIC OCEAN

ARCTIC CIRCLE

RUSSIA

SIBERIA

Okhotsk
Sea

Bering Sea

ALEUTIAN
(U.S.)

CHINA

Japan Sea

Kuril IS.

JAPAN

BONIN IS.
(Jap.)

MIDWAY
(U.S.)

WAKE IS.
(U.S.)

MARIANAS
(Jap.)

SIAM

FRENCH INDO-CHINA

PHILIPPINE
(U.S. to 1946)
ISLANDS

GUAM
(U.S.)

China Sea

MARSHALL IS.
(Jap.)

CELEBES

PELEW IS.
(Jap.)

CAROLINE IS.
(Jap.)

GILBERT IS.
(Br.)

HOWLAND IS.
(U.S.)

BORNEO

BISMARCK
ARCHIPELAGO
(Br.)

BAKER IS.
(U.S.)

DUTCH EAST INDIES

NEW
GUINEA

SOLOMON IS.
(Br.)

ELLICE IS.
(Br.)

TIMOR

SAMOA
(Br.)

INDIAN

NEW HEBRIDES
(Br. and Fr.)

FIJI IS.
(Br.)

TUTUILA
(U.S.)

OCEAN

NEW CALEDONIA
(Br.)

FRIENDLY
(Br.)

AUSTRALIA

NORFOLK

Scale of Miles

0   500   1000   1500   2000

TASMANIA

NEW ZEALAND